The Decline of Sterling

The demise of sterling as an international currency was widely predicted after 1945, but the process took thirty years to complete. Why was this demise so prolonged? Traditional explanations have emphasised the British effort to prolong sterling's role on the grounds that it either increased the capacity to borrow, enhanced prestige or supported London as a centre for international finance. This book challenges this view by arguing that sterling's international role was prolonged by the weakness of the international monetary system and by collective global interest in its continuation. Using the archives of partner countries in Europe, the United States and the Commonwealth, Catherine R. Schenk shows how the United Kingdom was able to convince other governments that sterling's international role was critical for the stability of the international economy and thereby attract considerable support for managing its retreat. This revised view has important implications for current debates over the future of the US dollar as an international currency.

CATHERINE R. SCHENK is Professor of International Economic History at the University of Glasgow. She has held academic posts in the United Kingdom, New Zealand and Malaysia and has been a visiting researcher at the Hong Kong Institute for Monetary Research and the International Monetary Fund. Her previous books include *Hong Kong as an International Financial Centre* (2001) and *Britain and the Sterling Area* (1994).

The Decline of Sterling

Managing the Retreat of an International Currency, 1945–1992

Catherine R. Schenk

CAMBRIDGE
UNIVERSITY PRESS

CAMBRIDGE UNIVERSITY PRESS
Cambridge, New York, Melbourne, Madrid, Cape Town,
Singapore, São Paulo, Delhi, Mexico City

Cambridge University Press
The Edinburgh Building, Cambridge CB2 8RU, UK

Published in the United States of America by Cambridge University Press, New York

www.cambridge.org
Information on this title: www.cambridge.org/9780521876971

First published 2010

A catalogue record for this publication is available from the British Library

Library of Congress Cataloguing in Publication Data
Schenk, Catherine R. (Catherine Ruth), 1964–
The decline of sterling : managing the retreat of an international currency, 1945–1992 / Catherine R. Schenk.
p. cm.
ISBN 978-0-521-87697-1 (hardback)
1. Pound, British–History–20th century. 2. Monetary policy–Great Britain–History–20th century. 3. International economic relations–History–20th century. I. Title.
HG939.5.S343 2010
332.4′94109045–dc22
2009053760

ISBN 978-0-521-87697-1 Hardback

For Duncan and Margaret and Archie

Contents

Figures

Tables

Acknowledgements

This book has been very long in the making, and I have drawn on the experience and expertise of many scholars and students in the process. I would particularly like to thank the archivists of the Bank of England, the International Monetary Fund, the Bank for International Settlements, the Reserve Bank of Australia, Arkib Negara Malaysia, HSBC Group and Australian National Archives, who were extraordinarily helpful in tracking down relevant material. This project has been supported by the Economic and Social Research Council (grants RES-165-25-0004 and R000223973), by the British Academy, by the Centre for Business History in Scotland and by the research leave programme of the University of Glasgow. I am also grateful to those who read parts of the manuscript, including Jim Tomlinson, B. J. Cohen, Forrest Capie, Neil Rollings and Duncan Ross. All errors of fact and interpretation remain, of course, my own.

Acknowledgments

1 Introduction

The role of sterling and the management (or mismanagement) of its retreat from an international to a national currency has been a central issue in the post-war history of the United Kingdom. Politically as well as economically, sterling's international role has helped to define Britain's place in the world. From the earliest days of post-war western European integration, sterling's place in the global international monetary system distinguished Britain from other European countries. In terms of the 'special relationship' with the United States, the international status of sterling alongside the US dollar created a forum for Anglo-American cooperation and an opportunity for the United Kingdom to exercise strategic influence. In Commonwealth relations, the problems of sterling were an important shared concern that defined the economic dimension of the new Commonwealth and the British Empire after the war. Given Britain's greatly reduced position in the international economy after 1945 and its relatively poor economic performance in the following decades, however, supporting an international currency seemed to many critics to pose an unacceptable burden. In this context, why was sterling's international role as a reserve currency and a commercial currency prolonged for so long? The literature notes that there is considerable inertia in the use of international currencies, but this is not easily explained.[1] Network externalities may delay switching from a currency used by a wide group of traders and states, and this would suggest that a tipping point will arise at some point that will lead to a rapid transformation, but what will prompt this event? The historical process of how states and markets adapt to the erosion of global economic leadership and how the use of international currencies is determined in this context is not clearly

[1] Chinn, M., and J. Frankel, *Will the Euro Eventually Surpass the Dollar as Leading International Reserve Currency?*, Working Paper no. 11510 (Cambridge, MA: National Bureau of Economic Research [NBER], 2005), contains a review of the literature. See also Kindleberger, C., *International Money: A Collection of Essays* (London: Allen & Unwin, 1981), and Eichengreen, B., *Sterling's Past, Dollar's Future: Historical Perspectives on Reserve Currency Competition*, Working Paper no. 11336 (Cambridge, MA: NBER, 2005).

Table 1.1 *International currency roles*

Role	Governments	Private	Determinants
Unit of account	Defining exchange rate parity	Denomination of merchandise trade	Stable value, size of issuing country in international trade and payments
Means of payment	Intervention currency in foreign exchange market	Vehicle currency: foreign exchange market	Depth and efficiency of the issuing country's financial markets
Store of value	Denomination of reserves	Denomination of deposits, loans, bonds	Stable value, depth and efficiency of country's financial markets

understood. To understand this phenomenon better we need to move beyond the British economy to examine how sterling's status fitted with the structure of the international monetary system and the commitment of almost all post-war governments to stable exchange rates.

The international role of sterling comprised its use as a reserve asset for other countries and its use commercially both as a unit of account and a settlement currency for international trade and investment.[2] It thus relates to the portfolio choices of both state and private market actors, as shown in table 1.1. This leads to a set of determinants for international currency status, including: the size of the issuing country; its relative importance in global trade and investment; the location of an international financial centre; and confidence in the stability of the currency's value.

The combination of a rapidly growing international economy with the pegged exchange rate system of the post-war decades required central banks to hold significant working reserves of foreign exchange as well as precautionary reserves to defend exchange rate parities. Although gold formed the foundation of the Bretton Woods arrangements and the US dollar's value was defined in terms of a fixed value of gold, as the system developed foreign exchange made up an increasing share of world reserves. In this context, many countries accumulated US dollar assets, but substantial reserves of sterling were also held by central monetary authorities, and many currencies were pegged to sterling rather than to the US dollar until the early 1970s. The denomination of commercial transactions in sterling was related not only to Britain's own trade but to

[2] This typology follows Kenen, P. B., *The Role of the Dollar as an International Currency*, Occasional Paper no. 13 (New York: Group of Thirty, 1983).

the institutions of the City of London, which re-emerged as the centre for many commercial and financial transactions unrelated to Britain's own commerce. Thus the insurance, shipping, commodity trading, banking and investment business located in London encouraged the use of sterling as the unit of account and the currency of settlement in a wide range of global commercial activities. These two functions of reserve and transactions currency are, of course, related through the efficiencies of retaining working reserves in the currency in which most transactions take place, but they are not mutually dependent, and we shall see that the importance of sterling to the activities of the City declined before sterling was able to be retired from its reserve currency status.

Despite profound changes in the way that the international monetary system functioned and a dramatic shift in the United Kingdom's global economic and political position during the decades after the war, there is a striking continuity in the historiographical tradition to the effect that successive governments promoted sterling as an international currency at the expense of national economic interests because of delusions of imperial grandeur right through to the 1970s. In 1954 Day warned that 'to lay emphasis on re-establishing sterling as an international currency … can involve Britain in taking up an excessively large part of the burden of world payments disequilibrium', given Britain's relative economic weakness compared to the United States and the shallowness of international liquidity. For these reasons, he argued that 'serious doubt should be thrown on the desirability of re-establishing the position of sterling as an international currency' in the 1950s.[3] The Suez Crisis of 1956 forced a reassessment of the United Kingdom's strategic power, after which the status of sterling became closely linked with the perception that British governments had overreached the limits of their global influence, with disastrous results. In 1958 Shonfield wrote a vigorous and influential criticism of British economic policy, asserting that 'there is no doubt that the Government has allowed its domestic policy since 1955 to be determined largely by the movement in international confidence in the pound sterling', which he judged 'tragic and absurd'.[4] The promotion of sterling's international role was 'an extraordinarily hazardous venture' that made the economy vulnerable to speculative exchange crises, necessitating damaging 'crisis measures of restriction' on the domestic economy.[5] Additionally, the sterling area system on which the international role of sterling depended caused a drain of scarce capital

[3] Day, A. C. L., *The Future of Sterling* (Oxford: Clarendon Press, 1954), pp. 8–10.
[4] Shonfield, A., *British Economic Policy since the War* (London: Penguin Books, 1958), p. 218.
[5] Ibid., p. 151.

from home industry. For Shonfield, sterling policy, along with excessive overseas military spending, was evidence of a costly failure on the part of the Conservative government between 1951 and 1957 to grasp Britain's true (reduced) international position.

In 1971 Strange reiterated many of Shonfield's arguments in her critique of the Labour government's sterling policy in the 1960s. Like Shonfield, she related the promotion of sterling as an international currency to misguided efforts to prolong the United Kingdom's great power status from the late nineteenth century, stressing that 'it has been the misfortune of British policy since the Second World War to have inherited from this distant imperial hey-day, associated ideas which no longer apply to Britain's changed situation, but have nevertheless proved remarkably hard to shed or modify'.[6] In an article published the same year as her seminal book she blamed the decline of Britain's economic power on successive governments 'clinging to traditional roles outside Europe, as world policeman and as universal financial uncle, and for putting before other considerations and objectives the prestige of sterling and the solidarity of the sterling area as the main prop of the commonwealth system'.[7] The inducements necessary to encourage countries to hold sterling had become a burden on the British economy through defence spending, high interest rates and excessive outward flows of investment. This interpretation of UK sterling policy has become entrenched in the post-war economic history of Britain.[8] For example, James repeats Strange's view of sterling policy as 'a British attempt to reassert the nineteenth-century role of world banker that it could in reality no longer afford'.[9] Cain and Hopkins describe the British authorities as 'intent upon restoring sterling to its rightful position in the world' and say that 'international economic policy [in the 1950s] was largely decided by gentlemen who clearly believed that re-establishing sterling internationally was more important' than export competitiveness or the fate of the empire.[10] Sir Alec Cairncross, a senior Treasury official during the 1960s and 1970s, is one of the few historians to emphasise the external constraints on British

[6] Strange, S., *Sterling and British Policy: A Political Study of an International Currency in Decline* (Oxford: Oxford University Press, 1971), p. 47.

[7] Strange, S., 'Sterling and British policy: a political view', *International Affairs*, 47(2), 1971, pp. 302–15, p. 304.

[8] Alford, B., *Britain in the World Economy since 1880* (London: Longman, 1996); Burk, K., 'Introduction', in K. Burk (ed.), *The British Isles since 1945* (Oxford: Oxford University Press, 2003), pp. 1–17, p. 6.

[9] James, H., *International Monetary Cooperation since Bretton Woods* (Oxford: Oxford University Press, 1996), p. 100.

[10] Cain, P., and A. J. Hopkins, *British Imperialism: Crisis and Reconstruction 1914–1990* (London: Longman, 1993), p. 274.

policy options, observing (without elaboration) that 'sterling remained a reserve currency largely because Britain was in no position to liquidate the balances in which other countries' reserves were held'.[11]

Whether or not sterling policy drained the domestic economy of vigour is not the main focus of this book. I have argued elsewhere that this case is overstated for the 1950s; investment in the sterling area was more a trickle than a flood, short-term sterling liabilities were not very liquid and the sterling area was not a safe market that postponed innovation in uncompetitive British industry.[12] Total net long-term capital flows never exceeded an amount equivalent to 1.6 per cent of gross domestic product (GDP) in the 1950s, and the problem for the British economy was not the amount of investment but the fact that the impact of investment on growth was much weaker than most of the United Kingdom's competitors.[13] Secondly, capital flows to the sterling area were restricted. Until 1952 all overseas investment was subject to the condition that it must promise to assist the UK balance of payments, and until 1954 sterling area governments could float loans only for specific development projects. Access to the London market, however, depended on the appetite for such loans in London (which declined) and the cost of borrowing (which increased). About one-quarter of private UK investment in the sterling area was for oil exploitation, and a significant additional portion was for mining, which promised to deliver scarce raw materials to the British economy.[14] It would be hard to make a case that restricting this category of investment would have benefited British industry. Reddaway has shown that direct investment in the sterling area generated substantial exports (on average £47 for every £100 invested for five years).[15]

Certainly, the pegged exchange rate system of the 1950s and 1960s constrained domestic economic sovereignty; this is the essence of a fixed exchange rate system. That this inflexible system struggled to adapt to the adjustments that were necessary after the end of the Second World War and the transition of global economic power to the United States and then western Europe is also uncontroversial. Rather than looking at the impact of sterling's international role, however, this book focuses on

[11] Cairncross, A. K., *The British Economy since 1945: Economic Policy and Performance, 1945–1995*, 2nd edn. (Oxford: Blackwell, 1995), p. 320.

[12] Schenk, C. R., *Britain and the Sterling Area: From Devaluation to Convertibility in the 1950s* (London: Routledge, 1994).

[13] Ibid., pp. 98–101.

[14] Ibid., pp. 96–7.

[15] Reddaway, W. B., *Effects of UK Direct Investment Overseas: Final Report* (Cambridge: Cambridge University Press, 1968).

the reasons why sterling persisted as an international currency, outliving the repeated predictions of its imminent demise so that, even in the late 1970s, its use as a reserve currency was still considered a multilateral responsibility that attracted financial support from the United States and western Europe. We need surely to look beyond lingering delusions of imperial grandeur for an explanation, and to view sterling in a wider context than just British policy.

Within the international monetary system, sterling was embedded in broader global and regional economic and political relations, with the result that the options available to UK governments were more complex than is usually acknowledged. Existing studies have noted this wider context, but none has fully integrated these global aspects using archival sources. The evidence suggests the need for a re-examination of the constraints on British policy and a reassessment of the common characterisation of it as an incompetent failure. An earlier devaluation and/or the elimination of sterling as a reserve or transactions currency were not easy solutions to the problem as it had emerged by the 1950s. The advent of a floating exchange rate in the 1970s and 1980s did not deliver the freedom from balance of payments constraints promised by critics of the pegged rate, nor did it rid the exchange rate of its political and economic importance. With simple unilateral fixes beyond the reach of successive governments they undertook a multilateral negotiated approach to sterling's international role.

Rather than cooperation, British governments could have opted unilaterally for a 'Little Britain' solution, defaulting on debt and retreating to national autarky, but there are few who would have proposed this as a realistic alternative.[16] British prosperity depends on international trade, and, in the era of the 'long boom' from 1955 to 1973, opting out of the international economic system would have been costly indeed. Instead, governments sought to internationalise the resolution of the vulnerabilities posed by sterling's use overseas by shifting some of the burden to other countries. They identified the international use of sterling as part of the wider global monetary system in which all major trading states had a vested interest. This strategy did involve a sacrifice in terms of national policy sovereignty, particularly to the International Monetary Fund (IMF) but also in other forums such as the European Economic Community (EEC), but it was clearly a better alternative than the other extreme. To understand the management of sterling's retreat, therefore, it is important to view it in the context of the evolution of the international monetary system in which it operated.

[16] This approach was supported by Tony Benn, for example.

Evolution of the international monetary system

The history of the international economy in the twentieth century can be interpreted in a stylised way through the framework of the Holy Grail of international economics; to achieve the impossible trinity of stable exchange rates, free capital flows and monetary independence.[17] The premise of the trilemma is as follows

(a) To keep exchange rates pegged with free international capital flows, governments must coordinate their economic policies with those of other countries or risk persistent and unsupportable imbalances in the balance of payments.
(b) If pegged exchange rates are abandoned, then countries can pursue independent national policies in an open economy.

In essence, only two out of the three options are sustainable: fixed exchange rates, policy sovereignty, free capital flows.

For the forty years before the First World War the international economy operated under the gold standard, which delivered stable exchange rates and rising volumes of world trade and investment. This is often characterised as the first era of globalisation, although the breadth of international transactions was narrower than during the second era a century later.[18] After the end of the nineteenth century

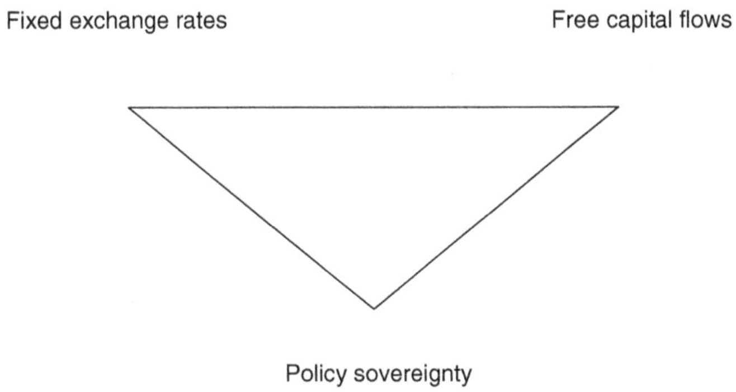

Figure 1.1 Policy trilemma

[17] Obstfeld, M., and A. Taylor, *Global Capital Markets: Integration, Crisis and Growth* (Cambridge: Cambridge University Press, 2004); Obstfeld, M., and K. Rogoff, 'The mirage of fixed exchange rates', *Journal of Economic Perspectives*, 9(4), 1995, pp. 73–96.

[18] Bordo, M. D., B. Eichengreen and D. Irwin, *Is Globalization Today Really Different than Globalization a Hundred Years Ago?*, Working Paper no. 7159 (Cambridge, MA: NBER, 1999).

and the horrors of the First World War, popular expectations of the government's responsibility for domestic economic affairs increased, and domestic monetary policy sovereignty gained priority. This left the choice between stable exchange rates and free capital flows. The perils of making the wrong choice about international monetary policy were made clear in the attempt to re-establish a fixed exchange rate system through the interwar gold exchange standard. There were a variety of problems with this system that drove it apart, including inappropriate exchange rates that necessitated pro-cyclical contractionary policies in the United Kingdom. War debt and reparations weakened the international financial system, and damaging international short-term capital flows culminated in the international financial crisis of 1931 that heralded the end of the gold standard, widely fluctuating nominal exchange rates and competitive devaluations. The downward spiral of international trade and payments as countries resorted to economic nationalism in an attempt to insulate their domestic economies from this unprecedented international crisis was symptomatic of the Great Depression of the 1930s.

During the Second World War the United States and the United Kingdom together designed a system to avoid a repeat of the failures of the 1919 Versailles peace settlement and the ensuing economic disasters of the interwar period. To this end, they sought to ensure multilateral trade and pegged exchange rates, combined with controls on capital flows to deliver national policy sovereignty. This reflected the contemporary view that the problems of the 1930s were caused by open capital markets that left countries vulnerable to contagion due to fickle and irrational investors with short-term horizons. As well as increasing risk in international trade and payments (thereby inhibiting growth), the consensus was that floating exchange rates undermined international political and economic cohesion by contributing to excessive nationalism. The response of states to the crisis in the 1930s had been to close borders to trade as well as capital, which prolonged and spread the Great Depression. The focus of policy-makers after the war, therefore, was on the multilateral liberalisation of international trade combined with a framework of stable exchange rates policed by the new International Monetary Fund. To this end, the IMF also provided short-term support for temporary disequilibria to give governments the confidence to free up trade and make their currencies convertible for current account transactions at a pegged exchange rate. This solution emphasised the right of states to pursue national policies of expansion to ensure the prosperity of their beleaguered populations. Freedom to invest overseas, particularly in the short term, was considered a small price to pay for the achievement of these cornerstones of growth and international harmony after decades of depression and war.

In the 1950s, therefore, free capital flows were sacrificed in order to gain exchange rate stability and policy sovereignty. The Bretton Woods institutions advocated current account currency convertibility to facilitate multilateral trade, but given the imbalance in the global economy after the war even this could not be achieved until the end of 1958. With the help of US aid, a restocking boom associated with the Korean War, and regional payments systems, national economies eventually recovered and world trade increased in volume. Regional payments solutions replaced the global multilateralism that the Bretton Woods system had been supposed to create. Britain coordinated the sterling area group of countries, which pegged their exchange rates to sterling, held sterling as their main foreign exchange reserve, imposed common exchange control against the rest of the world and enjoyed relatively unfettered capital flows from London.[19] Western European states (including the United Kingdom) devised the European Payments Union (EPU) in 1950, with US support, to allow the multilateral settlement of trade and payments among themselves before full current account convertibility.[20] International economic diplomacy became focused on visible trade, and this yielded spectacular results in the reduction of quantitative restrictions and tariffs, particularly in western Europe with the development of the European Coal and Steel Community (ECSC), and then the EEC in 1957, and also through successive rounds of the General Agreement on Tariffs and Trade (GATT).[21]

Current account convertibility was finally introduced at the end of the 1950s, while capital flows continued to be controlled. As the 1960s progressed, flows of long-term capital were liberalised in recognition of the fact that foreign direct investment (FDI) is conducive to growth and that investment for development is beneficial for the international economy as a whole.[22] This was an era that saw the dramatic expansion of multinational companies (particularly from the United States), prompting concerns in France and some less developed countries (LDCs) about

[19] Schenk, *Britain and the Sterling Area*.

[20] Kaplan, J. J., and G. Schleiminger, *The European Payments Union: Financial Diplomacy in the 1950s* (Oxford: Oxford University Press, 1989); Eichengreen, B., *Reconstructing Europe's Trade and Payments: The European Payments Union* (Manchester: Manchester University Press, 1993).

[21] Asbeek Brusse, W., *Tariffs, Trade and European Integration, 1947–1957* (London: Macmillan, 1997); Milward, A. S., *The European Rescue of the Nation-State, 2nd edn.* (London: Routledge, 2000).

[22] The 1960s were designated the first United Nations Development Decade, and the United Nations Conference on Trade and Development (UNCTAD) was founded in 1964.

cultural as well as economic imperialism, but American companies were generally welcomed in their largest target, the United Kingdom.[23] The combination of trade liberalisation and the expansion of long term investment delivered the 'long boom' for industrialised countries. Organisation for Economic Co-operation and Development (OECD) economies grew at an annual average rate of 5.4 per cent from 1958 to 1971. Almost as soon as the fixed exchange rate system devised at Bretton Woods started to work as planned (i.e. with current account convertibility and relatively free trade), however, it began to fall apart. From 1960 the United States and the United Kingdom both began to run persistent current account deficits while West Germany (the Federal Republic) ran surpluses, bringing pegged exchange rates into doubt and drawing currency speculators into a one-sided sure bet.

Meanwhile, financial innovation allowed short-term capital flows to evade the control of regulators, undermining the post-war solution to the trilemma. Although Obstfeld and Taylor use empirical tests on interest rates to conclude that capital controls in the Bretton Woods era were effective in isolating national capital markets, the rise of offshore markets infringed on national policy sovereignty as the decade progressed.[24] The offshore US dollar market (the Eurodollar market) grew rapidly in response to the increasing fragility of the pegged exchange rate system and the chronic imbalance between deficit and surplus countries. Freer capital flows left governments with the remaining choice in the trilemma: between monetary independence or fixed exchange rates. Under the pegged exchange rate system only the United States, as the anchor, could pursue an independent monetary policy, and other countries became increasingly dissatisfied with the sacrifices they had to make to retain their dollar exchange rate. The growing unease with the status quo was intensified by the United States' expensive involvement in the unpopular Vietnam War, which, combined with domestic expansion, contributed to the chronic balance of payments deficit and exported inflationary pressure. Unable to contract the domestic economy for political reasons and unable to control overseas expenditure for strategic reasons, the Americans restricted outflows of long- and short-term capital, relying on the offshore dollar market to meet the capital needs of US multinational corporations (MNCs) abroad. The tension between surplus and deficit countries eventually provoked a crisis, in which stable exchange rates between the United States and western Europe were sacrificed so

[23] The annual flow rose from $3 billion in 1960 to $7.6 billion in 1970.

[24] Obstfeld and Taylor, *Global Capital Markets*, ch. 5.

as to restore policy independence and to adjust to freer capital flows through the 1970s and 1980s.

Because of the high degree of openness between their economies, western European countries meanwhile moved unsteadily towards the sacrifice of domestic policy sovereignty among themselves in order to retain stable exchange rates. Their solution to the trilemma was different from that of the United States and the United Kingdom, but it was not achieved until almost thirty years years after the collapse of Bretton Woods. Institutional obstacles to a single European financial market persisted, however, and exchange controls were only fully abandoned by the core members of the European Union (EU) in 1990. The commitment first to the exchange rate mechanism (ERM) and then to the euro as a single currency in the European Union in 1999 reflected the openness between European countries, with the attendant high transactions costs of fluctuating exchange rates. The sacrifice of national sovereignty remains a contested issue in European politics, however. Elsewhere, too, the benefits of stable exchange rates meant that intermediate solutions were sought in an attempt to combine sovereignty with stability.

In the late 1980s and into the 1990s there were renewed efforts to 'square the triangle' through pegged exchange rate systems, currency boards or 'dollarisation' in developing countries and through official intervention to stabilise exchange rates among the major industrial countries, achieved through the Plaza Agreement in 1985 and the Louvre Accord of 1987. Obstfeld has identified seven coordinated interventions by the United States with other central banks with respect to the yen between the beginning of 1993 and the end of 1995.[25] Catte, Galli and Rebecchini identified nineteen such episodes in the seven years 1985 to 1991.[26] In 1997, on the eve of the east Asian financial crisis that erupted that year, the finance ministers of the G7 countries (the seven biggest industrialised economies: the United States, Japan, Germany, France, the United Kingdom, Italy and Canada), noted that 'close monitoring and coordinated responses may be required' to correct misaligned exchange rates, since 'exchange rate misalignments can heighten uncertainty in the global economy and can be detrimental to growth and trade'.[27] At the G7 meeting at the beginning of October 2004 finance ministers used a form of words that has been repeated almost annually since that date, to the effect that 'excess

[25] Obstfeld, M., 'International currency experience: new lessons and lessons relearned', *Brookings Papers on Economic Activity*, 1, 1995, pp. 119–220, pp. 178–82.

[26] Cited in Obstfeld, 'International currency experience', p. 178.

[27] June 1997 report of G7 finance ministers, as quoted in Clarida, R. H., *G3 Exchange Rate Relationships: A Recap of the Record and a Review of Proposals for Change*, Working Paper no. 7434 (Cambridge, MA: NBER, 1999), p. 19.

volatility and disorderly movements in exchange rates are undesirable for economic growth [and we] continue to monitor exchange markets closely and cooperate as appropriate', but they also called for greater exchange rate flexibility for some countries, particularly China, which moved to a more flexible system in July 2005.[28] Meanwhile, from 2002 the US dollar was allowed to decline against most currencies, in its most sustained fall since 1945, but it continued to accumulate in the reserves of surplus countries in Asia.

The role of reserve currencies has again become controversial, as the global imbalance between the United States on the one hand and economies in east Asia on the other generated huge accumulations of US dollars in their reserves, particularly in China and Japan.[29] Since 2001 US current account deficits and budget deficits have been funded by the massive accumulation of dollar liabilities in foreign exchange reserves globally, generating an enormous 'overhang' in terms of the ratio of official liabilities to official assets and giving rise to concern as to the impact on the international financial and monetary system if they were liquidated. This prompted Eichengreen to draw a comparison between the external position of the United States after 2002 with that of the United Kingdom in the 1950s.[30] In both cases the amount of national currency in overseas foreign exchange reserves led to doubts about the ability of the issuing country to sustain their external position and seemed to threaten the stability of the international monetary system.

The shift from sterling to the dollar that occurred during the post-war years offers a few insights into the future of the dollar as a reserve asset. A major reason for diversification away from sterling, in addition to the risk of its external value (which the dollar came to share), was the diversification of trade and national debt portfolios from sterling to the dollar, and then in the 1960s to the Deutschmark and other western European currencies. The pressure for diversification from sterling thus arose from the decline in its use as a commercial currency and the falling share of sovereign debt denominated in sterling as well as worries about its external value. The dollar shares the exchange rate risk but not yet the rapid decline as a unit of account and settlement or as a denominator of foreign debt. In the 1960s there was an obvious alternative to holding

[28] Statement on G7 finance ministers and central bank governors, Washington, DC, 1 October 2004.

[29] Dooley, M. P., D. Folkerts-Landau and P. Garber, 'The revised Bretton Woods system', *International Journal of Finance and Economics*, 9(4), 2004, pp. 307–13. See also the Federal Reserve Bank of San Francisco, *Proceedings*, February 2005, for a group of conference papers on this topic.

[30] Eichengreen, *Sterling's Past, Dollar's Future.*

sterling as a main reserve currency, although doubts about the dollar exchange rate had reduced its attractions by the late 1960s. In the current crisis, the euro may become a viable alternative international reserve to the dollar, but it has limitations, including the depth and liquidity of euro financial markets. Finally, while there are some a priori parallels, the UK situation in the 1950s was not nearly as fragile as that of the United States in the 2000s.

UK current account deficits were nothing like as large in relation to GDP, nor was the governments' budget deficit as large as that of the United States. In 2004 the US current account *deficit* was equivalent to 5.7 per cent of GDP, rising to 6.4 per cent in 2005, whereas in the United Kingdom in the 1950s the current account balance was on average a *surplus* equivalent to 0.8 per cent of GDP. The largest UK current account deficit in the period (during the Korean War bust of 1951) was only 2.1 per cent of GDP. In the 1950s and 1960s the United Kingdom had more influence over the holders of sterling reserves, and the majority of their trade was with Britain since many were colonies. The United States has less influence over the reserves policy of China and Japan and their trade is more diversified. Another key aspect is that the United States has increased its borrowing to fund higher levels of current expenditure, while in the 1950s British external liabilities were stable in nominal terms and fell in real value. With the current account in overall balance during the 1950s, short-term overseas liabilities helped to support British residents' acquisition of longer-term foreign assets through foreign investment. The comparison between the United Kingdom and the United States accentuates how the recent globalisation of the international economy has enhanced the ability to finance internal and external deficits in the longer term, which sustained a much larger global imbalance than in the 1960s.

Britain in the world economy

The evolution of sterling as an international currency was, of course, closely related to Britain's own international economic relations. Currencies perform three main tasks in both the domestic and international context: as medium of exchange, store of value and unit of account. In international terms, sterling developed these roles in the early nineteenth century, when British producers dominated manufacturing trade and services, particularly the financial and commercial services associated with the first era of globalisation. Sterling's international role thus derived originally from Britain's economic might. From 1860 to 1914 60 per cent of world trade was invoiced and settled in sterling even though Britain accounted for only 30 per cent of world trade.[31] In the interwar and post-war periods, however, the international use of sterling was determined by the organisation of the international monetary system and the need for reserve assets denominated in foreign exchange and acceptable currencies for international commerce. Britain's return to the gold standard under the guidance of Winston Churchill in 1925 at the pre-war exchange rate showed the perils of 'overvaluation' and the importance of an appropriate exchange rate for domestic prosperity. The abandonment of the interwar gold standard in 1931 was the first of many blows to British monetary supremacy in the twentieth century, and it ushered in a new framework for sterling's reserve role that reduced it from a global presence to a smaller and clearly identified group of countries known as the sterling bloc, with a core of Commonwealth countries and additional traditional trading partners of the United Kingdom. This group was formalised at the outset of the Second World War by a new exchange control system, which persisted into the post-war years. A similarly narrower approach to international trade focused on preferential tariffs for imperial trade, including the colonies and the Commonwealth.[32]

The centrality of the United Kingdom as a key combatant in the Second World War, leading a collective Commonwealth effort that extended through all major theatres of the war, increased the importance of sterling as a means of settlement during the war years and left a legacy of overseas sterling liabilities that persisted into the post-war period. As part of the effort to restore international monetary stability after the war, the global strategic as well as economic leadership of the United Kingdom and the United States determined that both countries were prominent in planning to reform the system from its ad hoc disorganisation in the interwar period, although the clear trajectory of the United States as the leading post-war industrial economy meant that the US dollar became the foundation of the Bretton Woods fixed exchange rate system devised in 1944. Nevertheless, the financial chaos left over from the war meant that sterling persisted as a major international currency in the context of a widespread belief that global peace and prosperity could best be achieved through maximising the extent of multilateral trade and payments. The Bretton Woods system established foreign exchange in the form of national currencies as the main reserve asset for countries other than the United States, but exchange controls limited the number of national currencies that could be used effectively as an international medium of exchange and

[31] Ibid.

[32] Drummond, I. M., *The Floating Pound and the Sterling Area, 1931–1939* (Cambridge: Cambridge University Press, 1981); McKenzie, F., *Redefining the Bonds of Commonwealth, 1939–1948: The Politics of Preference* (Basingstoke: Palgrave, 2002).

unit of account, and the shortage of dollars meant that sterling retained prominence as a means of settlement.

In the Bretton Woods system, using sterling as an anchor currency was a proxy for pegging to the US dollar since sterling was pegged to the dollar, which was in turn pegged to gold. A sterling anchor had the advantage of not requiring substantial reserves of scarce US dollars for intervention purposes. This benefit was particularly important in the 1950s, when dollars were scarce, but it had receded by the 1960s, when the United States began to run persistent deficits. Paradoxically, of course, this undermined the attractions of the US dollar as an alternative anchor, because the stability of the gold value of the dollar came under suspicion. Thus, as the benefits of the sterling peg eroded, so too did the attractions of the main alternative. West German exchange controls prevented the Deutschmark, as the strongest currency in the system, from becoming a major international currency until the 1970s.

The failure to address the transition from wartime chaos to 'equilibrium' in international payments meant that the Bretton Woods system did not operate as planned. Instead, as noted above, regional solutions to international payments imbalances were necessary, including the European Payments Union and the sterling area. The failure of Bretton Woods, therefore, might be credited with reinvigorating and prolonging the sterling area after the immediate post-war necessities had eroded by the mid-1950s.

Figure 1.2 shows the changing relative size of international trade to the British economy. Total trade (imports plus exports) amounted to about 30 per cent of GDP during the Bretton Woods period, compared to some 50 per cent at the end of the gold standard era. After the first oil crisis and the advent of floating exchange rates in 1973 international trade stabilised at a new higher level of about 40 per cent of GDP. The deficit in merchandise trade was considerably larger in the first half of the century, ranging from 6 to 10 per cent of GDP in the years 1900 to 1918 compared to 0 to 2 per cent of GDP after 1950.

While the value of trade (imports plus exports) relative to British economic activity was relatively stable at some 30 per cent from 1955 to 1973, and again at 40 per cent after the oil price shock of 1973, the steady decline of the United Kingdom's share of global trade is emblematic of Britain's relative economic decline from 1950 to 1974. Figure 1.3 shows this trend and also that, with the outset of the oil crisis and British entry to the EEC, this decline was halted, so that the United Kingdom maintained about 5 per cent of world merchandise trade to the end of the millennium – a remarkable achievement considering the rise of newly industrialising economies in east Asia and South America during these decades. This emphasises that the thirty years after 1945 were clearly critical to the

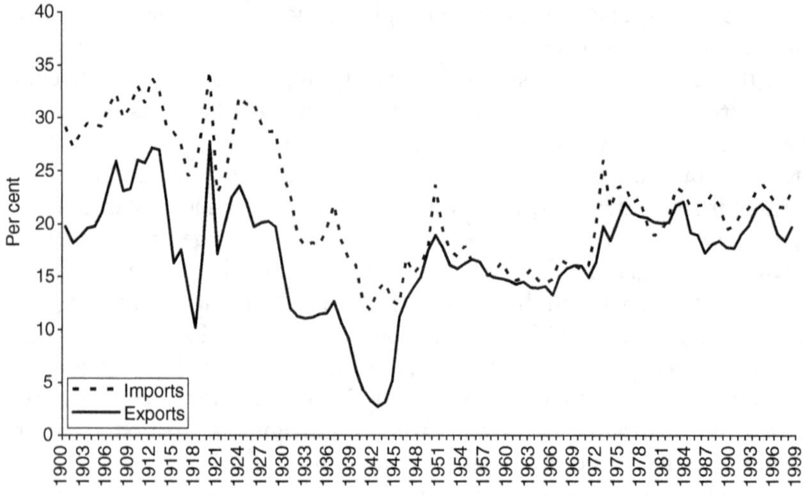

Figure 1.2 Goods trade as a percentage of UK GDP, 1900–99
Source: Mitchell, B. R., *British Historical Statistics*, 2nd edn. (New York: Cambridge University Press, 1988), for 1900–45, then Office for National Statistics (ONS).

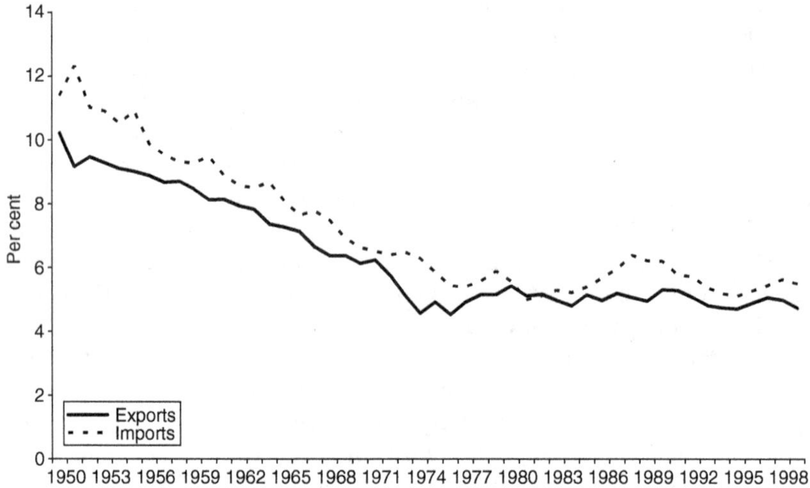

Figure 1.3 UK share of world merchandise trade, 1950–99
Source: UNCTAD.

prolonged transition from economic leadership that mirrored the decline in the prominence of sterling as an international currency.

Figure 1.4 shows the balance of the current account as a percentage of GDP for twelve countries to gauge the relative openness of the British

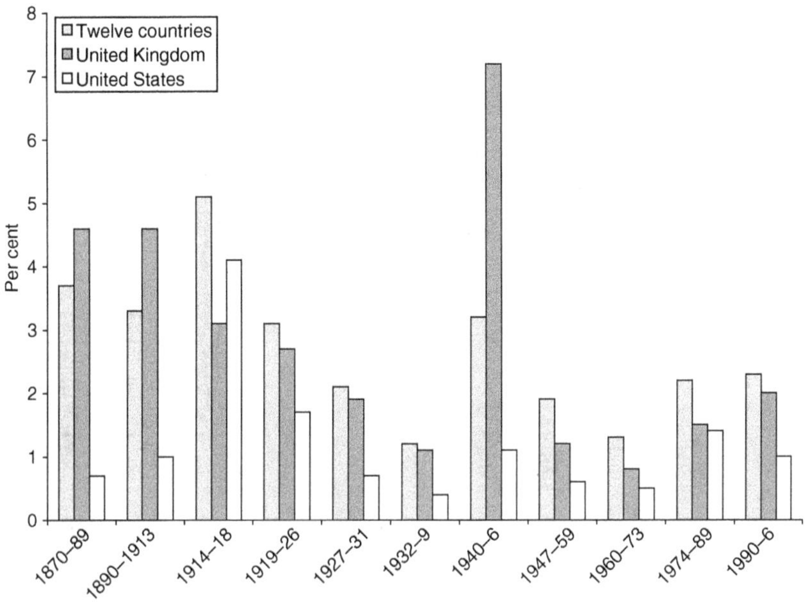

Figure 1.4 Mean absolute value of current account balance as a percentage of GDP, 1870–1996

Note: The twelve countries are Argentina, Australia, Canada, Denmark, France, Germany, Italy, Japan, Norway, Sweden, the United Kingdom and the United States.

Source: Obstfeld, M., 'The global capital market: benefactor or menace?', *Journal of Economic Perspectives*, 12(4), 1988, pp. 9–30.

economy and the capital balance. Net capital flows never returned to the high levels relative to GDP achieved during the gold standard era even during the second globalisation of the 1980s and 1990s. Figure 1.4 also emphasises the relatively closed nature of the US economy and the extraordinary impact of the Second World War on Britain's external position, which is considered in greater detail in chapter 2. Moreover, during the gold standard overseas net capital flows were much higher for the United Kingdom than the other countries on average, but were lower than the average after 1947.

Figure 1.5 shows that during the Bretton Woods era the UK current account was usually in surplus and averaged about 1 per cent of GDP. This ratio increased from 1973 so that the current account was about 1.5 per cent of GDP from 1974 to 2004 and was persistently in deficit, except during the second oil crisis, when North Sea oil generated surpluses.

While the evidence for the United Kingdom's relative decline in international trade during the Bretton Woods era is clear, the way that

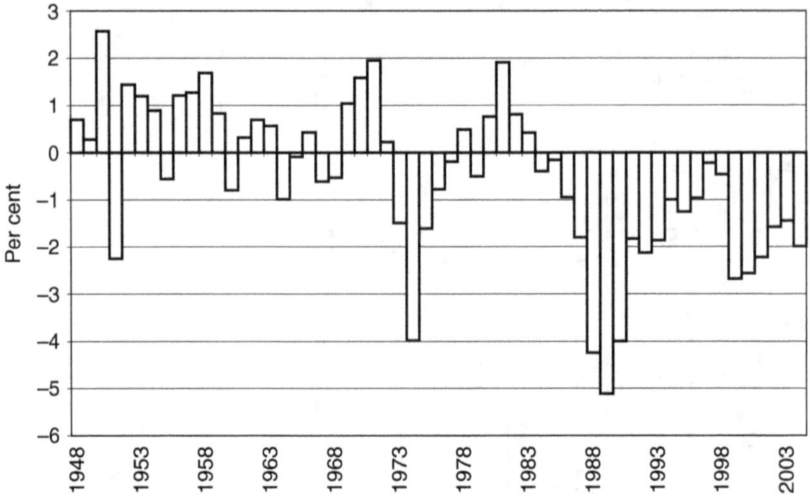

Figure 1.5 UK current account balance as a percentage of GDP, 1948–2004
Source: ONS.

the British economy engaged with international capital flows is quite different. Britain was the major target for US companies, partly because of its advantages in terms of language and culture compared with other European countries. The inflow of US firms was particularly striking in the banking industry, where the culture of the City of London was rudely shaken out of its traditional values by the arrival of the more aggressive and competitive practices of American bankers. By 1971 almost 10 per cent of US outward FDI was in banking and insurance. During the 1950s the value of US FDI in the United Kingdom grew from $542 million to $1.6 billion, and of the 230 new subsidiaries of foreign companies that were opened in Britain 187 (81 per cent) were American.[33] By 1963 it was estimated that foreign companies accounted for about 10 per cent of the net output of British manufacturing.[34] The globalisation of production was sustained over the following decades, with the result that, while the stock of inward FDI in the United Kingdom amounted to about 6.5 per cent of GDP in 1960, it had risen to 27 per cent by the end

[33] Bostock, F., and G. Jones, 'Foreign multinationals in British manufacturing 1850–1962', *Business History*, 36(1), 1994, pp. 89–126.

[34] Steuer, M. D., P. Abell, J. Gennard, M. Perlman, R. Rees, B. Scott and K. F. Wallis, *The Impact of Foreign Direct Investment on the UK* (London: Her Majesty's Stationery Office [HMSO], 1973), p. 189.

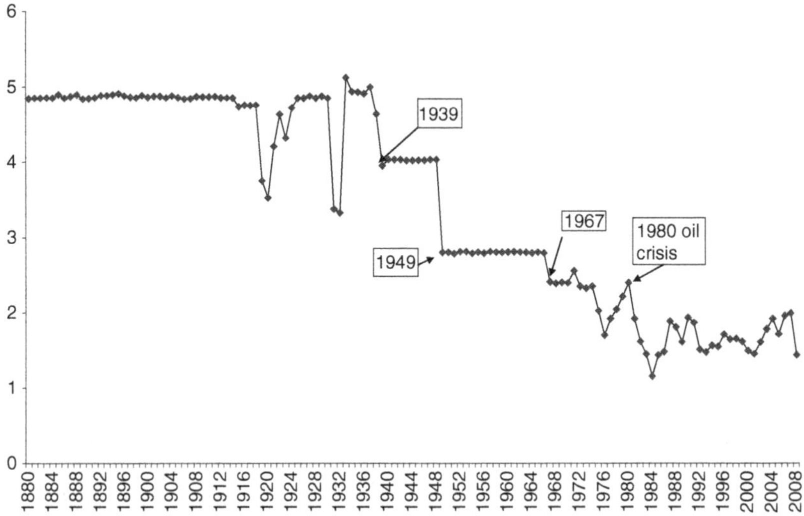

Figure 1.6 US dollar/pound exchange rate, 1880–2008

of 1999.[35] In terms of outward flows, British companies were responsible for about 13 per cent of global FDI in the 1960s, well behind the United States, which was the source of almost two-thirds of world FDI, or $57 billion, from 1960 to 1971. Although the absolute amount of UK FDI was smaller, it amounted to 5 per cent of British gross domestic capital formation on average, compared to only 3.5 per cent for the United States in these years.[36] Britain also had a much higher share of both inward and outward FDI than other European countries and accounted for about 40 per cent of all outward FDI from western Europe in the 1960s. Although no longer at the pinnacle of the international hierarchy, the United Kingdom was clearly still closely linked with the international economy.

Figure 1.6 shows the decline in the nominal dollar exchange rate for sterling, which reflected Britain's declining competitiveness compared with the US economy. The Bretton Woods period was characterised by two major devaluations, in 1949 and 1967, before sterling was floated in June 1972 in advance of the collapse of the pegged exchange rate system

[35] Pain, N., 'The growth and impact of inward investment in the UK: introduction and overview', in N. Pain (ed.), *Inward Investment, Technological Change and Growth* (London: National Institute of Economic and Social Research [NIESR], 2001), pp. 1–33, p. 6.

[36] UN Centre on Transnational Corporations, *Salient Features and Trends in Foreign Direct Investment* (New York: UN, 1983).

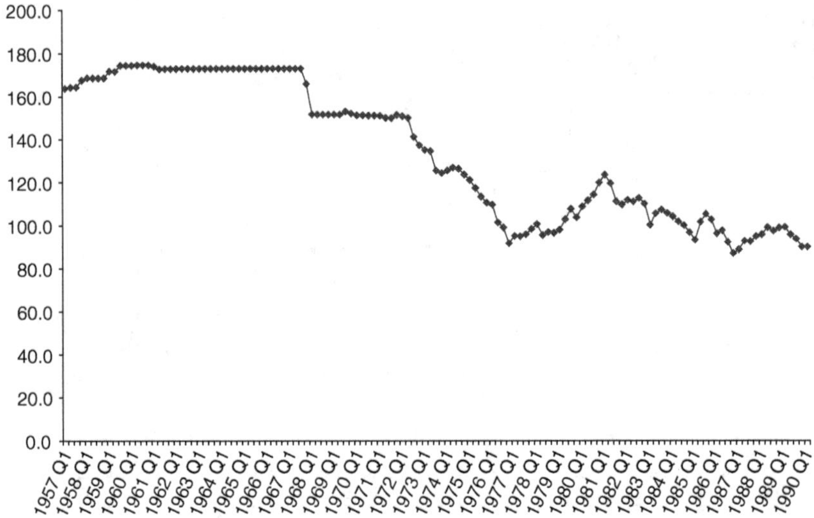

Figure 1.7 Sterling's nominal effective exchange rate (2000 = 100), 1957–90
Source: IMF, *International Financial Statistics.*

in early 1973. The last peak was during the second oil crisis in 1980, before the fall in the oil price and uncontrolled appreciation of the dollar brought the rate back to close to \$1 = £1 in 1984. The appreciation of sterling to \$2 = £1 from 2001 was partially reversed in the third quarter of 2008.

Figure 1.7 shows the nominal effective exchange rate from 1957, which is weighted according to the importance of the United Kingdom's trading partners. After a slight appreciation in the late 1950s the effective rate was stable until the devaluation of 1967. During the early and mid-1970s there was a steady depreciation, which was particularly marked during the crisis of 1976 that prompted a major IMF package, after which the depreciation was halted.

The real effective exchange rate in figure 1.8 gives a better impression of the movements in the exchange rate during the period of floating rates from 1975, when this official series begins. This index is adjusted for inflation and shows the exchange rate against twenty-one currencies weighted by the amount of goods trade with these countries. The appreciation of sterling during the North Sea oil boom in the early 1980s was followed by a generally declining trend through to mid-1996, when sterling began to appreciate against western European currencies and the US dollar.

Figure 1.8 Sterling's real effective exchange rate (1990 = 100), January 1975–May 2006

Measuring sterling's international role

The legal basis for the international use of sterling in the post-war period was exceedingly complex.[37] On the outbreak of war the 1939 Defence (Finance) Regulations established the sterling area group of countries, which were allowed to transfer sterling freely between themselves while imposing strict exchange controls on the transfer of sterling to other countries and strict controls on foreign currency transactions with the rest of the world. The aim was to maximise the international use of sterling while preserving the central reserves. During the post-war period other countries could use sterling only in bilateral transactions with members of the sterling area; they were not free to transfer sterling among themselves because they did not agree to impose common exchange control against the rest of the world. Monetary agreements signed with European states during 1946 and 1947 extended the transferability of currently earned sterling within Europe. This created four areas: the sterling area, the transferable sterling area, the bilateral area and the American or dollar area.

[37] For detail on the complexity, see Economic Cooperation Administration (ECA), *The Sterling Area: An American Analysis* (Washington, DC: ECA, 1952), and Bell, P. W., *The Sterling Area in the Modern World: Internal Mechanism and Cohesion 1946–1952* (Oxford: Oxford University Press, 1956).

In October 1947 the Defence (Finance) Regulations were replaced with the Exchange Control Act, which formalised the rules for the use of sterling. The act identified members of the sterling area as 'scheduled territories', which had the greatest freedom in their use of sterling for commercial and capital transactions and, in return, were expected to impose common exchange controls against payments with the rest of the world. By 1949 this had created 'the largest multilateral trading system in the world', including 606 million people, twelve countries and thirty-seven colonies and protectorates covering all continents of the globe.[38] The sterling area countries included all members of the Commonwealth except for Canada, all British colonies and Iraq, Kuwait, other Persian Gulf sheikhdoms, Libya, Jordan, Burma, Iceland and Ireland. The rest of the world was categorised as 'prescribed territories', and strict controls were imposed to prevent the conversion of sterling to US dollars and other American account currencies. In December 1958 the advent of the formal current account convertibility of sterling to the US dollar pertained only to residents of countries outside the United Kingdom and the sterling area. The distinction between the sterling area and the rest of the world persisted until June 1972.

The most obvious measurement of sterling's international role is how much was held overseas, although this stock measurement does not capture the medium of exchange role. During the post-war decades the nature of international reserves was transformed by the accumulation of foreign exchange assets by countries other than the United States. Gold dominated global liquidity in the 1950s, and foreign exchange reserves exceeded gold holdings for the first time only in 1970. Figure 1.9 includes only foreign exchange so as to show the fall in the relative use of sterling as a reserve asset over the course of the post-war decades.

In 1950 over 55 per cent of foreign exchange reserves were still held in sterling, but this share fell quickly, partly as a result of the Korean War boom of 1951–2 as rearmament pushed more dollars overseas. Sterling then declined at a steady rate for the rest of the decade as countries accumulated dollars, and then recovered slightly after sterling convertibility in 1958. In 1970 there appears to be a sharp increase in other currencies at the expense of sterling, but there are problems here with data coverage that make the pre-1970 and post-1970 figures difficult to compare. What is clear, however, is that by the mid-1970s the position of sterling as a reserve currency had been almost completely replaced by the

[38] Shannon, H. A., 'The British payments and exchange control system', *Quarterly Journal of Economics*, 63(2), 1949, pp. 212–37, pp. 216–17.

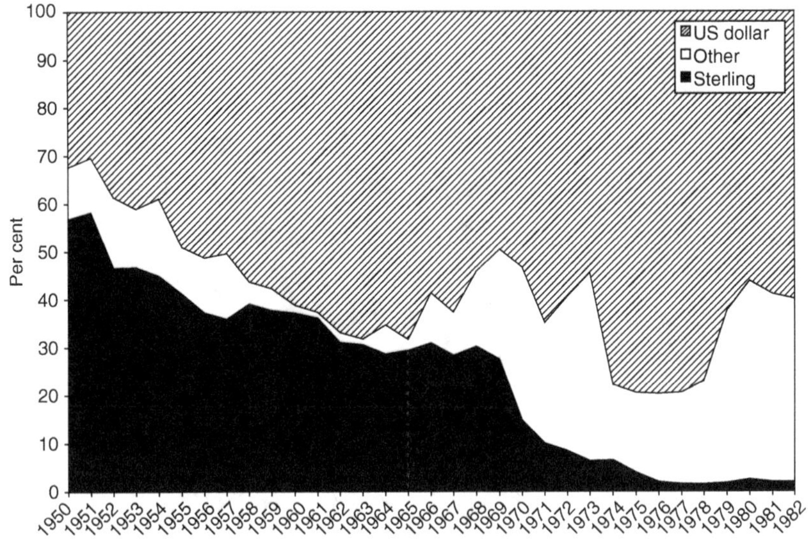

Figure 1.9 Denomination of foreign currency reserves, 1950–82
Source: IMF, *International Financial Statistics.*

US dollar. Thereafter, the Deutschmark eroded the dollar's dominance until the 2000s.

While the relative position of sterling as a reserve currency declined, figure 1.10 shows that the amount of sterling reported by official and private institutions was remarkably steady through the 1950s, rose in the early 1960s but then declined until the raw material boom of the early 1970s.[39]

The patterns of sterling holdings in the sterling area and elsewhere were very different, as can be seen in the following charts. Figure 1.11 shows that official sterling reserves of sterling area countries were fairly stable until the inflationary period at the start of the 1970s, while figure 1.12 shows that other countries ran down their sterling assets almost continuously throughout the post-war decades.

In both cases the nominal value of private holdings increased, although the impact of the devaluation of 1967 is clearly apparent for both groups of states. The overall decline in the real and nominal value of sterling

[39] There is a break in the series in 1962, which accounts for a one-off £97 million drop. The new series excludes some special funds that did not comprise liquid liabilities on the part of the United Kingdom – e.g. pensions funds, sinking funds and holdings of other Commonwealth securities.

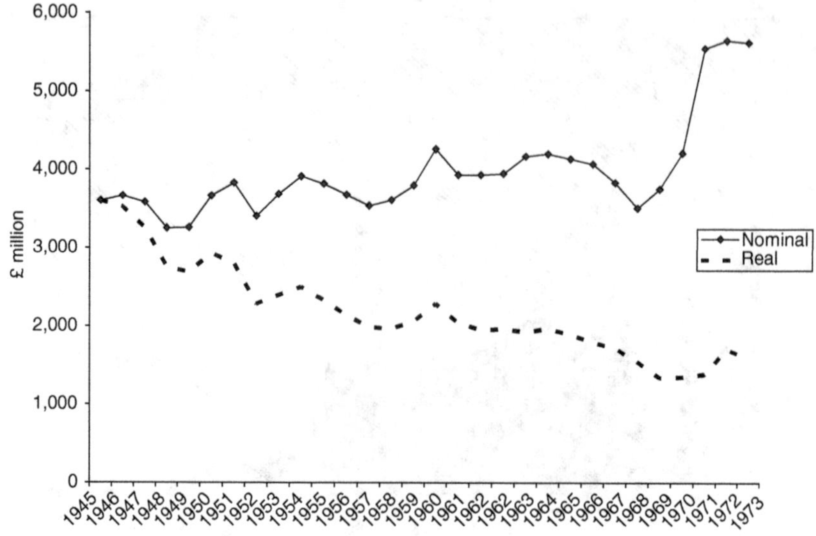

Figure 1.10 Real and nominal values of total sterling liabilities overseas, 1945–73

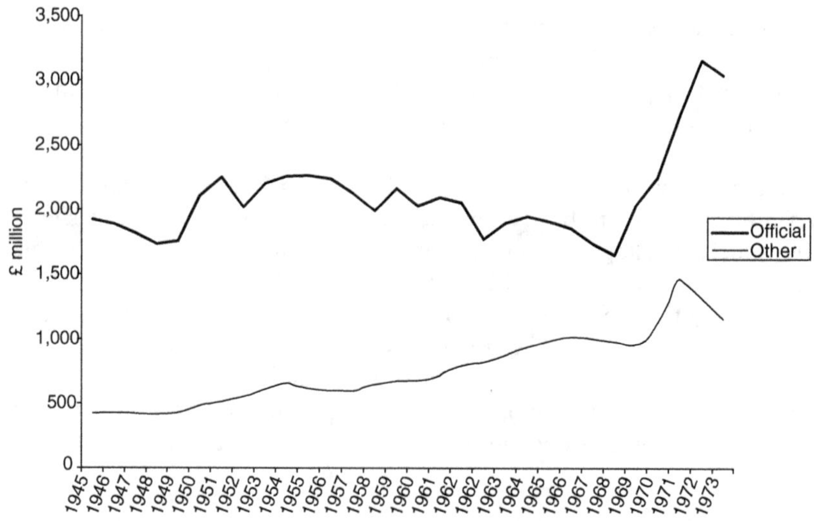

Figure 1.11 Sterling liabilities to the overseas sterling area, 1945–73

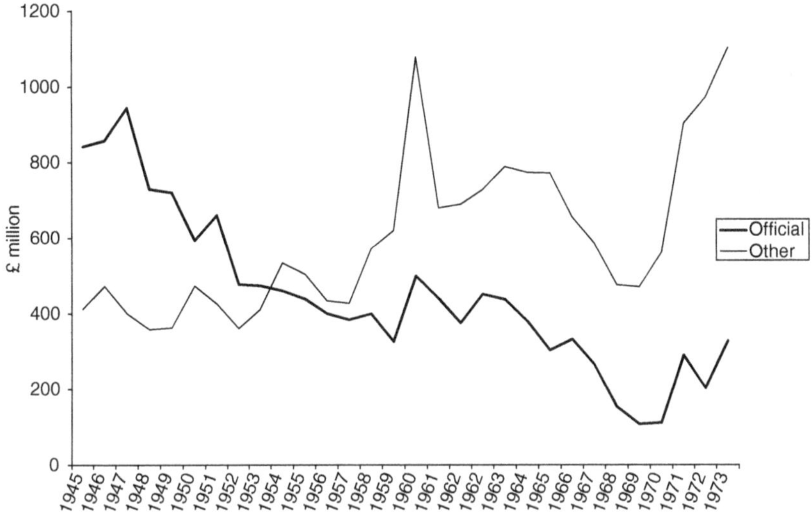

Figure 1.12 Sterling liabilities to countries outside the sterling area, 1945–73

reserves held by central banks and other official organisations from the 1950s is shown in figure 1.13. Figure 1.14 shows that, as a share of world trade, private reserves of sterling were a fairly steady 3 to 4 per cent of world trade but then fell steadily during the confidence crises of the early 1960s.

Within the nominal stability of sterling reserves in the sterling area, figure 1.15 shows that there was a dramatic geographical shift. At the end of the war the Indian subcontinent accounted for 58 per cent of total sterling liabilities to the overseas sterling area (OSA). These assets were accumulated during the war in lieu of payment for Britain's war-related expenditure in the region.[40] Almost immediately, however, the dominance of these balances was challenged by accumulations in Australia and New Zealand and by colonies in the Far East and Africa, so that by the end of 1952 the Indian subcontinent accounted for only a quarter of sterling area balances. From the mid-1950s oil sales in the Middle East and economic growth in east Asia led to a further redistribution of

[40] Tomlinson, B. R., 'Indo-British relations in the post-colonial era: the sterling balances negotiations, 1947–49', *Journal of Imperial and Commonwealth History*, 13(3), 1985, pp. 142–62.

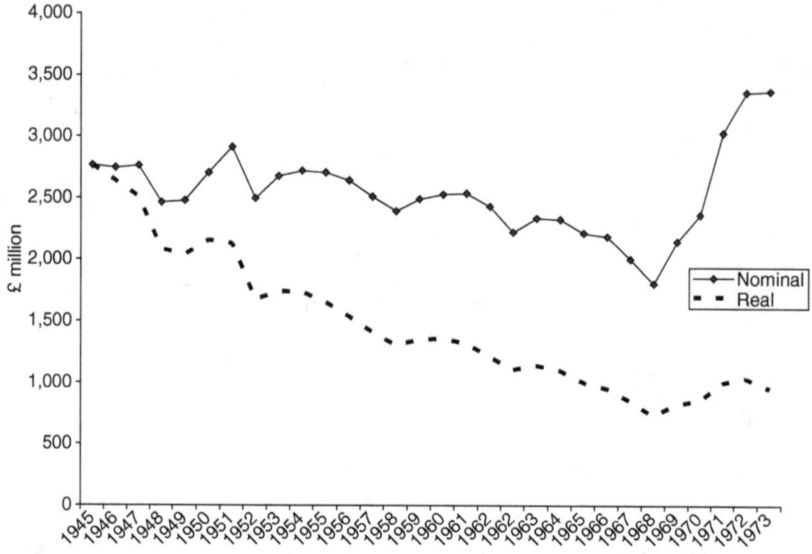

Figure 1.13 Sterling reserves of state institutions, 1945–73

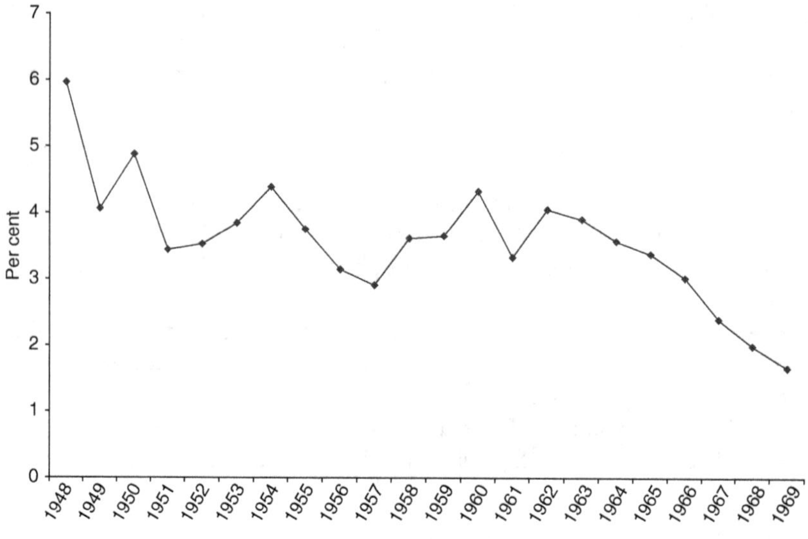

Figure 1.14 UK sterling liabilities to private holders as a percentage of world trade, 1948–69

Source: Treasury Historical Memorandum no. 16, 'Sterling balances since the war', 1972, the National Archives (hereafter TNA) T267/29.

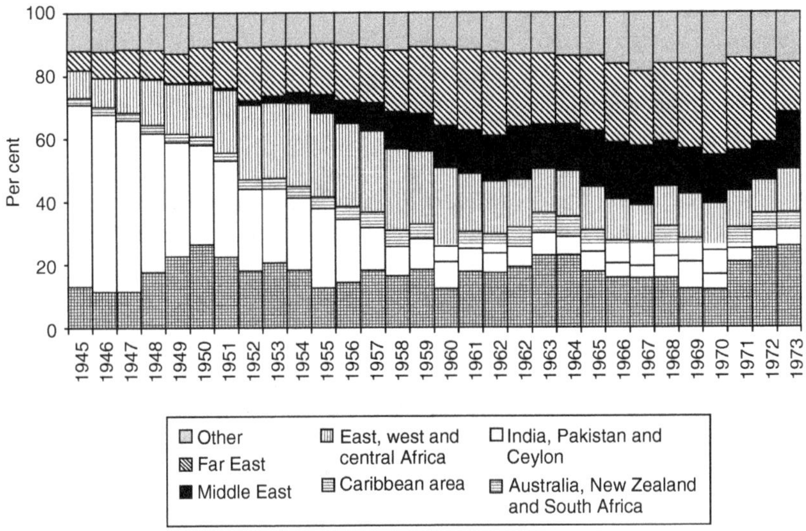

Figure 1.15 Distribution of sterling held by members of the sterling area, 1945–73

Note: There is a slight change in the data definition in 1962. Data are entered for this year both before and after the change.

sterling's reserve role, such that by November 1968 Hong Kong was the largest single official holder of sterling, followed closely by Australia and then Kuwait. After the oil boom of 1973 Nigeria and Saudi Arabia joined the group of major holders of sterling reserves.

These developments all show that the distribution of sterling reserves was profoundly affected by the pattern of economic development on the geographical edges of the United Kingdom's former formal and informal empire. The new distribution of sterling in the 1960s subsequently affected the international political economy of the devaluation and the negotiations to manage the end of sterling's reserve role, which are discussed in chapters 5 and 8. In this way, sterling was affected not only by the changes in the international monetary system but also by the new patterns of global development.

Summary and outline of the book

In 2009 the global reserves system came under increased scrutiny, both as a contributor to the global financial crisis and as a threat to future stability. The US dollar's role as primary international reserve asset combined with the accumulation of substantial reserves in east Asia, it is argued, contributed to the United States' ability to accumulate large balance of payments deficits and cheapened government borrowing. Depressed

US interest rates may have fuelled the consumer and mortgage debt boom. The sustained decline in the value of the US dollar from 2002, meanwhile, prompted a reconsideration of how long it could remain the world's primary reserve asset and if, when and how it might be overtaken by another currency, such as the euro. The prospect of more countries accumulating precautionary reserves in the wake of the crisis, thereby renewing the cycle, has prompted questions about the costs and benefits of issuing an international currency, how international currencies emerge and how they can be replaced without disrupting the global economic system. Joseph Stiglitz put the extreme case at the United Nations (UN) in February 2009:

> The system in which the dollar is the reserve currency is a system that has long been recognized to be unsustainable in the long run. It's a system that is fraying, but as it frays it can contribute a great deal to global instability, and the movement from a dollar to a two-currency or three-currency [system] is a movement that will make things even more unstable.[41]

The Stiglitz panel of experts reported to the UN Commission on 26 March 2009, calling for a new international reserve asset to forestall the instability arising from a transition away from the US dollar as the dominant reserve currency.[42] This view was endorsed by the UN Department of Economic and Social Affairs (DESA) in March 2009 when it called for a system to pool reserves to discourage national precautionary accumulations, and for a reserve asset separate from the US dollar that could be issued in response to the demand for liquidity.[43] The other major contributor to calls to replace the dollar as global reserve currency was Zhou Xiaochuan, governor of the People's Bank of China (PBC), whose huge dollar holdings make this opinion highly influential.[44] These proposals to create a new international reserve asset are similar to

[41] See www.unmultimedia.org/tv/unifeed/detail/10803.html, lecture by J. Stiglitz, 24 February 2009, part of the United Nations University series 'Emerging thinking on global issues', supported by the Office of the President of the 63rd session of the United Nations General Assembly.

[42] This recommendation echoed earlier proposals, such as that by Ocampo, J. A., *The Instability and Inequities of the Global Reserves System*, Department of Economic and Social Affairs Working Paper no. 59 (New York: UN, 2007). See also Stiglitz, J., *Making Globalization Work* (New York: Norton, 2006), ch. 9, for his proposal for 'global greenbacks'.

[43] DESA, 'Background note on the global financial and economic crisis, its impact on development, and how the world should respond' (New York: UN, 2009), interactive thematic dialogue of the UN General Assembly on the 'World financial and economic crisis and its impact on development', 25–7 March 2009, United Nations headquarters.

[44] Zhou, X., 'Reform the international monetary system', 23 March 2009, www.pbc.gov.cn/english//detail.asp?col=6500&ID=178. The recommendations were repeated in the PBC *2009 Financial Stability Report*, published in June 2009.

the suggestions put forward to resolve the challenges of the 1960s, when the system also appeared to be unsustainable on account of persistent American deficits and declining confidence in the dollar. In the 1960s these problems proved intractable, and in the end they were resolved – for a time – by the advent of floating exchange rates (for core global currencies) and financial innovation, which together reduced the need for national precautionary reserves. In the process, the secondary international reserve currency, sterling, was retired. The case of sterling in the post-war decades provides an opportunity to examine the process of a reserve currency in decline.

Although the demand for reserve currencies can be modelled with a range of variables, including issuing-country size, the share of world trade and the return on assets, these exercises have reinforced the importance of institutional rather than economic determinants. The important role of inertia is usually attributed to network externalities that prolong reserve currency status beyond the time predicted by economic fundamentals.[45] These externalities point to the danger of a tipping point or landslide effect should one major creditor switch reserve assets, with the result that the retirement of a reserve currency is likely to be non-linear. Eichengreen and Flandreau cast doubt on the strength of inertia, however, by showing that the dominant reserve currency shifted from sterling to the dollar and back again during the interwar period.[46] The case of sterling after 1945 helps in the exploration of the determinants and timing of shifts from one major reserve currency to another. Like the dollar today, the demise of sterling was widely predicted, but the process proved to be more gradual than was anticipated at the time, and an abrupt collapse, although forecast by many, was avoided. A major source of inertia in this case was institutional support mechanisms, which delayed the tipping point for the pound.

We have seen that, at the end of the Second World War, it was clear that the US dollar would be the dominant international currency in any global economic reconfiguration, and this became the core of the Bretton Woods system. Nevertheless, there continued to be a role for a secondary international currency to be used as a reserve asset, as an anchor currency and as a currency of settlement, because the supply of dollar assets and gold was likely to be restricted in the immediate post-war

[45] Chinn, M., and J. Frankel, 'Why the euro will rival the dollar', *International Finance*, 11(1), 2008, pp. 49–73.

[46] Eichengreen, B., and M. Flandreau, *The Rise and Fall of the Dollar, or When Did the Dollar Replace Sterling as the Leading International Currency?*, Working Paper no. 14154 (Cambridge, MA: NBER, 2008).

period by US balance of payments surpluses. The system therefore assumed a form that some economists suggest is impossible: more than one major reserve currency being able to operate at the same time over a prolonged period.[47] In the 1950s the sterling area (thirty-five countries and colonies pegged to sterling and holding primarily sterling reserves) accounted for a half of world trade, and sterling accounted for more than half the world's foreign exchange reserves. In the early post-war years this share had been even higher; the IMF estimated that official sterling reserves, excluding those held by colonies, were four times the value of official dollar reserves and that by 1947 sterling accounted for about 87 per cent of global foreign exchange reserves.[48] It took ten years following the end of the war (and a 30 per cent devaluation of the pound) before the share of dollar reserves exceeded that of sterling. This rather contradicts Chinn and Frankel's assertion that 'by 1945 the dethroning [of sterling] was complete'.

How do we explain the gradual nature of the decline of sterling – what Krugman refers to as a 'surprising persistence'?[49] Krugman asserts that 'the pre-eminence of sterling and its displacement by the dollar [after 1945] were largely the result of "invisible hand" processes, ratified more than guided by international agreements'.[50] Eichengreen has argued that the main causes were the loyalty of the Commonwealth countries and the unwillingness of any individual holder to 'aggravate the problems of the British economy, on which they depended as an export market'.[51] Closer examination of archival evidence shows that sterling's role was prolonged both by the structure of the international monetary system and by collective global interest in its continuation rather than by loyalty to a former imperial leader. As the market-based network externalities for sterling reserves eroded with the diversification of trade and debt, collective interest in the stability of the international monetary system beyond the sterling area produced a further set of

[47] See, for example, Krugman, P., 'The international role of the dollar: theory and prospect', in J. F. O. Bilson and R. C. Marston (eds.), *Exchange Rate Theory and Practice* (Chicago: University of Chicago Press, 1984), pp. 261–78, p. 261.

[48] IMF Staff, 'International reserves and liquidity: a study by the staff of the International Monetary Fund, 1958', reproduced in Horsefield, J. K. (ed.), *The International Monetary Fund, 1945–1965: Twenty Years of International Monetary Cooperation*, vol. III, *Documents* (Washington, DC: IMF, 1986), p. 371. At this time foreign exchange constituted only about 30 per cent of global reserves, but gold holdings were highly concentrated in the United States, so that foreign exchange made up about a half of global reserves excluding the United States.

[49] Krugman, 'The international role of the dollar', p. 274.

[50] Ibid., p. 261.

[51] Eichengreen, B., *Global Imbalances and the Lessons of Bretton Woods* (Cambridge, MA: MIT Press, 2007), p. 135.

incentives to support the continuation of sterling's international reserve role from the mid-1950s.

This book approaches the management of sterling's retreat as an international currency in a global context. From the 1940s onwards British governments engaged in bilateral and multilateral negotiations in order to gather international support to mitigate the perceived burdens of sterling's international role. The end of the Second World War left a legacy of hostility and suspicion in connection with both the official and private holding of sterling assets overseas, prompting repeated initiatives to reduce them and providing evidence of, at best, an ambiguous commitment to sterling as an international currency even in the 1950s. This contradicts the popular characterisation of British governments as being locked in a pursuit of lost imperial grandeur through the promotion of sterling's international role. Certainly, sterling was an important international currency, particularly in the immediate post-war period, and this delivered a special role to the United Kingdom in international relations. The international status of sterling was more often identified as a drain on British economic power rather than as a potential source of strength, however, and so sterling was often a point of friction rather than common purpose in relations with the Commonwealth, the United States and Europe. The Bank of England sought to restore sterling as a trading and commercial currency in the hopes that this would promote the commercial and financial activities of the City of London, but it was often stymied by the Treasury, and eventually it abandoned the effort as the US dollar gained ascendancy in the 1960s. On the other hand, from the first IMF stand-by in 1956 to the final Bank for International Settlements (BIS) Group Arrangement of 1977, successive British governments were able to use sterling's weakness and the threat this posed to the international monetary system to garner substantial support first to prevent a collapse of sterling's exchange rate and then to share the burden of retiring sterling as a reserve currency. This outcome suggests that the United Kingdom's sterling policy was more strategic and successful than it has hitherto been judged.

The book is structured into three key chronological periods: the post-war settlement and the re-establishment of international economic relations, 1945–59; the critical years of negotiating sterling's decline as a reserve currency, in the 1960s; and finally the persistence of sterling as an international currency, through the 1970s. Chapter 2 establishes the terms on which sterling participated in the international monetary system in the immediate post-war period, examining the years of crisis in which US support was sought to sustain the British economy at the cost of adopting the American vision of sterling's international role.

The disastrous 1947 convertibility attempt led to a reassessment of the Bretton Wood system and the transition to regional payments systems rather than a global one. Chapter 3 looks at how British governments tried to restore their monetary leadership by pushing forward plans for greater convertibility, partly under pressure from sterling area countries. These efforts foundered because of the lack of support from the United States and western Europe, without which the threat that convertibility posed to domestic price and incomes stability was too great. This established the principle that domestic priorities prevailed over the international status of sterling and that managing sterling's role in the international economy required international coordination.

The end of empire in this decade heralded a reorientation both economically and politically, and chapter 4 discusses how sterling fitted into the repeated attempts to join the European Economic Community in the 1960s, when it became clear that British accession to the EEC was predicated on a reduction of sterling's international role. The seminal event of the decade was the 14.3 per cent devaluation in November 1967, and chapter 5 approaches this controversial episode from an international angle, focusing on the role of the United States in the run-up to devaluation and on the intervention of the IMF in the aftermath. Chapter 6 examines the changing role of sterling in the City of London both before and after the devaluation, arguing that new exchange controls deliberately undermined the commercial use of sterling in the 1950s and that financial innovation in the form of the Eurodollar market reduced the interest of the banking community in the international role of sterling. British governments did not support the international commercial use of sterling at the expense of domestic interests. As early as the 1950s many politicians and bureaucrats stopped struggling to keep key currency status, and turned to trying to reduce or even eliminate sterling's role without damaging the international monetary system, British economic prospects or political relations with, first, the Commonwealth and, second, the United States and western Europe. The rhetoric of restoring sterling's traditional global prominence did not disappear, but the policies that were adopted and internal planning show that this goal was no longer consistently pursued in the 1950s. The Bank of England's further priority was to retain the commercial use of sterling as a medium of exchange and unit of account, but this was not supported by the Treasury at the expense of domestic interests, and was quickly overridden by the rise of the US dollar as the currency of the City from the early 1960s.

The 1960s was clearly a critical decade for the decline of sterling, not only because of the reorientation of Britain from Commonwealth to

Europe but because, at the same time, the international monetary system gradually crumbled. The international community proposed, debated and ultimately procrastinated over major reforms, and opted instead for ad hoc 'plumbing' solutions such as the Gold Pool and bilateral currency swaps. From 1965 more concrete proposals for a new reserve asset emerged, which eventually established the special drawing right (SDR) in 1967. Chapter 7 shows that British negotiators were active participants in these often acrimonious discussions, and that they hoped that the problems of sterling would eventually be resolved through these global efforts to replace key currencies and by persuading other industrialised countries that it was in their interests to support the elimination of sterling as a reserve asset.

While the plans for longer-term reform were stalled the perceived importance of sterling to the stability of the international monetary system resulted in repeated credit arrangements among G10 central banks to manage the retreat of sterling from its role as a reserve currency. Chapter 8 shows how, from 1968, this support was predicated on formal agreements with official overseas holders of sterling that controlled the diversification of their reserves even when the pegged exchange rate system was abandoned. The end of the Bretton Woods system, discussed in chapter 9, was prolonged and messy, particularly for sterling, which floated in advance of the rest of the developed world. The enthusiasm for pegged exchange rates within western Europe on the one hand and for floating rates in the United States and the United Kingdom on the other was clearly revealed. The international status of sterling was still strong enough to distinguish the United Kingdom from its European partners in their quest for monetary integration from 1969. Chapter 10 shows how the floating exchange rate regime of the 1970s and the commodity booms of these years changed the international role of sterling and how a final G10 central bank support package aimed at completing sterling's retreat was an integral part of the much more popularly discussed 1976 IMF rescue package. Chapter 11 discusses the brief resurgence of sterling as a petrocurrency in the wake of the second fuel crisis in the 1980s and sterling's role in Britain's troubled relationship with western Europe during the 1980s until the crisis of 1992. A final chapter concludes.

Part I

Reconstructing the International Monetary System 1945–1959

Planning during the Second World War for the organisation of the international monetary system helped to identify the key challenges that would face sterling at the end of hostilities. The accumulation of sterling debt and the increasing influence of the United States, with the emphasis on multilateral non-discriminatory trade, had a profound impact on sterling's role as an international currency. The next two chapters discuss the role that sterling played in the international monetary system and how it evolved during the prolonged rebuilding of the international monetary system from 1945 to 1959. These years were crucial to the retreat of sterling as an international commercial currency, and this was also the period when various solutions were proposed to end sterling's international reserve function. Although not publicly stated, these policies revealed that ministers and officials viewed sterling's international role with deep distrust, leading to various plans to curtail both its private and its official international functions.

2 The post-war international monetary system 1945–1950

Much of the terminology and discourse relating to sterling throughout the post-war period was forged during the crisis years of the 1940s. The 'overhang' of overseas sterling liabilities over assets was clearly identified in wartime planning to reconstruct the international economy once hostilities had ended. The high profile that Britain's wartime debts developed in the public and government psyche in the 1940s made it difficult to recognise that the international use of sterling in the 1950s was fundamentally different from that in the immediate post-war period. They were not referred to as 'war debts' but, rather ambiguously, as sterling balances, partly no doubt because of the bitter memories of the interwar war debt debacle and the agreement between the United States and the United Kingdom in 1941 not to burden another peace with such a network of liabilities. Nevertheless, Britain had offered these government securities in part-payment for wartime expenditure. As a result, there is a surprising continuity in the identification of sterling's weaknesses from the 1940s through to the 1970s, despite fundamental changes both in the international monetary system in which sterling operated and in the distribution of sterling holdings internationally. In these crucial years the post-war international monetary system was reformed after the failed attempt at sterling convertibility in 1947 postponed global multilateralism for a further eleven years. The exchange controls imposed subsequently in 1947 established the legal framework for the post-war sterling area. This chapter reviews the post-war settlement and identifies the key features that laid the foundations for the evolution of sterling's international role over the next thirty years.

The post-war settlement

If ever there was a chance to shape the role that sterling was to play in the international economy under the Bretton Woods system it was, arguably, in the chaos and repeated crises of the late 1940s. The United Kingdom emerged from the war victorious but bankrupt. Rather than capitalising on this weakness to divest itself of wartime burdens, British governments chose to struggle through with short-term support. The international role of sterling as a secondary global reserve was an important element of this strategy, although there was a lack of clear thinking about how sterling would regain its previous usefulness given the dramatic changes in the British economy and in the international economic system.

The most immediate issue, which had been recognised as a looming problem during the war, was the accumulation of sterling assets by overseas countries, mainly in the British Empire and Commonwealth, but also in South America and Europe. These liabilities were well in excess of the foreign exchange assets that could be used immediately to liquidate them. Nor was the British economy in a position to produce enough exports for creditors to spend them. In order for sterling to regain its international role in the post-war period, some solution needed to be arranged for these wartime debts to allow greater convertibility on the current account.

Table 2.1 shows the distribution of the wartime balances accumulated as of the end of 1945. Almost 84 per cent of the liabilities were to sterling area countries as defined at the time, although Egypt and Palestine were excluded from the sterling area in 1946, reducing the sterling area share to 69 per cent. The most outstanding feature of the table is the dominance of India (pre-partition) as the major creditor. Among non-sterling area (NSA) countries, the largest creditor was Argentina (with assets of £105 million), which had been an important source of wartime food imports. Lengthy bilateral negotiations with Argentina concluded with a transfer of British assets (mainly railway) against wartime sterling liabilities. The case of India was more complicated, since a formal agreement for burden sharing had been negotiated with the colony in 1940, under which India paid for its own defence and the United Kingdom met capital costs for Indian forces overseas. Under this agreement, India, a poor colony, spent £1,450 million on the war effort out of its own resources, or more than a half of the total war expenditure in the colony.[1] Britain's share ballooned beyond what had been contemplated in 1940 once the theatre of the war spread to east and south-east Asia. Egypt had more sterling in private hands than many other holders, and it was believed that Egyptians had benefited more from charging higher prices for their sales to the United Kingdom. This supported the case for the cancellation of some of the assets as a contribution to the collective war

[1] Treasury Historical Memorandum no. 16, TNA T267/29.

Table 2.1 *Distribution of gross sterling liabilities, December 1945*

	Amount(£ million)	Percentage of total gross liabilities
India/Pakistan	1,300	36.91
Eire	190	5.39
Australia	110	3.12
New Zealand	80	2.27
Ceylon	70	1.99
South Africa	70	1.99
Burma	25	0.71
Colonies	515	14.62
Egypt/Sudan	400	11.36
Palestine/Trans-Jordan	120	3.41
Iraq	70	1.99
Argentina	105	2.98
Norway	80	2.27
Brazil	35	0.99
Sweden	30	0.85
Subtotal: 15 holders	3,200	90.86
Total gross liabilities	3,522	100.0
Total OSA as of end 1945	2,950	83.76

Note: Egypt/Sudan left the OSA in July 1946, Palestine/Trans-Jordan in February 1948 and Iraq in 1959. The figures differ slightly from the Bank of England regional series.
Source: Treasury Historical Memorandum no. 16, 'Sterling balances since the war', TNA T267/29, 1972.

effort. Dealing with India, however, was clearly the crucial element in any settlement of the sterling balances.

A wholesale unilateral cancellation of sterling war debts was never seriously considered. This would have threatened to freeze international trade, as well as provoking insurmountable political conflict with creditors overseas and attracting criticism at home. Unilaterally dishonouring these debts would undermine the prospects for future borrowing as well as undermining Britain's strategic and moral leadership of the Commonwealth at a time of decolonisation in India, a strategically important colony. The assets had been accumulated in a variety of ways and through a variety of institutional arrangements, which complicated the application of equal treatment. Many had been accumulated by very poor developing economies in the British Empire, to which successive British governments and the public felt a moral obligation. As the official historian of the Bank of England put it in mixed metaphors, 'The Bank did not seriously entertain the idea that this entire living structure should somehow be put into an abrupt receivership.'[2] To the extent that the debts could be considered the outcome of a common war effort, however, it seemed reasonable to expect some multilateral support for repaying them and some cancellation from richer creditors. The approach of the British authorities was clearly to try to reduce their liabilities within a framework of 'business as usual' in order to retain the United Kingdom's creditworthiness, in political as well as economic terms.

The threat the debts posed to achieving the post-war goals of multilateral trade and payments suggested that they could logically be linked to the broader post-war settlement that had been agreed between the United States and the United Kingdom in 1942. A solution to the liquidation of these debts was part of the wartime planning for rebuilding the international monetary system. John Maynard Keynes' plan for an International Clearing Union (ICU) in 1942 drew attention to the difficulties that 'abnormal balances' would pose during the transition period, and suggested that the ICU should carry the burden of allowing these balances to be liquid and convertible.[3] On the American side, Harry D. White's plan more boldly included extended reference to this problem, noting that '[t]he unblocking of these sterling funds is highly to be desired. Probably, no single action would do more to stimulate world trade, prevent pressure on numerous exchanges, and reduce the probability of widespread depreciation of currencies.'[4] White developed transitional arrangements for his Stabilization Fund to buy part of the wartime sterling balances in order to provide immediate liquidity. The United Kingdom would pay 1 per cent interest and repay 80 per cent of the principal over twenty years, starting after three years. By June 1943, on the eve of meetings in Washington, Keynes became worried that the size of the wartime balances would swamp the quotas being discussed, but he still supported White's plans.[5]

[2] Fforde, J. S., *The Bank of England and Public Policy, 1941–1958* (Cambridge: Cambridge University Press, 1982).

[3] Proposals for an International Clearing Union, April 1943, paragraph 34; in Horsefield, *The International Monetary Fund, 1945–1965*, vol. III, p. 32. Lord Keynes added this to the ICU plan after reading Harry D. White's proposals.

[4] Preliminary draft proposal for a UN Stabilization Fund and a Bank for Reconstruction and Development of the United and Associated Nations, April 1942; in Horsefield, *The International Monetary Fund, 1945–1965*, vol. III, p. 55. The proposals were also included in the final draft discussed by the US Treasury in July 1943.

[5] Letter from Keynes to Sir David Waley, 22 June 1943; in Moggridge, D. E. (ed.), *The Collected Writings of John Maynard Keynes*, vol. XXV (Cambridge: Cambridge University Press, 1971), pp. 305–7. This document is also cited in Horsefield, J. K., *The International Monetary Fund, 1945–1965: Twenty Years of International Monetary Cooperation*, vol. I, *Chronicle* (Washington, DC: IMF, 1986), p. 52.

Back in London, the Cabinet disagreed and wanted the wartime accumulations dealt with separately, perhaps in the hopes of a better settlement and also in view of the damage that might be done to the international reputation of sterling as an international currency if all the balances were blocked. The Bank of England was particularly vehement that the wartime balances could not be blocked wholesale but, rather, had to be dealt with in bilateral negotiations with the holders according to prevailing economic and financial circumstances.[6] The Bank hoped to avoid relying on US assistance and instead advocated a programme of reinforcing the sterling area into a more formal bloc and pursuing external balance through austerity – what Keynes described as 'winning the war and putting on a hair shirt'.[7] The Washington delegation discussing these affairs in September 1943 was advised 'to go slow until we know more precisely what the financial conditions of the post-war period would be'.[8] The White proposals did not then appear in the first draft of the joint statement by the United States and United Kingdom, dating from October 1943. By January 1944 both sides had formally agreed that the resources of the Fund were explicitly not to be used for the post-war transition and that the goal was the convertibility of currently earned currencies only. Wartime debts were not included in the Joint Statement of Experts that formed the basis of the Bretton Woods negotiations in July 1944.

The Egyptian and Indian delegations to the Bretton Woods conference (as the two largest creditors) fought hard to have some transitional funding for the sterling balances included in article I of the IMF articles of agreement. A. D. Shroff, of the Indian delegation, made a particularly impassioned plea that the IMF should take over a proportion of India's sterling balances for conversion to other foreign currencies in order for India to fulfil its development ambitions.[9] The United Kingdom, United States and France all protested that this issue was 'not appropriate for the operations of the Fund' and the proposal was summarily rejected.[10] Pressnell relates the importance of the 'Keynes pledge' on 10 July, which

[6] Note by Sir Wilfred Eady, 19 January 1944; in Moggridge, *The Collected Writings of John Maynard Keynes*, vol. XXV, pp. 395–8. See also Fforde, *The Bank of England*, ch. 3.

[7] Letter from Keynes to Lord Beaverbrook, 8 March 1944. Keynes described the Bank's approach as 'sheer rubbish from beginning to end'; in Moggridge, *The Collected Writings of John Maynard Keynes*, vol. XXV, pp. 415–17.

[8] Quoted in Horsefield, *The International Monetary Fund, 1945–1965*, vol. I, p. 52.

[9] Speech by A. D. Shroff, 6 July 1944, in US Department of State, *Proceedings and Documents of the UN Monetary and Financial Conference*, vol. I (Washington, DC: Government Printing Office [GPO], 1948), document 251, pp. 424–6. The similar statement by the Egyptian delegate was also made on 6 July 1944, ibid., document 167, pp. 185–7.

[10] Ibid., document 267. p. 433.

promised the Indian delegation publicly that the United Kingdom would engage in negotiations and honour its sterling debts to India after the end of the war.[11] After noting that 'in respect of overseas assets the end of the war will find the UK greatly impoverished and others of the United Nations considerably enriched at our expense. We make no complaint of this provided that the resulting situation is accepted for what it is', he states:

> [T]he settlement of these debts must be, in our clear and settled judgement, a matter between those directly concerned. When the end is reached and we can see our way into the daylight we shall take it up without any delay, to settle honourably what was honourably and generously given.[12]

'Daylight' still seemed very distant in mid-1944.

The sterling assets held outside the sterling area were dealt with separately. During the summer of 1944 the British government embarked on discussions with the Dutch and Belgian governments in exile to 'bring order into financial relations' immediately after the war, and a similar format was applied later for other countries.[13] These three- or five-year agreements included pledges to exchange sterling at the official exchange rate and aimed to facilitate the restoration of international trade by providing small margins of credit in bilateral trade and a limited transferability of sterling.[14] Beyond the set margins – £5 million in the case of Belgium – settlement was made in gold or dollars. The right to transfer sterling within the European country (and its monetary area where relevant) and to anywhere in the sterling area or beyond (provided the UK government approved) was the foundation of the 'transferable sterling' group that would emerge after 1947. The agreements did not make any provision for the liquidation or blocking of wartime balances. They were designed in the expectation that the United Kingdom would be in surplus with most European states after the war, so the credit element was limited. Indeed, the British rejected a Belgian offer of a £10 million margin for fear they would be accumulating too many Belgian francs. As it turned out, the United Kingdom

[11] Pressnell, L. S., *External Economic Policy since the War*, vol. I, *The Post-war Financial Settlement* (London: HMSO, 1987), p. 166.

[12] Statement by Keynes on behalf of the UK delegation at meeting of Commission I, in Moggridge, D. E. (ed.), *The Collected Writings of John Maynard Keynes*, vol. XXVI (Cambridge: Cambridge University Press, 1971), pp. 86–7.

[13] The first agreement was with Belgium in October 1944. Agreements were also signed with France, the Netherlands, Sweden, Norway, Denmark, Czechoslovakia, Portugal, Switzerland and Spain.

[14] Cairncross, A. K., *Years of Recovery: British Economic Policy 1945–51* (London: Methuen, 1985), pp. 123–6.

was in persistent deficit with all these countries except for Denmark and France.

Britain hoped to achieve more advantageous agreements with Sweden and Switzerland, which had been neutral during the war and had required Britain to pay gold for wartime expenditure – £50 million worth in the case of Sweden. The agreement signed in March 1945 with Sweden was for the exchange of currencies at the official exchange rate combined with a secret limit on sterling accumulations of £40 million – in effect an offer by Sweden to give credit for up to this amount in bilateral payments. Switzerland tried to press a loan in Swiss francs or US dollars on the British instead of an agreement to exchange and hold sterling, but was 'sternly rebuked for making such an improper suggestion' that would be 'derogatory to the status of sterling'.[15] The Swiss were eventually brought around to a payments agreement after prolonged negotiations, which ended in March 1946. This provided a formal arrangement to hold £5 million in sterling plus a secret agreement to hold a further £10 million.

Sir Hugh Ellis Rees, a main negotiator of these agreements, wrote later that, while the terms were not very attractive to Britain's European partners, they were accepted 'for political considerations; no doubt they thought it worthwhile to make concessions and to cooperate with the UK … In 1945 it seemed reasonable to argue that the countries of Europe had been saved by our efforts, and they should now rally round us; it needed only a little persuasion for this to happen.' In the United Kingdom, supporters of the Bretton Woods schemes viewed these preliminary agreements as a way to deal with the transitional period by helping to restore multilateral trade and the international use of sterling without full convertibility, while critics of Bretton Woods could view them as a British-led solution to post-war payments problems without resort to American influence. Moreover, the ongoing consultations built into these agreements enhanced Britain's leadership of cooperation and coordination among European states.[16]

For the sterling area, Keynes' 1944 pledge that the sterling balances would be released on mutually agreed terms was not immediately fulfilled. Australia began informal discussions in March 1944 and the Commonwealth Bank received permission from the Bank of England to build up a gold reserve of £10 million from early June, but these talks did not result in firm proposals. Instead, the sterling balances quickly became inseparable from the prospect of American post-war financial

[15] Ellis Rees, 'The convertibility crisis'.

[16] Ibid.

assistance, which began to be planned in detail in the spring of 1945, culminating in the Anglo-American Financial Agreement in December of that year.[17]

From the British side, an American support package was a prerequisite for the repayment of the sterling balances. This was a view that had developed during the Anglo-American discussions in the run-up to Bretton Woods, and it played its part in the disappearance of wartime balances from the articles of agreement. It was hoped that the Americans might be persuaded to take over some of the liabilities, or at least provide funds to retire them. On the American side, these debts were an obstacle to Britain adopting freer payments and they provided an additional incentive for discriminatory trade against the United States, since they were not convertible. As in the mutual aid agreement during the war, the conditions for US help for Britain after the war hinged on Britain helping to achieve the US goal of non-discrimination and multilateralism. The sterling balances were therefore tied firmly into Anglo-American negotiations rather than bilateral negotiations between Britain and its main creditors, as had been promised at Bretton Woods just a year earlier.

At first both sides seemed to be in general agreement about the role of the sterling balances in the loan agreement. The Americans viewed cancellation of at least part of the wartime debts as a necessary prerequisite to US support. This coincided with British hopes to make any cancellations appear forced on a reluctant Britain by the Americans.[18] Keynes' initial planning for the post-war financial recovery in May 1945 famously posited either a future of 'Starvation Corner', with the United Kingdom in economic isolation and repudiating its debt, or the 'Temptation' of accepting large US dollar debt, which would entail a crippling service burden, or 'Justice', which provided for a cancellation of a quarter of the sterling balances, funding a half, a $3 billion grant from the United States to repay pre-lend-lease British expenditure, plus a loan of $5 billion. The labels given to each of these scenarios clearly identified the last as the most desirable alternative. As the British position developed in the summer of 1945, the proposed total value of cancelled sterling balances increased optimistically, from £750 million ($3 billion) to £1.25 billion ($5 billion), while the amount to be immediately released was reduced from £750 million ($3 billion) to £200 million ($800million).[19]

By the time the negotiations in Washington commenced in September 1945, however, the British had moved away from the inclusion of

[17] See correspondence in Australian National Archives (hereafter ANA) A571 1944/1660.
[18] Pressnell, *External Economic Policy*, pp. 279–81.
[19] Ibid., p. 244.

a specific formula for the sterling balances as part of the loan agreement without first consulting creditors. The Bank of England agreed with Keynes that it was impossible to treat all creditors on an equal basis, since they had different economic relationships with the United Kingdom and the balances had been accumulated in different ways. A unilateral approach could damage the reputation of sterling in the future, which would undermine the business of the City of London. Ever since the nineteenth century the British balance of payments had traditionally depended on invisible earnings arising from the activities of the City that related to sterling's international roles as a reserve and trading currency, and it was expected that this pattern would need to be restored in the post-war period. The Labour government that came to power in July 1945 was less interested in promoting international finance and more concerned with developments in the national economy, however. The Treasury agreed that treating sterling creditors uniformly was inappropriate but it was more worried about avoiding an acrimonious multilateral conference of major creditors, which would be required to conclude any all-encompassing agreement. The Chancellor of the Exchequer, Hugh Dalton, instructed the Washington mission that details of a sterling settlement were to be kept formally out of the discussions, although it would be understood that part of the US loan would be used to help solve this problem.

American negotiators pressed for more specifics, since resolving the sterling balances was an important presentational issue for the US public, who already viewed themselves as having supported the United Kingdom through lend-lease instead of allowing the accumulation of war debts when Britain's Commonwealth creditors had not. What was feasible for an unsympathetic US Congress to approve was a driving factor for the US side of the Washington talks. At the meeting of the Finance Committee on 19 September, Keynes offered two alternatives. The first was that the United Kingdom could receive minimum assistance from the United States and try to muddle through on a similar basis to what it had done during the war, operating the sterling area in combination with payments agreements with other countries. Wartime controls would be difficult to continue in peacetime and creditors might not be as willing to accumulate sterling assets under these circumstances. This outcome would also increase preference in trade among sterling countries. This was more of a threat than a genuine alternative from the American point of view, for which non-discrimination and multilateralism constituted an overriding goal. Keynes then presented a more liberal alternative, which combined allowing new current earnings of sterling to be freely convertible with a package of blocking, cancelling and releasing wartime balances, backed by substantial US financial assistance. Keynes tried to resist offering specific amounts for each category of solution for the balances, but Treasury secretary Fred Vinson insisted. The next day Keynes offered his 'personal view' orally, that it should be possible to cancel one-third, free 10 per cent and release the rest over a period of about fifty years, starting in five years' time. This solution, Keynes informed the Americans, would require a line of credit from the United States of about $5 billion over three to five years, although actual drawings would be kept as small as possible.[20] The Americans appeared to find these proposals broadly acceptable but asked for further detail, although Keynes complained to Dalton of 'a good deal of play acting, slow motion and poker playing'.[21]

The following day *The New York Times* published statistics provided by the British to the 'top committee' of negotiations. The leak of sensitive data spooked London, and the British authorities advised Keynes not to give any details in writing on plans for cancelling the sterling balances. They hoped instead that the Americans could be manipulated into initiating proposals, and said that Keynes should seek a US statement that any assistance was conditional on resolving the sterling balances problem, so as to put pressure on creditors. This approach seemed to bear fruit quite quickly, as on 5 October Harry White informally put forward a complicated formula to block, cancel and release balances on slightly more generous terms to the United Kingdom than Keynes' plan. The United States would offer to buy part of the sterling balances at a discount, thus reducing the overall amount by a further $2.5 billion. Keynes observed that 'Harry's point is, of course, to make the whole affair so complicated that the average Congressman has no idea what it amounts to'.[22]

The overriding issue in the negotiations by this time, however, was whether Britain could accept assistance if it entailed interest payments, which threatened to bring the British to the brink of suspending negotiations. On 20 October the Americans finally made their definitive (and, for the British, disappointing) offer of $3.5 billion at 2 per cent interest in exchange for a commitment to reduce the sterling balances. Keynes managed to push Vinson to $4 billion and then agreed to put this offer to London. A sterling balances settlement was implicit in the ensuing

[20] Minutes of US–UK economic negotiations, Finance Committee, 20 September 1945, in Moggridge, D. E. (ed.), *The Collected Writings of John Maynard Keynes*, vol. XXIV (Cambridge: Cambridge University Press, 1971), pp. 492–8.

[21] Letter from Keynes to Hugh Dalton, 1 October 1945, ibid., pp. 512–17.

[22] Letter from Keynes to Eady, 5 October 1945, ibid., pp. 531–5. White's plan is detailed in Pressnell, *External Economic Policy*.

wrangling, but the details were not made explicit, and White's proposals did not resurface.

In the long lull while waiting for instructions from London on how to respond to the Americans, Keynes devised a draft on 'sterling area arrangements' to form the basis for an exchange of letters between the two states, and sent it to Harry White before it had been agreed in London.[23] At the time Keynes considered this aspect of the loan agreement uncontroversial compared with the problems of the amount and terms of repayments. The draft repeated his offer to make all currently earned sterling in the sterling area and an unspecified portion of wartime accumulations freely convertible by the end of 1946 in exchange for US 'aid on a scale appropriate to the size of the problem'. The memo was vaguer than Keynes had been previously on the sterling balances, merely recognising the need to cancel some wartime balances on the principle of sharing the war burden, combined with some blocking. He made clear that Britain could not act unilaterally but only by mutual agreement with creditors, but he also committed the United Kingdom to enter into such negotiations 'at an early date'.

In London, ministers were appalled by the negative portrayal of the sterling area, and Eady responded to Keynes by sending him a substantial redraft rather than merely corrections. This recast the sterling area as a traditionally non-discriminatory and voluntary institution, which had been transformed temporarily towards discrimination by wartime exchange controls and the persistent dollar shortage. It retained the vague proposals to resolve the sterling balances problem through negotiation with creditors but omitted the paragraph referring to the 1946 deadline for sterling area convertibility. On the question of convertibility for non-sterling countries, Eady advised Keynes 'to shun debate about European payments agreements or special account agreements as you would shun the devil'.[24] The Americans took the issue up, however, proposing on 18 November that convertibility by the end of 1946 should include not just those countries with payments agreements but also the sterling area – a commitment that the Keynes mission recommended should be rejected.

On 6 November the Cabinet met to consider a final offer to the Americans. Hugh Dalton presented a proposal for a loan of $2.5 billion repayable at 2 per cent over fifty years, starting in five years, with an option on a further $2 billion interest-free 'as backing for an offer to

[23] Letter from Keynes to H. D. White, 5 November 1945, in Moggridge, *The Collected Writings of John Maynard Keynes*, vol. XXIV, pp. 570–7.

[24] Eady to Keynes, 6 November 1945, ibid., pp. 581–3.

members of the sterling area to make their sterling as freely available for current expenditure outside the area as inside'.[25] If this proved unobtainable, the limit was $4 billion at 2 per cent with an option of a further $1 billion at the same interest rate. Keynes would also be asked to negotiate a waiver on the payment of interest and capital triggered by a scarcity of dollars, or depression in trade flows, and a waiver on interest payments if UK exports fell below a given target. In return, 'we should agree to use the assistance given to us for progressive removal of discrimination and to secure writing down of sterling balances by voluntary agreement with each creditor'. Moreover, the United Kingdom would support the US proposals for an International Trade Organisation (ITO) and ratify the Bretton Woods Agreements. It was these latter commitments that proved most controversial in the Cabinet.

When the Cabinet discussed the proposals, Dalton tried to reassure his colleagues that ratifying the Bretton Woods Agreements would be in Britain's interests.[26] Stable exchange rates were 'clearly to our advantage' given the lesson learned during the competitive devaluations in the interwar period. The agreement would allow some flexibility in the sterling exchange rate and the possibility of greater movement in times of 'fundamental disequilibrium'. He dismissed objections to the relaxation of exchange restrictions on the current account as commitments that need be actioned only after a transition, 'which must be of several years' duration'. Nevertheless, Dalton aimed to get a separate formal assurance that the IMF board would agree to 'any change proposed in the par value of a member's currency which is necessary to protect that member from unemployment of a chronic or persistent character' and that each country should be able to determine the length of its own transition period.

Emanuel Shinwell and Aneurin Bevan were the most vociferous objectors, on the grounds that accepting the Bretton Woods Agreements implied the end of the sterling area. Their attitude to the United States was deeply affected by their antipathy to the entire multilateral payments project that the Americans had been driving since the mutual aid agreement of 1942. Shinwell argued that, 'in his view, the objective which the US government had in mind in the course of these negotiations was to break up the Sterling Group. If we allowed them to succeed in this aim, we should be entirely at their mercy in matters of world trade. Why, therefore, should we play into their hands by allowing them to

[25] Paper by Dalton for the Cabinet, Washington financial talks, 6 November 1945, TNA CAB129/4.

[26] Cabinet conclusions confidential annex, 6 November 1945, 4:30 p.m., TNA CAB128/4.

make it, in effect, a condition of their loan to us that we should ratify the Bretton Woods Agreements and thus destroy the coherence of the Sterling Group?' Bevan agreed that 'it was to our advantage to maintain that system; for our creditors in the Sterling Group were anxious to trade with us in order to get our goods'.

Both Shinwell and Bevan also believed that Britain was taking too humble a position in the negotiations and asserted that the United States depended on British markets for their own industrial recovery and could ill afford not to give assistance. The First Lord of the Admiralty, A. V. Alexander, agreed that the United Kingdom should not abandon its longer-term interests in order to achieve short-term US help. He noted that in 1931 Britain had 'refused to accept American dictation and had largely restored our position by our own efforts, within two years, in developing our Empire trade. If we could not get better terms from the Americans than those indicated in the memoranda now before the Cabinet, was it not worth considering whether we could not do the same again?' Dalton tried to disabuse his colleagues of the fantasy that the United Kingdom could retreat into a cosy arrangement with sterling countries. He noted that 'the Sterling countries were already showing signs of anxiety to discontinue these special war-time arrangements, which involved them in very great difficulties; and it was likely that, whatever happened about the American settlement, some countries would wish to break away very soon from the Sterling Group.' Moreover, Stafford Cripps (president of the Board of Trade) agreed that 'the suggestion that we should aim instead at consolidating the Sterling Group and retaining our power to apply discriminatory policies in our foreign trading was inconsistent with the declared policy of the Labour Party, which was committed to making a sincere attempt at securing, in cooperation with other countries, a multilateral basis for world trade'. In terms of national politics, Ernest Bevin, the foreign secretary, warned that refusing US assistance 'involved asking the British people to endure, for perhaps another three years, standards of living even lower than those to which we had been reduced at the end of six years of war'. Dalton predicted that the nation would have to reduce consumption of all food except bread and potatoes and cut imports of key raw materials, which would threaten industrial recovery. On the international stage, the Secretary of State for war warned that, 'if we now turned away from Anglo-American cooperation, the moral shock to the people of this country would be even greater than the material loss … [I]f we took the lead in disrupting Anglo-American economic cooperation, we could not expect the US to continue for long to shoulder their international responsibilities in political affairs.' On the weight of opinion (although without persuading Shinwell and Bevan), the Cabinet agreed to put forward Dalton's proposal to the Americans.

The final American response was delayed for almost three weeks, but the option of an interest-free portion was quickly dismissed. In the midst of this uncertainty, on 26 November, the Chancellor confirmed that ministers were not, after all, prepared to release all sterling area current earnings by the end of 1946. Keynes had been of the opinion that this had been agreed almost from the outset of the negotiations, and the apparent reversal threatened to crush hopes for any US assistance just at the last hurdle. For the mission in Washington the issue was moot, since the United Kingdom would in any case be forced to allow future sterling area earnings to be convertible, as otherwise these countries would no longer accept sterling in payment. On the other hand, this commitment was held in huge importance by the Americans. On both sides, therefore, it was impossible to drop this aspect now.

On 28 November Dalton presented what were expected to be the final US proposals to the Cabinet, although they had not yet been confirmed by American negotiators.[27] Cabinet members were asked to approve a draft financial agreement for a line of credit of $4.5 billion available until the end of December 1951, repayable over fifty instalments at 2 per cent interest. The British government would support the ITO proposals and the Bretton Woods Agreements would be ratified before the deadline of the end of 1945. Britain would not discriminate against the United States in any exchange controls, nor introduce discrimination against any country in any new quantitative restrictions that might be imposed during the transition. Under a section on 'Sterling Area Exchange Arrangements', Britain committed itself to making sterling receipts from current transactions by sterling area countries convertible into any currency for current payments by the end of 1946. In addition, the government committed itself to seeking 'by voluntary agreement with the countries of the sterling area an early settlement, varying according to the circumstances of each case, covering their accumulated sterling balances' through a combination of blocking, freeing and cancellation. This section concluded that 'the effect will be that when the arrangements contemplated above are completed any discrimination arising from the so-called dollar sterling pool will be entirely removed and that each member of the sterling area will have its current sterling and dollar receipts at its free disposition for current transactions anywhere'.

At the Cabinet meeting on 29 November, Dalton warned that the total might end up at $4 billion, of which $750 million would be to cover

[27] Washington financial talks by Dalton, 28 November 1945, TNA CAB129/5.

Lend-Lease goods in the pipeline, leaving 'new money' of $3.25 billion.[28] He downplayed the commitment on sterling balances as 'merely undertaking to carry out, without committing ourselves to an absolutely rigid time limit for completion, the negotiations which it had always been our intention to undertake with the sterling area countries'. Shinwell and Bevan reiterated their position that introducing current account convertibility for the sterling area, thereby dismantling the sterling group, would threaten Britain's recovery and longer-term economic and commercial interests. Shinwell argued that 'it would be better for HMG [Her Majesty's Government] to borrow from the US at 3, 4 or even 5% than to accept the conditions attaching to the credit which had been offered'. They both wanted the Washington mission to take a harder line with the Americans, again on the grounds the United States needed British markets for its exports. Again, though, they were outvoted by the rest of the Cabinet, who feared the economic hardship and political damage that would result if the negotiations collapsed. There had been little change of opinion in the Cabinet since the beginning of the month.

It seemed that the British government's view was set, but the next day it was agreed that Sir Edward Bridges should be sent to Washington to take over the leadership of the UK mission, arriving on Saturday 1 December. The disagreement in the Cabinet over the loan terms leaked out in Washington and was relayed over the newswires early in the morning of Sunday 2 December, to the effect that 'the Cabinet had felt it necessary to send Sir Edward Bridges to Washington with instructions which would virtually disown the recent conversations between the British and American delegates in regard to the liberalization of the sterling'.[29] The Americans responded to this about-turn with a hardening of their own position, and the provisions for current account convertibility for newly earned sterling were to be extended beyond the sterling area to all countries. On 5 December Dalton reported back to the Cabinet.[30] Once more, he tried to minimise the negative implications for the United Kingdom of effectively reducing the period of the transition under the Bretton Woods arrangements to fifteen months, while stressing the dangers of not reaching an agreement at all. The commitment was already agreed with respect to the sterling area and other IMF signatories, and so would only additionally affect countries with which the

[28] 57th Cabinet conclusions – minute 3 confidential annex, 29 November 1945, 11 a.m., TNA CAB128/4.

[29] 'Monday tape: the loan talks 12.21 a.m. Washington, Sunday', included with 58th Cabinet conclusions – minute 2, 3 December 1945, 11 a.m., TNA CAB128/2.

[30] 59th Cabinet conclusions confidential annex, 5 December 1945, noon, TNA CAB128/4.

United Kingdom had monetary agreements; Spain, Portugal, Argentina, Sweden and Switzerland. The Cabinet reluctantly agreed that the period of the transition should not be a breaking point for the negotiations. The Anglo-American Agreement was finally signed on 6 December.

The settlement came closest to Keynes' 'Temptation' scenario, with a $3.75 billion loan at 2 per cent interest, but it went beyond even Keynes' predictions about the cost of this assistance, as it was conditional on the introduction of current account convertibility within one year without resolving the underlying global imbalance. In other words, the UK government was pledged to convertibility but without resolution of the sterling balances problem, which was merely postponed. The Cabinet discussions reveal the persistence of outdated views over the reliability and cohesion of the sterling group of countries after the war. As was the case after 1931, some ministers expected these countries to continue to see their interests as tied closely to those of the United Kingdom; in the new environment of the post-1945 world, however, the United States was an alternative focus. The dominions had matured during the war, now sought greater autonomy from Britain and were less willing to follow British dictates. Dalton managed to convince the prime minister that these countries (India, Australia and New Zealand in particular) could not be persuaded to continue to use sterling if it were not liberalised, at least on the current account. As argued strongly and persistently by Keynes, the only hope for a future international role for sterling, and for preserving the sterling area, was therefore to move towards convertibility. Shinwell and Bevan warned of the dangers of 'throwing the USA open to the sterling area' but the costs were not well quantified, and their objections were dismissed by Dalton as a striving for cohesion in the sterling area that was no longer possible.[31] By the time Bridges tried to withdraw this aspect of the conditions it was too late; the Americans already considered it a 'done deal'. The introduction of sterling convertibility for countries outside the sterling area at the same time was a late addition to the conditions for the loan and ended up attracting remarkably little debate, because of the monetary agreements already in place in Europe. The United Kingdom was in any case already committed to the Bretton Woods institutions, and shortening the transition period was presented as more of a technical than a fundamental issue.

A major obstacle to a quick sterling balance settlement, according to both the Bank of England and the Treasury, was that it was impossible to have a common deal for all creditors. There were various political

[31] 57th Cabinet conclusions – minute 3 confidential annex, 29 November 1945, 11 a.m., TNA CAB128/4.

issues, particularly with India, which was at that time going through the process of gaining independence and preparing for partition. Any deal that did not include India was not going to help the overall problem very much, since the Indians held close to 40 per cent of all sterling balances. For Britain to repudiate debts unilaterally at this juncture would have been politically difficult, though perhaps not impossible. Informing creditors that a third of their assets had been cancelled and others frozen at the same time that Britain announced a large loan from the United States might well have made it more difficult to justify. Once a unilateral across-the-board solution had been abandoned, the basis for dealing with the sterling balances moved from what was affordable to what was negotiable.

The variety of ways that the balances had been accumulated did seem to suggest that Britain's creditors might react differently to calls for sacrifice. On 1 May 1946, in line with article 10 of the loan agreement, the Chancellor asked Australia and New Zealand each to cancel a half of their wartime sterling assets, mainly in order to provide an example to other larger creditors, such as India and Egypt. They refused, however, undertaking instead only to examine the positions of their respective countries and report back in due course. Eady rather bluntly told the Australian prime minister, J. B. Chifley, that, 'while from a legal point of view the creditors were free to use [the sterling balances], in practice there was no opportunity for spending on such a scale and they were therefore largely useless'.[32] Eady further explained that the debt to India had arisen from the generous Chatfield Agreement to apportion costs because of India's relative poverty. That agreement had been 'not inequitable' at the time of signing, but as it had been based on an assumption that the war would remain a European conflict the burden had become unexpectedly large. When the theatre moved closer to India the costs had multiplied, and the liabilities had accumulated much more rapidly than expected once India had become a base for British forces. Dalton recognised that the liabilities to Australia and New Zealand were 'negligible' compared to those to India and Egypt but argued that any approach to large creditors would have to have a wider basis in principle. He suggested that the principle should be that all future earned sterling should be freely convertible for current purposes but that 'a proportion of the existing unreal balances should be written off'. The phrasing of this claim for 'unreal' balances is particularly striking, and it is underlined in the Australian archive record. Not surprisingly, Chifley protested that Australia's external reserves were

[32] Note of a conversation between Chancellor and J. B. Chifley, 1 May 1946; drafted by the British and agreed by Chifley; ANA A571 1944/1660.

not in excess of their needs. His adviser, Herbert C. Coombs, who was also at the meeting, described a 50 per cent cancellation as unrealistic and insisted that any agreements had to be on the basis of each country's likely future requirements. In the end Chifley agreed only to 'consider what the Chancellor had said, although he was not prepared to hold out any hopes of accepting the suggestion' of cancellation. As John Fforde rather modestly observed, 'The appealing tactic of seeking first a favourable agreement with one's closest friends had not been a success.'[33] In fact, it is more likely that this tactic antagonised the Australians.

In the end, the pause for reflection extended to almost a year. Negotiations began with New Zealand in August 1946 but no agreement was reached, and discussions with Australia were delayed by the formation of a new national government. Dalton's letter to New Zealand, sent also to Chifley for information, is revealing of how the UK argument had changed. It set out in considerable detail how Britain's wartime sacrifice had been greater than elsewhere but concluded that 'comparisons are invidious and for our part we are prepared to let the matter rest there'.[34] Nevertheless, the paper went on to stress how Britain's financial position had changed from creditor to debtor over the course of the war while New Zealand's external financial position improved by £100 million (a combination of accumulated sterling balances of £64 million and repaid debt). The British estimated that the war had cost the country £5,000 million, of which £1,500 million had arisen from the loss of export earnings, £500 million was net government overseas expenditure since VJ Day (in West Germany, for example) and £3,000 million had been incurred for direct current war expenditure on supplies, troops, munitions, etc. Because of the loss of invisible earnings, Britain would be able to restore this imbalance only by increasing the volume of exports by a heroic 50 per cent above pre-war levels. This left no margin for repaying debt or contributing to Commonwealth defence. Reducing the burden of the sterling balances needed to be considered in this context. Not surprisingly, this claim of financial sacrifice did not find a very sympathetic audience. On 22 January 1947 Dalton wrote to Chifley politely asking him for his government's views on the sterling balances on the eve of sending a mission to India to discuss cancellation there.[35] Australia's attitude was clearly central to the UK bargaining position in India, where the stakes were

[33] Fforde, *The Bank of England*, pp. 102–3.

[34] UK memorandum for New Zealand negotiations, 14 August 1947, ANA A571 1944/1660.

[35] Note from E. J. Williams, UK high commissioner in Canberra, to J. B. Chifley, enclosing letter from Chancellor, 22 January 1947, archives of the Reserve Bank of Australia (hereafter RBA) S-a-1500; also in ANA A571 1944/1660.

much higher. Moreover, Australia was not only Britain's largest export market but also a substantial holder of sterling balances.

From September 1939 to September 1945 Australia's net sterling reserves increased from £60 million to £120 million, and by February 1947 they had risen further, to £170 million. In addition, Australia redeemed £12 million of debt and repatriated a further £53 million of assets. In June 1945 the Australians privately expected that access to wartime sterling balances would have to be restricted, including the freezing of any 'abnormal' balances, but they hoped that all future current earnings of sterling would be freely convertible.[36] This initially sanguine attitude to the freezing or funding of balances reflected a general view, most vibrantly stated by L. G. Melville of the Commonwealth Bank, that 'Australia would be like the dog that grasped for a reflection of its bone, if it forced on Britain "favourable" financial arrangements with regard to sterling balances which compelled Britain, in order to solve her own problems, to curtail drastically her purchases of Australian raw materials and foodstuffs'.[37] As the prospects for a large UK loan from the United States began to brighten, the Australians took a tougher line.

In a paper for consideration by the Australian Cabinet in February 1946 Chifley admitted that Australia had accumulated sterling assets during the war because of cash exports (particularly food and wool), a reduction in cash imports (partly as a result of procurement through mutual aid and Lend-Lease) and the equivalent of £113 million in US military expenditure in Australia.[38] Chifley considered the last category ineligible for cancellation or blocking because the US dollar proceeds had already been sold to the Bank of England for sterling. The Commonwealth Bank and the Australian government considered the issue of their sterling assets several times during 1946 and early 1947. The principle they adopted was first to determine how much foreign exchange Australia was likely to need over the next few years and then to consider how much of the 'surplus' might be frozen – an approach that did not bode well for identifying a large blocked element. At the end of September 1946 the Advisory Council of the Commonwealth Bank 'tentatively considered' that the sterling balances were not so large in

[36] Telegram from S. G. McFarlane in Canberra to F. Wheeler in London, 5 June 1945, ANA A571 1944/1660. L. F. Giblin was chair of the influential wartime Advisory Committee on Financial Economic Policy. L. G. Melville of the Commonwealth Bank and Roland Wilson were the other members tasked with examining the external economic impact of the war on Australia.

[37] Memo by L. G. M[elville], 14 February 1945, ANA A571 1944/1660.

[38] Chifley paper for Cabinet, February 1946, RBA S-a-1500. See also Australian position paper on Chifley's visit to London, 5 April 1946, ANA A571 1944/1660.

relation to requirements as to allow any to be 'reasonably written off'.[39] On the other hand, 'it would be equitable to assist the UK by agreeing to effect some writing down' if other countries did the same. They suggested either freezing some proportion of the surplus over a reasonable working balance, or taking over some of the United Kingdom's sterling liabilities elsewhere, such as from India.

In early March 1947 Chifley wrote to Dalton that his government had agreed to a gift of £A25 million (£20 million) to the UK government, in line with the UK request in January to cancel £20–30 million.[40] Chifley noted that this action would be presented 'as a contribution to the war costs of the UK in and around the Pacific' for local political purposes so that there would be no specific reference to the cancelling of any sterling debts. Nevertheless, Chifley hoped that it would 'help you [Dalton] in discussion with other sterling holders', and said that he had been in close consultation with New Zealand to ensure a simultaneous announcement of their 'gift' of £10 million. Chifley further recognised that more arrangements would need to be made over Australia's sterling balances, and he asked Dalton to discuss this with his adviser, Coombs, in London.[41] Eady announced the two gifts in parliament on 5 March 1947. They ended up being the only outright cancellations of wartime sterling balances, despite the Chancellor's edict in March 1947 that no sterling agreement should be concluded without an element of cancellation.[42]

Meanwhile, Coombs and Walter Nash (the deputy prime minister and finance minister of New Zealand) were in London as part of their countries' trade missions for the ITO negotiations. While there, Chifley suggested that they should informally discuss the prospects for some kind of agreement to restrain the expenditure of sterling balances with Hugh Dalton and other members of the Treasury, as well as Sir Wilfred Eady.[43] Australia and New Zealand were treated together, even though Australia was a much more important creditor and trading partner for the United Kingdom. By the end of March they had come to an agreement that formal contracts such as those being prepared for India, Pakistan and the Middle East would not be appropriate for Australia. Instead, Canberra was ready to commit informally to cap their drawings for current account purposes. Formal agreements would not be accepted by public opinion in Australia, and Canberra appears to have been granted this concession

39 Extract from minutes of the Advisory Council, 23 September 1946, RBA S-a-1500.
40 H. C. Coombs to Chifley, 15 January 1947, ANA A571 1944/1660.
41 Undated draft letter from Chifley to Dalton [March 1947], ANA A571 1944/1660.
42 Ellis Rees, 'The convertibility crisis', p. 22.
43 Letter from Chifley to Walter Nash, 20 February 1947, ANA A571 1944/1660.

as a quid pro quo for the Australians' willingness to cancel at least a small part of their accumulated assets. With this agreement confirmed, Coombs asked that Treasury officials be sent from Canberra to embark on formal negotiations, and in June 1947 the Australian treasurer, Stuart G. McFarlane, was sent to London.[44]

The British negotiator, Ernest Rowe-Dutton, hoped that Australia would agree to keep its sterling balances at the current level (£130 million according to Australia, £125 million of official balances according to the United Kingdom) for the next six months, which would mean living within current earnings. McFarlane countered with a request for a £40 million 'reserve and working balance' that could be drawn on (and replenished) freely over the next two years to allow for some fluctuation (taking the core down to £90 million), but this magnitude evoked 'shock' from the British side, and McFarlane was ready to reduce it to £25 million (although the Commonwealth Bank considered £40 million to be an absolute minimum).[45] During the negotiations the sterling convertibility crisis struck, and it changed the urgency of the British position. Under these circumstances, on 18 August 1947 Chifley agreed to hold a minimum of £125 million in sterling (the status quo for official balances), although part of this amount could be used to repay Australian debts in the United Kingdom.[46] Chifley also agreed to maintain 'uniformity of trade policy with the UK's as far as possible', and he reiterated his intention to sell Australia's gold output for 1947/8 to London. He resisted calls to commit Australia to spend no more US dollars than it earned over the next twelve months.[47] The British prime minister, Clement Attlee, expressed his appreciation in fulsome terms, both publicly and privately.[48]

Like the appeal to Australia and New Zealand, Britain's plea to India to cancel part of its balances in February 1947 fell on deaf ears, given India's urgent development needs and its forecast balance of payments deficit. In July an initial six-month deal was agreed that blocked the bulk

[44] Telegram 31 March 1947 from Coombs in London to Treasurer, Canberra, ANA A572, 1944/1660.

[45] Letter and enclosed record of meetings in London from S. G. McFarlane to Chifley, 23 June 1947, RBA S-a-1500.

[46] Correspondence in RBA S-1-1501. The agreement was formalised in a letter from Chifley to Clement Attlee on 5 September 1947; ANA A571 1944/1660; Rooth, T., 'Imperial self-sufficiency rediscovered: Britain and Australia 1945–51', *Australian Economic History Review*, 39(1), 1999, pp. 29–51; Lee, D., 'Protecting the sterling area: the Chifley government's response to multilateralism 1945–49', *Australian Journal of Political Science*, 25(2), 1990, pp. 178–95.

[47] W. C. Hankinson, UK high commission, to Chifley, 5 September 1947, ANA A571 1944/1660.

[48] Attlee to Chifley, 11 September 1947, ANA A571 1944/1660.

of India's balances and released £65 million, of which £30 million was to constitute 'working balances' that would not be spent outright. This agreement was concluded in the midst of the convertibility crisis, on 14 August, four days before the Australian agreement and a mere six days before the suspension of convertibility.

Would greater cancellation and funding have affected the longer-term UK external position? It can be speculated that the ratio of sterling area liabilities to reserves could have been reduced from 4:1 to 3:1 in 1946 under Keynes' plan, which might have improved short-term confidence in sterling, but the 'overhang' would still have been huge and the commitments for immediate release considerably larger than those actually negotiated. Moreover, the problems of 1947 were not primarily of confidence in sterling alone. The drain arose from currently earned sterling rather than wartime balances, so blocking or writing off more wartime debts would not have forestalled the crisis of 1947. Most of the wartime accumulations had been blocked into formal agreements by July 1947, and only £156.5 million of blocked balances were released in the year as a whole (not all of which was converted to US dollars). As is shown below, this was relatively insignificant compared to the overall drain. The run on sterling arose from the prolonged imbalance in the international economy that led to the dollar shortage, combined with Britain's own balance of payments problems after the fuel crisis, bottleneck problems and rising global prices. Once the deadline for sterling convertibility had been set there was an incentive for third countries to accumulate sterling in anticipation of converting it to desperately needed US dollars as soon as possible. During 1946 and 1947 non-sterling area countries accumulated £90 million of sterling assets, while the sterling area reduced its balances slightly. Repudiating the sterling balances would not have forestalled the 1947 convertibility crisis, which was part of a global problem.

One of the main rationales for negotiating with India rather than acting unilaterally was the need to keep India in the sterling area, which Tomlinson argues was vital both politically, for keeping India and Pakistan in the Commonwealth, and economically, so as to retain supplies of essential imports, in particular tea, which dominated Indian exports to the United Kingdom.[49] It must also be remembered that partition and its bloody aftermath occurred just at the time of the suspension of sterling convertibility. At the same time, though, Tomlinson shows that India was a drain on Britain's scarce capital goods in the late 1940s, in particular exports of machinery, which was by far the largest single category of

[49] Tomlinson, 'Indo-British relations'.

products exported to India. If trade with India had been cut off (the most extreme consequence of ejection from the sterling area) then capital goods exports could have been reduced, but imports of essentials would also have ceased. The resulting tea shortage and political break with India might not have been considered a reasonable price to pay by the beleaguered British public.

On the other hand, in the longer term, the cancellation of one-third of the wartime accumulation instead of the negotiated blocking that was finally implemented may not have affected the sterling balances problem as it emerged in the 1950s. From 1950 the decline in overall sterling balances that had proceeded from 1945 was reversed, as primary product producers began to earn large surpluses due to rearmament. By 1953, as figure 2.1 shows, east Asia and Africa held 40 per cent of the £2.8 billion in outstanding sterling liabilities, compared with 15 per cent in 1945, and so they had replaced India as the major sterling holders.

In sum, it is difficult to see even in hindsight that implementing Keynes' proposals would have fundamentally altered the post-war evolution of sterling, although it would have relaxed the pressure of external demand on British production. The 'overhang' would still have been considerable, and negotiated releases would still have posed a strain on scarce resources in these years of austerity. The difficult negotiations with Australia, traditionally a close partner in the Commonwealth, show the sensitivity to the political as well as the economic cost of alienating important raw material and food suppliers in the immediate post-war period.

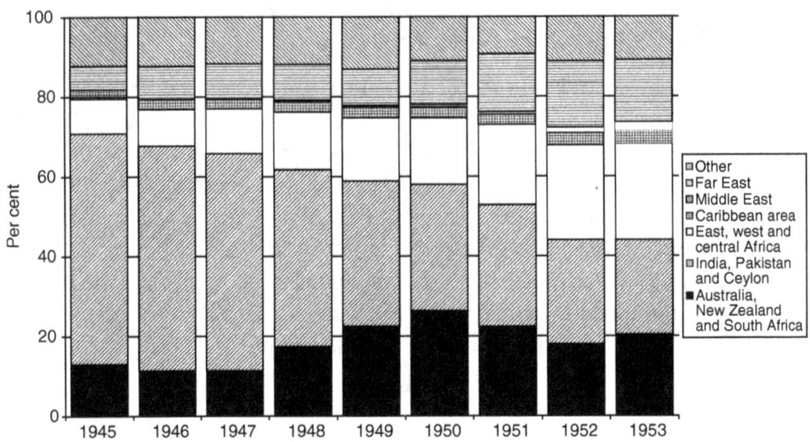

Figure 2.1 Distribution of sterling area balances, 1945–53

Nonetheless, wartime accumulations were not part of sterling's traditional reserve or trading currency role, so cancelling these obligations would not necessarily have signified reneging on commercial debt or seizing the foreign exchange reserves of sovereign states. Although in the late 1940s the Bank of England refused to accept efforts to distinguish between wartime and post-war balances, because this would damage the reputation of sterling, the justification for cancellation could probably have been interpreted by financial markets as an appropriate reallocation of the burden of Britain's wartime expenditure among the Commonwealth rather than as a retreat from sterling's role as an international currency. Cancellations and blocking agreements alone would not have prematurely ended sterling's reserve and trading currency roles, particularly at a time when the US dollar was in short supply and there was no other viable alternative international currency. This is made clear by the fact that the formal and informal blocking that did occur in the late 1940s did not eliminate the usefulness of sterling in the international economy in the longer term nor prevent the accumulation of sterling assets by other countries. While it is interesting to speculate on a counterfactual, in the event the efforts to conclude agreements were quickly overrun by the sterling crisis of 1947, which was not caused by the failure to freeze or write off the wartime sterling balances. By the time of convertibility, in July 1947, most wartime sterling balances had been negotiated into at least interim agreements following a common framework of blocked 'number 2 accounts' at central banks, while new current earnings and carefully negotiated working balances accumulated in more freely convertible 'number 1 accounts'.

The 1947 convertibility crisis

The Anglo-American Loan Agreement was finally ratified in July 1946 and sterling current account convertibility was introduced for all currencies a year later, on 15 July 1947. In preparation for this event, from November 1946 supplementary agreements were negotiated between the Bank of England and various European central banks under which the countries agreed to accept sterling from any country, and in return sterling currently earned was transferable to third countries, including the dollar area.[50] Agreements with Belgium, the Netherlands and Portugal came into force in January 1947 anticipating the 'transferability' of sterling to US dollars that would prevail from July. Belgium promptly began to accumulate

[50] Switzerland refused to accept sterling from any source and did not sign a supplementary monetary agreement. Agreements with Norway and Sweden that included minimum

sterling, selling £4 million for US dollars by the end of February 1947, rising to £15 million worth by the end of May. Ellis Rees believed it was a mistake for the Bank of England to introduce these concessions for some sterling holders before July 1947, because it provided a distraction from more fundamental work to prepare for the advent of convertibility, such as informing the Americans sooner of the unexpectedly perilous state of the balance of payments when this became clear in the spring of 1947.[51]

Dalton considered asking the Americans to postpone the date for convertibility in February 1947, in the midst of the winter crisis and the disappointing negotiations with India and Egypt, but the Treasury did not believe this would save many dollars, since Britain's trading partners would in any event demand payment in gold or dollars. The Bank of England believed that the US administration and the newly Republican-dominated Congress would reject such a request.[52] The Bank also assigned greater priority to restoring the international role of sterling, and this required convertibility, sooner rather than later. Fforde describes the Bank's aims in negotiating supplementary monetary agreements with Europe in these terms: to retain close relations with European countries, to allow greater transferability of inconvertible European currencies and to prevent New York from taking over the bulk of foreign exchange transactions pending the reopening of a London foreign exchange market. He also concludes that, if the monetary agreements had been allowed to lapse earlier, sterling could have been devalued or floated in July 1947 instead of being returned to inconvertibility, because Britain was obliged to give three months' notice before abrogating the agreements.[53] It is hard to view Britain's commitment to the European monetary agreements as a major factor preventing devaluation, however, given the willingness to abrogate agreements with other countries, such as India.

There is some doubt whether those at the highest level expected that convertibility could be sustained. As Fforde argues, Sir Wilfred Eady, the influential head of the Finance Office of the Treasury, expressed his doubts in the spring of 1947 as to whether convertibility could be maintained, although he also believed that the United Kingdom could not avoid taking the step to which it was committed. Meanwhile, the Bank was committed to convertibility but had no strategy for how to maintain it.[54] These positions smack of complacency about the potential pace of a

balances to be held in sterling were concluded on the eve of convertibility in June and July 1947. Negotiations with Denmark and France, begun in July, were not concluded.

51 Ellis Rees, 'The convertibility crisis', pp. 50–1.

52 Fforde, *The Bank of England*, pp. 140–3.

53 Ibid., pp. 129–31.

54 Ibid., p. 144–6.

run on sterling that would inhibit an orderly and negotiated retreat from convertibility.

During the first six months of the Anglo-American loan, drawings were on schedule for a proposed total for the year of $1.5 billion; thus about $800 million was drawn between July 1946 and January 1947. In February the Bank of England warned the Treasury that the dollar deficit was growing and that the rate of drawings would have to rise, although the Treasury resisted because of fears about the negative publicity that drawing more than $100 million per month would generate. The pressure on the balance of payments accumulated during the first half of 1947 as a result of the fuel crisis, payments to support West Germany, and inflation. In March the drawing was twice the usual amount, and in April there was an extraordinary drawing of $450 million, related partly to payment for ships. The drawing in May returned to a lower level, at $200 million, but in June a further $300 million was drawn, prompting questions about the potential exhaustion of the line of credit on the eve of convertibility.

The European payments agreements were meant to anticipate most of the effects of the actual introduction of full current account convertibility on 15 July and so avoid a sharp shock. Nevertheless, despite reassuring the House of Commons on 29 July that there was no extraordinary dollar drain as a result of convertibility, Dalton was forced to draw a further $175 million in July, leaving only $1 billion of the loan, while a further $300 million drawing was planned for August (of which half was drawn on 11 August). On 6 August the House of Commons was warned that the dollar deficit for the first half of 1947 was estimated to be the equivalent of £405 million, of which almost 75 per cent was the UK trade deficit with the United States and other dollar area countries. Only £68 million had been spent on sterling area purchases from the dollar area, and a further £43 million for dollar imports into Europe (including £29 million worth of food for West Germany). Attlee announced a range of initiatives to conserve dollar expenditure and increase exports during the state of the nation debate on the afternoon of 6 August but the exhortation to increase production, reduce defence expenditure, increase exports and reduce imports of luxuries and timber did not convince the House or the markets. Although he began by asserting that 'there is a difference between gravity and panic. It [the current situation] is a matter of gravity', he concluded with an alarming if eloquent call to the British public echoing Churchill's 'never was so much owed by so many to so few' speech of August 1940.

In 1940 we were delivered from mortal peril by the courage, skill and self-sacrifice of a few. Today we are engaged in another battle for Britain. This battle cannot be won by the few. It demands a united effort by the whole nation. I am confident that this united effort will be forthcoming and that we shall again conquer.[55]

This rhetorical flourish prompted a run on sterling on Friday 7 August, which was not stemmed by Hugh Dalton's more prosaic speech when the House resumed the state of the nation debate later that day. From 10 to 15 August there was a drain of $175 million from the reserves, and the Cabinet met on Sunday 17 August to discuss suspending convertibility – a debate that moved quickly on to when and how to inform the Americans. Further delay would allow the run to accelerate, but unilateral action would antagonise the Americans and perhaps prompt them to hold back further instalments of the loan, which still had $700 million outstanding to be drawn. After some debate there was a compromise, and Eady (by then in Washington) was instructed to advise the Americans immediately of the government's decision to suspend convertibility as a temporary measure on the evening of Tuesday 19 August.[56]

The Cabinet reconvened that Tuesday to discuss the bad news that the Americans were disappointed and relatively unsympathetic, on the one hand, but that, more positively, the drain on sterling on Monday had been somewhat less than anticipated ($16 million). A further twenty-four hours was allowed for negotiations with the Americans to try to save access to the loan. Since only 20 per cent of the drain appeared to be coming from the sterling area, convertibility for these countries was not formally suspended, but instead they were asked to exercise restraint. The continuation of current account convertibility within the exchange controls operated by each monetary authority, reinforced by collective agreements over dollar spending targets agreed in late 1947, became the cornerstone of the post-war sterling area system. The following day the Cabinet met again to consider a US counter-proposal to suspend the loan for two months. Cabinet members agreed that time had run out and that they needed to go ahead with the announcement as planned, at 9 p.m. on 20 August. They also agreed to promise not to draw on the loan beyond the tranches already notified to Washington.

The main sources of pressure on sterling during 1947 arose from the current balance of payments of Britain and the sterling area and from conversion by non-sterling area countries, partly due to the monetary agreements with Europe. At the Commonwealth economic meeting Eady blamed the crisis on Argentina, Brazil, Mexico, Peru, Chile and Sweden for converting sterling and thus prompting a run on the Bank of England.

[55] Hansard, House of Commons debate, 6 August 1947, col. 1492 and col. 1511.
[56] Transcript by Norman Brook of Cabinet meeting, 17 August 1947, TNA CAB195/5.

Table 2.2 *UK balance of payments with the dollar area (£ million), 1946–9*

	1946	1947	1948	1949
Current balance	–299	–506	–241	–291
Transfers to dollar area for rest of sterling area	–73	–299	+15	–53
Transfers to dollar area for non-sterling, non-dollar area	+37	–263	–102	–93
US loan	+247	+776	+82	+75
Gold and dollar reserves (+ signifies drawing)	–54	+152	+55	+3
Rest of sterling area net sales of gold in UK	+82	+77	+55	+68
Net drawings on IMF	0	+60	+15	0
Other (net long-term capital, balancing item, sterling holdings)	+60	+3	–23	+47
Marshall Aid (less US share of counterpart)	0	0	+144	+244

Source: UK Balance of Payments Yearbook: The Pink Book.

Eady asserted that the convertibility clause in the loan agreement was 'not a vicious thing and not of itself [the] cause of trouble', in an effort to deflect blame from both the United States and the United Kingdom.[57] Instead, he claimed that the problem had been slower than expected global recovery, which prolonged the dependence on US goods. This is somewhat disingenuous, since it had been clear in 1946 that the dollar shortage would extend beyond mid-1947.

Table 2.2 shows the UK balance of payments with the dollar area for 1946 to 1949. It is clear that the primary source of the drain was Britain's own current account deficit with the United States and Canada in 1947, which ballooned to the equivalent of over £500 million. A further £300 million of foreign exchange was transferred to the dollar area on behalf of the overseas sterling area countries to cover their deficits. The transfers on behalf of the non-sterling, non-dollar world (primarily western Europe and including £44 million in payments on behalf of West Germany) also increased enormously, showing a swing to the value of £300 million between 1946 and 1947. These dollar outgoings were paid for by drawing most of the US loan, selling South African gold, drawing on the IMF and reducing the gold and dollar reserves by $612 million (£152 million). Ellis Rees concluded that the crisis happened not because of the convertibility of sterling per se but because of the speed with which the loan was exhausted by current payments in the

[57] As reported by McFarlane, 27 August 1947, RBA S-a-1501.

months running up to convertibility. Transfers on behalf of European and sterling area countries that benefited from convertibility were only a secondary problem.

Britain was not able to increase exports to Organisation for European Economic Co-operation (OEEC) countries at all in 1947, which Cairncross attributes more to supply problems than a deliberate policy by these countries to run surpluses that they would soon be able to convert to US dollars. The United Kingdom was able to sell to all other groups of countries, however, so total exports increased by £245 million in 1947. It seems more likely that European countries were keen to accumulate sterling for conversion in 1947, since the UK trade surplus with the OEEC countries fell from £114 million in 1946 to £20 million in 1947. As noted above, in the six months between signing the loan agreement and the onset of convertibility Belgium purposefully accumulated sterling, and promptly converted it to US dollars under the terms of their bilateral monetary agreement with the United Kingdom. This process accelerated after convertibility, and the total conversions for 1947 amounted to $208 million (£50 million), which represented over a quarter of the loan drawn in 1947.[58]

The sterling balances of India, Pakistan and Ceylon fell by almost £100 million, and were responsible for almost the entire decline of sterling area assets, but most of this was spent in the United Kingdom rather than converted to US dollars. Countries outside the sterling area increased their sterling assets slightly overall, particularly western European official holdings, which rose by some £100 million. India drew down more of its balances than agreed, which shows how difficult the agreement was to enforce in this case. Bell notes that this was 'a matter of considerable concern to the British', but it did not provoke retaliation or reprimand because of India's bargaining power.[59] In 1949 Sir Leslie Rowan, Attlee's principal private secretary, admitted to the Americans that 'political and strategic considerations had made the UK liberal in releasing sterling balances' in the late 1940s.[60] There was particular sensitivity over India and Pakistan, since partition occurred on 15 August 1947 and was followed by a huge internal migration that cost hundreds of thousands of lives and provoked severe hardship. In these circumstances it is hard to envisage that India and Pakistan could have been refused access to their assets.

[58] Cairncross, *Years of Recovery*, p. 128.
[59] Bell, *The Sterling Area*.
[60] W. D. Matthews, Canadian embassy in Washington, DC, to Wynne Plumptre, 29 December 1949, 'Documents on Canadian external relations', vol. 15, 605.

Once the sterling crisis had necessitated the reintroduction of exchange controls outside the sterling area it was clear that the transition period of the Bretton Woods international monetary system was going to be extended indefinitely. In the short term, the run on the reserves during August 1947 prompted London to try to ration US dollar expenditure by the sterling area, and to this end the Chancellor called for an immediate Commonwealth conference. India refused to attend except as an observer, since it had signed an agreement to release £65 million just six days earlier (including the conversion of £15 million to dollars) and was reluctant to re-engage. Australia refused to make any minister available to attend, sending J. B. Brigden, financial counsellor of the Australian embassy in Washington to represent the government. Both Australia and New Zealand agreed to make every effort to contain US dollar expenditure but refused to accept formal targets; the internal UK Treasury history of the sterling balances deemed this first conference 'not a great success'.[61]

European nations reacted with varying degrees of anger and frustration to the suspension of the supplementary monetary agreements. New arrangements were negotiated with creditors through the second half of 1947 and the beginning of 1948, which took the form of a combination of continued blocking (Sweden), minimum balances to be preserved in sterling (Norway, Australia), some releases (Egypt, Iraq) and agreements to invoice trade in sterling (Egypt, Brazil, Argentina).[62] By the start of 1948 the United Kingdom was back to similar terms to the monetary agreements and payments agreements negotiated from 1944 to 1946 with many countries, sometimes with larger credit margins and in a couple of cases with more firm exchange guarantee provisions.

The case of Belgium was particularly bitter, as the Belgians had been using their supplementary monetary agreement to the full.[63] Table 2.3 shows the extent of their conversion of sterling earnings, mainly from Italy and the Netherlands, under their agreement in the run-up to July 1947. When convertibility was suspended they were left with £18 million of sterling and demanded settlement in gold or dollars for all but £5 million in fulfilment of the original monetary agreement, which was still in force. Maurice Frère, governor of the National Bank of Belgium,

61 Treasury Historical Memorandum no. 16, TNA T267/29. Brigden died a few months later, in November 1947. For Australia's response, see correspondence between Chifley and Hankinson 29 and 30 August 1947, ANA A571 1944/1660.

62 For details of the negotiations with Brazil, see de Paiva Abreu, M., 'Brazil as a creditor: sterling balances 1940–52', *Economic History Review*, 43(3), 1990, pp. 450–69.

63 This account comes from Sir Hugh Ellis Rees, who was personally involved: 'The convertibility crisis'.

Table 2.3 *Belgian conversion of sterling earned from third countries, November 1946–May 1947*

Amount	Date	Source
£2.5 million	November 1946	Norway
£1.5 million	January 1947	Italy
£2.2 million	February 1947	Italy and the Netherlands
£1.0 million	March 1947	Italy
£2.25 million	April 1947	Italy and the Netherlands
£4.0 million	May 1947	Norway
£1.5 million	May 1947	The Netherlands
Total: £15 million ($60 million)		

Source: Sir Hugh Ellis Rees, 'The convertibility crisis of 1947', Treasury Historical Memorandum no. 3, 1962, PRO T267/3, p. 24.

threatened immediately to stop buying sterling from Belgian banks, and the Foreign Office had to ask the prime minister, Paul-Henri Spaak, to intervene to ensure that banks would continue to accept sterling from customers. Belgium used the ensuing negotiations to make a further claim for an exchange guarantee and for the right to accept sterling in payment from a wide range of countries, thus increasing its potential sterling holdings to the level at which the United Kingdom would have to settle in gold or US dollars. After prolonged negotiations that were 'far from pleasant' and in which the Belgians 'did not hesitate to exploit our weakness to further their own interests', the British side had to concede a mutual exchange guarantee in terms of Belgian francs (not US dollars) and the expansion of transferability for Belgium in return for increasing the credit margin to £27 million instead of £5 million, to postpone the liability to settle in gold. Dalton resisted signing this agreement for several days, and then was on the verge of doing so when he abruptly resigned. By the time the agreement was signed, on 14 November, by the new Chancellor, Stafford Cripps, Belgian sterling balances had risen to £30.5 million and a gold payment of £3.5 million was due to Belgium. Immediately after the signing the Treasury served the appropriate notice under the new agreement that transfers of sterling to Belgium from several countries would be blocked as of the beginning of 1948, in order to stem their accumulation and the related UK gold liability.

Negotiations with the Indians proved difficult and prolonged, and they deserve some extended discussion, given the size of their balances and their importance in the immediate post-war period.[64] As India's balance

[64] Tomlinson, 'Indo-British relations'.

of payments deteriorated during 1947, a further release of £18 million for India (and £16 million for Pakistan) was agreed in February 1948. Negotiations for a final settlement began in June 1948, at which the British still hoped to arrange to cancel some liabilities against stores and other British assets in India. India demanded higher rates of immediate release, both to import British goods and to convert to US dollars. While the negotiations were under way India was also accumulating fresh sterling assets (amounting to £80 million in June 1948), which reduced their incentive to reach an agreement, since they were not as desperate for current releases from the blocked balances. The problem from the British side was that, if the United Kingdom refused an agreement, India would start to contravene the rules of the sterling area, prompting its expulsion. In the Cabinet, Cripps described this outcome as 'disastrous', partly because of the diversion of India's export trade to the dollar area.[65] In contrast, the departure of Egypt and Palestine from the sterling area was greeted with equanimity.

At last, a conservative valuation of stores and payment of an annuity for pensions absorbed £270 million of the assets, and a three-year scheme for releases was agreed. This was quickly overrun by India's balance of payments problems in 1949, which led to the rapid liquidation of sterling assets in advance of the agreed reduction. A new agreement in the summer of 1949 was then undermined by the subsequent devaluation of sterling in September. A final agreement on sterling balances was signed in February 1952, which set a minimum amount of sterling currency reserves to be kept in London over the next five years (£310 million) and rolled the releases from blocked accounts into the Colombo Plan for development in south Asia. In 1951 similar schedules to liquidate the wartime balances by 1957 were signed with Pakistan and Ceylon.[66] By this time, however, the international monetary and economic system had been transformed by the devaluation of sterling, the Korean War, the end of the dollar shortage and the establishment of the EPU.

Devaluation, 1949

One response to the convertibility crisis of 1947 might have been to devalue or float sterling rather than suspend convertibility. Marcus Fleming and James Meade, in the Economic Section of the Cabinet secretariat, had

[65] Transcript by Brook of Cabinet meeting, 17 June 1948, TNA CAB195/6.

[66] The schedule was £35 million per annum for India, £4 million per annum for Pakistan and £3 million per annum for Ceylon. In addition, minimum balances were to be kept in London as currency reserves. The agreements are to be found in Cmnd 8472 for India, Cmnd 8350 for Pakistan and Cmnd 8165 for Ceylon.

argued for greater flexibility in the exchange rate since 1944, but the idea was dismissed by the Treasury and the Bank of England as too much of a departure from the Anglo-American post-war vision.[67] Nevertheless, in June 1947 contingency planning began in the Bank and the Treasury to consider policy if Marshall Aid were not forthcoming and the Anglo-American Loan Agreement expired too quickly after convertibility, and this included a possible devaluation from US$4.04/£ to US$3.00/£. The timing was vital, however.

In the crisis of August 1947, floating would have antagonised the Americans and threatened access to the last US$700 million of the loan. Marshall Aid was announced in June 1947 and negotiations were planned for Paris in September to determine the distribution of the aid. Washington's emphasis on a joint European solution to trade and payments problems through economic integration was clearly in the foreground of their largesse, making this a most difficult moment to move to a floating sterling exchange rate. Moreover, withdrawing from the IMF at this stage would eliminate a key source of medium-term support.[68] Of course, with a free float there would be less need for credit, since the rate would take the burden of adverse movements, but there was hardly any discussion of a free float. 'Floating' throughout the post-war period really meant flexibility within wide margins.

On the other hand, given the experience of the 1930s, when the economy recovered after sterling had been floated in 1931, it is worth considering why this alternative was not considered more seriously. Initially there was no clear consensus that sterling was overvalued. After the First World War the huge debacle of the 'return to gold' at the pre-war parity, $4.86, in 1925 was widely criticised (most publicly by Keynes) as an 'overvaluation' that contributed to the weak performance of the British economy from 1925 to 1931.[69] To avoid a similar mistake after the Second World War, sterling was depreciated by 17 per cent against the US dollar, from $4.86 at the end of 1938 to $4.04, to compensate for the shift in the economic fortunes and competitiveness of the United States as against the United Kingdom. Rising prices in the United States compared to controlled prices in the United Kingdom and Europe led

[67] Burnham, P., *Remaking the Postwar World Economy: Robot and British Policy in the 1950s* (Basingstoke: Palgrave, 2003), pp. 23–4.

[68] The IMF declared France ineligible for access to the Fund after it devalued and implemented multiple exchange rates at the beginning of 1948. Aldcroft, D. H., and M. J. Oliver, *Exchange Rate Regimes in the Twentieth Century* (Cheltenham: Edward Elgar, 1998), pp. 98–9.

[69] Keynes, J. M., *The Economic Consequences of Mr. Churchill* (London: L. and V. Woolf, 1925); Moggridge, D. E., *British Monetary Policy 1924–31: The Norman Conquest of $4.86* (Cambridge: Cambridge University Press, 1972).

Keynes and other economists, such as Roy Harrod, to believe that the US dollar rather than the pound was slightly overvalued after the war.

Most at the Bank of England, where official expertise in exchange markets rested, were consistently against floating sterling, arguing that it would be impossible to manage with thin reserves assuming that some intervention would be required. During the 1930s float the newly established Exchange Equalisation Account (EEA) had intervened substantially. Given the imbalance between the United States and the rest of the world in the 1940s, intervention was likely to require sales of scarce gold and dollars to support the pound. Their concerns confirm that they did not actually consider a genuine free float with no intervention but, rather, a flexible policy. Even this would eliminate sterling's role as one of the two major reserve currencies in the proposed Bretton Woods system, which had only recently been ratified. There may have been an option to return to the sterling bloc era of the 1930s, with countries pegged to a flexible pound, but this was not likely to appeal to countries in the Commonwealth and beyond in the same way that the system had in the 1930s. These countries had development ambitions that could not be served by trade and investment from the United Kingdom alone, and the balance of global economic influence had shifted much more dramatically towards the United States than had been the case after the First World War. Calls for a closed imperial monetary and trading system were considered by Keynes and others as merely harking back to a past that was unrecoverable. Commonwealth countries would hold sterling only if it served their purposes of stability, liquidity and widespread acceptance in global (not just imperial) trade, and these attributes were likely to be undermined by a flexible rate in the context of the Bretton Woods system.

A stepwise devaluation might have been possible in 1947 within the existing commitment to stable exchange rates, especially since the rate survived only another twenty-four months. This option was not considered seriously, however. Cairncross details the repeated campaigns by Sir Richard 'Otto' Clarke, a civil servant at the Treasury, in June 1945 and again in February 1948 calling for a modest devaluation to correct the balance of payments.[70] At the time, however, direct controls rather than the price mechanism were the main policy instrument. Devaluation, it was argued, would not resolve the shortages and fundamental imbalance in production that plagued the post-war years. Increasing exports

[70] Cairncross, *Years of Recovery.* See also Cairncross, A. K., and B. Eichengreen, *Sterling in Decline: The Devaluations of 1931, 1949 and 1967* (Oxford: Blackwell, 1983), pp. 112–13, where the account is almost identical.

required expanded capacity rather than enhanced price competitiveness. Given the supply shortages, higher import prices would be felt more directly and quickly as a result of devaluation than any increase in export earnings, and this would necessitate even tighter quantitative controls and domestic restraint. The effect on import prices would be lessened if sterling area countries followed the pound, since many categories of food and raw materials came from the empire and the Commonwealth, but prices of essential machinery and manufactures from the dollar area would rise. Following the devaluation of the French franc in January 1948 there was a brief flurry of interest within the Treasury and the Economic Section in devaluing or floating sterling in the spring of 1948, even though France's actions attracted sanctions from the IMF, but there is no evidence that this debate ever reached ministers, and the idea was quietly abandoned.[71] The urgency was in part lessened as the current account returned to balance.

The decision finally to devalue in September 1949 had less to do with the specific problems of the British external position and was more the result of a gradual build-up of evidence and opinion, in the United Kingdom and in the rest of the world alike, that the US dollar was undervalued in comparison with all the main European currencies, not just the pound. European countries could not initiate an adjustment themselves without sterling leading the way, however, because of the important role that sterling played in intra-European payments. As James puts it, the view in the IMF was that 'a British devaluation was needed to clear the way for a general European adjustment'.[72] At the beginning of 1948 the United States and the IMF considered a general devaluation of European currencies, but ended up declaring that the time was not yet ripe. A year later, however, opinion in the IMF and Washington had hardened, and in March 1949 Frank Southard, the US executive director at the IMF, called for a general enquiry into the appropriateness of exchange rates across a range of European currencies.[73] Although it was not in the IMF's remit to suggest appropriate rates or initiate devaluations, the Fund wanted to be in a position to give informed advice.

Instead of a formal enquiry the managing director, Camille Gutt, arranged informal discussions with European members about exchange rate issues in May and June 1949, and he concluded that any general change of rates would have to be led by a devaluation of sterling, so

[71] Cairncross, *Years of Recovery*, p. 168.
[72] James, *International Monetary Cooperation*, p. 92.
[73] Horsefield, *The International Monetary Fund, 1945–1965*, vol. I, pp. 234–7; James, *International Monetary Cooperation*, p. 94.

that others could adjust their rates appropriately. In August an ad hoc committee of the IMF board began to examine a range of policies to restore equilibrium, including devaluation. The UK executive director (Geoffrey Tansley) had dissented from Southard's initial suggestion to establish this committee, though George Bolton eventually attended as a UK representative. The committee met intensively nineteen times from 18 August until it submitted its report on 8 September, by which time the British government had already secretly come to the conclusion that it would devalue. The report concluded that 'the Committee is convinced that taking Western Europe as a whole, adjustments of exchange rates varying in degree but in most cases substantial, are opportune and essential'.[74] The formal involvement and encouragement of the IMF in the general devaluation of 1949 rather contradicts Gavin's conclusion that the devaluation was an 'open violation of the rules of the International Monetary Fund'.[75] Instead, the sterling devaluation of 1949 needs to be viewed in a global context as part of a wider consensus about how to resolve the imbalance between the United States and the rest of the world, and the leadership of sterling in European monetary affairs at this time. In London, however, the enthusiasm for devaluation was slow to gather pace.

In March 1949, as the US recession began to take hold, Sir Robert Hall, director of the Economic Section, initiated a campaign to change minds in the Treasury and Foreign Office in favour of devaluation. The Board of Trade and the Bank of England remained resistant, and the decision was delayed while speculative pressure began to mount. Adding to the pressure were public claims from the US secretary to the Treasury, John Snyder, and the United Nations Economic Commission for Europe that European currencies were overvalued. Cairncross relates the details of the increasing insistence from the US administration at official and then ministerial level during May and June 1949 as planned tripartite discussions between the United States, Canada and the United Kingdom in September loomed.[76]

As Chancellor, Cripps remained solidly against devaluation, preferring to rely on direct controls and planning as he grew increasingly suspicious of his official advisers' commitment to Labour Party policy. Towards the end of June he won the Cabinet's support for a package of measures as an alternative to devaluation, including a dramatic 25 per cent cut in

[74] Horsefield, *The International Monetary Fund, 1945–1965*, vol. I, p. 237.

[75] Gavin, F. J., *Gold, Dollars, and Power: The Politics of International Monetary Relations, 1958–1971* (Chapel Hill: University of North Carolina Press, 2004), p. 167.

[76] Cairncross, *Years of Recovery*, pp. 172–5.

dollar expenditure and a special Commonwealth conference in July to coordinate further cuts in dollar imports. His call for a rise in bank rate, however, was roundly dismissed as ineffective in a planned economy. The debate also teased out a persistent thread of argument about the sterling exchange rate that would reappear over the next two decades. Devaluation was viewed by some as a tempting short-term solution to indulge market pressure but one that would not deliver lasting effects, particularly in an inflationary context when competitive gains for exports would quickly be eaten up by wage and price inflation. If devaluation was to be effective it had to be accompanied by stringent fiscal policies or price controls, but if these were adopted then there might be no need for devaluation in the first place. This was the position taken by the Bank of England, for which the negative impact on the future reputation of sterling weighed heavily, but it was also persuasive among officials in the Treasury.

Cripps' stubborn resistance meant that an opportunity for progress came about only when he left London on 19 July for a month in Switzerland to convalesce from exhaustion, leaving Hugh Gaitskell (minister of fuel and power) in charge. In Cripps' absence, Gaitskell, Douglas Jay and Harold Wilson met on 21 July and decided to recommend devaluation to ministers. A week later the Cabinet dodged the issue by giving the prime minister carte blanche to make the decision on his own. Attlee wrote to Cripps to advise him that sterling would be devalued on the grounds that speculative pressure was mounting, which discouraged exports and undermined willingness to hold sterling, and, secondly, that short-term aid to support the rate was unlikely to be forthcoming from the trilateral talks planned for September. Nor could any substantial aid arrive in any case before the reserves were exhausted.[77]

The trilateral talks had been called to discuss the payments imbalance between the dollar and sterling worlds. The United Kingdom hoped to gain reductions in US tariffs, relaxations on the use of Marshall Aid and Canadian and American acquiescence to strict sterling area cuts in dollar imports.[78] Initially, London sent a rather vague and academic agenda for the meeting, but the Canadians and Americans pressed for

[77] Cairncross, *Years of Recovery*, p. 183; Cairncross and Eichengreen, *Sterling in Decline*, p. 127.

[78] Cairncross, *Years of Recovery*, p. 185. The Canadians were asked to 'lend support to U.K. appeals to the U.S. to desist from devaluation talk'. Telegram from A. E. Ritchie, Canadian high commission in London, on a meeting with Oliver Franks, Leslie Rowan and others of the United Kingdom with N. A. Robertson, secretary to Canadian Cabinet, W. C. Clark, Canadian deputy minister of finance, and others, 7 July 1949; 'Documents on Canadian external relations', volume 15, 565.

more specifics in early August. The Americans wanted to discuss British domestic policies to increase the competitiveness of British exports and the role of the exchange rate, as well as ways that the United States and Canada could increase sterling imports.[79] With the exchange rate on the agenda, Attlee wanted the decision to devalue to be taken before officials gathered in Washington for the pre-conference meeting rather than bargain it for some sort of concession from the United States, as Cripps and Bevin had suggested.

From here on, Cripps sought firmer control of the process. He insisted that the announcement should come from him personally after he returned from the trilateral talks on 18 September (rather than 24 August, as Gaitskell suggested), thus prolonging the drain on the reserves. He was adamant that he would break the news, to the extent that the British Broadcasting Corporation (BBC) was not to mention it until he had got to that part in his live broadcast speech. This introduced a good deal of uncertainty, as embassies, consulates, etc. overseas could not reliably be informed at exactly the same time that Cripps spoke the actual word 'devaluation', with the result that there was a danger that the news would bounce back to London over newswires before Cripps had addressed the British public.[80] Cripps' tactics ended up prolonging the crisis and drawing considerable public criticism, which would have a lasting impact on the Labour Party's assessment of the economic and political costs of devaluing sterling.

At the beginning of September the Treasury drafted a long paper on the inflationary impact of devaluation on prices and wages, but this was dismissed by Cripps, who did not want the Cabinet to see it (although Attlee had a copy). Instead, Cripps asked for a legislated one-month freeze on all prices after the devaluation, except for bread.[81] The prime minister and his advisers resisted a wage and price freeze because it would require complicated new legislation and would create an anticipation of large price increases after the month-long freeze had expired.[82] As with future devaluations, the accompanying measures proved to be as difficult to agree as the decision to devalue itself.

The prime ministers of Australia, New Zealand and South Africa (the 'old dominions') had been told about the decision to devalue by Tuesday 13 September, but they were not advised of the rate until it was finally

[79] Telegram from Canadian ambassador to Washington, DC, to secretary of state for external affairs, 2 August 1949; 'Documents on Canadian external relations', vol. 15, 572.

[80] Telegram from Sir Edward Bridges to Sir Stafford Cripps, 15 September 1949, TNA PREM8/973.

[81] 'Price structure after devaluation', 9 September 1949, TNA PREM8/973.

[82] Telegram from Attlee to Cripps, 15 September 1949, TNA PREM8/973.

agreed in London. The advance notice was partly to ensure that they could arrange a simultaneous devaluation of their currencies, and also to secure their cooperation at the IMF board of governors' meeting on Friday 16 September. Ministers agreed that 'it was very desirable that the Commonwealth presented a united front' at this meeting, and to this end the 'new dominions' – India, Pakistan and Ceylon – were also to be informed a day or two before the IMF meeting.[83] The managing director of the IMF was told on Thursday 15 September and secret applications to alter exchange rates began to come forward to the IMF from various countries from 12:22 a.m. on Saturday, starting with the United Kingdom and South Africa.

On the afternoon of Saturday 17 September, once Cripps had returned from Washington, a special, secret, meeting of Cabinet was held to announce the devaluation to ministers and to go over Cripps' speech, which was scheduled for 9:00 p.m. on Sunday night. Ministers were led stealthily through no. 11 Downing Street, on foot, to the garden gate at the back of no. 10, and through the Old Treasury Building, in order to avoid attracting press attention.[84] Once assembled, members of the Cabinet challenged Cripps over his interpretation of devaluation as a response to speculators rather than as a longer-term adjustment intended to increase dollar earnings. Cripps replied that he believed the devaluation was indeed driven mostly by the need to calm speculation and that 'it was not at all clear that the devaluation, while it might increase the volume of this country's exports to the dollar area, would be sufficiently great (in view of the smaller number of dollars which would be earned) to help close the gap'.[85] He was still not persuaded by opinion in the United States and the IMF that a realignment of exchange rates would restore global balance. He also made clear his belief that devaluation would be inflationary and require greater sacrifice from the British public to contain wage demands. Clearly, Cripps was not convinced of the longer-term benefits of devaluation, even on the eve of the announcement, but viewed it as a short-term expedient.

Attlee and Cripps interpreted the initial public reaction to the devaluation as 'relief rather than apprehension, tempered by some slight feeling that the operation was a blow to national prestige. It enjoyed, generally speaking, a far better press than could, on Sunday night, have been anticipated.'[86] There was no sign, then, of the Labour Party

[83] Minute of a meeting of ministers, 14 September 1949, TNA PREM8/973.
[84] Memo by A. Johnston, 17 September 1949, TNA PREM8/973.
[85] Cabinet minutes CM 55 (49), 17 September 1949, TNA PREM8/973.
[86] Telegram from Cripps and Attlee to Secretary of State, UN delegation in New York, 21 September 1949, TNA PREM8/973.

being haunted by the spectre of being 'the party of devaluation' – the preoccupation of the Labour government in 1967. Public concern centred instead on Cripps' worries about the inflationary effects and the need for wage restraint. Unlike the devaluation of 1967, the 1949 policy reflected the accumulation of both market and official opinion in Europe, the United States and the IMF that devaluation was appropriate. There was also plenty of time for advance notice to be given to American, European and sterling area leaders, which reduced the political fallout.

During the tripartite talks in Washington the Americans received Cripps' advance notice of the proposed devaluation with palpable relief.[87] The meetings of officials prior to the announcement had been cordial but somewhat frosty and unproductive, as they waited for decisions to be made by the Cabinet in London. The Canadians reported back to Ottawa that the UK leader of the official talks, Henry Wilson-Smith, had not been able to meet with Cripps before leaving for Washington and found it 'rather embarrassing stalling for time until he gets word from the British Cabinet'.[88] On 3 September, just before Cripps met with his counterparts, Secretary of State Dean Acheson warned Oliver Franks, the British ambassador in Washington, that, unless further action was taken by the British to address the imbalance between the dollar area and the sterling area, the Americans could not be counted on for continued support. Bevin's speech at the opening of the ministerial talks was met warmly by Snyder, who described Bevin's praise for the Marshall Plan rather effusively as 'beautiful expressions of a great soul'.[89] At the time, Franks jubilantly credited the devaluation decision with restoring Anglo-American relations to the point that the United Kingdom was no longer viewed as merely another European nation, but was redeemed as the primary partner in reshaping the entire global trade and payments order. Milward agrees that the Washington talks 'mark[ed] the end of the American pressure to force Britain into taking the lead in the economic and political integration of Europe', but disagrees with Franks' conclusion that they restored the predominance of Anglo-American relationship over Washington's desire for European integration, since the US

[87] Telegram from Oliver Franks in Washington, DC, to Bridges in London, 20 September 1949, TNA PREM8/973.

[88] Canadian deputy minister of trade and commerce (in Washington, DC) to minister of trade and commerce, 29 August 1949, 'Documents on Canadian external relations', vol. 15, 585.

[89] Ed Ritchie, first secretary at high commission to the United Kingdom, to Secretary of State for external affairs, 8 September 1949, 'Documents on Canadian external relations', vol. 15, 591.

administration still expected Britain to support (if no longer lead) this campaign.[90]

Although the Americans did not offer advice on the precise rate to which sterling should be devalued they did impress upon Cripps the need for the devaluation to be substantial enough to preclude another change in the near future. Relations between Cripps (who still appeared unwell) and Snyder were not warm, and the Canadians reported a sharp exchange between them over the sterling balances during which Snyder complained that the overall total of the balances had not been reduced and very little was firmly blocked.[91] Cripps replied that the releases allowed under India's agreement were only equal to India's purchases of sterling capital goods and he and Bevin both stressed that if the Indian Congress government agreed to block or cancel more of the balances it would promptly be replaced by a left-wing government less amenable to Anglo-American strategic priorities. The meeting concluded with a commitment to ongoing trilateral discussions on the issues of trade and payments, including the sterling balances.[92]

Opinion in the rest of the sterling area was muted, and in the spirit of the general realignment all followed sterling. On the eve of the devaluation John Dedman, the Australian minister for post-war reconstruction, questioned Australia's membership of the sterling area.[93] Frederick Wheeler, secretary to the Treasury, responded that the system was still in Australia's national interest, as withdrawal would result in the country's substantial remaining sterling reserves being blocked. This gave Australia 'the strongest interest in supporting sterling and assisting in restoring its convertibility, if only as a means of protecting the value of her own sterling reserves'. Australia was a net drawer on the dollar reserves of the sterling area, peaking at US$164.8 million in 1947/8 and estimated at US$73 million in 1948/9, so the system allowed these dollar imports to continue. Australian exports might be diverted from sterling markets to US dollar markets to make up the dollar deficit, but the prospects for this were uncertain and such a strategy was unlikely to generate more dollars than the sterling area system did. The United Kingdom was the most reliable market for Australian production, and 'restoration of the widest possible multilateral trading system based on sterling offers the best

90 Milward, A. S., *The Reconstruction of Western Europe 1945–51* (London: Methuen, 1984), pp. 294–5.

91 H. H. Wrong, Canadian ambassador to United States, to minister of finance, 14 September 1949, 'Documents on Canadian external relations', vol. 15, 593.

92 Official meetings duly took place in November/December 1949.

93 F. H. Wheeler to J. J. Dedman, 17 August 1949, Australian Department of Foreign Affairs and Trade historical documents.

hope of promoting economic development and higher standards of living throughout the world', including Australia. Wheeler viewed the sterling area system as an alternative to a retreat to bilateralism in the short term and a pathway to achieving further multilateralism in the longer term. These internal discussions confirmed Keynes' and Dalton's conviction that Australia would reject proposals to restrict the sterling area to an inconvertible sterling bloc.

The economic impact of the devaluation is difficult to disentangle from other events surrounding it. Cairncross and Eichengreen, echoing Dow, have argued that devaluation five months earlier in April 1949, 'could have been represented as a considered move, inevitable in the long run and necessary in the general interests of the world economy. It certainly would have been a good deal smaller and less disruptive.'[94] In terms of size, Cairncross suggests that a 20–25 per cent devaluation, to a rate of $3.20 or $3.00 rather than $2.80, would have sufficed if the decision had been taken earlier in the year.[95] Although the actual rate was a 30 per cent devaluation against the US dollar, the trade-weighted devaluation was of the order of only 9 per cent, because most European and sterling area countries also devalued to some extent.[96] It is certainly possible that other countries would not have followed the pound if a smaller adjustment had been made, as Milward suggests, and so the effective devaluation could have been greater.[97] This would also have lessened the general readjustment of the dollar/non-dollar world partly achieved through the exchange rate changes in 1949, however.

The devaluation did achieve Cripps' goal of stemming the speculative drain of US dollars, but the longer-term economic impact was obscured by the advent of the Korean War restocking boom nine months later, which generated primary product price inflation, particularly for sterling area exporters, and reduced the global dollar shortage. As predicted, the devaluation had a quicker and more significant impact on imports than on exports. In the twelve months leading up to the outbreak of the Korean War, in June 1950, British import prices rose by 17 per cent while export prices rose only by 5 per cent.[98] Nevertheless, domestic inflation was contained partly through continued controls and

[94] Cairncross and Eichengreen, *Sterling in Decline*, pp. 116–17. See also Dow, J. C. R., *The Management of the British Economy, 1945–60* (Cambridge: Cambridge University Press, 1964), p. 41

[95] Cairncross, *Years of Recovery*, p 188.

[96] Cairncross and Eichengreen, *Sterling in Decline*, p. 153. Pakistan did not follow sterling.

[97] Milward, *The Reconstruction of Western Europe*, p. 292.

[98] Cairncross and Eichengreen, *Sterling in Decline*, p. 154.

the Labour Party's ability to garner trade union cooperation on wage demands.

On the other hand, it is important to assess the political and symbolic importance of the devaluation for Anglo-American relations. Restoring the US government's confidence in the United Kingdom's commitment to the path of opening up to global payments rather than retreating into a sterling area bloc was probably as important as the economic effects. Although trade controls were reimposed in the wake of the end of the Korean-War-induced boom, in 1951, the path to freer payments had been established and a closed sterling area system could no longer be interpreted realistically as a longer-term alternative to freer global payments. This was especially evident in the strong pressure on Britain to restore sterling convertibility from key members of the sterling area, such as Australia, which led to the 'collective approach' to convertibility from 1952. The combined European devaluations against the US dollar in September 1949 also laid the foundations for the establishment of the European Payments Union in 1950 with American support.[99]

What lessons were learned from the 1949 devaluation? Certainly, the speculative run meant that neither the IMF nor the United States ever publicly suggested that sterling should be devalued again. In the 1950s the US position over exchange rate flexibility – and, indeed, convertibility – hardened, so that they no longer supported either and moved towards encouraging the EPU as a means to promote European integration, even at the cost of discrimination against the United States. When the United Kingdom made plans to move towards convertibility in the early 1950s they were immediately discouraged by the US administration. By the 1960s, when the market periodically acted on the belief that devaluation was imminent, the United States was committed to sustaining the sterling exchange rate as a defence against subsequent speculation against the dollar. As a result, the Americans appreciated successive British governments' struggles during the 1960s to sustain the fixed rate and did not greet the devaluation of 1967 with the relief that had accompanied the 1949 move. Once the dollar shortage had disappeared, the IMF, Europe and the United States blamed British governments' inability to contain excessive domestic demand for the pressure on sterling and fought hard to force the United Kingdom to adapt its domestic policy to reflect the exchange rate rather than adapt the exchange rate to relative international prices.

[99] Eichengreen, *Reconstructing Europe's Trade and Payments*.

Conclusions

Although the period dealt with by this chapter was only five years long, it was a crucial period for setting the foundations for sterling policy for the next three decades. The debate about the sterling balances brought the external position clearly to the forefront of British government planning, and they became a focus of advice and criticism from the United States and Europe that was to continue through to the 1970s. The term 'sterling balances' persisted, as did reference to the 'overhang' of these liabilities over reserve assets and the need for a solution to the 'sterling balances problem'. Although from 1945 to 1948 the bulk of the sterling balances could legitimately be claimed to have arisen from the abnormal financial exigencies of wartime, by the end of the decade this was no longer the case. Nonetheless, for the next thirty years sterling assets held overseas were perceived both within the United Kingdom and by the United States and Europe as extraordinary accumulations that burdened the British economy and threatened the international monetary system as a whole, and so required special action by the United Kingdom or the international community – despite the fact that the wartime accumulations were replaced in the 1950s by new assets held by central monetary institutions of new territories for a variety of different reasons.

Negotiations over how sterling assets would be spent pulled the overseas sterling area countries closely together (although sometimes in acrimonious relations) during the late 1940s. The Labour government sought to identify an ongoing common interest in supporting sterling as an international currency, thus sharing the burden of Britain's wartime and postwar difficulties. This effort to carry the overseas sterling area along in common purpose was not as successful as was hoped. Australia and India were quick to identify their own national interests as being separate from those of Britain. By the early 1950s the willingness of the overseas sterling countries to sacrifice their own interests to those of the United Kingdom had receded further, and the sterling area system came to rely more on the colonial use of sterling.

The European monetary agreements highlight the important role that sterling played in restoring international payments during the early years of the dollar shortage, but the climacteric of 1947 had long-lasting implications for the evolution of the international monetary system. The lesson drawn by Europe was that a quick dash to convertibility had to be abandoned, and slower progress on a regional basis was pursued instead. The way forward was cleared by the devaluation of sterling, which led the global realignment against the US dollar. That European states could not readjust on their own is testament to Britain's monetary leadership in these years and the importance of sterling in the international monetary system, but the key policy platform soon moved to the European sphere, with US support.

Along with the rhetoric and stylised understanding of the sterling balances 'problem', the early years after the Second World War also established the involvement of the United States, and to a lesser extent the IMF and Europe, in the direction of British sterling policy. The international role of sterling was central to the very origins of the IMF in the run-up to Bretton Woods. One of the key weaknesses in the Bretton Woods institutions was the failure to resolve the transition from the immediate post-war global imbalance to an environment in which controls on trade and payments could be relaxed within a pegged exchange rate system. Excluding a resolution of wartime liabilities from the articles of agreement was part of this lacuna. From the 1950s, British governments and officials sought to reverse this outcome by developing schemes for the IMF to take over Britain's overseas sterling liabilities.

For Washington, sterling policy was of vital importance in two respects. First, the 'key currency' scheme that emerged after 1944 required sterling to be a secondary reserve asset, which encouraged the State Department to seek to restore sterling's traditional international role even if at a reduced level compared to the US dollar. The Americans' preoccupation, and later frustration, with the persistence of the sterling balances arose from their view that the 'overhang' had to be reduced in order to restore confidence in sterling and thereby provide the foundation for its rehabilitation. Second, and more directly, these liabilities were believed to constrain Britain's ability to adopt the liberal, multilateral tenets of America's post-war vision for the international system. This prompted strong pressure on British governments to agree to eliminate the threat that these liabilities posed by reducing the total and (paradoxically for the US liberal vision) restricting the convertibility of the rest. The inability to deliver the strict freezing or cancellation of these liabilities prior to July 1947 was a great disappointment to the United States, but it was not in the end the main cause of the collapse of the convertibility trial of 1947, which was primarily attributable to the UK current account.

In the following year recognition that the threat to multilateralism was the global imbalance, rather than just the United Kingdom's external position, led to an emerging consensus that the whole system of Bretton Woods exchange rate pegs needed adjustment. By this time, however, Britain's Labour government (and Cripps in particular) had become wedded to direct controls and had lost faith in the ability of the price mechanism to deliver the root and branch reform of British industry that would restore its competitiveness. Public assertions by the IMF and the United States that European currencies, including sterling, were overvalued served to precipitate a change of view, although Cripps never believed (correctly, as it turned out) that devaluation would resolve the underlying problems of the UK economy. British governments' lack of faith in the ability of exchange rate adjustment to improve Britain's international performance is another persistent theme throughout the post-war period.

In sum, many of the themes of the external pressures on British sterling policy found their origins in the first years after 1945, as the United States, the IMF, the sterling area and Europe all grappled with the apparently parlous position of the British external position. International opinion about sterling was set to evolve over the following decades, but the initial five years of crisis after the war definitely left their mark on the pattern of what was to come. Indeed, so scarred were many policy-makers and commentators by this period that they often continued to view sterling as still being caught in the difficulties of the immediate post-war period. Sterling was persistently believed to be overvalued, the ratio of sterling liabilities to foreign exchange reserves was often cited and sterling held in foreign exchange reserves was described as precarious and extraordinary, making sterling vulnerable to speculation. Overseas sterling holdings continued to be a 'problem' for the international monetary system, requiring both vigilance by British governments and international cooperation. Nevertheless, the actual international role of sterling was to be transformed in the 1950s – as the next chapter shows.

3 The return to convertibility 1950–1959

The turbulent international monetary relations of the late 1940s established the discourse of the burden of the sterling balances and the 'overhang', which persisted in characterisations of sterling's international role throughout the 1950s. Despite the continuity in how sterling's international status was interpreted, during the 1950s the actual role of sterling changed dramatically, as the wartime accumulations were exhausted and replaced by the official reserves of Commonwealth and colonial territories. During this decade the relatively weak performance of the British economy and the identification of 'stop-go' in the domestic policy cycle intensified public controversy over the constraint imposed on British policy-making by sterling's international role. The United Kingdom seemed to some commentators to be pursuing an ambitious global strategic and economic role that was detrimental to the national economic interest. This debate was both a prism for a reassessment of what Britain's global position should be, both economically and politically, and marked the beginning of the 'declinist' approach to assessing the performance of the British economy. After a bold scheme for the United Kingdom to lead an attack on the flawed Bretton Woods system was abandoned in early 1952, British governments learned that the management of sterling as an international currency was constrained by American and European attitudes.

Sterling as a reserve currency

The international monetary system in the 1950s was very different from what had come before and from what followed in the 1960s. At the start of the decade the recovery of western Europe and the dominance of the US economy created a shortage of dollars that was only partly relieved by $13 billion of Marshall Aid, which began to flow out of America from 1948. With the United States the main source of the machinery and consumer goods necessary to restore the living standards of other countries, there was a scramble to increase dollar earnings and restrict dollar expenditure. The contractionary impact of such policies was ameliorated by the intra-European payments agreements and the sterling area arrangements discussed in chapter 2, and in the 1950s about 40 per cent of world trade was still denominated in sterling. This climate changed with the onset of the Korean War in June 1950, which generated a global demand for raw materials for rearmament, increased US spending and redistributed dollars towards Europe and developing countries. From 1950 to 1954 western European monetary authorities and governments doubled the value of their holdings of US dollars, from $2.4 billion to $5 billion. These developments in the international economy had profound effects on the role of sterling as a reserve currency and as a commercial currency.

Figure 3.1 shows that, during the 1950s, the proportion of global foreign exchange reserve held in sterling gradually declined, particularly during the Korean War boom, when the US dollar recovered as a reserve asset. All the same, sterling remained the only major reserve currency other than the dollar, accounting for one-third of global foreign exchange reserves, and it was clearly vital to the operation of a fixed exchange rate regime that required ample reserves to manage the pegged rates. Gold still comprised two-thirds of global reserves, with the rest being foreign exchange. The gold was unevenly distributed, with the United States holding two-thirds of world gold reserves at the start of the decade, because the Bretton Woods system depended on the fixed US dollar price of gold. Britain also held the bulk of its reserves – some 90 per cent – in gold during the 1950s. By the end of the decade other countries had accumulated

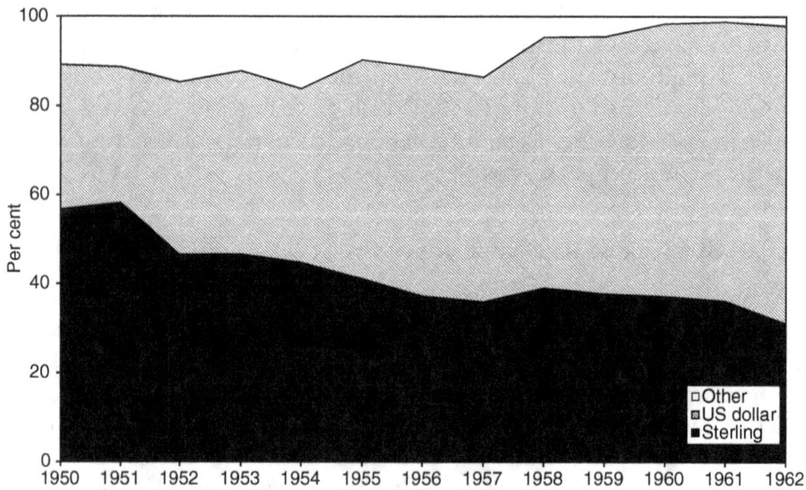

Figure 3.1 Distribution of foreign exchange reserves, 1950–62

substantial gold reserves, so that the US share had fallen to a half, while foreign exchange reserves grew more rapidly than gold reserves.

Figure 3.2 shows that, while the nominal value of overseas sterling holdings increased slightly, the real value declined rapidly at the end of the 1940s, recovered briefly during the Korean War and then resumed the decline for the rest of the decade. This trend was interrupted only in 1960, by a one-off accumulation of sterling (£131 million) by Ford Motor Co. of America in preparation for a minority purchase into its UK subsidiary. It is also clear that the British domestic economy grew much more rapidly than the value of foreign sterling liabilities, so that, whereas in 1950 the value of net overseas sterling liabilities amounted to 26 per cent of British GDP, by 1962 this ratio had fallen to 12 per cent – the same as the average proportion from 1931 to 1938.[1]

The preoccupation of governments and critics at the time was not the volume of overseas sterling liabilities, however, but the ratio to 'assets', which were narrowly defined as official holdings of gold and foreign exchange. Figure 3.3 shows that this ratio declined from the very high level of the immediate post-war years to about 3:1 by the end of the decade. Although the ratio improved, therefore, the 'overhang' was still

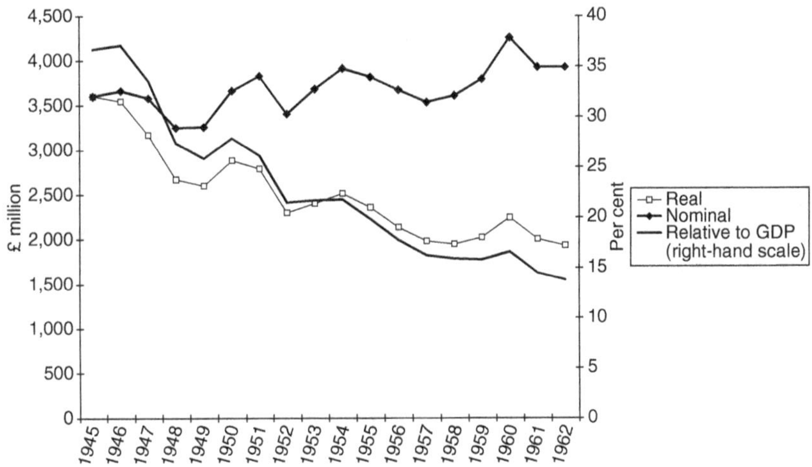

Figure 3.2 Real and nominal value of net overseas sterling holdings of countries and relative to UK GDP, 1945–62

[1] Data from *Reserves and Liabilities 1931–1945*, Cmnd 8354 (London: HMSO, 1951). GDP in current prices from www.measuringworth.com. Officer, L. H., 'What was the UK GDP then?', MeasuringWorth, 2009, www.measuringworth.org/ukgdp.

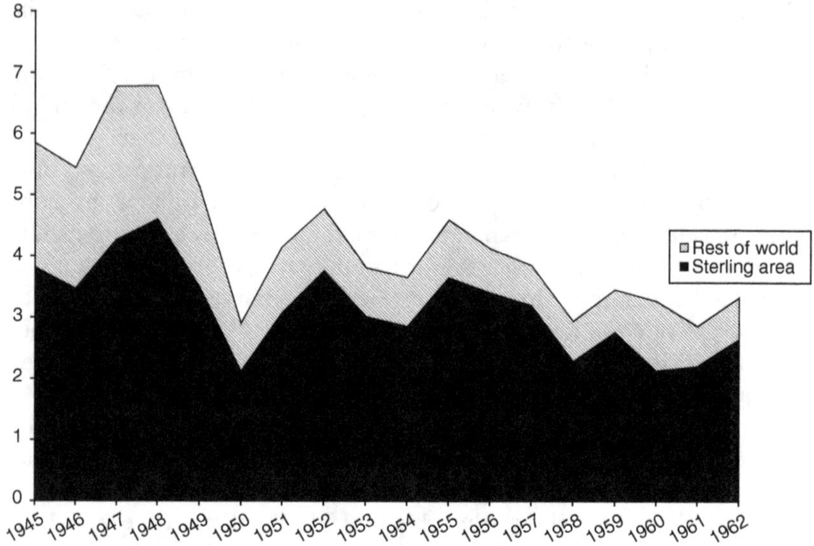

Figure 3.3 Ratio of overseas net sterling liabilities to reserves, 1945–62

substantial throughout the 1950s, and an increasing share of British overseas sterling liabilities was held in sterling area countries, mainly as foreign exchange reserves. The threat was that, if these reserves were all presented for conversion to US dollars at once, the Bank of England would not be able to honour them. Of course, the likelihood of this happening was very small, but the ratio suggested that even a 25 per cent liquidation would exhaust Britain's foreign exchange reserves.

In part, this interpretation rests on the calculation of the ratio.[2] The ratio of sterling balances to foreign exchange reserves tends to include illiquid liabilities and exclude substantial liquid assets. In the event of a run on the pound, the reserves would be the first area to feel the strain, but the government had other liquid assets at its disposal. A substantial sum of US equities, mainly General Motors and Shell Oil, had been accumulated during the war (valued at $875 million in 1958), and in addition IMF resources could be accessed in an exchange crisis, as was clear during the 1956 Suez Crisis. Adjustments to take account of a broader definition of 'assets', including the reserve position in the IMF and a conservative valuation of $700 million for the equities, is shown in figure 3.4. On this reckoning, the ratio of liabilities to assets was more

[2] Conan suggests changing the ratio by including OSA non-sterling holdings and national assets. He also casts doubt on the liquidity of colonial liabilities. Conan, A. R., *The Rationale of the Sterling Area: Texts and Commentary* (London: Macmillan, 1961), pp. 12–14.

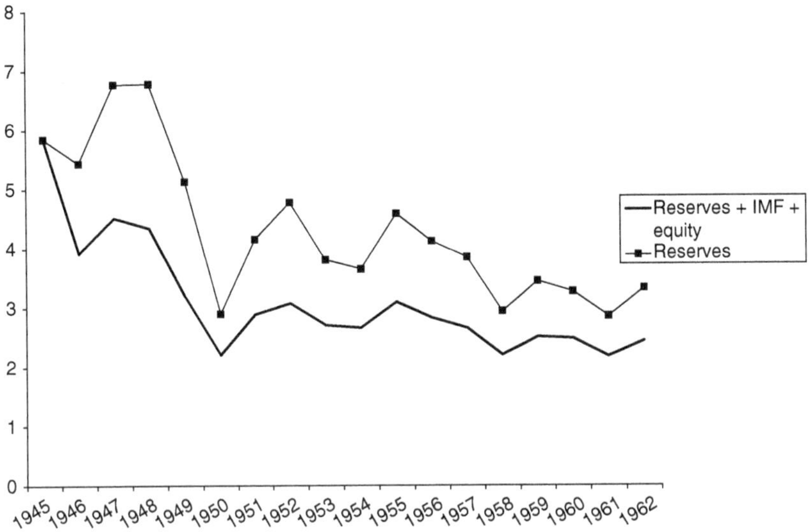

Figure 3.4 Ratio of net sterling liabilities to reserves and total assets, 1945–62

stable at a lower level, below 3:1, from 1950. It might be argued that these were not all liquid assets, since sales of equity could reduce their value and drawings on the IMF took time, but a substantial proportion of the sterling liabilities was also illiquid.

The liquidity of Britain's overseas sterling liabilities was determined largely by who held these assets and for what purpose. We have seen that during the 1940s a range of agreements were reached with the major holders of sterling that limited liquidity. The extent to which these agreements were enforceable varied, and it was shown that, particularly in the case of newly independent India and Pakistan, the government was not willing to take punitive measures when spending exceeded agreed amounts. In the 1950s the situation changed, as the value of sterling assets held by British colonies more than doubled, from £673 million in 1950 to £1.45 billion in 1958, by which time colonies accounted for about a half of the total overseas sterling reserves.[3]

The longer-term impact of the sterling 'overhang' should not be overlooked, however. The balances did, ultimately, represent claims on British production or foreign exchange if they were all to be redeemed, which would represent a burden on British resources even if this was

[3] The composition of colonial sterling balances and their implications is covered in greater detail in Schenk, *Britain and the Sterling Area,* pp. 20–5.

achieved gradually. In fact, although the geographical distribution of this debt shifted, the total value of sterling liabilities did not decline during the post-war period, so there was no net drain on the reserves or the economy other than the cost of borrowing. The British economy was able to sustain a higher level of overseas debt than otherwise, and, when the sterling balances were rising, they financed British balance of payments deficits. Nevertheless, the perception that the accumulation of sterling by central monetary authorities was in some way extraordinary, dependent on the habitual but waning loyalty of Commonwealth countries and colonies, led to the conviction that the sterling balances would sooner or later be replaced by other forms of reserves. This shows an underlying assumption that the reserve role of sterling would decline.

The choice of reserve asset in the pegged exchange rate Bretton Woods system was determined primarily by the anchor currency and the denomination of trade and debt. As trade and debt became more diversified, the reserve currency had to be convertible against a more diversified portfolio. For sterling area countries, most of their trade was with the United Kingdom, and London was the main source of borrowing. This reflected both the legacy of pre-war imperial and other traditional economic and political relationships and also the global imbalance after the end of the war. This situation changed as the decade progressed, but the costs of switching from one reserve currency to another prolonged the process into the 1960s.

The use of sterling as a reserve currency is often attributed to the lingering impact of British imperial relations. Eichengreen has argued that 'after World War II sterling was not held because of any lingering incentives conferred by network externalities but mainly as a matter of loyalty by members of the Commonwealth and the colonies with limited choice in the matter'. The power of Commonwealth loyalty as the primary explanation must be drawn into question by the fact that Canada was a leading member of the Commonwealth but was not part of the sterling area, and, on the other hand, Iraq, Kuwait and other countries outside the Commonwealth did hold their reserves in sterling. There was certainly a remnant of imperial feeling after the war, but most states had emerged with clear priorities of pursuing full employment and economic development. The difficult negotiations with Australia, New Zealand and India in the 1940s showed that they had become adept at exercising their own interests when they conflicted with those of the United Kingdom. Nor did the Commonwealth buy into British efforts to use the sterling area as a triangular system of complementary trade, with the developing economies producing primary products for the United Kingdom and the rest of the world and buying manufactured goods from the United

Table 3.1 *Percentage share of sterling in total reserves, 1950–8*

	1950	1951	1952	1953	1954	1955	1956	1957	1958
Iraq	95	80	81	86	91	84	80	71	66
Ceylon	89	73	78	67	73	67	56	53	47
Australia	82	66	65	70	64	49	58	65	55
Pakistan	78	79	52	57	59	62	53	50	44
India	73	69	69	97	97	98	56	44	33
New Zealand	64	61	62	73	69	61	72	63	66
South Africa	24	22	23	8	19	7	8	—	—

Source: Schenk, *Britain and the Sterling Area*, p. 30.

Kingdom to support British deficits elsewhere.[4] After the emergency trade restrictions of 1951, they refused to participate in coordinated trade programmes and sought to accelerate the British programme for restoring sterling convertibility. As Eichengreen acknowledges, the persistence of using sterling as a reserve asset was the result not just of symbolic or emotional allegiance but of a rational understanding that diversification would disrupt the entire sterling system of exchange rate stability and damage the British economy (and perhaps the global monetary system) in ways that were not in the interests of its trading partners. These factors can be interpreted as network externalities, being part of the benefits of sticking with an established collective system.

Nonetheless, during the 1950s most independent members of the sterling area that had control of the denomination of their reserves did diversify from the high levels of sterling that they had held at the start of the decade, mainly by spending their sterling on British goods while they held their US dollar assets and gold constant. Table 3.1 shows that South Africa, as a major gold producer, had completely eliminated its sterling reserves by mid-1957, while Australia, Britain's largest export market, had reduced the sterling share of its reserves to 55 per cent by the time of convertibility. India, Pakistan and Ceylon (renamed Sri Lanka in 1972) completed the process of diversification to the global average of reserves in sterling. From the mid-1950s oil revenues led to a steady increase in the amounts of sterling held in non-Commonwealth countries in the Middle East, in particular in Iraq and the Persian Gulf. Kuwait's sterling assets grew from £3 million at the end of 1952 to £260 million by the

[4] For the erosion of trade relations within the sterling area, see Schenk, *Britain and the Sterling Area*, ch.3.

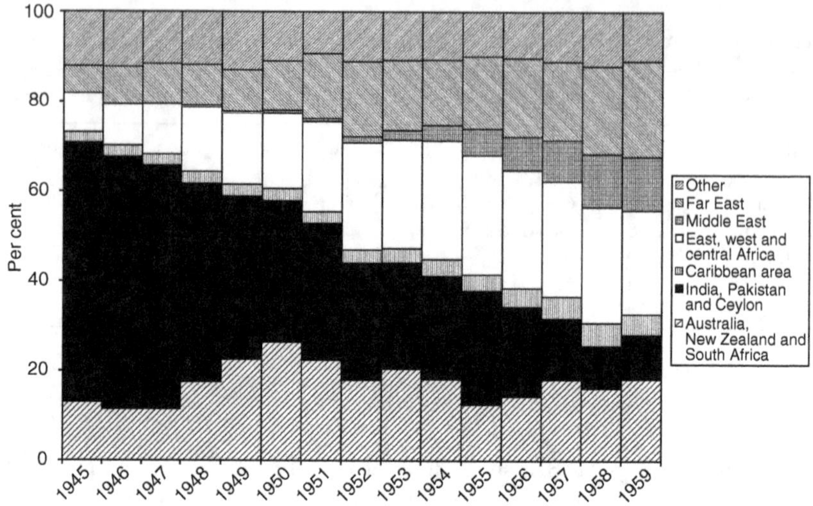

Figure 3.5 Geographical distribution of sterling assets held by sterling area countries, 1945–59

end of 1958, bringing them nearly to the level of Australia, which held £295 million of sterling by that time.

While Commonwealth loyalty was not a driving factor in sterling's reserve status, British dependent territories were vital to the transformation of the international role of sterling in the 1950s. Figure 3.5 shows a redistribution of sterling reserves from the independent members of the sterling area to colonies, particularly in Africa and the Far East, which benefited from high raw material prices in the early 1950s.

Figure 3.6 shows that the share of Malaya and Singapore, as major tin and rubber exporters, grew especially quickly, and they comprised 24 per cent of colonial balances by 1952, compared with 16 per cent in 1949. During the Korean War boom the balance of trade for Malaya and Singapore went from a deficit of £92 million in 1949 to a surplus of £431 million in 1951. Although this surplus receded in subsequent years, Malaya and Singapore's cumulative trade surplus from 1949 to 1957 was still £674 million. West Africa was the other region that was a major holder of sterling, due to sustained high cocoa prices during this decade. Here we see that the imperial system was a major factor in the geographical redistribution of overseas sterling liabilities.

One-third of colonial sterling assets arose from currency boards that required 100 per cent sterling backing for local currency. They could be liquidated quickly only in the event of a dramatic monetary contraction

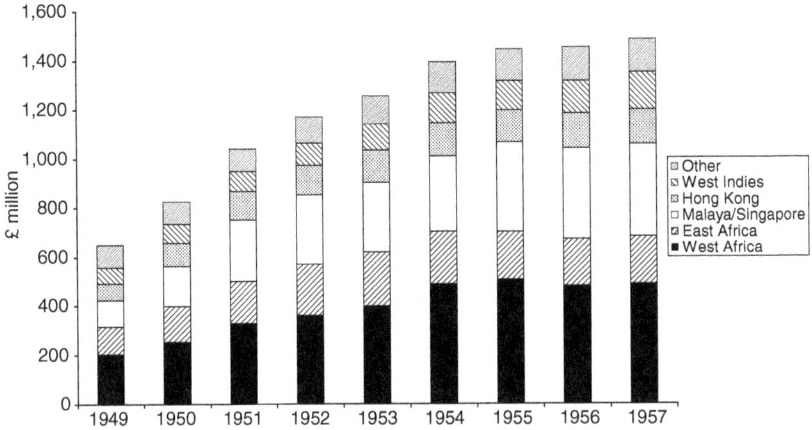

Figure 3.6 Colonial sterling balances, 1949–57

caused by a severe balance of payments deficit. A further third were held by colonial governments as reserves arising out of budget surpluses accumulated in response to the volatile nature of international primary product markets. The low market price of many British government securities, which traded at about one-sixth below their face value in the 1950s, further reduced their liquidity except in a crisis. The most liquid portion was the 20 per cent of colonial balances that consisted of commercial bank assets held in cash or UK Treasury bills. Disaggregating the sterling balances in this way, rather than treating them as a homogeneous mass of short-term liquid liabilities, reduces the threat that they could realistically pose to the central reserves. In a severe crisis, the United Kingdom could control their liquidation and subsequent impact on the central reserves. Rather than a short sharp shock, the danger of large overseas liabilities was that they would pose a more prolonged drain on the reserves if there was an overall decline. In the meantime, they could sap confidence in the sterling exchange rate whenever market sentiment turned against the pound.

The sterling balances that continued to preoccupy policy-makers and commentators were therefore no longer the same as the wartime balances that had captured the public imagination in 1946. The debt burden was successfully reduced during the 1950s through a combination of inflation and the redistribution to more reliable holders resulting from the regional development of the world economy. This transformation of the international role of sterling should be seen as a defining feature of Britain's international economic position during the 1950s, which underlay the progress towards sterling convertibility. The colonial accumulations in the 1950s arguably did not reflect a genuine restoration of sterling as a reserve asset, since they did not have a free choice over the determination of their reserves, but, on the other hand, Britain's control over its dependent territories was eroding during the 1950s as trade preferences waned and decolonisation progressed. Once Malaya, Ghana and Nigeria had gained independence, towards the end of the decade, they continued to use sterling as their reserve currency and to keep 100 per cent sterling backing for their local currencies.

There are several strands to the argument that the interests of the colonies were sacrificed to support sterling. The colonial monetary system was clearly central to the transformation of the sterling balances from wartime debt to foreign exchange reserves, but did this represent exploitation, as was argued by Hazlewood at the time?[5] The key strand to this critique is that colonial development needs were thwarted by import controls and the currency board system, which stopped colonies from spending their sterling reserves, and that they were forced to concentrate on expanding primary production to meet the needs of the British balance of payments. Hinds identifies the 1947 sterling crisis as a 'landmark' in imperial policy that prompted Britain to view the colonies as central to the support of sterling, as they could produce goods that earned scarce US dollars to pay for British imports from the United States. From this date, he argues, the empire was brought more firmly into serving metropolitan economic priorities, to the detriment of the prospects for the colonies. Krozewski, Hinds and Fieldhouse emphasise the period from 1950 to 1952, when the raw materials boom prompted by the Korean War created a brief period of importance for the colonies in the sterling area.[6] As primary product prices boomed, the opportunity for the empire finally to generate a surplus focused the attention of the Colonial Office and the Treasury on developing the export potential of the colonies.

The hopes that the colonies would generate a sustained surplus were soon ended, however, by the slump in primary product prices from 1952 onwards. Nevertheless, we have seen that the surpluses that the colonies accumulated had a profound longer-term impact on the geographical distribution of the sterling balances. For Krozewski, this coloured events for the next decade, because the colonies were prevented from spending

[5] Hazlewood, A., 'Sterling balances and the colonial currency system', *Economic Journal*, 62, 1952, pp. 942–5. Other contemporary critics include Polk, J., *Sterling: Its Meaning in World Finance* (New York: Harper, 1956), and Newlyn, W. T., and D. C. Rowan, *Money and Banking in British Colonial Africa: A Study of the Monetary and Banking Systems of Eight British African Territories* (Oxford: Oxford University Press, 1954), pp. 201–4.

[6] Fieldhouse, D. K., 'The metropolitan economics of empire', in J. Brown and W. R. Louis (eds.), *Oxford History of the British Empire*, vol. IV, *The Twentieth Century* (Oxford: Oxford University Press, 1999), pp. 88–113.

these surpluses through trade controls that provoked tensions between the Colonial Office, which sought to sustain reserves, and the Treasury, which aimed to reduce sterling balances. He argues that it was only when the colonies could no longer cushion British balance of payments deficits either through accumulating reserves or through trade that the end of empire was gradually accepted.

From a political point of view, both Hinds and Krozewski contend that the need to maintain control of colonial sterling reserves affected British engagement with nationalist movements in Africa, both through local colonial administrators and via the Colonial Office and Treasury in London.[7] It must be remembered, however, that India, Pakistan and Sri Lanka achieved independence in the 1940s notwithstanding the fact that they were the largest sterling creditors after the war. There was clearly more at stake in decolonisation than vulnerability to reserves diversification. Moreover, as Hinds notes, the threat of diversification by the major colonial holders nearing independence in the 1950s was never that serious. There were few realistic alternatives, and newly independent states continued to rely on the UK market for investment. Sterling is also viewed as central to the timing of decolonisation at the end of the 1950s. For Krozewski, and also for Cain and Hopkins, once the colonies no longer provided positive support to sterling and had become a potential drain on the British purse through their development aspirations, the process of decolonisation was accelerated.

Certainly, as we have seen, the colonial monetary system was an important element in the transformation of the sterling balances for Africa and the Far East. Of equal importance for the African territories were the marketing boards that built up considerable surpluses. An even larger accumulation was in the form of government reserves, which arose from taxes on exports and a conservative spending policy, encouraged by the fall in the market value of many British government securities through the decade. At the same time as they accumulated these sterling assets, colonial governments also increased their sterling debt through public issues in London. Colonies accounted for about 60 to 70 per cent of all public issues in London in the 1950s, using the funds for projects such as electricity and power generation, and railroad and port construction.[8]

[7] Hinds, A., *Britain's Sterling Colonial Policy and Decolonization, 1939–1958* (London: Greenwood Press, 2001); Krozewski, G., *Money and the End of Empire: British Economic Policy and the Colonies, 1947–1958* (New York: Palgrave, 2001).

[8] Sunderland argues that the Bank of England and the Treasury prevented the Crown Agents from raising these loans in the most efficient manner. Sunderland, D., *Managing the British Colonial and Post-colonial Development: The Crown Agents, 1914–1974* (Woodbridge, Suffolk: Boydell & Brewer, 2007).

It is becoming well established in the literature that the empire had a final moment of prominence in British policy-making during the dollar shortage from 1945 to 1951, but this position quickly receded. Hinds devotes over a half of his book to this brief and unusual period of external and domestic economic crisis, when the boom in colonial exports played a key role in the support of sterling. This threatens to distort his analysis of decolonisation as a whole, since this was a time when the United Kingdom could not afford generous spending plans, even for its poor colonial dependencies, and the rhetoric required to get any aid for colonies required reference to the British balance of payments even if the chief goal was the encouragement of local development. Moreover, he does not in the end provide much evidence that there were viable alternatives for colonial development in these years, or that different policies would have produced better results.

Krozewski argues that colonies were thwarted in their desire for independent monetary systems in the form of central banks in order to protect sterling. He fails, however, to make a case that a departure from monetary orthodoxy in the 1950s would have enhanced the development potential of the colonies; indeed, when Ghana eventually went down this road in the 1960s it was disastrous. Nor is there much evidence that the incoming post-colonial regimes themselves really wanted monetary independence. Currency board arrangements were continued by the newly independent states of Nigeria, Malaya and Ghana because they served their interests best, not Britain's.[9] Developing economies need stable currencies and exchange rates to attract foreign investment. While colonial and post-colonial administrations were reluctant to spend their reserves, their sterling assets were considered in London to be a burden rather than an advantage for sterling.

During the 1950s the government and the Bank of England devised various initiatives to encourage the spending of colonial sterling balances on development. This policy was as much a response to external criticism of poor colonies lending money to the United Kingdom by holding British government debt as it was a result of a desire to reduce the 'overhang'. A further factor was the increasing difficulty that colonies found in raising capital for development on the London market.[10] Using

[9] Schenk, C. R., 'Monetary institutions in newly independent countries: the experience of Malaya, Ghana and Nigeria in the 1950s', *Financial History Review*, 4(2), 1997, pp. 181–98; Stockwell, S., 'Instilling the "sterling tradition": decolonization and the creation of a central bank in Ghana', *Journal of Imperial and Commonwealth History*, 25(2) (special issue: 'Managing the business of empire: essays in honour of David Fieldhouse), 1998, pp. 100–19.

[10] Schenk, *Britain and the Sterling Area*, pp. 35–42.

the sterling balances to pay for development and thereby reduce British liabilities in a controlled way stemmed back to the 1940s. Leslie Rowan was encouraged by the American administration at the end of 1949 to believe that the US government would provide US dollar aid to India and Pakistan in return for them cancelling their sterling balances.[11] This idea was taken up with alacrity in London, but in the end it was rejected by the US Secretary of State, Dean Acheson, in May 1950, although releases of south Asian sterling balances subsequently formed part of the Colombo Plan.

The Treasury completed a review of possibilities for the local investment of colonial sterling assets in 1953. This concluded that the colonies should be encouraged to spend their sterling assets by introducing a fiduciary element of up to 20 per cent in their currency backing, which promised to release up to £70 million for development. When the colonial authorities were asked to take even this modest spending proposal forward in 1954, however, they were not enthusiastic. Bangura argues that, in Africa, this was due to the imminence of independent monetary institutions, but, since these successor institutions maintained the 100 per cent reserve ratio, this argument is not persuasive.[12] A more convincing explanation is that the additional development capital was deemed to be small relative to the increased risk to convertibility of local currencies to sterling. The conservatism of the colonial financial systems were arguably not driven from London but from the local administrations, which feared for their international credit rating and did not want to give London an excuse to constrain public borrowing further. All this suggests that, while sterling and empire were clearly linked in the 1950s, the relationship was a complicated one and that its strength had eroded by the end of the decade.

Sterling as a trading currency

The use of sterling for international commercial transactions declined during the 1950s according to estimates of the proportion of sterling area and non-sterling area trade conducted in sterling. Cohen summarised these in 1971 and determined that the amount of world trade for which sterling had probably been used had been a half in 1945 but only about

[11] Telegram from W. D. Matthews, minister, Canadian embassy in United States, to Wayne Plumptre, head, economic division, Ottawa, relating discussion among Labouisse, Rowan and Matthews in Washington, 29 December 1949. Documents on Canadian External Relations, vol 15, 605.

[12] Bangura, Y., *Britain and Commonwealth Africa: The Politics of Economic Relations 1951–75* (Manchester: Manchester University Press, 1983), pp. 47–8.

27 per cent by 1960, mainly because of the increase in European trade, of which almost none was sterling-denominated.[13] On the other hand, private holdings of sterling were a fairly constant share of world trade, varying between 3.0 and 4.5% from 1950 to 1962.[14] The breakdown for these liabilities to the private sector is available only from 1962, but at this point 71 per cent of privately held overseas sterling was in current and deposit accounts at UK banks, suggesting that they were mainly working balances related to commerce rather than forming part of an investment portfolio.

The decline in the commercial use of sterling in the 1950s was caused by the changing pattern of imperial and Commonwealth trade as European economies recovered and rivalled Britain as sources of manufactured goods. This in turn formed the background for the profound shift in British strategic and political as well as economic relations, which moved away from the empire and towards Europe and the United States. This culminated in the virtual end of empire by 1962 and the first application to join the EEC in the same year.[15] In 1950 the Conservative Party declared itself 'the Party of Empire', asserting in its manifesto for the 1951 general election, *This Is the Road*, that 'the greatest possible development of Empire Trade is our aim'.[16] By the time of the Conservatives' 1955 manifesto they had shifted ground from viewing sterling and empire as closely linked to emphasising 'the move towards a world-wide system of freer trade and freer payments' in order to 're-establish sterling in a position so strong and respected that it can play its full part as a major international currency'.[17] This decline in imperial pride and cohesion had political as well as economic motives, as the exploitative elements of empire became more widely criticised and the process of decolonisation advanced, but economic forces were also at work.

Britain's share of colonial exports fell from 31 per cent to 23 per cent between 1953 and 1958. The corresponding share of British exports in

[13] Cohen, B. J., *The Future of Sterling as an International Currency* (London: Macmillan, 1971), pp. 70–3. The 1960 figure was from *The Economist* based on 95 per cent of intra-sterling area trade, 70 per cent of trade between the sterling area and the rest of the world and 5 per cent of non-sterling area trade.

[14] Data from Treasury Historical Memorandum no. 16, TNA T267/29.

[15] The following section draws on Schenk, C. R., 'Shifting sands: the international economy and British economic policy', in W. Kaiser and G. Staerk (eds.), *British Foreign Policy 1955–64: Contracting Options* (London: Macmillan, 2000), pp. 19–32.

[16] Conservative and Unionist Party, *This Is the Road: The Conservative and Unionist Party's Policy* (London: Conservative and Unionist Central Office, 1950); Schenk, C. R., 'The sterling area and British policy alternatives in the 1950s', *Contemporary Record*, 6(2), 1992, pp 266–86.

[17] Conservative and Unionist Party, *United for Peace and Progress: The Conservative and Unionist Party's Policy* (London: Conservative and Unionist Central Office, 1955), p. 15.

Table 3.2 *Sources of manufactured imports in selected colonies (percentage of total manufactured imports), 1953 and 1959*

	United Kingdom		West Germany		France		Japan	
	1953	1959	1953	1959	1953	1959	1953	1959
East Africa	81.6	58.9	4.4	10.2	0.6	0.0	0.9	6.4
Ghana	74.4	60.0	4.6	14.1	0.0	1.5	8.4	13.0
Malaya	60.3	40.3	5.9	9.3	1.1	2.3	13.8	27.4

Note: East Africa includes Kenya, Uganda and Tanganyika.
Source: Wells, S. J., *British Export Performance: A Comparative Study* (Cambridge: Cambridge University Press, 1964), p. 17.

colonial markets fell from 29 per cent to 23 per cent in the same period. Table 3.2 shows the changing nature of trade in manufactures in major colonial and ex-colonial markets between 1953 and 1959.[18]

Britain's share was mostly replaced by increased imports from West Germany into Africa and from Japan into Malaya. By 1959 Malaya was importing half its iron and steel from Japan, as well as an increasing proportion of electrical and metal-working machinery, in addition to textiles. The increasing share of imports from West Germany into the colonies reflected a loss of competitiveness, particularly of British automobiles and capital goods.

The changing geographical distribution of trade was not the result of changes in discrimination, since most colonies had removed preferences in favour of British goods by 1952. Instead, British competitiveness in terms of price and quality declined as European producers recovered from the war and British exporters faced increasing resistance and competition to their goods in colonial markets.[19] The trade links of the empire were thus loosening naturally at the time of decolonisation, and by the mid-1950s the quantitative importance of imperial preference as the cornerstone of the imperial economic system for both the United Kingdom and its colonial trading partners had largely been eroded. Inflation erased much of the benefit that overseas producers enjoyed in the British market from specific duties. This effect was reinforced by the liberalisation of trade generally and changes in the composition of trade away from imports on which preference was given and towards goods such as raw materials, which carried no tariffs.

[18] Ghana and Malaya achieved constitutional independence during this period.
[19] See Schenk, *Britain and the Sterling Area*, ch. 3.

By 1953 the average preference margin on trade between the United Kingdom and the Commonwealth was only 5 to 6 per cent, or half the rate that had prevailed in 1937, although the levels of preference varied widely. [20] In 1958 the preference on colonial products ranged from 1 per cent on cocoa to 7–8 per cent on oranges, 10 per cent on bananas and 12 per cent on coffee.[21] In 1955 the United Kingdom exported £382 million worth of goods to the colonies, of which only 38 per cent went to colonies offering some preference; most of these exports were not subject to preferential tariffs, however. Malaya was the only important market for British exports in which preference was significant, and even here only a third of the goods were offered a preference margin, which averaged 13 per cent. The larger African and Asian markets did not offer any preference to British goods. The Board of Trade acknowledged in 1956 that the close commercial ties of overseas territories to the United Kingdom were not due to tariff preferences but, rather, to the influence of long-standing technical and commercial connections.[22] By the mid-1950s, as Europe recovered, even these informal ties were waning.

Evidently, imperial preference did not offer a future basis for UK export strength. There was no scope for turning back the clock and reinforcing the British Empire as an alternative to or a bulwark against Europe. Even in the midst of a collective balance of payments crisis at the end of 1951 the Commonwealth committed itself to freer trade and payments on a global scale and was unwilling even to consider reinforcing old imperial economic ties.[23] The public communiqué from the Commonwealth economic conference in January 1952 announced:

> A lasting solution of the sterling area's problems must be found in order to prevent the recurrence of crises, to make sterling strong and to establish the economies of member countries on a sound and stable basis. These aims can best be achieved when the world-wide trade of the sterling area is on a substantially higher level than at present, when sterling is freely convertible into all the main currencies of the world and its position need no longer be supported by restrictions on imports.[24]

In June 1952 Otto Clarke advised the Cabinet that 'the hard fact is that the US is economically more important to [the overseas sterling area]

[20] MacDougall, D., and M. Hutt, 'Imperial preference: a quantitative analysis', *Economic Journal*, 64, 1954, pp. 233–57, p. 256–7.

[21] Draft paper by Colonial Office for Secretary of State, 6 March 1958, TNA T234/227.

[22] Board of Trade paper, 30 November 1956, TNA T234/223.

[23] Cain and Hopkins, *British Imperialism*, p. 287. This is explored in greater detail in Schenk, 'The sterling area and British policy alternatives'. Existing preferences in the British market were, of course, vigorously defended by the Commonwealth.

[24] TNA T236/3086.

than the UK, for the USA can provide for their development while the UK cannot'.[25] The 'community of interest' for the sterling area was to make sterling stronger and convertible, attract US investment and increase world trade. Clarke and Commonwealth leaders clearly viewed convertibility as contributing to the strength and usefulness of sterling, thereby increasing their prospects for development through an increase in multilateral trade.

Constitutional independence did not, initially, affect the financial relationship between the United Kingdom and its ex-colonies fundamentally. Despite some threats to the contrary, the sterling assets of newly independent countries were not run down precipitously. As small open economies in a fixed exchange rate world, there was little scope for the operation of an independent monetary policy, and as a consequence new central banks had few discretionary policy instruments. In the extreme case of Malaya, the currency board system and 100 per cent foreign exchange cover for the local currency was prolonged until 1967, a decade after constitutional independence and eight years after the opening of the country's central bank.[26] Behind the rhetoric of fostering an independent monetary policy, these central banks served domestic political purposes primarily, by presenting the appearance of independence to the local population while maintaining a close link with sterling. Dependence on overseas investors dictated guaranteeing the convertibility of local currency to sterling at a fixed exchange rate by keeping 100 per cent sterling backing. The movement from currency boards to central banks, therefore, masked a continuation of the automatic relation between the balance of payments and the money supply. There was some political resistance to the continuation of the financial relationship with Britain. In 1960 Kwame Nkrumah, the president of Ghana, considered taking his country out of the sterling area – or, at least, used this threat to try to squeeze more aid out of the British government. His threats fell on unresponsive ground, however, and he was assured that the sterling area held greater benefits for Ghana than Ghana's membership offered to Britain. London offered competitive rates of interest on invested reserves, and, since 80 per cent of Ghana's trade was conducted in sterling, holding any other currency would introduce an exchange risk.[27] Furthermore,

[25] Report on external economic policy, 24 June 1952, TNA DO35/6488.

[26] Schenk, C. R., 'The origins of a central bank in Malaya and the transition to independence, 1954–60', *Journal of Imperial and Commonwealth History*, 21(2), 1993, pp 409–31; Schenk, C. R., 'Malaysia and the end of the Bretton Woods system 1965–72: disentangling from sterling', *Journal of Imperial and Commonwealth History*, 36(2), 2008, pp. 197–220.

[27] Telegram from Colonial Office to Snelling (UK high commissioner, Accra), 8 September 1960, BE OV69/5.

breaking the tie with sterling would hurt Ghana's prospects for borrowing abroad.[28]

The use of sterling both as a global reserve and as a commercial currency was, clearly, strongly affected by imperial and Commonwealth relations during the 1950s. It quickly became clear, however, that these ties were unlikely to sustain sterling in the longer term, as economic and political relations within the Commonwealth and empire eroded. As noted above, it became the conviction of the Conservative government, in power following the defeat of Labour in the 1951 general election, that retaining controls on the overseas use of sterling was not in Britain's longer-term interests, and restoring the convertibility of the pound became a central feature of Conservative Party policy.

The sterling exchange rate

Figure 3.7 shows the movement in the official exchange rate between the margins of US$2.78–2.82, which were set in place from December 1951. This period began just as the Korean War boom turned to a bust, which is reflected in the exchange rate until the end of the year. When Operation Robot was devised and the adoption of a floating rate seemed possible in early 1952, the exchange rate was at its lowest band, but by the end of the year and through the following two years the rate hovered

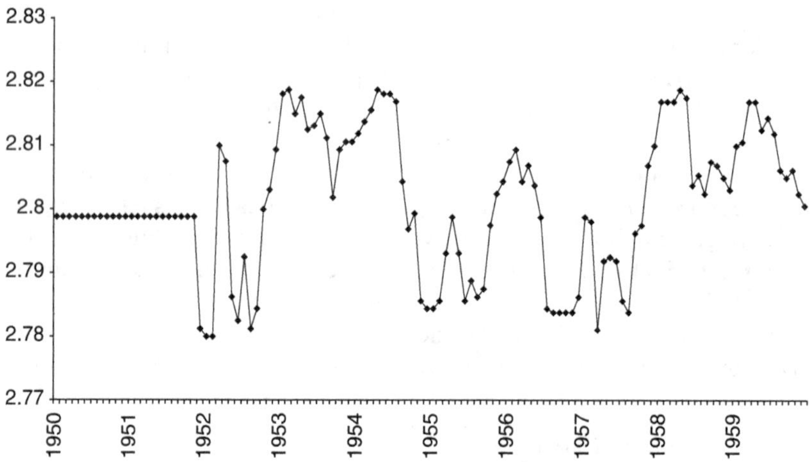

Figure 3.7 Official US dollar/pound market exchange rate (end-month), 1950–9

[28] Note by Loynes, 7 October 1960, BoE 69/6.

around the top band. Renewed speculative pressure and balance of payments deficits in 1955 drove the rate to the bottom band but there was some recovery during the first half of 1956 until the Suez Crisis led to a run on sterling. The improved conditions during 1958, which convinced the Treasury and the Bank of England to launch Operation Unicorn, are also evident in figure 3.7, with the rate falling to the par level only at the end of 1959, twelve months after 'C-day'.

Figure 3.8 shows the heavy discount on sterling in the early 1950s in Hong Kong and New York, where the impact of the Suez Crisis at the end of 1956 and of the confidence crisis of 1957 is clear. Hong Kong operated a freely floating exchange market as a legacy from its days as an entrepot for China. Because it was a colony, UK and other sterling area residents could evade their national exchange controls to convert sterling to US dollars through the free market in Hong Kong.[29] From March 1955, as is described below, the Bank of England kept the transferable sterling rate close to $2.80, and arbitrage between the Hong Kong rate and the security sterling rate kept these rates together.[30] Security sterling arose from sales of sterling assets that had been held privately overseas. Since the proceeds could be reinvested only in similar sterling assets, supply tended to exceed demand, and the rate was often at a discount

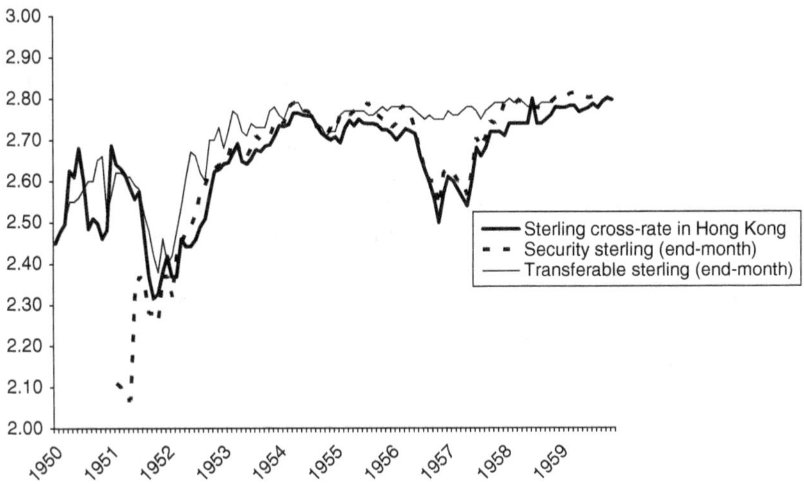

Figure 3.8 Alternative sterling exchange rates (US dollar/pound), 1950–9

[29] Schenk, C. R., 'Closing the Hong Kong gap: Hong Kong and the free dollar market in the 1950s', *Economic History Review*, 47(2), 1994, pp. 335–53.
[30] Ibid.

on the official exchange rate. The Hongkong and Shanghai Banking Corporation (HSBC) tended to buy in this market to feed demand from the Bank of China, and from the late 1950s this demand kept the Hong Kong and security sterling rates near the official rate.

The Treasury and the Bank of England believed that 'cheap' sterling, available openly in a range of offshore markets, undermined confidence in the official exchange rate as well as diverting foreign exchange away from the official reserves. This increased the incentive to eliminate these markets by unifying all sterling markets at the official exchange rate.

Convertibility on the current account

During the 1950s the pound was gradually and without great fanfare made convertible on the current account for those resident outside the United Kingdom or other sterling area countries. The process started at the end of 1951, when the Bank of England won its campaign to reopen both the spot and forward markets for sterling. Until this time the Exchange Equalisation Account offered forward services at a very cheap 1 per cent and the Bank of England engaged directly with authorised banks in the spot market within one cent of the official rate of $2.80/£1.00, but this exposed the EEA to risk from arbitrage. From December 1951 authorised banks were able to trade among themselves at greater margins of plus or minus two cents or a 1.4 per cent margin. The Bank hoped thereby to increase the risk of holding open positions in sterling and so reduce speculative leads and lags.[31]

Meanwhile, the Korean War generated surpluses for most sterling area countries, which reduced their willingness to keep tightening their belts in response to crises that seemed increasingly to be down to Britain's own inability to compete internationally. This new-found confidence on their part was combined with the development of increasingly ambitious industrialisation plans that required buying and borrowing in the cheapest market, which was often not the United Kingdom. As Robertson and Singleton show in the case of Australia, '[B]y turning to the World Bank [in 1949] Australia had shown that it was not prepared to allow the pace of its economic development to be constrained by the resources of the sterling area.'[32] The desire for greater convertibility for sterling was part of these internationalisation strategies, both to service non-sterling debt and to increase the range of import sources.

[31] Fforde, *The Bank of England*, pp. 414–15.

[32] Singleton, J., and P. L. Robertson, *Economic Relations between Britain and Australasia 1945–1970* (Basingstoke: Palgrave, 2002), p. 63.

In response to these pressures, at the end of 1951 the Bank prepared a paper for the Chancellor proposing a plan to achieve general current account convertibility. The Bank predicted that, with US financial assistance, convertibility could be introduced as early as 1953, giving two years for sterling area countries to correct internal inflationary situations and restore balance of payments equilibrium.[33] The expectation of American support was based on the enthusiasm in the US administration for the EPU, and the British perception that the Americans would go even further to hasten the advent of wider convertibility, which would finally allow the full implementation of the Bretton Woods system. This proved to be a costly misunderstanding of the US position.

Britain was also under external pressure to make progress towards convertibility. At the Commonwealth finance ministers' meeting in January 1952, representatives unanimously agreed that inconvertibility should not be continued indefinitely and that some movement towards liberalisation was required.[34] This forced the pace of British policy in this period and lent support to those in the Treasury and the Bank of England who sought to liberalise sterling payments. A change in approach also seemed desirable as the sterling area balance of payments moved from surplus to deficit, necessitating further cuts in imports by the United Kingdom and the rest of the sterling area. These developments added to the attractions of a more flexible system to cushion fluctuations in international trade and payments.

Lucius Thompson-McCausland and George Bolton at the Bank of England, along with Herbert Brittain, Leslie Rowan and Otto Clarke in the Treasury, all began to support early convertibility during the balance of payments downturn at the end of 1951 and early 1952. As Burnham notes, on 10 January, just after the Commonwealth Finance Committee preliminary meeting of officials and five days before the Australian finance minister's opening speech calling for convertibility to be the goal of the sterling area, the Cabinet rather ambitiously endorsed the Chancellor's call for a working party on convertibility and even agreed that the 'ultimate aim' of policy should be convertibility at a flexible exchange rate.[35] This planning resulted in the famous Robot plan, for convertibility at a flexible exchange rate combined with blocking most sterling balances. The plan was developed by a small group in the Treasury and the Bank of England in a panicked rush during February, because it had already been decided that any major policy departure must be announced in

[33] Fforde, *The Bank of England*, p. 424.
[34] Schenk, *Britain and the Sterling Area*, pp. 114–15.
[35] Burnham, *Remaking the Postwar World Economy*, p. 38.

early March at the same time as the budget. In the end, however, it was not just the rush that doomed the plan to failure.

Although he supported a move to convertibility, Cameron Cobbold, as governor of the Bank of England, resisted Clarke's enthusiasm for flexible exchange rates, arguing that this would undermine the acceptability of sterling as an international currency, which was one of the ultimate benefits to be derived from convertibility. The Treasury did not prioritise sterling's reputation, however. More fundamentally, Cobbold worried that floating the pound, or 'letting the rate take the strain', would relax the pressure on government to correct the internal economic position, which was required for longer-term sustainability. Others in the Treasury agreed and urged the immediate adoption of tighter domestic policies and import controls, so as to weather the current crisis, instead of convertibility, particularly as these measures would be needed in any case if the exchange rate were to be stabilised. Rather than an alternative to harsh domestic restraint, a flexible exchange rate would increase the need for controls, and this made the policy less appealing to ministers. The Robot plan was thus fundamentally illiberal and restrictive rather than a rush to free floating and deregulation.

By the time the decision had to be taken there was no official consensus for the Chancellor of the Exchequer, Richard 'Rab' Butler, to present to Cabinet, and this no doubt undermined the prospects for success.[36] The foreign secretary, Sir Anthony Eden (then negotiating in Lisbon over the ill-fated European Defence Community and close to European opinion), felt that the timing for a unilateral policy break was not opportune, stressed the international political disruption that would ensue and added his negative vote. So did Lord Cherwell, special economic adviser to the prime minister (Churchill), who stressed the domestic economic and political damage from the internal price instability and unemployment that would ensue from a substantial depreciation. Churchill described this threat as his 'main anxiety' over the plan.[37] On these bases, the Cabinet rejected the Robot scheme on 29 February 1952.

Fforde blames the failure of Robot on the haste with which the plan was devised, which made it an unappealing invitation to leap into a substantially unknown new environment, as against Cherwell's assertion that familiar tools such as the budget could stem the immediate crisis. Cherwell thus offered a comfortable adaptation of the status quo for risk-averse members of the Cabinet.[38] Burnham stresses Butler's tired

[36] Fforde, *The Bank of England*, p. 438.
[37] Winston Churchill to T. L. Rowan, 17 April 1952, TNA T236/3242.
[38] Fforde, *Bank of England*, pp. 449–51.

and lacklustre championing of the proposal in Cabinet but concludes that 'it is clear ... that Eden's opposition killed the February version of Robot'.[39] International political obstacles were thus crucial. Moving beyond these immediate circumstances, although the downturn in the balance of payments had provoked a reassessment of sterling policy, it also made it an unpropitious time to relax controls, paradoxically, as the weak economic environment exaggerated the risk to the domestic economy. In the context of an apparent economic emergency, the sacrifice to domestic stability was not deemed worth the 'shock and awe' benefits of freeing up sterling. As the emergency receded, however, the prospects for a revolutionary departure in sterling policy ebbed away, and a more gradual move to liberalisation from a position of strength rather than weakness became the agreed approach. A brief and abortive revival of the Robot plan based on a flexible rather than a floating rate in June 1952 was quietly shelved.

Recently, Newton and Burnham have resurrected the Robot episode, which was first amplified academically by Cairncross. They both see Robot as an important turning point that would have led to better national economic performance. Burnham makes the more extreme case, to the effect that the rejection of a floating exchange rate in 1952 was a mistake with profound long-term consequences for the UK economy. He argues that floating the pound would have released British governments from the constraints of the controls and interventionist economic policy that defined the post-war consensus, in particular with regard to industrial relations. With a more market-oriented international monetary policy, he asserts, British governments would have been free to introduce more market-oriented domestic economic policies, including an attack on welfare states and trade unions in the style of Margaret Thatcher. Because sterling was not floated in 1952, this breakthrough was delayed until the early 1980s. Floating the pound in the 1950s would have avoided, in his view, thirty years of institutional failure that held the British economy back from modernisation. His argument was echoed by Thatcher's former Chancellor of the Exchequer, Nigel Lawson, in the *Times Literary Supplement* in 2005 with the subtitle 'How Churchill might have made Thatcher unnecessary'.[40]

Even if depreciation had improved the price competitiveness of British exports in the short term, it is not clear that this alone would have increased productivity. Instead, Burnham views a floating exchange rate

[39] Burnham, *Remaking the Postwar World Economy*, pp. 81–5.

[40] Lawson, N., 'Robot and the fork in the road', *Times Literary Supplement*, 21 January 2005.

in February 1952 as a political opportunity for a raft of wholesale changes to economic policy-making – abandoning Keynesianism, 'checking' the nascent process of European integration and freeing British governments to restructure the economy and industrial relations. This seems a rather heroic set of assumptions. In 1958 Shonfield had a more apocalyptic view of the outcome of the Robot scheme, describing how 'with a slender gold reserve, and a pound sterling exposed in such a way that every breath of international rumour could be turned into a hurricane of speculation, there would have been only one course open to the defenders of the pound – to cut and cut expenditure at home, until we had built up a siege economy which could withstand any violence that might come from abroad'.[41] This interpretation hinges on there being 'defenders of the pound', implying only flexible rates, but this is a much more likely scenario than a free unilateral float.

Broadberry and Crafts, following arguments similar to those of Burnham, blame Britain's long-term productivity losses partly on British governments' preoccupation with short-term pressures such as the balance of payments and monetary overhang. For them, the need to respond to these immediate pressures prevented the development of a different industrial relations framework, which could have generated improvements in productivity to close the gap between the United Kingdom and the United States and West Germany.[42] They identify a gradualist strategy comprising the 'continued use of controls, non-convertibility, pegging the exchange rate, appeasement of the TUC [Trades Union Congress]' that the Conservative government used to defend against the threat of inflation and unemployment.[43] This 'gradualism implied that opportunities to increase competitive pressures on managers of British firms were forgone – there would be no Thatcher-shock and industrial relations would not be reformed'.[44] They conclude, however, that this outcome was 'unavoidable' in the post-war period, and that 'early liberalisation of the economy, which would have entailed a spectacular appreciation of the price level and depreciation of the pound, ... would have been a high-risk strategy' that was rejected by 'virtually all commentators', and so 'the macroeconomic strategy was rational' despite its longer-term drawbacks.

Changing the foreign currency price of British production would not have helped in the longer term unless it enhanced productivity,

[41] Shonfield, *British Economic Policy*, p. 218.

[42] Broadberry, S. N., and N. F. R. Crafts, 'British economic policy and industrial performance in the early post-war period', *Business History*, 38(4), 1996, pp. 65–91.

[43] Ibid., p. 76.

[44] Ibid.

perhaps through eliminating trade union obstacles. Conversely, price and exchange rate instability might have enhanced the calls from labour for protection, and we have seen that convertibility in the Treasury's mind was not linked to general economic liberalisation. Indeed, Milward has argued that the costs of increased trade restrictions and retaliation would have far outweighed any advantage from a depreciation of sterling under Robot.[45] In the 1980s there was much more consensus about the drain that poor industrial relations placed on the economy and on public living standards. The experience of the 1970s made Thatcher's reforms politically possible in ways that could not have been envisaged in the 1950s. Furthermore, the UK government was not alone in shifting its economic priorities in the 1980s; the administration of Ronald Reagan in the United States was also on board. Broadberry and Crafts also acknowledge that, even in the more favourable environment of the early 1980s, Thatcher's reforms would have resulted in a political backlash for the Conservative government had it not been for the distraction of the Falklands War.[46] This all suggests that such a policy would have been extremely unlikely to have been successful in the less supportive policy environment of the 1950s. The importance of international support was soon revealed to be an important element of British strategy.

After an immediate move to convertibility had been abandoned in February 1952, there still had to be some progress to meet the demands from the rest of the sterling area for liberalisation in time for a Commonwealth economic conference, which was promised by the end of the year. This led to the development of the 'collective approach to convertibility' in the summer of 1952.[47] This was a rather complicated scheme along the lines of the planning at the time of the Commonwealth finance ministers' meeting; to replace the EPU by making sterling freely convertible on the current account, along with other European currencies, in a programme supported by a new pool of $5 billion provided by the United States. The plan had the benefits of Robot in terms of greater flexibility but added a cushion for the domestic economy of financial support and reduced the risk for sterling by bringing other major European currencies along at the same time. Kaplan and Schleiminger describe the plan, in comparison with Robot, as 'more like a trot than a headlong dash'.[48] Unfortunately, the cooperation and enthusiasm of both Europe and the

[45] Milward, *The European Rescue of the Nation State*, pp. 352–78.
[46] Broadberry and Crafts, 'British economic policy', p. 86.
[47] For detailed evidence on the development of this policy, see Schenk, *Britain and the Sterling Area*, Burnham, *Remaking the Postwar World Economy*, and Fforde, *The Bank of England.*
[48] Kaplan and Schleiminger, *The European Payments Union*, p. 168.

United States was seriously overestimated, and the initiative was quickly rebuffed. Although Burnham argues that the United States and Europe (or at least France) would have accepted Robot in 1952, by early 1953 they were certainly not ready to entertain the more modest collective approach.

First, though, the scheme had to gain the acceptance of the Commonwealth economic conference. The officials' meeting in September 1952 revealed some disquiet about a flexible exchange rate and disappointment that the convertibility would be only for residents outside the United Kingdom and the sterling area, but there was general agreement that the policy marked a positive step, and the United Kingdom was tasked with approaching the United States and Europe to get the project off the ground. In advance of the ministerial meeting, Commonwealth officials amended the scheme to shift the support fund from the United States to the IMF, as this seemed more likely to be successful, although the Americans would still need to put up most of the funds. They were also concerned about the dangers of removing quantitative trade restrictions at the same time as liberalising payments, and so trade liberalisation was moved into the longer term.[49] This revealed the contradiction between attitudes to current account payments and trade. The liberalisation of sterling was deemed to require tighter, or at least prolonged, trade controls, which proved to be a key aspect that undermined the international acceptance of the British concept of convertibility. The American and European priority was to restore the progress towards trade liberalisation that had been suspended during the downturn after the Korean War.

The optimism of the Commonwealth economic conference soon gave way to disappointment when it became clear in the initial discussions in Washington in early March 1953 that the US Treasury and State Department would not support the plan.[50] Eden and Butler sailed for Washington against the advice of the US Secretary of State, John Foster Dulles, who thought that an official approach was premature. Their abrupt arrival may have 'bounced' the newly elected Republican administration of Dwight Eisenhower, which promptly rejected the idea of contributing to a stabilisation fund. Recalling memories of the 1930s, when floating exchange rates were accompanied by economic nationalism, the administration was also hostile to the idea of flexible or floating exchange

[49] Schenk, *Britain and the Sterling Area*, pp. 119–21; Burnham, *Remaking the Postwar World Economy*, pp. 119–22.

[50] Schenk, *Britain and the Sterling Area*, pp. 121–2; Kaplan and Schleiminger, *The European Payments Union*, pp. 174–8.

rates, and put greater priority on European integration and maintaining the EPU. British hopes that American support for the EPU would segue neatly to support for full convertibility spearheaded by sterling were dashed. The Americans had come to view convertibility as a threat to trade liberalisation, since, without exchange controls to retain a stable exchange rate, countries would rely more on trade restrictions. Indeed, it was part of the collective approach that, while quotas would eventually be abandoned, other trade restrictions would not. More fundamentally, the Americans did not believe that the British economy was resilient enough to support convertibility. For them, the order of liberalisation should be to strengthen the domestic economy, then liberalise trade and only at the final stage move to the payments system, rather than either going for convertibility at a floating rate to avoid strengthening the domestic economy, or using convertibility at a stable exchange rate as a lever to force the government to introduce effective domestic economic policies. Trade liberalisation needed to precede convertibility.

The American attitude was confirmed by the report of the Commission on Foreign Economic Policy, headed by Clarence Randall, which was submitted in January 1954.[51] This stated that American policy

> does not favour a 'dash' for convertibility, or letting the currency 'find its own level', since such a method presents the danger of a vicious circle of inflation and would require larger reserves than may be available to prevent currency depreciation from getting out of hand.

In phrases that would become familiar to British governments in the 1960s, the report was vehement in saying that the onus of adjustment should be on internal domestic price stability rather than letting the exchange rate take the burden. In a thinly veiled reference to the need to get Britain's own house in order, the report concluded:

> A strong internal economy, willing and able to control its money supply and its budget as safeguards against inflation, sufficiently mobile to make the best use of its resources, and able and willing to save in order to increase its productivity and improve its competitive position in world markets, is a prerequisite to convertibility.

The final nail in the coffin of the collective approach was the blunt statement that, 'to restore full convertibility in sterling, Britain's reserves must be strengthened'.

When Britain approached the OEEC for its views a few weeks after the ill-fated visit to Washington, the Europeans were also hostile to

[51] Commission on Foreign Economic Policy, *Report of the Commission on Foreign Economic Policy* ('Randall Commission') (Washington, DC: GPO, 1954).

floating exchange rates, preferring to continue to pursue progress on trade liberalisation and embark on their own European approach to convertibility through the evolution and eventual replacement of the EPU. Their attitude should not have been a surprise, given the preoccupation on the Continent with economic integration at this time. As Kaplan and Schleiminger relate, '[A]fter the Washington rebuff in March 1953, little scope was left for anything more than a stately walk [towards convertibility], at a carefully measured pace'.[52] Britain had enormously misinterpreted the mood in the United States and Europe and overlooked how their priorities did not match those embodied in the collective approach. A key lesson from this painful episode was that the United Kingdom could not go it alone in sterling policy, but had to cooperate and collaborate with other countries.

Instead of a 'dash' or a 'trot', the 'stately walk' over the next eighteen months delivered the benefits of greater sterling convertibility for non-residents and some limited flexibility of the exchange rate through the introduction of a series of administrative measures. Rather than responding to a crisis, these technical changes established the basis from which a general move towards convertibility could be made from a position of strength once the rest of Europe was ready to embrace convertibility and flexibility. The discussion of ambitious initiatives by officials and ministers during the internal debates in the 1951–3 period no doubt contributed to the relatively smooth introduction of de facto convertibility on the current account, with the unification of the transferable sterling accounts in 1954 and the beginning of official support for the transferable sterling rate in New York in February 1955. The new system meant that sterling was freely transferable between some forty-eight countries outside the sterling area and convertible to US dollars through the transferable sterling market in London and New York at or near the official rate. Meanwhile, within Europe, the EPU settlements were hardened and OEEC countries began more concerted planning for generalised convertibility to succeed the EPU.

The achievement of de facto convertibility was partly aimed at increasing the usefulness and reputation of sterling as an international currency, which the Bank of England deemed was profoundly damaged by 'cheap sterling' traded outside London below the official rate and by the persistence of bilateral account countries that could not transfer their sterling other than to the United Kingdom. The Bank thus pursued its priorities by maintaining a stable exchange rate but enhancing the usefulness of sterling for non-resident traders. The first stage, unifying all

[52] Kaplan and Schleiminger, *The European Payments Union*, p. 180.

transferable account sterling on 22 March 1954, was combined with the opening of the London gold market, further emphasising the fact that it formed part of the restoration of the status of the City of London and of sterling.

The Bank was able to persuade the Treasury partly because the official market rate had risen from its lowest threshold of $2.78 in the autumn of 1952 to over $2.81 by the beginning of 1954, so the time was ripe to make a move from a position of strength. As the Bank had promised, the transferable rate in New York promptly strengthened during March 1954, from $2.75 to $2.78, but it started to slip in June as the balance of payments worsened and rumours began to circulate about a possible devaluation. By the end of the year the rate was down to $2.75 and the Bank of England renewed its campaign to support the rate to stop cheap sterling deals and commodity shunting. The Treasury was eventually convinced, not least by the stories of London merchant banks and even foreign central banks using the discounted market, and the decision was taken in February 1955 to intervene in the transferable sterling market.[53] The rate was successfully raised from $2.72 in January 1955 to $2.77 by the end of February, and de facto convertibility at a stable exchange rate had been achieved. The cost of supporting the transferable sterling rate was predictably smaller than protecting the official rate in London. For 1956, a year that included the Suez Crisis and a major IMF drawing, net sales of US dollars in support of the transferable rate were $146 million, while net sales in the official market amounted to $446 million.[54]

The advent of informal convertibility prompted a major reconsideration of the role of the sterling area and its future. The Treasury–Bank of England report on the future of sterling was completed in July 1956 and considered by the Cabinet Economic Policy Committee in February 1957.[55] Among the conclusions it was noted that the sterling area had evolved from being a post-war 'economic bloc' and returned to a 'banking group' that was more similar to the inter-war sterling bloc. It was agreed that little could or should be done to change the sterling area relationships, although it was recognised that the nature of the system was changing in the absence of a deliberate policy. Instead, the priority for British governments should be to strengthen the British economy itself.

[53] Schenk, *Britain and the Sterling Area*, pp. 127–8; Burnham, *Remaking the Postwar World Economy*, pp. 146–54; Fforde, *The Bank of England.*

[54] 'Gold and dollar reserves', 5 February 1957, BE EID3/114.

[55] 'Problems of the sterling area; report by a working party of the Treasury and the Bank of England', 25 June 1956, TNA T236/3935.

Hillier of the Colonial Office summed up the approach for the rest of the decade when he predicted in October 1956

> [j]ust as it [the sterling area] has grown up...like Topsy, rather as the result of many varied circumstances, so its future will reflect the result of stresses and strains rather than of a planned attitude to the 'system' as a whole.[56]

The sterling area was no longer central to the management of the future of sterling.

Over the next three and a half years progress towards formal current account convertibility for sterling was merged into the European process of planning for the end of the EPU and the establishment of the European Monetary System (EMS). Annual negotiations to renew the terms of the EPU alongside OEEC trade discussions allowed ongoing and close discussions between European countries on the evolution of international monetary relations at a time when the Continental governments were developing their plans for greater economic integration.[57] The European Monetary Agreement of August 1955 set the blueprint for common progress towards legal convertibility, with a European Fund to support weaker members and a settlements system that provided a safety net in the case of devaluation of a member's currency. The system required narrow bands around pegged but adjustable rates so that, in the end, the Continental preference for stable exchange rates superseded the British desire for greater flexibility.[58] The lack of flexibility in the system also meant that the United Kingdom could lead a European move to convertibility only from a position of strength, which did not arise for another three years. As in 1949, sterling was the cornerstone in the reform of the European exchange rate system, but this did not really strengthen Britain's bargaining position or leadership.

The estrangement between the US and the UK governments over the Suez Crisis in 1956, and the drain of $650 million from the reserves that ensued, increased Britain's dependence on European joint action and further undermined the likelihood of a unilateral approach. The ill-fated military expedition to seize the Suez Canal from Egyptian control in October 1956 prompted a run on sterling and revealed in the clearest possible way the political and strategic effects of Britain's financial weakness. Indeed, Kunz has argued that 'economic diplomacy defined the course of the Suez crisis from beginning to end'.[59] Peden shows how

[56] Letter from Hillier to Rowan, 9 October 1956, TNA T236/4304.

[57] Kaplan and Schleiminger, *The European Payments Union*, pp. 237–8.

[58] Ibid., pp. 218–25.

[59] Kunz, D. B., *The Economic Diplomacy of the Suez Crisis* (Chapel Hill: University of North Carolina Press, 1991), p. 2.

Harold Macmillan as Chancellor and Eden as prime minister ignored the Treasury's warnings of the dangers of engaging in an expensive campaign when domestic inflationary pressure was undermining confidence in sterling.[60] Klug and Smith have confirmed that pressure on sterling began in July, when Egypt nationalised the canal, and that the Bank of England spent $360 million supporting the market rate during November 1956 alone because the market anticipated devaluation.[61]

Officials and ministers believed that devaluing sterling so soon after 1949 would destroy the current sterling payments system, break up the EPU and end any prospect for the future of sterling as an international currency. Countries would quickly wish to divest themselves of the remainder of their sterling reserves, which would be insupportable. Britain would have to block these balances unilaterally, creating even greater international political problems for the British than they were currently experiencing, while not avoiding an ignominious retreat from Suez. As in 1952, devaluation also raised the prospect of uncontrolled domestic inflation. A more rational strategy was to treat the crisis as the short-term problem that it was (the balance of payments in the first half of the year was in surplus) and to look to the IMF for near-term support. This required American agreement, which was finally forthcoming only on 3 December, when Eden announced his intention to withdraw by the 22nd of that month.

During November Macmillan had tried to rattle the sterling sabre, threatening the US Treasury secretary, George Humphrey, that a collapse of sterling would lead to a triumph of communism, but Humphrey was not persuaded; the Americans would not be drawn into support for sterling so easily.[62] After the military withdrawal was successfully agreed the IMF granted an unprecedented 100 per cent of the UK quota in a $1.3 billion stand-by arrangement, breaking its own rules, which forbade providing support for capital outflows. The United States offered an additional $500 million from the Export-Import Bank.[63] The incoming director of the IMF, Per Jacobsson, exceeded even the ambitious expectations of the Bank of England and the Treasury by announcing that he intended to commit the full 100 per cent of Britain's quota even before he took office, on 3 December. In the event, the economic and financial

[60] Peden, G. C., *The Treasury and British Public Policy* (Oxford: Oxford University Press, 2000), p. 446.

[61] Klug, A., and G. W. Smith, 'Suez and sterling 1956', *Explorations in Economic History*, 36(3), 1999, pp. 181–203.

[62] Boughton, J., 'Northwest of Suez: the 1956 crisis and the IMF', *IMF Staff Papers*, 48(3), 2001, pp. 425–46.

[63] Boughton, 'Northwest of Suez', p. 440.

impact was quickly reversed, reinforcing the view that it was merely a speculative crisis. The political and strategic break with the United States and the humiliation of the negotiations made this the seminal event of the decade, however. It also set the precedent for the central role of sterling in the Cold War politics that would emerge in the 1960s. As the first major IMF credit operation, it also led the way for the IMF to be much more involved in sterling policy through the 1960s, and established the special support that the United Kingdom could attract as an issuer of an international currency. The rationale for breaking the rules and supporting a speculative capital outflow was explicitly because sterling's international status meant that its collapse would have important implications for world trade. While sterling's international status did not make Humphrey blink in the face of Macmillan's threats, it was vital to the actual amount and terms of IMF support.

Progress towards convertibility was stalled while the balance of payments recovered from yet another crisis of confidence in 1957, but through the first half of 1958 reserves were rising and confidence was restored. Rowan at the Treasury urged the new Chancellor, Peter Thorneycroft, to take the opportunity of this improved environment to move to formal current account convertibility by the end of the year, with the support of Cobbold at the Bank of England.[64] First, it was necessary to secure the agreement and cooperation of European partners to ensure a smooth transition from the EPU to the European Monetary Agreement. Cobbold was authorised to approach the governors of the French and West German central banks in early November. The looming French presidential election and the collapse of the European Free Trade Area (EFTA) talks threatened to derail the timetable, but momentum was regained in early December. By the 14th the economic ministers of France and West Germany had agreed to synchronise the move to convertibility by the start of 1959. Emissaries from the Treasury visited the major European capitals from 19 December, receiving a 'frosty reception' only in Oslo.[65] Operation Unicorn, as it had become known, proceeded smoothly, with the announcement on 27 December of the unification of transferable and dollar area sterling into 'sterling for overseas account'. Although the move was viewed in the Bank at the time as less important than the 1954 and 1955 unification of sterling, the breakthrough of de jure current account convertibility across Europe was about to usher in a new era of accelerated integration of payments, as we shall see in chapter 4.

[64] Fforde, *The Bank of England*, pp. 595–605.

[65] Ibid., p. 601.

Conclusions

During the 1950s sterling emerged from its wartime constraints and began to operate more as a reserve currency for colonial and Middle Eastern states as traditional Commonwealth countries diversified their reserves. In the process, the proportion of world reserves denominated in sterling declined slowly, but the total nominal value of Britain's overseas sterling liabilities remained fairly constant. The use of sterling as a commercial currency also fell as Commonwealth and imperial trade became more diversified and British exports declined as a share of world trade. Nevertheless, the private accumulation of sterling overseas kept up with the rate of growth of world trade until the end of the decade. The extraordinary circumstances of the post-war years had clearly disappeared, and this prompted British and sterling area governments to reconsider longer-term sterling policy. By this time, however, opinion in the United States and Europe had moved away from convertibility and towards trade liberalisation.

The devaluation of 1949 and the volatility of the balance of payments arising from the Korean War ushered in several years of active official and ministerial interest in evolving the international role of sterling beyond the straitjacket of inconvertibility, and even beyond the confines of the Bretton Woods pegged exchange rate system. In the end, these ambitions foundered on the political priority of domestic economic stability and the lack of sufficient international or domestic support for a departure from the status quo. The proposals and negotiations reveal an unresolved conflict about the sequencing of convertibility for sterling, how it related to trade liberalisation, or even what the ultimate aim was. On the one hand, some, such as Clarke, hoped for a floating or flexible rate to 'take the strain' and relax the pressure on the domestic economy so as to correct balance of payments problems. Others, such as Cobbold, wanted to ensure a stable if flexible exchange rate to maintain discipline on domestic economic policy and encourage greater international use of sterling. For most in Britain, convertibility did not represent a move towards a free market policy, since it would require prolonged trade controls or even further retreat into discrimination and stronger imperial preference. Moreover, convertibility was only for current account transactions and only for non-resident sterling, excluding capital flows and current account payments of residents of the United Kingdom and overseas sterling countries, who would continue to be subject to exchange controls. The resistance both from the Bank of England and from the United States, the sterling area and Europe to a floating or flexible rate meant that this element was abandoned as the process moved into the European forum.

Unlike the 1940s and the 1960s, during the 1950s sterling was not high on the international agenda. The Americans lost interest in the sterling balances as they turned their attention more forcefully to trade liberalisation and promoting European integration as part of their global strategic vision. This process also preoccupied European states as they successfully organised the European Coal and Steel Commission and then followed deliberate steps that culminated in the Treaty of Rome in 1957. After the failure of convertibility in 1947 and the readjustment of exchange rates in 1949, American enthusiasm for a dash to convertibility evaporated. The British government's concentration on convertibility as a way to restore its international financial leadership at the same time as undermining the regional approach of Europe reinforced Britain's peripheral status during this decade. That neither the United States nor Europe was willing to forgo the process of European integration and trade liberalisation for the doubtful benefits of limited current account convertibility was made bluntly clear in the rejection of the collective approach in 1952. The strategy of the British then returned to trade liberalisation with Europe in 1953, although they rejected participation in the development of a European Economic Community.

The process of achieving formal convertibility was deferred to the European forum, although the commercial importance of sterling meant that the United Kingdom had considerable control over timing. In the run-up to 1958 the technical foundations for external current account convertibility were established by supporting the exchange rate for transferable sterling in New York, essentially uniting transferable sterling with American account sterling under the guise of simplifying the complex exchange control arrangements devised in 1947. Harder EPU settlements also led to the gradual liberalisation of payments between the dollar area and the rest of the world, until the final step at the end of 1958 towards formal current account convertibility to US dollars for sterling and other European currencies was a small one.

Part II

Accelerating the Retreat: Sterling in the 1960s

The reduction of sterling's international role as a reserve currency was an underlying feature of British policy throughout the 1960s, although no effective way was found to achieve this until the Sterling Agreements of 1968. The crumbling of the pegged exchange rate system, multilateral efforts to replace or reform it and the reorientation of Britain's external focus from empire to Europe and the United States all underlay the development of sterling policy. The great turning point seemed to be the dramatic devaluation of sterling in 1967, but in the end it was EEC membership that prompted the public acknowledgement that the reserve role of sterling would be actively reduced as a matter of official policy. Internally there is clear evidence that voices at the highest level of the Treasury and the Bank of England had come to this view at the beginning of the decade, but there seemed little scope to achieve this in the pegged exchange rate regime. Successive British governments pursued a strategy of gathering multilateral support to reduce the risk of a sudden diversification of global reserves away from sterling, which allowed a fairly smooth reduction in sterling's share of global reserves to a mere 7 per cent by 1970.

As an international commercial currency, sterling's relative position also declined. This process was most closely related to the United Kingdom's relative decline in world trade, but it was also a by-product of continued and intensified exchange controls on the international commercial use of sterling during the 1950s and 1960s. These controls were vigorously, if unsuccessfully, resisted by the Bank of England, which sought to protect the interests of the City of London. From the early 1960s, however, changes in the City due to financial innovation and the large-scale entry of banks from abroad, particularly the United States, changed the emphasis of the City's activities and reduced the importance of sterling-denominated commercial business. In terms of both the reserve and the international commercial role of sterling, therefore, the 1960s are the crucial decade for the retreat of sterling as an international currency.

4 Sterling and European integration

The troubled path of the United Kingdom's accession to the European Economic Community in the 1960s has been vigorously researched by political and economic historians.[1] The major economic obstacles revolved around how the common external tariff would affect Britain's trade with the Commonwealth and the impact on British producers. Other challenges included fisheries policy, budget contributions and the Common Agricultural Policy (CAP). The monetary institutions of the EEC were in the process of development during the years when Britain sought unsuccessfully to join, but progress was slow and uneven because of the lack of consensus within the original six members (West Germany, France, Italy, Belgium, the Netherlands and Luxembourg). Nevertheless, although it was trade that overwhelmed the negotiations, the issue of sterling as an international currency did emerge as an important symbol of the distinctive character of Britain's relations with the rest of the world, complicating its transformation to EEC membership.

The issue of sterling has been a major theme in the United Kingdom's relations with Europe. It can even be argued that the exchange rate regime between sterling and the European currencies has become the defining feature of Britain's attitude to Europe, since fixing sterling into

[1] For recent treatments, see Rollings, N., *British Business in the Formative Years of European Integration, 1945–1973* (New York: Cambridge University Press, 2007); Ludlow, N.P., *Dealing with Britain: The Six and the First UK Application to the EEC* (Cambridge: Cambridge University Press, 1997); Wilkes, G. (ed.), *Britain's Failure to Enter the European Community 1961–63: The Enlargement Negotiations and Crises in European, Atlantic and Commonwealth Relations* (London: Routledge, 1997); Daddow, O. J. (ed.), *Harold Wilson and European Integration: Britain's Second Application to Join the EEC* (London: Routledge, 2003); Ludlow, N. P., *The European Community and the Crisis of the 1960s: Negotiating the Gaullist Challenge* (London: Routledge, 2006); and Parr, H., *Britain's Policy towards the European Community: Harold Wilson and Britain's World Role 1964–67* (London: Routledge, 2006). There were also many contemporary accounts, including those of Kitzinger, U., *Diplomacy and Persuasion: How Britain Joined the Common Market* (London: Thames & Hudson, 1973); Camps, M., *Britain and the European Community 1955–63* (Princeton, NJ: Princeton University Press, 1964); and Camps, M., *European Unification in the Sixties* (Oxford: Oxford University Press, 1967).

a European system of stable exchange rates in an environment of open capital markets requires the erosion of British policy sovereignty. Sterling policy is therefore fundamental to Britain's commitment to the European integration project. Most of the trade aspects of European integration quickly became uncontroversial after Britain joined the Community (the major exception is the CAP), but the monetary obligations continue to provoke strong reactions and have separated Britain from the core of European countries. Sterling policy in the 1980s and 1990s, as we see in chapter 10, was dominated by the decision over whether to join the ERM and then the euro, and debate over the appropriateness of the abdication of policy sovereignty this required.

As in the 1990s, so in the 1960s sterling was symbolic of the extent of Britain's commitment to common European goals and priorities, and this was clearly seen in Britain's three attempts to join the EEC. The international use of sterling was emblematic of the United Kingdom's alliances and responsibilities beyond Europe, to the United States and the Commonwealth/sterling area, which were important obstacles to Britain being absorbed into the European integration process. In order to accord with the priorities of the Six, Britain had to divest sterling of its role as an international reserve asset. The two major issues related to sterling that featured in the accession negotiations were the sterling balances and the preferential capital flows, which were seen as the quid pro quo for sterling area members to keep their reserves in sterling. The rhetoric from Europe (and France in particular) also centred on the potential drain that the decline of sterling's international status might pose to EEC resources.[2] The Six were already heavily engaged in multilateral support for sterling through the Bank for International Settlements (BIS), as is described in chapter 8. This chapter shows how the management of sterling became an integral part of the reorientation of Britain as a European nation.

Sterling increased in prominence through the three rounds of negotiations. In 1962 Meade warned that the 'financial-policy problem of the UK balance of payments and of the position of sterling' was 'equally important' to the commercial issues, but the nature of the Treaty of Rome with its concentration on the common market meant that the negotiations were dominated by trade issues, and in particular by the impact of the Common External Tariff on Commonwealth trade with Britain.[3] By

[2] Under the provisions of the Treaty of Rome, exchange rates were considered a matter of common interest (article 107) and members were committed to mutual support in times of balance of payments crisis (article 108).

[3] Meade, J. E., *UK, Commonwealth and Common Market* (London: Institute of Economic Affairs [IEA], 1962), p. 38.

1967 Strange went so far as to suggest that there was a 'conspiracy of silence' about monetary issues in the accession negotiations, although the archival record shows that sterling was discussed.[4] By the time of the final application, Christopher Soames, British ambassador to France, asserted that 'the monetary question will be regarded as a touchstone of our seriousness'.[5] Sterling was never the most prominent or intractable subject of negotiation, but the British government was forced to commit itself publicly to ending sterling's reserve role before entry into the EEC could be ensured. This chapter also emphasises that the EEC's attitude to sterling was affected by its own progress towards economic and monetary union (EMU) in the context of the crumbling of the Bretton Woods pegged exchange rate system.

Erosion of traditional relationships in the 1960s

An important feature of this decade, which helps to explain the growing commitment to EEC membership by British governments, is that many of the United Kingdom's traditional special relationships eroded during the 1960s. Britain's relations with the Commonwealth became strained; especially with major sterling holders such as Hong Kong, Singapore and Australia. For these countries, the decline of sterling was wrapped up with the withdrawal of British military forces in the Far East and the imposition of controls on overseas investment. The government began to discuss reducing UK defence expenditure abroad from the early 1960s, in recognition of the burden of the financial costs involved.[6] In the end, however, the withdrawal from Singapore and Malaysia could not take place until after the successful conclusion of the military confrontation between Malaysia and Indonesia. This was finally considered imminent during the sterling crisis of mid-July 1966, when planning for withdrawal accelerated. The agreement ending the confrontation was signed in August, paving the way for serious defence cuts in south-east Asia in the 1967 Defence White Paper.[7]

The new military strategy in the 1960s also alienated Hong Kong (the world's second largest sterling holder). As part of the redeployment of

[4] Strange, S., *The Sterling Problem and the Six* (London: Political and Economic Planning [PEP]/Chatham House, 1967), p. 7.

[5] The 'monetary question' referred to non-discrimination in capital flows and ending sterling's reserve role; Christopher Soames to Sir Con O'Neill, 23 December 1970, TNA FCO59/664.

[6] Jones, M., 'A decision delayed: Britain's withdrawal from south east Asia reconsidered, 1961–68', *English Historical Review*, 117, 2002, pp. 569–95.

[7] Note by secretary of the Cabinet (Burke Trend) on the economic situation, 18 July 1966, Cabinet Memoranda CAB129/126.

forces, the British government insisted in 1966 that Hong Kong take over more of its own defence costs.[8] This smacked of the abandonment of imperial responsibility in Hong Kong, as well as posing an unwelcome burden on local resources in a dependent territory with low per capita income and no prospect for full independence. After the decision to withdraw forces east of Suez, in August 1966, Harold Wilson, the prime minister, instructed the Secretary of State for the colonies, Frederick Lee, to approach the governor of Hong Kong about increasing the local contribution to the cost of the garrison. After a series of ill-tempered negotiations Hong Kong agreed from April 1967 to pay £4.245 million per year, plus local works, for the maintenance of the garrison, taking the annual total to about £5 million, or nearly a half of UK defence expenditure.[9] This was not an easy negotiation, and it generated considerable heat in Hong Kong's Executive and Legislative Councils.[10] In his tour of the Far East at the beginning of 1967, the Commonwealth secretary noted that 'the Government of Hong Kong have done so much for themselves that they tend to feel forgotten by us'. Secret contingency planning in the Cabinet for abandoning Hong Kong during the communist unrest in the colony in May 1967 seems to confirm this assessment.[11] The process of decolonisation was therefore reflected even in those few territorial ties that remained.

Australia was the largest sterling balance holder throughout most of the 1960s and was traditionally Britain's largest and closest sterling area trading partner, but economic relations here also came under strain from the early 1950s. On the one hand, Australia was very protective of its position in the London capital market, and thus a strong supporter of the sterling area, but it also objected to Britain's cautious approach to sterling in the 1950s. As Australia's goals for diversifying its industrial structure developed, it became clear that Britain could not be relied on as the sole provider of capital or as a preferred supplier, and Australia renegotiated its trade relations with Britain in the 1950s to reduce the preference offered to British products.[12] More emphasis was placed on relations with the United States and the multilateral institutions that the

[8] This issue is treated in greater detail in Schenk, C. R., 'The empire strikes back: Hong Kong and the decline of sterling in the 1960s', *Economic History Review*, 57(3), 2004, pp. 551–80.

[9] Ministry of Defence paper, 'Defence estimates 1967'; draft white paper, 2 February 1967, TNA CAB129/128.

[10] Telegram from secretary of state for the colonies in Hong Kong to John Stonehouse in London, 6 December 1966, TNA T317/1067.

[11] Schenk, 'The empire strikes back'.

[12] For Australia's commercial relations with the United Kingdom, see Singleton and Robertson, *Economic Relations between Britain and Australasia*.

United States dominated as sources of capital. Australia was also affected by the dramatic recovery and then acceleration of industrial expansion in the Far East, so that by the late 1960s Japan had become a more important market for Australian products than the United Kingdom.

The growing estrangement between Australia and the United Kingdom was enhanced by the conflicts that arose over Britain's applications to join the EEC. From the first application, in 1961–3, the countdown to the end of the special economic place of Australia and New Zealand in Britain's international economic relations began. In 1964 sterling comprised 79 per cent of Australia's official foreign exchange reserves, but this was reduced to 60 per cent by October 1967 after the Reserve Bank of Australia sold off just over £200 million of its sterling assets. The Australians were fiercely protective of their preferred access to the UK capital market for official borrowing and to the private capital market for other investment, both of which were threatened by the preference that might have to be granted to European borrowers under the EEC arrangements.[13] The precarious nature of Australia's preferred status was further revealed in March 1966, when, under balance of payments pressure, the United Kingdom imposed voluntary controls on reinvested profits by overseas companies in the developed sterling area, including Australia. A surge of outward portfolio investment at the end of the 1960s prompted the Treasury to seriously consider imposing exchange control on Australia and perhaps the rest of the sterling area (code-named Operation Brandon). In the end the plans were rejected, because of the danger of generating such ill-will in Australia that the Sterling Agreements system would collapse.[14] As will be seen in chapter 8, the Australians linked their reserves policy closely with continued free capital flows from the United Kingdom.

Outside the sterling area, relations with the United States also became strained during the 1960s. On the one hand, the crumbling of the international monetary system provided opportunities for bilateral British–American negotiations. Both sides saw advantage in this approach as a way to provide agreed initiatives to guide the G10 (the Group of Ten leading industrial countries) discussions on the future of the international monetary system. The close contact also generated friction, however. In the early 1960s members of the US administration often viewed the 'special relationship' as a burden and were resistant to pressure from

13 Schenk, C. R., 'The UK, the sterling area and the EEC, 1957–63', in A. Deighton and A. S. Milward (eds.), *Widening, Deepening and Acceleration: The European Economic Community 1957–63* (Baden-Baden: Nomos, 1999), pp. 123–37.

14 See correspondence in TNA T312/2909.

the United Kingdom to equate the problems of sterling with those of the dollar. In 1963, for example, when Sir Denis Rickett and Sir Alec Cairncross from the Treasury and Sir Maurice Parsons from the Bank of England visited for informal bilateral financial talks, the US Secretary of State, Douglas Dillon, refused to have lunch or dinner with them and would agree only to meet with them 'once *briefly*'.[15] The repeated calls from the United Kingdom for American support for sterling also increased bitterness between the two administrations.[16]

These irritations underlay a variety of strategic issues on which British and American policy diverged, including the US State Department's efforts to cancel the Skybolt programme and stymie Britain's nuclear development. Later, Britain's unwillingness to contribute to military efforts in Vietnam and then the decision to pull forces out of south-east Asia altogether disappointed and antagonised the Americans as we shall see in chapter 5. A further complication was that, while the United States supported British applications to join the EEC, Britain's 'special relationship' with the United States was an obstacle to the success of these applications, particularly for the French.

The first application, 1961–1963[17]

The underlying theme of the British position in the first application to join the EEC in 1961 was that the Six would not force the United Kingdom to do anything that undermined the position of sterling, since this threatened the integrity of the international monetary system as a whole. In April 1961 the Treasury asserted, rather naively: 'It seems reasonable to expect that the other members would not want to push us into policies which we believed to be unwise and which could be damaging to sterling.'[18] In July 1961 A. G. Perrin of the Bank of England went further and advised that '[w]e must assume that, as a Member, the Community will recognise the value (to them) of the sterling system and make

[15] Italics in the original. Dillon's pencil memo on note from Robert Roosa to Douglas Dillon, 18 March 1963, USA National Archives and Records Administration (hereafter NARA) RG69-A-407, Box 106. See also Pagedas, C. A., *Anglo-American Strategic Relations and the French Problem, 1960–1963: A Troubled Partnership* (London: Frank Cass, 2000); Dumbrell, J., *A Special Relationship: Anglo-American Relations in the Cold War and After* (London: Macmillan, 2001); and Dobson, A. P., *The Politics of the Anglo-American Economic Special Relationship, 1940–1987* (Brighton: Wheatsheaf, 1988).

[16] Gavin, *Gold, Dollars, and Power*, pp. 130–3.

[17] The following two sections draw on Schenk, C. R., 'Sterling, international monetary reform and Britain's applications to the EEC in the 1960s', *Contemporary European History*, 11(3), 2002, pp. 345–69.

[18] Paper by the Treasury for the Inner Group, 6 April 1961, TNA T236/6553.

provision accordingly. If we cannot make this assumption or if in negotiations it becomes apparent that it is invalid, we had better not join.'[19] The Treasury and Bank believed that sterling's role as a trading and reserve currency was vital to the stability of the international monetary system, particularly at a time when the dollar was under considerable strain. By extension, they assumed that the international role of sterling would be recognised and supported by Britain's European partners.

The Bank also had vague hopes that sterling would become the currency used for settlements within and outside Europe, and that the City of London would be Europe's financial centre. Perrin optimistically noted, 'Such a development, though likely in some degree to come about of itself, is highly desirable and ought to be an object of policy.'[20] Since no other European state promoted its currency as an international vehicle or reserve unit, it seemed natural that sterling was most likely to take on this role in the EEC. This view later received some support on the Continent. In 1966 Hermann Abs, the influential director of Deutsche Bank, suggested that, 'if the UK joins the EEC, sterling will have a chance to preserve and indeed strengthen its position in Europe and in world trade' by becoming a key currency for Europe.[21] The Treasury anticipated that, 'with the UK a member of the club, the Community would, in a sense, be committed to the support of sterling', and it did not expect this to be a major obstacle at the beginning of the negotiations. The mutual support schemes of the Community were seen as an advantage of membership for the United Kingdom, even though they would require closer consultation on internal and external economic policies and therefore some loss of sovereignty.[22] In hindsight, this seems remarkably complacent, but the British were encouraged in this view by European attitudes to the sterling crisis of early 1960/61.

In the five months before the United Kingdom officially launched its application in July 1961, sterling received $900 million worth of multilateral support, and Britain negotiated a drawing of $1,500 million from the IMF to repay these obligations by the end of September. This episode gave the European central banks their first taste of coordinated support for sterling outside the IMF. Initially, it seemed that this precedent would

[19] A. G. Perrin to Luce and J. Rootham, 6 July 1961, Bank of England (hereafter BE) OV47/39.

[20] Ibid.

[21] Hermann Abs writing in an article published by *The Times* and *Die Welt*, 28 October 1966; quoted in Strange, *The Sterling Problem and the Six*, p. 39.

[22] 'The position of sterling and the future of the sterling area', 8 May 1962, paper by the Bank of England/Treasury Long Term Policies Group, TNA T230/673; see also note of a meeting to discuss a draft of this paper, 6 October 1961, TNA T230/668.

not affect the prospects for Britain's application. In March 1962 Franco Bobba, head of the Monetary Division of the European Commission, pointed out in discussion with representatives of Lazard Brothers that, 'if the EEC countries had taken these steps to help sterling when Britain was not a member of the Community, it could be safely assumed that they would do so when Britain was a member of the Community'.[23] It was noted in the Treasury that 'something very similar was said by members of the Commission when we discussed some of these questions with them in February'.[24] More publicly, Andrew Shonfield of the Royal Institute of International Affairs also reported that in 1962 Europeans were ready to 'pass the hat round' to help defend the sterling exchange rate should it come under pressure from speculators.[25]

Despite these optimistic signals, other less favourable opinions were also forming in Europe. At the end of 1961 Leonhard Gleske, director of the Monetary Questions Division of the European Commission, reported that there was a divergence of views among the Six on how much of a strain UK membership would pose for sterling.[26] In June 1962 the 'question of the sterling area' was raised by the French foreign minister, Maurice Couve de Murville, and by President Charles de Gaulle in discussion with British representatives. Their concern stemmed from fears that the UK balance of payments would deteriorate on accession to the EEC and that the Community would be obliged to engage in costly support for sterling through the mutual aid provisions of the Treaty of Rome.[27] In response, the British assured the Europeans that the UK foreign exchange reserves and IMF drawing rights would be sufficient to support the British economy through any transitional difficulties after accession.[28] Before any drawing on the IMF they agreed to discuss their options with EEC partners after accession, but devaluation was out of the question. In order to counter claims that the sterling area biased Britain towards global rather than European priorities, the French were reassured that the sterling area was now a

[23] J. A. Robinson (UK delegation to Brussels conference) to J. G. Owen (Treasury), 29 March 1962, BE OV47/54.

[24] Sir Douglas Allen (Treasury) to G. de Moubray (Bank of England), 4 April 1962, BE OV47/54.

[25] Shonfield, A., 'The economic implications of the Brussels breakdown', in K. Younger (ed.), *Implications of the Brussels Breakdown* (Oxford: Oxford University Press, 1963), pp. 15–23, p. 16.

[26] G. R. Bell record of a conversation with Leonhard Gleske, 15 December 1961, BE OV47/51.

[27] E. Roll memo of a conversation with Robert Marjolin, 30 June 1962, BE OV47/56.

[28] Brief for Edward Heath's meeting with Maurice Couve de Murville, 'Monetary aspects of the UK's accession to the European Common Market', by M. E. Johnston, 6 July 1962, OV47/57.

'banking nexus' rather than a tight economic/financial bloc. Leadership of the sterling area was therefore compatible with joining the EEC in the same way that French colonial monetary relations were compatible with its own membership. Essentially, the British line was that sterling was not (and should not become) an EEC problem, although the internal correspondence showed some hope that accession would increase support for sterling. By ruling out devaluation, the British signalled their intention to correct the underlying problem of competitiveness through domestic policy. The credibility of this commitment was soon in doubt, however.

At a strategy meeting at the Treasury to design the response to French concerns, it was agreed that Edward Heath, the United Kingdom's chief negotiator, should not raise monetary issues himself, in the hope that any confrontation on this topic could be avoided until after UK accession was assured.[29] In conversation with Eric Roll, Robert Marjolin, the influential French EEC commissioner, agreed with this approach and offered to urge the French to postpone discussion of financial questions.[30] His efforts were only partly successful, as by November 1962 it was reported that 'the Finance Ministers [of the Six] did not discuss the position of sterling, but that there is a growing feeling in the Community that some long-term consolidation of sterling balances will be necessary, if the UK is to be a stable partner in the enlarged Community and to achieve satisfactory growth'.[31] The Europeans interpreted the sterling balances as an insupportable short-term debt that constrained expansionary growth policies. 'Consolidation' meant turning these short-term liabilities into more predictable and less liquid longer-term debt. Since the monetary authorities had to hold liquid assets as foreign exchange reserves, consolidating the sterling balances in this way would eliminate the reserve role of sterling to which the French in particular objected. With sterling a mere national currency, its management would no longer threaten to set British priorities against those of Europe, and Britain would not have as much vested in the Anglo-American alliance.

In his memoirs, Couve de Murville recalled that his concerns about the sterling exchange rate and the sterling balances were received with annoyance and surprise by the British. This attitude encouraged him not to persist with this line of questioning (although he considered it

[29] Note of a meeting at the Treasury, 6 July 1962, BE OV47/57. This was reconfirmed at the Common Market Negotiations (Official) Committee meeting of 21 December 1962, BE OV47/62.

[30] Telegram from Roll to Frank Lee, 13 July 1962, BE OV47/57. Marjolin had particular responsibility for economic and financial affairs in the European Commission.

[31] Extract of a memo from the UK delegation to Brussels, 1 November 1962, BE OV47/62.

fundamental), given the range of other difficulties already pressing on the negotiations.[32] In hindsight, H. L. Jenkyns of the Treasury also remarked, in 1965, that 'it is probable that this [sterling] would have played a prominent part in negotiations in 1963 if they had not been terminated abruptly at the beginning of that year'.[33]

Interestingly, British official and ministerial opinion was fast moving towards that of Europe in the 1960s, as enthusiasm for retaining sterling as an international currency waned. In the 1950s the strength of the economy was sometimes expressed as dependent on the strength of sterling. By the early 1960s confidence in sterling was considered to be dependent on the strength of the economy rather than vice versa. In December 1962, weeks before the failure of the first application, the Chancellor of the Exchequer, Reginald Maudling, asserted: 'I regard it as a major aim of policy to free the UK economy from the inhibitions of reserve currency status.'[34] In response, Humphrey Mynors (deputy governor of the Bank of England) argued that monetary authorities and others held currencies because they were useful in trade. The reserve role of sterling thus derived from its transactions role, so it was the costs and benefits of sterling as a trading currency that needed demonstrating and 'not the difficulty of "funding the sterling balances", which is but an echo of lost causes'.[35] Given the lack of confidence in the dollar and the shortage of gold, there was no alternative to sterling as a reserve asset for many countries, and so eliminating its vehicle or reserve role would contract international liquidity and threaten the growth of world trade and payments. The time was not ripe for unilaterally ending the international reserve role of sterling until an alternative source of international liquidity could be devised through international negotiation.[36] Nevertheless, this was clearly a longer-term goal.

During the accession negotiations, the Six moved forward with plans for economic and monetary union. In October 1962 the European Commission launched its 'Action Programme' on the creation of a

[32] In his memoirs, Couve de Murville recalled that he raised the issue of sterling only once during these negotiations; Couve de Murville, M., *Une Politique Etrangère, 1958–1969* (Paris: Librairie Plon, 1971), p. 419.

[33] H. L. Jenkyns to D. Hubback, 20 December 1965, BE OV47/63; Jenkyns was in the UK delegation to the OECD in 1961–3.

[34] Quoted on top of Humphrey Mynors' reply dated 3 January 1963, BE OV47/63.

[35] Mynors paper, 3 January 1963. This paper was circulated to the Bank of England Common Market Committee for consideration on 18 January 1963 and sent to Reginald Maudling on 22 January; BE OV47/63.

[36] Chancellors continued to be tempted by a quick solution, however, and by the end of 1964 the new Labour government was again looking for ways to transform the sterling balances into longer-term debt. L. P. Thompson-McCausland to Lord Cromer, 11 December 1964, BE OV53/30.

common market.[37] The proposals aimed at coordinating national policies while falling short of full economic and political union, about which there was considerable disagreement among the Six. The Action Programme called for a new council of central bank governors, and prior consultation on various aspects of economic policy, such as bank rate, minimum reserves, open market policy, exchange rate changes and applications to the IMF. The memorandum also called for a common European attitude in international organisations, a plan for mutual assistance credits for currencies under pressure and a commitment to relax existing capital controls by the end of 1965. Monetary union merely 'could' be a goal of the third stage of integration (i.e. after 1966) and was justified primarily as a measure necessary to protect the Common Agricultural Policy.[38]

The Bank of England and the Treasury both found little in this document with which the UK government needed to disagree.[39] It was assumed that the council of central bank governors would merely run parallel with existing finance ministers' meetings or the informal consultations among central bank governors at the BIS. In any case, the existing European Monetary Committee and Committee on Policy Relating to Economic Trends already brought the Six close to prior consultation. Some new difficulties might be raised over policy changes that affected sterling, as secrecy was of paramount importance to avoid leaking rumours to the market. Günther Schleiminger of the BIS reassured the Bank of England that prior consultations would be confined to 'les grandes lignes de la politique' rather than operational details.[40] The British attitude was generally in line with that of other European central bankers, who submitted their misgivings to the European Council in July 1963.[41] The Committee of Governors of the central banks of the member states was formally established on 13 April 1964, but prior consultation on sensitive policies such as the exchange rate was never enforced.

37 *Memorandum of the Commission on the Action Programme of the Community for the Second Stage*, Brussels, 1962.

38 Maes, I., *Macroeconomic and Monetary Thought at the European Commission in the 1960s*, RSCAS [Robert Schuman Centre for Advanced Studies] Working Paper no. 2004/1 (Florence: European University Institute [EUI], 2004), p. 12.

39 Summary of the Community's programme of action during the second stage, 30 October 1962, BE OV/47/60. This conclusion was agreed formally with the Treasury; paper by W. D. Pattison (Treasury) for Common Market negotiations (Steering Committee), 8 January 1963, BE OV47/63.

40 Note of a discussion between Schleiminger and de Moubray in Brussels, 15 January 1963, BE OV47/63.

41 On the German point of view, see also Bernholz, P., 'The Bundesbank and the process of European monetary integration', in Deutsche Bundesbank (ed.), *Fifty Years of the Deutsche Mark: Central Bank and the Currency in Germany since 1948* (Cambridge: Cambridge University Press, 1999), pp. 731–89, p. 745.

Another forum for potential conflict was over the relaxation of capital controls. In 1959 Marjolin, through the European Commission, had proposed a fast track towards capital liberalisation as part of the creation of the Common Market, but only West Germany was enthusiastic. The other members of the EEC were more cautious, mainly because of their fears of destabilising short-term capital flows, but also because of the desire to retain monetary policy sovereignty.[42] This caution was reflected in the limited range of relaxations in the First Directive on capital controls, in 1960. Only capital flows linked to trade within the EEC, direct investment, and investments in listed shares were to be liberalised.

The initial British response was that, if after accession the UK balance of payments was too weak to relax controls, Britain should be exempted, since the British 'were responsible for the management of an international currency'.[43] In any case, Britain would have a veto on such changes in policy until the beginning of 1966. Since the special position that the United Kingdom had as a provider of an international currency was one of the major objections among the Six to bringing the United Kingdom and sterling into the EEC, the British position was at best naive.

Discussion of the appropriate British response to the First Directive continued into the summer of 1961. Noting that 'The first Directive and the broader provisions of the Treaty itself suggest that the Six are ready to move faster towards complete liberalisation of capital movements than we have felt able to afford', J. M. Forsyth of the Treasury argued that 'our prime objective in the financial field must be to maintain the strength of sterling and we ought not to accept obligations which seem likely to make it more difficult to attain that end'.[44] In contrast, her colleague in the Treasury, J. S. Owen, suggested that the British negotiators should accept the First Directive and leave until later the details of how far the United Kingdom would actually go to adhere to it.[45] The Bank of England and Forsyth thought that such a postponement of financial problems was dishonest, but this view prevailed as the general pattern: that monetary and financial matters were left unresolved while the thorny issues of agriculture and commonwealth trade preoccupied the negotiators.[46]

In September 1961 the Six investigated the extent to which UK exchange control accorded with the First Directive. Discussion between the Six and the United Kingdom on capital movements then took place

[42] Bakker, A. F. P., *The Liberalization of Capital Movements in Europe: The Monetary Committee and Financial Integration 1958–1994* (Dordrecht: Kluwer Academic, 1996), pp. 80–5.

[43] Paper on capital movements for submission to ministers, 12 April 1961.

[44] Treasury brief on capital movements, 16 August 1961, BE OV47/46.

[45] Memo, 23 August 1961, BE OV47/46.

[46] Memo by J. H. H. (Bank of England), 23 August 1961, BE OV47/46.

in February 1962, but the discussions were general and mainly related to points of information.[47] In April the Chancellor was advised to begin relaxing existing exchange controls on capital flows to make it clear that Britain had no reservations about the First Directive during the EEC negotiations.[48] It was clear that preferential access of the sterling area to the London capital markets was not to be allowed to obstruct British membership of the EEC.

Again, British complacency was partly justified by the attitudes of the Six. The enthusiasm of European governments for uncontrolled short-term investment had been extinguished by the currency pressures of 1960/1, which prompted the reintroduction of capital controls even in West Germany. In December 1962 the European Council adopted a weak Second Directive on capital controls. Bakker describes how this document was of little substance, but was promoted in order to sustain some semblance of momentum over liberalisation.[49] A proposed Third Directive foundered on the increasing caution of the European partners and the disintegration of the international monetary system.

The accession negotiations were abruptly terminated by de Gaulle's press conference of 14 January 1963. As others have noted, this first veto arose mainly from strategic conflict with the United States, and the inability of the British to convince de Gaulle of their genuine willingness to adapt their policies on agriculture and trade to the Treaty of Rome.[50] Sterling had been successfully kept in the background of the first set of negotiations, but French objections had been aired, as had the division among the Six. This meant that sterling was likely to become more prominent in the second round of negotiations.

The second application, 1967

The failure of Britain's effort to gain entry to the EEC did not end British interest in monetary developments among the Six. Ministers decided almost immediately that, despite the breakdown, policy should be developed so as to be consistent with eventual membership of the EEC. This

[47] Summary record of a meeting between UK delegation and Commission on Capital Movements, Economic Policy and the Balance of Payments, 19 February 1962, BE OV47/52.

[48] Sir D. Rickett to Lee for Chancellor of Exchequer, 13 April 1962, BE OV47/54.

[49] Bakker, *The Liberalization of Capital Movements in Europe*, pp. 92–4.

[50] Kaiser, W., *Using Europe, Abusing the Europeans: Britain and European Integration 1945–63* (London: Macmillan, 1996); Vaisse, M., 'De Gaulle and the British "application" to join the Common Market', in Wilkes, *Britain's Failure to Enter the European Community*, pp. 51–69; Bange, O., *The EEC Crisis of 1963: Kennedy, Macmillan, de Gaulle and Adenauer in Conflict* (New York: St Martin's Press, 2000).

was for two reasons. First, EEC accession continued to be the avowed policy of the British government, and moving in parallel on monetary matters would ease the eventual adjustment to membership. Second, recent experience had suggested that the United Kingdom was likely to require rapidly arranged and substantial external credits, such as had characterised the early 1960s. The Six were the most obvious source of such credits, and so, 'if for no other reason, therefore, we cannot afford to weaken our contacts with them in this field'.[51]

On the other hand, closer cooperation with the Six on reforming the international monetary system was rejected, and instead it was agreed that collaboration with the United States should continue.[52] On the global scene, the United Kingdom saw its interests most closely linked with those of the United States, and British policy with regard to international monetary reform focused on developing a joint Anglo-American view rather than engaging more deeply with the Six. Partly this was because both were 'key currency' countries, but a further consideration was that the British hoped to influence US policy by convincing them to abandon their plans to extend their system of bilateral swaps as a solution to the problems of the international monetary system. Instead, chapter 7 will show that Britain sought to encourage the US administration to take a longer-term view of the problem and to devise a multilateral and permanent solution within the IMF.[53] The British also, of course, relied on American support for future drawings on the IMF, so they could not afford to abandon their 'special relationship' with the United States. British governments continued to walk the fine line between maintaining close and separate ties to the United States and showing willingness to prepare for eventual membership of the EEC.

At the beginning of 1965 the Treasury began to encourage the new Labour government to develop a coherent external economic policy, especially with respect to the EEC.[54] As the Bank of England reported, '[I]n so far as there are ministerial ideas about external economic policy, a number of them contain dangerous illusions.'[55] In March 1965 the Foreign Office presented a paper to the External Economic Relations Committee recommending that eventual membership of the Common

[51] Bank of England paper, 'Monetary cooperation after Brussels', 6 June 1963, TNA T230/641.

[52] See correspondence in BE OV53/16.

[53] Bank of England brief for April talks in Washington, 27 March 1963, BE OV53/16.

[54] The Labour Party was elected in October 1964, and Harold Wilson replaced Sir Alec Douglas-Home as prime minister; James Callaghan replaced Maudling as Chancellor of the Exchequer.

[55] Rootham to governors, 29 January 1965, BE OV52/2.

Market should be the major aim of external policy, and the Treasury followed up with a series of papers on the various aspects of UK membership. This time it was recognised that, because of the ongoing discussions about the future of the international monetary system, financial and monetary matters were likely to be much more prominent and that 'it would take considerable negotiations to fit sterling into the monetary framework of the Six'.[56] By the end of 1965 it was generally recognised that sterling and the sterling balances were 'bound to come under close scrutiny'.[57]

The second application to join the EEC was formally announced in May 1967.[58] In the meantime, the international financial system had undergone a major boom with the explosion of the Eurodollar market, the 'invasion' of US banks into London and the faltering international status of the US dollar. During the 1960s the sterling area gradually disintegrated as the benefits of pegging to sterling eroded. Nigeria and Ghana broke their fixed rate to sterling in 1962 and 1965, respectively. Other sterling area countries, such as Australia, also diversified their reserves. At the end of 1964 sterling still made up 83 per cent of the official reserves of overseas sterling countries, but this share had fallen to 75 per cent at the end of 1966 and 65 per cent at the end of 1967.[59] As the monetary links of the sterling area relaxed, so too did the capital market links, culminating in the announcement of a voluntary restriction on British investment in the developed sterling area countries in March 1966. British leadership of the sterling area as an obstacle to entry to the EEC was on its way to resolving itself.

Nevertheless, the British position on the role of sterling in the EEC was remarkably unchanged from the arguments that had been used in the 1961–3 application. The briefing papers for negotiators in 1967 followed very closely the conclusions of the working parties in 1961/2. Because of the impact that sterling policy had on the US dollar and the international payments system, sterling was a global problem that crucially involved the United States and sterling holders, not a European problem, so the

[56] Note of a meeting of the External Economic Relations Committee, 12 April 1965, BE OV52/2.

[57] Jenkyns to Hubback, remarks reflecting general feeling in Treasury, 20 December 1965. This view of the Treasury's policy papers was echoed by D. F. Stone to Rootham, 17 January 1966, BE OV47/63.

[58] In November 1966 Wilson announced his intention to make high-level contact with the Six about accession. For the causes of the government's delay in applying again, see Gowland, D., and A. Turner, *Reluctant Europeans: Britain and European Integration 1945–1998* (London: Longman, 2000), pp. 154–8.

[59] The 1967 figure is at the new devalued rate of exchange; Bank paper on 'The future of the sterling balances', March 1968, BE OV53/38.

proper forum for reform was the G10 or the IMF.[60] This, of course, was at the root of the French objections to UK accession, since the reserve currency problem tied the United Kingdom and United States more closely together in a partnership outside the Six. Again, agreeing to devalue sterling before entry was not a possible option, because even discussing it publicly would prompt damaging speculative pressure.

The British negotiating brief for 1967 called for exactly the same arguments as in the 1961–2 talks: that the sterling balances were stable, that the sterling area did not contribute to instability in the UK balance of payments and that its reserves were more likely to be diversified through the accumulation of non-sterling assets than by selling sterling assets, so the direct impact on the United Kingdom would not be so great. In making this last argument the UK position implicitly acknowledged that the reserve role of sterling was set to decline, but that this process should be allowed to evolve gradually rather than be hastened by design. By 1967 the French were preparing to establish Paris as an international financial centre, so the brief added that '[i]n the minds of some Frenchmen, fear of British dominance in the financial field may be a reason for wanting to see us excluded from the Community, but this is not likely to be said openly'.[61] In response, the United Kingdom hoped to appease the French by arguing that linking London with the rest of Europe might consolidate a stronger European banking network that would more effectively balance the power of New York. All references to sterling as a key currency for Europe had disappeared under the weight of the proposals to reform the international monetary system.

Some greater realism was reflected in the conclusion to the brief, which admitted that 'when all this has been said, however, we have to acknowledge that there is a sterling problem'. The United Kingdom would continue to need short-term facilities for periodic crises of confidence in sterling and some long-term arrangement for the sterling balances, and, ultimately, to relieve sterling of its reserve role. For the short term, the British continued to try to convince their partners that they would not invoke article 108 of the Treaty of Rome to garner support for sterling during a crisis resulting from pressure from the sterling area (rather than from the UK balance of payments itself). In the House of Commons, on 8 and 9 May 1967, the prime minister pledged to use the BIS facilities for confidence crises and not to make recourse to EEC arrangements.

[60] Brief for the Economic Committee, EEC negotiating brief, by W. S. Ryrie, 'The international role of sterling', 17 May 1967, TNA T230/955.
[61] Ibid.

As will be seen in chapter 8, the Treasury and the Bank of England hoped that the sterling balances problem might be resolved through a permanent and longer-term G10 central bank support scheme for the diversification of the sterling reserves. Because of the impact of sterling policy on the US dollar and the international monetary system generally, sterling was not primarily a European problem. The UK negotiators were nonetheless advised that it was preferable to express their willingness to discuss these issues with the Six *after* entry, from the British point of view.

Part of the weakness in the British proposals on sterling policy was due to a failure to understand the strength of the objections of the Six. In May 1967 W. S. Ryrie observed:

> One of the difficulties we face in dealing with this subject is that it is hard to be certain how far the argument that the international role of sterling is incompatible with our membership of the Community is genuine, and how far it is being blown up for political reasons to provide a possible pretext for excluding us.[62]

In February 1967 Gerard de la Martiniere of the French Ministry of Finance remarked to Cairncross, rather ominously, that 'the British authorities were not sufficiently alive to the genuineness of the French concern about the sterling balances'.[63] One explanation for the complacency was that other members of the EEC were not believed to share the French view. In March, David Hubback of the Treasury noted: 'The present position seems to be that all Members of the Six, with the exception of the French, are prepared to accept our thesis that sterling in its international role does not present the EEC with any serious problem if and when we join.'[64] The other members of the Six emphasised the dangers posed by the general weaknesses of the British economy, but they had no fatal concerns about sterling.

By June 1967, when Harold Wilson was preparing to go to Paris to rescue the British application, de Gaulle was known to expect a devaluation of sterling before British entry.[65] On the one hand, he 'disliked' reserve currencies because they unfairly created an artificial market for that country's debt and so allowed their governments to borrow cheaply by issuing securities held in central banks overseas, but, conversely, he also believed that the sterling balances were a millstone around Britain's neck. He was not convinced that the British could distinguish between

62 Ibid.

63 A. K. Cairncross to D. H. Rickett, 6 February 1967, TNA T230/955.

64 Hubback to Rickett, 20 March 1967, TNA T230/955.

65 The British assessment of de Gaulle's views are set out in the draft for the prime minister's visit to Paris on 19 June, by Ryrie, 7 June 1967, TNA T230/955.

their international balance of payments and their national balance of payments, so he did not believe British assurances that article 108 would not be invoked in order to protect sterling in a crisis. Finally, he believed that the Americans were able to exert pressure on Britain because of the weakness of sterling. This suspicion that Britain was a Trojan horse, preparing to deliver the EEC to American domination, had already been expressed in de Gaulle's rejection of the first British application.[66]

On 25 September James Callaghan, the Chancellor of the Exchequer, published an article in *Le Monde* aimed at the French audience, in which he argued that the sterling balances should not be an obstacle to UK membership of the EEC. He confirmed that, 'so far as the role of sterling is concerned, we are ready for change', and suggested that there might be a common European currency in the future.[67] Callaghan's public hint that the United Kingdom was happy to see the decline of sterling's reserve status did not achieve its goal. Five days after the *Le Monde* article appeared the European Commission published a highly critical 'Opinion' on the British and other applications to join the EEC, in which it sided publicly with the French view that the weakness of sterling and the potential volatility of the sterling balances was indeed an obstacle to British membership of the EEC.[68] The Opinion criticised both Britain's unwillingness to discuss the 'sterling problem' in the EEC negotiations and the British preference to 'seek a solution to the problem of sterling as an international currency in a framework wider than that offered by the Community'. The Commission insisted that, since a global solution did not seem imminent, these issues had to be dealt with in the European context. The existing Basle Agreements were too small and impermanent to be relied on. Finally, sterling's international reserve role had to be eliminated *before* membership by stopping any growth in existing overseas sterling balances and, indeed, reducing their total value. This would require exchanging them either for some other currency or for a longer-term UK liability. A meeting was scheduled for 14 November 1967 to discuss the issue, but in the meantime Couve de Murville expressed

[66] Quoted in Nicholson, F., and R. East, *From the Six to the Twelve: The Enlargement of the European Communities* (London: Longman, 1987), p. 31. Cairncross notes that Michel Debré, French minister of economic affairs and finance, also believed there was a US imperialist plot: 'From the Treasury diaries of Sir Alec Cairncross: four Anglo-French conflicts 1967–8', *Contemporary European History*, 6(1), 1997, pp. 117–31, p. 188, entry of 2 February 1967. For the views of the Six, see also Ludlow, N. P., 'A short-term defeat: the Community institutions and the second British application to join the EEC', in Daddow, *Harold Wilson and European Integration*, pp. 135–50.

[67] 25 September 1967, BE OV53/36.

[68] *Opinion on the Applications for Membership received from the UK, Ireland, Denmark and Norway*, Commission of the European Communities, Brussels, 29 September 1967.

France's worries about sterling in a separate interview, thus increasing pressure on the exchange rate.[69] Wilson was forced to accept the need for devaluation, and the exchange rate was duly changed from $2.80 to $2.40 on 18 November 1967.

In a press conference on 27 November de Gaulle announced his second rejection of a British application to the EEC. With respect to sterling he stated:

> The Common Market, finally, is incompatible with the state of sterling – as revealed again by the devaluation and by the loans which preceded and accompanied it. Moreover, in view of the pound's position as an international currency and the enormous external balances which weigh it down, the state of sterling would not allow it at present to become part of the solid, interdependent, and assured society in which the franc, the mark, the lira, the Belgian franc, and the guilder are joined.[70]

The French were roundly criticised for their rejection of the application. Otmar Emminger of the Deutsche Bundesbank speedily sided with the British, criticising the French attacks on sterling and agreeing that the sterling balances were not a major problem for Britain.[71] In any case, the Six soon found themselves in disequilibrium, and the 'solidity' of their currencies so proudly noted by de Gaulle was quickly challenged by the international monetary crisis of 1968. A general change of European parities ensued in 1969, which had a profound impact on the approach to exchange rate stability in the EEC.

The realignment of European exchange rates proved particularly costly because of the compensation payments necessary under the new Common Agricultural Policy. This encouraged the Six to accelerate planning for economic and monetary union while the rest of the world moved towards greater flexibility of exchange rates. In February 1968 the European Commission drafted a short 'Memorandum sur l'action de la Communauté dans le domaine monétaire' calling for the elimination of fluctuation margins between member exchange rates, a single unit of account and a system of mutual assistance, but this initiative foundered in the gold crisis of March 1968 and 'les événements' of May 1968 in Paris.[72] The initiative was renewed by the Barre Plan of February 1969, which called for greater consultation on economic policy and laid the foundations for the commitment to economic and monetary union agreed

[69] Cairncross and Eichengreen, *Sterling in Decline*, p. 188.
[70] Quoted in Nicholson and East, *From the Six to the Twelve*, p. 52.
[71] Text of speech by Otto Emminger to Currency, Credit and Monetary Committee of the Federal Association of German Industry in Frankfurt, 28 November 1967, BE OV53/37.
[72] Maes, *Macroeconomic and Monetary Thought*, p. 15.

at the Hague summit in December 1969. There was no consensus about the method to be adopted to achieve this goal, however. The dispute focused on disagreement between the French, who wanted to impose the single currency first, which would then force policy convergence, and the West Germans, who aimed at achieving convergent macroeconomic policies before the introduction of a single currency. These details were left to the Werner Committee, which reported its blueprint in October 1970 for economic and monetary union, to be achieved by 1980. The Werner Report left the final details for coordinated policy-making unclear, and so did not finally resolve the Franco-German disagreement. In practice, it was easier for governments to make commitments to exchange rate policy in the context of the collapse of Bretton Woods in 1971 than to create an independent unified macroeconomic policy, so it might be argued that the French position prevailed.[73] On the other hand, the tighter bands for European currencies (the so-called 'snake in the tunnel') proved difficult to operate, and few currencies were consistent members of the snake once it came out of the tunnel in March 1973.[74] In this context of conflict and instability over exchange rate policy, Britain began its final approach to the EEC.

The final battle for accession, 1970–1972

Sir Con O'Neill, a primary negotiator for the final application, recalled after the successful conclusion of the accession negotiations that 'no subject which entered into the negotiations was more elusive and mysterious, both in the way in which it developed and in the way in which it was solved, than the problem of sterling'.[75] Given the controversy over international monetary reform after 1967, it is not surprising that sterling was prominent in the final accession negotiations in the early 1970s. Europe's plans for economic and monetary union helped to make the future role of sterling in the development of the integration project more urgent. In addition, the final resolution of the sterling issues took place at a time of turmoil in the international exchange markets in the summer of 1971, which culminated in the 'Nixon shock' of August that year. The fragility of the fixed exchange rate system and the importance of stability among European currencies were evident in these events, so monetary

[73] Peeters, T., 'EMU prospects and retrospect', in M. T. Sumner and G. Zis (eds.), *European Monetary Union: Progress and Prospects* (London: Macmillan, 1982), pp. 1–17.

[74] Giavazzi, F., and A. Giovannini, *Limiting Exchange Rate Flexibility: The European Monetary System* (Boston: MIT Press, 1989), pp. 25–7.

[75] Hannay, D. (ed.), *Britain's Entry into the European Community: Report by Sir Con O'Neill on the Negotiations of 1970–1972* (London: Frank Cass, 2000), p. 124.

issues were at the forefront of European officials' minds. Certainly, the international monetary environment of 1971 was different from that of 1961 and 1967, but each of these years was plagued by serious global payments imbalances. This perhaps helps to explain the extraordinary continuity in the approach to sterling in discussions with the Europeans.

As in the discussions in 1967, France was still the main protagonist on the European side, and there were still contradictions in the French position that confused the British team. The French continued to argue both that sterling as a reserve currency offered the United Kingdom the chance to run balance of payments deficits and, on the other hand, that the sterling balances weakened the British economy.[76] Ten years of accession negotiations had not brought the two sides closer together on the diagnosis of the problem. As in 1961 and 1967, the British viewed the resolution of sterling as a reserve currency as part of global planning for the future of the international monetary system, and not as an issue that could be resolved in a European context. As O'Neill put it, 'It was perfectly evident to us that this was a process which would not only involve more Governments than merely those of the Community but would above all take much more time than was available for our negotiations.'[77] Sterling still distinguished Britain's international relations from those of other European states.

In the final accession negotiations there were two main issues related to sterling, both of which had been raised in earlier applications: non-discrimination in capital flows and the reserve role of sterling. Acceding to the EEC's rules on capital account liberalisation would mean that British policy could no longer discriminate in favour of the sterling area. This was a very delicate point of the negotiations for Britain, since preferred access to the London capital market was a cornerstone of the sterling area system and had been formalised in the 1968 Sterling Agreements with several countries, including Australia and New Zealand.

Curtailing sterling's reserve role was another way of saying that Britain needed to run down the sterling balances in a way that did not put undue strain on the British economy. There were no illusions in Europe about the future of sterling's reserve role once the Basle Agreements of September 1968 had removed the 'voluntary' aspect of holding sterling. On the other hand, the French did not want the remnants of reserve currency status to encourage the use of sterling as the new European reserve currency under the terms of European monetary integration.

[76] Meeting in Allen's room, Treasury, with Bank of England and Cabinet Office representatives, 14 January 1971, TNA FCO30/1136.

[77] Hannay, *Britain's Entry into the European Community*, p. 127.

On the British side, as we have seen, there was a growing consensus by the early 1970s that reducing the use of sterling as a reserve asset was desirable. On this question, therefore, there was scope for agreement so long as a firm commitment about how this would be achieved could be delayed until after accession. The issue was complicated by the increase in the nominal value of sterling balances from 1969 to 1971 as the foreign exchange reserves of many economies rose due to the inflationary global boom of these years. The rise in the absolute value of the sterling balances is shown in figure 4.1.

France was still the most vociferous and persistent critic of the Bretton Woods international monetary system and the role of reserve currencies in particular. For Georges Pompidou, the French president, however, sterling did not figure in this general critique, as he did not view sterling as a genuine reserve currency, so his criticisms were aimed at the United States rather than the United Kingdom. On the other hand, Pompidou believed that entry to the EEC threatened to enhance sterling's reserve role and/or accelerate monetary union. In November 1970 Pompidou told Soames that his main concern was 'how to avoid the entry of sterling in to the EEC leading automatically to the establishment of a new European reserve currency aligned against the dollar'.[78] Pompidou was

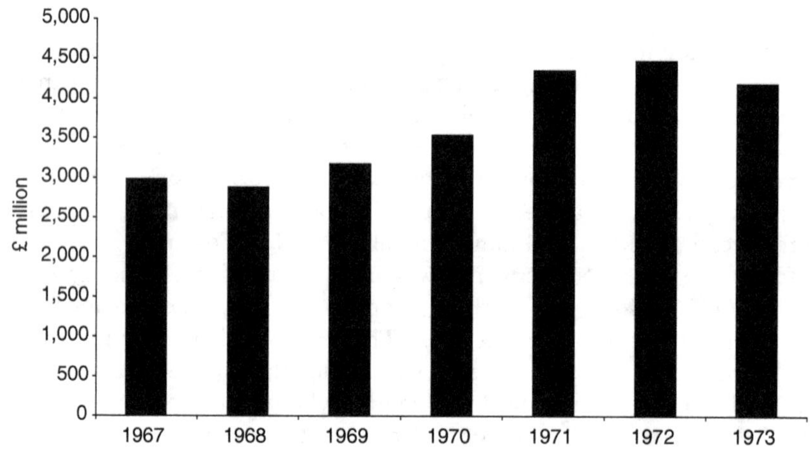

Figure 4.1 Value of sterling assets held by sterling area countries, 1967–73

[78] Soames to O'Neill, 30 November 1970, TNA FCO59/664. O'Neill refers to this correspondence in his account of the accession negotiations in Hannay, *Britain's Entry into the European Community*, pp. 125–6.

sensitive to antagonising the Americans if Europe proposed an alternative or rival reserve currency to the dollar or SDR.[79] The question of sterling was therefore part of the internal debate among the Six over progress towards monetary union, and for this reason Pompidou wanted a commitment that the reserve role of sterling would be phased out as part of the terms of British accession. In addition, this would remove any benefit that Britain gleaned from the sterling area and at the same time minimise the strain on the EEC's resources if it had to support sterling in the future.[80]

Towards the end of December 1970 Raymond Barre, the vice-president of the European Commission for Economic and Financial Affairs, devised six questions on the British economy and sterling to form the basis of discussions in Brussels. The questionnaire posed some problems for the British team, as they assumed that any answers would leak to the press or otherwise be published in due course. Since exchange rate policy and discussion of the reserves were sensitive both politically and financially, the responses had to be fairly general.[81] Question 5 asked how the rise in sterling balances from 1969 to 1970 would affect Britain's obligations under the 1968 Sterling Agreements with the sterling area.[82] The Treasury wanted to emphasise that, despite the absolute increase in sterling balances, the international role of sterling was in decline. Sterling had fallen as a share of world reserves from 12 per cent in 1960 to 7 per cent in 1970, and the sterling balances had fallen from an amount equivalent to 15 per cent of UK GNP in 1964 to 10 per cent in 1969. The sterling balances were thus declining relatively even though they increased in nominal terms. Moreover, the rate of increase was expected to slow after 1970. Edward Heath, now prime minister, insisted that this entire section be deleted so as not to emphasise the decline of sterling.[83] At this point Heath was not ready to embrace this negative view of sterling publicly by acknowledging this obvious trend. Instead, the reply sent to Barre merely reviewed recent movements in the balances and asserted that the renewal of the 1968 Sterling Agreements was a matter for the countries concerned, not the EEC.

[79] Soames to O'Neill, 23 December 1970, TNA FCO59/664.
[80] Ibid.
[81] Anthony Barber to Edward Heath, 8 February 1971, FCO 30/1136.
[82] Draft reply to question 5, February 1971, FCO 30/1136. Total OSA sterling balances increased by £300 million from 1969 to 1970.
[83] PM's Office to Chancellor of Exchequer, 12 February 1971. The change was reluctantly agreed by the Treasury on 16 February 1971. Memo by M. R. Morland, 16 February 1979, FCO 30/1136. This correspondence contradicts O'Neill's claim that the answers were complete at the end of January; Hannay, *Britain's Entry into the European Community*, p.130.

Question 6 was concerned with how the United Kingdom viewed its obligations to Europe compared to its responsibilities to the sterling area, 'in particular preferential relations in the financial and monetary fields, and in the matter of foreign exchange systems and markets and exchange control'.[84] The British side believed this reflected an outdated misunderstanding of the nature of the sterling area by the early 1970s. They responded that 'the UK's position in the sterling area system does not lead to the range of preferential relationships implied in the question' other than for capital flows. The answer then repeated the British position on capital flows stated by the UK delegation in Brussels on 18 December 1970, and based on the principle established as early as the first application – i.e. that the United Kingdom would accede to European rules on capital flows at the end of the transition period.

At the beginning of February, before the questionnaire was returned, O'Neill asked for permission to approach Valéry Giscard d'Estaing, the French minister of economy and finance, on the issue of sterling so as to get a better idea of his thinking, in the hopes of heading off further difficulties and misunderstandings. The Treasury refused to allow this, preferring to wait for the Six to take the initiative on sterling, and because the Chancellor wanted to approach Giscard himself in a few months' time.[85] The strategy, as in the first and second applications, was to hope that detailed discussions on sterling could be avoided prior to accession. As things turned out, it might have been useful to make such a contact, because in mid-March 1971 the French turned again to the offensive on sterling. As G. R. Bell noted in correspondence with O'Neill, 'The answers to the Barre questions do not really of themselves afford a good opportunity for engaging in a useful dialogue. They answer the questions blandly, and without revealing anything that the Six do not already know.'[86] Heath was warned that there might be criticism that the answers were not very forthcoming, but that given the potential for leaks no further detail could be committed in writing.[87] These concerns proved accurate. Barre was disappointed and reportedly was 'persuaded from the vagueness of the British answers that the British were not ready for a serious discussion on sterling'.[88] Disappointment and suspicion brought him and the French back to the offensive at the meeting of the Committee of Permanent Representatives to the EEC Council on 18 March.

[84] Draft reply to question 6, February 1971, FCO 30/1136.
[85] Bell to O'Neill, 17 February 1971, TNA FCO59/664.
[86] Ibid.
[87] Barber to Heath, 8 February 1971, TNA FCO 30/1136.
[88] Crispin Tickell note of conversation with Georges Berthoin, deputy head of delegation to the European Communities in London, FCO59/664.

O'Neill relates in his recollection of events that, on 17 March, Pompidou decided that the problem of sterling would need to be raised immediately, and the French representative, Jean-Marc Boegner, was instructed to make a speech to the Committee of Permanent Representatives the next day.[89] Boegner set out three issues to be considered before the next meeting of the Council of Ministers, scheduled for two weeks later on 30 March. The first was the contradiction between sterling as a reserve currency and the progress towards economic and monetary union in Europe. Second, he called for a progressive reduction in the sterling balances during the transition period after accession; and, third, France insisted on ending discrimination in capital flows.[90] On the first point, the British viewed the reserve role of sterling as a longer-term problem that did not require immediate action. On the second, deliberately running down sterling holdings by independent central monetary authorities during the transition after accession would be costly at a time when the pressures on British finances were most acute, and therefore this suggestion was to be resisted. The third issue was more controversial, because it involved either relaxing controls on capital flows to Europe, which would be costly, or imposing new controls on the sterling area, which would threaten relations with these states and their willingness to retain their sterling reserves.

In subsequent discussions with members of the French government and bureaucracy, Boegner's statement was described as the result of a characteristic volte-face by Pompidou that was mishandled in the haste to draft the statement, resulting in a text that was more obstructive than intended.[91] The Chancellor of the Exchequer, Anthony Barber, tried to reassure Heath that Boegner's statement was not a surprise to the Treasury and should not be interpreted as evidence of new intransigence on the part of the French to the whole British application.[92] Barber claimed that he had not believed that the British answers to the questionnaire answers would satisfy the Six and expected to be questioned further on sterling, so that 'I do not feel that the tone of the French statement was either unreasonable or hostile'. Nor did he believe 'that

[89] Hannay, *Britain's Entry into the European Community*, p. 131.

[90] Text of Jean-Marc Boegner's statement, telegram from Brussels, 18 March 1971, TNA FCO 59/664.

[91] D. M. D. Thomas (British embassy, Paris) to Norman Statham, Foreign and Commonwealth Office (FCO), 24 March 1971. Morland to O'Neill and Tickell, 26 March 1971. J. E. Galsworthy, 'Note for the record', 23 March 1971. A. M. Palliser to Soames, 23 March 1971, TNA FCO59/664.

[92] Barber to Heath, 24 March 1971, FCO 59/664. This letter is discussed also by O'Neill in Hannay, *Britain's Entry into the European Community*, pp. 131–2.

the French have introduced these questions now in order to disrupt or delay the negotiations'.[93] France's resolve not to use sterling to delay the negotiations was confirmed by Michael Palliser of the British embassy in Paris in discussion with Pompidou's adviser Simon Nora, who had been present when Pompidou decided to instruct Boegner to make the intervention.[94] Sir Geoffrey Rippon, the chief UK negotiator, also wrote to the prime minister to support the Chancellor's reassurances. He suggested that he should continue to insist that the capital flows issue could form part of the negotiations but that the reserve role of sterling and the sterling balances could not.[95]

This skirmish speaks to the opaque nature of the negotiations, the unpredictable role that sterling played in Anglo-French discussions and the lack of communication between the French and the rest of the Six. The rest of the Six were surprised by Boegner's statement and did not support the French position. It did achieve the French goal of bringing the sterling discussions out into the open, however, especially as Boegner's text was leaked to the press. The British strategy had been to sideline sterling as a topic for 'discussion' rather than 'negotiation' and so avoid firm commitments and publicity that might undermine confidence in the exchange rate, and the British believed that the Six understood and accepted this approach. Despite subsequent reassurances, Boegner's statement did reflect a change in the French position that required a firmer commitment to the reduction of sterling balances before accession could be agreed.[96]

Once public, the French statement also made it necessary to communicate British policy to the rest of the sterling area. On 29 April 1971 sterling area ministers of finance were advised that the United Kingdom had no desire to reverse the decline in sterling's reserve role, but neither did the United Kingdom want to accelerate this process. Moreover, 'we could not simply decide to run down the reserve role of sterling without having a clear idea of what to put in its place'. Any solution in the context of the EEC would need to avoid excessive drains on the United Kingdom or damage to the international monetary system, and 'it would have to be acceptable to the official holders of sterling'. The Chancellor concluded with an assurance that 'there is no question of discussions on concrete arrangements for the reserve role of sterling in the longer

[93] Barber to Heath, 24 March 1971, FCO 59/664.

[94] Palliser to Soames, 23 March 1971, TNA FCO59/664.

[95] Geoffrey Rippon to Heath, 26 March 1971. Heath minuted that he agreed with Rippon's strategy; 20 March 1971, TNA FCO59/664.

[96] Meeting between Rippon and Baron Geoffroy de Courcel (French ambassador to London), 26 March 1971, TNA FCO50/664.

term taking place without full consultation with you'.[97] This ruled out a British commitment on the sterling balances before accession, or, at least, a public commitment.

At the meeting of the Council of Ministers on 30 March an ad hoc group was set up to discuss the issues raised by Boegner. Sir Jeremy Morse of the Bank of England and Bell of the Treasury attended the meeting on 21 April, which Bell described as 'courteous and friendly'.[98] They made a statement to the effect that Britain was willing to participate in a scheme to reduce the sterling balances in the longer term, but that this was to be discussed only after accession. They were pressed hardest on the large volume of British capital exports to the sterling area, which the Six interpreted as a drain on the British economy.[99] The Dutch member of the group, A. Looijen, later reported to the British team on the discussions after the British representatives had left the meeting. The 'Five' opposed French suggestions that the United Kingdom should impose controls on capital exports to the sterling area, since this was not within the terms of the treaty, which said little about capital flows. On the other hand, there was unanimous agreement on the need to reduce the sterling balances, particularly because no member should have a reserve currency in the final phase of European monetary union.

At the next meeting of the ad hoc group, on 28 April, the French became even more specific about extracting a commitment from Britain to reduce the sterling balances. They proposed a 5 per cent annual reduction and an undertaking that the total amount should not rise above the value as at the end of 1970.[100] The rest of the Six unanimously agreed that the sterling balances should not be part of the negotiations for accession. There was consensus that the United Kingdom should stop discriminating in favour of the sterling area with respect to capital flows after accession, although a French proposal for specific limits on British net investment was not supported because it was deemed unworkable and beyond the powers in the treaty. At their meeting the next day the split between the French and the others over sterling's reserve role became more firm, and the drafting of an agreed report for the Committee of Permanent Representatives meeting on 6 May was postponed.[101]

[97] Text of message from the Chancellor, 29 April 1971, TNA T312/2815.
[98] Bell for Ryrie, 23 April 1971, TNA FCO 30/1140.
[99] Bell to Ryrie for the Chancellor, 16 April 1971, TNA T295/800.
[100] Telegram from Kenneth Christofas in Brussels, 29 April 1971, TNA T295/800.
[101] Telegram from Christofas in Brussels, 1 May 1971, TNA T295/800.

The report of the ad hoc group as finally submitted on 4 May set out more areas of disagreement than agreement.[102] On the role of sterling and the sterling balances, the Six agreed in principle to the need for discussions before accession over 'the case for stabilisation and even for a certain reduction of the sterling balances held by official bodies, in accordance with provisions, and in a manner, to be decided within the ambit of the enlarged Community'. The final phrase implied action *after* accession. There was no consensus, however, over whether there should be a firm undertaking that from the date of signing the treaty of accession the sterling balances should be capped and progressively reduced, or whether there should merely be 'consultations within the enlarged Community and at the international level with the purpose of gradually phasing out the reserve currency role of sterling in the context of the final stage of economic and monetary union'. The sterling balances question, therefore, was not going to be completely pushed under the carpet, but it seemed possible that the British could avoid a firm unilateral commitment to dispose of sterling's reserve role before they joined the EEC. Moreover, there was recognition that this was not exclusively a European problem, but one that needed to be discussed 'at the international level'. This was reconfirmed later in the report, where it was agreed that, 'inasfar as difficulties were to arise from a massive conversion of sterling balances, the solution to this problem would in principle have to be found in an international context other than that of the Community'. This approach accorded with the British view that sterling's problems needed to be resolved in the context of the international monetary problem more generally. It also confirmed that the EEC mutual support mechanisms were insufficient for this purpose.

A stickier problem than the sterling balances was the way that British policy regarding capital flows did not accord with European rules. The report of the ad hoc group showed that the Six agreed that Britain's balance of payments suffered from excessive capital outflow, but they did not agree about the implications of this or about possible solutions (either restricting capital outflows or enlarging the current surplus). The British believed Europe's concern was based on a fallacy, since *net* outward investment was well within the current account surplus in 1969 and 1970 and was expected to be so again in 1971. This applied both to the global balance and the balance with the sterling area. With respect to

[102] 'Summary of report of "ad hoc" group following the Council's decision of 30 March 1971', 4 May 1971. The covering note to the translation by J. F. Slater urged that 'our possession of this document should on *no account* be divulged' (emphasis in the original); TNA T295/800.

the sterling area, much of the 'outflow' was reinvested profits rather than capital drained from the United Kingdom per se.[103] Moreover, there was no mention of capital flows to third countries in the Treaty of Rome, so the British did not believe that this was a legitimate topic for negotiation. Finally, the British doubted that French ministers or officials really understood the costs that their 'special preoccupation' with non-discrimination would pose to the British economy.[104] The Treasury viewed ending discrimination in favour of the sterling area as 'unthinkable', since it would either require the United Kingdom to liberalise all short-term and long-term capital flows to Europe, which went well beyond existing liberalisation among the Six, or require new controls on outflows to the sterling area, which would prompt large-scale diversification of reserves by these countries under the terms of the 1968 Sterling Agreements.[105]

Figure 4.2 shows the downward trend of net private investment in the sterling area as a proportion of total private overseas investment, which seems to support the British view. Only for issues on the London capital

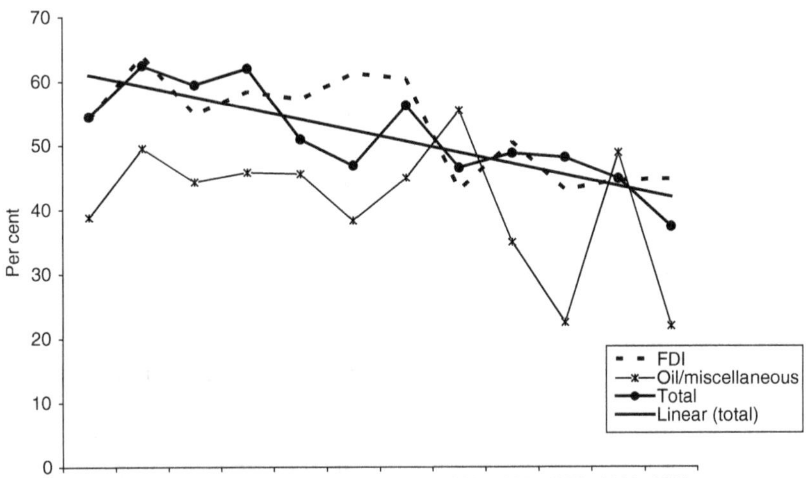

Figure 4.2 Private investment in sterling area as a percentage of total overseas private investment, 1959–70
Source: TNA T296/800.

103 Treasury brief for visit of the prime minister to Paris 19–21 May 1971, 13 May 1971, TNA T295/868.
104 P. E. Thornton to R. T. Armstrong, 2 June 1971, TNA FCO30/1141.
105 Treasury brief for visit of the prime minister to Paris 19–21 May 1971, 13 May 1971, TNA T295/868.

market did the net outflow to the sterling area contrast sharply with a net inflow from the rest of the world, and even this pattern ended from 1965. The value of these portfolio flows was relatively small, however: £17 million to the sterling area from 1959 to 1970, or 0.7 per cent of total net flows to these countries.

The Six disagreed over whether discrimination in favour of the sterling area needed to be abandoned before or after accession. Here, however, a compromise was suggested in the report: that the United Kingdom should delay full liberalisation of flows to the rest of the EEC and treat the EEC at least as favourably as the sterling area for all capital transfers specified in Community directives. The United Kingdom would therefore conform to more directives before the end of the transition period than had been planned. Adopting the directives on accession would cost about £100 million annually, 'thus seriously worsening the burden in the early years of Britain's membership'.[106] Although the United Kingdom could privately agree in principle to non-discrimination, any specific moves in that direction would have to be at Britain's discretion in negotiation with the overseas sterling area countries.

Meanwhile, the closure of the West German foreign exchange market on 5 May and then the floating of the Deutschmark on 10 May again pitched the French against the Germans. The position of the Treasury and the Bank of England in this dispute was to remain aloof, since 'we have nothing useful to contribute and would be very ill-advised to involve ourselves in what looks like being a pretty nasty row between the Germans and the French'.[107] At the Council of Ministers meeting on 10 May the French revealed themselves as still intransigent – demanding a reduction in sterling balances and an immediate end to discrimination in favour of the sterling area on accession. The continuing stalemate pointed to a meeting of Heath and Pompidou as the only way forward.

On 20 and 21 May 1971 Heath met with Pompidou to discuss the key obstacles to British accession, particularly agriculture and sterling. Pompidou kept the meeting very secret from even his own prime minister, but viewed personal contact with Heath as vital to overcome the impasse.[108] At this meeting, a secret agreement was reached to eliminate

[106] Ibid.

[107] J. R. A. Bottomley reporting views of Treasury and Bank of England, 6 May 1971, TNA FCO30/1140. Young identifies Anglo-German disputes over CAP, the relief floating offered to the United States and the postponement of narrower exchange rate markets during this crisis; Young, S. Z., *Terms of Entry: Britain's Negotiations with the European Community, 1970–1972* (London: Heinemann, 1973), p. 191.

[108] Dispatch from Paris, British embassy (Soames), to Douglas-Home on the prime minister's visit to Paris 19–21 May, 9 June 1971, TNA PREM15/374. Campbell details the growing consensus from early 1971 that a bilateral meeting between Heath and

sterling as an obstacle to British accession. In return for Pompidou lifting his specific proposals to reduce sterling balances, Heath committed to 'take measures which would tend to stabilise the level of official sterling balances between 30 June 1971 and the date of our accession to the EEC'.[109] This went further than the Five had claimed in the ad hoc committee report, which had merely asked for stabilisation after accession, and pushed forward the initial baseline by six months. Pompidou did not raise the issue of capital flows, and so this was not discussed.[110]

Heath made a statement in the House of Commons on his return on 24 May, explaining in general terms that the major obstacles had been resolved. He also wrote to Pompidou to confirm that 'we presume that following the talks between the President and the Prime Minister this matter [sterling] will now be put aside [in deliberations of the Six in Brussels] at least to the extent that any further questions on sterling will be dealt with after the conclusion of an accession agreement in the context of progress towards European economic and monetary union', adding that the French negotiators should be so instructed.[111] The next day the foreign secretary, Sir Alec Douglas-Home, reported to the Dutch permanent representative to the EEC, Looijen, in The Hague that 'we are confident in the light of the Prime Minister's talks with President Pompidou that the French Government will not wish to press for further discussion of sterling questions before the negotiations are concluded'.[112] Nevertheless, at the permanent representatives' meeting the next day, 27 May, the French tabled a paper that restated the line they had taken in the Council of Ministers – i.e. Britain had to cease discriminating in favour of the sterling area on capital flows, and the sterling balances should be reduced according to a fixed annual schedule. They did not get support from the rest of the Six, but the intervention did throw a further spanner into the works.[113]

The French negotiator, Michel Jobert, who was a close confidant of Pompidou and had helped to pave the way for the secret Paris summit, claimed he had not received the new instructions from Pompidou in time for the European Council meeting, and he subsequently sought advice

Georges Pompidou would be necessary; Campbell, A., 'Anglo-French relations a decade ago: a new assessment', *International Affairs*, 58(3), 1982, pp. 429–46.

109 Armstrong to Ryrie, 3 June 1967, TNA PREM15/373.

110 Thornton to Armstrong, 2 June 1971, TNA FCO30/1141.

111 Armstrong to Soames, 25 May 1971, enclosing letter from prime minister to Pompidou, TNA PREM15/373.

112 Telegram from Douglas-Home to The Hague, 26 May 1971, TNA FCO30/1040.

113 Telegram from Brussels to O'Neill, 27 May 1971, TNA FCO30/1040. O'Neill describes this episode in some detail in Hannay, *Britain's Entry into the European Community*, pp. 135–8.

from the British over how to proceed.[114] Withdrawing the paper was not a possibility, since this would indirectly reveal that a secret agreement had been forged between Heath and Pompidou. Heath agreed instead that Jobert should encourage the Six to discuss the French paper but that UK representatives would be invited to the meeting of deputies to make a statement about the place of sterling in the enlarged community. This statement would be made by Rippon, who would explain that the British

> have always said that we should be prepared to envisage an orderly and gradual rundown of official sterling balances after our accession. We should be ready to discuss after our entry what measures might be appropriate to achieve a progressive alignment of the external characteristics of sterling with those of other currencies in the community in the context of progress toward economic and monetary union in the enlarged community, and we are confident that official sterling could be handled in a way which would enable us to take our full part in that progress. In the meantime we should manage our policies towards the official sterling balances in a way which would be consistent with these longer-term objectives.

The main goal was to sidetrack the French away from their demand that Britain had to eliminate discrimination in capital flows immediately upon entry to the EEC.[115] The French side tinkered with the wording of Rippon's statement, but, more importantly, claimed that they could not ignore the capital flow issue now that it was on the negotiating table in Brussels. The British countered that Pompidou had not raised this issue with Heath and that they could make no additional commitments on this matter. Finally, after five days of frantic correspondence, on 4 June a compromise was reached in which Rippon would publicly assert the British intention to achieve 'alignment of the external characteristics of, *and practices in relation to*, sterling' with that of the EEC. The French and British agreed privately that the 'practices' referred to 'steady progress towards non-discrimination in capital movements in compliance with our [UK] obligations under the Treaty of Rome' after accession.[116] This final bilateral skirmish paved the way for Pompidou to instruct Giscard to cede the issue of sterling to post-accession discussion.

The European Commission duly met on 7 June, but, before Rippon could make his agreed speech, Raymond Barre as chairman circulated a new initiative that he hoped would overcome what was still believed to

[114] Soames to Armstrong, telegram from Brussels, 28 May 1971, TNA PREM15/373.
[115] Telegram from Armstrong to Soames, 29 May 1971 (cleared with prime minister), TNA PREM15/373.
[116] Armstrong to Tickell, FCO, 5 June 1971, PREM15/373.

be a gulf between France and Britain. Rippon then made the following statement and withdrew from the meeting.

> We are prepared to envisage an orderly and gradual run-down of official sterling balances after our accession.
>
> We shall be ready to discuss after our entry into the communities what measures might be appropriate to achieve a progressive alignment of the external characteristics and practices in relation to sterling with those of other currencies in the community in the context of progress towards economic and monetary union in the enlarged community, and we are confident that official sterling balances can be handled in a way which will enable us to take our full part in that progress.
>
> In the meantime we shall manage our policies with a view to stabilizing the official sterling balances in a way which would be consistent with these longer-term objectives.
>
> I hope that the community will regard this statement as disposing satisfactorily of the question of sterling and associated matters, leaving only the arrangements for UK compliance with the directives relating to capital movements under the Treaty of Rome to be settled in the course of the negotiations.

Giscard d'Estaing's immediate and full acceptance of the British position was greeted with incredulous laughter by the other delegates. The Commission was indignant at having been sidelined by secret bilateral meetings between the British and the French.[117] Barre told Rippon that his statement amounted to 'zero plus zero' and 'he could not understand why Giscard had agreed to it'.[118] Although the national delegations of the Six were expecting a statement, having been warned over the previous weekend, the Commission was not alerted, and bridges needed to be built to restore goodwill. With this final wrinkle ironed out, though, the issue of sterling's future in Europe ceased to be an obstacle to British accession. Rippon formally sent the text of his statement to the EEC on 22 January 1972 and it was published in March as an 'Exchange of letters on monetary questions'. Six months later sterling was floating and the sterling area itself was abolished.

Conclusions

Paradoxically, as the reserve role of sterling declined, it gained more prominence as a European issue, particularly for France. This preoccupation

[117] Telegram from Rippon in Luxembourg to London, 7 June 1971, FCO30/1141 and PREM15/374.

[118] Telegram from Rippon in Luxembourg, 7 June 1971, FCO30/1141. See also R. C. Beetham's account of the aftermath of the meeting, in which he describes Raymond Barre as 'livid'. Churchill Archives Centre, British Diplomatic Oral History Programme, interview with R. C. Beetham, News Department, Foreign and Commonwealth Office.

can be explained by the collapse of the international monetary system and the associated controversy among the Six over European monetary integration. It is clear from earlier historical studies that de Gaulle personally posed a major stumbling bloc for British accession and that, once he was no longer in power, the course of enlargement would be smoother. Nonetheless, the negotiations proved difficult and were still subject to errors and misunderstandings that provoked last-minute skirmishes.

The future of sterling appeared in a variety of guises through the accession negotiations. It had a symbolic importance first as an excuse for rejection of the early applications, and as a test of genuine 'Europeanness' for Britain. It was also a preoccupation of the French arising from their general critique of the international monetary system in the contemporaneous G10 negotiations that split the Six, which are discussed in chapter 7. Ending sterling's reserve role occasionally loomed large in the negotiations, but this was not ultimately resolvable in a European context because any reform required global support and the cooperation of the overseas sterling area. This was finally recognised by the Six, who accepted a firm commitment from the British about their intentions after accession rather than action to reduce sterling balances as a condition of accession. All the same, France was able to extract a commitment from Heath to try to contain the increase in sterling's use as a reserve currency in the months leading up to accession.

The discussions about sterling through the decade of negotiations confirmed the realities of sterling as a reserve currency and forced the government to be public about the intention to reduce that role. The first major public statement to this effect (a decade after it had been accepted privately) was forced in response to the leaking of Boegner's statement. In the House of Commons, on 27 April 1971, Barber set out his willingness to phase out sterling's reserve role 'provided that means could be found which avoided an unacceptable burden on the UK, promoted the healthy development of the international monetary system, and protected the interests of the sterling holders'.[119]

In mid-June 1971 the Foreign and Commonwealth Office (FCO) commissioned an opinion poll by the European Movement on the question 'There is discussion about whether or not the pound sterling should be a reserve currency. Do you understand what this means?'. Only 25 per cent of respondents answered 'Yes' (which the Foreign and Commonwealth Office thought was a very high number). Of these, only 28 per cent believed that sterling should be a reserve currency and

[119] Hansard, 27 April 1971. This was labelled as a 'Major statement of future policy with regard to sterling' by the Treasury in 1972; TNA T312/2815.

40 per cent believed this was an issue 'best left to the experts'. The FCO concluded that 'at least we can safely deduce that the vast majority of the British public does not look upon sterling as being a particularly important subject of negotiation'.[120]

Barber, as Chancellor of the Exchequer, was not so sanguine about reaction on the Conservative back bench, where he believed there was 'a good deal of sentimental attachment to the idea that the reserve currency role of sterling is good for this country – good for prestige and good for business', although he recognised that this was no longer the view in the City.[121] The Treasury set the case out clearly for Barber to use with his colleagues: sterling constituted only 7 per cent of global reserves and financed less than 20 per cent of world trade. 'Two world wars, three devaluations, the rise of the dollar, and the decline of sterling ... have eaten away the foundations of the prestige argument and the UK would be foolish not to recognise the fact.'[122] Moreover, sterling business in the City was relatively small. On the negative side, interest payments on the sterling balances cost about £200 million every year, and the balances were a constraint on policy-making, since overseas holders of sterling responded to adverse economic developments in Britain by diversifying their reserves.

At the September 1971 meeting of Commonwealth finance ministers in Nassau, the Chancellor had an opportunity to reassure sterling holders about the commitments that Britain had made in the course of the accession negotiations. In his opening statement, he emphasised that 'there should be no cause for alarm' and stressed that Britain had given the EEC 'no undertaking on how fast or by what means changes in sterling's reserve role would be brought about'.[123] He then repeated the assurances given at the end of April that any arrangements to reduce the sterling balances would be made in consultation with the overseas sterling area and with their agreement. His audience was not fully convinced. In his closing remarks, the Chancellor repeated his assurances and 'asked the meeting to bear in mind and take quite literally the assurances he had given earlier'. In response to suggestions from the developing countries of the sterling area, the Chancellor conceded that 'there might be

120 'Public opinion and sterling', S. A. Budd, 25 June 1971, TNA FCO59/666.

121 Ryrie, passing on Chancellor's views to Sir Alan Neale, 25 May 1971, TNA T312/2815.

122 Memo by J. A. Marshall, 26 May 1971. Barber minuted: 'This is a v. useful note. When we come to debate the CM in the House we must consider a passage which makes some of these points in a direct way.' 29 May 1971, TNA T312/2815.

123 Chancellor's opening remarks to Commonwealth finance ministers' meeting, September 1971, TNA T312/2815.

bilateral discussions with the official holders of Sterling, or there might be a gathering together of a number of them', but he forestalled any immediate moves on the basis that 'there would be ample time for real and meaningful discussion before any decision was taken'.[124] By this time the priority for Britain was the renegotiation of the Sterling Agreements (discussed in chapter 8), which did bring greater consultation with the sterling area over sterling policy. After the breakthrough with the French in May/June 1971, the challenge for managing the decline of sterling shifted from the European context back to the sterling area – which is discussed in chapter 8.

[124] Chancellor's closing remarks at Commonwealth finance ministers' meeting, September 1971, TNA T312/2815.

5 The 1967 sterling devaluation: relations with the United States and the IMF 1964–1969

The devaluation of 1967 is often interpreted as a failure of economic policy, and it has become emblematic of the inability of the Labour Party to cope effectively with the reduction of sterling's international role. It therefore constitutes a key episode in sterling's post-war retirement. On taking office in October 1964, the new Labour government discovered that the prospective deficit in the balance of payments was much worse than it had anticipated: £800 million rather than £400 million. Nevertheless, one of its first decisions was to reject devaluation as a way out of this imbalance, in favour of a supply-side modernisation of industry so as to enhance competitiveness. The Labour government's postponement of devaluation through repeated annual speculative crises in 1965 and 1966 has been widely criticised.[1] By delaying the decision to devalue, it is argued, the prime minister, Harold Wilson, and the Chancellor of the Exchequer, James Callaghan, set in train three years of recurring speculative crises that cost the central reserves millions of dollars and required repeated emergency constraints on the domestic economy. The reluctance to change sterling's exchange rate is interpreted as arising partly from Wilson's pride (dubbed by Stewart as 'Yorkshire obstinacy') and partly from his fears for the political reputation of the Labour Party because of the memory of 1949. A more practical political consideration was that the Labour government had a majority of only five members, which would have made it politically very difficult to carry successfully both the devaluation and the deflationary measures that would have had to accompany it.

Callaghan has also been criticised for the inadequacy of the domestic economic measures taken to restore the balance of payments to

[1] Ponting, C., *Breach of Promise: Labour in Power, 1964–70* (London: Hamish Hamilton, 1989); Strange, *Sterling and British Policy*; Stewart, M., *The Jekyll and Hyde Years: Politics and Economic Policy since 1964* (London: J. M. Dent and Sons, 1977); Brittan, S., *Steering the Economy: The Role of the Treasury* (London: Penguin Books, 1971). Alford, *Britain in the World Economy since 1880*, refers to Wilson's sterling policy as 'dithering and delay'; p. 281.

equilibrium in the first years of the Labour government until devaluation was forced on him in November 1967. Cairncross and Eichengreen, for example, note:

> The Labour government, on taking office, came down firmly against devaluation. But it did so without giving much consideration to the alternative. It contented itself with ruling out devaluation as 'unmentionable' but devised no coherent strategy for avoiding it.[2]

Callaghan's successor as Chancellor, Roy Jenkins, described the defence of the $2.80 parity as 'a sort of British Dien Bien Phu', in reference to France's doomed two-month defence of a strategic position in Vietnam in 1954.[3] As Newton summarises the traditional view, 'The picture which emerges is of a somewhat disorganised government unwilling to take hard decisions concerning the economy, its policy in the end governed by a political rationale rather than an economic one.'[4] Newton himself goes on to argue that on taking office in 1964 the government's policies were appropriate to the situation, that the response to the first round of the crisis in October 1964 was successful and that the fresh crisis three weeks later was the fault of irrational newly liberalised capital markets. He argues that both the 1964 and 1967 crises were essentially speculative, since 'there was no insurmountable problem with Britain's trading position'.[5] This follows previous revisionist accounts, such as those by Cairncross and Oliver and Hamilton, who show that the option of devaluation was not completely ignored and that there was considerable contingency planning in the Labour government during the 1960s.[6] The rehabilitation of Wilson and Callaghan over the devaluation is part of a more general critique of the 'declinist' or pessimistic view of British relative economic performance in the post-war decades, spearheaded by Tomlinson.[7] Bale has argued that Wilson, Callaghan and George Brown (Secretary of State for economic affairs) acted rationally to a collection of constraints, including the stringent domestic measures that would need to accompany devaluation, a lack of consensus that devaluation would solve the fundamental problems of British competitiveness and a

[2] Cairncross and Eichengreen, *Sterling in Decline*, p. 166.

[3] Jenkins, R., *A Life at the Centre* (London: Macmillan, 1991), p. 214.

[4] Newton, S., 'The two sterling crises of 1964 and the decision not to devalue', *Economic History Review*, 62(1), 2009, pp. 73–98. See also Cairncross, *The British Economy since 1945*, p. 154; Cairncross was a Treasury official during these years.

[5] Newton, 'The two sterling crises of 1964', p. 25.

[6] Cairncross, A. K., *The Wilson Years: A Treasury Diary 1964–1969* (London: Historians' Press, 1997); Oliver, M. J., and A. Hamilton, 'Downhill from devaluation: the battle for sterling 1968–72', *Economic History Review*, 60(3), 2007, pp. 486–512.

[7] For a succinct account of the argument, see Tomlinson, J., 'Economic growth, economic decline', in Burk, *The British Isles since 1945*, pp. 63–90.

sense of obligation in the face of international pressure from the United States and Europe to hold the rate at its current level in order to protect the international economic system.[8] Tomlinson concurs, but identifies the political damage from harsh deflationary measures and the credibility of Wilson's economic management as paramount for ministers, and concludes that 'politics was in command' despite calls from some in the Treasury, such as Nicholas Kaldor, advocating devaluation.[9]

While the domestic economic and political context has already attracted considerable attention from historians, this chapter addresses the international perspective on the sterling exchange rate in these years by focusing on the external consultations and expectations regarding a possible devaluation and how this affected British policy. We will see in chapter 7 that the management of reserve currencies was part of ongoing multilateral discussion during this period, which many in the government hoped would resolve the pressure on sterling. Consistent with the theme that sterling policy was affected by outside pressures, this chapter explores relations with the United States and with the international community through the IMF. Sterling's fortunes were of crucial importance in bilateral relations with the administration of Lyndon Johnson in Washington because of the potential for contagion from speculation on sterling to spread to the US dollar, and because of the link between defence of the sterling exchange rate and the Wilson government's commitment to the overseas strategic reach of the British armed forces. This chapter ends with an account of the shifting balance of power between London and the IMF and the longer-term implications of the IMF's involvement in the devaluation and its aftermath.

Devaluation and Anglo-American relations

The prospects for devaluing sterling were considered by the Johnson administration from the first days of the Wilson government. When Wilson took office in October 1964 and promptly had to introduce restrictive policies to support sterling, Johnson's reaction was cool, although he did welcome Wilson's decision not to raise interest rates, which would have put pressure on US markets. On the other hand, Wilson's defence of the balance of payments included a 15 per cent surcharge on manufactured and semi-manufactured imports and a system of export rebates

[8] Bale, T., 'Dynamics of a non-decision: the failure to devalue the pound 1964–67', *Twentieth Century British History*, 10(2), 1999, pp. 192–217.

[9] Tomlinson, J., *The Labour Governments 1964–70: Economic Policy* (Manchester: Manchester University Press, 2004), p. 50.

that could be considered hostile to the United States. Johnson did not comment on Wilson's forthright assurance that devaluation was 'rejected now, and for all time'. Publicly he welcomed Wilson's policies, but US embassies, consulates, etc. overseas were advised that this was because the president had been faced with a fait accompli and had little other option than to acquiesce quietly. These overseas posts were advised to be more circumspect in their public support.[10]

Within a month the government's initiatives were shown to be inadequate, and so began a period of prolonged frustration in Washington and New York over Wilson's failure to take the decisive action that the Johnson administration believed was necessary to convince the markets of the British government's ability to avoid devaluing the pound. Callaghan reassured Robert Roosa, the US Treasury undersecretary for monetary affairs, at an introductory meeting in 11 Downing Street in November 1964, that devaluation was 'out of the question'. He also tried to convince Roosa that he was truly committed to bringing the balance of payments into line, noting that '[h]e felt like he had felt when he was a young man and had an overdraft at the bank, and in those days his banker was very concerned about such an overdraft. He did not like this position and this in fact was a strong incentive to take steps to improve their position and get out of the situation.'[11] He was soon to recover from his embarrassment and extend the overdraft.

On 19 November 1964 Wilson wrote to Johnson asking for his support if an appeal was made to the IMF for a further stand-by arrangement.[12] With the current account stable, sterling's problems were still viewed in London as short-term and suitable for resolution by recourse to international credit. Bank rate was increased to 7 per cent, but it took the announcement of a \$3 billion multilateral support package (including the IMF stand-by arrangement) to stem speculative pressure on sterling. William McChesney Martin, the chairman of the US Federal Reserve (the 'Fed'), believed that the move in UK bank rate had come too late, 'and then they made a good many foolish statements about how they didn't really need it', sparking a run on the pound on 24 November that was stemmed only by a hasty multilateral operation agreed by telephone

[10] Letter from Wilson to President Johnson, 24 October 1964; telegram from secretary of state to certain posts, 26 October 1964, Foreign Relations of the United States (hereafter FRUS), 1964–68, vol. VIII, 'International monetary and trade policy'.

[11] Meeting in 11 Downing St between Callaghan and Roosa, US undersecretary of the Treasury, 7 November 1964; this was Roosa's first meeting with the new Labour government. National Archives and Records Administration (hereafter NARA) RG56, Records of the Under Secretary of State for Monetary Affairs (hereafter USSMA), Box 22.

[12] Message from Wilson to Johnson, 19 November 1964, FRUS 1964–68, vol. XII.

the following day. Martin called the Earl of Cromer, the governor of the Bank of England, pledging US support, and the European central banks were brought in on a substantial package, which succeeded in steadying the market.[13]

In the wake of the successful $3 billion multilateral operation, Wilson paid a visit to Washington in early December, at which Johnson hosted an off-the-record meeting on the British economic situation.[14] In the long term Wilson agreed that the 'basic solution has to lie in improving Britain's competitive position both with respect to exports and to manufactured imports', but he also mentioned that he was considering some defence cuts – an issue that would become a central source of conflict in Anglo-American relations. He blamed speculation against the pound on the 'unfortunate effects of having to explain and defend British policies before a whole series of international meetings, each generating leaks which agitated those in other countries who were already antagonistic toward a Labour government'. This diverted the blame for a lack of confidence from his own government to malicious perceptions in Europe. Douglas Dillon, the US secretary of the Treasury, and Martin of the Fed both retorted that the British government was itself to blame in the presentation of the October and November measures, which 'played down the effectiveness on the domestic economy of the measures they were taking. He [Dillon] reviewed several such incidents in detail, and expressed the hope that in the future, statements about the British situation and policy measures would be limited, and would be designed to inspire the confidence of foreign businessmen and governments.' No response from the British side is recorded to this very forthright (and, from the record, prolonged) criticism, and the frustration felt in Washington over British economic policy continued to resurface.

The Chancellor tried to cement his personal relations with Johnson by discussing his April 1965 budget with American officials in the run-up to its presentation domestically.[15] Frederick Deming, the new Treasury undersecretary for monetary affairs, was in London at the end of March, and Callaghan assured him that he would be 'pleased' by the budget. Deming took the opportunity to stress how important it was

[13] Telephone conversation with Johnson: report on continuing UK monetary crisis, 25 November 1964, http://fraser.stlouisfed.org/martin/record.php?collection_references_id=4893.

[14] Record of meeting, Washington, 7 December 1964, FRUS 1964–69, vol. XII, 'Western Europe/UK'. The minute starts: 'It was agreed to begin with that this was a meeting which never occurred.'

[15] Telegram from the US embassy in the United Kingdom to the Department of State, 6 April 1965, FRUS 1964–69, vol. XII.

to President Johnson that the budget should contain strong measures to convince public opinion that Wilson intended to defend sterling, and Wilson responded 'without qualification that he intended to defend the sterling rate'. Deming also reassured Callaghan that, 'if the budget was strong but still not well received and trouble developed, the President felt that the US and the UK should stick together and that the US would be as helpful as we could'.[16] At this point the Americans were still engaged in supporting the British if they could be prevailed upon to take firm domestic measures, but the offer reduced the pressure on Callaghan to adopt such measures.

This cooperative attitude was quickly challenged when the April budget proved insufficient and sterling again came under pressure in the summer of 1965. At this point, as chapter 7 shows, the administration began to engage more actively in the reform of the international monetary system in a multilateral way rather than concentrating on Anglo-American cooperation. At the same time, Johnson's advisers began to recommend a firmer attitude to American support for sterling. As pressure in the exchange markets mounted, Callaghan had a visit to Washington scheduled for the end of June, at which the US Treasury expected to be asked again for short-term credit. Merlyn Trued, the assistant secretary of the Treasury for International Affairs, advised the Treasury secretary, Henry (Joe) Fowler, 'In my view, your meeting with Callaghan is a decisive moment. I would hope that your line will be firm so that no illusions are harboured when Callaghan returns to the UK.' Fowler was advised to make it clear that the United States 'simply cannot afford to do any more than we are now doing'.[17] Fowler agreed, and urged the president to resist discussing further bilateral support and instead to encourage Callaghan to consider a longer-term multilateral solution to sterling's difficulties covering the next two to three years.[18] Rather than coming cap in hand, however, Callaghan took the offensive by opening discussions with his proposals to reduce Britain's overseas military commitments, noting that 'the U.K. cannot continue to carry the present foreign exchange burden and it must come down' either through reductions in Europe or the Far East, or both.[19] This raised vigorous protests from Robert McNamara, the US secretary of defense, and the undersecretary, George Ball, who responded firmly that 'we recognize the British problem, but we cannot accept a further extension of our own [military]

[16] Memo for Treasury secretary Henry Fowler from Frederick L. Deming, 1 April 1965, NARA RG56 Records of USSMA, Box 22.
[17] Merlyn Trued to Fowler, 28 June 1965, NARA RG56 Records of USSMA, Box 22.
[18] Memorandum from Fowler to Johnson, 28 June 1965, FRUS 1964–69, vol. XII.
[19] Memorandum of conversation, 30 June 1965, FRUS 1964–69, vol. XII.

commitments'. McNamara had stressed from the time of Wilson's first visit to Washington, in December 1964, that the United States viewed the continuation of Britain's global presence as vital to the interests of the free world.[20]

Barely a month after his visit to Washington, Callaghan was forced by pressure on sterling into a further austerity budget. This time Wilson reassured Johnson that the measures 'showed the Government's determination to put the strength of sterling before politics' and that, despite domestic political objections, 'I am determined to face up to our overriding problem of maintaining confidence to the limit', but his protestations lacked credibility in Washington.[21] The same day as this message was sent from London, Francis Bator, the deputy national security advisor, began to press the president to begin contingency planning for a sterling devaluation.[22]

The seriousness of the August 1965 crisis on Anglo-American relations is revealed in a telephone call between Fed chairman Martin and President Johnson on 5 August.[23] Martin advised Johnson that he believed that the United States had come to a 'crossroads' on supporting sterling in the wake of the complacency exhibited in London. In Martin's opinion, the United Kingdom had taken a 'shot-gun approach rather than rifle approach', introducing many technical measures rather than a few clear cuts, so the psychological impact was not enough to calm the markets. Support from Europe was not likely to be forthcoming and so the United States would have to bear the full burden of any new operation. Martin remarked that 'most of the world has lost confidence in their [the British] ability to manage their affairs', to which Johnson replied: 'I have too, and never have had any confidence from the time that they started.' He asked Martin what the impact would be be if the United States said 'You haven't followed our advice so we can't help you'. Martin agreed: 'We don't want them to devalue, that's the last thing we want them to do but we simply can't just go on bailing them out if they won't actively take steps to help themselves.' In these circumstances the United States would need to protect the dollar in conjunction with Britain's European counterparts – a formula he believed possible.

20 For an account of the strategic negotiations in the 1960s, see Jones, 'A decision delayed'.

21 Message from Wilson to Johnson, 29 July 1965, FRUS 1964–69, vol. XII.

22 Memorandum from Francis M. Bator of the National Security Council Staff to the president's special assistant for national security affairs (McGeorge Bundy), 29 July 1965, FRUS 1964–69, vol. XII.

23 Telephone conversation with Johnson: discussion of British sterling crisis and devaluation, 5 August 1965, http://fraser.stlouisfed.org/martin/record.php?collection_references_id=4895.

Martin suggested putting all pressure possible on the Wilson government to introduce a more comprehensive and effective package of domestic restraint, but added that if this failed there was no point in going to Canada and Europe to seek a support package. Instead, Martin suggested abandoning sterling and going to the IMF to work out a framework to protect the dollar.

Johnson described his frustration with Wilson in colourful and patronising terms: 'I have this feeling that just like a reckless boy that goes off and gets drunk and writes checks on his father, and he can honor 2 or 3 or 4 of them and finally [you] call him in and just tell him, now we've got to work this out where you live off what you're making ... and if you don't I can't come to your rescue any more and he just goes on and ignores it and writes another one. Now the time is come that we've got to turn him down.' Johnson continued that 'I was convinced some time ago that they are not going to protect the pound', and suggested that Martin needed to take steps to protect the dollar. Johnson then reiterated that 'I've had very little confidence in that administration'. Martin complained that the State Department had encouraged the United Kingdom to believe that it would get support for sterling. Johnson concluded that Martin should talk to Fowler to devise ways to 'protect the dollar and let them go their way'. Johnson and Martin seemed to have come to the end of their patience, but the US Treasury had a different point of view, based on the actual costs to the United States of letting sterling fall.

The next day, Treasury secretary Fowler put his own views directly to the president: that the cheapest policy in the short term was for the United States to keep contributing to multilateral support.[24] The best scenario was that the United Kingdom would hold the sterling exchange rate. This would require further support of about $2.5 billion, of which the United States should put up $700 million (28 per cent), and in return demand that the United Kingdom enforce a wage/price/dividend freeze. If sterling were devalued, the costs to the US gold reserves would be $1 to 2 billion – i.e. much more than the cost of short-term support. A larger devaluation would prompt the United States to suspend gold convertibility and effectively end the Bretton Woods system. All the same, Fowler did not want to give support unconditionally. At the Dillon Committee hearings in mid-August Fowler warned that 'it would be a mistake for the British to assume that they could count on US assistance in developing a multilateral

[24] Fowler to Johnson, 6 August 1965, FRUS 1964–69, vol. XII. Roy suggests that American views on a sterling devaluation softened only in January 1967; Roy, R., 'The battle for Bretton Woods: America, Britain and the international financial crisis of October 1967–March 1968', *Cold War History*, 2(2), 2002, pp. 33–60.

rescue package without taking satisfactory measures themselves'.[25] Such measures should stem domestic inflationary pressure and encourage confidence in the government's ability to increase export competitiveness. Unlike Martin, Fowler was not yet ready to abandon support for sterling as the first line of defence against the US dollar, and Johnson was sufficiently convinced by the argument to continue.

Another point of view came from the influential American ambassador to London, David Bruce, who argued that any assistance to Wilson should be conditional on the United Kingdom maintaining its strategic commitments East of Suez and on the Rhine.[26] He interpreted public opinion in Britain as oblivious to the looming crisis in colourful terms: '[T]he general atmosphere here is euphoric, beneath the surface on which float the *Economist*, the *Financial Times*, the politicians, the daily denizens of the City, the mass of the population here are as unconscious of impending disaster as if they were deep water jumbo shrimps in the Gulf of Mexico... [I]f balance of payments were a phrase as familiar in the UK as fish and chips, one could expect a sense of national cohesion with attendant readiness to accept personal sacrifices and austerity programs. Such is not the case.' He warned that public opinion would turn against America if the United States did not support the pound, but he stressed that the United States should not act unilaterally but, rather, participate in a multilateral package, and then only if the United Kingdom retained its commitment to defending the free world.

Throughout the summer, despite some contingency planning for a sterling devaluation, the Americans continued to put pressure on Britain not to devalue. Sir Burke Trend, the Cabinet secretary, was sent to Washington at the end of July for secret talks with Fowler and Bator on behalf of Wilson, and returned 'with clear-cut understanding that the US would not stand still for a unilateral move by the UK to devalue – that retaliatory action would be taken and that devaluation was out'.[27] Sir William Armstrong, permanent secretary to the Treasury, reassured Deming that Wilson believed that devaluation 'would do the UK no good and might do positive harm'. Wilson resisted this option out of concern for the international monetary system, but,

> of equal importance, he remembered the last devaluation by a Labour Government. Therefore, Sir William [Armstrong] believed, sterling would be

[25] Record of 2nd meeting of Dillon Committee, 13 August 1965, NARA RG56, Dillon Committee Box 15.

[26] Incoming telegram to the State Department from David Bruce, 6 August 1965, NARA RG59 1964–66, Box 919.

[27] Note of a meeting between Fred Deming and John Stevens (Treasury), 11 August 1965, NARA RG56 Records of USSMA, Box 22.

> defended to the last gasp – all reserves would be thrown into the fight – and anything else the Prime Minister could lay his hands on. Only when there was nothing left and no resources to turn to would the Prime Minister countenance devaluation, and he would not really countenance it then – he would be forced to it. In such a case, sterling obviously would have to float rather than to get a definite devaluation, because there would be no reserves.[28]

Since a sterling float was considered much worse than devaluation to a new parity, Armstrong's interpretation of Wilson's position served to encourage further US support, rather than reassuring them that a tidy 10 to 15 per cent devaluation could be achieved.

Meanwhile, Martin at the Fed began to devise plans for longer-term multilateral support for sterling, in what came to be termed in Washington the Martin–Cromer plan. The scheme pulled together a syndicate of participating countries to support the sterling exchange rate through concerted market intervention in a way analogous to the Gold Pool. The United States, Canada, West Germany, Italy and Switzerland, plus the BIS, were likely members, with a total of $1 billion in resources. Other members of the G10 could be added once the programme had been launched, adding a probable further $500 million.[29] Along the lines of Fowler's advice to the president, in order to access the support the British government would have to announce a wage, price and dividend freeze to restore market confidence. Directly afterwards, the participating central banks would publicly express confidence in sterling and privately begin to accumulate sterling balances through market purchases up to a possible ceiling of 5 per cent of their reserves, in order to make the official market rate more robust. The Bank of England would offer an exchange guarantee in terms of participant currencies in the form of six to ten months' forward cover, although the Americans noted that it was likely that Cromer would need also to consider a US dollar guarantee for existing official sterling balances. The market intervention could either be gradual or a coordinated, massive 'anti-bear squeeze' to punish speculators. The outcome would transfer sterling from less reliable holders in the sterling area to the G10 in return for an exchange guarantee, but with limited liquidity for these sterling assets.

Callaghan was intrigued by the plan, but recognised that a commitment to a wage and price freeze would be a major stumbling block, since the Cabinet would be unlikely to accept these terms.[30] The whole proposal

[28] Memo of Deming conversation with Sir William Armstrong, 5 August 1965, NARA RG56 Records of USSMA, Box 22.

[29] Drafts of Martin–Cromer Plan, 4 and 20 August 1965, NARA RG56, Records of USSMA, Box 22.

[30] Memo of conversation at 11 Downing St. by Deming with Callaghan, Cromer, Parsons, Armstrong, 6 August 1965, NARA RG56 Records of USSMA, Box 22.

can be interpreted as a way for the central banks (including the Bank of England) and the US administration to force Callaghan to introduce the controls on the domestic economy that they believed were necessary to stem inflationary pressure and restore confidence. As Fowler advised Callaghan when discussing the timing of the Martin–Cromer initiative on 21 August, 'Manifestation on part of the UK to deal with wage-price problem is [the] heart of [the] problem.'[31] By the end of August this strategy seemed to be working, as a statutory programme for wage and price restraint was prepared for the Cabinet meeting on 9 September, but Wilson made it clear that, to get through the Cabinet, any programme would need to be voluntary for the trade unions. A White Paper on prices and incomes had recently been agreed in April that set the conditions when incomes might rise above 3 to 3½ per cent, but there was no compulsion and trade union adherence was voluntary.

On 24 August 1965 Fowler optimistically wrote to the president that he hoped that the statutory programme would be enough to activate the Martin–Cromer plan in early September, but European central bankers were more sceptical.[32] Originally, Martin and Cromer had agreed that the United States would approach potential European participants, but Callaghan and Wilson overturned this proposal unilaterally and ordered the deputy governor of the Bank of England, Leslie O'Brien, to approach Louis Rasminsky, the governor of the Bank of Canada. They also sent telegrams to European finance ministers outlining the proposal on 28 August.[33] The Americans had tried to insist that the exchange guarantee should cover a float of sterling as well as devaluation to another pegged rate but they were outmanoeuvred by the British, who put their own version to potential participants. The two sides also disagreed over the extent of the convertibility of the accumulated balances, with the British insisting on limiting convertibility to thirty days' notice. These two caveats to the scheme reduced its attractions for potential participants and reduced the chances of successful negotiations, leaving the Americans feeling bitter at being outmanoeuvred by Wilson and Callaghan.

The initial response from Rasminsky was negative, because the British insisted that the accumulated sterling would have limited convertibility and because he believed the plan was better suited to intergovernmental operation than to central banks. Central bankers did not express

[31] Note of telephone conversation, 21 August 1965, Callaghan and Fowler, NARA RG 56, Records of USSMA, Box 21.

[32] Memorandum for president from Fowler, 24 August 1965, NARA RG56, Records of USSMA, Box 22.

[33] Memo by Charles Coombs, 21 September 1965, NARA RG56, Records of USSMA, Box 22.

opinions on the economic policy of other governments, as required by the scheme. The British insistence on restricting convertibility and the guarantee proved to be critical to the rejection of the plan, and heightened suspicion in Europe that it was a clandestine way to secure longer-term support for the sterling balances. Nevertheless, O'Brien believed that the Europeans would be forced to acquiesce if they were threatened with the alternative of a floating pound; described by O'Brien as 'put[ting] a pistol to their heads'.[34] Toniolo describes how Rupert Raw of the Bank of England toured the Continent to raise support for the plan but 'met with a frosty reception', similar to that in Ottawa.[35] The French and Italian central bank governors (Bernard Clappier and Guido Carli, respectively), who were approached first, objected to commenting publicly on another state's economic policy and protested that, legally, they could not tie up their liquid reserves in assets with limited convertibility. Charles Coombs, vice-president of the New York Fed, and a key architect of the plan, had grave misgivings about Raw's negotiations, worrying that 'the negotiating approach being employed by the British would not only fail to bring about any agreement, but might so poison the atmosphere with suspicion of British motives that we might find it extremely difficult to rescue them'.[36] The plan seemed to be backfiring.

As the meetings got bogged down, Carli and Karl Blessing, president of the Deutsche Bundesbank, called an extraordinary meeting of the governors at the BIS on Sunday 5 September to discuss sterling. Here, Cromer and Alfred Hayes, president of the Federal Reserve Bank of New York (FRBNY) were unable to overcome the European suspicion that the plan was really a medium-term vehicle to fund the sterling balances, despite Cromer dropping the limitations on convertibility.[37] The threat of a float did result in an offer of more orthodox short-term support, however, in the form of a new multilateral arrangement announced on 10 September. The US contribution was almost a half of what Fowler had predicted, at only $400 million, but this represented 40 per cent of the total package rather than 28 per cent. In addition, the Fed implemented its end of the Martin–Cromer plan by buying up sterling in the markets despite the fact that no strict wage/dividend/price freeze had been announced. The TUC had merely agreed to refer wage increases to the Prices and Incomes Board, but in the end the bill was not passed until

[34] Ibid.

[35] Toniolo, G., *Central Bank Cooperation at the Bank for International Settlements, 1930–1973* (Cambridge: Cambridge University Press, 2005), pp. 392–5. Toniolo credits Coombs of the Federal Reserve Bank of New York with the plan rather than Martin.

[36] Memo by Coombs, 21 September 1965, NARA RG56 Records of USSMA, Box 22.

[37] Ibid.

July 1966. Under Martin's scheme the Exchange Stabilisation Fund had presidential authority to purchase up to $300 million in sterling, which had an exchange guarantee. This coordinated market assault successfully restored confidence in the market; as Toniolo relates, 'Speculators ran for cover,' and funds flowed back to London.[38]

A month later Cromer met with Martin, along with John Stevens of the UK Treasury and Treasury secretary Fowler. They agreed that the September operation had been very useful, but Martin was 'convinced that most of the central bankers still worried about the eventual success of the Martin–Cromer arrangement', although the only realistic doubt that he entertained was the risk of 'back-sliding by the UK'.[39] His doubts seemed well justified. The UK National Plan had been published in the interim, setting an unrealistic target of 25 per cent growth in output by 1970 with no effective policies to achieve it. The plan was subsequently abandoned in the crisis of July 1966. There was no evidence that Callaghan would be able to deliver the firm commitments necessary for the multilateral Martin–Cromer scheme. It was in this context that discussions began in Basle about a longer-term solution for the sterling balances – discussed in chapter 7.

The September 1965 crisis revealed that the Americans were still more willing than the Europeans to provide long-term support for sterling even if Wilson did not meet their conditions in domestic economic policy. Part of the explanation is that, behind the scenes, the US State Department linked this support to Britain's overseas presence in south-east Asia.[40] In talks in London during the sterling crisis at the start of September with George Ball and David Bruce, Wilson initially rejected the link between military commitments and sterling support. He was particularly firm that there would be no link between US support for sterling and UK support for involvement in Vietnam, but, according to the Americans, he eventually accepted that the two issues were related with regard to the British presence in Singapore and Malaysia. The British record of the meeting noted that Wilson affirmed rather vaguely that 'Her Majesty's Government were quite clear that finance, foreign policy and defence must hang together particularly East of Suez'.[41] Ball's

[38] Toniolo, *Central Bank Cooperation at the Bank for International Settlements*, p. 393. Toniolo describes Cromer as being embarrassed at the 'dramatic' meeting on 5 September.

[39] Meeting of Cromer and Stevens with Fowler, Martin and Deming, 4 October 1965, NARA RG56 Records of USSMA, Box 22.

[40] For an extensive discussion of the link between military commitments and sterling support, see Coleman, J., *A Special Relationship? Harold Wilson, Lyndon B. Johnson and Anglo-American Relations 'at the Summit', 1964–1968* (Manchester: Manchester University Press, 2004), ch. 4.

[41] Quoted in Jones, 'A decision delayed', p. 582.

report on his private meetings with Wilson stated that he and Bruce had 'made emphatically clear that the U.S. Government considered that the Anglo-American relationship must be regarded as a totality, in which each element of the relationship should be given weight and each related to the other. Thus it would be a great mistake if the United Kingdom failed to understand that the American effort to relieve sterling was inextricably related to the commitment of the United Kingdom to maintain its commitments around the world.' As McGeorge Bundy, the US national security advisor, told Johnson, 'George Ball really put it to the British on Singapore and our support of the pound.'[42] Earlier in the summer Johnson had rejected a formal link between protecting sterling and British support in Vietnam, choosing instead to focus on Britain's wider commitment to south-east Asia rather than making Vietnam a breaking point.[43] In his enthusiasm, Bundy had already informally suggested to a member of Wilson's staff that 'a battalion would be worth a billion' dollars of sterling support, 'a position which I [Bundy] explicitly changed later'.[44]

American imperatives in south-east Asia thus provided the British with some leverage for future financial negotiations, as was noted by Sir Burke Trend in a memo to Wilson after the September package had been concluded.[45] Fielding and O'Hara have also shown clearly that the Wilson government recognised the potential strength of their bargaining position as the Vietnam War became a major political as well as economic issue in the United States.[46] O'Hara notes that 'the weakest partner in any system can acquire a great deal of power if its collaborators are unwilling to let it disintegrate'.[47] Ponting has gone further, arguing that there was a formal quid pro quo between financial support for sterling and Britain's continued presence east of Suez, on which Wilson later reneged. From the archive record, it seems that the understanding may have seemed clearer on the US side than on the British. The commitment by the British seems to have been contingent on events rather than a fait accompli, although the trade-off between

[42] Memo from Bundy to Johnson, 10 September 1965, enclosing telegram from George Ball in London dated 9 September 1965; FRUS 1964–69, vol. XII.

[43] Fielding, J., 'Coping with decline: US policy toward the British defense reviews of 1966', *Diplomatic History*, 23(4), 1999, pp. 633–56, pp. 643–4.

[44] Memo from Bundy to Johnson, 10 September 1965, enclosing telegram from Ball in London dated 9 September 1965; FRUS 1964–69, vol. XII.

[45] Jones, 'A decision delayed', p. 583.

[46] Fielding, 'Coping with decline'; O'Hara, G., 'The limits of US power: transatlantic financial diplomacy under the Johnson and Wilson administrations, October 1964–November 1968', *Contemporary European History*, 12(3), 2003, pp. 257–78.

[47] O'Hara, 'The limits of US power', p. 259.

defence expenditure and sterling was invoked repeatedly over the next few years in order to retain American interest in participating in multilateral support packages.

What seemed to Bundy a breakthrough in understanding between London and Washington in 1965 proved elusive. When Wilson returned to Washington at the end of the year he carefully avoided a commitment to conform to American priorities on defence while welcoming ongoing talks on the issue. He referred vaguely to his plan to make 'readjustments in the British defence posture East of Suez' but indicated that the British 'would maintain their presence'.[48] British representatives subsequently visited Washington very briefly in January 1966 before putting the defence review draft to the Cabinet in February, and their plans were generally welcomed in Washington, particularly because of the continued (albeit reduced) commitment to south-east Asia, which was so important for public opinion and for strategic reasons in the United States as it remained ensnared in the Vietnam War.[49]

Vietnam became a greater source of conflict across the Atlantic as pressure mounted on the Labour government to break with the United States over this issue. Wilson tried to support American policy diplomatically and made several efforts to broker a peace, but public opinion and opposition within his own party constrained his efforts to be supportive. On 24 May 1966 Wilson warned Johnson that he would have to criticise publicly any US bombing near urban populated areas and he urged Johnson to rethink his strategy, but this did not prevent the bombing of oil refineries in Hanoi and Haiphong. On 29 June Wilson was forced to dissociate himself publicly from the American air strikes.[50] Dumbrell and Ellis have described how 'the Americans were deeply unhappy with this public show of disagreement from their closest ally and indeed had spent many weeks prior to the bombing attempting to persuade Wilson not to take such a step'.[51] While new initiatives to support the United States in Vietnam were off the table, the British continued to meet the State Department's minimum hopes for the UK commitment in south-east Asia.

[48] Memo prepared by the executive secretary of the Department of State (Benjamin Read), 'Visit of Wilson 15–19 December 1965', FRUS 1964–69, vol. XII.

[49] Fielding, 'Coping with decline', p. 651.

[50] Telegram from the Department of State to the embassy in the United Kingdom, enclosing letter from Wilson to Johnson dated 24 May 1966; FRUS 1964–68, vol. XII.

[51] Dumbrell, J., and S. Ellis, 'British involvement in Vietnam peace initiatives 1966–67: marigolds, sunflowers, and "Kosygin Week"', *Diplomatic History*, 27(1), 2003, pp. 113–49, p. 121. Young discusses Wilson's efforts to broker a peace in 1965 in Young, J. W., 'The Wilson government and the Davies peace mission to North Vietnam, July 1965', *Review of International Studies*, 24(4), 1998, pp. 545–62.

Wilson's public criticism caused a cooling of relations just as another crisis hit sterling in the summer of 1966. Johnson was inclined to refuse Wilson's request to visit Washington in July unless he undertook not to repeat the statement or otherwise embarrass the president, but Wilson reassured him that 'he does not believe in making a mess on another fellow's carpet' and begged the president to see him.[52] Callaghan told Fowler that he finally planned to introduce tough new measures, including a National Board for Prices and Incomes, and to enforce a temporary standstill in wages, and this prompted a reconsideration of the appropriate US position between Treasury, Department of Defense, White House and Fed officials.[53] The wage/price freeze the Americans had hoped to force on Callaghan in the summer of 1965 finally seemed in sight, but confidence in Wilson's ability to make it effective had now waned. A repeat of the pattern of summer sterling crises in an environment of greater tension over Vietnam might have presented the Americans with an opportunity to exert leverage on Britain, but in fact it was exactly the opposite: US vulnerability to Britain's strategic policy increased Wilson's bargaining power.

In advance of Wilson's visit, the US Cabinet worried that, even if Callaghan's domestic policies were effective in the short term, they would involve sacrifices that might drive the government to retreat from east of Suez and West Germany to assuage public opinion, which was hostile to overseas military expenditure. In this case Wilson 'might face us with an implicit "more money" or "cut East of Suez" choice'. For McNamara, keeping Britain in south-east Asia was paramount, but, for the Treasury, the priority was to use the current crisis to drive the British to resolve sterling's long-term problems, even if this meant withdrawing from military commitments. Ball took a different tack altogether and argued that the United Kingdom should be asked to sign the Treaty of Rome immediately and retract its global role into leadership within Europe – a solution that implied a devaluation as the quid pro quo demanded by the French. The president was initially non-committal when faced with these options.

In London, Callaghan clearly understood the pressure he was under from overseas. In mid-June 1966 he remarked rather wearily to Cromer:

> I have no doubt that if devaluation of sterling were to come about serious antagonism would be generated world wide against this country for jeopardising the international payments system through failing to pursue domestic policies of

[52] Telegram from the embassy in the United Kingdom to the Department of State, 4 July 1966, FRUS 1964–69, vol. XII.

[53] Memorandum from Fowler to Johnson, 18 July 1966, FRUS 1964–69, vol. XII.

a type acknowledged universally by individual countries and the international institutions as appropriate to a situation which has been clear to all to see.[54]

On 20 July 1966 Callaghan introduced a raft of stringent measures to contain inflation, including higher taxes, cuts in government expenditure and a six-month wages, salaries and dividends freeze, which steadied the exchange market. A week later Wilson arrived in Washington and 'reiterated his belief that there was absolutely no point in devaluation. It would solve nothing.'[55] He resisted Ball's suggestion to consider joining the EEC and received some support from Fowler, who argued that Britain should enter the EEC from a position of strength and not have its terms dictated by the French, which would include devaluation. Instead, Wilson signalled that, although military cutbacks would be required, they would begin in Europe and extend to south-east Asia only after the confrontation with Indonesia had been concluded.

On 24 August 1966, in the midst of the crisis, the US ambassador, Bruce, met with Wilson to discuss British overseas military commitments, and he reported back to the US Cabinet the next day that 'Prime Minister regards East of Suez as more important than Europe, even though in the long run he wants to fall back for his major base from Singapore and Hong Kong to Australia'. Rusk and McNamara strongly objected to letting the United Kingdom withdraw from south-east Asia so long as the Vietnam conflict continued, but Fowler warned that if too much pressure was put on the British to keep their presence then 'we would have open-end commitment for financial support'.[56] Johnson concluded that the United States could safely 'give more direction to the UK ... Don't offer UK anything, but may have to give something.' It seemed that muddling through would continue pending 'an imaginative solution'.

Ball used the Cabinet meeting to reiterate his view that Britain should be pushed into Europe, noting that the 'UK is living in two centuries. It is not a big power now and it must enter Europe; it must modernise its economy.' Coombs suggested that the US swap system could be expanded to allow more credit for the United Kingdom, as a crisis for sterling loomed in the run-up to the September IMF meetings, which

[54] Letter sent to the Chancellor by Cromer, 15 June 1966, BE OV44/124.

[55] Memorandum of conversation, 27 July 1966, prime minister, Chancellor of the Exchequer, Sir William Armstrong of the Treasury, and the prime minister's private secretary; Fowler, Ball and Deming; FRUS 1964–69, vol. XII.

[56] Deming to undersecretary about Cabinet meeting of president, Fowler, Robert McNamara, Dean Rusk, Ball, Walt Rostow, Bator, Gardner Ackley, Bruce and Deming, 25 August 1966; NARA RG56 Records of USSMA, Box 22.

regularly prompted speculation about changes in exchange rates.[57] Gavin recounts how, after the summer sterling crisis of 1966, the Fed was considering a broad range of options if sterling should devalue, but that there was consensus that devaluation would be disastrous for the international monetary system.[58]

In a separate memo dated the same day as the Cabinet meeting, Fowler recommended to the president that Coombs should contact European central bankers with a view to pulling together a $1 billion 'war chest to defeat a possible bear raid on sterling during September' – a scheme similar to the Martin–Cromer plan of 1965.[59] The United States would initially offer to put up 40 per cent, but would agree to shoulder 60 per cent of the burden if this was rejected, and in the end this was the formula concluded. As confidence continued to ebb away from sterling, on 4–5 September the G10 central bankers met again in Basle. Toniolo describes the proceedings as 'quite acrimonious. [Marius] Holtrop [president of the Nederlandsche Bank] and [Hubert] Ansiaux [director of the Banque Nationale de Belgique] almost exploded with fury when Coombs pressed them to sign up to a new credit arrangement.'[60] No agreement could be reached, and the negotiations were continued by telephone over the next nine days. In the end, total US swap facilities were increased from $2.8 billion to $4.5 billion in total to allow an increase in the US–UK swap by $600 million (bringing the UK limit to $1,350 million). At the same time, other European central banks reluctantly agreed to extend swaps of $300 million, bringing the total line of new credit to $900 million. During the negotiations O'Brien was forced to acknowledge that, if another request for assistance were necessary, 'it would be disastrous'. Patience in Europe was clearly running out, and the cost of supporting what increasingly seemed to be an unrealistic exchange rate began to outweigh the threat to the international system should the pound be devalued. The Americans, with more to lose in terms of confidence in the dollar and leverage over defence policy, remained firm supporters of the $2.80 exchange rate, and, indeed, Coombs did a lot of the running in the negotiations with Europe.

One of the outcomes of the 1966 crisis, which coincided with the end of the confrontation with Indonesia in August, was a reassessment of Britain's overseas defence commitments, culminating in the decision to

[57] Coombs to J. Dewey Daane, 15 August 1966, NARA RG56 World/1/550, Deming Group Box 157.

[58] Gavin, *Gold, Dollars, and Power*, pp. 168–70.

[59] Memorandum for Johnson by Fowler, 25 August 1966, NARA RG56, Records of USSMA, Box 22.

[60] Toniolo, *Central Bank Cooperation at the Bank for International Settlements*, p. 395.

withdraw forces from south-east Asia completely by the mid-1970s. This marked an important break in Anglo-American defence policy, which had been founded on a continued but reduced British presence in the region. In April 1967 Secretary of State Dean Rusk wrote in strong terms to George Brown, now foreign secretary, that the United States was concerned not only by the actual policy choice of reducing troops by one-half over four years but also by the possibility of announcing a full-scale withdrawal by the mid-1970s.[61] Jones relates a meeting between Johnson and Wilson in Bonn four days later at which Johnson light-heartedly asked if Wilson was 'going crazy' by withdrawing from south-east Asia and went on to offer to solve 'all ... Britain's financial worries' if Wilson sent two batallions to Vietnam – an offer cheerfully rejected by Wilson, who claimed that this would put his government out of office.[62] For the Wilson government, the domestic political importance of making a public commitment to reducing overseas military expenditure was clearly of overriding importance.

When the withdrawal east of Suez was finally announced publicly in July 1967, Wilson told Johnson firmly: 'The British Government have had to reach their decisions, after the fullest consultation with their friends and allies and taking due account of their views, on the basis of their own best judgment of what is politically and economically right for this country.'[63] This admitted to no quid pro quo over previous financial support in other areas. He concluded that

> I am convinced that, if this country is in the future to be the same kind of effective partner for her friends and allies in the world as she has, I hope, been in the past, the political and economic realities must be faced and not fudged; and, in particular, that our essential objective of building an unshakeable economic base for Britain is the right one not only for this country but for all our allies as well.

This did not console the Americans, who expressed themselves 'very disappointed' when the defence White Paper was delivered to them.[64]

This, then, was the political context in which the final battle for sterling took place in the autumn of 1967. Repeated bouts of support from the United States, as part of bilateral and then multilateral schemes, had sustained sterling from the early 1960s. By the middle of the decade the willingness of the Americans to continue to 'ante up' to maintain the

[61] Memorandum from Rusk to George Brown, 21 April 1967, FRUS 1964–69, vol. XII.
[62] Jones, 'A decision delayed', p. 588.
[63] Telegram from Wilson to Johnson, 13 July 1967, FRUS 1964–69, vol. XII.
[64] Memorandum of conversation, British ambassador Sir Patrick Dean with under secretary of state Nicholas Katzenbach, 17 July 1967, FRUS 1964–69, vol. XII.

sterling exchange rate was wearing thin and they began to request more explicit quid pro quos in other areas, first in domestic policy and then strategic policy. The international use of sterling and the dollar made the two powers vulnerable in similar ways, and they were also tied together strategically in south-east Asia and West Germany. When the cards finally began to drop in the middle of 1966, the commitment to maintain a presence east of Suez was sacrificed to ameliorate the balance of payments in the longer term and to appease public opinion as domestic spending cuts and wage and price freezes hit voters.

Meanwhile, in the summer of 1967 pressure on sterling began again, due to a range of factors that affected confidence. In October Walt Rostow, Johnson's special assistant for national security affairs, rather generously blamed the turnaround in sterling's fortunes on 'bad luck': the Middle East war and closure of the Suez Canal, rising interest rates globally when British rates were falling, and poor export performance due to recession in Europe.[65] By 7 November Fed chairman Martin was sufficiently alarmed to telephone O'Brien at 3:15 p.m. New York time to ask if there was anything that he could usefully do to help steady the market. O'Brien replied that 'probably the only form of help that was likely to be effective would be massive purchases of guaranteed sterling', which would essentially mark a return to the successful Martin–Cromer operation of 1965. This time Martin demurred, noting that it was unlikely that he could get approval to further increase the US facility.[66] This exchange was received with disappointment and concern in London, and a more formal approach to the United States for support was launched as a matter of urgency, including a visit by Denis Rickett, a senior civil servant, within the week.

In the midst of this building sterling crisis in early November, the Parliamentary Labour Party increased its pressure on Wilson to demand that the Americans cease their bombing campaign in Vietnam immediately.[67] Fearing that Wilson might fly across the Atlantic to confront him, the president sent a firm message that the prime minister would not be welcome in Washington to discuss Vietnam, and that if he came 'it would wreck the existing personal relationship' between the two men. Nevertheless, the next day Sir William Armstrong and Sir Paul Gore-Booth (permanent undersecretary of state in the Foreign Office) drafted a personal message from Wilson asking to visit Washington in

[65] Memorandum from Rostow to Johnson, 19 October 1967, FRUS 1964–68, vol. XII.

[66] Telegram from Foreign Office to Maude in Washington, 7 November 1967, TNA PREM13/1854.

[67] Telegram from Washington to Foreign Office,.'Secret for Sir Burke Trend and Sir P. Gore-Booth only', 8 November 1967, TNA PREM13/1854.

December so as to have decisive discussions on the Anglo-American monetary and strategic partnership.[68]

The Foreign Office/Treasury draft drew attention to the dangers to the relationship between the United States and the United Kingdom and, by extension, to world peace if a solution could not be reached for the problems in the international economy, and warned that, 'if the attack on the pound were allowed to succeed, it would merely be the prelude to an attack on the dollar itself… [A]s a result of the strains which would then develop, a whole chain of political reaction would be touched off, the results of which would pass out of our control and could do permanent damage to the whole system of the free world's cooperation.' The draft warned Johnson that, without support, Wilson would be forced into deflationary policy that would have to include further reductions east of Suez, the Middle East 'and even in Europe itself'. The implications were clear: the free world was at stake if monetary cooperation between the United Kingdom and the United States was not secured. This was only the first draft of the message, but Gore-Booth and Armstrong believed it urgent and uncontroversial enough to plan to send it to Washington that very evening. Wilson was prepared for a final effort to invoke the centrality of Anglo-American strategic interests in the Cold War to gather long-term support for sterling in response to the speculative pressure that was expected to escalate once poor trade returns had been published on 14 November.

Instead of a direct message to the president, a telegram was sent on 9 November to Sir Patrick Dean, the UK ambassador.[69] Dean was reminded of the hardening of public and political opinion against the government's policy on Vietnam, the drain on sterling and recent reports from Emile van Lennep, chairman of the EEC Monetary Committee, that Europe was unlikely to provide assistance this time. The message continued: 'Ministers feel that the period of existing from hand to mouth must be brought to an end and a secure basis provided for the place of sterling in the international monetary system.' Rickett was on his way to Washington with a proposal that would give 'real security to sterling for a long period ahead, including British immunity from the effects of changes in the sterling balances'. If he got a positive reaction, a team would be sent to Washington to negotiate for about a month, 'during which period interim help would also be needed from the Americans. If at the end of the talks no agreement could be reached H.M.G. would have to take whatever action seemed appropriate in all the circumstances',

[68] Gore-Booth to Trend, enclosing draft telegram, 9 November 1967, TNA PREM13/1854.
[69] Telegram from Foreign Office to Washington, 9 November 1967, TNA PREM13/1854.

including further defence cuts, with implications for the future of the North Atlantic Treaty Organization (NATO). Dean was advised that 'we can quite see that, at first blush, the proposals suggested above may seem so far-reaching as to be very difficult of adoption by the US government. If so, however, they would have to ask themselves whether they would prefer to face the probable consequences, for themselves and for the rest of the world, of the only alternative course which, as we see it, would be open to us.' Further threats were implied in the observation that 'as a loyal disciple of Roosevelt the President would be aware from his memories of the economic cut-throat of the '30s where this might lead'. The message concluded that the 'simultaneous rise in the temperature on both Vietnam and sterling that has made the Prime Minister feel that it would be highly desirable for him to confer with President Johnson without delay'.

Wilson was clearly prepared to exert the power he derived from Johnson's weak position in Vietnam and the dollar's vulnerability to sterling's weakness to engage longer-term support for sterling, but in Washington the time for this strategy was deemed premature. Dean replied the next day that he and Rickett (who had since arrived in Washington) agreed that a direct meeting between Wilson and Johnson should not be attempted for a few days yet. The United States seemed ready to provide short-term support for the current crisis along the lines of previous credits but any longer-term scheme depended on the cooperation of the West Germans and Italians at least. A US loan, or even an increase in purchases of guaranteed sterling, would require at least informal approval from Congress, which was not minded to increase overseas commitments given the current political climate over Vietnam. Moreover, Johnson was under siege at home and unlikely to take further risks with presidential and congressional elections only about a year away. Wilson acquiesced to the delay but sent a copy of a personal letter to Johnson, to be passed on by Dean when the time came. This closely followed the lines of the Gore-Booth/Armstrong text but added explicitly that military cutbacks would ensue if sterling were forced to devalue.

On 11 November Rickett called on Fowler to report his government's views on the sterling crisis and to draw the United States into considering longer-term support, and he came out of the meetings believing that the 'talks with Fowler ... got off to a good start'.[70] Indeed, Rickett suggested that Fowler would put the case so well to Johnson that no direct communication from Wilson would be necessary. They met next with

[70] Telegram from Washington to Foreign Office, 11 November 1967, TNA PREM13/1854.

Deming, who suggested that the bulk of the $3 billion target of longer-term support could be met by $500 million purchases of guaranteed sterling by the United States plus $250 million each by West Germany and Italy and an IMF stand-by arrangement of $1.4 billion. The rest could be collected from other central banks holding guaranteed sterling and medium-term commercial bank loans. Rickett reported that Fowler was also favourable and vowed to take 'a very affirmative and positive attitude'. The scheme was essentially a repeat of the Martin–Cromer plan of 1965 with a more limited group of countries.

Fowler's memo for the president reported that 'the message was that they [the United Kingdom] were at the end of the line, unless they have assurance of substantial long-term credit soon. They may be forced to devalue – perhaps within a week.' Fowler advised that a devaluation 'might seem tempting' but it would be desirable only if the devaluation were modest, if others didn't follow, if Wilson was also able to keep up his military commitments overseas, if the government didn't fall and, finally, if inflationary pressures didn't undermine the impact. This was a rather formidable list of caveats, and Fowler advised that 'the risks for us are just too great to take this gamble if we can find another alternative', because the dollar and gold market would come under attack and a modest devaluation to a new rate might not be enough to stem the pressure.[71] Fowler relayed Deming's suggestion of a $1.4 billion IMF credit and persuading Italy and West Germany to join the United States in holding $1 billion in guaranteed sterling (of which the United States would take a half).

The initial optimism quickly evaporated when O'Brien reported from Basle that the European central banks had refused to hold guaranteed sterling even before Fowler had a chance to meet with Johnson. Instead, the Basle group suggested that Britain should apply to the IMF for the full $3 billion in the form of a stand-by arrangement. Fowler did not support this plan, since such a large stand-by would use almost all the IMF's General Arrangements to Borrow (GAB) facilities, would make it difficult for the United States to borrow from the IMF and would take five to six weeks to negotiate, by which time sterling would be finished. Fowler continued to stress that it was important to resist devaluation even for the next two months and perhaps through 1968, after which 'either they could hold longer or take the plunge under better circumstances'. Rostow supported US participation in a multilateral package, and on

[71] Memorandum for the president, from Fowler, 12 November 1967, NARA RG56 Records of USSMA, Box 22 (reprinted without underlining in FRUS 1964–68, vol. VIII).

13 November he urged the president to have a 'last try at supporting sterling'.[72] Rostow was further buoyed when he received positive reports from Deming, by then lobbying in Europe on Britain's behalf.[73]

On 14 November Deming worked the corridors of the OECD Working Party no. 3 meeting as central bankers struggled to make the trip from their inconclusive meeting in Basle.[74] Wilson and Callaghan cabled Rickett urging him to 'do your utmost in conjunction with Deming to persuade continentals to cooperate in securing something on the lines of the Fowler package you discussed in Washington', and added that, while contingency planning for devaluation had begun, 'we do not, repeat not, accept that 12 o'clock has struck'.[75] Deming negotiated vigorously on behalf of the United Kingdom for $1.6 billion in new central bank credits to add to the $1.4 billion from the IMF, while Rickett reassured him that the British intention was to maintain the parity if sufficient support could be found. Morgan notes that Callaghan later recalled that Wilson and he had 'decided finally' at 11:15 p.m. on 13 November that the devaluation had to go ahead, so the continued efforts to gather a support package were somewhat disingenuous.[76]

Back in Washington the British received further clear messages that the US administration did not want sterling devalued.[77] Deming told Rickett that, at a meeting with the president just before he left Washington, '[t]he president had then made it clear that he thought it most important that we [the United Kingdom] should be given every help in avoiding a change in the rate. Deming had told the President that the chances of getting the Europeans to hold guaranteed sterling were not very good. The President had told him to "go at them"' and do his best to get an agreement.[78] Everything seemed to rely on negotiations with Europe, and Rickett and Deming agreed that their tactic would be to 'work on the Germans and the Italians before the matter was raised in any wider circle', since Otmar Emminger, of the Deutsche Bundesbank, and Rinaldo Ossola, of the Banca d'Italia, were key leaders in Europe and the G10. Emminger was delayed by weather on his trip from Basle but Ossola met with Rickett on the 14th and did not rule out taking guaranteed sterling, although it would have to be approved by the Italian Treasury rather than

[72] Memorandum from Rostow to Johnson, 13 November 1967, FRUS 1964–68, vol. VIII.
[73] Memorandum from Rostow to Johnson, 16 November 1967, FRUS 1964–68, vol. VIII.
[74] Memo by George Willis, 'Brief chronology of pre-devaluation events', 2 December 1967, NARA RG56 Records of USSMA, Box 22.
[75] Telegram to Paris for Rickett from Wilson, 14 November 1967, TNA PREM13/1854.
[76] Morgan, K. O., *Callaghan: A Life* (Oxford: Oxford University Press, 1997), p. 271.
[77] Telegram from Washington to Foreign Office, 14 November 1967, TNA PREM13/1854.
[78] Telegram from Rickett in Paris to Armstrong, 14 November 1967, TNA PREM13/1854.

having the low profile of a central bank operation. He also told Rickett that no EEC country was likely to follow sterling if the devaluation could be kept below 15 per cent.

The next day, Wednesday 15 November, the circus moved to Paris, where the Economic Policy Committee meeting took place, followed by an informal G10 dinner. Deming continued his personal conversations with his European counterparts to ascertain whether they would follow a sterling devaluation and how much they would put up to support the current rate. Rickett reported that 'Deming and I again urged Emminger and Ossola to work out some form of central bank support as a vital element in package. This needed not merely to increase amount but to provide something which would be available immediately.' Van Lennep, a senior Dutch official, reported that the discussion at lunch among the Six about sterling had been inconclusive.[79]

Despite slow progress, on 16 November Sir Patrick Dean reported from the British embassy in Washington that 'the feelings of the administration against our making a move seem to have been steadily strengthening in the last 48 hours' and that he feared for the future of Anglo-American relations on a wide range of fields if sterling was devalued.[80] On the morning of the 16th Fowler called Dean to his office to tell him to urge the Chancellor to submit an application to the Fund immediately for a credit facility of at least $1.4 billion, and preferably more.[81] He didn't care if it was a stand-by arrangement or a drawing, just that the amount was large and the application was immediate. This shows Fowler's desperation to restore confidence in anticipation of the G10 deputies' meeting on the morning of 17 November.

On 16 November the European Commission formally passed on its view of sterling's difficulties to the US State Department. Raymond Barre, the European commissioner for economic and financial affairs, visited the US ambassador in Brussels, who reported directly to Rusk and Fowler.[82] By this time Barre and van Lennep believed that 'the British have lost their nerve and have decided to devalue', and the Commission members wanted to impress the US administration that they 'believe devaluation to be a wrong and dangerous course of action', because it would give British exports an unfair competitive edge against European and American manufactures, which would cause economic distress in five of the six EEC countries (West Germany being the

[79] Telegram from Rickett in Paris to Armstrong. 15 November 1967, TNA PREM13/1854.
[80] Telegram from Washington to Foreign Office, 16 November 1967, TNA PREM13/1854.
[81] Ibid.
[82] Inward telegram to Department of State from US embassy Brussels, 16 November 1967, NARA RG59 SN Files 1967–69, Box 833.

exception). Given this, the Commission felt that a 15 per cent sterling devaluation was the maximum that could be accepted without triggering an adjustment in European exchange rates, but the members did not believe that this would be enough to stem speculative pressure on sterling. Finally, the Commission feared that a sterling devaluation would lead to speculation against the dollar at a time when the US balance of payments figures were going to be announced, and 'the confluence of these two phenomena could shake the foundations of the world monetary system'. For these reasons the Commission was ready to bring together aid of about $3 billion from the IMF, the BIS and European and American governments, but the United Kingdom would have to commit itself firmly to wage controls and other internal restrictive measures. As well as setting out Europe's fears and the amount they were willing to pay to avoid devaluation, this communication confirmed the outer limit of a devaluation that would not trigger competitive devaluations elsewhere. This figure was also clearly understood in London.

The next day, Friday 17 November, West Germany and Italy agreed to offer short-term credit at a lunch attended by the G10 deputies at the Château de la Muette, part of the OECD's headquarters in Paris, where they had gathered for a regular meeting on SDR matters, and other countries followed their lead. The package to forestall devaluation seemed assured, but by this time the Cabinet had decided to devalue sterling anyway, having reached the decision at an acrimonious meeting on the evening of 14 November.[83] By the time he left for London on the evening of the 17th, Deming had collected pledges of $1.375 billion in bilateral short-term support for sterling, including the US contribution.[84] When Deming arrived in London, at 9:30 p.m., he was driven directly to the Treasury, where he was told that sterling would be devalued to $2.40, by 14.3 per cent, just within the 15 per cent trigger for other European countries. Fowler and Johnson had been told in Washington early that afternoon (UK time) and Johnson had accepted the news 'without animosity'.[85] Sir William Armstrong advised Deming that the United Kingdom still needed short-term credit as the IMF stand-by arrangement could not be activated for a further week, and he hoped

[83] Morgan, *Callaghan*, pp. 271–2.

[84] Telegram from London to State Department, 24 November 1967. These details are from a memorandum of Deming's conversation with Armstrong on the evening of 17 November; NARA RG56 Records of USSMA, Box 22.

[85] Wilson sent a personal message to Johnson announcing the decision earlier in the day on 17 November in advance of the formal notification at 14:55. Personal message from PM to President Johnson, 17 November 1967, TNA PREM13/1854.

that the support offered in Paris would be forthcoming even though the basis for it had changed.

The original letter from Wilson to Johnson drafted by the Foreign Office and the Treasury on 9 November, which raised the spectre of the collapse of the world economic and political order if sterling was devalued, was never sent. The message from Wilson on 17 November was of a much different character. Wilson referred to his belief only 'a week ago' that he could not see how he would be able to ask for further sacrifice from the UK public without drastically reducing military expenditure, but said he now believed that the United Kingdom could remain committed to the principles of the defence White Paper. Dean made clear in his meeting with Johnson when this message was conveyed that Wilson meant that there would still be cuts in overseas expenditure but that there would be no drastic change in foreign or defence policy.[86] The threat to break NATO was empty but the commitment to south-east Asia was soon abandoned, in January 1968, when Wilson committed to withdraw British troops east of Suez by the end of 1971 as part of the additional measures to support the new devalued rate. The general tenor of Wilson's message was to blame sterling's difficulties on 'events over which we could exert little or no control', such as the Middle East crisis, dock strikes, rising world interest rates and French antagonism, and to stress the sacrifices that the British people had endured over the past eighteen months of restrictive economic policy. Wilson likened sterling's problems to 'the misery of the abscess which breaks out, is temporarily healed, then breaks out again. Each of us has shrunk from having the tooth pulled out. But when we finally decide to do so, the feeling of relief is not simply an illusion. The removal of a certain poison from the system purges the whole system itself.' He claimed that, even if more short-term support had been forthcoming, the 'exceptionally ghoulish package of further measures' that accompanied the devaluation would have had to be implemented in any case. Without devaluation these policies would have been 'out of the question politically'. This corresponds with Wilson's later recollection that he chose devaluation over muddling through with further short-term credit because of the onerous conditions that were expected to be attached to such assistance by the IMF.

Unlike 1949, the devaluation was not welcomed in Washington, particularly since it followed repeated and substantial allocations of short-term credit from the United States and others that had been designed to avoid this very outcome. It was clear in any case that financial support would still be required to support the new rate, at least in the short

[86] Telegram from Dean to Foreign Office, 17 November 1967, TNA PREM13/1854.

term. When formally told of the decision by Dean, Johnson replied that he was 'distressed at the decision' to devalue, and 'distressed and disturbed' that the meetings to garner multilateral support had failed, but that 'as a politician he had felt in his bones from the moment that the crisis first blew up a week ago that we [the British] should be forced to take the decision to devalue'.[87] The Treasury secretary, Fowler, likewise received the news 'calmly and with an indication of regret but no animosity'.[88]

The British public and overseas governments were not as restrained. Wilson's efforts to reassure the public that devaluation 'does not mean that the pound here in Britain, in your pocket or purse or in your bank, has been devalued' suggested that he either did not fully understand the implications of devaluation or that he believed the British public were not smart enough to fathom the real implications in terms of their purchasing power. These comments would haunt his political memory. The Australian high commissioner, Sir Alexander Downer, was particularly scathing in his report to Harold Holt, the Australian prime minister, noting that 'the government has received as bad a press as can possibly be imagined', and he described Wilson as 'a master of expediency, a tightrope dancer, a temporiser, rather than a national figure'.[89]

The gloomy predictions for the dollar in the wake of the sterling devaluation seemed justified when the markets opened after the weekend. US gold sales totalled $28 million on Monday 20 November, $45 million on Tuesday and $104 million on Wednesday.[90] These losses loosened the cohesion in the Gold Pool, although the members were successfully brought together to make a joint statement in support of the $35 per ounce price on 26 November. By mid-December the losses following devaluation amounted to $1.5 billion.[91] By this time the United States was in what Gavin refers to as 'the most severe monetary crisis the United States faced in the postwar period',[92] and it had (in part) the Wilson government and sterling devaluation to blame. The pressure on the dollar continued to increase through the first quarter of 1968, as Congress refused to pass tax increases, culminating in the collapse of the Gold Pool in mid-March 1968. Two weeks later Johnson announced that he would not be contesting the next presidential election.

[87] Ibid.
[88] Ibid. Maude took the message to Fowler after notifying Pierre-Paul Schweitzer.
[89] Letter from Sir Alexander Downer, Australian High Commission, to Harold Holt, Canberra, 28 November 1967; Australian National Archives, M1002, 290.
[90] Telegram from the president's special assistant (Rostow) to Johnson in Texas, 22 November 1967, FRUS, 1964–68, vol. VIII.
[91] Gavin, *Gold, Dollars, and Power*, p. 172.
[92] Ibid., p. 173.

In London, the devaluation prompted the government to announce in January 1968 that troops would be completely withdrawn east of Suez by 1971. This led to great disappointment in the State Department but, in the end, little reaction from President Johnson.[93] The analysis here supports Jones' contention that the abrupt abandonment of the British presence in Singapore, Malaysia and the Persian Gulf was not triggered by the devaluation, but should, rather, be viewed as part of a gradual process of reducing the commitment once the decision that Britain's overseas defence expenditure was not supportable in the long term had been taken back in 1964.

The devaluation of 1967 did not end the pressure on sterling, on account of a combination of global instability in the international monetary system, failure to constrain demand effectively and the time lag for the effects to be felt on the balance of payments. The resultant pressure on the US dollar over the ensuing months culminated in the gold crisis of March 1968. From the devaluation of sterling on 18 November to the end of December the Gold Pool sold nearly $1.5 billion to support the US dollar price, but the US gold stock fell by almost $1 billion, to $12.07 billion.[94] Confidence was restored by the determination of the Gold Pool, but it remained 'brittle'. At the beginning of 1968 Wilson was advised that the Americans were toying with the idea of suspending convertibility of the US dollar to gold altogether, or perhaps limiting sales by the Gold Pool to official rather than private buyers. The United Kingdom considered both options disastrous and strongly supported the continuation of the Gold Pool.

At the end of February the ceiling for the Gold Pool was raised by $200 million, and half of this was used up within two days as a run developed in response to comments in the United States by Senator Javits and others calling for a rise in the price of gold.[95] O'Brien at the Bank of England called the Fed chairman, Martin, to try to get him to refute Javits' position publicly, but Martin refused, claiming that he could not intervene until after the Senate had voted on releasing the statutory gold backing for the US currency issue the following Tuesday.[96] The next day the governor of the Bank of England called Martin again, who confirmed that the United States was determined to continue with the defence of the dollar. The governor pledged his support, and his belief that the

[93] Jones, 'A decision delayed', p. 592.

[94] Treasury brief for prime minister's visit to the United States, 30 January 1968, BE OV53/37.

[95] Note of a conversation between Radice and deputy governor of the Bank of England, 1 March 1968, BE OV53/38.

[96] Note for the record, 1 March 1968, BE OV53/38.

other members of the pool would also continue to support the US policy after their affirmation on 10 March during the BIS meetings, 'to which they subscribed knowing full well that this week might be a bad one'.[97] The next morning, however, Martin called Cromer to say that the US authorities were thinking of withdrawing from the Gold Pool and starting new arrangements to sell gold at $35 only to those central banks that undertook to buy and sell at this price.[98] As the drain reached a torrent, the Bank of England closed the London market and Martin gathered the Gold Pool central bankers in Washington to restore some stability to the market.

Sensing an opportunity to link the problems of sterling again with those of the dollar, and seeking to attract the attention of the world's central bankers to the importance of sterling's stability for the greater good of the international monetary system, Cromer arrived at the Washington summit with a brief to gather $5 billion of support for sterling, with the underlying threat that sterling would be floated or that convertibility would need to be suspended. His pleas were 'politely rejected' by his colleagues.[99] Britain was not able to take advantage of the moment of crisis to frighten Europe into a major support scheme, although there was some sympathy for the country's plight and expressions of good intentions for future cooperation towards a longer-term and more considered solution to sterling's repeated bouts of weakness. Hamilton argues that the gold crisis was more important for sterling than the 1967 devaluation, because it prompted consideration of a more radical departure in policy – i.e. floating or retreating into isolationism through suspending the convertibility of the pound.[100] These plans were hasty, however, and did not necessarily represent realistic threats at this point. Cromer came away with pledges of $1.175 billion in new short-term credits, which were added to existing lines of credit from the IMF and central banks to make up a headline total of $4 billion. Chapter 8 puts this episode into the context of the development of multilateral support for sterling in the 1960s.

The summer of 1968 saw a minor repeat of the sterling crises of the previous three summers, and Britain drew on the $1.4 billion IMF stand-by arrangement to repay short-term debt to Europe and the United States. Part of the repayment of Fed swaps was 'funded' by the United States

[97] Note for the record, 13 March 1968, BE OV53/38.

[98] Telegram from Foreign Office to the Washington embassy (for Maude, UK trade and supply delegation), 14 March 1968, BE OV53/38.

[99] Roy, 'The battle for Bretton Woods', p. 53.

[100] Hamilton, A., 'Beyond the sterling devaluation: the gold crisis of March 1968', *Contemporary European History*, 17(1), 2008, pp. 73–95.

buying up guaranteed sterling, which it proposed to hold for up to three years. In this way short-term bilateral central bank credits were funded into longer-term debt to the IMF and the United States. At the same time, much more fundamental plans were finally afoot to shore up the sterling balances in the longer term under the Basle Agreements, as discussed in chapter 8.

Devaluation and the IMF

The IMF took a keen interest in sterling policy as part of its commitment to the stability of the Bretton Woods system. With both parties working for a strong pound, we might expect a warm and supportive relationship between the Labour government and the IMF, but Britain's susceptibility to the IMF's evolving conditionality principle poisoned relations and led to greater prominence for the BIS in resolving sterling's longer-term role. In the first massive drawing of $1.3 billion in December 1956, Britain had established a special relationship with the IMF at a time when this institution was still setting its operating procedures and principles.[101] The drawing was allowed on the basis of a general agreement that there was nothing fundamentally wrong with the British balance of payments position (indeed, there was a current account surplus) but that the international role of sterling made the economy vulnerable to short-term speculative pressures that could appropriately be funded through IMF facilities. The special international status of sterling thus allowed the executive board to overturn the rule that the Fund should not lend to offset large and sustained capital outflows. With this precedent, in subsequent years IMF stand-by arrangements were regularly used to combat speculation against sterling and to convert short-term bilateral central bank credits into medium-term debt.

Table 5.1 shows the amounts of stand-by credit arranged with the IMF and highlights that it was only from the August 1965 stand-by that the credit was actually drawn. In the crises of the 1950s and early 1960s, the announcement that a stand-by arrangement was available appears to have been enough to affect market confidence. Table 5.2 shows the drawings made by the United Kingdom in addition to the stand-by arrangements. Drawings were considered a softer option in terms of conditionality and the ability of the IMF staff to monitor policies, since stand-by arrangements could be phased and were subject to more prolonged scrutiny

[101] The total was equivalent to 100 per cent of the UK quota, comprising a drawing of $561,470,000 plus a stand-by arrangement of $738,530,000. For a full account, see Boughton, 'Northwest of Suez'.

Table 5.1 *UK stand-by arrangements with the IMF (SDR million), 1956–77*

Date of inception	Date of expiration or cancellation	Amount approved	Amount drawn	Undrawn balance at end of term	
22 Dec. 1956	21 Dec. 1957	738.53		738.53	
22 Dec. 1957	21 Dec. 1958	738.53		738.53	
22 Dec. 1958	21 Dec. 1959	738.53		938.53	Includes augmentation by repurchase of 200.00.
8 Aug. 1961	7 Aug. 1962	500.00		1,270.00	Includes augmentation by repurchase of 770.00.
8 Aug. 1962	7 Aug. 1963	1,000.00		1,000.00	
8 Aug. 1963	7 Aug. 1964	1,000.00		1,000.00	
8 Aug. 1964	7 Aug. 1965	1,000.00	1,000.00		
30 Nov. 1967	29 Nov. 1968	1,400.00	1,400.00		
20 Jun. 1969	19 Jun. 1970	1,000.00	1,000.00		
31 Dec. 1975	30 Dec. 1976	700.00	700.00		
3 Jan. 1977	2 Jan. 1979	3,360.00	2,250.00	1,720.00	Includes augmentation by repurchase of 610.00.

Source: IMF, *International Financial Statistics Supplement on Fund Accounts* (Washington, DC: IMF, 1982).

Table 5.2 *UK drawings on the IMF, excluding stand-by arrangements (US$ million), 1956–70*

Date	Amount drawn
1956	561.50
1961	1,500.00
1964	1,000.00
1965	1,400.00
1966	122.50
1968	1,400.00
1969	850.00
1970	150.00

in terms of performance criteria.[102] Up to 1964, although no stand-by funds were used, the United Kingdom did draw over $2 billion from the IMF in immediate drawings within its quota. The largest drawings were during the crises of 1965 and 1968, and they were used in part to repay stand-by obligations and other multilateral support when they came due.

In the crisis of August 1961 the UK IMF executive director, David Pitblado, requested a stand-by arrangement of $500 million and a drawing of $1.5 billion in order to fortify the reserves and help overcome speculation, as well as using $200 million to repay central banks. This support did not come without strings, and as part of his presentation to the executive board Pitblado responded to the IMF staff's criticism of excessive overseas spending in their first article VIII consultations by giving reassurances that the defence and aid budget were under review. In addition, an anti-inflationary plan was submitted to the IMF management. The US representative (soon to be deputy managing director), Frank Southard, strongly supported the British request on the grounds that, '[i]n view of the importance of sterling as one of the two leading reserve currencies, there was a clear and evident common interest in assisting in its strengthening in time of weakness'.[103]

When Pitblado returned for a further stand-by of $1 billion almost exactly a year later, he again invoked the special circumstances of sterling as a reserve currency. He argued:

> Even though there was good reason to hope for a continuing improvement in the balance of payments soon, sterling as a reserve currency was exposed to shifts in sentiment which could put pressures on the reserves, and the existence of a stand-by would help to deal with and even forestall these pressures by evidencing the Government's determination both to maintain these policies and the strength of sterling and the Fund's support.[104]

This special pleading drew support from the West German representative, Wilhelm Hanemann, who acknowledged that he thought 'it was quite clear that the stand-by with the Fund was required because sterling was a reserve currency and, therefore, exposed to special strains'. The stand-by arrangement was approved unanimously and was renewed each of the following two years, with little discussion, although the Chancellor each

[102] J. A. Whittome to Schweitzer, 1 May 1969, IMFA C/UK/810, 'Mission Goode and staff, April–May 1969'.

[103] IMF executive board minutes, 4 August 1961, IMFA C/UK/420.2.

[104] IMF executive board minutes, 27 July 1962, IMFA C/UK/420.2.

time submitted a letter of intent to the executive detailing his proposed policies.[105] The letter of intent for the 1964 renewal, coming just before a general election (in which the government changed from Conservative to Labour), put particular emphasis on the need to consult with the IMF over any major change in economic policy (made for economic or non-economic reasons) before drawing on the stand-by. Perhaps anticipating his imminent removal from office, Reginald Maudling, the Conservative Chancellor of the Exchequer, cheerfully agreed that, 'if a stand-by had been given to support certain policies, any government ought to feel that it had to inform the Fund fully if there was any major shift of policy and that it should not use the Fund's resources until, if need be, consultations had taken place and new understandings reached'.[106]

As we have seen in the Anglo-American discussions above, the IMF was to play a more central role in the crisis of the summer of 1965, with an immediate drawing (as opposed to a stand-by arrangement) of $1.4 billion arranged in May. This time the GAB had to be invoked and there was much more discussion of the content of the Chancellor's letter of intent. The US representative, W. B. Dale, drew attention to three innovations in this operation: that the Chancellor had undertaken to consult regularly with the Fund while the drawing was outstanding; that the letter of intent was formally embodied in the IMF executive board's decision; and that there would be quantitative targets related to British credit policy.[107] The letter of intent reported 'estimates' for increases in bank lending to the private sector of 5 per cent (£230 million) for the year ending March 1966, and Callaghan undertook 'to consult with the Fund if the estimates of movements in the banking figures should be materially exceeded'.[108] For the Fund staff, restraining domestic credit expansion was the most important component of the letter of intent, and at the meeting to ratify the drawing in mid-May they warned that the pace of bank lending was already outstripping these estimates, prompting the Bank of England to call in special deposits and formally request the banks to restrict their lending to the 5 per cent target. Dale's reference specifically to the innovation of 'quantitative targets related to credit policy in the UK' confirms that the board viewed the 'estimates' in Callaghan's letter of intent rather firmly.

Considerable emphasis was also placed on the requirement for ongoing consultation and a further undertaking by the Chancellor 'to take such

105 IMF executive board minutes, 29 July 1963 and 27 July 1964, IMFA C/UK/420.2.

106 Note of a meeting with the Chancellor of the Exchequer, 26 June 1964, report by Irving Friedman (IMF), IMFA C/UK/810 missions.

107 IMF executive board minutes, 12 May 1965, EBM 65/25, IMFA C/UK/420.2.

108 Letter from Callaghan to Schweitzer, 27 April 1965, IMFA EBS/65/69.

further action as may be necessary to ensure the success of these policies and intentions'. This reflected the lack of confidence, particularly in Europe, over the credibility of the government's deflationary programme as it stood.[109] The French representative, René Larre, concluded rather fatalistically that 'the proposed drawing would exhaust the resources to be expected by the UK authorities from multilateral co-operation. From now on, they would be on their own, and he wished them luck in making the right decisions.' He also characterised the drawing as 'rescuing a reserve currency', but added that this alone would not cure the weaknesses of the international monetary system. In the end, the pessimists were proved right and the government's policies were insufficient to stem speculative pressure against sterling later in the summer, forcing the United States and Europe again to supply short-term multilateral support through the BIS in November. The IMF's procedures for monitoring British economic policy lacked an effective enforcement mechanism, which left the IMF staff in the unenviable position of being an irritant to the British but unable actually to influence British policy.

The first staff visit related to the new practice of consultation took place a year later, in May 1966, on the eve of the next summer sterling crisis.[110] The mission was highly critical of the implementation of the letter of intent and pessimistic about the future. Unemployment was falling (signalling economic growth), incomes policies were taking too long to implement and, while private credit expansion had remained within target, this had been offset by huge increases in public borrowing from banks, so that overall bank credit had increased by about £250 million. Jacques Polak, the economic counsellor of the IMF, who led the mission, observed: 'I have little doubt that the feelings of disappointment with respect to the past, and unease to the future which we expressed are widely shared in the Bank of England and the Treasury... There is no indication, however, that these views are shared by the Chancellor', who 'takes the position that the trend in the balance of payments is satisfactory; that the disappointing out-turn in 1965 can be attributed to special factors; that there is therefore no particular need for concern about equilibrium being reached a bit later than expected'. Callaghan clearly bristled under the scrutiny, and Polak reported that he 'showed little willingness to listen to Fund comment on what he termed "the UK government" way to run its own affairs'. The mission's report called for

[109] See comments by Pieter Lieftinck of the Netherlands and S. Siglienti of Italy, IMF executive board minutes, 12 May 1965, IMFA EBM 65/25.

[110] The mission was in London from 3–14 May, just after the UK budget had been announced. For an informal report, see Polak to managing director, 16 May 1966. The official report is dated 14 June 1966: IMFA C/UK/420.2.

much tighter fiscal policy and a continuation of tight money, although the UK representative on the executive board, John Stevens, asserted that it was up to the United Kingdom to decide where the burden of adjustment should fall and referred optimistically to the recent tight budget, the incomes policy and controls on overseas investment. The IMF staff received general support for their critical view when the report was discussed by the executive board on 1 July 1966. The imminent crisis led to the Chancellor's 20 July special measures to curb demand, and by the time of the next visit to London, in May 1967, the IMF staff reported that 'the authorities have moved closer to the Fund's position on major policy issues during the past year'.[111]

It is clear from this account that the British Labour government chafed under the IMF's persistent pressure to impose contractionary domestic policies, and the annual open discussions of domestic British policy failures at the IMF executive board meetings were no doubt embarrassing. Sterling's weakness made British governments vulnerable to Washington's vision of how to return the international economy to equilibrium without disturbing the pegged exchange rate system, with the particular emphasis on monetary policy and credit control rather than the industrial policy favoured by Labour. The debacle over the devaluation of sterling in November 1967 and its aftermath greatly intensified these tensions and was instrumental in pushing the United Kingdom to opt for using the BIS to find a long-term resolution for sterling's weaknesses.

Along with most outside observers, the IMF actively prepared for a possible sterling devaluation during 1966 and 1967. Preliminary studies included the likely amount of a sterling devaluation, effects on other countries, the likelihood of other countries following sterling and how the management of the IMF might influence the decisions of those other countries. In September 1967 Jean-Paul Salle, at the European office of the IMF, reported from the Basle central bank governors' meeting that O'Brien was informally taking soundings of the maximum sterling devaluation that was possible without others following, and the feeling was that 10 to 15 per cent was the appropriate amount.[112] The planning gained new urgency at the beginning of November 1967, when the governor of the Bank of England asked L. A. Whittome, a senior official of the IMF, who was then visiting London, to tell Pierre-Paul Schweitzer, the IMF's managing director, that the United Kingdom no

[111] Report by Richard Goode to managing director on staff mission to London 2–12 May 1967, 15 May 1967, IMFA C/UK/420.2.

[112] J.-P. Salle to Schweitzer, 12 September 1967, IMFA C/UK/320, 'Economic conditions 1966–70'.

longer considered itself bound by an undertaking given in June 1967 not to devalue within six months.[113] This prompted urgent work on a contingency paper back in the IMF offices in Washington. Schweitzer and the deputy managing director called on the US Treasury secretary on Tuesday 7 November to discuss the possibility of a new UK drawing to forestall devaluation. Fowler was later reported to be frustrated by the cautious attitude of Schweitzer and his unwillingness to contemplate facilities larger than 200 per cent of the United Kingdom's IMF quota. On Saturday 11 November Schweitzer told US officials that he would be willing to arrange a new stand-by of $1.4 billion, which would take the United Kingdom up to the maximum 200 per cent of sterling's quota in the Fund, as the May 1965 drawing of $1.4 billion was still outstanding. Schweitzer was clearly prepared to take relatively strong measures in the hope of avoiding a devaluation that might disrupt the international monetary system more generally. At this time the United Kingdom already had outstanding drawings of $1.4 billion, plus $122.5 million that had been drawn to finance the gold part of the increased quota in March 1966 plus $101.8 million in charges.

On the same day, 11 November, Sir Denis Rickett of the Treasury and Jeremy Morse, an executive director of the Bank of England, arrived in Washington to discuss strategy. As noted above, in the morning they met with Deming and Fowler to set out their case for a $3 billion long-term credit package as the minimum required to prevent devaluation. In the afternoon they met with Schweitzer, who said he would be happy to put a proposal for a $1.4 billion stand-by arrangement to his board to avoid devaluation.[114] Given the United Kingdom's indebtedness, however, this would require activation of the GAB, which would delay the final decision by a few days. In addition, Schweitzer warned that the Chancellor would have to deliver a very firm letter of intent to convince the board that the rate could be sustained.

The next day Morse returned with the G10 central bankers' proposal that the IMF provide a stand-by arrangement for the full $3 billion, which would take sterling to an extraordinary 266 per cent of its quota. Schweitzer's initial reaction was positive, although he warned that such an extreme level of support would require the UK government to make a very robust commitment to monetary and fiscal retrenchment and introduce an incomes policy.[115] After consultation with his senior staff that evening, however, Schweitzer turned Morse down, offering support

[113] Memo for files by Albin Pfeifer, 2 February 1968, IMFA S121, 'Devaluations – 1967'.
[114] Telegram from Washington to Foreign Office, 11 November 1967, TNA PREM13/1854.
[115] Telegram from Washington to Foreign Office, 12 November 1967, TNA PREM13/1854.

only up to 200 per cent of quota. To go any further was too much of a departure from the policy and practice of the Fund, 'amounting to a distortion of its character', and Morse telephoned O'Brien in Basle at about midnight with the bad news. The next morning, 13 November, O'Brien passed the news on to his colleagues in Basle.

Back in Washington, Schweitzer had lunch with Fowler, Deming and Martin, and they all agreed that a $3 billion stand-by arrangement was not feasible and urged the British to have another try to get Ossola and Emminger to agree to a 'Fowler package' of buying up and holding guaranteed sterling, even though the prospects of success were 'very slender'.[116] At this point the IMF managers appear to have abandoned hope that they might avoid devaluation and began to polish up their contingency planning for the 'dissuasion' of other countries from following sterling. This appeared to be justified when, in the afternoon, Morse gave Schweitzer his personal opinion that the government would probably decide to devalue during the weekend of 18–19 November.[117]

Over the next twenty-four hours the IMF staff worked on a programme for a stand-by with or without devaluation and a GAB package. Early on the morning of Wednesday 15 November Evan Maude, the UK representative on the IMF executive board, told Schweitzer that, contrary to his advice the previous day, opposition to devaluation in London was strengthening and that further attempts were being made to assemble a package to defend the rate. Schweitzer warned that the accompanying measures for a stand-by arrangement without devaluation would need to be 'stiff'. It was clear that, whether sterling was devalued or not, any recourse to the IMF would require a firm and resolute letter of intent, but Schweitzer established that, if there was no devaluation, the United Kingdom had to 'make it clear that H.M.G. was girding itself for what Southard called a "thorough re-examination of the efficacy of the whole British economic effort"'.[118] The terms of a stand-by without devaluation were likely to be more difficult than those accompanying devaluation. On the other hand, Dale called Maude that evening to report 'that his authorities were more than ever anxious that we [the United Kingdom] should not move'.[119] Frustrated by Schweitzer's refusal to allow

[116] Telegram from Washington to Foreign Office, 13 November 1967, TNA PREM13/1854.

[117] Memo for files by Albin Pfeifer, 2 February 1968, IMFA S121, 'Devaluations – 1967'. James asserts that, by 13 November, Schweitzer and the IMF staff believed that sterling should (not just would) be devalued: James, *International Monetary Cooperation*, p. 189.

[118] Telegram from Maude in Washington to Foreign Office for Armstrong, in Wilson's papers, 15 November 1967, TNA PREM13/1854.

[119] Ibid.

a $3 billion stand-by arrangement, Dale suggested circumventing the managing director by asking for a drawing rather than a stand-by, since a drawing proposal would go directly and more quickly to the executive board for a decision. Maude did not encourage him, as the United Kingdom would need Schweitzer's goodwill, but he did report the plan and the US position back to Wilson in London.

The following morning Maude spoke to Schweitzer again to report that, while no decision had yet been made, devaluation might be announced in London on 18 November. Schweitzer warned that it would take some time for the accompanying stand-by to be arranged, and it was agreed that an IMF mission would be sent to London the following evening. Early the following morning, 17 November, Maude told Schweitzer that the decision to devalue had finally been taken. Schweitzer received the news 'without surprise and with little comment'.[120] The official request for approval was received at the Fund at one o'clock that afternoon and the IMF mission left for London at 7:00 p.m. At 8:00 a.m. on Saturday 18 November, Washington time, the IMF board members were issued with the paper proposing sterling devaluation, and the board met at eleven o'clock to approve it. In the three hours in between, Schweitzer and his deputy, Southard, phoned around European capitals and Ottawa to confirm that they did not also intend to devalue. This was important to ensure that sterling's move was as effective as possible in improving Britain's competitive position.

At the executive board meeting, Maude first apologised for meeting on a Saturday morning at short notice and then announced the new parity, adding that 'this represents a downward adjustment in the parity of the pound – or a devaluation – I don't want to flinch from the word – of 14.3%'.[121] Dale quickly rose to offer unequivocal support but other members of the executive board were less gracious. Georges Plescoff (France) remarked critically that he 'considered that the failure of the policies to restrain internal consumption and the fragility inherent in sterling's role as a reserve currency had made it increasingly evident that the British authorities were unable to restore the external position of sterling without drastic measures' and he called for strong internal controls to protect the new rate and the abolition of the export tax rebate. Horst Ungerer (West Germany) and Pieter Lieftinck (the Netherlands) agreed with Plescoff. Ungerer worried that there was insufficient public urgency

120 Telegram from Dean, 17 November 1967, TNA PREM13/1854.
121 IMF executive board minutes, EBM67/86 18, November 1967; IMFA S121, 'Devaluations – 1967'.

about the need to contain domestic demand in the United Kingdom, but Lieftinck was more supportive, remarking that 'a decision to apply surgery to an ailing patient always caused anxiety in the immediately preceding period, but once the operation had taken place and the patient was on the road to recovery, then there was reason for rejoicing'. Maude calmly acknowledged these comments and agreed to convey them to the Chancellor, but he warned that the impact of the devaluation would take time to be felt on the balance of payments, so changes to taxes would not be rapid.

As part of the devaluation package the United Kingdom formally requested a twelve-month stand-by arrangement of $1.4 billion, and this drew the IMF into close inspection and monitoring of British economic policy. Unlike other stand-by arrangements, the full amount was made available immediately, in order to support confidence in the new rate, rather than in phases, as was the usual practice.[122] The IMF insisted that the United Kingdom agree to a suitable programme of policies to improve the balance of payments, however, and also required a more intensive series of surveillance during the term of the stand-by. Reviews of progress were scheduled for February, July and November 1968, with the threat that, if the IMF did not consider that the desired improvement in the balance of payments was being made, the UK government would be asked to consult formally with the Fund.

The terms of the letter of intent began to be drafted by the IMF on 13–14 November, before the devaluation was announced, and put particular emphasis on credit controls. The IMF staff calculated that, in order to achieve a current account improvement of £300 million, the expansion of domestic bank credit would need to be limited to £500 million. This implied a ceiling on government borrowing from the banking sector of £250 million, to leave £250 million for the private sector.[123] Real GDP was predicted to grow by 3 per cent, of which half would need to be diverted from the domestic sector to exports and import substitution. The brief for the staff mission to London therefore focused (as in 1965) on monetary and fiscal restraint through quantitative targets – an approach that had already proved impossible for the IMF to enforce throughout 1966 and 1967. To achieve the fiscal restraint and meet the credit ceiling, the IMF staff calculated that the government's borrowing requirement would need to be reduced by £400 to £500 million out of

[122] Statement by chairman of executive board of IMF at the board meeting 29 November 1967, IMF C/UK/1760 'Stand-by arrangements 1967'.

[123] Draft notes concerning a program, 14 November 1967, IMF C/UK/1760, 'Stand-by Arrangements 1967'.

the forecast £1 billion.[124] In addition, the IMF wanted a commitment that the new rate would be maintained without recourse to current account controls or new capital account restrictions. Moreover, the terms of the stand-by arrangement included the provision that frequent discussions were to be held so long as sterling exceeded 125 per cent of its quota in the fund. With the UK position strengthened by the decision to devalue finally having been taken and the IMF already publicly committed to some kind of help, the stage was set for a confrontation.

The IMF mission, led by Richard Goode, director of the fiscal affairs department, arrived at Heathrow airport at 8:00 a.m. on 18 November and got directly down to work.[125] The team was scheduled to depart London at 2:00 p.m. on 23 November, leaving only six days to conclude the negotiations. At a meeting on the afternoon of his arrival, Goode expressed his doubts about the adequacy of the UK programme to Treasury officials. Later in the evening Maurice Parsons of the Bank of England warned him that, although reducing government spending was desirable, it was impracticable to impose a limit on Exchequer borrowing from the banking system, or on total bank credit. Meeting with Sir William Armstrong and Denis Rickett the next morning, Goode threatened that if quantitative ceilings were not agreed this would delay the announcement of the stand-by arrangement. The negotiations then dragged on through Monday 20 November, and that evening Schweitzer told Goode on the telephone to continue to press for a quantitative limit on the Exchequer borrowing requirement. Schweitzer also appeared that evening on the BBC's *Panorama* programme to express his confidence that a deal would be successfully concluded. Goode reported from London on 21 November that, 'in general, [UK] officials are agreed that the measures already taken are not adequate. They have recommended further measures and intend now to work in terms of a Stage 2 operation', but he warned Schweitzer that quantitative targets were likely to be rejected.[126] By this time the Cabinet had agreed that the measures that accompanied the devaluation were inadequate to restore confidence and hold the rate, and the Treasury was busy devising new policies.

On the morning of Wednesday 22nd Goode met for about forty-five minutes with the Chancellor and Armstrong. Whittome reported

124 Briefing paper by Goode and Pfeifer, 17 November 1967, IMF C/UK/810, 'Missions'.

125 The other members of the team were David Finch (an Australian who later led the 1976 IMF mission to Britain), Brian Rose and Bo Karlstroem. Unless otherwise noted, this account is from Goode's own report of his mission, dated 11 December 1967: C/UK/810, 'Mission Goode and staff, November 1967'.

126 Whittome to managing director, 21 November 1967, reporting a phone conversation with Goode in London; IMF C/UK/810, 'Missions'.

to Schweitzer that 'Mr Goode said, to his great surprise, Sir William Armstrong [secretary to the Treasury] told the Chancellor that, in his personal view, the government should forgo the standby arrangement rather than agree with the quantitative commitments which the fund was insisting on. The Chancellor replied, "Well, let's not be hasty." Mr Goode says that in his opinion the British are confident that the Fund cannot afford not to lend.'[127] The Chancellor explained that strict public quantitative targets were unsuitable given economic uncertainties and were incompatible with the parliamentary system, and he could not agree. Goode began to get cold feet at this point and reported to Whittome in Washington that 'he could not foresee the consequences of a firm stand by the fund and did not feel in a position to give advice'.[128] He received some support from Nicholas Kaldor, special adviser to Callaghan, who expressed his personal support for the mission – 'three cheers for the IMF'. In the face of British intransigence, Goode had to telephone back to Washington for new instructions.

Schweitzer then tried a direct appeal to Callaghan to call his bluff. That afternoon Schweitzer cabled the Chancellor to insist on a quantitative target to ensure that specific measures were taken, and to advise Callaghan that he was instructing his mission to return to Washington with no agreement. He concluded: 'I cannot fail to mention that I am concerned that unless this central point is met [quantitative targets] we would all be courting a new crisis before too long for sterling and the world monetary system as a whole.'[129] Callaghan responded that he would be willing to make a general commitment that additional measures would be taken but argued again that it was not practicable to produce a figure for the magnitude of additional fiscal measures.[130] He argued that, 'as the Fund Board will be aware, calculations of the effect of a change in the parity of a currency, and still more of the timing of such effects, are necessarily extremely speculative. This makes it difficult to decide precisely, in the initial stages, on the scale and timing of the measures that are required to make sure that the improvement in the [government's – crossed out in ink by Callaghan] competitive position is not lost through insufficient capacity at home being available to meet the expected increase in demand as it builds up over time.' He was

[127] Whittome report to managing director on a telephone conversation with Goode, 22 November 1968, IMF C/UK/810, 'Missions'.

[128] Ibid.

[129] Message from Schweitzer to the Chancellor of Exchequer, 22 November 1967, IMFA C/UK/1760, 'Stand-by arrangements 1967'.

[130] Letter from the Chancellor of Exchequer to Schweitzer, 23 November 1967, IMFA C/UK/1760, 'Stand-by arrangements 1967'.

clearly worried about prompting a recession through excessive restraint if the devaluation were quickly effective. The Cabinet was due to meet at 11:30 a.m. and Callaghan hoped that Schweitzer would reply in time for this to be reported to Cabinet. Early next morning Schweitzer replied that Callaghan's vague assurances were not adequate and suggested a statement either that the Exchequer borrowing requirement should be reduced to £1 billion in 1968/9 or that the next budget would include measures making an additional £300 million of resources available for the balance of payments. Meanwhile, the clock was ticking for the departure of the mission at 2:00 p.m. Failure to announce an agreement would have profound consequences for confidence in the new sterling exchange rate.

At 10:00 a.m., four hours before the IMF mission was due to depart, the representatives of the UK Treasury finally agreed to Schweitzer's first suggestion, that Callaghan would make a statement that the borrowing requirement for 1968/9 would be no more than £1 billion. There followed some squabbling about the definition of the borrowing requirement but the IMF's broader definition prevailed, requiring a reduction of £500 million. The letter of intent also committed Britain to improving the balance of payments by at least £500 million per year, so as to generate a surplus in the second half of 1968 of £200 million. The IMF mission finally left Heathrow airport three and a half hours late, at 5:30 p.m.

The executive board met to consider the application for a stand-by arrangement on 29 November but the meeting did not go completely smoothly.[131] Dale was predictably supportive, noting that 'he believed that the stabilisation program was necessarily flexible and one that inspired confidence'. Plescoff (equally predictably) disagreed, arguing that the supplementary measures to support the devaluation were 'inadequate', and he expressed himself 'somewhat disappointed by the letter of intent', and he considered that 'the Staff Report did not go far enough in pursuing the commitments which should have been undertaken by the British government'. The perception that the deal with the United Kingdom had been excessively 'soft' was also held by many developing countries, which began to resent a rich country such as Britain being treated more favourably than poorer countries with regard to the phasing of drawings and the terms as well.[132] Nevertheless, the record shows that the IMF

[131] Minutes of the IMF executive board, 29 November 1967. Kafka and Phillips also expressed their disquiet about the terms of the letter of intent; IMFA C/UK/1760, 'Stand-by arrangements 1967'.

[132] De Vries, M. G., *The International Monetary Fund, 1966–1971: The System under Stress*, vol. I, *Narrative* (Washington, DC: IMF, 1976), pp. 341–3; James, *International Monetary Cooperation*, pp. 189–90.

had played a hard game in London and pushed the British government beyond their initial intentions.

Sir William Armstrong's effort to call the IMF's bluff did not work in this instance and the Chancellor was required broadly to accept the terms that the mission had arrived with. Schweitzer was not susceptible to the threats about the impact on the international monetary system and held firm to his belief that the United Kingdom could not afford to forgo IMF assistance, or even a prolonged delay in negotiations. The Chancellor's weakness was enhanced by the recognition in the Treasury and the markets that the initial accompanying measures to support the devaluation were inadequate. If on top of this the IMF mission had failed, the impact on sterling could have been disastrous.

The day after the IMF's apparent victory, Southard sent a self-congratulatory message to Schweitzer over the Fund's role, which was 'in sharp and refreshing contrast to the experience in 1949 when events unfolded so rapidly that the Fund as an organization was really able to play no effective role. We must also recognize that our capacity to play an effective role resulted from the fact that the UK did keep in close touch with you for about a week as their thinking developed. This enabled us to make our plans and to bring the Fund staff into the picture early enough so that they could play an effective role.'[133] The negotiations of 1967 were a precursor for those of 1976, when quantitative targets again became a stumbling block that drove negotiations down to the wire. While the week of 18–23 November was critical in the short term, it also set the scene for a longer-term struggle between the IMF and successive British governments over the terms of stand-by arrangements and the IMF's view of the importance of domestic credit expansion (DCE) as a tool of policy aimed at both inflation and the external balance.[134] Meanwhile, the main protagonist, James Callaghan, was replaced as Chancellor by Roy Jenkins a week after the IMF mission's departure.

The visit of the first IMF surveillance mission took place in February 1968, at a delicate time for the planning for Jenkins' first budget, which was due to be announced on 19 March. The intense secrecy surrounding the budget interfered with the mission's ability to get details of the government's fiscal plans and with the timing of the publication of the mission's report.[135] The mission was restricted to questions of economic analysis and estimation but it returned later in March, when more detailed

[133] Frank Southard to Schweitzer, 24 November 1967, IMFA C/UK/1760, 'Stand-by arrangements 1967'.

[134] James, *International Monetary Cooperation*, pp. 190–1.

[135] Briefing paper 14 February 1968, IMF C/UK/810, 'Missions'.

discussions could take place. In their report to the executive board, the IMF staff expressed themselves satisfied with the fiscal constraint in the budget, although the situation was complicated by the global gold crisis. They concluded optimistically that, 'so far as can be judged at the present time, the policies now in force will establish conditions in the domestic economy appropriate to the achievement of a surplus of £500m or more in 1969'.[136]

This optimism had evaporated by the time Goode returned to London in May for the scheduled article VII consultation, when he reported 'an atmosphere of gloom and uncertainty' due to financial upheavals and the political situation.[137] Government expenditure was running well above expected levels (£700 million to £750 million rather than £500 million, on account of new and increased spending programmes and rises in wages and prices), and so was bank lending, particularly that related to export finance, which was outside the controls announced in November. Schweitzer came to London on 23 May for exploratory talks with Jenkins on these issues and urged restraint, but made little tangible progress. He was alerted that Jenkins planned to draw the full $1.4 billion stand-by amount in June.

The deteriorating prospects for meeting the targets in the letter of intent prompted David Finch, a member of the IMF mission, to suggest that Schweitzer should invoke article XVI, which required the United Kingdom to consult again with the Fund if the terms of the letter were not being honoured, but Schweitzer decided in the end that 'he did not think invoking it would help anyone'.[138] The situation had not improved by June 1968, and on the 19th the United Kingdom drew the full $1.4 billion of the stand-by arrangement. The British managed to convince Schweitzer and the IMF staff to state in their report that the borrowing requirement would reach £650 million with the possibility of a further £70 million, rather than a headline figure of £700 million to £750 million, in order to coincide with the government's public commitment. In the end, however, the fine details did not fool the executive board when it discussed the British position in early July. The IMF staff report optimistically concluded that, although bank credit was still growing too rapidly and the spending and borrowing of the public sector was too high, 'there is at present no reason to change the judgement that if the UK holds firmly to its present policies respecting bank credit to the private sector and prices and incomes, and acts more

136 Report of staff mission for the executive board, 26 March 1968, IMFA C/UK/810, 'Missions'.

137 Goode to managing director, 23 May 1968, IMFA C/UK/810, 'Missions'.

138 Goode to Schweitzer and Southard, 28 June 1968, 'Note of a meeting of Schweitzer with Maude and Guy Huntrods, 16 July 1968 (UK)', IMFA C/UK/810, 'Missions'.

vigorously to check public spending and borrowing, a satisfactory surplus in the balance of payments can be obtained in 1969'.[139] The executive directors were not convinced. Lieftinck expressed his opinion that devaluation had not been accompanied by sufficiently strong domestic measures. John Stone, of Australia, remarked that the Fund's conclusion 'had in it a large element of whistling in the dark' and should have been more explicit on the budget strategy.

When Schweitzer agreed not to invoke the article XVI consultation requirements of the stand-by arrangement in July, he warned British officials that the next review would 'have to be taken seriously'. To this end, he asked that the Chancellor be officially included in the deliberations and present for the report of the next mission in late July, at which minutes would be taken that could be quoted publicly in order to tie the government to its commitments.[140] The UK Treasury response was not promising; it was claimed that it would be embarrassing for the Chancellor to have to make quotable commitments to the IMF. Schweitzer insisted that he was not asking for new commitments, just some reassurance that policies were in place to meet the promises in the letter of intent.[141] Ultimately, Jenkins did meet with the mission, on 5 August, and he submitted a report but asked not to be quoted directly. At this meeting he predicted a surplus of £250 million in 1969, which the IMF considered inadequate. On the other hand, the IMF did not recommend further measures, because they thought that the Treasury's estimate of the surplus was too modest.[142] The government's borrowing requirement was now estimated at £560 million rather than £700 million.

Even with this more optimistic prediction there was considerable dispute within the mission over whether the United Kingdom should be deemed to have failed to meet the terms of the letter of intent and be forced to introduce fresh measures. Marcus Fleming, the British head of the IMF research department, was among the most vociferous voices against this strategy, noting that the mission brief calling for new measures 'appears to bear out the worst suspicion of our critics as to the crudity and dogmatism of the Fund approach to the problems of a complex economy'.[143] He acknowledged that 'no doubt some of us may feel that

[139] Discussion of the IMF report 3 July 1968,IMFA 1963 C/UK/420.2.

[140] Meeting of Schweitzer with Maude and Huntrods – memo by Southard, 16 July 1968. Minutes were not taken at previous meetings with the Chancellor present; IMFA C/UK/810 'Missions'.

[141] Southard to Whittome and Goode, 22 July 1968, IMFA C/UK/810, 'Missions'.

[142] Draft report of mission to managing director from Goode and Whittome, 16 August 1968, IMFA C/UK/810, 'Missions'.

[143] Fleming to Goode, 22 July 1968, IMFA C/UK/810, 'Missions'.

the UK authorities have, in the past, been too prone to give priority to domestic over international objectives. My own criticism would rather be that they have been stupid in their approach to both sets of objectives. However that may be, any one-sidedness on the British part is no excuse for one-sidedness on ours.' The targets were too precise because they were not all within the government's power and depended on external factors and policies in other countries. Schweitzer appears to have agreed, and Jenkins again avoided article XVI. Altogether, the outcome of the mission was not as bad as either side had anticipated, both sides agreeing to a continuation of existing policies.

The final surveillance mission related to the 1967 stand-by arrangement was scheduled for 21–30 November 1968. In August the United Kingdom repaid $85 million of the stand-by arrangement, and it was committed to repaying a further $100 million by the end of November, reducing the Fund's holding of sterling back to 193 per cent of quota. This time the talks were influenced by the Deutschmark crisis and the extra measures that the Chancellor announced on 22 November, such as increased indirect taxes, import deposits and a revised ceiling on bank lending.[144] The balance of payments forecast for 1969 had improved to £300 million, and the IMF mission merely urged the continuation of existing policies.[145] In these circumstances the United Kingdom decided not to ask for a new stand-by arrangement after the twelve months had expired. This seemed to bring an end to the ongoing tensions of IMF visits, but Britain's continued need for short-term credit meant that this was merely a lull in the pressure.

Adherence to article VII of the IMF required annual missions, and the next was scheduled for 16 April–6 May 1969, by which time the predictions of November appeared excessively optimistic. Nevertheless, the IMF staff expected the Treasury to ask for a new stand-by arrangement of at least $1 billion. They proposed that the terms should include a firm credit ceiling and a target of a £300 million balance of payments surplus in financial year 1969/70. When Jenkins tried to insist that the mission should complete its work before he was scheduled to leave London on 27 April, Schweitzer refused on the grounds that this left insufficient time for his staff to prepare their report, especially since the mission

[144] In the first three weeks of November 1968 there was a huge speculative inflow into Deutschmarks in the expectation of revaluation, prompting an emergency meeting of finance ministers in Bonn from 20 to 22 November. For details and implications, see Gray, W. G., 'Number one in Europe: the startling emergence of the Deutsche Mark 1968–69', *Central European History*, 39(1), 2006, pp. 56–78.

[145] Goode to managing director, report of mission, 2 December 1968, IMFA C/UK/810, 'Missions'.

wanted to arrive after the budget. He insisted that Jenkins be present at the meeting at which the team summed up its visit and recommendations in order to get a clear government commitment to the mission's report, so he suggested either that Jenkins postpone his trip or that the IMF would postpone the first drawing on a stand-by arrangement until July. Faced with this choice, Jenkins agreed to return to London from Washington for a few days in early May.[146]

Predictably, the British had difficulties with the IMF staff's insistence again on publishing quarterly credit ceilings, and they sought a compromise whereby the commitments would be made by British representatives at the IMF rather than by the Chancellor, and that they would not be published. Schweitzer objected, on the basis that other countries had had to conform to such commitments and that 'performance criteria of this kind were the essence of conditionality'.[147] The IMF staff clearly had in mind that other countries had criticised the November 1967 package as being too relaxed and favouring the United Kingdom over other borrowers. After discussion with British officials the mission leader, Richard Goode, 'had a suspicion, which their informal comments had in no way allayed, that they would not implement the policies necessary to make the ceilings stick. In effect this would postpone a showdown with the Fund to after June. From the British view more time was a gain; moreover, if their reserve figures continued to be good then perhaps they would not need to take further drawings after the first.'[148] This shows how sour relations had become between the IMF and the United Kingdom.

When the IMF staff finally met with Jenkins, the British held firm to their position that targets were politically and technically impossible for the United Kingdom and suggested the possibility that no help was taken from the IMF, with thinly veiled threats to Schweitzer. Sir Douglas Allen, permanent secretary at the Treasury, warned that 'it was not attractive to contemplate the world if there were no transaction. Jenkins said that this would inevitably involve risks for the whole International Monetary System (that would be a heavy responsibility for the Managing Director) and he would of course have to explain to parliament how the whole situation had arisen. Schweitzer said he understood that and might of course be called upon himself to answer questions.'[149] This time it was the IMF's

[146] Goode, director Fiscal Affairs Department memo for file, 20 March 1969; memo 21, March 1969, IMFA C/UK/810, 'Missions'.

[147] Managing director and Chancellor of Exchequer meeting, 29 April 1969, IMFA C/UK/810, 'Missions'.

[148] Whittome report on Goode's meetings for managing director, 5 May 1969, IMFA C/UK/810, 'Missions'.

[149] Managing director and Chancellor of Exchequer meeting, 29 April 1969, IMFA C/UK/810, 'Missions'.

turn to back down, and a stand-by was finally arranged for $1 billion in four drawings, starting at the end of June 1969. The United Kingdom set quarterly objectives for domestic credit expansion in a memorandum of understanding included in the IMF staff report, but they would comprise a commitment by UK representatives to the IMF rather than by the Chancellor of the Exchequer.[150] As in their relations with the United States, British negotiators were able to exploit their weakness and the threat of disorder in the international monetary system if sterling was pushed to a float to extort concessions from their creditors. This was despite widespread criticism of British policy, not only by the IMF staff, whose report at the end of May 1969 stated 'The balance of payments problem of the UK has proved to be more intractable than was earlier recognised', but also by the OECD Working Party no. 3, which reported at the end of May that 'progress towards a substantial balance of payments surplus since the 1967 devaluation has been disappointingly slow' and 'it may be doubtful whether the policies at present announced will keep domestic demand sufficiently in check'.[151]

At the executive board meeting in June to agree the $1 billion stand-by arrangement, the chairman was forced to acknowledge that the letter of intent did not have the usual trigger clauses, or performance criteria related to credit or fiscal policies, but he said: 'I personally am satisfied that there is no departure in substance from the policy on stand-by arrangements as set out at that time.'[152] Schweitzer tried to reassure the board by saying: 'The UK has adopted a quantified financial program but, for reasons of its own, has preferred in the letter of intent and the stand-by arrangement a clause providing for the full-scale review of performance.' As a quid pro quo, the IMF had made no commitment to allow purchases of the second $500 million of the $1 billion total without further review, unlike cases when, if performance criteria were set out and met, the IMF was then committed *ex ante* to agree the drawing. Schweitzer confirmed that this new, more flexible form of agreement would be made available to other applicants to the IMF, in order to divert claims that the United Kingdom was getting special treatment. This did not convince the executive directors. John Stone, the Australian representative, remarked drily that, 'had he wished to take a cynical course, he would have said that the transactions which Directors were discussing

150 Managing director meeting with deputy managing director, Gold, Goode and Whittome, 10 May 1969, IMFA C/UK/810, 'Missions'.

151 IMF staff report on UK for executive board, 29 May 1969, IMFA C/UK/420.2; OECD Working Party no. 3 report on UK economy, 28 May 1969; IMFA C/UK/320, 'Economic Conditions 1966–70'.

152 Executive board minutes, 20 June 1969, IMFA C/UK/420.2.

had already been approved, and that nothing was to be gained by saying anything further'. The executive board was presented with a fait accompli as a result of the hard bargaining in London and the unwillingness of the IMF management to abandon sterling because of the threat to the international monetary system.

Conclusions

What does the international perspective on the 1967 devaluation add to our understanding? This account of intense and often acrimonious negotiations reinforces the domestic policy evidence, from Newton and others, that there was a rigorous and wide-ranging analysis of various options rather than a sloppy muddling through on international monetary policy. The commitment to reform was much greater among officials than ministers, however. The key role of sterling in the international monetary system did allow Wilson and his Chancellors of the Exchequer to garner repeated large doses of international support for the sterling exchange rate both before and after the devaluation of 1967. From its first emergency drawing in 1956, the international status of sterling laid the foundation for special treatment by the IMF, which was sustained, albeit reluctantly, over the next fifteen years. The threat that sterling might be floated, with disastrous consequences for the international monetary system, was repeatedly invoked to strike fear in the heart of the IMF and the Johnson administration. On the other hand, there were times when Britain's creditors called the United Kingdom's bluff, and in return for support the Labour government was forced to accept a range of deflationary measures to which it had little ideological commitment. Given this lack of faith, it is not surprising that the terms of these credits were not consistently adhered to. The evidence presented here shows that sterling's weakness could be an effective source of bargaining power for Britain, in international financial relations and in Anglo-American strategic negotiations alike.

Moreover, the hard bargains driven by British negotiators and the evidence that the contractionary terms of IMF or American credits were not honoured rather contradicts the usual interpretation, that the interests of the domestic economy were sacrificed to the international status of sterling. Instead, the Wilson government is shown to have argued strongly, and usually successfully, that contractionary domestic measures were not appropriate, and, even when they were adopted, the commitments were not honoured. Access to credit to support confidence in sterling does not appear to have been a binding constraint on public sector borrowing, incomes policy or domestic credit expansion. The Americans were unable to force Wilson to adopt a wage/price freeze in 1965 and unable to enforce their wish for continued domestic restraint in 1966/7 in the run-up to the devaluation. Nor did they succeed in stopping the United Kingdom from reducing its military presence in south-east Asia and the Middle East. Similarly, the IMF was unable to enforce the terms of the 1967 stand-by arrangement or to implement successfully the conditions on the subsequent facilities offered to the Labour government in the 1960s by invoking article XVI.

This evidence does not fit the characterisation of Dumbrell and Ellis that 'London's attitude towards Washington was shaped by a humiliating economic dependence and by Wilson's desire to establish a close personal relationship with the American leader'.[153] Certainly, Johnson never felt warm towards Wilson personally, and so little progress was made on the latter front, but to characterise the economic relationship as 'humiliating' is going too far. Boyle has also emphasised the economic dependence of Britain on the United States as the key determinant of Anglo-American relations in this period.[154] The analysis presented here suggests that a better characterisation of the relationship is one of interdependence rather than viewing the United Kingdom as a mere supplicant.

The Anglo-American axis needs to be viewed in the context of the wider G10 and IMF discussions about the weaknesses of the international monetary system to understand the motivation and willingness of the United States to support sterling. Chapter 7 shows that, from mid-1965, as the US administration came to terms with the chronic nature of its own balance of payments deficit, it became more committed to the multilateral approach to resolving the problems of the international monetary system, which implied a multilateral solution to interim crises. From this time onward as well, Johnson and Fowler became more focused on a long-term solution to what they saw as a sterling balances problem analogous to that of the 1940s, and they sought ways to 'fund' the sterling balances. This pushed them into the discussions in the G10 and the BIS, starting in 1965, that sought to shore up the use of sterling as a reserve currency in a parallel but separate forum from the resolution of the problems of the US dollar as a reserve currency.

[153] Dumbrell and Ellis, 'British involvement in Vietnam', p. 147.

[154] Boyle, K., 'The price of peace: Vietnam, the pound, and the crisis of the American empire', *Diplomatic History*, 27(1), 2003, pp. 37–72.

6 Sterling and the City

> The empire may have disintegrated and the UK may now be a third-rate military power, but the City of London has staged a comeback which would be the envy of any child movie star reaching maturity.
>
> I. O. Scott, quoted by R. J. Clark of Natwest in 1970[1]

Much of the criticism of the management of the retreat of sterling as an international currency has focused on a perceived contradiction between the City of London's financial interests in free trade and a strong and convertible pound as against the interests of industry in cheap money, a low exchange rate and protection.[2] At the time of the post-war international monetary settlement, the interests of the City and the economy as a whole were usually seen as overlapping or even identical, particularly given the traumatic experience of British industry during the floating exchange rate era of the 1930s, when financial instability and disrupted trade patterns accentuated the impact of the depression on domestic producers. The traditional dependence of the balance of payments on invisible earnings was another key factor. In the planning for the post-war period, Keynes argued vehemently and persistently that the restoration of sterling as an internationally acceptable currency was a prerequisite to the re-establishment of the City of London as an international financial centre. Only if sterling were convertible would Commonwealth countries continue to bank in London. If sterling were not convertible then the sterling area arrangements would collapse, to the great detriment of both the British economy and the City of London.[3] His proposals for the International Clearing Union argued:

[1] The comment was written by Scott in 'That controversial eurodollar market', *Natwest Bank Review*, August 1969, pp. 2–22; quoted in Clark, R. J., 'The evolution of monetary and financial institutions', in D. R. Croome and H. G. Johnson (eds.), *Money in Britain, 1959–1969* (Oxford: Oxford University Press, 1970), pp. 131–49, p. 138.

[2] This dichotomy has also been identified for the nineteenth century to explain Britain's longer-term relative economic decline: Pollard, S., *Britain's Prime and Britain's Decline: The British Economy 1870–1914* (London: Edward Arnold, 1989).

[3] Keynes' speech in the House of Lords, in defence of the IMF proposals, 23 May 1944.

The sterling area, if we mean by this the system under which the members of the British Commonwealth do their international banking through London, grew up under conditions of freedom. It lives and breathes by being a voluntary system. It is only in that same atmosphere of the City of London as Liberty Hall dealing in a currency of general acceptability that we can expect to preserve it.[4]

The 'dollar pool' did not arise from, say, an Australian exporter earning dollars and depositing them in his or her central bank, which transferred them to the Bank of England in exchange for sterling Treasury bills or other interest-bearing sterling assets. Rather, the usual practice related to the denomination of trade in sterling. Thus the Australian exporter would sell his or her goods for sterling to an American buyer either directly or in London. The American buyer would sell the equivalent US dollars in London to get the sterling. These dollars would then end up in the central reserves through the British banking system. In this way, the dollar pool, London's international financial and banking services, and sterling as an acceptable trading currency were closely linked.[5] The benefits arising from the City's dominance of international finance were usually considered self-evident, mainly because invisible earnings had traditionally been a vital support to the balance of payments.

During the 1950s it was widely asserted that the international role of the City was dependent on the strength of sterling. Without an international currency, it was argued, the lucrative operations of the City would wither away and with them would go the exports of services that helped strengthen the balance of payments. This was to change in the 1960s, as the international financial system evolved in ways that increased the use of the US dollar in London, through the Eurodollar market. British merchant banks rose to the challenge, but the opportunities also sparked an influx of new foreign banks that competed vigorously for business and for staff. Despite the new dollar business, banks lobbied fretfully against new exchange controls on sterling introduced in the 1950s and the periodic intensification of these controls in the 1960s, arguing that they pushed business away from the City. Despite consistent rhetoric about the links between sterling and the City, however, by the 1960s the City was no longer dependent on the status of sterling as a global reserve currency.

Clarke argued cogently in a widely read study in 1965 that the link between reserve and transactions currency had eroded: 'It is the

[4] Plan for an International Currency (or Clearing) Union, 25 January 1952; in Moggridge, *The Collected Writings of John Maynard Keynes*, vol. XXV, p. 124.

[5] This practice is described by Sir Wilfred Eady to J. M. Keynes, 6 November 1945; in Moggridge, *The Collected Writings of John Maynard Keynes*, vol. XXV, p. 582.

City's usefulness both to Britain and to the world that attracts pounds to London, not the prestige surrounding a reserve currency.'[6] As he noted, this was also the conclusion of the government's 1958 Radcliffe Committee investigation into the working of the monetary system. While 'prestige' may not have been important, confidence in the exchange rate was. A survey by the Economists Advisory Group concluded in 1971 that the confidence of private traders in sterling was important to the earnings of the City, directly for bankers who held the deposits and indirectly for agents, brokers and insurance firms.[7] They cited ship brokering and commodity trading as two examples in which the use of sterling as a unit of account encouraged the invoicing and settlement of transactions in sterling in ways that generated ongoing direct and indirect earnings for the City. In these cases, the brokers and merchants claimed that if this business was denominated in other currencies their connections with their clients would be threatened and their business would be more easily drawn to other financial centres.[8] Cohen writing in the same year also argued that, 'in my opinion, British policy ought to be directed toward the maintenance of the pound's role as a transactions currency', because of the net invisible earnings the City generated for the balance of payments.[9] He saw the appeal of sterling as an intervention currency, and therefore as a reserve currency, as deriving substantially from its private trading role rather than the other way around.

Measuring sterling as a commercial currency

The proportion of trade invoiced and settled in sterling has never been firmly ascertained. Estimates on the basis of guesses as to the proportion of intra-sterling area trade and trade between the sterling area and the rest of the world were used by the Bank of England, although they also commissioned spot checks from trade returns. An enquiry in 1952 by the exchange control authorities determined that only about 5 per cent of trade between non-sterling countries was in sterling. This may have increased slightly with the recovery of London commodity markets and the relaxation in the use of transferable sterling, although there were countervailing pressures. In the early 1950s the main contributors were Egypt's trade with Russia and Iraqi trade, which was settled in sterling and estimated at about £3 billion annually. From the 1950s sterling's

[6] Clarke, W. M., *The City in the World Economy* (London: Pelican Books, 1965), p. 245.
[7] Economists Advisory Group, *An Economic Study of the City of London* (London: Allen & Unwin, 1971), pp. 250–1.
[8] Ibid., pp. 251–2.
[9] Cohen, *The Future of Sterling as an International Currency*, p. 239.

commercial role was thus determined mainly by the share of the United Kingdom and the sterling area in global trade.

A further enquiry in 1960 suggested that 70 per cent of trade between the sterling area and the rest of the world was still settled in sterling. Exchange controls meant that almost all intra-sterling area trade was in sterling, the main exception being trade between Singapore and Malaysia after 1965, which was denominated in Malaysian dollars, so sterling's share of intra-sterling area trade was estimated at 90 per cent. This formula generated a global total of about 26 to 30 per cent of world trade in 1966, a figure the Bank gave to the Treasury, where it became the official estimate.[10] At the same time, Mendelson of *The Economist* approached the Bank of England, which told him the formula off the record. He then published his estimate of 27 per cent of global trade in June 1966, which was subsequently widely cited, for example by Cohen and Clarke. In November 1968 the Bank of England revised its formula to take account of greater diversification by sterling area countries, and the results of Export Credits Guarantee Department (ECGD) and HM Customs investigations in 1967. The outcome was a reduction from 70 per cent of trade between sterling area and non-sterling area countries in 1964 to 60 per cent by 1967, giving an overall total of 21 per cent of world trade settled in sterling by 1967. These proportions were then published by the Economists Advisory Group in their study of 1971.[11]

An important observation of the 1960s data is that there was very little provision for a decline in the sterling proportion of intra-sterling area trade except for the integrated market of Malaysia and Singapore. By June 1965, however, 89 per cent of New Zealand's imports from Australia were settled in Australian dollars, and this proportion rose to 98 per cent by 1967, suggesting that there may have been diversification elsewhere.[12] For sterling area trade with other countries, an estimate of 55 to 60 per cent denominated in sterling by the late 1960s might be considered high. New Zealand was one of the most closely linked independent members of the sterling area, with a high proportion of sterling reserves, but the share of New Zealand's imports from the United States settled in US dollars rose from 72 per cent in 1965 to 80 per cent in 1968, and 93 per cent of imports from Japan were settled in yen.[13] This suggests that only about two-thirds of New Zealand's trade was still settled in sterling

[10] Bank of England, EID memo, 27 November 1968, TNA T312/2305.

[11] Economists Advisory Group, *An Economic Study of the City of London*, p. 251.

[12] Data from British high commission, commercial department, Wellington, 19 June 1969, TNA T312/2304.

[13] Ibid. The share of export receipts from the United States settled in dollars increased from 72 per cent in 1965 to 80.4 per cent in 1968.

Table 6.1 *Sample of export invoices, June 1969*

Destination	Sterling invoices	Foreign-currency invoices	Total	Percentage in sterling
Ireland	53	0	53	100
Sterling area	157	6	163	96.3
Rest of the world	326	55	381	85.6
Total	536	61	597	89.8

Source: TNA T312/2639.

by 1968. Most other sterling countries had reduced their dependence on British and sterling area trade even more.

There was some frustration at the lack of accurate data, but the technical obstacles to collecting it seemed insurmountable. Table 6.1 shows the breakdown of 597 export consignments in 1969. This is the number of invoices rather than an amount, but it does suggest that sterling still dominated British exports. In May 1970 a further sample of one week of UK export invoices confirmed that 89 per cent of 525 consignments were invoiced in sterling.

In 1975 HM Customs sampled 1 per cent of items in the UK trade accounts for imports and exports, other than oil, for one month. The results showed that 90 per cent of UK exports and 30 per cent of UK imports were then being invoiced in sterling, although Customs thought their sampling might overestimate the import proportion. Similar samples taken in 1971 and 1973 both confirmed that, in these years, 90 per cent of UK exports and 50 per cent of imports were invoiced in sterling. The decline was greater therefore in the invoicing of imports than exports. By 1975 Customs estimated that only 8 per cent of non-oil world trade was invoiced in sterling. In addition, 11.5 per cent of oil revenues to producing countries were paid in sterling. This compared to one-third of oil revenues in 1971 and 1973, although oil accounted for a smaller slice of world trade in these years. On this basis, the Bank of England considered that there had been a significant decline in non-UK trade invoiced in sterling, leading them to conclude that not quite 10 per cent of total world trade including oil was settled in sterling in 1975 – a 63 per cent fall since 1960. By 1976 only about 5 per cent of oil revenues were paid in sterling, suggesting that the share of world trade denominated in sterling was falling quickly by the middle of the decade.[14] The

[14] EID paper on commercial use of sterling, 30 March 1976, BE 3A38/4.

Table 6.2 *Share of currencies in invoicing of world trade, 1979*

	US dollar	Deutschmark	Pound	Franc
Exports	54.8	14.4	7.5	6.1
Imports	54.3	13.9	6.9	6.4

Source: Page, 'The choice of invoicing currency in merchandise trade'.

general picture is of a predictable and fairly steady decline in the use of sterling as the currency of trade settlement as Britain's share of world exports declined. This was encouraged from 1977 by rules that increasingly required foreign-currency financing for export credit. In the London foreign exchange market, by 1979 99 per cent of turnover was via the US dollar in the first instance.[15] By 1989 sterling was the fourth most traded currency, behind the US dollar, the yen and the Deutschmark, but the Deutschmark and yen were both well ahead, with 27 per cent of turnover each on one side of the transaction, compared with sterling at 15 per cent. About 90 per cent of all foreign exchange transactions were made with the dollar.[16]

The National Institute of Economic and Social Research investigated the choice of invoicing currency in merchandising trade at the end of the 1970s, bringing together a range of estimates from the developed and developing world.[17] They found that most developed countries (other than Ireland) tended to use their national currency to invoice their exports but tended to use US dollars more for imports. This reflected a desire to avoid exchange risk in exports and the fact that the global markets in most primary products were based on the dollar, particularly oil. A major exception was Japan, which invoiced 62 per cent of its exports and 93 per cent of its imports in dollars in 1980, and Australia, which invoiced 70 per cent of its exports and 52 per cent of its imports. On this basis Page concluded that the dollar was 'the only currency with a major role in trade between other countries'. The results are summarised in table 6.2, which reports that about 7 per cent of world trade was invoiced in sterling in 1979, when the United Kingdom accounted for 5.9 per cent of world exports. Most of this was trade between the United Kingdom and Ireland, while the only

15 Group of Thirty, *The Foreign Exchange Markets under Floating Rates* (New York: Group of Thirty, 1980).

16 BIS, *Central Bank Survey of Foreign Exchange and Derivatives Market Activity 1995* (Basle: BIS, 1996).

17 Page, S. A. B., 'The choice of invoicing currency in merchandise trade', *National Institute Economic Review*, 98, 1981, pp. 60–72.

countries that invoiced more than 10 per cent of their trade in sterling were Norway, Finland and Sweden (data for 1968).

Sterling in banking and finance

There are a range of ways to examine the international financial use of sterling. Figure 6.1 shows that the weakness of sterling in the 1960s did not dramatically affect the level of private holdings of sterling in London by residents of the sterling area. Although the annual data disguise a reduction by £60 million in liabilities to the sterling area in the first nine months of 1967, that was reversed by the end of the year.[18] Residents of the rest of the world, by contrast, reduced their sterling assets in London steadily during the crises of 1966 to 1968, though the nominal value recovered in the inflation of the early 1970s. This suggests that private sterling area holdings were more robust to confidence in sterling,

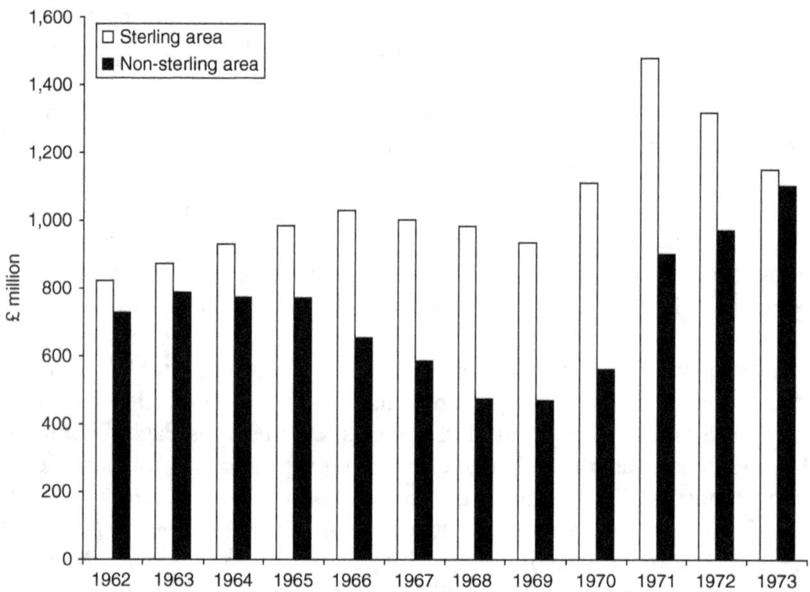

Figure 6.1 Overseas private holdings of sterling, 1962–73
Source: Bank of England Quarterly Bulletin.

[18] The sterling area was disbanded at the end of June 1972. The data for 1972 and 1973 include countries in the sterling area before the change; this series is discontinued from 1973 onward.

confirming the Bank of England's conclusion that the devaluation had not affected the commercial use of sterling in the medium term. This seems not to have been the case for the rest of the world, however.

On the basis of intelligence from the City, in 1969 the Bank of England estimated that there was a core of about £500 million that comprised the working balance for traders in the sterling area and a further £350 million for residents of the rest of the world, which had remained substantially unchanged for several years.[19] In addition, what was termed the 'investment' element came to London to earn higher returns. This was more volatile and prone to withdrawal in times of crisis, and it was the main source of decline in the second half of the 1960s.

Figure 6.2 shows that from 1975 to 1978 sterling held in official foreign exchange reserves overseas contracted, but banking and money market liabilities to private holders in sterling continued to increase exponentially. The contraction in liabilities to overseas central monetary institutions was due to the decline in the sterling reserves of the Organization of the Petroleum Exporting Countries (OPEC) in these years, from £3 billion in 1973 to £1 billion in 1978, as they switched to European and other currencies. From 1979 OPEC countries' reserves recovered,

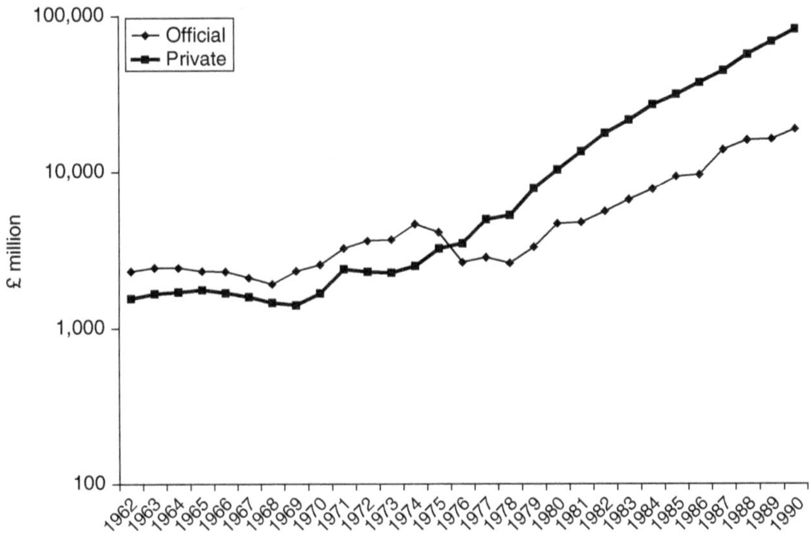

Figure 6.2 UK overseas sterling liabilities, 1962–90
Note: Scale is logarithmic.
Source: Bank of England Quarterly Bulletin.

[19] Group on the International Monetary System, memo, 24 October 1969, TNA T312/2639.

although they did not increase the proportion of their reserves held in sterling.

The end of exchange controls in 1979 increased lending by UK banks to banks overseas, as well as sterling deposits in London from overseas. From October 1979, when exchange controls were lifted, to June 1981 sterling lending by UK banks to overseas banks increased by £3 billion. In 1980 only 7 per cent of UK banks' liabilities to non-residents was denominated in sterling but, by 1990, this share had doubled to 14 per cent, mainly due to sterling deposits of foreign banks in London. Sterling then retained its share of total liabilities to non-residents through to 2001.

After the relaxation of exchange controls from October 1979 the eurosterling market also expanded and became more integrated with the domestic interbank sterling market.[20] The share of sterling in international banks' foreign currency liabilities actually fell after 1980, however, as is shown in figure 6.3. The share in the total was affected by

Figure 6.3 Sterling's share of global banks' foreign currency liabilities, December 1977–June 2008
Source: BIS Quarterly Review, December 2008.

[20] McMahon, C. W., 'The UK's experience in winding down the reserve role of sterling', in Group of Thirty, *Reserve Currencies in Transition* (New York: Group of Thirty, 1982), pp. 42–9.

variations in the exchange rate against the US dollar, but it is clear that while sterling increased its share it was never very prominent in banks' foreign currency positions. Sterling benefited only in a small way from the diversification away from the dollar, which accounted for 75 per cent of total liabilities at the start of the period and only 43 per cent by 2008, mainly replaced by the euro, which had a 25 per cent share in 2008.

On the other hand, sterling has become somewhat more important for foreign banks' assets held in the United Kingdom, as is shown in figure 6.4. This share peaked in 1990, when sterling joined the ERM, and then was built back up from a low point in 1994 to 16.5 per cent in June 2008. Along with exchange rate volatility and the share of the UK in international trade, an important determinant of sterling's international financial and commercial role was the extent of exchange control.

Capital controls on sterling

The use of sterling as a commercial currency was affected not only by the relative decline in the share of the United Kingdom and the sterling area in world trade but also by controls imposed on sterling to bolster the

Figure 6.4 Share of foreign banks' assets in the United Kingdom denominated in sterling, December 1977–June 2008
Source: BIS Quarterly Review, December 2008.

balance of payments.[21] While the Bank of England sought to encourage the commercial use of sterling as part of its general support of the City, ministers and Treasury officials often viewed these transactions as avenues for speculation against the sterling exchange rate through leads and lags. The result was a series of battles over the use of sterling, which reveals the lack of support for sterling's international commercial role from the 1950s.

In 1957 the use of sterling to finance trade between third countries was withdrawn to conserve foreign exchange. Over the next two years Parsons of the Bank of England wrote to Rowan at the Treasury passing on the complaints from the City over restrictions on these usance facilities.[22] The City believed that continuing the restrictions harmed sterling because third parties turned permanently to other currencies to finance their trade. Moreover, this was 'traditional business for London, and, although the facility is not greatly used, it has considerable prestige value'. The pressure from the Bank often stressed that such controls brought sterling into disrepute (an issue close to the heart of the Treasury), as well as hampering the activities of the City (which did not have as great a priority for the Treasury). Many in the Treasury had little sympathy for the City. David Bensusan-Butt, for example, responded that prestige and tradition were not a good enough reason to relax controls that might cause a drain on the reserves if confidence in sterling waned.[23] This view prevailed through a series of repeated pleas from the governor of the Bank of England on behalf of the City.[24] Reflecting on the Bank of England's position during this period some decades later, R. S. Symons of the Treasury (who was in charge of the exchange control division in 1954/5) identified three themes in the Bank's lobbying for reducing exchange controls: that exchange control was 'an unreasonable interference with personal freedoms' in peacetime; that it was expensive because it was so complicated; and that its effectiveness was eroded by the gradual easing of administration and enforcement, and by the gaps that had emerged, as in Kuwait and Hong Kong.[25]

[21] This section draws on material published in Schenk, C. R., 'The new City and the state in the 1960s', in R. Michie and P. Williamson (eds.), *The British Government and the City of London in the Twentieth Century* (Cambridge: Cambridge University Press, 2004), pp. 322–39.

[22] Parsons to Rowan, 22 August 1958, TNA T231/1034. The controls were introduced in September 1957 in response to a balance of payments crisis.

[23] D. M. Bensusan-Butt to Rudd, 29 August 1958, TNA T231/1034.

[24] Parsons to Rickett, 24 November 1958; Cobbold to Makins, 15 January 1959, and to Chancellor of the Exchequer, 28 January 1959; TNA T321/1034.

[25] Symons, R. S., 'Exchange control 1959–1972: UK attitudes and actions', Treasury Historical Memorandum no. 23, April 1975, TNA T267/34.

At the end of April 1959 Cobbold began a sustained campaign to remove the ban on refinance credit. He made repeated and increasingly urgent demands that 'the desire of the market to be able to grant refinance credits arises partly from the feeling that it ought to be able to give the full service that is traditional and partly from its wish to increase its business'.[26] Roger Makins and A. W. France at the Treasury were not convinced. France noted: 'It seems to me that the case for doing this is simply not enough and that we should continue to refuse. There are better candidates [for liberalisation].'[27] At the end of June the Bank of England and Treasury met to discuss the issue. Treasury officials suggested that the relaxation should wait until after the general election, which was held in October, and the Chancellor, Derick Heathcoat-Amory, agreed. Cobbold was incensed and demanded that he be allowed to quote the Chancellor that it was he who refused to relax these restrictions, thus making public the split between the Bank and the Treasury.[28]

By October 1959 the Treasury and the Bank were finally agreed that the ban on refinance credits should be lifted, since sterling appeared strong, the business was an essential part of trade finance and, crucially, such a move was unlikely to have a big impact on the reserves. The Chancellor continued to refuse to act, however, despite pointed questions asked in parliament.[29] Although his Treasury advisers no longer believed there was a case for singling out this form of credit for a ban, Heathcoat-Amory contended that 'I have a feeling that our short-term trade credits are likely to continue to rise and that together with our other overseas commitments are likely to make quite big enough inroads into our reserves'.[30] The ban was not finally lifted until May 1963.

This did not mark the end of the Treasury's suspicion over the international commercial use of sterling, but the danger that new controls themselves would undermine confidence in the exchange rate by signalling the government's own fears outweighed the short-term gains to the balance of payments. At the beginning of 1965 James Callaghan, as Chancellor, began a general review of ways to tighten exchange control. In mid-January he told the prime minister of his intention to collect a package of measures to tighten up the supply of sterling to the switch market, but he decided not to rush new controls while sterling was weak

26 Governor of the Bank of England to the Chancellor of the Exchequer, 13 November 1959, TNA T231/1034.

27 A. W. France minute on a brief by F. W. Glaves-Smith, 12 May 1959, TNA T231/1034.

28 Minute of a Bank/Treasury meeting by Roger Makins, 8 July 1959, TNA T231/1034.

29 Glaves-Smith to France and Rickett, 9 October 1959; Chancellor minute, 6 November 1959; TNA T231/1034.

30 Chancellor minute, 24 November 1959, TNA T231/1034.

for fear of further disrupting international confidence.[31] By the end of the year a special committee chaired by Dennis Rickett was investigating ways to stem the outflow of capital from the United Kingdom. Again, the Treasury and the Bank of England agreed to take no action, although a Bank of England representative was instructed to go to Hong Kong to assess the possibility of tightening exchange control in the colony to stop leaks in sterling controls.[32]

In October 1968 the Treasury again withdrew the use of sterling for financing trade among non-sterling countries. The rationale given to the IMF was that 'there had been a marked increase in the amount of such credit outstanding and, since sterling advanced under this facility involved a more or less immediate claim on the reserves, it was considered that its continuance could not be justified. Withdrawal should result in a benefit to the reserves of some £50m over 6–8 months as existing credits fall due.'[33] The Treasury did not expect much reaction to the reimposition of controls, but the IMF objected to the failure to consult it in advance. Unlike in 1957, when the controls were first introduced, the United Kingdom was now under article VIII supervision, and since sterling and the US dollar were trading currencies any restrictions on their commercial use required the permission of the IMF. As the United Kingdom was likely to come under pressure to repay a 1965 drawing and thus arrange a new stand-by in 1969, the government acquiesced to the IMF's request and retrospectively applied for approval. This episode shows that the British government was more willing than the IMF to forgo the international commercial role of sterling.

The reimposition of controls provoked outrage within the City and from the Conservative opposition (particularly Reginald Maudling, who had been the Chancellor from 1962 to 1964). This episode was widely interpreted as exposing an important breach between the Bank of England and the Treasury.[34] During a speech a few weeks later, the governor of the Bank of England, Leslie O'Brien, was critical of Labour's policies and claimed that the City had lost faith in the government. This prompted seventy-six Labour backbenchers to sign a motion to ask for his resignation and prompted the Conservative opposition to defend O'Brien vociferously.[35]

[31] Note from the Chancellor to the prime minister, 13 January 1965, TNA T295/65.

[32] Minutes of Sir Dennis Rickett's Investment Group, attended by representatives of the Treasury and the Bank of England, 3 December 1965, TNA T295/123.

[33] Answer to IMF consultation on exchange control policy, 18 April 1969, TNA T312/2897.

[34] *The Economist*, 1 November 1968, p. 65.

[35] *The Economist*, 16 November 1968, p. 64.

The evidence presented here contradicts Strange's assertion that the government promoted the use of sterling as an international transactions currency in the 1960s.[36] Instead, it seems that the Treasury resisted relaxing controls on short-term capital flows despite pleas by the Bank of England and the City. From 1964, as sterling came increasingly under pressure in international markets, the Treasury became deaf to the pleas from the City for relaxations that could offer a potential leak should confidence worsen, and the Bank of England was unable to push the Treasury to change its decision despite the personal intervention of the Bank's governor. Policies that sought to support the balance of payments and the exchange rate were no longer consistent with the interests of the City. The balance of power appears to have swung rather against the Bank of England in these matters in the 1960s.

Another case of controversy over controls on sterling was over security sterling. The supply of security sterling arose from sales of US securities, foreign property and repatriated FDI that had been made before February 1950. These proceeds were ring-fenced in order to prevent disinvestment by non-residents from being a drain on the UK reserves. Security sterling could then be invested in UK securities with at least a five-year maturity or transferred to a blocked sterling account. The transferability of sterling between blocked accounts led to a market in security sterling, mainly against US dollars in New York, where security sterling traded at a discount on the official rate. At the end of 1959 the assistant secretary in charge of the exchange control division of the Treasury, F.W. Glaves-Smith, completed a paper on the future of exchange control, which advocated eliminating security sterling since the rate was at that time close to the official rate and the balance of payments was strong. This reflected a more general consensus developing among officials in the Treasury and the Bank of England, to the effect that the effectiveness of exchange control was diminishing and that ministers should be made aware that controls could not be relied upon to protect sterling in a crisis.[37] As the balance of payments position deteriorated in 1960, this advice did not find agreement higher up in the Treasury, and this paper was never given to the Chancellor. During the summer sterling crisis of July 1961 the Chancellor turned to controls on outward direct investment as a tool to prop up the balance of payments in the short term, despite the benefits that such investment might deliver in the longer term.[38]

36 Strange, *Sterling and British Policy*, p. 236.

37 Symons, 'Exchange control 1959–1972', TNA T267/34.

38 Stricter criteria were applied to outward FDI to allow only projects that promised to deliver current account benefits within two to three years – in practice, sales subsidiaries and local assembly plants abroad. Symons, 'Exchange control 1959–1972', TNA T267/34.

In March 1962 the permanent undersecretary to the Treasury, Sir Frank Lee, prepared a paper for the Chancellor proposing relaxations of exchange control in the context of plans ultimately to join the EEC, and suggested that security sterling should be abolished immediately regardless of whether the application was successful.[39] The Bank joined the campaign to eliminate security sterling, on the basis that a widely quoted discounted rate for sterling undermined confidence in the official rate.[40] The Chancellor, Selwyn Lloyd, resisted this suggestion and instead took the opportunity to ease some of the effects of the July measures on FDI, by allowing firms to acquire foreign exchange in the switch sterling market to invest overseas (thereby facilitating a transfer of assets from foreign securities to UK FDI). Although Treasury officials and the Bank of England were agreed that the security sterling market should be eliminated, they found it difficult to convince ministers, who were reluctant to relax controls, particularly when sterling was under pressure. By the mid-1960s purchases of security sterling by Hong Kong on behalf of the Bank of China kept the rate at or near the official rate. Annual turnover in the market was estimated at about £100 million by April 1967.[41] Callaghan, as Chancellor, finally initiated another investigation into unblocking security sterling in February 1967, and it was then eliminated in the budget of April 1967, mainly because it was not effective in preventing the repatriation of sterling securities, and removing the control might encourage more inward investment.

Despite this progressive move to rationalise exchange control, the incoming Labour government in 1964 generally turned away from liberalisation as the balance of payments situation worsened.[42] The Treasury's Working Party on Overseas Investment in October 1964 advised the new government that large balance of payments deficits were expected, and suggested a range of ways to tighten controls on outward investment. In addition, the Chancellor's personal adviser, Thomas Balogh, developed his own proposals to restrict overseas investment, and various tax and other amendments were made to stem outflows of portfolio and direct investment, including the May 1966 voluntary programme of restraint on investment in the developed overseas sterling area. Oliver and Hamilton have described in detail how the Treasury, as well as actually introducing new controls, considered extending exchange controls to the sterling area as part of a series of code-named contingency plans in the months

[39] Symons, 'Exchange control 1959–1972', TNA T267/34.

[40] Sir D. Rickett to Frank Lee for Chancellor of Exchequer, 13 April 1962, BE OV47/54. He also advocated relaxing the voluntary July 1961 controls on outward FDI.

[41] 'Budget changes 1967', 24 April 1967, BE 4A165/3.

[42] Symons, 'Exchange control 1959–1972', TNA T267/34.

following the devaluation of November 1967.[43] In the midst of the gold crisis in March 1968 the Treasury proposed Operation Brutus, to block overseas-held sterling so as to prevent a drain of reserves. This would have represented a drastic departure from current policy and betrayed the remaining trust of overseas holders of sterling (like Brutus' betrayal of Julius Ceasar), causing disruption to the international monetary system that could have been seriously considered only at a time of grave crisis. The Bank of England objected and sought to protect not only its customers (overseas central banks) but also the interests of the City. Oliver and Hamilton note that the Bank argued that blocking the balances would 'close the door on the inflow of foreign capital to London and undermine the sustainability of the UK's investment banks'.[44] Instead, the Bank suggested that floating sterling would be preferable (an indication of the seriousness of their objections to blocking, since floating was anathema to the Bank), but the Treasury agreed that this would prompt the collapse of the international monetary system as a whole, and the plan was abandoned as the immediate crisis receded.

In 1968 a large outflow of portfolio investment, mainly to Australia, prompted Treasury officials again to consider imposing exchange controls on investment in the overseas sterling area. The voluntary controls on direct investment in the developed Commonwealth since May 1966 had not inhibited banking flows. During 1968 the Treasury estimated that individuals in Britain had sent about £200 million to Australia alone through portfolio investment. Operation Brandon, in late 1968 and early 1969, investigated the possibility of introducing exchange controls on portfolio investment to all sterling area countries, either by mutual consent or unilaterally, but this policy was in the end dismissed. Again, the initiative came from the Treasury and was firmly resisted by the Bank of England, partly on the grounds that it would damage the interests of banks in the City. The Treasury took more seriously their argument that, if new controls were imposed on private capital outflows from London, overseas banks would hasten the diversification of their private holdings, which would outweigh any benefits to the capital account of a reduction in portfolio investment abroad.[45] Even opening discussions with overseas sterling countries on a voluntary scheme was expected to put the Sterling Agreements in jeopardy, so the Bank and Treasury rejected 'any plan for extending exchange controls to the OSA in the near future, except in circumstances of catastrophe'.[46] The reasons that persuaded

[43] Oliver and Hamilton, 'Downhill from devaluation'.
[44] Ibid., p. 490.
[45] Sterling Area Working Party report, 12 February 1969, TNA T312/2766.
[46] Ibid.

the Treasury were not to do with the interests of the City but with the wider implications for sterling and the international monetary system. In the end, exchange controls were extended to the sterling area only when the sterling float in June 1972 signalled a departure from the post-war orthodoxy.

The Treasury continued to believe that the international use of sterling to invoice and settle trade provided dangerous opportunities for commodity shunting, and leads and lags that increased speculative pressure on the exchange rate during successive bouts of crisis. In the wake of the Basle Agreements of 1968, and their success in stemming the diversification of sterling as a reserve currency, the Treasury began to consider in more depth the international role of sterling and what the government's goals should be in the longer term. This followed Clarke's influential 1965 study on *The City in the World Economy*, which had concluded that 'the evidence strongly suggests that the City will continue to attract business even in the face of a decline in the use of the pound in the world's exchange reserves', but predicted that external competition was likely to challenge the City's prospects.[47] In March 1969 A. Mackay, undersecretary at the Treasury, wrote to Frank Figgures, second secretary to the Treasury, suggesting that an interdepartmental investigation be launched into the trading role of sterling and how this was related to sterling's reserve role and to the invisible earnings of the City.[48] Figgures turned to the Bank of England for a first indication of how dependent invisible earnings were on the trading role of sterling.

By this time the Bank was not concerned about the impact that a decline of sterling as a commercial currency would have on the City's invisible earnings, although it acknowledged that there might be some losses for banking services due to lower private sterling balances. Most other markets, such as the foreign exchange market, commodity markets and brokerage, would continue to flourish using other currencies. The Bank concluded that the bulk of invisible earnings had not been affected by the declining role of sterling over the past few years, concurring with Clarke that 'the trading role of sterling does not depend directly on its role as a reserve currency but is more a matter of habit and convenience'.[49] The Bank also reassured the Treasury that there was no evidence that the devaluation of 1967 had had a large lasting impact on invoicing and settlement in sterling. A few commodity dealers began settling in other

[47] Clarke, *The City in the World Economy*, p. 211.

[48] Alastair Mackay (Treasury) to F. E. Figgures, 13 March 1969, TNA T312/2304.

[49] Roy Fenton (Bank of England) to Figgures, 22 August 1969; R. E. J. Gilmore minute for W. S. Ryrie of a meeting at the Bank of England with the Treasury, 25 September 1969; TNA T312/2305.

currencies, but most had reverted to sterling within a few weeks. On the other hand, W. S. Ryrie of the Treasury argued that there had to be an indirect link between the reserve role and the trading role, since the latter depended on the sterling area exchange control that prohibited the use of NSA currencies on intra-sterling area trade. This common exchange control was, in turn, related to the commitment to the sterling area system and sterling's reserve role. In response, the Bank argued that countries with low sterling reserves, such as India, continued to conduct almost all their trade in sterling.[50] By the 1960s the intra-sterling area exchange control was in any case already becoming more relaxed.

A joint Bank/Treasury paper in October 1969 concluded that, while the trading role of sterling generated only small net invisible earnings, there would be no benefit from actively reducing this role.[51] The proportion of trade financed in sterling was expected to continue to fall, although the nominal amount of such trade would remain constant. The balances held for trading purposes amounted to just under a half of all private sterling balances, or £825 million, and British banks paid rates of interest that were about two percentage points lower on these trading balances than they would on other sources of funds to replace them. In summary, sterling's trading role was declining, was not directly linked to the earnings of the City overall but probably did generate some net invisible earnings, partly because of the low cost of this kind of borrowing, and no policy was recommended to affect this trend.

Despite this passive conclusion, the next year the Treasury began to consider ways actively to reduce the proportion of trade denominated in sterling. In 1970 it sought to increase the non-sterling finance of British trade with the non-sterling area, in particular foreign-currency invoicing of UK exports, to generate improvements in the balance of payments. To meet this end the ECGD was allowed to provide cover in non-sterling currencies. At the time, the Treasury wanted this facility extended to trade with the sterling area (i.e. non-sterling financing of sterling area trade), but the Bank of England resisted on the grounds that this would reduce the use of sterling as a commercial currency too far.[52] The Treasury revived the Bank's earlier argument that the City's earnings were not closely related to the commercial use of sterling. Indeed, insurance was the fastest-growing sector, and its business was unrelated to sterling. On the other hand, the Treasury estimated that the finance of trade in

[50] Ryrie to A. K. Rawlinson, undersecretary at Treasury, 29 September 1969, TNA T312/2305.

[51] Group on the International Monetary System, 'Costs and benefits of the international role of sterling and its reduction', 24 October 1969, TNA T312/2639.

[52] Mackay to Fenton, 25 June 1970, TNA T312/2639.

sterling cost the balance of payments about £100 million annually. The Bank responded firmly that its assessment of the importance of sterling invoicing had been made on the basis of continued exchange control restricting intra-sterling area trade settlement to sterling area currencies, of which sterling was the most liquid.[53] Using non-sterling currencies to finance trade would ultimately lead to the settlement of trade in these currencies and thus the elimination of trading balances in London (then estimated at some £500 million), which formed a cheap form of borrowing for banks. The Bank therefore disputed the overall saving to the balance of payments predicted by the Treasury and defended the continued restrictions on the finance of sterling area exports.

In summary, the Treasury and the Bank of England separated the reserve role from the commercial role of sterling by the early 1960s, and both viewed the decline of sterling's importance in world trade with equanimity, since it did not seem to be seriously challenging the competitiveness of the City or its invisible earnings. Where the Treasury differed was that, from the 1950s, it actively sought to introduce policies to hasten this decline in an effort to protect the balance of payments from the opportunities for speculative pressure offered by third-party financing of international trade. The Bank of England did not believe that the savings from these restrictions outweighed their disadvantages in terms of reputation, and consistently – and often vigorously – objected, though not very successfully. By the early 1960s its attitude to sterling as an international currency was affected by the huge growth of non-sterling business in the City and the accelerating pace of financial innovation – discussed in the next section.

The eclipse of sterling, 1958–1970

During the 1950s the City was constrained by tight exchange controls on trade and payments, both in sterling and foreign currencies. Domestically, the banking system also wallowed in a comfortable uncompetitive environment of interest rate cartels and tight government control of competition.[54] From the end of the 1950s, with the advent of non-resident current account convertibility, the opportunities in London for international commercial business for residents outside the United Kingdom increased. Even before December 1958 the gradual liberalisation of sterling controls set the scene for the most important financial innovation of the era, the Eurodollar market, which transformed the business

[53] Fenton to Mackay, 28 June 1970, TNA T312/2639.
[54] Clarke, *The City in the World Economy*, p. 22.

of the City by creating an explosion in offshore business denominated in foreign currencies, in particular the US dollar. Despite the common understanding that the market emerged because of Cold War worries among Russians and others that the US authorities would block their US dollar accounts, the origins of the market lay in the innovative approach of a single clearing bank responding to tight domestic liquidity within the cosy cartel that restricted competitive bidding for domestic retail deposits. The growth of the market owed much to limits on interest payable in the United States and the unwillingness of the financial authorities in the United States or in Europe to allow the growth of foreign-owned, foreign-currency deposits in their own jurisdictions for fear that the resulting short-term capital flows would undermine their monetary sovereignty. Thus regulatory constraints in other markets greatly increased the advantages of the City of London as a host to this, the most quickly growing financial market in the world in the 1960s. In the process it transformed the nature of the City and diminished the relative importance of traditional sterling business compared with the offshore US dollar market.

The Eurodollar market began to emerge in 1955, when the Midland Bank bid for overseas dollar deposits to overcome the local liquidity shortage by evading the UK interest rate cartel. In June the bank offered rates of 1⅞ per cent for US dollars from non-residents, compared with 1 per cent available in New York under Regulation Q.[55] This tactic was immediately successful, attracting $80 million within a few months, most of which Midland switched into sterling assets. The Bank of England was surprised by this innovation, but decided to allow it after considering the possibility of imposing further controls, noting that, 'whilst the Bank would much prefer to see non-resident access to London money rates through the medium of sterling held on the appropriate types of non-resident account, they would raise no objections to banks accepting deposits from non-residents and converting these to sterling through swaps in the London market'.[56] Swapping the US dollars into resident sterling investments created an inflow of foreign exchange through the capital account of the balance of payments. Figure 6.5 shows the accumulation of US dollar deposits by the Midland Bank in the first year. Figure 6.6 shows the subsequent rapid increase in all UK banks' holdings of US dollar deposits. In mid-1956 Midland still accounted for at least

[55] Schenk, C. R., 'The origins of the Eurodollar market in London, 1955–1963', *Explorations in Economic History*, 35(2), 1998, pp. 221–38.

[56] Note by L. T. G. Preston to Robert Menzies confirming the content of a conversation, 22 July 1955, BE C43/111.

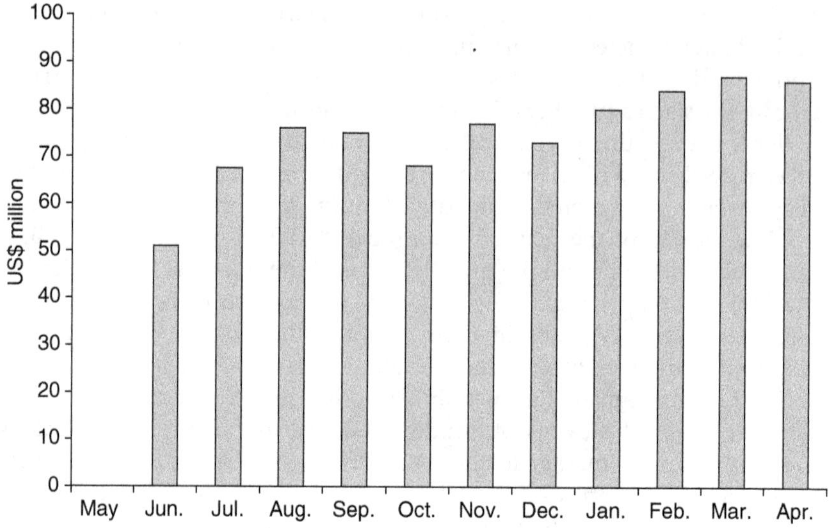

Figure 6.5 Midland Bank's US dollar deposits, May 1955–April 1956
Source: BE C43/111.

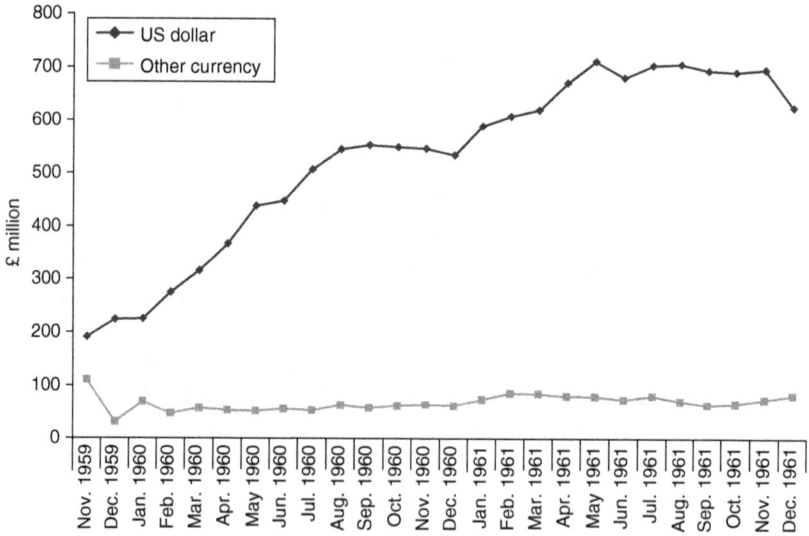

Figure 6.6 UK authorised banks' US dollar deposits by NSA foreigners, November 1959–December 1961
Source: BE EID10/21.

a half of total Eurodollar deposits, but by the end of 1962 it held only 3 per cent. American banks in London, British overseas banks, accepting houses and Japanese banks quickly took over the market. Liabilities denominated in US dollars accounted for 85 per cent of the total.

The principal use of US dollar deposits by 1962 was for the finance of trade, replacing sterling finance, which was either not available or too expensive.[57] Canadian banks tended to relend their assets to New York security dealers and brokers while American banks transferred their assets back to head office in the United States.[58] Japanese banks in London were particularly active in attracting Eurodollar deposits, and by September 1960 they had obtained liabilities amounting to more than $200 million, most of which was converted to yen to finance Japanese industrial expansion. Because of higher perceived risks, Japanese banks offered interest rates two percentage points over the usual rate to obtain the funds, but this was still cheaper than borrowing in Japan.[59]

The innovation was taken up quickly as a reserves management tool by central banks. From 1959, for example, the Bundesbank and the Banca d'Italia engaged in swaps between local currency and US dollars at rates that encouraged their banks to place Eurodollar deposits abroad. By 1962 commercial banks seeking to employ liquid funds were believed to be the main sources of deposits, and some of these were the product of swaps with their central banks. The second largest category of depositors was the European central banks directly (and the BIS), which sought to deposit their US dollar surpluses abroad in order to manage their official reserves.[60] From as early as July 1958 the BIS requested permission to make dollar deposits with banks in London up to a total of $30 million. By October 1960 this limit had been increased to $100 million and in January 1963 the limit was raised further to $150 million. By this time the BIS had total Eurocurrency deposits of $400 million in Canada, France, Switzerland, Belgium, Scandinavia and Italy as well as London.[61] Lucius Thompson-McCausland of the Bank of England estimated that, of the $2.5 billion to $3 billion in the Eurodollar market, $1.5 billion to $2 billion was directly or indirectly 'pushed out' by central banks, leaving about $1 billion for other sources, such as US corporations. The

[57] 'UK banks' foreign currency assets and liabilities', 29 January 1962, BE EID10/21.

[58] Low of the Bank of London and South America suggested in October 1962 that more American banks' deposits were being used in Europe rather than being channelled to head office. Report of a discussion by L. P. Thompson-McCausland, 4 October 1962, BE EID10/21.

[59] Note from G. W. Lucas to R. L. Workman (Treasury), 21 July 1961, BE EID10/21.

[60] Paper for the Committee on Overseas Figures, 11 May 1962, BE EID10/15.

[61] Note by R. A. O'Brien, 16 January 1963, BE EID10/22.

innovation of Eurodollar deposits turned out to be the beginning of a much larger acceleration in financial innovation that profoundly changed the City of London's operations.

Figure 6.7 shows the annual rate of growth of the global Eurocurrency deposits from 1965 to 1979. The rapid growth in this source of funding attracted attention from the public as well as policy-makers. In 1969 *Time Magazine* described it as 'the genie that escaped from the bottle', noting its usefulness for finance but also that such large and liquid offshore funds threatened the policy sovereignty of states.[62] Many commentators have suggested that a desire to sustain the status of London as an international financial centre was the major reason why the Bank of England, and later the Treasury, let the market find a home in London.[63] As officials at the Bank of England stated in 1961, 'However much we dislike hot money we cannot be international bankers and refuse to accept money.'[64] The explanation needs further elaboration, however. Certainly, in the late 1950s, much public and official opinion still believed that the international activities of the City generated prestige and current account earnings, although the extent of these benefits and their

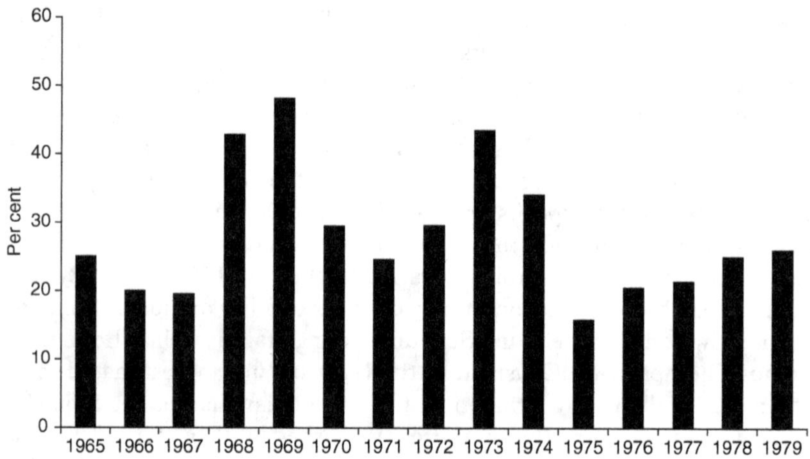

Figure 6.7 Annual growth in Eurocurrency market (net of interbank holdings), 1965–79

[62] *Time Magazine*, 16 May 1969.

[63] Rajan, R., and L. Zingales, *Saving Capitalism from the Capitalists: Unleashing the Power of Financial Markets to Create Wealth and Spread Opportunity* (New York: Random House, 2003), p. 261; Helleiner, E., *States and the Reemergence of Global Finance: From Bretton Woods to the 1990s* (Ithaca, NY: Cornell University Press, 1994), p. 84; Burn, G., *The Re-emergence of Global Finance* (Basingstoke: Palgrave, 2006).

[64] Report by J. M. L. for Hamilton, 19 Oct. 1961, BE EID10/19.

opportunity cost regularly attracted criticism. The Treasury's intensification of controls on many financial transactions in the late 1950s and through the 1960s show that hurting the interests of the City was not an obstacle to imposing controls if they were deemed necessary for balance of payments purposes. As Burn notes, of more immediate importance in 1955 was that the initial growth of US dollar deposits generated a net inflow of dollars that helped reduce Britain's persistent balance of payments deficits.[65] The fact that the dollars attracted by Midland Bank reduced the recorded fall in the United Kingdom's central reserves in June 1955 from $56 million to $6 million carried considerable weight in the Bank of England and the Treasury. In a time of balance of payments deficits, the United Kingdom did not want to introduce new controls on capital *inflows*.

By August 1962 the market had spread more widely and the danger of a maturity mismatch between short-term deposits and longer-term lending prompted the Bank of England to reassess its regulatory stance. The Eurodollar market attracted foreign banks (particularly US banks) into the City, and in this context the Bank decided that requesting bankers to exercise voluntary self-restraint 'would be embarrassing to apply'. Suspicious or dangerous dealing would not be conducted by the big operators with which the Bank had most contact and influence, so 'moral suasion' was unlikely to work. The Bank also considered imposing separate higher liquidity ratios for Eurodollar loans, but it was not confident that it would be able to enforce such discrimination between items in the banks' accounts. Even gathering information on the maturity spread of deposits was considered too onerous for the banks to report. The only positive action was that the governor of the Bank of England was instructed to approach the leading six or so banks in the market and warn them to keep their positions liquid by maintaining adequate reserve ratios.[66] By 1973 US banks held about 40 per cent of Eurodollar deposits, British banks about 25 per cent and consortium banks 8 per cent.[67]

An important reason for the continued domination of London was the reluctance of other regulatory authorities to permit this offshore business, for fear that it would disrupt national monetary independence. It was also aided by controls in the United States on capital outflows to protect the balance of payments, particularly the US interest equalisation

[65] Schenk, 'The origins of the Eurodollar market in London'; Burn, *The Re-emergence of Global Finance*, p. 127.

[66] Summary of a meeting at the Bank of England, 16 August 1962, BE EID10/21.

[67] *Bank of England Quarterly Bulletin*, 14(1), 1974.

tax in 1963, which discouraged borrowing in the United States and pushed customers to use offshore facilities. The outcome of the different regulatory environments in the United States and the United Kingdom was a reallocation of international banking activity. In this way the Bank of England promoted the retirement of sterling from the centre of the City's business, and in the process restored its global competitive position. Figure 6.8 shows how Britain dominated global foreign bank assets at the expense of the United States by the late 1960s.

Despite the early acceptance of the initial innovation, the ongoing toleration of the market was not merely the outcome of institutional inertia. The market was the subject of close scrutiny on both sides of the Atlantic, and also among European central bankers. Even while imposing the Interest Equalization Tax (IET), the US Treasury agreed with the Bank of England that there was no immediate need for external supervision or new regulation of the Eurodollar market in London.[68] Burn describes the slow realisation in the United States of the importance of

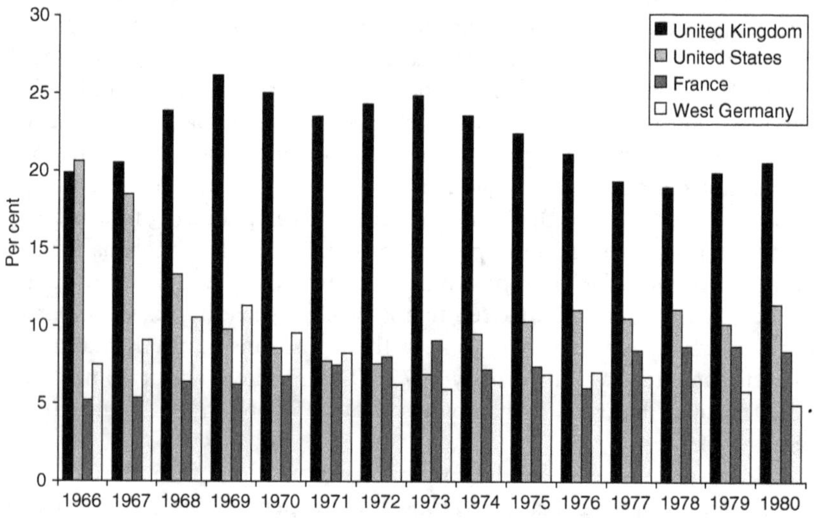

Figure 6.8 Banks' foreign assets as percentage of world banks' foreign assets, 1966–80
Source: IMF, *International Financial Statistics Yearbook 1981* (Washington, DC: IMF, 1982).

[68] At the beginning of 1963 the US Treasury reassured banks that it did not object to their participation in the market. Memo of conversation with W. B. Eagleson, vice-president of the Girard Trust Corn Exchange Bank of Philadelphia, with Daane, Trued, Schott, 30 January 1963; NARA, USSMA, Box 105, RG69-A-407.

the market and confusion over its impact in the early 1960s. Underlying this confusion, however, was a conviction that the market was useful for the international financial system and, indeed, for US corporations operating overseas, although US banks' involvement through their overseas branches might undermine the Fed's efforts to restrain domestic liquidity.[69] A further danger was that the regulatory and supervisory lacunae in London might enable reckless behaviour by lenders and borrowers. The risks of currency mismatch, the term structure of liabilities and assets and the opacity of final borrowers in the market all seemed to make it ripe for crisis. The undersecretary of state for monetary affairs, Robert Roosa, told Parsons of the Bank of England early in 1963 that he 'was certain that the Eurodollar market would continue to be a feature of the international financial situation. It was potentially a vehicle for instability but also an important part of liquidity', at a time when the perceived shortage of international liquidity was an important preoccupation.[70] In talks with US banks, Roosa

> reminded them that although there is no question of imposing exchange control, they should, in his words, ask themselves whether they are serving the national interest by participating in this sort of activity, which adds to the volume of short-term capital outflow from the US. Mr Roosa was not too optimistic about the outcome.[71]

In 1963, however, some major US and European banks did agree among themselves to restrict the interbank market and avoid the 'pyramiding' of deposits through interbank lending, because of fears over the market's stability.[72]

At the end of November 1963 a fraudulent food oil scam in the United States (dubbed the 'Great Salad Oil Flap' by *The Economist*) brought down the broker Ira Haupte and generated a series of defaults on Eurodollar loans. This sent shock waves through the market and brought monetary authorities back to the question of regulation and supervision.[73] The increasing volume of short-term cross-border interbank flows raised the

[69] Burn, *The Re-emergence of Global Finance*, pp. 151–62.
[70] Memo of meeting of Roosa with Rickett and Parsons, 9 April 1963, NARA, USSMA, Box 106, RG69-A-407.
[71] Note by S. Goldman of a conversation with Roosa, 1 May 1963, BE EID10/20.
[72] Andrew L. Gomory, executive vice-president of Manufacturers Hanover Trust, New York, to Roosa, 1 November 1963, NARA, USSMA, Box 105, RG69-A-407. Hermann Abs of Deutschebank to Gomory, 5 September 1963. The director of the Bayerische Vereinsbank told Gomory the same, 1 September 1963; NARA, USSMA, Box 105, RG69-A-407.
[73] Note by Preston to Bridge, circulated to Selwyn, O'Brien and Parsons, 4 December 1963; BE EID10/22. Losses totalled $100 million; *The Economist*, 25 January 1964.

spectre of the financial crisis of the 1930s, but, unlike the 1930s, this did not lead to a reversal of policy.[74] In London, the system of informal supervision continued. As Cromer told Holtrop, now the chairman of the BIS, 'If in an individual case it appeared to us that an unsound situation was developing, we would then discuss the matter with the bank in question.'[75] Dewey Daane, the Fed governor, worried about the possibility that 'unsound lending' might to lead to a chain of defaults that would cause a banking crisis similar to that of 1933.[76] He was reassured by arguments that the Eurodollar market represented a small proportion of banks' total liquidity and that the market was sensitive to the risks of geographical concentration.[77] Like the Bank of England, the Fed used its contacts to obtain more information about the market by asking a small number of leading US corporations why and how they used the Eurodollar market, but it did not put any obstacles in the way of such transactions.[78]

Burn is critical of the late interest the Fed took in the Eurodollar market, noting that it was only in 1960 that it sought to gather intelligence about how the market worked in Europe.[79] The result of this study led it to consider ways to insulate the United States from the Eurodollar market 'by prohibition or patriotic persuasion', or by altering incentives or reserve requirements. The main goal was to curtail the evasion of tight domestic monetary policy through the Eurodollar market, not to eliminate its usefulness for the international financial system generally. The Fed initially focused on ways to withdraw US banks from the market, but by 1967 it clearly recognised the limitations of its regulatory reach. The report concluded:

(a) Prohibition might stimulate innovation in methods of avoidance.
(b) Efforts at persuasion might bring counterproductive psychological reactions.
(c) It would not be sound policy to make what might have to be a permanent change in the framework of reserve requirements for transitory reasons.[80]

Two years later, after the 1968 gold crisis had shown the vulnerability of the US dollar to persistent balance of payments deficits, the Fed finally moved to discourage foreign branches of American banks from

[74] Bridge to Parsons and O'Brien, 5 December 1963, BE EID10/22.
[75] Cromer to Holtrop (BIS), 31 March 1964, BISA FER8 7.18(10).
[76] Note by Henry N. Goldstein for Mr Young, 17 February 1964, NARA, RG82, Box 76.
[77] An example was the inability of Italian banks to borrow in the market in November 1962; ibid.
[78] Note for the files by Alfred Hayes re conversation with W. Braddock Hickman, president of the Federal Reserve Bank of Cleveland, 13 April 1964, NARA, RG82, Box 76.
[79] Burn, *The Re-emergence of Global Finance*, pp. 140–4.
[80] A. B. Hersey to Robert Solomon, 19 October 1967, NARA, RG82, Box 76.

repatriating Eurodollars, in an effort to make its tight monetary policy more effective. In September 1969 the Fed imposed a 10 per cent reserve requirement on net liabilities to foreign branches of US banks in excess of the average amounts outstanding in May 1969. The Fed estimated that some 30 per cent of foreign branch resources were used to supply parent offices in 1969 but that in 1970 this level fell to 2.7 per cent.[81]

Despite taking steps to insulate the US economy, there is no evidence that the Americans tried to push the Bank of England or the UK Treasury to impose controls in London. Burn interprets the evidence that the US authorities were concerned by the market in the early 1960s as suggesting that they were frustrated by British reluctance to curtail it, but it is not clear from his account what the United States wanted Britain to do.[82] The official US view was that the American economy was vulnerable to short-term capital movements of many kinds, including the Eurodollar market, and that this problem could not be contained effectively through further restrictions. On the plus side, the market had increased overseas borrowing of US dollars, thus relaxing pressure on direct borrowing from the New York market. By 1970 the president's National Advisory Committee on International Monetary Affairs viewed the market as a symptom rather than a cause of instability and concluded that

> it would not be possible to achieve tight controls on the access of US banks, companies, or investors to foreign short-term financial markets (including the Eurodollar market).[83]

The Fed was uncertain about the net impact of the market on the balance of payments, but found that London's facilities were a useful way to ease domestic pressure to relax capital controls and tight money in the United States, since large American corporations could borrow in this offshore market.

In London, the cosy informal networks that had developed since the nineteenth century encouraged the Bank of England to continue to rely on personal contacts and 'moral suasion' rather than directives, despite the fact that the market was changing dramatically with the establishment of US banks in the City. Both sets of regulators also recognised that this innovation marked a new era of complexity in international finance that was no longer as amenable to national controls. Moreover, the Bank

[81] Kelly, J., *Bankers and Borders: The Case of American Banks in Britain* (Cambridge, MA: Ballinger, 1977), p. 101.

[82] Burn, *The Re-emergence of Global Finance*, pp. 163–7; Burn does not refer to discussions at the BIS detailed below.

[83] Frederick L. Springborn, report for IMF questionnaire, 4 November 1970, NARA, RG56, entry 360D 'NAC actions'.

of England was clearly sensitive to the dangers of regulatory competition between international financial centres. The overriding priority for both governments was minimising balance of payments deficits, and the market had a role to play in this campaign on both sides of the Atlantic.

European opinion was more suspicious, and the Bank of England came under increasing pressure in Basle to impose controls. These efforts foundered over the conflict between national sovereignty and international cooperation, the interests of London and Washington in the continuation of the market, the danger of pushing it to a less well supervised offshore financial centre and a lack of consensus over its impact on national and international economic stability. Efforts to improve transparency and supervision were stymied by the priority that central banks gave to the privacy of their clients' business. It would take the 1982 Latin American debt crisis for central banks and the banking community to begin to overcome this inhibition and start to embrace transparency, although obstacles to communication between national financial regulators continue to plague efforts at prudential supervision, as was starkly revealed in the 2007–9 global financial crisis.

The BIS was the ideal forum for this discussion. It used the market in its banking relations with member central banks, and it was a regular meeting place for central bankers away from their governments.[84] In June 1962 Guillaume Guindey, the general manager of the BIS, invited member central banks to meet to discuss the Eurodollar market. The BIS observed that, 'looked at strictly as a competitive phenomenon and as a service to both the lenders and borrowers who use it, the Eurodollar market would appear a useful development. Are there disadvantages or dangers which should be set on the other side of the ledger?' – such as counteracting monetary policy, the dangers of a liquidity crisis in the market or the impact on forward exchange markets. The BIS concluded with the question: 'Is it right for the central banks to leave the Eurocurrency markets without supervision or management?'[85] Rather than grappling with policy issues, however, the meeting of experts merely skated over these fundamental questions and concentrated instead on the exchange of statistics.[86]

[84] The involvement of the BIS in the discussions over the eurocurrency markets is described in Toniolo, *Central Bank Cooperation at the Bank for International Settlements*, pp. 465–71.

[85] Short paper by BIS as basis for discussion of eurodollar market at meeting of experts on 6–8 October 1962, 31 August 1962, BIS, 1/3A(3) 'meeting of experts', vols. 1–2.

[86] The Americans were particularly keen to see the BIS collect data on the market to help them trace its movements and potential impact on the United States. Fred H. Klopstock, manager of research department of Federal Reserve Bank of New York, to M. Gilbert, 28 May 1962, BIS, 1/3A(3) 'meeting of experts', vols. 1–2.

Central bank governors met in December 1963 just after the Ira Haupte crisis, and their views reveal a lack of detailed understanding combined with general suspicion of the market. Alfred Hayes, the New York Fed president, worried about the overextension of credit to a few borrowers and 'inadequate checking between countries of the credit-worthiness of borrowers'.[87] He was still uncertain of the impact on the US balance of payments. Blessing noted that 'the Bundesbank was not concerned about the participation of the German commercial banks in the Eurodollar market'. He felt that the market had similar problems to those affecting all short-term international credit, but also that 'the Eurodollar market had encouraged foreign bankers to be less cautious than they would normally be in granting foreign credits'. Jacques Brunet, governor of the Banque de France, remarked that he 'could not say whether the market was good or bad but that the central banks were justified in regarding it with a certain amount of suspicion.' On the other hand, he also thought that 'there was no necessity for rigid controls'.[88] Cromer of the Bank of England was unworried by the market. Summing up the discussion, Holtrop concluded that 'the general view seemed to be that there might be problems in connection with the Eurodollar market but that they were not essentially different from the problems that existed in relation to international short term capital movements in general'. The BIS initiative then focused on the collection of statistics for the next couple of years.

This account of the reactions to the rise of the Eurodollar market in the 1960s shows the Bank of England's growing commitment to this new enterprise in the City of London, which sustained and encouraged its re-emergence from the doldrums of the post-war years and provided market opportunities that offset the impact of continued exchange controls on sterling and the relative decline of British trade in the global economy. The resurgence of the City was not due to British banks themselves, but this did not seem to bother the regulators. In the process, therefore, the character of the City was transformed by these offshore activities as sterling receded and foreign banks were attracted to London. From 1962 to 1970 the number of foreign bank branches or subsidiaries increased from fifty-one to 129, and then to 214 in 1979, by which time

[87] The following account comes from Letter Ferras to the governor of the Bank of Japan, Masamichi Yamagiwa, who was not present at the meeting; 23 January 1964, BIS, FER8 7.18(10).

[88] G. Lefort, of the Banque de France, later corrected the French position by emphasising the need to encourage banks to be more prudent in their lending. Lefort comments on the 'Report of experts' draft, 19 December 1963, BIS, 1/3A(3) 'meeting of experts', vols. 1–2.

the United Kingdom accounted for some 20 per cent of global foreign banking assets.[89] As predicted by the Bank of England and other contemporaries, the decline of sterling clearly did not mark the end of the City of London's leadership of international banking, although it probably did contribute to the domination of US and other foreign banks in London.

The return to the pinnacle of international banking was short-lived. In the 1970s London's relative position declined again, as a consequence of the proliferation of international financial centres in response to the liberalisation of capital controls (especially in the United States after 1974) and innovations in products and communications. In 1970 London ranked first in the world in terms of head offices and being host to branches, subsidiaries and representative offices of the world's major banks, but it had fallen to third place by 1980, behind New York and Tokyo.[90] Nevertheless, foreign assets as a share of total assets of banks in the United Kingdom leapt from 46 per cent to 68 per cent between 1970 and 1981.[91] Among industrialised countries, only Luxembourg banks had a greater share of foreign assets. While the relative position of London may have receded, the City continued to be an international resource.

In October 1962 the governor of the Bank of England called for more foreign borrowing in London, and in December Iceland was the first non-sterling country to be able to borrow sterling in London for over ten years. The Japanese government followed, raising £5 million in sterling in August 1963, but this was the last foreign bond issue in sterling for the next year, as dollar-denominated Eurobonds began to appear. At the same time as the Iceland sterling issue, the Bank of England and the Treasury were working with British investment banks, including S G Warburg & Co., to arrange a US$30 million loan for the Belgian government.[92] Kynaston describes how the close relations that George Bolton, of the Bank of London and South America, had with the Bank of England, on the one hand, and with Warburg, on the other, led Bolton

[89] Pecchioli, R. M., *The Internationalisation of Banking: The Policy Issues* (Paris: OECD, 1983), p. 69.

[90] Choi, S. R., D. K. Park and A. E. Tschoegl, 'Banks and the world's major banking centers, 1990', *Weltwirtschaftliches Archiv*, 132(4), 1996, pp. 774–93.

[91] Pecchioli, *The Internationalisation of Banking*, p. 19.

[92] See correspondence in BE C40/773. I. de L. Radice draft letter to Sir A. Rumbold of Commonwealth Relations Office, 13 December 1963, BE C40/1213. See also telegram to Commonwealth posts, 25 January 1963, BE C40/773. On the origins of the Eurobond market, see Kerr, I. M., *A History of the Eurobond Market: The First 21 Years* (London: Euromoney, 1984); Burk, K., 'Witness seminar on the origins and early development of the eurobond market', *Contemporary European History*, 1(1), 1992, pp. 65–87; Burn, G., 'The state, the City and the Euromarkets', *Review of International Political Economy*, 6(2), 1999, pp. 225–61; Kynaston, D., *The City of London*, vol. IV, *A Club No More 1945–2000* (London: Pimlico, 2001).

to obtain permission for a group of investment banks to develop London market loans denominated in foreign currencies.[93] After appearing to fall through in February 1963, the bond was finally issued, for US$20 million, in May, but it was fully subscribed by a consortium of banks out of their holdings of Eurodollars and did not generate a secondary market. The July 1963 Autostrade issue for $15 million was the first quoted Eurobond issue, listed in London and Luxembourg, issued by Warburg, Banque de Bruxelles, Deutschebank and Rotterdamsche Bank.

The Treasury and the Bank of England viewed these new forms of loans as important enough to require reassurance for sterling area governments and central banks, which were jealous of their preferred access to the London capital market. The Treasury advised sterling area posts that 'the object of these loans is to make the facilities of the London capital market more widely available and to mop up some of the very volatile Euro-dollars at present in London'.[94] The market was at first used mainly by state borrowers; European state-owned enterprises and public sector borrowers raised $44.4 billion on the Eurobond market between 1963 and 1980.[95] American corporations entered the market in 1965, and in that year private borrowers almost matched public borrowers in terms of the money raised, quickly taking the dominant share of the market from then on. From 1963 to 1967 S G Warburg and Hambros led in terms of lead or co-lead managers for new issues, participating in twenty-five issues each. In the period from 1968 to 1972 their position was overtaken by Deutschebank, with seventy-five new issues, and then the US investment houses Morgan and Co. and White Weld, with fifty-seven and forty-three, respectively. British investment banks appeared content to let the Americans take the lead.[96]

In April 1968, just after the March gold crisis, the Fed publicly acknowledged that the London Eurobond market was an integral part of its balance of payments policy: 'It has always been clear that part of the required adjustment in international payments would have to come through increased European financing of capital investment in Europe and elsewhere.'[97] This tendency had been reinforced, of course, by the

[93] Kynaston, *The City of London*, vol. IV, p. 276. The other banks were Barings, Samuel Montagu and, later, Hambro.

[94] I. de L. Radice draft letter to Sir A. Rumbold of Commonwealth Relations Office, 13 December 1963, BE C40/1213. See also telegram to Commonwealth posts, 25 January 1963, BE C40/773.

[95] In April 1974, for example, the UK government borrowed $2.5 billion from a banking syndicate that included the Chase Manhattan Bank.

[96] Kerr, *A History of the Eurobond Market*; Kynaston, *The City of London*, vol. IV, p. 326.

[97] *Federal Reserve Bulletin*, April 1968, p. 353.

IET of 1963, which raised the cost of borrowing in New York. In 1968 new issues of securities in foreign markets by US corporations soared to $2.1 billion from $450 million the previous year.[98] The US money supply was insulated from the Eurodollar deposit market by reserve requirements imposed in 1969, and at the same time offshore borrowing of US dollars by foreign companies was encouraged in order to ease the pressure on domestic capital markets. British companies also turned to the Eurodollar market to raise funds to invest overseas in the wake of the Labour government's intensification of controls on outward FDI. The total borrowing on the Eurodollar market by companies from UK banks was estimated to have risen from £6 million in 1965 to £63 million in 1968 – an outcome that was viewed with satisfaction by the Chancellor of the Exchequer.[99] International financial markets were thus recognised by governments as forming part of the solution to the global payments imbalance.

Conclusions

In the immediate aftermath of World War Two, the fortunes of the City of London and the international role of the pound sterling were believed to be closely intertwined. The rhetoric used to persuade the public of the need for exchange controls to protect the exchange rate certainly invoked the importance of the international role of sterling as part of the United Kingdom's rightful leadership in international economic (and, by tacit extension, political) affairs. As British economic performance faltered, however, a debate arose over whether the benefits to the City that derived from the strength of the pound were worth the perceived damage that pro-sterling policies posed to other areas of the economy during the 1950s and 1960s. This chapter has emphasised that this discourse and the debate that it prompted took place in an environment of intense capital controls, not only in the United Kingdom but globally as well, and that these controls had little to do with supporting the interests of the City of London. Indeed, many of the exchange controls imposed by the Treasury to support the sterling exchange rate were vigorously opposed by the City and by the Bank of England during the 1950s and 1960s. If sterling devalued, the City stood to lose from uncovered positions and the potential diversion of some traditional commercial business to other centres, but a greater risk was the longer-term viability of the international financial centre due to the skein of increasingly complex capital

98 *Federal Reserve Bulletin*, October 1969, pp. 774–5.
99 Symons, 'Exchange control 1959–1972'.

controls. Rather than a coincidence of interest between supporting the sterling exchange rate and supporting the City, therefore, the two often pulled in opposite directions, until the City escaped the tangle of controls by launching into the offshore market.

The shift from sterling to the US dollar in international commercial and financial transactions heralded the resurgence of the City of London rather than its demise. If sterling had remained the dominant currency, it is possible that British institutions might have retained their prominence rather than giving way to American ones, but this is by no means assured. Globalisation provoked supervisory and regulatory challenges, but also generated renewed overseas earnings potential. Figure 6.9 shows the rapid growth in banks' earnings from non-residents in the 1980s and again from the mid-1990s, and that foreign exchange business constituted a declining share of revenue.

Cain and Hopkins and Kynaston have argued, with hindsight, that the link between the interests of sterling and the interests of the City was fallacious.[100] The evidence presented in this chapter shows that this was recognised at the time, both in the Bank of England and in the Treasury. Cain and Hopkins, in common with Strange, argue that government and Treasury policy in the post-war period was aimed primarily at promoting

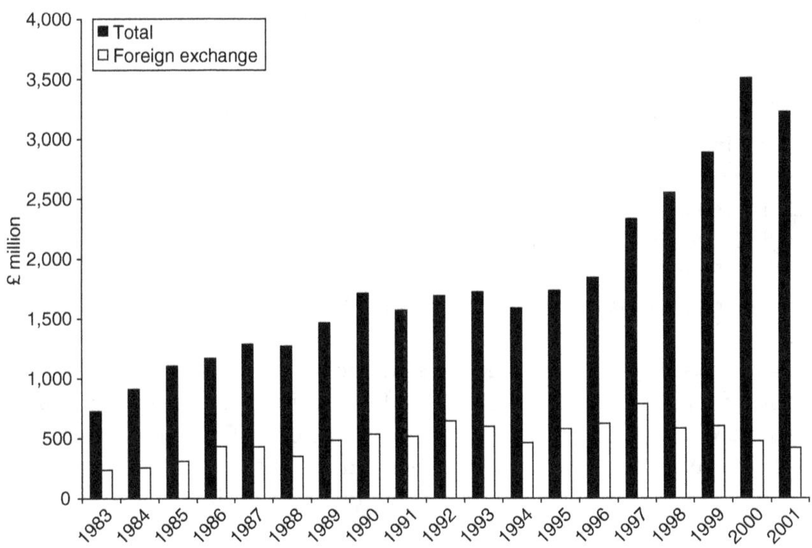

Figure 6.9 UK banks' service earnings from non-residents, 1983–2001

[100] Kynaston, *The City of London*, vol. IV, p. 4; Cain and Hopkins, *British Imperialism*, pp. 265–6.

the international use and status of sterling. Krozewski goes so far as to state that, 'in the late 1950s, Britain attempted to re-establish sterling as the dominant international currency'.[101] This chapter has argued, in contrast, that the governments of the 1950s and 1960s were not committed to promoting the interests of the City of London by supporting a strong sterling exchange rate or encouraging the international use of the pound. Ministers and Treasury officials were often hostile to the use of sterling in international trade, and even the Bank viewed the decline of the commercial use of sterling with equanimity by the 1960s, although it resisted new controls on the City's business. This was a natural outcome of Britain's declining share of world trade. On the other hand, resources and effort were devoted to maintaining the exchange rate, not for the City's glory but for a range of sound financial reasons, including the centrality of sterling to the international monetary system as a whole, fear of what would happen to the domestic economy in the event of a devaluation or float, and the attendant risks to the successive governments' domestic political fortunes.

Despite the handicaps besetting sterling, London was able to continue to exploit the historic advantages of scale and scope developed in the nineteenth century, in large part because of even tighter controls on capital inflows imposed in competing international financial centres such as New York and Frankfurt during the post-war decades. During the 1970s the increasingly global nature of international banking and financial markets, combined with innovations in communication, led to a dispersion of global finance, but London continued to punch well above Britain's weight in the international economy even without having an international currency. London continued to host more foreign banks than any other international financial centre throughout the half-century after 1945. In terms of banks from the top thirteen international financial centres, Choi, Park and Tschoegl have shown that London dropped from first rank in 1970s to third rank (behind New York and Tokyo) in 1980, but also that it had recovered first place again by 1990.[102] This shows the remarkable consistency in the attractions of the City of London for international banking despite repeated global financial crises and ongoing financial innovation. This performance also confirms the irrelevance of an international currency to the location of international banking once commercial finance had been overtaken by other business.

[101] Krozewski, *Money and the End of Empire*, p. 186.

[102] Choi, S. R., D. K. Park and A. Tschoegl, 'Banks and the world's major banking centers 2000', *Review of World Economics*, 139(3), 2003, pp. 550–68.

7 Multilateral negotiations: sterling and the reform of the international monetary system

A vital feature of the management of the retreat of sterling was the continuing effort to engage the rest of the world's economic leaders in resolving the problems that the reserve currency role of sterling appeared to pose for domestic economic policy. Indeed, as the 1960s progressed, waiting for a global solution to weaknesses in the international monetary system emerged as a cornerstone of British sterling strategy, allowing ministers to postpone unpalatable decisions about achieving this on their own. Certainly, there was a legitimate a priori case for viewing sterling's problems as part of the wider weaknesses in the Bretton Woods system as it functioned in the 1960s. Much ink and effort was spent on analysing the n–1 problem of using national currencies as reserve currencies in the context of the US dollar, famously identified by Robert Triffin. Increased demand for reserves that arose from growth in world trade could be met only if the issuing countries ran persistent balance of payments deficits. This was the diagnosis of part of the United States's economic problems in the 1960s, but it was not as easy to apply in the case of the United Kingdom, since official sterling balances did not increase overall, although the geographical distribution did shift – as we have seen. Nevertheless, sterling remained a primary reserve asset for a broad range of developing countries.

Figure 7.1 shows IMF estimates of the currency distribution of foreign exchange reserves, which reveal that sterling accounted for a remarkably stable 30 per cent of global foreign exchange reserves from 1964 to 1969 despite the devaluation of 1967 and the upheavals in the international monetary system during this period. After 1967 there was a diversification away from the US dollar and towards other currencies (primarily the Deutschmark), but sterling's share was stable despite the devaluation in November that year. This trend reflected waning confidence in the gold value of the dollar, on account of persistent US deficits and the accumulation of dollar liabilities in excess of US reserves. After continually battling with claims that the excess of foreign, official short-term liabilities

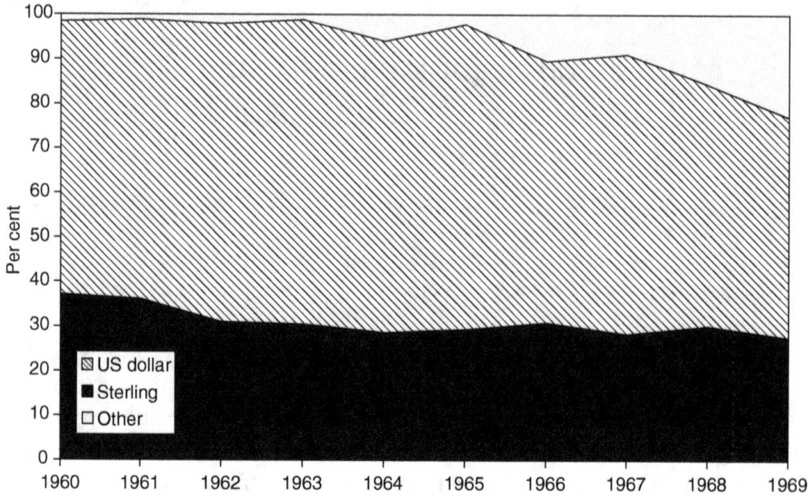

Figure 7.1 Denomination of global foreign exchange reserves, 1960–9

over assets was unsustainable, and with bouts of speculation against sterling when the house of cards seemed ready to fall, British governments took heart from what they viewed as similar problems emerging for the United States. With the Americans 'onside', a global solution to replace reserve currencies (and thereby relieve both the United States and the United Kingdom of their burdens) might be found.

This interpretation did not find consistent support outside Britain. In February 1965 Robert Marjolin remarked to Salle of the IMF that he 'recognized that the problem of sterling was something quite different from that of the dollar, and that it was very difficult to have a clear view of what the British government should do'.[1] Bussière states more firmly that, after devaluation in 1967, 'sterling and the British monetary authorities were not able to influence the system and its dynamic anymore' and that sterling was 'not taken into account by the French authorities as a crucial element of the debate'.[2] Because of the importance of France as a key protagonist in the multilateral negotiations, this effectively sidelined Britain. One of the key differences between the dollar and sterling was

[1] J.-P. Salle – note of interview with Marjolin on 27 February 1965, recorded 3 March 1965, IMFA, S370 'Liquidity, international'.

[2] Bussière, E., 'France, European monetary cooperation, and the international monetary system crisis, 1968–1973', in H. Haftendorn, G. H. Soutou, S. F. Szabo and S. F. Wells (eds.), *The Strategic Triangle: France, Germany, and the United States in the Shaping of the New Europe* (Baltimore: Johns Hopkins University Press, 2006), pp. 171–87.

that the total value of Britain's sterling liabilities to monetary authorities overseas was not growing as quickly as those of the United States. Instead, the UK situation was generally interpreted as a legacy of wartime and pre-war imperial relations that required a negotiated settlement between the United Kingdom and its creditors to resolve. The United States, on the other hand, was seen to be reaping the benefits of the evolution of the Bretton Woods system to a dollar standard by running persistent balance of payments deficits that spread inflation to surplus countries. At the same time, however, there were important similarities.

Throughout the 1960s and 1970s the governments of both countries vigorously resisted external pressure to adopt domestic economic policies that would reduce their balance of payments deficits. The European focus was clearly on the United States rather than the United Kingdom, but it should be remembered that the resolution of the sterling balances 'problem' was a central obstacle to Britain's accession to the EEC. In both cases, Europe claimed that the use of national currencies as reserve assets generated gains for the donors at the expense of increased risks for the international monetary system. The willingness of countries to accumulate sterling- and dollar-denominated assets increased the ability of the United Kingdom and the United States to sustain their balance of payments deficits. On the other hand, when the willingness to hold dollars or sterling was brought into question, the system became unstable, since a change in sentiment could threaten to bankrupt each country's core reserves.

The disappointing outcome of the prolonged multilateral negotiations in the G10 and the IMF to reform the international monetary system was the introduction of the special drawing right to supplement reserve currencies in 1967. The constraints on SDR operations and the lack of consensus make it a symbol of the failure of the leading countries of the world to agree either on a diagnosis of the problem or the solution.[3] Nevertheless, this disappointment was not a certainty at the outset, and a close study of the negotiations shows how British governments hoped to use them to resolve the burden of sterling's reserve currency status.

The negotiations over reform of the international monetary system were prolonged and at times ill-natured, because of the strategic and political context in which they took place. British applications to join the EEC were repeatedly rejected during this period, NATO was under threat after France withdrew from the organisation's integrated military command structure, the empty chair crisis damaged the effectiveness of the EEC, and British and American contributions to military

[3] James, *International Monetary Cooperation*, p. 172. Callaghan's biographer refers to the SDR as 'by general consent' Callaghan's 'greatest achievement' as Chancellor: Morgan, *Callaghan*, p. 284.

expenditure in West Germany were a source of ongoing disagreement that was 'inextricably linked', in Gavin's words, to international monetary problems.[4] Throughout the decade the Kennedy and Johnson administrations joined with British governments to urge an increasingly reluctant West Germany to offset the foreign exchange costs of the Anglo-American military presence in the country, culminating in the tripartite talks in 1966 and 1967.[5] The balance of payments weaknesses of the two strategic leaders of the free world were shown to threaten global security through these disputes. Meanwhile, the assassination of President Kennedy in November 1963 had left the US administration in disarray, prolonging internal US disagreements as changes in personnel ensued. In October 1964 the Conservative government in Britain was replaced by a new Labour government with its own agenda. As John Fforde remarked in 1963 (the governor of the Bank of England minuted his approval),

> We all know quite well that intruding deep into contemporary payments problems are the wider issues of foreign policy which are currently a source of dissension within the Western Alliance. We also know that these wider issues cannot be accommodated within our system of monetary logic. It is precisely this intrusion which now makes the international payments problem so defiant of systematic solution. For it is impossible to devise a monetary system, with rules and regulations, suited to 'normal' times, which can cope with 'structural' problems vitally affecting Western defence arrangements, the balance of power within the Alliance, and the political position of the USA in the whole world. But the payments problem has, of course, to be handled somehow or other; or else very unacceptable economic and monetary consequences must ensue.[6]

The complexity of the interlinked security and monetary issues of these crucial years reinforced Britain's belief that the interests of sterling and the dollar were tightly intertwined, and this created both synergies and tensions between the United States and the United Kingdom (which are dealt with in greater detail in chapter 5).

During the 1960s Britain's position in the international system changed, both economically and politically, in ways that profoundly affected the British attitude to sterling as an international currency. Consistent with realignment towards Europe and the dismantling of imperial obligations, during the 1960s British policy aimed to manage sterling's decline with the minimum of impact on the domestic economy. This could best be achieved not through unilateral action, which would invite retaliation and increase the domestic burden of adjustment, but by garnering the

4 Bussière, 'France, European monetary cooperation', p. 137.
5 For a thorough account of these negotiations see Gavin, *Gold, Dollars, and Power,* ch. 6.
6 Note by J. S. Fforde, 13 March 1963, BE OV53/22.

support of the international community, emphasising the importance of a stable pound to the stability of the international monetary system as a whole and linking the resolution of the burden of sterling to a general reassessment of the role of reserve currencies.

The G10 negotiations to reform the international monetary system

Underlying the efforts to reform the international monetary system was the growing tension in the Bretton Woods system, as capital flows became freer and national economies grew out of the exchange rates set in 1949. As exchange controls became less effective, the choice was between stable exchange rates and monetary independence. In the 1960s most bankers and almost all central banks and governments were still unwilling to accept floating exchange rates, with their echoes of 1930s economic nationalism. On the other hand, governments sought independence to achieve national goals of full employment and growth at an inflation rate of their choosing. For the United States (and, to a lesser extent, the United Kingdom), this was compounded by their pursuit of extraterritorial ambitions, such as the Vietnam War. Under Bretton Woods, only the United States, as the anchor of the system, could pursue an independent monetary policy, and other countries became increasingly dissatisfied with the sacrifices they were making in order to retain exchange rate stability. The United States could continue to borrow so long as creditors would accept US dollars. In this sense, the adherence to the fixed exchange rate system meant that surplus countries were funding American overseas expenditure and substantial long-term private capital outflows in the form of FDI.[7] If creditors stopped accepting dollars this would precipitate the devaluation of their existing assets. Instead, they exerted pressure on the United States to correct their balance of payments, and spent many hours devising ingenious proposals to replace the dollar with another international asset linked to gold.

The diagnosis of the flaws in the international monetary system was as controversial as the choice of remedy. The process of negotiating the successful introduction of the SDR has been described by Keith Horsefield, the official IMF historian, as an 'unremitting struggle', and he seemed grateful to leave the details of the complex negotiations to his successor, Margaret de Vries.[8] The second series of official history of the IMF traces

[7] Eichengreen, B., *From Benign Neglect to Malignant Preoccupation: US Balance of Payments Policy in the 1960s,* Working Paper no. 7630 (Cambridge, MA: NBER, 2000).

[8] Horsefield, *The International Monetary Fund, 1945–1965*, vol. I, pp. 586–7; de Vries, *The International Monetary Fund, 1966–1971*, vol. I, pp. 11–208.

in exhaustive detail the toing and froing between different plans. The positions of the protagonists were remarkably consistent, however.

The major focus of the debate in the 1960s was international liquidity, described by Galbraith to President Kennedy as 'a fashionable conversation piece of the economists' union'.[9] The debate ranged over two main areas. First, what did 'liquidity' mean – the absolute amount of international reserves or their distribution? Second, was there too little liquidity, as argued by the United States and the United Kingdom, or was there too much, as argued by France and other members of the EEC? In fact, the liquidity debate was really about adjustment, not reserves. Deficit countries sought more credit to prolong their adjustment, and so argued that there was inadequate liquidity in the system. On the other hand, the surplus countries, suffering from inflationary pressure, urged the deficit countries to adjust and asserted that there was adequate liquidity. At the Bretton Woods conference in 1944 the United States pushed through a system that put the onus of adjustment on debtors (the United Kingdom and Europe), and in the 1960s the United States and the United Kingdom sought to shift the burden back to creditors. This dispute over the diagnosis of the problem was a major reason why the technical discussions about liquidity in the 1960s failed to resolve anything. Even when the terms of the special drawing right were agreed, there was still no consensus on how it related to liquidity. The United States viewed the SDR as a new source of international reserves, while the Europeans insisted that a country had to be in balance of payments equilibrium before it could be issued.

The multilateral approach to reforming the international monetary system was launched by Per Jacobsson, the managing director of the IMF, in 1958, when he published a report asking how to increase international reserves to accommodate the expansion of the global economy. The short-term outcome was an increase in IMF quotas in 1959, but this was recognised as no more than an interim solution. A series of 'plumbing patches' followed through the early 1960s. In 1960 the major central banks agreed not to push the London gold market price up with their purchases. This informal pact was institutionalised in the Gold Pool in 1961. We have seen that the Fed and other leading central banks developed a system of bilateral currency swaps to provide short-term support for currencies under speculative or seasonal attack. In September 1961 the ten major industrial economies agreed to lend to the IMF, if this was required to deal with pressures that would destabilise the international

[9] Letter from John Kenneth Galbraith to President Kennedy, 28 August 1963, FRUS, 'Foreign economic policy', section 3.

monetary system, through a scheme known as the General Arrangements to Borrow.[10] After the scheme had been announced, in January 1962, these countries became known as the G10, and subsequently they took the lead away from the IMF in international monetary reform for the next few years. Outside these arrangements, academics and politicians soon began to turn their minds to imaginative ways to overcome imbalances and inequalities in the system. The many stages on which the issue was considered added to the complexity of the process, causing some confusion and repetition.

At the beginning of 1961 the British priority in Anglo-American discussions was to get agreement that there actually was a longer-term, systemic problem in the international monetary system, that the stability of both the dollar and sterling was important to the Western powers and that the role of the IMF should be expanded to ameliorate the present situation.[11] The American side tended to view the US deficit position as temporary and strongly resisted any proposals that might undermine the global role of (and confidence in) the dollar. For the Americans, the problem was the distribution of reserves rather than overall liquidity, and the distributional problem could be solved by the ad hoc system of bilateral currency swaps already developed by the Fed. From 1961 the Fed accumulated foreign currencies to buttress its diminishing gold reserves in defence of the dollar, but it continued to argue that the imbalance in the international monetary system could be overcome by short-term measures.[12] The US position was obscured by internal conflict within the administration, between the Treasury (led by Douglas Dillon and Robert Roosa), which favoured stopgap measures such as the swap scheme, and the Council of Economic Advisers (CEA – led by Robert Heller), which preferred more ambitious, long-term structural plans.[13] The US Treasury countered that any American proposal to overhaul the entire system was unlikely to attract the support of Europeans, while even suggesting major changes would undermine confidence in the dollar.

In the United Kingdom, a new Chancellor of the Exchequer, Reginald Maudling, took office in July 1962 as the momentum towards reform stalled, and there seemed to be an opportunity for a new initiative. At the IMF meeting in Washington on 19 September 1962 Maudling presented

[10] James, *International Monetary Cooperation.*, pp. 161–5.

[11] Paper by Frank Lee for UK representatives heading for Washington, 2 February 1961, TNA T236/6427.

[12] See, for example, the record of US–UK talks in London in January 1963; BE OV53/15.

[13] Memo for Kennedy by Carl Kaysen, deputy special assistant for national security affairs, 6 July 1962, FRUS 1961–63, vol. IX, 'Foreign economic policy', section 4.

his plan for mutual currency accounts (MCAs). The planning in London had leaked to the Americans, which Roosa described in August as 'trying to get something fancy to fulfil the "great expectations" set off by the change in command', and he predicted a run on sterling or the dollar if the plan was ill-conceived.[14] At this time, Roosa was trying to promote his own idea of swaps of national currencies, whereas the British were thinking of transferable IMF accounts as a way to increase liquidity and reduce reliance on reserve currencies and gold.[15] The idea of the MCA originated with L. P. Thompson-McCausland and F. J. Portsmore at the Bank of England and was then taken up in the Treasury. Despite early indications of American disapproval (and some internal criticism, from Alec Cairncross, for example) the Treasury pressed ahead, and the plan announced by Maudling in September provided for the IMF to create a separate pool to which countries in surplus would contribute currencies in return for claims on the account. These claims would form interest-bearing assets with a gold value guarantee that would be part of the donors' national foreign exchange reserves. The goal was to increase liquidity (deficit countries would be able to draw on the MCA more freely than on IMF quotas) while stemming the accumulation of US dollars and sterling held in overseas official reserves and slowing the conversion of excess holdings of reserve currencies into gold.[16] The plan reflected the British priority of finding a solution that made the resources of the IMF more easily accessible rather than creating new reserve assets outside the IMF, and it also promised to resolve the sterling balances problem, by allowing countries to exchange sterling for MCA credits. Underlying this latter priority was Maudling's view, expressed at the end of 1962, that sterling's reserve role needed to be ended. As he told the Cabinet in advance of his IMF speech in September, 'The long term problems for the UK arose from the gold exchange system and the use of sterling as a reserve currency.'[17]

From the outset Maudling's proposal did not meet with approval, either in Washington or in Europe, and it was therefore dead in its tracks. Jacobsson described it as 'half-baked'. Roosa published a rebuttal of the plan even before it was publicly announced, arguing that no institutional

[14] Note from Roosa to Robert W. Bean, US Treasury representative, US embassy in London, 21 August 1962, NARA RG56, records of undersecretary of state for monetary affairs, Box 111.

[15] Treasury Historical Memorandum no. 25, 1975, 'International liquidity: an account of the negotiations leading up to the creation of special drawing rights in the International Monetary Fund 1962–1968', TNA T267/35.

[16] Solomon, R., *The International Monetary System, 1945–81* (New York: Harper & Row, 1982), pp. 63–5.

[17] Treasury Historical Memorandum no. 25, 1975, TNA T267/35.

reform was needed as the US balance of payments deficit would soon be remedied.[18] The Americans objected particularly to the new assets having a gold guarantee, since this would bring them into competition with the dollar and might undermine confidence. Dillon was so suspicious of the Maudling proposals that he advised Kennedy not even to mention the possibility of reforming the international monetary system in his speech to the IMF board, for fear of appearing to be implicitly supporting Maudling's scheme. Dillon argued that 'our analysis of these proposals is that they are extremely dangerous to the US dollar. This view is shared by those continental European officials to whom the British have confided the general outlines of their scheme. In short it seems to us that the British proposals fit in very well with the constant long-term effort by the United Kingdom to undermine the dollar and force its eventual devaluation.'[19] As suggested by Dillon, the Europeans were no more enthusiastic than the Americans, as they worried that the scheme would lead them to be persistent creditors.[20]

In retrospect, the Treasury and the Bank of England agreed that the MCA scheme had not been a serious proposal but merely a way to draw the interested parties into tangible discussion after the momentum towards reform had been lost. As Thomson-McCausland optimistically explained to the governor of the Bank of England,

> The Chancellor's chief point in launching the MCA was that thought should be given to the longer-range problems of international liquidity. MCA was not put forward as the particular solution which he was pressing but as a contribution to the discussion he wanted to get going. So far as the Americans and ourselves are concerned MCA has served this purpose excellently. We have established very good relations and, starting from MCA, have gone on on both sides to consider more important and fundamental things.[21]

Over the following months, during bilateral discussions of the MCA scheme, British negotiators were able to get the American side to agree that there was *potentially* a need for a fundamental change in the international monetary system in the longer term, beyond the mere continuation of currency swap arrangements.[22] The British strategy of engaging

[18] Roosa's article was published in the *Business Review* of the Federal Reserve Bank of Philadelphia: Solomon, *The International Monetary System*, p. 64. For Jacobsson's response, see James, *International Monetary Cooperation*, p. 166.

[19] Memo from secretary of the Treasury Dillon to President Kennedy, 18 September 1962, NARA RG56, records of undersecretary of state for monetary affairs, Box 111, and FRUS, 1961–63, vol. IX, 'Foreign economic policy', section 5.

[20] Governor Carli of the Banca d'Italia showed some support. Treasury Historical Memorandum no. 25, 1975, TNA T267/35.

[21] Thompson-McCausland to governor, 28 January 1963, BE OV53/22.

[22] Final report of Anglo-American working party on MCA, 7 May 1963, BE OV53/18.

in close consultation with the United States thus seemed to have borne fruit in pushing the Americans towards longer-term planning.

At the end of the Anglo-American talks over the MCA scheme, the United States agreed to renew bilateral discussions with the United Kingdom in May 1963 about medium- and long-term solutions, and also to engage in four-party talks in June with the United Kingdom, West Germany and France – an outcome considered a victory by Maudling and the prime minister, Harold Macmillan.[23] Even Roosa later accepted that the MCA initiative had provided a 'valuable catalyst' for the process of longer-term planning.[24] Maudling hoped that this series of meetings would produce a firm set of proposals in time for the ministerial meeting of the G10 in September 1963, but in the end the Paris talks disappointingly merely set out a series of questions, and so the initiative fell back to the Anglo-American axis, where a secret Task Force on International Liquidity was set up. Meanwhile, Kennedy began to hint publicly that the United States would consider more fundamental reform when he gave a speech in Frankfurt in June 1963, and again a month later in a major speech on the balance of payments. Maudling hoped to take advantage of this mood to engage Dillon in a bilateral meeting but Dillon replied that he did not want the G10 to perceive of the United States and the United Kingdom as 'ganging up' and refused to meet.[25] The Anglo-American rapprochement was certainly not complete and Maudling seemed prone to overestimate the American enthusiasm to push forward reform.

The final report of the secret US/UK task force arising from the May meetings was completed in early September 1963, in time for the G10 meeting that month, but it was inconclusive.[26] The two sides agreed that there was no immediate shortage of liquidity but that one might emerge in the future. The best way to approach the longer-term problem was to improve the facilities of IMF by increasing quotas, making the gold tranche transferable and perhaps by arranging for the Fund to engage in long-term borrowing from creditor countries. Another priority, particularly for the Americans, was to ensure that new gold flowed into central banks rather than the market. At British urging the Task Force also suggested that ways to increase cooperation between the dollar and sterling should be studied, although this was never a priority to the Americans, and their enthusiasm for bilateral discussions waned as

[23] Note by Parsons for Cromer, 20 May 1963, BE OV53/18.

[24] Quoted in Solomon, *International Monetary System*, p. 65.

[25] Meeting in Chancellor's room with Bank of England and Treasury, 24 July 1963; Dillon to Chancellor, 9 August 1963, BE OV53/20.

[26] Final report of US/UK Task Force on International Liquidity, 6 September 1963, BE OV53/21.

their commitment to actually achieving reform of the international monetary system increased. The immediate Anglo-American goal at the G10 meetings was reduced from proposing fundamental reform to merely trying to get agreement for a substantial increase in IMF quotas.[27] In line with these plans, at the September G10 meeting ministers duly agreed to establish a working group of officials to report to ministers on possible improvements to international liquidity. The group, comprised of twenty deputies representing member countries, the IMF, the BIS and the OECD, and known as the Committee of Twenty, met monthly over the next nine months before submitting its report in June 1964.

The G10 deputies were unable to overcome the differing views on the diagnosis and the remedy, particularly with regard to the French, who abhorred reserve currencies and favoured a scheme based on gold, and the Americans, who sought to supplement rather than replace reserve currencies with a reserve asset that would approximate money rather than credit.[28] As Sir Denis Rickett advised Sir William Armstrong in April 1964,

> There is a clear-cut division between those who regard the subject of the enquiry as being what steps should be taken to increase international liquidity (the US, UK, Canada, Japan and Sweden) and those [the Six] who consider that the main problem is how to restrict international liquidity or at least prevent any further expansion of it for some time to come.[29]

These differences in interpretation also existed at central bank level, as Cromer reported from the central bank governors' meeting in Basle in January 1964:

> The Governors' dinner was largely taken up by a verbal sparring match between Holtrop [of the Nederlandsche Bank] on the attack and Hayes [representing the Fed] on the defence on the subject of the failure of the Americans to cure their balance of payments deficit, on the forbearance of the Europeans in holding so much in the way of key currencies in their reserves and some pretty general discussions and misgivings around the table on the activities of the G10.[30]

Meanwhile, the British sought to develop a joint Anglo-American position within the G10 through bilateral working parties, but little progress was made because of the lack of consensus within the US

[27] Sir Eric Roll (Washington) to Rickett, 21 September 1963, BE OV53/22.

[28] For an account of the meetings, see Solomon, *The International Monetary System*, pp. 65–9.

[29] Rickett to Armstrong, 9 March 1964, BE OV53/27.

[30] Governor Cromer's note on G10 central bank governors' dinner in Basle 12–13/1, 14 January 1964, BE OV53/25.

administration.[31] Even the IMF urged the G10 to slow down its proceedings, agreeing, on the one hand, that the real problem was the US deficit, but on the other hand, in support of the US position, that any talk of replacing reserve currencies threatened confidence. At the executive board meeting in January 1964 Schweitzer urged that '[t]he present adequacy of international liquidity is not, I think, a matter of concern ... We are dealing with a problem – to the extent that it is a problem – for the longer run ... The deadlines that we set ourselves to make sure that the work gets done may run the risk of creating expectations in broader circles of proposals for specific action by a particular date ... [W]e must be careful when we discuss revolutionary proposals lest we undermine the present monetary system and confidence in the reserve currencies.'[32]

In the spirit of this go-slow approach, the G10 deputies' report to ministers in June 1964 proposed two spin-off working groups: one to be undertaken by Working Party 3 of the OECD on correcting balance of payments disequilibria, and one chaired by Rinaldo Ossola on creation of reserve assets (the Ossola Group). Roosa and Dillon stressed that the Ossola Group could investigate new assets but was not to take a view on whether they were necessary. The deliberations were to be strictly on a contingent basis, 'just as in military sphere governments prepare for contingencies they hope will never materialize'.[33] Dillon reaffirmed that there should be no suggestion that any scheme would replace rather than buttress existing reserve assets. In recognition of the French desire for more coordination and discipline over deficit countries such as the United States, the G10 deputies' report also promoted the idea of 'multilateral surveillance', which was rather vaguely defined and in practice limited to the exchange of statistical information through the BIS, to allow transparency about the level and direction of bilateral short-term support operations. The British, in particular, as recipients of short-term credits, resisted any infringement of their national sovereignty that might result. [34] Multilateral surveillance remained a loose arrangement devolved to the BIS.

Even on increasing IMF quotas there was no agreement. The French and the West Germans remained vehemently opposed, although the Dutch and Italians supported a more modest increase while at the same

[31] See correspondence in early 1964 in BE OV53/25.

[32] Executive board minutes, statement by managing director, 10 January 1964, IMFA S370.

[33] Telegram from the US embassy in France to the Department of State, Paris, 16 June 1964, 7 p.m., FRUS 1964–68, 'International monetary and trade policy'.

[34] Ibid.

time wanting to increase their voting rights through larger selective increases.[35] Furthermore, the Six insisted that 25 per cent of any increase would have to be deposited in gold – a solution resisted by both the United States and the United Kingdom, which could not afford it. The United States wanted a 50 per cent increase and Maudling expected to be able to negotiate agreement from the Six for a 33.3 per cent increase, but in the end only a 25 per cent rise was achieved, and even this was delayed until February 1966.

The pursuit of reform through the G10 rather than the IMF reflected distrust among the French and some other members of the Six of the governance of the IMF, which they considered dominated by the United States and the United Kingdom.[36] This approach sidelined countries outside the G10 and prompted vigorous protests, from Australia and Egypt in particular. It was up to the IMF executive to protect its interests, and in July 1963 Frank Southard, deputy managing director of the IMF, wrote in strong terms to the incoming managing director, Pierre-Paul Schweitzer (who replaced Jacobsson after his death in May 1963):

> We are aware of the reasons that induce the Ten to consult among themselves at the senior official level on what they wish to do on these matters of major policy, but this should not be done in a way which would give the Fund only a subordinate role in this vital field. The Ten should not undermine the Fund, which they and others have created and developed as a working institution with world-wide membership, jurisdictional powers, huge resources, and public and parliamentary recognition … It would not be possible to avoid permanent damage to the Fund if the G10 were to evolve their proposals in isolation and were then to put them into force through the Fund without due regard to the sensitivities and legitimate interests of others.[37]

Despite his previous post as deputy governor of the Banque de France (an institution not sympathetic to the IMF), Schweitzer was convinced that the IMF should be the vehicle for any reform of international liquidity.[38] This was supported by the non-G10 members of the IMF as well as the United Kingdom and the United States. At the October 1963 IMF meetings, therefore, the board of governors agreed that they would begin their own study of international liquidity problems in parallel with the G10. The IMF staff drafted papers and proposals for the managing

[35] Rickett to Armstrong, telegram from Washington G10 deputies, 13 April 1964, BE OV53/27.

[36] Bordo, M. D., D. Simard and E. White, *France and the Bretton Woods International Monetary System: 1960–1968*, Working Paper no. 4642 (Cambridge, MA: NBER, 1994). This was also the view taken at the time by Strange, in *Sterling and the Six*, p. 54.

[37] Southard to Schweitzer, 26 July 1963.

[38] Selected remarks on the international monetary system and liquidity at the Fund and Bank, October 1963 annual meetings, filed 31 December 1963, BE OV53/24.

director, but any papers submitted to the G10 group had to be passed through the executive board first, which slowed the interaction between the two efforts. The process of determining firm, workable proposals was thus complicated even further.

Progress was slow as the Ossola Group began to meet in late 1964 to prepare its report to ministers in May 1965, although Robert Solomon, one of the American team, remembered the meetings as warm and friendly.[39] At the outset, the French and the Dutch were the most supportive of introducing a new reserve asset that would replace the dollar and sterling. The United States hoped to stall any long-term reforms in the expectation that the US deficit would contract, making the problem disappear. The United Kingdom, Canada, Sweden and Japan were willing to see a new reserve asset supplement, but not replace, reserve currencies.[40] The Americans' position by the end of 1964 was that the proposed 25 per cent increase in IMF quotas would meet the immediate need for international liquidity. They hoped to prolong the discussion of longer-term proposals but favoured a solution that operated through the IMF rather than the narrower G10 membership and insisted upon supplementing rather than replacing reserve currencies.[41] It was not until July 1965 that the Americans came around firmly to the need for a supplementary reserve asset administered through the IMF.[42] The Treasury Historical Memorandum on the negotiations (written in 1975) states that, when the G10 deputies were meeting, 'there was no thought in their [the UK Treasury's] minds that it would be advantageous if sterling could divest itself of its reserve role'.[43] In fact, we have seen that this was a prominent feature of Maudling's original approach, and the incoming Labour government would follow his lead.

The change in government in Britain from Conservative to Labour in October 1964 occasioned a reassessment of sterling as a reserve currency – particularly from Harold Wilson's controversial economic adviser, Thomas Balogh, who sought to segregate sterling balances held by other central banks by 'funding' them into longer-term debt, effectively ending sterling's role as a reserve currency. In the Treasury, too, Alec Cairncross, head of the government's economic service, recommended in October that the reserve role of sterling should be phased

[39] Solomon, *The International Monetary System*, p. 75.

[40] Thompson-McCausland on 'Ossola Group; UK aims', 19 October 1964, BE OV53/30.

[41] The US position was set out in time for Harold Wilson's first visit to the United States as prime minister in early December 1964; FRUS 1964–68, vol. VIII, briefing paper prepared by the Department of State and the Department of the Treasury, 4 December 1964.

[42] See correspondence in July–September 1965; BE OV53/33.

[43] Treasury Historical Memorandum no. 25, 1975, TNA T267/35.

out, albeit over ten to twenty years.[44] Some in the Bank of England agreed. In December Fforde argued strongly that, 'unless the UK manages to undergo profound economic changes within a very few years, it is apparent to me that "running a reserve currency" is positively bad for us', because it allowed the United Kingdom to borrow too much in the early stages of a deficit, thereby postponing corrective measures and then necessitating drastic measures later, while also precluding any change in the exchange rate. His view was that the IMF should issue an international paper currency with a gold value guarantee in exchange for existing sterling reserves; the United Kingdom could then disband the sterling area and eliminate discrimination in exchange control.[45] Fforde's *cri de coeur* provoked reconsideration within the Bank. Thompson-McCausland resurrected his original proposal for an International Settlement Account, which would allow future accruals of sterling and dollars in national reserves to be converted to International Reserve Units. Lord Cromer, governor of the Bank of England, advised caution, however, as 'it would be wrong and impracticable to aim at wholly replacing the reserve currencies with some new international unit', despite the ongoing negotiations to achieve this very outcome within the G10.[46]

The prospect of somehow painlessly shifting Britain's overseas liabilities from the reserves of many countries to a single more reliable holder and thereby ending sterling's reserve role remained compelling. At the end of 1964 Callaghan was attracted by Balogh's funding proposals to reduce the liquidity of these liabilities but recognised that any such scheme would require multilateral support, which might prove difficult to negotiate. Callaghan decided first to approach Douglas Dillon, US Treasury secretary, about the prospects for a funding scheme for the sterling balances, but he was rebuffed. Dillon's view was similar to that of Cromer: that it would be impossible to negotiate successfully with the Six at this point and so both sterling and the dollar had to remain as reserve currencies for the time being.[47] Given the disagreements within the G10, there seemed little prospect of a new initiative for sterling, although Balogh and Callaghan remained interested in a funding scheme and received some quiet encouragement from Otmar Emminger, a manager of the Deutsche Bundesbank, and Guillaume Guindey, of the French Ministry of Finance. Rumours that the G10 would 'consolidate' the sterling balances reached the IMF managing

[44] Ibid.
[45] Fforde to Thompson-McCausland, 2 December 1964, BE OV53/30.
[46] Thompson-McCausland note for the record, 28 December 1964, BE OV53/30.
[47] Hubback to S. Goldman, 21 December 1964, BE OV53/30.

director in June 1965, when Marcus Fleming reported that this had been discussed at the Ossola Group meeting.[48] Frederick Deming, who had by now replaced Roosa as US undersecretary of state for monetary affairs, discouraged Sir Denis Rickett from the idea, however, pointing out that the official sterling balances had not been a source of instability over the past year; Rickett agreed. More importantly, he stated that funding the sterling balances was not an issue for the G10 to consider.[49] In the end, the Treasury recognised the disadvantages of transforming the most stable part of overseas sterling liabilities from debts that might never have to be repaid into a fixed liability, but, clearly, it would not have got far in the G10 negotiations without US support. What these discussions show is that, in 1964, the Treasury was actively pursuing ways to divest sterling of its reserve role by transforming the sterling held by central monetary institutions from the liquid assets that define national reserves to illiquid assets that would no longer be used in this way.

Into the midst of the Ossola Group's deliberations, in February 1965 de Gaulle announced that he wanted a 50 per cent increase in the price of gold and a return to the gold standard – ideas that drew on the views of Jacques Reuff, one of the French president's chief economic advisers. Wilson as prime minister was advised by the Bank of England and by Balogh not to take this proposal too seriously, but merely to interpret de Gaulle's outburst as a signal that progress towards general reform was likely to be even slower than hitherto. For them, the main thrust of de Gaulle's speech was an attack on the US dollar and US FDI into Europe.[50] Giscard d'Estaing later reassured London that the criticism of reserve currencies was not directed at sterling, which the French considered mainly a payments currency rather than a reserve currency.[51] De Gaulle interpreted sterling as a natural reserve currency for the sterling area group of countries in the same way that the franc was useful for the franc area. His objection to reserve currencies was directed specifically at the way the international monetary system led to unwanted accumulations of US dollars by surplus countries in Europe and funded 'le défi Américain'. Three months later Guindey confided to the British representative in Paris that 'General de Gaulle did not

[48] Thompson-McCausland reports that Cromer had overtures from Guindey, Brunet and Emminger about funding the sterling balances; 17 June 1965, BE OV53/32. Memo to Schweitzer from J. Marcus Fleming, 14 June 1965, IMF Archive, C/UK/315 'Credit arrangements and maintenance of balances within reserve currency area 1965–1969'.

[49] Note for the record, Rickett speaks with Deming, 13 October 1965, BE OV53/33.

[50] Thomas Balogh to prime minister, 9 February 1965, BE OV53/31.

[51] Note by Patrick Reilly (UK embassy, Paris) to Charles Johnston (FO) re meeting with Valéry Giscard d'Estaing on 15 February 1965, BE OV53/31.

really understand the subject. M. Rueff had a prophet-like certainty of the rightness of his own views' and 'there was still complete confusion about the French Government's position on this issue'.[52] Nevertheless, these remarks rocked confidence in the US dollar price of gold, which was the foundation of the pegged exchange rate system, and increased pressure for reform.

The Ossola Group submitted its report on the advantages and disadvantages of various proposals to ministers in May 1965, but their remit (and ongoing disagreement) prevented them from advocating one solution over the others, so the process of reform was not taken much further forward. In April Wilson and Callaghan had tried to take leadership of the process by devising new proposals, but the Treasury was unable to come up with any workable schemes.[53] Nevertheless, Callaghan made plans to visit Paris and Washington in June to take advantage of any momentum from the Ossola Group report. This time, the Johnson administration was more receptive.

In order to break the deadlock within his administration, President Johnson convened a group, chaired by Deming, to determine a coherent American position and negotiating strategy. The remit of the Deming Group also referred specifically to the link between the fortunes of the pound and American strategic interests by considering 'what steps the United States could take to arrange for a relief of pressure on sterling, so as to give the UK the four- or five-year breathing space it needs to get its economy into shape, and thereby sharply reduce the danger of sterling devaluation or exchange controls or British military disengagement East of Suez or on the Rhine'.[54] In early July 1965 Johnson also appointed a high-level study group (the Dillon Committee) to firm up the US view and advise his new Treasury secretary, Henry Fowler, who had succeeded Dillon in April 1965. The group included Roosa and Dillon from the previous administration, Edward Bernstein (the former IMF director of research), Kermit Gordon (of the Brookings Institution), Andre Meyer (the director of Lazards in London), David Rockefeller (usually represented by Paul Volcker) and Charles Kindleberger (of the Massachusetts Institute of Technology). This allowed Dillon, who had been hostile and suspicious of British initiatives, to continue to have direct influence over US policy. The Dillon Committee convened in the mornings in closed session and then met in the afternoon with a group of top officials from the Treasury, the

[52] Patrick Reilly note of meeting with Guindey, 25 May 1965, BE OV53/31.

[53] Treasury Historical Memorandum no. 25, 1975, TNA T267/35.

[54] Letter from Johnson to Fowler, 16 June 1965, quoted in Solomon, *The International Monetary System*, p. 82.

Fed, the White House and the CEA, along with the US representative in the IMF.[55] Movement at last seemed possible, but Callaghan was increasingly sidelined as Johnson's views coalesced.

As the American administration became committed to achieving tangible reform, the bilateral relationship with Britain receded in importance. It was clear that France was the most important protagonist and that the key to a global solution was agreement with Europe, not with the United Kingdom. When Wilson was about to arrive in Washington in December 1965, Joseph Barr, acting secretary to the Treasury, complained to Johnson that 'the British tend to link the dollar with sterling in considering special arrangements for dealing with volatile balances. We believe, however, that European countries are not strongly interested in reducing existing dollar holdings and are not likely to consider such arrangements on terms which would be attractive to us.'[56] The president was advised to rebuff any suggestion by Wilson to renew bilateral discussions or to link the issue of sterling and the dollar, partly to avoid antagonising the Six with secret talks and partly because the American position was that the way forward was to create a new reserve asset and that existing holdings of reserves constituted a separate issue. Certainly, the United States did not want to develop a scheme that would see its dollar liabilities stop growing or, in an extreme case, be presented for payment in gold.

While sterling and the US dollar could not, therefore, be treated together, sterling was still an important feature of longer-term solutions to the international monetary system. The Dillon Committee's first meeting, in July 1965, coincided with a sterling crisis, and this led the committee to agree that 'long-range monetary problems might be difficult to solve if there were a recurrent threat of a sterling crisis. A long-term loan of reserves to the UK would be more helpful than a mere conversion of existing sterling balances into another form of reserve asset, because the former would augment total world liquidity and the latter would not.'[57] The recurring problems of sterling were therefore another important delaying factor in the resolution of the general weaknesses in the international monetary system, alongside persistent US balance of payments deficits.

[55] Advisory Committee on International Monetary Affairs (Dillon Committee) 450/80/23/4–7, NARA RG56.

[56] Brief delivered by Barr to the White House, 15 December 1965, NARA RG56, undersecretary for monetary affairs, Office of the Assistant Secretary of Intenational Affairs, Advisory Committee on International Monetary Arrangements and the Balance of Payments, Box 22.

[57] Meeting of Dillon Committee with officials, 16 July 1965, NARA RG56, Advisory Committee on International Monetary Affairs 450/80/23/4–7, Box 15.

As well as setting up internal committees, Johnson's desire for the United States to take the lead in breaking through the deadlock also prompted Fowler to call in July 1965 for a world monetary conference, but his naive initiative fell on unresponsive ground. The probability of a successful conclusion was too small to warrant the risk such a public meeting would pose to international confidence, and the British and Europeans were surprised that he went public on this without prior consultation. The West Germans and Italians did not agree that the situation was urgent enough to merit such a conference.[58] The French rejected the overture outright, because there was insufficient consensus either on the nature of the problem or on the direction of a solution for such a conference to be successful. They did recognise the signal of a freshening of the US position, though, and agreed that it might be picked up again by discussions among the G10.[59] The G10 duly met at the beginning of August, to discuss Fowler's proposal for a global conference, but they agreed merely to renew discussions among themselves.[60] Towards the end of that month Fowler began to tour the capitals of Europe (starting in Paris and finishing off in London, on 8 September) to promote another G10 initiative at official level to devise proposals to put to the IMF for a new reserve asset, perhaps by combining the G10 with the executive board of the IMF as a 'preparatory committee'.[61] Predictably, the executive board also agreed (against resistance from members of the Six) to renew its own work on devising a new asset.[62]

The British persisted in seeking bilateral agreement with the Americans on a scheme that would use the reform of the international monetary system to resolve the sterling balances by linking together the use of the US dollar and sterling as reserve currencies. The UK Treasury had come firmly to the view that existing holdings of reserve currencies would have to be part of the solution to prevent the increase in liquidity from the new assets being undone by conversion of existing reserve currency holdings to gold.[63] In December 1965 the British submitted a paper to the US Treasury that emphasised the vulnerability of reserve currencies to speculative conversion and the need to consider strengthening existing reserve currencies at the same time as introducing new reserve assets.

[58] Hubback to Rickett, 14 July 1965, BE OV53/32.

[59] Note of a meeting of Chancellor with Giscard, 22 July 1965, BE OV53/32.

[60] Note of G10 meeting, telegram from Paris to Foreign Office, 4 August 1965, BE OV53/32.

[61] Record of a meeting between Schweitzer, Southard, Fowler and Deming, 15 September 1965, IMFA S370, 'Liquidity, international'.

[62] Telegram from Washington to the Foreign Office, 6 November 1965, BE OV53/33.

[63] Memorandum from Rickett to Callaghan, 2 November 1965, Treasury Historical Memorandum no. 25, 1975, TNA T267/35.

The paper then outlined a plan that would allow countries to exchange their existing holdings of sterling and dollars for a new reserve unit issued by the IMF and linked to gold, in this way transferring the British/US liability from various creditors to the IMF.[64] Callaghan took up the idea with enthusiasm, but reintroducing the problems of sterling and the dollar was not welcomed by Europe or the United States.

The Americans rejected the whole premise of the plan. They did not see the problems of the dollar and sterling as identical, there was at present no apparent desire to convert existing holdings of either sterling or dollars and it would eliminate the dollar as a reserve currency, thus removing the ability of the United States to finance its short-term balance of payments deficits. Tactically, the British scheme was unlikely to appeal to the Europeans and would tend to reinforce their view that the whole enterprise of reform was designed to relieve the particular balance of payments problems of the United States and the United Kingdom. For this reason, the British were dissuaded from putting their paper before the G10. In a parallel paper, the US Treasury advised that it would support plans to deal with sterling balances so long as they did not involve the dollar or could possibly be used for the dollar. This excluded exchanging sterling balances for gold-guaranteed liabilities of the IMF, which could be used for the dollar.[65] On the other hand, the US Treasury could support a longer-term loan of reserves to the United Kingdom.

After the September 1965 sterling crisis, the era of Anglo-American bilateral cooperation appears to have given way to the imperative of gaining acceptance by Europe, and the Americans became unwilling to link the reform process to sterling's particular problems. At the G10 deputies' meeting on 14–15 December, the US representative stated clearly that the United States did not want a new reserve asset to replace existing assets. Parsons, representing the United Kingdom, disagreed, remarking that 'if we can find a reserve asset that serves both purposes, so much the better', but he received no support.[66]

As the G10 deputies returned to their study in 1966, the main points of disagreement were over how and in what circumstances a new reserve unit would be issued, and whether it would be restricted to the G10 or available to all members of the IMF. The Six were strongly against any

[64] UK paper, 'Use of a new reserve asset in relation to existing holdings of reserve currencies'; Draft position and comments on British paper, 10 December 1965, NARA RG56 World/1/550 Deming Group, Box 162.

[65] Treasury paper 10 December 1965, NARA RG56 World/1/550 Deming Group, Box 162.

[66] Record of G10 deputies meeting 14–15 December 1965, NARA RG56 World/1/550 Deming Group, Box 162.

move to use a new unit to support balance of payments deficits, and the French in particular wanted any solution to be limited to the G10. In January Hayes, president of the Federal Reserve Bank of New York, told the Dillon Committee that he preferred a scheme that would create reserve assets in the form of unconditional drawing rights on the IMF rather than a new reserve unit linked to gold. The other members of the committee disagreed and continued to hope for a new reserve unit representing a claim on a pool of currencies paid in by a group of advanced countries but not linked to gold. Realising that this might be difficult to negotiate, the agreed strategy that emerged was a dual approach comprising special drawing rights for all members of the IMF plus a new reserve unit for a narrower group of countries, such as the G10.[67]

At the start of 1966 the position of the British was that they hoped reform would provide additional reserves, protect against reductions of the existing stock of reserve currencies (i.e. diversification from sterling) and include countries outside the G10 (which tended to hold sterling). These goals required a new reserve asset, which could be unconditional drawing rights in the fund or some new instrument, and the UK side was ready to support both initiatives. Any new reserve unit should be transferable between central banks and the IMF, linked but not convertible to gold, bear low – if any – interest, be located within the IMF, include the G10 plus Switzerland and be managed, in association with the IMF, along the same lines as the GAB.[68] The British continued to hope that the new reserve unit could be used to protect sterling from a diversification of reserve holdings despite resistance from the United States and Europe.

At the G10 deputies' meeting at the end of January 1966 the members discussed slightly different US and UK proposals for reserve units, as well as a more broadly distributed scheme of drawing rights (termed 'special reserve drawing rights' in the US plan).[69] The reserve unit part of the proposals did not generate much support among the G10, particularly from the French, and the chairman, Emminger, tried to bring the different positions together in a compromise proposal, which sparked some disquiet in New York and Washington. In response, in March Hayes

[67] Minutes of the Dillon Committee, 21 and 25 January 1966, NARA RG56, Advisory Committee on International Monetary Affairs (Dillon) 450/80/23/4–7, Box 15. James states that the term 'drawing right' was adopted in July 1967 at the insistence of the French, but this term was clearly used much earlier and the title 'special drawing right' was agreed by the G10 deputies in April 1967: James, *International Monetary Cooperation*, p. 170.

[68] UK position paper for the G10, to be submitted in Paris on 31 January 1966, dated 20 January 1966; BE OV53/34.

[69] De Vries, *The International Monetary Fund, 1966–1971*, vol. I, p. 80.

reiterated his fears to Deming that a new reserve unit would threaten the US dollar, stating: 'As you know, I have been particularly concerned that a small coterie of ultraconservative European central bank officials would seize upon a reserve unit proposal as a means of imposing severely restrictive controls over the financing of such US deficits as will inevitably appear from time to time.'[70] Hayes argued that Emminger was siding too much with the French in his efforts to bridge the gap between Paris and Washington, and concluded: 'The main problem is with the French and the Dutch, and I would prefer to see the negotiations stretch out over a lengthy period rather than make costly compromises with their intransigence.'

While a reserve unit was blocked by the French, the IMF and central bankers were reported to be sympathetic to the drawing rights approach.[71] Another consequence of the January G10 deputies' meeting was that members of the IMF executive board became nervous about the pace of progress and called for the IMF staff to develop their own proposals to counter the trend towards limited solutions that excluded most members of the IMF.[72] Schweitzer persistently pushed for a scheme that was universal, and the IMF staff devised two plans for reserve creation through the Fund that would be open to all members (although all might not choose to participate): quasi-automatic drawing rights through the Fund, and the creation of a new affiliate of the IMF (an International Reserve Fund) that would issue gold-guaranteed reserve units transferable between countries as well as to and from the Fund.[73] The British believed it very unlikely that universal drawing rights would be accepted by the EEC countries, which would anticipate that they would be the major funders, and so Douglas Wass, the UK representative on the executive board, was advised to be non-committal.[74] The board discussed the plans in March and April but was unable to determine a preference between the two plans, and so they remained personal proposals of the managing director rather than being endorsed by the IMF board as a whole.

A solution through the IMF implying greater access to increased resources and wider membership suited the British, but their priority was

70 Minutes of the Dillon Committee, 25 January 1966 and 18 November 1966, NARA RG56, Advisory Committee on International Monetary Affairs (Dillon) 450/80/23/4–7, Box 15. Letter from A. Hayes, Federal Reserve Bank of New York, to Deming, 1 March 1966, NARA RG56 World/1/550, Deming Group papers, Box 161.

71 Minutes of the Dillon Committee, 21 March 1966, NARA RG56, Advisory Committee on International Monetary Affairs (Dillon) 450/80/23/4–7, Box 15.

72 De Vries, *The International Monetary Fund, 1966–1971*, vol. I, pp. 86–91.

73 Executive board minutes, 3 March and 15 April 1966, IMFA S370, 'Liquidity, international'.

74 Memos 10 and 15 March 1966, BE OV53/34.

to get a quick agreement so that it might be implemented by 1968, when another sterling crisis was anticipated.[75] The Europeans were not keen to rush any reforms until the US balance of payments deficit had been reversed, however. Callaghan's frustration with the process was clearly expressed in May 1966. He was asked by the Treasury and the Bank of England to 'call round his colleagues' in the G10 to try to get up some momentum, but he refused, since 'he suspected that progress was not going to turn out to be adequate, and he wished to keep his hands free to criticise the whole exercise. He added that he had no feeling of solidarity with or loyalty to the rest of the Group of Ten countries. If the Deputies report turned out to be as disappointing as he feared, it was his inclination to criticise it severely in public.'[76]

In mid-June 1966 Emminger, in his capacity as chair of the G10 group, suggested a joint meeting of IMF executive board and the G10 to try to break the stalemate. The British were not enthusiastic, and agreed with the United States that there were practical obstacles to bringing such a large group together and that this would merely prolong the talks.[77] Nevertheless, at the G10 ministerial meeting at The Hague in July, it was agreed to go forward with joint meetings, despite the opposition of the French. Making progress without France was viewed as a breakthrough, and when Fowler visited London just after the meeting Callaghan suggested that a strategy of trying to isolate the French from the rest of the Six should continue so that progress might ultimately be made with only the French opting out.[78] The format of joint meetings made it much more likely that Schweitzer's preference for a universal reserve asset rather than one purely for the G10 would be adopted. Conversely, this condition also undermined the prospects for a new reserve unit rather than an adjustment of drawing rights. By this time another sterling crisis loomed, and the Americans believed that this would further delay progress. The Dillon Committee, after discussing sterling's weakness and the need for the United Kingdom to contain inflationary pressure, concluded: 'The Committee was not optimistic that under these circumstances a satisfactory agreement could be reached on international monetary reform during the important second stage of negotiations.'[79] Sterling's weakness

[75] Whittome report of meeting at UK Treasury and Bank of England, 25 May 1966, IMFA S370 'Liquidity, international'.

[76] Meeting of Chancellor with Treasury and Bank of England representatives, 12 May 1966, BE OV53/34.

[77] Telegram from Washington to Foreign Office, executive board meeting, 18 July 1966, BE OV53/35.

[78] Treasury memo of a meeting with Fowler, 28 July 1966, BE OV53/35.

[79] Minute of Dillon Committee meeting, 11 June 1966, NARA RG56, Records of undersecretary of state for monetary affairs, Dillon Committee, Box 15.

and the multilateral efforts to support it were a genuine impediment to longer-term progress.

As we shall see in chapter 8, the July 1966 sterling crisis prompted a major multilateral support package, arranged through the BIS. International monetary reform was pushed further down the agenda of European states as they increased pressure on the United Kingdom and the United States to rectify their balance of payments positions. In August 1966 Harold Wilson briefly considered taking a fresh approach (at George Bolton's suggestion) by starting separate negotiations between the United States, Canada and Australia (which had been vociferous in rejecting the G10 forum, from which they were excluded).[80] This was quickly rejected as impractical politics given the hostility that would be raised in Europe, but it shows the pessimism at the time about the ongoing G10/IMF negotiations. The bleak outlook was confirmed when the September EEC finance ministers' meeting failed to deliver an agreed position on reform, with the French continuing to insist that the US balance of payments needed to be corrected before more ambitious contingency planning could be undertaken. In this unpromising environment, the first joint meeting of the deputies of the G10 and the executive board of the IMF did not take place until November 1966, followed by an equally inconclusive meeting in January 1967.

By the end of February, however, progress seemed more possible. Rickett reported that the Americans were committed to achieving an agreement by the September IMF meetings in Rio de Janeiro, which required a firm plan at least a few months in advance. The Six were split between the French and the Belgians, who wanted to delay any reforms and concentrate on forcing the United States to correct its deficit, and the Dutch and the Italians, who were ready to go ahead with proposals for a new reserve unit. The West Germans were undecided and trying to play the honest broker.[81] The overriding priority of the Europeans was to gain an internal consensus rather than allow this issue to divide them. Because Europe was the main obstacle to progress, West Germany was the key to delivering an agreement.

In early April 1967 Daane of the Fed reported from the G10 central bankers' meeting in Basle that the United States and the United Kingdom were the only supporters of early reform, the Europeans preferring to suspend negotiations for up to two years.[82] The IMF staff fleshed

[80] Letter from Bolton to prime minister, with minute asking for comments as Wilson planned to take this forward, 10 August 1966; BE OV53/35.

[81] Telegram from Rickett to Stevens (Washington), 20 February 1967, BE OV53/36.

[82] Minutes of Dillon Committee, 11 April 1967, NARA RG56, Advisory Committee on International Monetary Affairs (Dillon) 450/80/23/4–7, Box 15.

out their two approaches of a Reserve Unit Fund and a Special Reserve Facility based on drawing rights in the IMF, and they were discussed in separate meetings of the G10 deputies and the executive board at the end of March and early April.[83] Internally in Washington, Dillon viewed a drawing rights outcome as not bad in principle, but he feared that the IMF proposal was likely to be further watered down in negotiations and therefore concluded that the United States should continue to press for a reserve unit 'so as to draw the Europeans toward a reasonably meaningful drawing right approach. Perhaps an impasse and a negotiating crisis is necessary before eventual agreement can be reached. This is frequently necessary in international negotiations.' The minute of the Dillon Committee meeting on 11 April 1967 noted that '[o]ther members of the Committee supported this view'. Walter Heller, an adviser to Johnson and formerly chairman of his Council of Economic Advisers, was among those to meet with the West German economics minister, Karl Schiller, in April to 'hammer home' the American message that 'failure to agree on a plan could lead to a crisis atmosphere, the establishment of bilateral defences rather than a collective approach, and various restrictionist measures', that '1967 is the year of decision' and that any further postponement would be viewed as failure.[84] Heller was also to make it clear that the Americans would not accept a compromise that gave the EEC states a veto on issuing SDRs, that they insisted the new reserve asset be unconditional, non-repayable and therefore permanent, and that the asset should be segregated from other rights and obligations in the IMF and not linked to gold. In the meantime, the Dillon Committee began to consider an acceptable form of drawing right.

Schiller's brokerage within Europe came to fruition at the EEC finance ministers' meeting in Munich on 17 and 18 April, at which, unexpectedly, they agreed unanimously (albeit with varying degrees of enthusiasm) to support a drawing right scheme. Schiller stressed to the Americans that he had worked hard to bring the French to agree that any reform should be undertaken and that no further movement was going to be possible, but Fowler was disappointed that a new reserve unit was off the table, and the Dillon Committee recommended that pressure be put on the West Germans to shift the EEC towards a more substantial solution.[85]

[83] G10 deputies discuss the Fund's two illustrative plans 31 March and 1 April 1967, executive board has informal meetings on 20, 22 and 23 March and 10 April 1967; IMFA S730, 'Liquidity, international'.

[84] Briefing paper for Heller by F. Deming and G. Willis, 3 April 1967, NARA RG56, Deming Group, Box 161.

[85] Minutes of Dillon Committee, 28 June 1967, NARA RG56, Advisory Committee on International Monetary Affairs (Dillon) 450/80/23/4–7, Box 15.

The Economist in London also viewed the outcome as a sell-out by the West Germans.[86] Nevertheless, France's willingness to engage in reform planning did mark a vital breakthrough.

In May IMF staff quickly began to draft outline proposals for a drawing right scheme through the IMF to put to ministers for agreement in Rio in September.[87] The G10 deputies and the executive board considered the draft at their last joint meeting, in Paris in June that year. Just before the meeting Fowler and Bator tried to persuade Schiller that, if the Six isolated the French at the meeting, the French would eventually join them, asserting that this 'was a historical pattern'.[88] Schiller made it clear that,

> [w]hile Chancellor [Ludwig] Erhard [the head of the West German government until late 1966] had often been willing to agree with conflicting propositions made by the US and France, thus putting himself in an awkward and helpless position, Chancellor [Kurt] Kiesinger [Erhard's successor] wanted to 'win the French to a common solution with you [the United States].' The present German regime did in fact want to revive the Franco-German Treaty. He said that Germany was taking a 'loyal Triangular position'. There might be another way – to let the French go to Rio alone in splendid isolation but the German people would not understand this. They would view it as a failure of government policy.

Johann Schoellhorn, state secretary of the West German Ministry of Economics, who was also present, stressed that the mandate of the European Monetary Committee had been amended to call for the Six to act together on international monetary matters so that the Americans would not be able to break their solidarity. Fowler retorted that 'at the time of Bretton Woods, western Europe was a wrecked battle ground. US blood and treasure had helped revitalize it. Was it asking too much of western European nations now to play by the rules of the game?' Schiller reassured Fowler of the consistent German loyalty to the United States, and the meeting ended inconclusively.

As Albin Pfeifer of the IMF reported, while the joint ministerial meeting began well, 'the setbacks had come on the third day when the

[86] Cited in Cohen, S. D., *International Monetary Reform 1964–69: The Political Dimension* (New York: Praeger, 1970), p. 125.

[87] Outline of a reserve facility based on drawing rights in the Fund, 29 May 1967, put to executive board meeting on 5 June 1967. The outline was written by Polak, Fleming, Nicoletopoulos and Gold; IMFA S730, 'Liquidity, international'.

[88] Memo of conversation in Fowler's conference room, 19 June 1967, Fowler, Francis Bator (White House), Arthur Okun (CEA), assistant secretary Knowlton, with German finance minister, Karl Schiller, Ernst Jirka, first secretary, Baron Herbert van Stackelberg, Johann Schoellhorn, state secretary at the Ministry of Economics; NARA RG56 World/1/550, Deming Group, Box 157.

French – apparently largely for the record – started proposing amendments on practically every other paragraph and the US delegates felt obliged to propose counter-amendments. The text emerging from this third day was so riddled with proposed amendments that the [IMF] staff had no longer seen fit to issue it as a Fund paper.'[89] There was no agreement on the key controversial issues of voting or 'reconstitution' (i.e. the extent to which drawings would need to be repaid), which in turn determined how closely the rights resembled 'money' rather than 'credit'. By this time Fowler was prepared to protest publicly at the Rio meeting, and threaten a return to discrimination and bilateralism if agreement was not reached.[90]

The completion of an agreed outline plan became embroiled in the efforts of France, with support elsewhere in the EEC, to link the issue of special drawing rights to reforming the voting procedure and weightings in the IMF, effectively to give the Six a veto. The reconstitution issue – whether SDRs would have to be repaid – was potentially a breaking point for the United States, and Deming and Fowler hoped that if there was no agreement the exact details could be left to be negotiated later, so as to prevent a failure of the whole scheme at Rio. Fowler was also firm that he would not accept an EEC veto.[91] The US Treasury considered a contingency whereby the United States would table its own plan unilaterally at Rio, but this was discouraged by the chairman of the Fed. Instead, the Americans hoped to achieve a vague resolution at Rio that could be refined later. As predicted, the issue of reconstitution was left unresolved by the G10 ministerial meeting in London on 18–19 July 1967 and through two subsequent meetings of deputies, and a make or break ministerial meeting was scheduled for 25 August.

The combination of the ongoing impasse and the looming deadline led to high-level negotiations. On 15 and 16 August President Johnson met with Chancellor Kiesinger to impress upon him the importance of finalising an agreement in time for the Rio IMF meetings in September, in the hope that this would strengthen the West German resolve to bring France into line. On 22 August, three days before the key ministerial meeting in London, Schweitzer went to the US Treasury offices with his advisers to meet with Fowler and explain that the draft outline, as it stood, blurred the issue of whether the wider reform of the IMF being sought by the French would precede the adoption of SDRs, and therefore

89 Pfeifer to Whittome, 28 June 1967, IMFA S730, 'Liquidity, international'.

90 Meeting of Dillon Committee, 10 May 1967, NARA RG56, records of OASIA, records of the NAC, NAC minutes entry 350A, Box 3.

91 These views were expressed at a meeting of the US delegation to the G10 ministers' meeting, 10 July 1967; NARA RG56 Deming Group, Box 157.

that the United States should be able to accept the text. The final technical details were left to be decided after Rio in order that some agreement could be announced. Here again, it is clear that the weakness of sterling and the importance of the EEC as a bloc meant that Washington emphasised West Germany as the key broker rather than the United Kingdom as a strategic partner.

The ministerial meeting on 25 August in London, chaired by Callaghan, was heated and prolonged, starting at 10:00 a.m. and finishing shortly before midnight. In the end, Fowler had to concede the European veto, and some form of reconstitution or repayment once 70 per cent of a country's allocation of SDRs had been exceeded within five years. This was less than the French had demanded and arose from a compromise suggested by Emminger and Carli.[92] For the Americans, this meant that 70 per cent of the SDR allocation represented a first-line reserve asset, whereas the Six could continue to characterise the outcome as a signal that the rights were analogous to credit. In a personal meeting in Rio, Callaghan and Fowler congratulated each other on outflanking the French. Callaghan noted that, once it had become clear that Michel Debré, the French minister of economics and finance, would not break with the rest of the Six, it was just a matter of waiting until all the pieces fell in place. Fowler replied that the tactics had worked because the reconstitution plans were authorised by Germany and Italy, 'and therefore it was their job to lead the debate with the French' while Fowler and Callaghan sat back.[93] This self-congratulatory meeting occurred just as the market and de Gaulle were poised to deliver the final blow to confidence in the sterling exchange rate. Callaghan's *Le Monde* article on sterling and Europe appeared on 24 and 25 September 1967, in which he stated publicly that, 'so far as the role of sterling is concerned, we are ready for change'. Clearly, he was not anticipating the change that would ensue in November 1967 with the forced devaluation of sterling.

The actual implementation and interpretation of the new SDR remained a source of conflict. Between Rio and the ministerial meetings in London at the end of March 1968, to finalise the terms of the SDR, the international monetary situation had changed dramatically. Sterling had been forced to devalue by 14.3 per cent, Johnson had introduced a new and more stringent programme to correct the US balance of payments and Wilson had imposed serious cuts in the UK budget, including accelerating the shrinking of Britain's global military presence. Despite

[92] Cohen, *International Monetary Reform 1964–69*, p. 140. The executive board of the IMF approved the text on 9 September.

[93] Meeting of Fowler, Rostow, Senator Javits and Bator with Callaghan and Rickett at US embassy in Rio de Janeiro, 24 September 1967; NARA RG56, OASIA, Box 22.

these efforts, the Gold Pool had collapsed in mid-March, leading to a two-tiered gold system essentially delinking the US dollar from gold and changing the fundamental structure of the international monetary system. In these circumstances, it is not surprising that the fine details of the SDR scheme remained controversial.

When the G10 ministers met in Stockholm at the end of March 1968 to agree the final terms of the SDR and amendments to the articles of the IMF, Debré interrupted proceedings at the very beginning to call for a general discussion on the international monetary situation. He was delayed slightly by the chair, but then launched into a vigorous call for an immediate rise in the price of gold and the end of the reserve currency system.[94] He concluded: 'Special drawing rights, if launched after the restoration of equilibrium in the US balance of payments, would be a psychologically interesting experiment; if launched earlier they would be disastrous.' Fowler responded that it was clear that SDRs were not to be used to fund US balance of payment deficits. Debré 'expressed disappointment that his remarks had not found a greater echo' but did not receive any support for his calls for a change in the gold price, and discussion turned to the details of the allocation mechanism. Again Debré protested, this time that the amendments effectively turned the SDR from a credit instrument (which he had agreed to in London) into a form of money. The record of the meeting notes Debré remarking that 'now – in a blinding flash – it was revealed that the [SDRs] were a reserve currency'. After vigorous debate over two days, in which Roy Jenkins, the new Chancellor of the Exchequer, did not take a prominent role, Debré announced that he would abstain from the draft agreed by the others in a statement that was subsequently issued to the press. His position was based on the shift in the status of SDRs from a credit facility to an international money and the fact that fundamental problems with the position of national currencies and gold in the international monetary system had not been addressed – something the British had pressed for at the outset of the negotiations.

The British effort to link the SDR to the retirement of sterling as a reserve currency might be interpreted as a failure, but hope did continue to flicker. Emminger had informal talks at the IMF about using SDRs to fund the sterling balances after the sterling devaluation of November 1967, with a suggestion to issue sterling holders with SDRs that the IMF would lend back to the United Kingdom.[95] In January 1968 Jacques Polak, the Fund's economic counsellor, discussed such possibilities with

[94] F. L. Hall's record of the Stockholm meeting, held 29–30 March 1968; IMFA S371.
[95] Jacques Polak to managing director, IMF, 24 November 1967; IMFA, C/UK/315, 'Credit arrangements and maintenance of balances within reserve currency area 1965–1969'.

Thompson-McCausland, Kit McMahon, economic adviser to the Bank of England, and Sir Jeremy Morse, although he advised Schweitzer that 'probably the most difficult aspect of this whole operation is not the manner of its financing, but the relations between the UK and the present holders of sterling'.[96] During the negotiations for the Basle Agreements in the summer of 1968, however, the Europeans insisted that SDRs would not be used to fund sterling balances, and Morse gave a firm undertaking to Michel Debré to this effect.[97] Nevertheless, the IMF staff continued to seek ways to link sterling and SDRs.

Polak proposed an issue of SDRs to fund the sterling balances again in March 1970, when the Sterling Agreements were coming up for renewal. For him, this would eliminate sterling as a reserve currency, which was desirable because 'the IMF works less effectively if there is a multiplicity of reserve currencies with official holders having the option to move from one into the other'. L. A. Whittome provided a counterpoint for Polak's enthusiasm and advised Schweitzer to be very cautious, since Polak's plan was unlikely to appeal to the United Kingdom, the EEC was currently discussing the sterling balances and getting rid of sterling as a reserve currency might be detrimental to the United States, and possibly France.[98] A plan for a special allocation of SDRs to replace sterling reserves, to be amortised by the United Kingdom over twenty to thirty years, resurfaced in a recommendation from an IMF working party on sterling in April 1971, and, while it was agreed that the 'time was not ripe', it was communicated to the British and was embraced by the Chancellor in September 1972 – by which time sterling was floating and the IMF was not as keen to intervene.[99]

The multilateral discussions on the reform of the international monetary system appear in retrospect confused and inconclusive, partly because they lacked urgency or political will from the Americans until 1965, and then because they became embedded in disputes within the EEC in the following years. In the early 1960s the Americans refused to recognise that that there was a long-term problem, partly on a doctrinal

[96] Polak to managing director IMF, 29 January 1968; IMFA, C/UK/315, 'Credit arrangements and maintenance of balances within reserve currency area 1965–1969'.

[97] Minute of a meeting on 14 June 1968 at Treasury with Jenkins, Morse (BE), Deming, Willis (US Treasury) and Griffen and Solomon (Fed); NARA RG56, 'Briefing books', Box 22.

[98] Polak to Schweitzer, 31 March 1970, and Whittome to Schweitzer, 1 April 1970; C/UK/315, 'Credit arrangements and maintenance of balances within reserve currency area 1970–July 1971'.

[99] Clark, P. B., and J. J. Polak, 'International liquidity and the role of the SDR in the international monetary system', *IMF Staff Papers*, 51(1), 2004, pp. 49–71, discuss other suggestions for the use of the SDR.

basis and partly because of the dangers to the dollar if there were plans to replace it as an international currency. In addition to internal American dissension, globally there was no consensus on the nature of the problem, and therefore no agreement as to solutions. Instead of building consensus, the negotiations in the G10 and in the IMF entrenched divisions between continental Europe, the British and the Americans, although the British fought hard to persuade the American administration to enter into a bilateral alliance. Although the discussion was mainly in the context of the international role of the US dollar, the British side aimed to devise a supplement for reserve currencies generally that would apply to sterling as well as the dollar.

The final compromise solution, in the form of the SDR, did not replace the use of national currencies as reserve assets, nor did it resolve the fundamental problem of the expansion of global dollar reserves backed by a shrinking ratio of gold, nor did it redistribute the burden of adjustment. Instead, solutions to the sterling and dollar problems were found outside the discussions for reforming the international monetary system. As Fowler acknowledged privately, the SDR did not provide a solution to the balance of payments problems of the United Kingdom or the United States: 'These problems must be met through strengthening of the adjustment process, for which countries experiencing prolonged surpluses as well as deficits must share responsibility. SDRs will, however, assist the US in protecting its gold reserves and in building up its reserves in a steady and orderly way when our balance of payments position is corrected. The plan will also strengthen the Fund and help keep that institution at the centre of the IMS.'[100] Indeed, just as the SDR was being finalised, the American administration began to plan for unilaterally breaking the link between the US dollar and gold as the Gold Pool crumbled.

Conclusions: the failure of multilateral negotiations in the 1960s

By the early 1960s many in the government and the Bank of England, including Chancellors of the Exchequer Maudling and his successor Callaghan, were seeking ways to end sterling's reserve role that would minimise the cost to the domestic economy without disrupting the international monetary system. Assertions that sterling's reserve role could

[100] Meeting of National Advisory Committee on International Monetary Affairs, 18 April 1968, NARA RG56, records of OASIA, records of the NAC, NAC minutes entry 350A, Box 3.

not be abruptly and unilaterally ended should not be interpreted as a desire to retain it for its own sake or to promote the prestige of Britain. In the 1960s the priority of the British was to stave off what they foresaw as a damaging reduction in international reserves in the future, and in this context retiring sterling as a reserve currency without replacing it with some other reserve asset would merely add to contractionary pressure in the international economy. Sterling had to remain a reserve currency in the interim until a multilateral solution for new reserve assets could be found. The Treasury's hopes that the new reserve asset would replace sterling as well as create new liquidity were not shared in the United States or Europe, but the Treasury's strategy makes it clear that sterling's reserve role was interpreted as a burden to be borne in the interests of the international monetary system rather than as a symbol of status.

The ten years of discussion and negotiation to reform the architecture of the international monetary system in the 1960s were a failure. They did not succeed in reforming the IMF, or preserving the fixed exchange rate system or preventing the ultimate crisis of confidence in the US dollar. The SDR was the flawed product of this failure. It was based on the idea that there would be too little liquidity, which in turn assumed that the US deficit would be corrected and even reversed – a very remote prospect by 1967. If SDRs were activated while there was an imbalance in the international payments system, it would imply that this imbalance needed to be supported by access to less conditional credit for deficit countries – something the French, in particular, found repugnant.[101] This failure of consensus delayed the activation of the SDR to the end of the 1960s, by which time the problem was a dollar glut and worldwide inflation, not a shortage of liquidity. Meanwhile, the retirement of sterling as a reserve asset was sought outside the IMF through the BIS.

[101] For an example of the French view, see note by F. Everson, UK embassy Paris, of a discussion with Duguen (French Ministry of the Economy and Finance), 8 February 1968.

8 The Sterling Agreements of 1968

Chapter 7 has established that successive British governments in the 1960s used multilateral frameworks to try to relieve the pressure that the reserve role of sterling posed. By identifying sterling as an issue of concern to the stability of the international monetary system as a whole, they sought to spread the burden of retreat. They met resistance from both the United States and Europe in the G10 context, but this did not imply an abandonment of this strategy. Although it failed in the G10 and the IMF, the United Kingdom was successful in engaging the Bank for International Settlements in sharing the risks inherent in reducing the reserve role of sterling, and this laid the prerequisite for bilateral negotiations with holders of sterling in the summer of 1968 that transformed the nature of official sterling reserves. The BIS provided a forum for negotiations among central bankers separate from the political wrangling of governments that so hampered the G10 negotiations.

The outcome was two sets of agreements. Under the Basle Agreement the G10 central banks agreed to provide a safety net line of credit of $2 billion on which the Bank of England could draw to offset declines in its central reserves due to the diversification of overseas-held sterling reserves. As a quid pro quo, they insisted that the United Kingdom negotiate bilateral Sterling Agreements with thirty-four countries to keep a minimum proportion of their reserves in sterling over the term of the Basle Agreement. In return, the United Kingdom offered holders a guarantee of the US dollar value of 90 per cent of each of these countries' official sterling reserves so long as the minimum sterling proportions were met. Countries could break the agreement and diversify, but they would lose the US dollar exchange guarantee. The goal of the two sets of arrangements was to manage the process of diversification away from sterling as a reserve currency. The Sterling Agreements were most important, since they reduced the exchange risk of holding sterling and thus reduced the incentive for countries to abandon sterling for speculative purposes. If overseas sterling reserves nevertheless fell due to an overall decline in these countries' reserves then the G10 central banks would provide credit to the Bank of England to support the liquidation of these liabilities. The arrangements thus transformed the nature of sterling as a reserve asset from a voluntary portfolio choice into a formal contractual commitment. During the late 1960s and early 1970s, however, the problem was not a decline in sterling assets held overseas but how to contain an increase in these UK liabilities. A further complication was the devaluation of the US dollar against gold and sterling in 1971, which undermined the value of the guarantee. The implications of this development are dealt with in this chapter.

The origins of the Basle Agreement

The arrangement of systems of multilateral support for the international monetary system was developed during the exchange crises of 1960 and 1961, when pressure on sterling led to concerted efforts by European central banks to support existing exchange rates. In March and June 1961 the United Kingdom garnered bilateral support totalling $904 million from European and US central banks in what became known as Basle Arrangements. As Toniolo relates, the Bank of England and the US Fed were enthusiastic about the ability of the combined forces of central banks to forestall short-term speculative pressure and sought to extend or formalise the arrangements. Creditors in Europe were less enthusiastic about extending the system, and the initiative was instead formalised through the BIS. Credits would remain bilateral but the BIS would inform each creditor of the details of the total operation, in what was termed 'bilateral concerté'.[1]

In March 1963, September 1964 and November 1964 Britain negotiated a series of lines of credit under the bilateral concerté scheme to cover short-term speculative attacks on sterling.[2] After the first operation, George Ball, the undersecretary of state for economic and agricultural affairs in the US State Department, was keen on a support arrangement for the dollar similar to that arranged for sterling, but he hoped to achieve an agreement among governments rather than through central banks. He couched his proposal to the president in terms of a 'reverse Marshall Plan' for the United States. Ball's view was to arrange $2 billion from the IMF and $2 billion from European governments. The

[1] Toniolo, *Central Bank Cooperation at the Bank for International Settlements*, pp. 381–5.

[2] M. J. Thornton (BE) to Conolly, 22 September 1964, BISA GILB9 7.18(23). The details of the deal as reported to the BIS were three-month deposits with the Bank of England by the central banks of West Germany ($150 million), France ($100 million), Switzerland ($100 million), Belgium ($25 million) and the Netherlands ($25 million), to a total of $400 million. Italy agreed to conclude a pound/lire mutual swap facility for $50 million for three months.

US Treasury thought this was a non-starter politically, as public opinion in Europe would not support it. Instead, the president introduced export incentives and the Interest Equalization Tax.[3]

Toniolo interprets the March 1963 operation as a test of the new arrangements, which appeared successful, since the entire line of credit – amounting to $250 million – was repaid within three months.[4] Pressure on sterling in September 1964 was more substantial, as the balance of payments deteriorated sharply on the eve of the general election. The BIS was disappointed not to have been included as a participant in the September package rather than just a reporter, particularly as it had offered to arrange a $250 million sterling swap for the Bank of England, which had been turned down in February 1964.[5] Roy Bridge, head of foreign exchange at the Bank of England, explained that the United Kingdom wanted currencies and not gold, and so had negotiated directly with the countries concerned, keeping the possibility of BIS support in reserve for the future. D. H. MacDonald, a manager at the BIS, expressed his view that '[i]t was not much fun always being a bridesmaid and never the bride' and said that the BIS would have been prepared to give a $450 million line of credit for three months if it had been asked. This exchange suggests that the Bank of England had access to ample short-term resources to shore up sterling in the early 1960s. It is also evident that the BIS played a proactive role in these arrangements and was jealous of its leadership in this new initiative.

In the last week of September 1964 the Bank of England negotiated total support of $1 billion, of which $500 million was from the United States and $50 million from Canada. Table 8.1 shows the breakdown of the European contributions, most of which had been drawn by the end of October during the crisis after the new Labour government took power. All the credit was repaid on 2 and 3 December 1964, by drawing on the IMF stand-by arrangement just after the conclusion of a further bilateral concerté on 25 November – shown in table 8.2.[6] This new facility, arranged after a 'frantic round of telephone calls' by Cromer, governor of the Bank of England, amounted to $3 billion, of which only $275

[3] George Ball memo for the president on negotiations at political level for supplementary financing of balance of payments deficit, 16 April 1963, NARA RG69-A-407, Box 105. Treasury paper on political negotiation of an overall financial arrangement, 5 April 1963, NARA RG69-A-407, Box 105.

[4] Toniolo, *Central Bank Cooperation at the Bank for International Settlements*, p. 385.

[5] D. H. MacDonald conversation in Basle with Bridge, 11 October 1964, BISA Registry Files – Bank of England Policy File 2/2, vols. 3 and 4 (1 April 1949–31 August 1968).

[6] Conversations with Preston and MacDonald, 27 November 1964. The BIS credit line was a $250 million stand-by in gold for three months to be implemented by three-month swaps. BISA Registry Files – Bank of England Policy File 2/2, vols. 3 and 4 (1 April 1949–31 August 1968).

Table 8.1 *European contributions to the bilateral concerté for the Bank of England (US$ million), September 1964*

	Total arranged	Drawn in September 1964	Drawn in October 1964	Drawn in November 1964	Total drawn
Belgium	25	25			25
France	100	30	50	20	100
West Germany	150	50	75	25	150
Italy	50		40	10	50
Netherlands	25	10	10	5	25
Switzerland	100	30	50	20	100
Total	450	145	225	80	450

Source: GILB9 7.18(23), BIS Historical Archive.

Table 8.2 *Bilateral concerté for the Bank of England (US$ million), November 1964*

	Amount arranged
Austria	50
Belgium	75
France	200
West Germany	500
Italy	200
Netherlands	75
Sweden	100
Switzerland	80
United States	1,000
BIS	250
Total	2,530

Notes: All deposits of US dollars, except swaps for national currency for France, West Germany and Switzerland. Other support from Canada and Japan brought the total to $3 billion.
Source: GILB9 7.18(23), BIS Historical Archive.

million had been drawn by the end of the year.[7] A further line of credit was concluded among European central banks in September 1965, in

[7] BISA FER9. Quotation from Toniolo, *Central Bank Cooperation at the Bank for International Settlements*, p. 391.

response to heavy pressure on sterling in the exchange markets, to which the BIS contributed $50 million on three-month stand-by in the form of a gold/sterling swap.[8] The situation was quickly reversed, and the markets steadied by October 1965. These arrangements show that the United Kingdom was juggling short-term credits to support sterling, drawing on the credits to intervene in the exchange market and also publicising the packages to stem speculation. By moving between multilateral support from Europe, the United States and IMF facilities, the Bank of England managed to keep the speculators at bay.

While the short-term facilities were successful in supporting sterling through a series of confidence crises, they did not amount to a long-term solution, which is what Britain's creditors increasingly preferred.[9] In mid-September 1965 Cromer rejected proposals made at a BIS meeting of central bankers to 'fund' sterling reserves into a longer-term and more predictable debt, effectively curtailing their liquidity and ending the reserve role. He explained that variations in overseas sterling area central banks' holdings did not contribute to the United Kingdom's balance of payments problems. Instead, it was private sterling balances that caused the difficulties. He therefore diagnosed the problem as related to sterling's trading role rather than its reserve role. More fundamentally, the United Kingdom's creditors in the sterling area would not accept the shifting of their existing liquid sterling exchange reserves into less remunerative and less liquid long-term assets.[10]

Although 'funding' was out, the Bank of England hoped that support might be found through the BIS network to cover potential diversification of the sterling area reserves. Rather than preventing the liquidation of sterling assets, the proposals sought to protect the UK reserves from the impact of future sales of sterling based on the model of short-term support already agreed under the bilateral concerté. In this way, the international community would ease the impact of the decline of sterling as a reserve currency on the United Kingdom, though this was not explicitly declared. It must be remembered that these central bankers were simultaneously involved in devising longer-term plans to replace reserve currencies in negotiations between the G10 and the IMF.

In London, the Bank's viewpoint was put more frankly by John Fforde in October 1965: 'Often in the past we have felt that whatever

[8] Memo by H. H. Mandel (manager BIS), 13 September 1965, BISA Registry Files – Bank of England Policy File 2/2, vols. 3 and 4 (1 April 1949–31 August 1968).

[9] For discussions during this period, see Toniolo, *Central Bank Cooperation at the Bank for International Settlements,* pp. 391–4.

[10] Cromer to Ferras (and copied to other central banks), 16 September 1965, BISA LAR2 F01 7.18(14).

the pros and cons of maintaining the status quo there was in practice no means of altering it. There are signs that we need no longer take that view, because the viability of the sterling system is now of more pressing importance to the stability of the entire international monetary structure than before.'[11] The alternative of a substantial devaluation of sterling had been ruled out not only by the British Labour government but also by most European countries and the United States, in the interests of the stability of the international monetary system.[12] To avoid devaluation, the United Kingdom needed a multilateral defence against speculative pressure that might force devaluation before longer-term domestic measures could correct the underlying balance of payments problems. On this basis, Fforde made a case to the UK Treasury that the Bank should take the BIS up on its offer to help coordinate European support for cyclical variations in sterling balances that adversely affected the British reserves. The choice was between an arrangement through the G10 or one through the BIS. The latter was favoured, since it would avoid intergovernmental wrangling and because '[i]t would be wise ... to see to it that any new arrangements for sterling ... are of a kind which foster a closer association between the UK and the Continent' in the context of European integration.

The case for a fresh multilateral approach to the sterling balances problem was set out at the BIS by Maurice Parsons, deputy governor of the Bank of England, in November 1965. He argued that, until 1964, speculation against sterling could be easily dealt with through short-term support but that UK deficits had become much larger and the available short-term credit had been fully exploited. The situation, therefore, called for a new and less ad hoc solution with a longer-term commitment. Parsons concluded, according to a handwritten note of the meeting by Michael Dealtry of the BIS, that the problem could be summarised as 'How can we give assurance to world at large that we're not in as exposed a position as we appear to be?'[13] This emphasises that the target of multilateral support was to counter speculative pressure due to a lack of market confidence in the exchange rate rather than to resolve the underlying weaknesses in the balance of payments. Parsons also carefully avoided explicitly asking for support for a permanent reduction of the sterling monetary reserves. In reality, however, if credit from the bilateral

[11] Solutions to the problem of the sterling balances, Fforde to Armstrong (Treasury), 19 October 1965, BE OV44/151.

[12] Toniolo, *Central Bank Cooperation at the Bank for International Settlements*, p. 393.

[13] Dealtry's handwritten record of the meeting of experts at the BIS to discuss sterling on 23 November 1965; emphasis in the original. BISA DEA13 7.18(12), 'Sterling balances 1965–1966'.

concerté were used to offset declines in sterling reserves, this would shift UK liabilities from the sterling area to the G10 central banks.

The opinions of other central bankers were split, mainly over the possibility of identifying those movements in reserves due to the United Kingdom's own balance of payments and those that were beyond Britain's control. More generally, the Belgian representative, Cecil de Strycker, a director of the Banque Nationale de Belgique, felt that the BIS should restrict itself to describing the problem rather than prescribing solutions. Otmar Emminger of Germany, Rinaldo Ossola of Italy and G. A. Kessler, a director of the Nederlandsche Bank, all supported more positive action, and in the end Milton Gilbert, the BIS economic adviser, was instructed to prepare a paper for the governors setting out the various pressures on sterling and to propose solutions.[14] The target of support was to be those drains that were likely to be reversible or cyclical rather than trying to counteract a long-term contraction of the sterling reserves. When Gilbert had visited the Bank of England to gather background earlier in November 1965 he had been warned that 'facilities usable only against movements in overseas sterling area balances would be unlikely to inspire sufficient confidence either in the holders of those balances or in the holders of non-sterling area private balances'.[15] The support could not, therefore, be directed exclusively at the sterling area monetary reserves. While offering credit was likely to be acceptable to most G10 central bankers only if the position was reversible (i.e. related to fluctuations in sterling reserves), the United Kingdom clearly viewed this as an opportunity to spread the risks of a more permanent diversification out of sterling. It is hard to conceive of the circumstances in which a diversification would be reversed.

The original BIS plan was for a line of credit of $1 billion, to which the BIS would contribute $75 million.[16] The European/BIS share of the credit was $600 million and the United States agreed to roll over its existing $400 million to make the $1 billion total.[17] The aim was to provide a facility large enough to 'convince those who hold their monetary reserves in sterling that the value of their assets could not be affected by events outside the control of the UK authorities'.[18] By 26 December the

[14] BIS paper 'Le problème des avoires en sterling', 13 December 1965; BISA DEA13 7.18(12), 'Sterling balances 1965–1966'.

[15] 15 November 1965, report of a visit by Milton Gilbert (of the BIS) on 12 November 1965 by Fforde; BE OV44/152.

[16] 'Balances sterling confidential', 22 December 1965, BISA DEA13.

[17] The final breakdown was slightly different, as shown below: United States, $310 million, and France, $90 million.

[18] Paper by Gilbert entitled 'The problem of the sterling balances', 13 December 1965; BE OV44/152.

proposed amount was down to $700 million, of which the BIS would contribute $70 million.[19] Credit would be available in the form of three-month renewable swaps that would cover twelve months in total.

The Bank of England was very disappointed that the arrangement was for only twelve months in the first instance and discussed various ways to refinance outstanding swaps after twelve months, either through the BIS or the IMF.[20] After much discussion the governors agreed that the United Kingdom should approach the IMF for a stand-by arrangement to refinance any outstanding swaps.[21] On 3 March 1966 Parsons met with Pierre-Paul Schweitzer, the managing director of the IMF, who agreed in principle to a refinancing stand-by arrangement of about $500 million. He noted, however, that this would require drawing on the GAB, which might be controversial, since it required government support rather than merely agreement by central bankers.[22] The French ultimately came up with a scheme to avoid this, by getting the British to agree not to draw on the IMF during the period of the BIS support, so that these facilities would be available at the end of the twelve months for refinancing. Cromer noted that 'this proposal would have the advantage of avoiding the publicity inherent in the UK applying for a standby and would also defer the question of further activation of the GAB. The fact that all this is very vague I think suits our present attitude of mind.'[23] The effect was, essentially, for the British government to earmark $600 million of IMF drawing rights to refinance the Basle funding. The twelve-month scheme was thus extended to twenty-four months.

At the meeting of experts in February 1966 it was agreed that there needed to be some contribution from the United Kingdom itself to finance the impact of 15 to 20 per cent of any reduction in the sterling balances, 'because the introduction of self-help by the Bank of England would make the whole arrangement presentationally more acceptable'.[24] This was not enough for some of the governors, such as Hubert Ansiaux of Belgium. The United Kingdom hoped to resist any element of 'self-help' above 15 per cent and responded with a plan to identify the amount

[19] English draft of paper, 26 January 1966, BISA Dealtry Papers DEA13 7.18(12).

[20] See discussion in Treasury and Bank of England, January–February 1966, BEOV44/153.

[21] Note of the meeting on 12–14 February 1966 of the BIS governors by M. H. Parsons; BE OV44/153.

[22] Meeting of Sir Maurice Parsons with the managing director of the IMF, 3 March 1966, BE OV44/154.

[23] Letter from Cromer to Armstrong (Treasury) regarding the discussions in Basle, 19 April 1966, BE OV44/154.

[24] Record of meeting of experts on sterling balances, 11 February 1966, BISA DEA 13.

of changes in the sterling balances that had a direct impact on reserves, based on a complex formula.[25] This assumed that 100 per cent of the movements in non-sterling area balances were reflected in falls in the value of British reserves but that only 66 per cent of reductions in sterling area balances cost the reserves, since about one-third might be used to buy British or other sterling area goods and services. Since the BIS had estimated that sterling balances overall were likely to fall by $1,250 to 1,500 million, the Bank of England expected the resulting burden on reserves over the next three to five years to be $900 to 1,100 million, neatly justifying the requested support of $1 billion.[26] After much wrangling, the final solution was that the United Kingdom was allowed to draw on the credit up to an amount of 50 per cent of its estimate of the drop in reserves attributable to a decline in the sterling balances. By this time it is clear that the arrangements were anticipating a permanent decline in sterling reserves.

Throughout these negotiations Jean-Paul Salle of the IMF attended meetings at the BIS as an observer, since the proposal included an IMF stand-by arrangement to the United Kingdom to cover part of the credits offered by the European central banks. Pierre-Paul Schweitzer, director of the IMF, did not want the IMF involved in the technicalities of the agreement, however.[27] In the end, as was explained above, a stand-by arrangement was not explicitly included in the agreement. Schweitzer insisted that any stand-by offered to the United Kingdom would have to be on the usual terms, which would require a firm letter of intent committing the British government to constrain fiscal spending and domestic lending.[28] The IMF was proving itself much less amenable to the British predicament than the BIS members.

The final outcome was the June 1966 'Group Arrangement', under which several European central banks agreed to offer up to $600 million in swap credits for nine months to support sterling in the event of a net reduction in overseas holdings of sterling below a base level of £4,300 million due to factors other than the United Kingdom's own balance of payments problems (the total at the time was £4,500 milion). The cut-off point was further divided into £3,080 million for OSA balances and £1,220 million for NSA balances.[29] A separate agreement with France

[25] Draft of paper by Hubback summing up the discussions with the BIS, 22 March 1966, BE OV44/154.

[26] Note from B. E. Parsons to Ferras enclosing a copy of letter to central bank experts, 18 March 1966, BISA DEA 13.

[27] Schweitzer to Salle, 31 March 1966, IMFA C/UK/315, 'Credit arrangements and maintenance of balances within reserve currency area 1965–1969'.

[28] Ibid.

[29] Telegram from Bridge to MacDonald (BIS), 3 May 1966, BISA LAR2 F01 7.18(14).

provided a further $90 million in swap facilities (unrelated to movements in sterling balances) and the US Fed agreed to hold up to $310 million in 'guaranteed sterling', bringing total support to the round number of $1 billion, equivalent to 8.3 per cent of outstanding sterling balances.[30] The arrangement was presented as a way of protecting against speculative movements that might disrupt the international monetary system by forcing a sterling devaluation, but, clearly, the assumption underlying the scheme was to ease the impact of a reduction in sterling reserves through diversification. It remained in place (despite the subsequent devaluation and the 1968 Basle Agreement) until it was finally liquidated on 29 January 1971.

The Treasury was not as enthusiastic about the Group Arrangement as the Bank was, particularly since it constrained the Treasury from drawing on the IMF. When the details were finalised at the end of May 1966 Sir William Armstrong of the Treasury wrote to Cromer:

> In giving his agreement to the new arrangements the Chancellor was moved less by enthusiasm for their quality and prospective benefits to us than by a consideration of the risks, particularly in confidence in sterling, that might be run in rejecting them. In particular, the comparatively modest scale of the facilities, their rigid link with movements in the sterling balances and the complex formulae by which recourse to them is to be calculated are all comparatively unsatisfactory features. However, even with these limitations, they do constitute a reinforcement for sterling, and there is no disposition here to underestimate the importance of being able to announce a replacement of the 10th September facilities.[31]

At the last minute the Bank of England had feared that the Treasury would reject the proposals once a link to an IMF stand-by arrangement to refinance them was dropped. In Fforde's view, 'In present circumstances, but particularly in the context of any future approach by the UK to the EEC, this could only be interpreted as an almost incomprehensible gesture of despairing defiance.'[32] Armstrong's remarks suggest that the Chancellor was persuaded on these grounds.

Nevertheless, the 1966 Group Arrangement did not inspire longer-term confidence in future collective support. Three days after the Arrangement was announced, on 13 June 1966, the Chancellor, James Callaghan, wrote to Cromer:

[30] Salle to Schweitzer, 18 April 1966. At the meeting in April the French expert explained that Banque de France would have less difficulty participating if it was not linked with the level of sterling balances, 'as the French Govt was opposed to any support of a reserve currency as such'.

[31] Letter from Armstrong to Cromer, 26 May 1966, BE OV44/155.

[32] Note by Fforde to Parsons, 2 May 1966, BE OV44/155.

In my opinion it would be unwise in the extreme to rely on the self-interest of others in their desire to maintain parity of sterling for a sufficiency of support in a future crisis. Since November 1963 other countries, including the United States, have given much thought as to how they would react if sterling were to be devalued and have, in my judgment, overcome the fears they then had. They would of course deplore such an eventuality which, after all the assistance they have given, they would feel was due to the inadequate financial and economic policies of HMG.[33]

Callaghan seemed to view the Arrangement as a last chance for British governments to get their house in order, without which the prospect of devaluation was becoming increasingly inevitable.

Despite its limitations, the 1966 Group Arrangement quickly became the foundation of British official hopes that the rest of the world would share the burden of ending sterling's reserve role. The Bank of England's Sterling Area Working Party of 1966 recommended in November that 'all possibilities be explored of extending the scope of any renewed Arrangement to include an element of longer-term credit'.[34] The working party feared that the confidence effects of the Arrangement would be undermined if it became public that it was of fixed duration. Other than exhortation to correct Britain's chronic balance of payments problems, and plans to use diplomacy to try to put a 'brake' on the process of diversification, this was the only positive recommendation of the report. Gradually, it became Callaghan's view that 'building on Basle' represented the most promising way to achieve medium- or longer-term reduction in the sterling balances.

As was the case for other schemes, the first Group Arrangement was not used as much as anticipated, partly because of its presentational impact on confidence and partly because, despite the informal undertaking, the United Kingdom negotiated a further IMF stand-by arrangement during the annual sterling crisis in September 1966.[35] In the first six months the BIS offered $400 million of sterling/dollar swaps but the Bank of England withdrew only $75 million, all of which was provided by the BIS, so that no individual country was called upon to contribute.[36] In January 1967 the United Kingdom began to test the waters over a renewal of the Group Arrangement, and got the impression from

33 Letter sent to the Chancellor by Cromer, 15 June 1966, BE OV44/124.

34 Working Party on the Future of the Sterling Area, 2 November 1966, final report, BE OV44/115. This was a Treasury/Bank of England working party. The members were Rootham, Heasman, Fenton, Haslam, de Loynes, McMahon, D. W. C. Allen and Hallows. It was to review events and prospects for the sterling area since the last report in 1956.

35 Toniolo, *Central Bank Cooperation at the Bank for International Settlements*, pp. 395–7.

36 Note of meeting of experts, 9 January 1967, BISA DEA 13.

the BIS that this was likely to be possible with little or no change in the terms.[37] In March 1967 the renewal was agreed, with little discussion, partly since it had been so little used. This was soon to change.

Up to the end of August 1967 only the BIS's $75 million had actually been drawn, but on 15 September 1967 (two months before devaluation) a further $150 million was drawn, necessitating a call on participating countries.[38] At the same time it was agreed that the United Kingdom could draw an amount up to 80 per cent of the cost to reserves, rather than the 50 per cent agreed earlier.[39] A further $100 million in October, in advance of the devaluation, and $525 million in November, in the wake of the devaluation, brought total drawings to the maximum. In February 1968 the governors of the BIS agreed to another renewal of the Group Arrangement, with the proviso that 'the Bank of England should, during the coming months, make new proposals aimed at replacing, if necessary, the existing facility by a more permanent arrangement'.[40] From March 1968 the entire facility was drawn, as was the full $90 million from France. The French contribution was completely repaid at the end of November 1968 but repayments to other countries did not begin until 16 September 1969, after which the United Kingdom repaid $75 million per month. The debt was retired with a final payment of $150 million on 29 January 1971. All countries participated and were repaid in equal proportions.[41]

Meanwhile, in October 1967 the BIS arranged multilateral support for a total line of credit of $250 million from European central banks and the Fed to repay the IMF stand-by arrangement drawn in December 1964, which was due on 1 December 1967. The BIS acted as principal and then negotiated bilaterally with other central banks to raise the funds needed, keeping the details of the participation of these

[37] Note on talks between personnel at the bank and various members of BIS concerning the renewal of the June agreement, 11 January 1967, BE OV44/156.

[38] Deposits with the BIS were as follows (all at 4⅞ per cent): West Germany, $42 million; Austria, $9 million; Belgium, $12 million; Canada, $17 million; Italy, $27 million; Japan, $11 million; Sweden, $6 million. Mandel minute, 13 September 1967, BISA File 2/2j2, 'Bank of England – sterling balances – group arrangement – policy'.

[39] Telegram 15 September 1967, from BIS to all central banks, BISA File 2/2j2, 'Bank of England – sterling balances – group arrangement – policy'.

[40] Minute of meeting of board of directors, 12 February 1967, BISA File 2/2j2, 'Bank of England – sterling balances – group arrangement – policy'. See also 13 February 1968, extract from Morse's memo to the governors concerning the Basle governors' meeting on 11 February 1968; BE OV44/159.

[41] The final schedule for the $525 million from countries was West Germany, $145 million; Italy, $95 million; Belgium, $42.5 million; the Netherlands, $42.5 million; Canada, $60 million; Switzerland, $50 million; Japan, $40 million; Sweden, $20 million; and Austria, $30 million. BISA File 2/2j2, 'Bank of England – sterling balances – group arrangement – policy'.

banks confidential.[42] The whole arrangement took a month to conclude, was finalised on 20 November 1967 (after devaluation) and began to be repaid in June 1968. This partly involved the British Treasury selling notes denominated in European currencies to the BIS.[43]

The second Group Arrangement, 1968

After the renewal of the 1967 Group Arrangement, the Bank of England began to devise plans for a medium-term support fund to offset the future diversification of sterling reserves.[44] This planning was interrupted by the devaluation, but finally, with the Chancellor's consent, the governor of the Bank of England, Sir Leslie O'Brien, proposed such a plan to his counterparts at their regular meeting in Basle in the second week of March 1968. Events soon overran this effort at forward planning, however. On 15 March the Gold Pool collapsed under speculative pressure, throwing the international monetary system into disarray and increasing speculative pressure against sterling. The London gold market was closed while central bank governors convened at an emergency meeting in Washington to determine the way forward. The outcome was a pledge among central banks not to deal in gold below the official price of US$35 per ounce, while the private market was allowed to fluctuate. In effect, the two-tiered gold market meant that the convertibility of the US dollar was suspended. At the meeting in Washington on 16–17 March, O'Brien tried to use the crisis environment to press for direct long-term support for sterling against possible diversification. On 16 March he asked for a package of $5 billion in credit through the BIS, but he was turned down. Roberto Carli of the Bank of Italy suggested a system of US dollar swaps, and others suggested various formulae for blocking parts of the sterling balances, but the governor resisted these proposals.[45] Instead, the central banks the following day offered pledges of $1.175 billion, mostly from the United States, as shown in table 8.3.

At this point existing unused facilities amounted to $1,436 million from bilateral and previous Basle facilities, plus $1,400 million in the IMF

[42] The United Kingdom had wanted $300 million, but since the actual repayment was only $251 million the European banks rejected this amount. The EEC contribution was $167 million in the end. BISA File 6/63, 'Refinancing arrangement for the UK – policy'.

[43] The BIS offered this plan at the IMF meeting in Rio and it was taken up in October 1967 and concluded on 13 November 1967. 16 October 1967, D. H. MacDonald conversation with Bridge, BISA.

[44] Bank of England, 'The future of the sterling balances', March 1968, TNA T318/191.

[45] Sir William Armstrong telegram to Chancellor of Exchequer from Washington, 16 March 1968, BE OV53/38. See also Hamilton, 'Beyond the sterling devaluation'.

Table 8.3 *New support for sterling arranged on 17 March 1968*

	US$ million
United States	700*
West Germany	150
Italy	75
Belgium	50
Netherlands	50
Switzerland	50
BIS	100
Total	1,175

Note: * $500 million of this was an increase in the Federal Reserve Board swap facility from $1,500 million to $2,000 million.
Source: Note for the record by R. J. Wiles, 19 March 1968, TNA T318/191.

stand-by arrangement, taking the total support available to sterling to a headline total of just over $4 billion.[46]

After the March crisis had receded, the governor returned to the negotiation of a medium-term facility to 'fund' the diversification of sterling reserves in the longer term. At the beginning of April the BIS devised a plan that involved $2 billion of credit that would be financed from deposits by sterling area countries with the BIS and by the BIS borrowing on the Eurodollar market, but this was soon abandoned as being technically too complex, and involving the BIS in excessively large commitments.[47] Nevertheless, this shows the enthusiasm within the BIS for it to be involved, and that the BIS viewed this as a key area in which it could be influential.

On 12 May 1968 the Bank of England submitted another plan for a medium-term facility of $2 billion to cover the diversification of sterling reserves, which was expected to be at the least £150 million per year and at the most £700 million per year over the next three years, but the response was unenthusiastic.[48] The feeling in Europe was that a further call on BIS central banks would have to be combined with some greater undertaking on the part of the sterling area. The Swedish and

[46] Note for the record by R. J. Wiles, 19 March 1968, TNA T318/191. See also telegram Armstrong to Chancellor of the Exchequer, 17 March 1968, BE OV53/38. CD2
[47] The MacDonald scheme, 10 April 1968, BE OV44/160.
[48] Reported at a meeting of Parsons and Maude of IMF with Deming at US Treasury, 4 June 1968, BE OV53/39.

Swiss representatives at the meeting of experts at the BIS to discuss the matter at the end of May suggested offering an exchange guarantee for the sterling balances so as to inhibit diversification.[49] This meeting was held the day that Hong Kong finally agreed to accept a scheme, which was a de facto exchange guarantee for half their sterling balances.[50] Hong Kong had been offered the Hong Kong dollar (not US dollar) guarantee of the value of half its reserves on the understanding that it was a special case, as a colony with very large sterling balances, holding 99 per cent of its reserves in sterling and having not followed the November sterling devaluation. The Hong Kong government had won the guarantee by threatening that large amounts of private sterling balances would be dumped by Hong Kong banks on the market unless some form of exchange rate guarantee was offered.

The Bank of England and the Treasury had been firmly against exchange guarantees for sterling throughout the 1960s. Not only would a guarantee be expensive if it were used, but it would undermine confidence in all unguaranteed sterling and so generate an unsustainable drain on the British reserves. The United States would also protest, since the move would lead to calls for exchange guarantees for official US dollar balances.[51] Major holders of sterling, including Malaysia and Australia, had asked for exchange guarantees prior to the 1967 devaluation, but they had been refused. Once raised by the Europeans as a necessary offset to multilateral support, however, and after the principle of no guarantees had been breached in negotiation with Hong Kong, opinion began to change. On 24 May 1968 O'Brien told Sir Douglas Allen at the Treasury that, while his public view at the moment on guarantees was that 'we are not prepared to entertain such a possibility', he wanted 'to be in a position, when our discussions are resumed in Basle on the 9th June, to be able to indicate to my colleagues that the provision of guarantees might be possible. This would undoubtedly be useful in my negotiations with them.'[52] Parsons in New York reported on 28 May that Emile van Lennep had also suggested that, if the sterling area countries accepted limits on the use of their sterling balances, 'they would be entitled to demand a guarantee for their sterling'.[53] Thus,

[49] 27–28 May 1968, unofficial summary of discussion at the experts meeting at the BIS, BISA STE1 F02. Also reported by C.W. Mynors, 29 May 1968, BE OV44/162.

[50] Telegram from Trench to Secretary of State for the colonies, 28 May 1968, TNA T312/1936. The Hong Kong deal had been leaking in the press since the UK government offered the deal at the beginning of May. Schenk, 'The empire strikes back'.

[51] Record of a meeting in Sir Douglas Allen's room between the Treasury and Bank of England representatives, 4 June 1968, BE OV44/162.

[52] O'Brien to Allen, 24 May 1968, BE OV44/162.

[53] Letter from Maurice Parsons to the governor, sent from the Sheraton, New York, concerning a talk with van Lennep, 28 May 1968, BE OV44/162.

while the Swedish and Swiss suggestion at the experts' meeting did not provoke explicit support from other representatives, opinion in London was already moving towards exchange guarantees as a counterpart of the Basle Agreements.

At the experts' meeting at the end of May, opinion strongly supported sterling area deposits of foreign exchange that could be used to finance the facility rather than drawing on European and American credit. These discussions reveal that Europe's patience with the continued calls to support sterling had worn thin and more inclusive solutions were being sought. Not only was the United Kingdom expected to share more of the burden, but the sterling area would also need to contribute to resolving sterling's reserve role on a multilateral basis. European central bankers were also mindful of the requirement to sell their continued support to their governments. At the 9 June governors' meeting in Basle, for example, Edwin Stopper of the Swiss National Bank observed that 'parliamentary sanction would be required', and he was doubtful whether the federal government would wish to place legislation before parliament unless 'it was sellable. The UK's willingness to offer guarantees was a great improvement. Diversification had to be reduced to a minimum, at least until the UK's own reserves could enable the balances to be repaid.'[54]

O'Brien's request to inject a guarantee into the Basle negotiations found support in the Treasury from W. S. Ryrie, a senior official there, who advised the Chancellor to agree, and the Bank of England began negotiations on this basis in early June.[55] After the Bank of England Sterling Area Working Party had confirmed in mid-June 1968 that an exchange guarantee would have to be offered to the sterling area in order to get European support for a BIS scheme, a scheme to offer a guarantee for 80 per cent of official sterling reserves in exchange for limits on diversification was quickly put to the Chancellor, Roy Jenkins, on 19 June, and it was then discussed in Amsterdam the next day with Jelle Zijlstra, managing director of the BIS, who welcomed the plan.[56] This substantially changed the nature of the 'funding' arrangement and really left the amount of support promised by BIS partners as a nominal confidence booster.

The addition of guarantees was not at first enough to persuade Britain's European partners. At the governors' meeting in July, Ansiaux

[54] Meeting in Basle of the governors, 9 June 1968, BE OV44/163.

[55] Paper by Ryrie for the Chancellor, 5 June 1968, BE OV44/163.

[56] Final report by the sterling area Working Party on Sterling Balances, 14 June 1968, BE OV44/117. Minute of meeting in Netherlands Bank, Amsterdam, on 20 June 1968 with BIS president Jelle Zijlstra, Ferras and MacDonald with Morse and Raw of BE; BISA STE1 F02.

of the Banque Nationale de Belgique, who claimed to speak on behalf of all EEC members, complained about the share of the burden placed on European central banks. His comments are worth quoting at some length, because they give a flavour of the frustration felt in Basle:

> [W]hilst the Central-bank groups were asked to enter into precise commitments concerning both the contingent amounts to be made available, the credit risk, the period and the rhythm of repayments, these obligations were not matched by similar commitments from the OSA central banks. Without a reciprocal gesture it was difficult to see how the Six could accept the present UK proposals. Consequently, some more specific commitment from the OSA countries was vital.[57]

In this way the Europeans put considerable emphasis on sterling area deposits at the BIS as a form of pooling arrangement to cover initial drawings by the United Kingdom on the facility. Ansiaux went further and proposed compulsory deposits by countries that diversified their reserves, although the BIS believed that asking for voluntary deposits would be more successful and desirable.[58] In the end, the Bank of England agreed to encourage sterling area countries to make voluntary deposits in the BIS that would be drawn on to support sterling diversification. In July 1968 the Chancellor asked finance ministers in the sterling area to make deposits with the BIS, concluding: 'I would strongly urge you to consider making such a move.'[59]

By the beginning of September, on the eve of the Basle meeting to conclude the arrangements, total sterling area deposits in the BIS amounted to $110 million, of which $50 million came in after the July governors' meeting, but only $20 million to $25 million could be attributed to the UK negotiations.[60] Table 8.4 shows the increase in deposits between July 1968 and March 1969, which bears little relation to the terms of the Sterling Agreements. India, with the lowest minimum sterling proportion (MSP) in its reserves, made the largest deposit, and Singapore, with large and problematic sterling balances, made no additional deposits. New Zealand, with a high MSP, made net withdrawals.

The Americans showed a considerable lack of understanding of the complexities of the sterling negotiations when they suggested at the end of June that the British might conclude the guarantee agreements within the ten days before the next Basle meeting at the beginning of July. They

[57] Minutes of meeting of central bank governors at the BIS, 7 July 1968, BISA GILB 5 7.18(23).

[58] D. H. MacDonald memo, 3 July 1968, BISA GILB 5 7.18(23).

[59] Chancellor of Exchequer to missions to pass to finance ministers, 5 July 1968, BE OV44/224.

[60] Progress report by Fenton, 3 September 1968. The low level of OSA deposits remained a disappointment for Ansiaux. BE OV44/171.

Table 8.4 *Money received by the BIS from sterling area central banks (US$ million)*

	Date of first deposit	Value at 5 July 1968	Position at 7 March 1969	Additional deposits after July 1968
India	9 Sep. 1968	0.0	67.0	67.0
Australia	before 1968	3.0	65.5	62.5
Malaysia	6 Apr. 1968	4.0	47.6	43.6
Ireland	before 1968	6.3	39.5	33.2
Pakistan	1 Sep. 1969	0.0	21.0	21.0
Uganda	21 Aug. 1968	0.0	12.5	12.5
Libya	12 Mar. 1968	0.0	10.0	10.0
New Zealand	before 1968	18.3	7.5	–10.8
Jordan	22 Sep. 1968	0.0	7.0	7.0
Malta	29 Nov. 1968	0.0	4.6	4.6
Tanzania	20 May 1968	2.5	1.6	–0.9
Jamaica	31 Jul. 1968	0.0	3.0	3.0
Zambia	before 1968	0.0	2.0	2.0
Cyprus	8 Aug. 1968	0.0	2.0	2.0
Singapore	26 Jun. 1968	1.0	1.0	0.0
Total		35.1	291.8	256.7

Source: FER9, BIS Historical Archive.

were told that this was completely out of the question, and that no negotiations could begin until the safety net was in place.[61] Deming of the US Treasury finally agreed to the plan on 3 July, on the conditions that there was general agreement from other countries, that the United States share was only one-quarter to one-third of the total and that the subject was discussed with some key congressional committee chairmen.[62] After a series of visits and discussions by the British financial secretary with his European counterparts, the BIS governors met in Basle on 7 July and agreed in principle (reluctantly, in the case of Belgium and France) to offer multilateral support. The amount and distribution were not to be set until the September Basle meeting, after the United Kingdom had concluded its negotiations with the sterling area.[63]

The terms were finally agreed at the beginning of September 1968, once agreements with thirty countries covering 77 per cent of official sterling

[61] Note by CJM (BE) of a telephone conversation between himself and Solomon of the Federal Reserve System, 27 June 1968, BE OV44/165.

[62] Meeting of the governor and Goldman with Deming and Daane, 3 July 1968, BE OV44/165.

[63] Meeting of the central bank governors at the BIS, 7 July 1968, BE OV44/167.

Table 8.5 *Contributions to Group Arrangement 1 (1966) and Group Arrangement 2 (1968)*

	Group Arrangement 1 (US$ million)	Group Arrangement 2 (US$ million)	Group Arrangement 1 (%)	Group Arrangement 2 (%)
BIS	75.0	80.0	8.2	4.0
Belgium	42.5	80.0	4.7	4.0
Canada	60.0	100.0	6.6	5.0
Denmark	0.0	37.5	0.0	1.9
West Germany	145.0	400.0	15.9	20.0
FRBNY	310.0	650.0	34.1	32.5
Japan	40.0	90.0	4.4	4.5
Italy	95.0	225.0	10.4	11.3
Austria	30.0	50.0	3.3	2.5
Switzerland	50.0	100.0	5.5	5.0
Netherlands	42.5	100.0	4.7	5.0
Norway	0.0	37.5	0.0	1.9
Sweden	20.0	50.0	2.2	2.5
Total	910.0	2,000.0	100.0	100.0

Source: GILB5, BIS Historical Archive.

assets had been concluded. The formula was an extension of the 1966 Group Arrangement in terms of length and size. If total sterling balances fell below £3,080 million (the level at 11 June 1966) there was a $2 billion safety net in place. Table 8.5 shows the contributions of the participating countries. Germany and the United States were the largest contributors, with Germany increasing its share slightly compared to the 1966 agreement. The shares of others were reduced somewhat to allow for the inclusion of other Scandinavian countries. France claimed that it could not contribute because of its own parlous balance of payments position.

In the end, the United Kingdom drew funds only from Austria, West Germany, Switzerland and Italy under the Group Arrangement 2, and only for a fraction of the $2 billion total line of credit.[64] In September 1968 $50 million was drawn, and then a further $550 million in October (partly to repay the Fed $300 million), but this was the peak.

64 On 25 April 1969, of the total line of credit of $2 billion, only $400 million was outstanding, of which $155.2 million was raised by deposits from the OSA and $244.8 million from withdrawals by other countries. The only countries involved are Austria ($3.8 million), West Germany ($120 million), Italy ($21 million) and Switzerland ($100 million). BISA STE1, F01 4/5/71, Table of 2nd Group Arrangement with Bank of England.

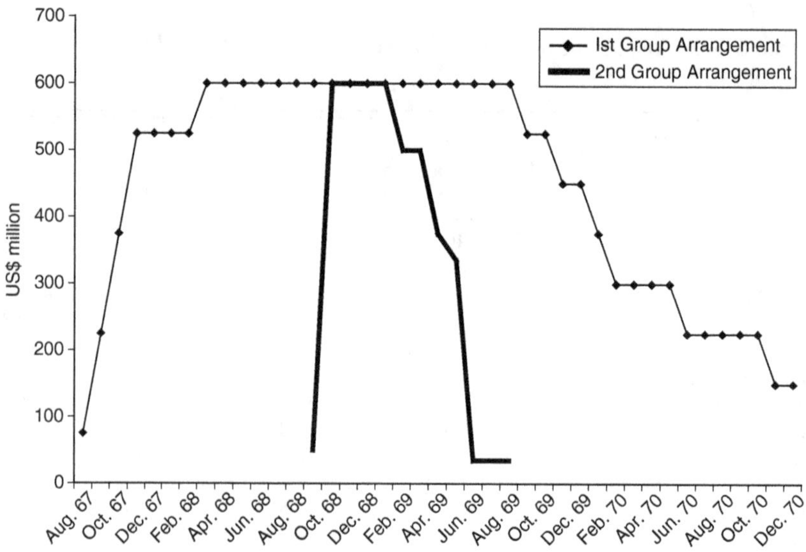

Figure 8.1 Outstanding drawings on Group Arrangements 1 (1966) and 2 (1968), August 1967–December 1970

From February 1969 the United Kingdom began to repay and in April there was only $500 million outstanding. This was covered by $236 million of sterling area deposits in the BIS, and $264 million drawn from other countries, comprising $15 million from Austria, $120 million from West Germany, $29 million from Italy and $100 million from Switzerland.[65] Ansiaux's emphasis on sterling area deposits thus bore dividends, in the form of reducing the claim on Europe by almost a half. The exchange guarantee, combined with balance of payments surpluses and the waning confidence in the exchange rate of the US dollar, meant that most of the hard-fought $2 billion line of credit was not in the end used. By insisting on a guarantee, the European central banks had avoided providing substantial support for the retreat of sterling as a reserve currency. The headline $2 billion support had its strength only in presentation.

The IMF could not endorse the Basle Agreement. Immediately after it had been concluded there was a flurry of advice to Schweitzer that the IMF should remain agnostic over the benefits of the agreements. David

[65] BISA STE1, Stevenson files, F01, 4/5/71, Table of 2nd Group Arrangement with Bank of England.

Finch, for example, argued that 'a segregated role for sterling countries does not seem to me to merit the support of the Fund which has consistently argued against any arrangement which separates countries, particularly any that discriminate against non-Ten [non-G10] members'.[66] In the end, however, the official advice was a bit more forthcoming. The IMF area groups were told: 'In any conversation with representatives of member countries care should be taken to avoid any judgement as to whether or not the proposed scheme or any provision in it should or should not be accepted by any member.' Instead, representatives should be told that the IMF supported anything that provided stability to the international monetary system and that the present proposal 'offers a practical means of achieving this end, subject, of course, to negotiations of terms acceptable to the parties involved'.[67] The IMF was thus caught between its desire for a resolution to the problem of the sterling balances and the potential that this solution would not be in the best interests of sterling holders, many of which were developing countries. The problems that the agreements posed for holders of sterling balances are discussed in the next section.

Negotiating with the sterling area: July–September 1968

The negotiations with overseas holders of sterling reserves constituted a challenging race to get agreement before the BIS meeting in September – described by Morse as 'a lightning tour of the overseas sterling area countries'.[68] The deadline left only three months to conclude the most important formal agreements relating to sterling's future. British negotiators were sent in small teams to the many official holders of sterling around the world, reporting back regularly to the Bank of England and Treasury on their progress. They were sent out to set minimum sterling proportions that countries would commit to hold in their reserves, to set an interest rate payable to the United Kingdom on these assets and to set the guaranteed exchange rate. In the end, the charge for the guarantee was reduced gradually, finally being abandoned in negotiations with Australia, and then with all the others at the beginning of September, at a cost of about £3.8 million.[69] The proportion of guaranteed sterling was

66 David Finch to Schweitzer, 22 July 1968, IMFA C/UK/315, 'Credit arrangements and maintenance of balances within reserve currency area 1965–1969'.

67 Memo to area departments from L. A. Whittome, 23 July 1968, IMFA C/UK/315, 'Credit arrangements and maintenance of balances within reserve currency area 1965–1969'.

68 Minute of meeting in Netherlands Bank, Amsterdam, on 20 June 1968 with BIS president Zijlstra, Ferras and MacDonald with Morse and Raw of BE; BISA STE1 F02.

69 Meeting in Chancellor's room with Snelling and governor of Bank of England, 4 September 1968, BE OV44/224.

initially offered at 80 per cent of reserves, but in mid-August this was increased to 90 per cent in negotiations with New Zealand, which was then offered to all countries. The MSPs ended up considerably lower than had been hoped. This was mitigated to some extent by secret side agreements about the level at which sterling would be held in excess of the formal agreement. The divergence between the public and private commitments shows the political need for sterling area governments to be seen to drive a hard bargain with the United Kingdom. The bitterness and stubbornness of some countries stemmed from the 1967 devaluation, which had created not just a sense of betrayal overseas but also a new balance of power between Britain and these Commonwealth countries, and even some colonial territories. The negotiations also identified the range of issues that complicated Britain's relations with these countries, including the applications to the EEC, development aspirations and (post-)imperialism.

Even before the final terms had been agreed in Basle the details were beginning to leak, and the British government had to reassure finance ministers. Australia and New Zealand were kept in closer touch with BIS negotiations than others, but in June 1968 the Chancellor sent a telegram to all Commonwealth finance ministers that 'I should like to emphasize that there is no question of any of the arrangements which we hope to make in Basle, interfering with the liquidity or usability of the sterling balances without the consent of the holders. The new facility should certainly do much to strengthen confidence in sterling and the sterling area system of payments which is of such value to all its members and to contribute to monetary stability generally.'[70] At the same time, the governor of the Bank of England wrote to his counterparts in the sterling area that 'the need for consultation with holders of sterling balances is fully recognised and to avoid any misunderstanding I should emphasise that the intention of the new facility is to strengthen confidence in sterling and to contribute to monetary stability generally. There is no question of any interference with the sterling area arrangements without the consent of the holders.'[71]

Table 8.6 shows the range of MSPs finally agreed. Colonies had the largest MSPs, reflecting the continuation of colonial monetary arrangements that required 100 per cent sterling backing for local currency issue and the denomination of most government reserves in sterling. Singapore and Malaysia both took their lead from Australia and negotiated the same

[70] Chancellor of Exchequer to Commonwealth finance ministers, 13 June 1968, BE OV44/224.

[71] Maurice Parsons to governors of sterling area central banks, 13 June 1968, BE OV44/224.

Table 8.6 *1968 Basle Agreements: final agreement of minimum sterling proportions*

East Caribbean Currency Authority	100
Gambia	100
Hong Kong	99
Barbados	97
Mauritius	95
British Honduras	90
Bahamas	80
Bermuda	80
Ceylon	80
Ghana	80
Guyana	80
Malawi	80
Trinidad	80
Malta	75
Bahrain	70
New Zealand	70
Sierra Leone	70
Zambia	65
Nigeria	60
Jamaica	57
Ireland	55
Uganda	51
Cyprus	50
Dubai	50
Iceland	45
Australia	40
Malaysia	40
Pakistan	40
Singapore	40
Jordan	25
Tanzania	25
Kuwait	25
Libya	18
India	13

40 per cent MSP. India had already diversified its reserves and had the lowest MSP.

Figure 8.2 shows the overall proportion of sterling in reserves of those countries that signed a Sterling Agreement. This shows the recovery of sterling in the first year of the agreements, and then again from the time of the primary product boom in 1971 and the steadily rising guarantee obligation if sterling depreciated.The most intransigent members of the

Table 8.7 *Proportion of sterling in official reserves (percentage), 1964–8*

	Australia	New Zealand	Malaysia	Singapore
1964	79	98	96	100
1965	70	97	96	98
1966	69	97	90	93
June 1967	64	80	87	74
October 1967	60	85	82	50
December 1968	46	76	58	44

Source: BE OV44/116, 1968, from TNA T312/2811, T312/2804, T312/2649 and T312/2312.

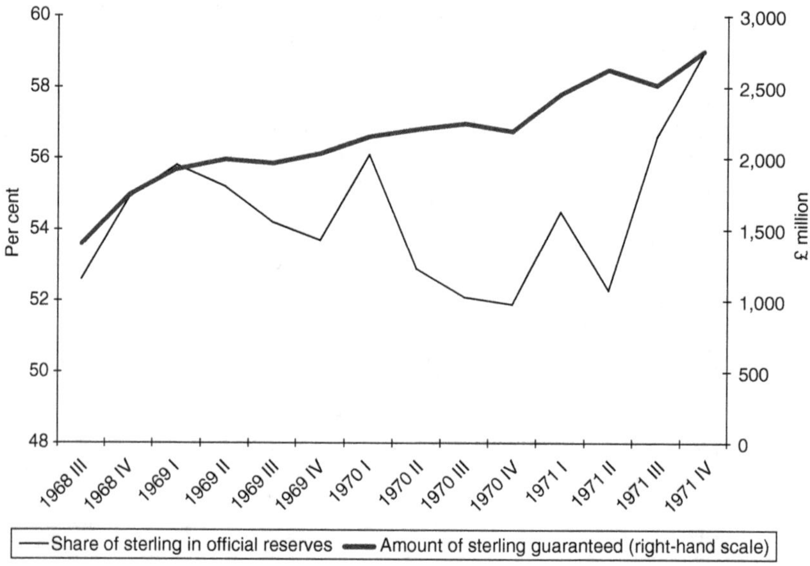

Figure 8.2 Sterling Agreements, quarter I 1968–quarter IV 1971

sterling area were Australia, Malaysia and Singapore, all of which had substantial sterling balances, as table 8.7 shows.

Singapore

The British felt the greatest sense of betrayal during the negotiations in Singapore, which is not surprising, as the negotiations came so soon after the announcement of the withdrawal of military forces from

Singapore, which (despite some mitigating aid) threatened to devastate the local economy. While relations with the prime minister, Lee Kuan Yew, had always been warm, Robert Haslam, a director at the Bank of England, described the Singaporean negotiators as 'tough, devious and self-centred'.[72] At the time of the devaluation the Bank of England assumed that sterling made up 88 per cent of the city state's foreign exchange reserves, but a week after devaluation the finance minister, Goh Keng Swee, announced that he had been diversifying the reserves and that the proportion was actually only about 50 per cent.[73] The Bank of England had not been aware of the diversification because the non-sterling assets had been accumulated secretly through new reserves rather than by the conversion of existing sterling balances in London. In December 1967, six months before the Sterling Agreement negotiations, Singapore converted a further £10 million into gold, prompting a letter from the Chancellor to Lee Kuan Yew regretting the diversification and asking for advice on his future plans. The reply from Goh suggested that this was an issue for Singapore only and gave no indication of future plans or willingness to negotiate. The British decided that any aid to mitigate the impact of the withdrawal of military forces would be conditional on the end of diversification, and this was relayed to Lee in a letter from the prime minister, Harold Wilson, in February 1968. Lee did not respond directly, but the British high commissioner, Sir Arthur de la Mare, understood Lee to have given a verbal undertaking to halt diversification. In the global crisis of March 1968, however, Goh converted a further £10 million in sterling to gold and US dollars. De la Mare was instructed to insist that Singapore buy back the sterling immediately but Lee asked for a deferral until April, after national elections and a possible shake-up of the Cabinet. Goh remained finance minister after April, though, and no action was taken, prompting negotiations between the Treasury representative in Asia, Christopher Fogarty, and Goh in May. Goh fought a hard campaign and Fogarty finally agreed to a compromise: that Singapore would put £10 million worth of gold on deposit in the United Kingdom for two years. Goh remained dissatisfied and the issue remained unresolved, and then it became tangled up in the Basle negotiations in the summer of 1968. Meanwhile, Lee visited Wilson in London in May 1968, but managed to avoid giving a firm assurance that the 50 per cent sterling component of reserves would be maintained.

After the Singapore elections there was a power struggle between Goh and Lee, in which the former continued to diversify the reserves,

[72] Haslam to Morse, 2 August 1968, BE OV44/242.
[73] For a summary of the episode, see BE OV44/247.

apparently without Lee's knowledge. After the Basle negotiations began in July 1968, therefore, London was playing a chasing game with Sim Kee Boon, joint permanent secretary of the Singapore Ministry of Finance, who had little sympathy for the British position. A major issue was the proposed 20 per cent of sterling balances that were left unguaranteed under the Basle arrangements (this amounted to about £47 million in Singapore's case) and the MSP. Neither Goh nor Sim had confidence in Britain's ability to hold to the new sterling parity.

The £10 million gold deposit re-emerged when the United Kingdom rejected Singapore's request to swap the gold for sterling, to be placed on the London money market to attract favourable rates and then used to repurchase the gold at the original price in two years' time. Sim even declared that Singapore would accept all the British terms of the Basle arrangement if the gold scheme were accepted and the gold was considered part of the sterling reserves. Sim also threatened that, 'in the absence of agreement to the Singapore scheme, the safeguards required "would be multiplied ten-fold", involving much arduous negotiation'.[74] Clearly, the Singaporean negotiators believed they had the upper hand, and this was confirmed when the Foreign and Commonwealth Office (FCO) instructed Fogarty to accept a compromise to designate the £10 million of gold as sterling, so long as a 50 per cent MSP – i.e. a commitment to the status quo – could be agreed. Once this had been offered, however, Sim and Goh rescinded their offer and pressed for a lower MSP.[75]

At this stage the British became suspicious and began to investigate Singapore's sterling reserves in greater detail. The conclusion was that sterling probably formed only about 39 per cent of the city state's total exchange reserves, since a further diversification of about £25 million appeared to have been made between May and August 1968, despite Lee's assurances. This was lower than the 43 per cent (excluding the £10 million of gold) or 47 per cent (including the gold) presented by Goh.[76] At this point Fogarty and Haslam recommended that 'the time has come to consider seriously the possibility of leaving [the] Singapore negotiations suspended and being prepared at the end of the day to exclude and block Singapore' – i.e. suspend convertibility of their remaining sterling reserves and arrange to release them slowly over the next few years.[77] Rather than call off the negotiations, the FCO advised

[74] Telegram from Fogarty and Haslam, 1 August 1968, BE OV44/247.

[75] Telegram no. 975 from Colonial Office to Fogarty, 9 August 1968. Telegram from Fogarty and Haslam to CO, 15 August 1968; BE OV44/247.

[76] Telegram no. 815 from Fogarty and Haslam to CO, BE OV44/247.

[77] Ibid.

Fogarty and Haslam to get a private interview with Lee in order to try to get him to intervene and overrule Goh.[78] De la Mare was dispatched to visit Lee.

Lee professed his surprise at and ignorance of the figures and agreed to try to challenge Goh, but de la Mare did not believe that Lee would be able to confront Goh successfully in the Cabinet. Goh had correctly predicted the British demilitarisation and then the devaluation while Lee had argued to his colleagues that Britain would not betray Singapore in these ways, leaving him with little political capital. After meeting with de la Mare, Lee confronted Goh, but, predictably, Goh returned to the offensive, arguing that he had not sold any sterling below the official exchange rate while agreeing that he had been hedging his sterling reserves against other currencies because he expected another devaluation. Lee then managed to get a commitment from Goh not to reduce sterling below its current proportion until after 1 October 1968, thus setting a deadline for the conclusion of a Basle arrangement.[79] De la Mare had little confidence that, if required, Lee would overrule Goh, and he asked that, if no agreement could be reached, the commander-in-chief should be consulted, since such a failure would adversely affect Singapore public opinion against the British and damage British commercial and business interests.

British observers in the Treasury and the FCO were not so pessimistic, and the prime minister and the Chancellor each wrote to Lee near the end of August, urging him to come to an agreement speedily in order to sustain stability in the international monetary system. At this time Singapore was aware of the agreement with Australia for an MSP of 40 per cent but not of Australia's informal side agreement to keep to a target of 47 per cent. This precedent allowed the British to offer a similar concession of 40 per cent to Singapore, which was in the end accepted on 6 September 1968, and letters were finally exchanged on 19 September.[80] Sim tried to get formal assurances that Singapore was not being treated any less favourably than any other sterling area member but the British team refused to accede. The British believed that the Singaporeans gave up once the terms of the deal with Australia had become known, as they did not think that they could get a better deal.[81]

78 Telegram from Commonwealth Relations Office secretary to Fogarty and Haslam, 19 August 1968, BE OV44/247

79 Telegram no. 841 from Colonial Office to de la Mare, 22 August 1968, BE OV44/247.

80 Telegram no. 898 from de la Mare to Colonial Office, 4 September 1968, BE OV44/247.

81 Summary of the entire negotiations, including the run-up to them, by R. Hay for Lee Kuan Yew's visit to the Chancellor on 16 January, 30 October 1968, BE OV44/247.

Australia

As with Singapore, there were special circumstances in the case of Australia. In the years up to 1967 British portfolio investment in Australia had increased considerably, and there were discussions in Whitehall and at the Bank of England about possible ways to stem this flow. The threat of introducing controls on investment provoked a fierce response from the Australian Treasury, and this conflict provided the background for the negotiations after devaluation. The Australians argued that the devaluation had reduced the foreign exchange value of their sterling reserves, and that, while portfolio investment had increased, FDI from Britain had declined because of the voluntary programme imposed in 1966. William McMahon, head of the Australian Department of the Treasury, advised the Chancellor of the Exchequer: 'I fear too that it [controls on British investment in Australia] would add strength to the considerable body of opinion in this country which favours an early and substantial shift of our overseas reserves out of sterling. That opinion I am bound to say is now held here by more than a few responsible people.'[82]

Australia was also strategically important, since other countries in the region with even greater sterling balances, such as New Zealand, Malaysia and Singapore, all looked to Australia for leadership and compared their settlements with that of Australia. In the end, New Zealand settled quite quickly with a relatively high MSP of 70 per cent, because it had such a high proportion of their reserves in sterling at the time the negotiations began. All the technical concessions made to Australia, however, were passed on by the United Kingdom to New Zealand, Malaysia and Singapore.

The Reserve Bank of Australia (RBA) was keen to diversify reserves out of sterling in the years prior to the devaluation of 1967, but the government resisted, and it remained official policy until November 1967 to retain the bulk of reserves in sterling. Periodically, however, the proceeds of gold sales and overseas loans had been kept in US dollars, so the share of sterling in gold and foreign exchange reserves had fallen from 77 per cent in June 1963 to around 60 per cent by October 1967.[83] The RBA's case for diversification was not simply because of the threat of devaluation but, more fundamentally, because of the shifting denomination of Australia's overseas debt, which had fallen from a level of 84 per cent in sterling to some 50 per cent on the eve of the devaluation, when sterling still accounted for over 60 per cent of reserves. In the weeks before the

[82] Letter from McMahon to Chancellor, 1968, BE OV44/225.

[83] Memo for the board, 31 October 1967, RBA, BM-Pe-87.

devaluation, however, the RBA rejected suggestions that it should further reduce sterling holdings, for fear that this 'would be likely to start a flood of speculation against sterling, which could lead to large disorderly competitive devaluations'.[84] After devaluation the board of the RBA returned to the question of diversification, and by the end of July 1968, just as the Sterling Agreement negotiations were about to begin, it was minded to recommend to the Treasury that the RBA should reduce its commitment to sterling, although it was recognised that this might disrupt political relations with Britain.[85] From the time of devaluation in November 1967 until July 1968 sterling was held at 57 per cent of the Reserve Bank's foreign exchange and gold reserves, but this proportion was reduced to 53 per cent in August and 52 per cent by 18 September, so it is clear that the RBA was diversifying during the Sterling Agreement negotiations.[86] Its preferred MSP during the negotiations was 35 per cent while the United Kingdom was pressing for 50 per cent, and it was reluctant to be committed for as long as the proposed seven years.

During the Basle negotiations from July to September, the Reserve Bank, through its new governor, John Phillips, was particularly forceful in its advice to the Treasury to diversify out of sterling. Phillips urged the Treasury to agree to hold reserves in three equal parts of gold, US dollars and sterling, and he had already arranged that gold could be bought from South Africa.[87] The RBA's view at the end of August was that asking Australia to relinquish control of its reserve policy 'is unreasonable and presses upon us difficulties far greater than the UK realises', because Australia's reserves were more volatile seasonally than was the case with more developed economies, and so required higher precautionary reserve levels, and the RBA was expecting persistent deficits in the years to come.[88] It also believed that there was a chance that the convertibility of the country's sterling reserves could be blocked at some time in the near future, and did not want to be tied into large holdings.[89]

The talks with the Australians dragged on through July and August, much to the frustration of the foreign secretary, Michael Stewart. He

[84] Memo by investment department, 6 November 1967, RBA, BM-Pe-87.

[85] Minutes of the Reserve Bank board, 3 July 1968, RBA, BM-Pe-95.

[86] Papers for the Reserve Bank board meeting, 4 September 1968, RBA, BM-Pe-96. The shift was achieved by selling UK Treasury bills, buying US Treasury bills and retaining the proceeds of a Deutschmark loan in Deutschmark. The MSP definition of sterling reserves was 47 per cent on 25 September due to slight differences in coverage.

[87] Telegraph from Canberra to Commonwealth Office from Mr Rooke to Ockley, 10 July 1968, BE OV44/225.

[88] Harold Knight (deputy governor) to J. G. Phillips (governor), 23 August 1968, RBA, GHK-68-1.

[89] H. Knight record of phone conversation with governor Phillips in Kuala Lumpur, 15 August 1968, RBA, GHK-68-1.

noted towards the end of August that '[m]inisterial dilatoriness in handling this matter has various causes, including Party difficulties. The Treasurer has only just given his mind to the matter and is concerned with tactical issues. There is irritation that we should have worked out this scheme with the Europeans without consulting the Australians in advance and some pleasure in keeping us waiting now ... Above all we are advised that Australian Ministers do not appreciate the risks to the whole international monetary system if the Basle Plan is not brought to fruition.'[90]

The British negotiating team also complained of a lack of urgency and concentration on the issue by the Australians, who were preoccupied with domestic economic concerns, such as their government budget.[91] R. P. Fenton, a senior official at the Bank of England, noted in mid-August that the negotiating process was plagued by political problems, 'compounded as it currently is of distrust of the UK and our capacity to manage our own housekeeping; internal political problems in Australia arising from Treasurer McMahon's steadily weakening position; the Australia first policy of their Prime Minister and the thought that he might well call an election within the next few months. On top of this there is the Reserve Bank's very firm position on seeking to diversify to a 35% level and Governor Phillips' recent accession to office.'[92]

On the Australian side, the Treasury and the Reserve Bank hoped to go slow on the negotiations, since the proposals were not appealing and they did not completely believe Britain's claims that the Basle Agreement would be jeopardised if Australia did not sign in time for the September meeting. In mid-August Phillips wanted to 'dig our heels in hard', and the Treasury secretary acknowledged with some satisfaction that 'the normal pace of Canberra decision making would prove a bit slow for the UK team'.[93]

In order to speed up the negotiations, they were lifted to prime ministerial level. In direct correspondence with Harold Wilson, the strongly nationalist Australian prime minister, John Gorton, emphasised the need to maintain free access for Australian goods to the British market and free flows of investment from Britain.[94] The Australians thus couched the Basle Agreement in terms of a quid pro quo for the continuation of the advantages of sterling area membership at a time when these were

[90] Telegram no. 816 to Chancellor, 22 August 1968, BE OV44/226.
[91] Ibid.
[92] R. P. Fenton note for governors, 13 August 1968, BE OV44/224.
[93] H. Knight record of conversations with Phillips and Sir Richard Randall, 14–15 August 1968, RBA, GHK-68-1.
[94] Telegram from Mr Gorton to Harold Wilson, 29 August 1968, BE OV44/226.

under threat from European integration and capital controls. Gorton proposed a package that was unacceptable to the British: a 40 per cent MSP and a unilateral right to rescind any agreement. This prompted Wilson, extraordinarily, to send the governor of the Bank of England, Leslie O'Brien, to negotiate personally. It was thought that this would be better than Wilson himself going out, since the governor could not engage in political discussions that might sidetrack negotiations.[95] At this point the Chancellor of the Exchequer, Roy Jenkins, also advised Henry Fowler at the US Treasury that the Americans might be asked to intervene in an attempt to bring about a reasonable and speedy conclusion with the Australians.[96] The Reserve Bank was certainly aware that pressure from the United States, an important source of investment, might increase, and this had factored into its attitude to the negotiations by the end of August.[97]

The Australians continued to drive a hard bargain. O'Brien was forced to abandon any charge in return for the exchange guarantee. He also accepted the 40 per cent MSP, with an informal understanding that Australia would in fact keep to 45 per cent. The termination of the agreement was also a compromise. One of the most important issues for the Australians was to commit the British not to constrain capital flows to Australia. As Gorton put it to O'Brien, 'The issue is you want a three-year minimum because the Basle countries insist on it: and I insist on getting out of the agreement if you put more controls on capital exports.'[98] Eventually, they settled on a three-year agreement with the proviso that, if the United Kingdom imposed capital restrictions, there would be 'immediate consultation'. Furthermore, the Australians would have access to the London market for refinancing existing sterling loans when they came due. If, because of market conditions or the state of the British balance of payments, conversion or refinance were not possible, this would be taken into consideration to reduce the MSP.[99]

All the same, the Australians drew out the negotiations to the wire (and beyond) in the hope of getting the commitment to access to the London market to refinance sterling loans made public rather than hidden in an unpublished private side agreement. On 23 September Ryrie advised Jenkins that 'the Australians are taking a line which is both pettifogging and unreasonable and the Chancellor is advised to take a

[95] Telegram sent from Sir C. Johnston to CO, 29 August 1968, BE OV44/226
[96] Telegram no. 6837 from Chancellor to Fowler, 30 August 1968, BE OV44/226.
[97] Memo by H. Knight for J. G. Phillips, 23 August 1968, RBA, GHK-68-1.
[98] Telegram from Johnston to Colonial Office concerning the meeting between the PM and the governor on 1 September, 2 September 1968, BE OV44/226.
[99] Telegram from Johnston to Colonial Office, 2 September 1968, BE OV44/226.

firm line with Mr McMahon' to settle the outstanding difficulties over the telephone the following day. In the end, the United Kingdom had to compromise and allow the Australians to publish the refinance proviso in an unclassified side letter. Even so, the formal documents were signed and exchanged only on 3 October 1968, over a week after the deadline. The United Kingdom had been forced to reduce the period from seven years to three, plus renewal by mutual agreement for two more years, and had been forced to agree that no charge would be made by the United Kingdom for the guarantee. The concession on the charge was then generalised to all agreements, and the three-plus-two formula was offered to all countries that had not yet concluded their agreements (fifteen negotiations were still to be completed at the beginning of September 1968).[100] The Australian MSP was 40 per cent, although there was a verbal undertaking to keep sterling at the present level of about 47 to 48 per cent of reserves, the difference comprising about £56 million.[101]

Malaysia

At first it seemed that negotiations with Malaysia would be quite straightforward, particularly in comparison with Singapore. Malaysia's sterling reserves had not been diversified to anything like the same extent, and the negotiating brief noted that 'apart from some relatively small-scale diversification in 1966 ... Malaysia have been co-operative in their sterling policy. Since 1966, although wishing to reduce their high sterling percentage of overall reserves, they have consulted us in advance over proposed diversification'.[102] Malaysia was deeply affected by events in Singapore, however, given the rivalry between the two states so soon after partition in 1965. The approach to sterling of the more self-interested and forward-looking Singapore embarrassed the Malaysian government when the extent of Singapore's diversification was revealed. By contrast with Singapore's 50 per cent of reserves in sterling, Malaysia held 77 per cent of its reserves in sterling at the time of devaluation, and suffered correspondingly larger losses. The British goal in the negotiations was to get an MSP of 73 per cent, to allow for some diversification that had already been agreed, and also to get Malaysia to deposit 40 to 50 per cent of its total non-sterling currency reserves with the BIS, where it would be available for the United Kingdom to borrow.[103]

[100] Progress report by Fenton, 3 September 1968, BE OV44/171.
[101] 'The sterling area negotiations', by Bank officials, 4 September 1968, BE OV44/171.
[102] Undated negotiating brief, BE OV44/242.
[103] Ibid.

The Malaysian finance minister, Tan Siew Sin, initially appeared favourable to the Basle Agreement, noting: 'This facility is a great step forward as it goes well beyond anything which has been agreed before, both in magnitude and in length of term ... It should give much greater confidence to holders of this currency.'[104] When the negotiations began in earnest on the Sterling Agreements, however, he quickly changed his tune. In common with the position adopted by other countries, he refused to accept an obligation to pay interest for the guarantee, and this was finally abandoned in all negotiations at the beginning of September. More fundamentally, he cast doubt on the whole international monetary system, and announced that he expected a US dollar devaluation in the near future. He scolded the leading countries, claiming: 'In Britain in particular and also in other developed countries, there had been a major failure of Governments resulting in labour indiscipline, continuous inflation, and general lack of confidence, which was now painfully justified, in any paper currencies.' On the Basle Agreement, he said: 'The US$2 billion was quite inadequate and could easily be frittered away in a couple of years on maintaining the UK standard of living.' These charges amounted to a serious criticism of British policy, and also showed considerable foresight for events to come over the next few years. Tan concluded that 'the scheme was not attractive to Malaysia and he would rather take a risk in diversifying further out of sterling – and indeed perhaps also out of dollars, it might be better to hold reserves in tin or rubber equities than in any of the traditional reserve media including gold'.[105]

After the 1967 devaluation, Malaysia had embarked on a programme of diversification, agreed with the United Kingdom, to aim at a sterling proportion in the reserves of about 50 per cent (£123 million), and this had largely been achieved by the summer of 1968. Malaysia was due then to receive part of the assets of the dissolved currency board it had shared with Singapore, which would raise its sterling share to about 55 per cent, and this was the British bottom line for the MSP after Tan Siew Sin's initial rejection of British proposals for a 73 per cent MSP. The Malaysians refused to agree, however, and fought hard for an MSP of just 30 per cent. Agreement could not be reached, and negotiations were suspended early in August to allow the conclusion of the agreement with Australia to take place, in the hope that Malaysia would follow Australia's lead.

As the Australians stalled, negotiations resumed in Kuala Lumpur on 21 August, but the disagreement dragged on, particularly on the MSP

104 Telegram no. 849 addressed to CO from Kuala Lumpur from Sir M. Walker, 11 July 1968, BE OV44/242.

105 Telegram from Walker to Commonwealth Office, 25 July 1968, BE OV44/242.

question. By September the Bank of England's view was that '[w]e all feel very strongly that the Malaysians are outdoing the Australians in their intransigence'.[106] They were insisting on a 30 to 35 per cent MSP, with various private agreements on exclusions and targets that would not be published.[107] The Malaysian Cabinet was due to discuss the agreement on 4 September, and the British made a final attempt to reach agreement in time for the Basle meeting on 7 September by offering greater flexibility on the MSP.[108] The Malaysian Cabinet stuck to the 35 per cent MSP, with an added private agreement to keep to an 'operating' proportion of 45 per cent. If Britain wanted an agreement signed before the Basle meeting, this was the only deal possible.[109] The British side could not accept such a low MSP, however, because it would also have to be offered to Singapore, and because it was considerably lower than the 40 per cent recently agreed with Australia.[110] The failure to reach agreement before the Basle meeting was deemed 'unfortunate but not disastrous', and consideration began as to possible sanctions or other pressure Britain might exert.[111] A week later, however, the Malaysians capitulated on the MSP and agreed to 40 per cent plus a private side agreement similar to that of Australia (although they quibbled over whether it would be in writing). They also asked for and got the Australian concession on future access to the London market to refinance debt. The agreement was finally concluded after a personal meeting between Jenkins and Tan at the end of September.

The two largest holders of sterling reserves in 1968 were Hong Kong and Kuwait – each of which presented its own special obstacles in the negotiations. On the eve of the November 1967 devaluation Hong Kong held £363 million of sterling and Kuwait £515 million.[112] During the March gold crisis Kuwait began to diversify its reserves, but it was still the second largest single sterling holder by the time of the Sterling Agreement negotiations.

Hong Kong

Negotiations with Hong Kong were quickly brought to an initial conclusion, partly because the United Kingdom had tortuously negotiated a

[106] Progress report by Fenton, 5 September 1968, BE OV44/171.
[107] Ibid.
[108] Telegram to Fogarty in Kuala Lumpur, 3 September 1968, BE OV44/242.
[109] Telegram no. 1014 from Kuala Lumpur to Commonwealth Office, 5 September 1968, BE OV44/242.
[110] Ibid.
[111] Meeting of the Sterling Negotiations Group, minutes by C. J. Carey, 5 September 1968, BE OV44/242.
[112] BE OV444/116.

Hong Kong dollar exchange guarantee for half Hong Kong's reserves in May 1968, just as the decision to offer exchange guarantees to other sterling holders was made.[113] From the comfort of the Mandarin Oriental Hotel, the negotiator, R. Henry Turner, wrote to Fenton at the Bank of England at the end of July that

> on the whole the negotiations went reasonably well, and the general outcome was not in doubt. It became clear fairly early on that Hong Kong was likely to accept the new scheme as an improvement on the earlier facility; and that they would not make an issue of any of the various points they raised, since they felt that our negotiations with other Sterling Area countries would probably bring about the improvements they wanted. As a result, much of the haggling on details in the last few days has been in the nature of shadow-boxing ... so that the Financial Secretary could demonstrate to the Executive Council that he has put up a good fight on behalf of the Colony. A good deal of the persecution mania which appears to have afflicted Hong Kong since the November devaluation still persists.[114]

In November 1967 Hong Kong held about £400 million in sterling reserves, and the total cost of the devaluation was estimated to be £30 million for the government and a further £20 to 25 million for banks. The colony's governor, Sir David Trench, wrote passionately that 'I find it difficult to find words to express my feelings and those of my advisors, official and unofficial, on the manner in which Britain has now defaulted on its very large net financial obligations to Hong Kong'.[115] Many in the UK Treasury were unsympathetic to this plea from a colonial dependent, W. S. Ryrie remarking that 'the fact that the Governor and the Financial Secretary are indignant is neither here nor there and I am not sure that a certain amount of indignation in the Executive Council matters very much either'.[116] Hong Kong initially followed sterling down against the dollar but then revalued by 10 per cent a few days later, after local protests about the impact of devaluation on the cost of food imports from China.[117]

Hong Kong's position was heavily influenced by its colonial status. It was among the first to conclude negotiations with Britain and ended up with a much higher MSP for its reserves (99 per cent) than almost any other territory. It did, however, get an unusual concession, in that part of commercial banks' balances were brought into the exchange guarantee, along with government-owned sterling reserves.

113 The Hong Kong guarantee was in terms of the Hong Kong dollar/sterling exchange rate: Schenk, 'The empire strikes back'.

114 R. Henry Turner to Fenton, personal and confidential, 26 July 1968, BE OV44/261.

115 Telegram from the governor of Hong Kong to the Commonwealth Office, 28 November 1967, BE OV44/258.

116 Memo by W. S. Ryrie for Goldman and Wright, 6 December 1967, TNA T312/1934.

117 Schenk, 'The empire strikes back'.

The Sterling Agreement was complicated for Hong Kong because there was no central monetary authority. Note-issuing private banks had to hold sterling reserves, and special arrangements were negotiated to bring these reserves under the guarantee, which continued to evolve after the agreement was finally signed in September 1968. The commercial banks swapped some of their sterling with the Exchange Fund to bring it into 'official' hands, thus making it subject to the guarantee. The Exchange Fund then deposited this sterling back with the banks so that it was available for them to use freely. The situation was further complicated when the Hong Kong government itself offered a guarantee of 100 per cent of the Hong Kong dollar exchange value of commercial banks' sterling assets in January 1969. This greatly increased the importance of the Sterling Agreement for the Hong Kong government, as they depended on it to meet their own commitment to local banks.[118]

When, at the end of 1970, the time came to renegotiate the Sterling Agreements for those countries that had signed a three-year agreement, Hong Kong (which had signed a five-year agreement) tried to get 'most favoured nation' (MFN) status for itself in any concessions reached with other countries. This was refused, since, as Haslam noted, '[i]n the case of Hong Kong MFN treatment could open up enticing vistas of substantial diversification'.[119] At the end of March 1970 Hong Kong's sterling balances were £422 million and the colony was the largest single holder of sterling reserves.[120] In August 1971, after the renegotiation of the three-year agreements, Hong Kong was offered a reduction in its MSP by ten percentage points to 89 per cent, and this was accepted.[121] The later defection of the colony from sterling is discussed in chapter 10.

Kuwait

Middle Eastern countries drove a hard bargain and were among the last countries to sign agreements. They proposed very low MSPs (25 per cent for Kuwait, 18 per cent for Libya), which was clearly beyond what was desirable for the United Kingdom. Like Malaysia and Singapore, the Kuwaitis wanted to be among the last to sign, to make sure that

[118] Schenk, C. R., 'The evolution of the Hong Kong currency board during global exchange rate instability, 1967–1973', *Financial History Review*, 16(2), 2009, pp. 129–56.

[119] Minute on a note from RHT to Schofield/Fenton, 18 December 1970, BE OV44/264.

[120] Draft Sterling Area Working Party report, 18 June 1970, BE OV44/120.

[121] Telegram no. 560 from FCO to Hong Kong, 2 August 1971, BE OV44/264. It was formally agreed on 20 August 1971.

they could benefit from any concessions made to any other country.[122] This form of brinkmanship plagued the final weeks of the negotiations, as each country wanted to exert pressure on the United Kingdom for greater concessions. Kuwait was a substantial sterling balance holder as a result of earnings from oil exports, holding £499 million in sterling in November 1967.[123] The Kuwaitis were also among the largest diversifiers during the March 1968 gold crisis, reducing the sterling proportion of their reserves from 66 per cent to 47 per cent.[124] The first round of negotiations, in July, failed to bring agreement and a second round began at the beginning of August, with the British aiming for an MSP of 50 per cent, but the talks were abandoned after only a few days, as agreement was not likely to be possible and one of the teams of two negotiators was suffering from heat exhaustion.[125] The team reported that 'the Kuwaitis welcome the scheme in principle but say it will be impossible to persuade the national assembly to accept an MSP greater than 25%'.[126] Their position was interpreted as mainly political, stemming from public distrust of the British government.

At the beginning of September, as the deadline for formal agreement by the BIS approached, Jenkins sent a personal message to Kuwait urging the conclusion of the negotiations on the basis of a public 25 per cent MSP alongside a private statement of intent that they would not in practice go below 45 per cent.[127] The Kuwaitis finally accepted modified proposals of a 25 per cent MSP in addition to 'expressing their intention to use their best endeavours to maintain the end-June proportion (54%) in practice' on 5 September, in time for the Basle meeting.[128] The FCO explained the exceptional terms for Kuwait as follows:

> In the case of Kuwait, which is not in the Commonwealth, which is one of the very largest holders of sterling and which presents many special features as a member of the sterling area, no agreement will appear amongst the published documents, but adequate assurances have been given by Kuwait in an acceptable written form on the continued maintenance of sterling holdings; and it is this which is important for the success of the totality of the arrangements.

122 Progress report by Symons, 23 August 1968, BE OV44/170.
123 Brief for Chancellor of Exchequer, 10 January 1968, TNA T312/1955.
124 Sterling Area Working Party report, February 1969, BE OV44/119.
125 Sterling negotiations progress report for Mr Ryrie by A. R. H. Glover of the Treasury, 7 August 1968; R. P. Fenton note for governors, 13 August 1968; BE OV44/224.
126 Report by Commonwealth Office to teams in Kuala Lumpur and Singapore, 19 August 1968, BE OV44/224.
127 Progress report by Fenton, 22 August 1968, BE OV44/170.
128 Progress reports by Fenton, 3 and 5 September 1968, BE OV44/171. Quotation from Fenton report for governors, 6 September 1968, BE OV44/224.

Furthermore it will be made clear in public that separate and parallel arrangements have been made with Kuwait.[129]

For similar reasons, on 23 September Libya agreed to an 18 per cent MSP with an oral commitment to hold 50 per cent.[130]

Aftermath

The initial conclusion of the agreements, while tortuous, was not the end of the story. In February 1969 the Sterling Area Working Party reviewed the events and the prospects for the management of sterling. It acknowledged that, while the agreements had turned out to be effective in ending diversification, the negotiations had permanently altered the sterling area relationship by turning the official exchange reserves from 'banking liabilities' into 'contractual debts'.[131] In the future, the working party suggested, the management of sterling should be treated as part of the general reduction and restructuring of external debt. The short-term facilities that had supported sterling and the British balance of payments for the past decade would need to be paid off, however, before the sterling balances could be reduced. The working party did recognise the desire in the United Kingdom and elsewhere to reduce sterling's reserve role and not to increase sterling balances, but, rather rashly, it saw no alternative to encouraging an increase in private sterling holdings to help offset repayments of other debt, even at the cost of higher UK interest rates: 'It is better, despite possible criticisms, to acquire a banking liability and see the proceeds to meet a firm debt payment than to decline the former and seek to defer the latter.' It also recommended that when the Basle Agreements came up for renewal in 1971 they should be extended for a further two years. The working party concluded that 'unless or until a satisfactory international solution is found it would be better for the UK to continue a policy of debt repayment and consolidation; controlled run-down of official sterling balances; and the maintenance of sterling as a trading and financial currency'.[132]

On longer-term aims, the working party concluded that the status quo was unavoidable:

Although running a reserve currency has seemed something of an embarrassment, and indeed a burden, against the background of the UK's growing short-

[129] Commonwealth Office to overseas missions, 11 September 1968, BE OV44/224.
[130] Progress report by Fenton, 24 September 1968, BE OV44/173.
[131] Sterling Area Working Party report, 12 February 1969, TNA T318/192.
[132] Ibid.

term international indebtedness, running an international banking business has, on the other hand, proved a profitable undertaking in terms of the Balance of Payments. The Working Party would wish to see sterling's role as an international trading and financing currency maintained. Secondly, no plan could be put into effect without damage to the UK unless it were acceptable to the present holders of sterling. If some totally unattractive scheme were forced on the overseas sterling area the likelihood is that the alternative to their acceptance would have to be a severe curtailment of the use of their sterling holdings whose consequences could not but be contrary to the UK's long-term interests. Finally, because the UK does not have the political or financial strength to find a new solution unaided, the active participation of the other major financial powers is essential.

We have seen, however, that sterling's role as an international trading and commercial currency had already been much eroded by the end of the 1960s.

The Basle Agreements came up for renewal after three years in 1971, just when the United Kingdom was forced by its European partners to commit publicly to divest sterling of its reserve currency status as a condition of joining the EEC.[133] The publicity for the end of sterling's reserve status came at the behest of the EEC but it also fitted with the development of British policy priorities from the early 1960s. The United Kingdom's withdrawal from the sterling area system was part of a longer-term process that involved a gradual realignment of British policy priorities, starting with the hastening of decolonisation at the end of the 1950s, the first application to the EEC in 1963, the strategic withdrawal from east of Suez, and the break with the United States in the mid-1960s.

The coincidence of the commitment to Europe and the expiry of the Basle Agreements allowed the renegotiation at the BIS to take account of the need to reduce official sterling balances rather than try to sustain them. Unlike the situation in 1968, when an unsustainable rundown in balances was the threat, by 1969 Britain was battling to stop official sterling balances from increasing. Bank of England and Treasury officials leapt at the possibility of offering countries a ten percentage point reduction in the minimum sterling proportion that they had to hold. This would ensure rapid and relatively easy renewal by almost all the participants (except for Libya, which was likely to withdraw anyway for political reasons). In June 1970 the Conservative Party had gained power from Labour, however, and the new Chancellor of the Exchequer, Anthony Barber, needed to be persuaded that this offer would not lead to a precipitous fall in overall sterling balances that might put a strain

[133] Statement on sterling by Mr Rippon to the EEC ministers, 7 June 1971, BE OV44/191.

on the reserves.[134] In the end he was persuaded by the ease with which the renewals could be agreed (particularly with Singapore and Malaysia, as large sterling holders), the fact that hints had already been made to Australia (so they expected a reduction in MSP) and French expectations that some progress would be made in the renegotiations to reducing sterling's reserve role.

The prime minister, Edward Heath, also needed to be persuaded. In his meeting with Barber he argued that Georges Pompidou, the French president, was particularly concerned by the exchange guarantee aspects of the Basle Agreements. If some of the agreements could be allowed to expire, the amount of sterling covered by guarantee would be reduced, and so would France's objections. Barber countered that sterling balances were predicted to rise considerably, making it more difficult to keep them to the level of June 1971. In the end Heath was persuaded, and it was agreed to lower the MSP in the new agreements by ten percentage points overall to forestall future increases. This was not to be announced until parliament had risen for the summer break in August, however, so as to avoid controversy or the announcement being linked to the EEC commitment.[135] In the meantime, the international monetary system suffered a near-fatal blow with the suspension of convertibility, and then the devaluation of the US dollar, in August 1971, on the brink of the final conclusion of the agreements in September. The exchange guarantee, which was predicated on a devaluation of sterling rather than a devaluation of the US dollar, became effectively inoperable, and the United Kingdom gained the MSPs without a practical quid pro quo.

Conclusions

From 1961 to 1967 the United Kingdom came to rely on coordinated bilateral support for short-term sterling crises, which was used in conjunction with IMF stand-by arrangements. By collecting this support from central banks, the United Kingdom avoided direct intergovernmental discussions. Although it might be assumed that European central bankers discussed these arrangements with their governments, they did not need formally to seek ministerial or public approval. By the mid-1960s, however, the patience with short-term support arrangements was wearing thin among the Bank of England's creditors. As the

[134] Record of a meeting in the Chancellor's room, 23 June 1971, BE OV44/191.

[135] Memo of a conversation between Morse, Neale and Henly, 24 June 1971, BE OV44/191. Meeting on the 26th under Neale to take stock of the situation, 27 August 1971, BE OV44/192. Prime minister's views recorded in a note from Armstrong to Ryrie, 20 September 1971, BE OV44/192.

discussions to reform the international monetary system began to gain some momentum, as discussed in chapter 7, central bankers at Basle began to explore longer-term solutions to sterling's reserve role.

The precedent for medium-term lines of credit to pay for the diversification of sterling reserves was established under the first Group Arrangement of June 1966. The negotiations also gave European and US central bankers a much more detailed understanding of the sterling balances and the sources of their volatility. At this time the IMF confirmed that it was reluctant to help in the management of the decline of sterling as a reserve currency, while the BIS came forward to play a leading coordinating and policy-making role in devising and negotiating the European and American packages, as well as hosting the information-sharing meetings between central bankers and experts.

The Basle Agreement between G10 central banks in 1968 is much better known than the Sterling Agreements that accompanied it, but the latter were longer-lasting and had a more profound impact on the nature of sterling as a reserve currency. The agreements set minimum ratios for sterling reserves among the signatories, often below the status quo when the negotiations had begun. The US dollar value guarantee was not invoked in the first round of agreements, since the pound retained the \$2.40/£1 exchange rate until June 1972, but it was a necessary quid pro quo. The agreements also provided a framework for managing the share of sterling in global foreign exchange reserves in the future once they came up for renewal in 1971. The reserve role of sterling thus became formalised and negotiated, rather than voluntary and based primarily on market portfolio decisions.

The 1967 devaluation of sterling had exposed the vulnerability of sterling area countries to the weaknesses in the British economy, and the 1968 negotiations revealed a profound sense of betrayal among these states. Unlike the Group Arrangements, in which Britain was shielded from political discomfort by the relatively collegial central bankers' club, the Sterling Agreement negotiations exposed the British authorities to vigorous complaints and criticism from governments of a broad range of emerging and developing economies. British teams were left kicking their heels in the overseas capitals of former colonies, waiting for their creditors to accept compromise proposals. By the end of 1968 it was clear that there was no longer any prospect of relying on common purpose among the Commonwealth over this issue, and the balance of power had clearly shifted away from the United Kingdom. The tactic of moving towards integration with Europe was further vindicated.

Part III

Sterling's Final Retreat 1970–1992

The decade of the 1970s was a perilous time in the international economy, and it had a profound impact on the retreat of sterling. The period was plagued by destabilising international capital flows that pulled the Bretton Woods system apart in a series of shuddering wrenches. Flexible exchange rates were introduced sporadically from the late 1960s to deal with persistent imbalances, but the general consensus in favour of pegged exchange rates did not begin to falter until the early 1970s. After years of equivocating, in 1971 the US authorities took unilateral action to ameliorate the impact of the international role of the US dollar on their country's balance of payments, in a way that the British government was never powerful enough to do. The rush to accede to American demands shows the political as well as economic commitment to an international monetary system with collective rules. Coming so soon after the failure to find multilateral ways to reform the system, the outcome was another collaborative short-term scheme that was, in the end, insufficient to restore the confidence and flexibility required by international financial markets. The Smithsonian Agreement did, however, succeed in bringing Japan belatedly to its rightful place as a crucial player in the system, commensurate with its commercial influence in its region and beyond.

During the start of the decade British influence on international payments policy waned, on account of a variety of developments. West Germany became an even more important player as a major surplus country and a beneficiary of US military expenditure. France's intransigence enhanced its position in transatlantic as well as European negotiations. The relatively early float of sterling in June 1972 marked the effective fall of the United Kingdom out of the pegged rate system, while the final effort to join the EEC encouraged British governments to keep a low profile in any intra-European conflict. By the time of the 1973 oil crisis, Britain's accession to the EEC had to some extent restored its position vis-à-vis both Europe and the United States.

In 1970 it seemed that the ending of sterling's international reserve role had been completed, but the oil crisis temporarily reversed this trend. On top of this, the nominal increase in sterling reserves increased British vulnerability to external pressures and encouraged Britain to renew the Sterling Agreements that had been designed for a pegged exchange rate environment. The experiment with flexible rates from 1972 seemed to be containing the pressure until the persistent depreciation of sterling from 1975 intensified inflationary pressure. Ultimately, the flexible regime did not eliminate the constraint of the exchange rate on domestic policy sovereignty. The ensuing loss of market confidence required an emergency bail-out from the IMF and the G10 central banks analogous to the arrangements of the 1960s.

The third Group Arrangement, of 1977, was the final scheme to share the burden of ending sterling's reserve role. By the 1980s sterling's share of the world's foreign exchange reserves had fallen below 3 per cent. Sterling was no longer a primary international currency, although echoes of this historic role were felt in the second oil crisis in the 1980s, when sterling re-emerged as a petrocurrency. Political sensitivity to the exchange rate continued despite the end of its international status, and chapter 11 explores these events of the 1980s as an epilogue to the narrative of the retreat of sterling from its one-time position as an international currency.

9 Sterling and the end of Bretton Woods

During the first half of the 1970s the pegged exchange rate system finally gave way to a less coherent system that combined floating, flexible and pegged rates. International financial flows accelerated rapidly and volatile commodity prices (including oil) added to inflation and slowing growth, which proved to be the greatest post-war challenge for policy-makers and economists. Britain abandoned the sterling peg before most others, in June 1972, but this did not mean that the Sterling Agreements became less important to managing sterling's reserve role, and they were maintained until the end of 1974. This chapter examines these years of crisis and transformation in the international monetary system.

The Nixon shock and the Smithsonian Agreement, August–December 1971

With the advent of the administration of Richard Nixon in 1969 came a new and harder line attitude from the US government over international monetary problems, which culminated in the 'Nixon shock' of August 1971. The new economic policy announced at this time marked the end of the American administration's willingness to engage in prolonged negotiations to reform the international monetary system, and the end of their acceptance of the pegged exchange rate system as a constraint on their economic policy. During his first years in power Nixon was convinced that the United States' economic problems were the result of an excessive international defence burden and protectionist policies by its creditors, which pushed the American balance of payments into persistent deficit. After the end of the Vietnam War his attention turned to the responsibilities of surplus countries. Although the announcement in August 1971 surprised America's allies, it had had a long gestation period and marked the culmination of official planning in the United States rather than a break from that process.

In January 1969 Nixon established the Volcker Group, named for his undersecretary of state for monetary affairs, Paul Volcker, to develop policy in this area. The Group put emphasis on early activation of the SDR and a general realignment of exchange rates, and as early as March 1969 (before the exchange crisis of May) the Group was preparing a contingency policy in which the United States would unilaterally break the link between the US dollar and gold. The preference was still for a negotiated amendment to the international monetary system, but if this had not borne fruit within the next year or so then unilateral action was called for to increase pressure on the Europeans to adjust.[1] The most important countries to consider in forming policy, according to Nixon's special adviser on foreign affairs, Henry Kissinger, were Germany and France, while 'the UK is not a factor because it is financially prostrate'.[2] In the end, the devaluation of the French franc in August 1969 and the float upward of the Deutschmark from the end of September forestalled the more dramatic moves that the American administration had planned to achieve a general currency realignment.[3]

Once this immediate crisis had receded, Paul McCracken, chairman of the Council of Economic Advisers, and the Treasury secretary, David Kennedy, took the opportunity to push forward with their longer-term plans for greater exchange rate flexibility within the existing parity system.[4] Kennedy used his speech at the IMF meetings on 30 September to suggest a study of greater flexibility. Within the US Treasury, planning for a major realignment of international exchange rates had been renewed in late 1970, and it gathered pace during the huge capital outflow from the United States in May 1971.[5] At the height of the crisis, on 8 May, while exchange markets in Europe were still closed, the US Treasury devised a plan to force the international community to adapt their attitude to the global payments imbalance that presaged the Nixon shock of three months later:

1 'Summary of a possible US approach to improving international monetary arrangements', 17 March 1969, NARA, Department of the Treasury, Volcker Group Masters: FRC 56 86 30.

2 Memo from the president's assistant for national security affairs [Kissinger] to Nixon, 25 June 1969, NARA, Nixon Presidential Materials, NSC Files, Agency Files, Box 215, CEA.

3 Gavin, *Gold, Dollars, and Power*, pp. 191–2. The franc was revalued by 11.1 per cent on 8 August 1969. The Deutschmark was floated on 30 September and repegged with a revaluation of 9.29 per cent on 24 October 1969.

4 Memo from secretary of the Treasury (Kennedy) to President Nixon, 19 September 1969, NARA, Nixon Presidential Materials, NSC Files, Agency Files, Box 289, Treasury, vol. I. Memo from the chairman of the CEA (McCracken) to Nixon, 8 September 1969, NARA, Nixon Presidential Materials, NSC Files, Agency Files, Box 215, CEA.

5 Memo from the US executive director of the IMF (Dale) to the undersecretary of the Treasury for monetary affairs (Volcker), 23 November 1970, NARA, Department of the Treasury, Files of Under Secretary Volcker: FRC 56 79 15, '1971 contingency planning papers'.

(i) suspension of gold convertibility;
(ii) imposition of trade restrictions;
(iii) diplomatic and financial intervention to frustrate foreign activities which interfere with the attainment of our objectives; and
(iv) reduction of the US military presence in Europe and Japan.[6]

The Treasury viewed America's basic objective as 'to take advantage of the present crisis to achieve (i) a lasting improvement in the balance-of-payments position of the United States, (ii) a more equitable sharing of the responsibilities for world security and economic progress and (iii) a basic reform of the international monetary system'. It is clear that, from this point, the emphasis shifted even more firmly to adjustment by the rest of the world rather than ongoing multilateral negotiation.

These developments from early 1969 show that the suspension of gold convertibility in order to force a general realignment of exchange rates in favour of the United States had been discussed for over two years before it was implemented. While the final decision to break from a negotiated solution to international economic reform was rushed through in August 1971, the foundations had been laid over the previous months. The unilateral approach was given added impetus by the new Treasury secretary, John Connally, who took office in February 1971 and quickly built up his personal influence, developing a thread of economic nationalism that found a receptive audience in President Nixon.[7] Connally distanced himself from the Treasury Department and was heavily influenced by the protectionist advice of Peter Peterson, the head of Nixon's Council for International Economic Policy (CIEP), in the spring of 1971.[8] During the summer Nixon was convinced that America's global political and strategic dominance depended on economic hegemony and that economic nationalism would deliver political gains at home. Indeed, Becker has argued that the Nixon shock was an example of 'the relentlessness of Nixon's pursuit of domestic political advantage to the exclusion of almost all other considerations'.[9]

On the morning of 2 August 1971, in the midst of yet another run on the US dollar after the publication of a rising trade deficit, Connally met with Nixon and laid out his framework for a new economic policy: the

[6] Paper prepared in the Treasury, 8 May 1971, NARA, Department of the Treasury, Files of Under Secretary Volcker: FRC 56 79 15, '1971 contingency planning papers'.

[7] Gavin, *Gold, Dollars, and Power*, pp. 192–5; Solomon, *The International Monetary System*, pp. 190–1.

[8] Becker, W. H., 'The US and the search for a new monetary system', in H. Haftendorn, G.H. Soutou, S. F. Szabo and S. F. Wells (eds.), *The Strategic Triangle: France, Germany, and the United States in the Shaping of the New Europe* (Baltimore: Johns Hopkins University Press, 2006), pp. 189–206.

[9] Ibid., p. 203.

suspension of convertibility and a 10 per cent import surcharge on the external side, and a wage/price freeze, expenditure cuts and the reintroduction of the investment tax credit on the domestic side.[10] Nixon was initially most enthusiastic about the domestic components of the policy but was eventually persuaded that the international and domestic strikes should be made simultaneously. Connally warned that the convertibility of the dollar would not survive to the next congressional and presidential elections, in 1972, so it was better to close the gold window from a position of relative political strength. By Thursday 12 August Nixon was described as elated about the plan, equating the new economic policy with his diplomatic breakthrough in China. The final decision was taken at Camp David, the president's country residence, over the weekend of 14–15 August (in the absence of both Kissinger and the Secretary of State, William Rogers) and announced on the evening of 15 August.

The next afternoon, Volcker met with European Treasury and central bank representatives in London, including Sir Alan Neale of the UK Treasury and Jeremy Morse of the Bank of England.[11] Volcker started by being explicit that he was not in a position to begin negotiations but merely to explain the thinking behind Nixon's announcement. He described the internal domestic measures (the ninety-day wage/price freeze and the fiscal measures), which he claimed the administration believed would be enough to stem speculation against the dollar. The president had taken the external measures anyway, however, to help resolve the longer-term issues of exchange rates and the international monetary system. He asserted that 'the US, at this stage, had no program which it was going to spring on anyone', but added that 'we would not be satisfied without a reform that could repair the erosion which had taken place in the US position over the years'. Emminger, of the Bundesbank, Neale and Morse all tried to impress upon Volcker the need to reopen exchange markets within a few days at new parities, but Volcker would not be drawn into indicating what sort of adjustment the Americans were looking for other than that it had to be enough to allow the United States to run balance of payments surpluses over the next few years, and that changing the price of gold was neither necessary nor sufficient. Johann Schoellhorn, of the German Ministry of Economics, and the other Europeans advised Volcker that agreement was unlikely to be able to be achieved while the 10 per cent surcharge was in place,

[10] Account from Nixon Oval Office tapes, FRUS editorial notes 164 and 165.

[11] Germany, France, Italy, Japan and the United Kingdom were represented. Memo of conversation, 16 August 1971, NARA, Department of the Treasury, Files of Under Secretary Volcker: FRC 56 79 15, 'France'.

but Volcker reasserted that this measure would be kept in place until the US position had improved. In the meantime, before a general reform was accomplished, the US dollar would float in the same way as the Deutschmark and the Canadian dollar. He offered an informal meeting with Connally in Washington to the representatives of those countries present, but the Europeans didn't want to commit themselves, since a failed meeting would be disastrous for the markets. With that, the Americans left the meeting room.

After leaving London, Volcker visited Paris on 17 August to meet with Valéry Giscard d'Estaing, the French minister of the economy and finance. There, he blamed the August crisis mainly on the Germans selling US dollars during the summer, while thanking France for its cooperative attitude over speculation.[12] Volcker also reassured Giscard that, in terms of exchange rate adjustments, 'the burden of adjustment would lie less on Europe than on Canada and Japan'. The European Community ministers met on 19 August but could not devise a common response. France refused to revalue and resisted the German suggestion of a joint European float against the dollar.

The OECD Working Party no. 3 and the G10 deputies met in Paris from 2 to 4 September, and there was strong pressure on the United States to raise the price of gold in exchange for revaluing European and Japanese currencies. Volcker rejected this proposal and continued to play the game long, insisting on referring to the ongoing discussions as consultation rather than negotiation.[13] G10 ministers then met in London on 15–16 September and again tried to push the United States to lift the surcharge and raise the dollar price of gold before returning to new parities. They also complained that the US target for a $13 billion improvement in its balance of payments was unrealistic within the timescale proposed.[14] Connally responded that these issues needed to be addressed along with the reform of defence expenditure and protectionism outside the United States, and reasserted that the president was opposed to merely changing the gold price. The deputies were then charged with developing reform proposals.

Rather belatedly, after 20 September the US administration began to form concrete ideas about its specific objectives and how to achieve

[12] Memo of conversation, 17 August 1971, NARA, Department of the Treasury, Files of Under Secretary Volcker 1969–1974: FRC 56 79 15, 'France'. Volcker did not visit Germany or Italy.

[13] Memo from Robert Hormats of the National Security Council Staff to Kissinger, 6 September 1971, NARA, Nixon Presidential Materials, NSC Files, Agency Files, Box 218, CIEP.

[14] Telegram from the embassy in the United Kingdom to the US Department of State, 17 September 1971, NARA RG 59, Central Files 1970–73, FN 10.

them.[15] It is really very surprising that the administration had not developed a strategy before delivering its ultimatum to the United States' allies and trading partners, but it appears that Volcker and Connally hoped that the initiative would come from Europe or Japan and that the United States would merely be responsive, rather than proactive, in achieving a resolution. Solomon's opinion is that, while Connally's 'keen intelligence enabled him to grasp the substance of the economic problems he was forced to deal with, he brought to the job no broad vision of how to improve the economic welfare of his own country or the world'.[16] In the third week of September, over a month after the announcement of the new economic policy, a high-level coordinating committee was set up to define America's objectives for international monetary reform. It quickly decided that multilateral negotiations needed to take place within the next two months on monetary, trade and defence issues. The surcharge could be lifted in order to ensure progress at these meetings. There was no initial consensus, however, on whether the strategy should be a revaluation of other currencies to a new peg or whether it was better to continue to float.[17] By the time of the G10 meetings in Washington, a few days later, the coordinating committee was collectively advocating a general move to floating exchange rates, but Connally was not convinced that this would be politically possible, or that it would be acceptable to Europe. The surcharge was a 'wasting negotiating asset', since its impact was not as great as had been expected in August, so it should be bargained away quickly with the greatest effect possible.[18] There was no consensus, though, on how hard-line the negotiations should be.

This ambiguity was reflected in the American position at the IMF/World Bank meetings and G10 meetings in Washington from 26 to 28 September. Here, Connally broached the possibility of all currencies floating for a transition period and offered the carrot of lifting the import

[15] Memo from the president's assistant for international economic affairs (Peterson) to Nixon, 20 September 1971, NARA, Nixon Presidential Materials, NSC Files, Agency Files, Box 216, 'CEA'.

[16] Solomon, *The International Monetary System*, p. 191.

[17] Memo from Peterson to Kissinger, 24 September 1971, NARA, Nixon Presidential Materials, NSC Files, Agency Files, Box 218, 'CIEP'. The committee was chaired by Peter Peterson with representatives from the Treasury (Volcker and Petty), the Department of State (Samuels and Trezise), the CEA (Solomon), the Office of Management and Budget [OMB] (Dam) and the Federal Reserve Board and National Security Council [NSC] staff.

[18] Information memo from Robert Hormats of the NSC staff to Kissinger, 28 September 1971, NARA, Nixon Presidential Materials, NSC Files, Subject Files, Box 376, 'president's economic program'.

surcharge if real progress was made towards a solution.[19] France strongly resisted the suggestion of a float and continued to press for a change in the dollar gold price. The major outcome from the impasse came from an initiative by Arthur Burns, chairman of the Fed, who suggested that Jelle Zijlstra, president of the Nederlandsche Bank and the BIS, be selected as an honest broker to tour the world's major capitals and negotiate a general realignment of parities. He was chosen by the G10 central banks because of his good English skills, his political background and the trust that he commanded internationally.[20]

Meanwhile, the US administration continued to struggle to come to a consensus on the position to adopt.[21] The president was vehemently opposed to changing the price of gold, partly because of the need to go to Congress to achieve this. Volcker favoured a new pegged exchange rate system, but the director of the Office of Management and Budget, George Shultz, tried to persuade Nixon that floating rates were a better option.[22] In any case, restoring the convertibility of the dollar to gold was rejected. On 2 November Nixon directed that there should be no consideration of a change in the gold price or a return to convertibility in the US position.[23] The French were the main obstacle, since they refused to accept a revaluation of the franc without a rise in the dollar price of gold – a barrier solidified at the EEC finance ministers' meeting in Versailles on 4 November.[24] A proposed G10 meeting on 22 November was postponed for a week to allow more intra-European negotiation.

Zijlstra arrived in London on 10 November after visiting Bonn and Paris. The IMF and OECD suggestions for realignment left the effective rate for sterling practically unchanged, but the British hoped to take advantage of the situation to gain a competitive devaluation. Britain was running an annual current account surplus of about £800 million

[19] This was included in a public speech by Connally (quoted in Solomon, *The International Monetary System*, p. 195) and in private discussion with Karl Schiller (economics minister) and Karl Klasen (Bundesbank) of West Germany: Memo of conversation, 25 September 1971, NARA, Department of the Treasury, Files of Under Secretary Volcker: FRC 56 79 15, 'Germany general'.

[20] Letter from Leslie O'Brien to Chancellor of the Exchequer Barber, 4 October 1971, TNA T312/2939.

[21] Memo from Peterson to secretary of the Treasury Connally, 26 October 1971, NARA, Department of the Treasury, Records of Secretary Shultz: FRC 56 80 1, 'CIEP'.

[22] FRUS, 1969–1972, vol. III, 'International monetary policy', note 187.

[23] Memo from Nixon, 2 November 1971, NARA, Nixon Presidential Materials, NSC Files, Agency Files, Box 268, OMB, 'Secret'.

[24] Letter from Emminger, vice-president of Bundesbank, to Volcker, 12 November 1971, NARA, Department of Treasury, Files of Under Secretary Volcker: FRC 56 79 15, 'Germany general'.

but the Treasury expected the position to deteriorate over the next two years, because of policies to increase employment and cost-push inflation resulting from rising wages.[25] In the end, however, the British were unable to persuade Zijlstra to build in this extra advantage for the United Kingdom, and his report on 23 November left the sterling rate unchanged within a general system of realignments that would see a depreciation of about 10 per cent in the value of the US dollar. This would be achieved mainly through appreciation of the Deutschmark, the yen, the Swiss franc, the Belgian franc and the Dutch guilder and a depreciation of the US dollar by only 5.5 per cent, including a rise in the price of gold from $35 to $37 per ounce. There was to be no change to the parity of France, Italy, Sweden or the United Kingdom, while the Canadian dollar would continue to float.[26] Zijlstra also recommended new exchange controls, consultation on monetary policy, trade liberalisation and greater flexibility of parities while referring the issue of defence burden sharing to later negotiations.

Volcker and Connally found these proposals more of a hindrance than a help to negotiations, as they continued to reject a change in the gold price and the proposed improvement in the US balance of payments was well below the target of $13 billion.[27] During November signs of a general recession began to appear in Europe and pressure for an early settlement increased. At the G10 deputies meeting in Rome in advance of the ministerial meeting at the end of November, Volcker offered an 11 per cent average devaluation of the dollar if there was progress on trade issues (particularly reducing agricultural protection in the EEC) and defence burden sharing. In addition, exchange margins would be expanded to +/– 3 per cent, but there would be no return to the convertibility of the dollar to gold and no change in the gold price. Volcker threatened to publish this offer in advance of the ministerial meeting to turn up the heat on the negotiations, but was finally persuaded not to.[28]

Behind the scenes before the G10 meeting in Rome, Nixon and Connally had agreed that a change in the dollar price of gold might be offered in bilateral meetings with Pompidou scheduled to be held in the Azores in mid-December. This reflected the urgency of coming to an agreement and a change of heart in Washington about the political cost of a change in gold price if the dollar remained inconvertible. At the G10 ministers' meeting on 29 November, Connally and Volcker abruptly suggested a 10 to 15 per cent revaluation of the dollar gold price without the

25 Brief for Zijlstra's visit, 5 November 1971, TNA T312/2939.
26 Zijlstra's report, 23 November 1971, TNA T312/2939.
27 Solomon, *The International Monetary System*, p. 202.
28 Ibid.

agreement of the White House.[29] A dollar devaluation of even 10 per cent seemed excessive to the Europeans, who had been seeking a change of only about 5 per cent. Moreover, the French were still unable to commit themselves before the Pompidou–Nixon summit, and so the Rome meeting adjourned without coming to a resolution. The Americans believed that they had agreed that trade negotiations would go ahead between the United States and the EEC as part of the international monetary settlement, but the European Commission was subsequently unable to agree to this (primarily due to French resistance) at its meeting on 11 December.

The breakthrough finally came in the Pompidou–Nixon summit on 13–14 December, when Nixon agreed to devalue the dollar by raising the price of gold from $35 to $38 per ounce, and in return Pompidou agreed not to push for an early return of the convertibility of the dollar to gold. Through its intransigence, France had become the cornerstone for the eventual Smithsonian Agreement.[30] During the summit, Pompidou was able to reduce the proposed exchange rate margins from +/– 3 per cent to +/– 2.25 per cent and cut the rise in the price of gold from 10 per cent to 8.9 per cent, and the United States lifted the import surcharge. France agreed to retain the franc's parity with gold, and it was anticipated that sterling would also remain unchanged, while the Deutschmark would revalue by 5 to 6 per cent and the yen by 9 to 11 per cent. Pompidou also held the line on the return to fixed exchange rates, rather than the more open-ended objective of 'established' exchange rates that the Americans had wanted. The United States was also committed to 'assist in the stability of the system and the defence of the newly fixed exchange rates in particular by vigorous implementation of its efforts to restore price stability and productivity'. In return, France committed to supporting a European Commission mandate to engage in negotiation over trade, although the specific reference to agricultural trade in the American draft was deleted in the final version. Pompidou also managed to get a reference to gold convertibility as a future topic for discussion into the memorandum. The Americans conceded that the discussions at a recent NATO meeting met the requirements for defence burden sharing, so this was effectively shelved.

[29] An eye-witness account of this is in Solomon, *The International Monetary System*, p. 203. For the views of the White House (and the fact that Nixon had not agreed), see White House staff meeting chaired by Schulz, 2 December 1971, NARA, Nixon Presidential Materials, White House Special Files, Haldeman Notes, October–December 1971.

[30] 'Framework for a monetary and trade settlement', secret agreement between Nixon and Pompidou, Azores, undated, NARA, Nixon Presidential Materials, NSC files, Subject Files, Box 356, 'Monetary matters'.

The G10 ministerial meeting at the Smithsonian Institution in Washington on 17–18 December largely confirmed these bilateral commitments between the United States and France. The new parities were graduated, with the smallest appreciation by Italy and Sweden, followed by France and the United Kingdom, then Belgium and the Netherlands. Reflecting the underlying trade imbalance, the West German currency appreciated slightly more, and the largest increase was that of the Japanese yen.

Throughout these discussions the relationship between the United Kingdom and the United States was never very close or influential. Washington's main source of information was West Germany, and the main obstacle was France. Connally viewed the British application to join the EEC as compromising London's freedom of action, asserting that, until accession, Britain was likely to follow the French line. In discussions with Connally in Tokyo in November, the Japanese prime minister, Eisaku Sato, observed that the 'special relationship' with the United States ought to have made the United Kingdom more helpful in negotiations with France, but that 'these days, with its membership in the EEC pending, the UK could hardly be called helpful'.[31] There was some common ground between the United States and the United Kingdom over American calls for adjustments to the Common Agricultural Policy but it was not exploited, since the trade negotiations never became detailed. In contrast to the 1960s, during the 1970s the British were largely sidelined and preoccupied with EEC accession. Their efforts to gain a competitive devaluation failed and sterling was left at its old gold parity. Rather than strengthening the usefulness of the Anglo-American special relationship by giving the United States a more intimate window on Europe, the road to British accession to the EEC weakened the United Kingdom's links with the United States until after the treaty of accession had been signed, at the end of January 1972. After the float of sterling, five months later, Volcker remarked to the president that, 'in general, the British have been one of our major substantive antagonists, while maintaining a façade of wishing to cooperate closely as a mediator between the Common Market and the US'.[32] The special relationship was at a low ebb and Europe was cold comfort for sterling. Europe's narrow band framework, established in April 1972, allowed only a 2.25 per cent variation among member exchange rates, and sterling lasted only eight weeks in the so-called 'Snake in the Tunnel'.

[31] Memo of conversation, Tokyo, 12 November 1971, NARA, Department of the Treasury, Records of Secretary Shultz, FRC 56 80 1, Subject Files, '1971–74'.

[32] Memo by Volcker for Nixon, NARA, Department of the Treasury, Files of Under Secretary Volcker: FRC 56 79 15, 'UK British float'.

The Smithsonian Agreement parities never inspired full confidence. Immediately after the conclusion of the agreement there was considerable frustration in Europe over the passive approach of Connally, Volcker and Burns to the US dollar exchange rate, as they essentially left all intervention up to the European central banks.[33] Connally in particular took a very hard line on the limits to American responsibility for the stability of the system. This tension intensified in the summer after the float of sterling, when speculation against the dollar drove European central banks to absorb large dollar balances while the Fed and the US Treasury remained passive. From 28 June, when sterling floated, up to 17 July central banks outside the United States took in $4.925 billion, of which $2.5 billion was bought on 13 and 14 July alone.[34] At this point the Fed chairman was able to persuade the new secretary of the Treasury reluctantly to consider engaging in swaps with foreign central banks, up to a total of perhaps $2 billion, and using the borrowed foreign currency to buy dollars in the market in support of the rate.[35] President Nixon was persuaded of the merits of the scheme, and on 19 July the Fed intervened for the first time to support the Smithsonian rates by activating a Deutschmark swap and intervening to the extent of $50 million. This action was received with great relief in international markets and by Helmut Schmidt, the West German minister of economics and finance, who was under political pressure to cease buying dollars.[36] He put an ultimatum to Kissinger on 20 July that either the United States committed itself to support the dollar or Germany would impose new capital controls and cease buying dollars. This threat seems to have worked, and Burns and Shultz, by now the US Treasury secretary, agreed that the United States would support the dollar exchange rate, although the major burden was still expected to be borne by surplus countries.

The reorganisation of the international monetary system prompted by the Nixon shock and delivered through bilateral negotiation between the United States and France changed the tenor and pace of the wider reform discussions. On 22–23 April 1972 (on the eve of the launch of

[33] Letter from Pompidou to Nixon, 4 February 1972, FRUS, 1969–1976, vol, III, 'International monetary policy'.

[34] Memo from Secretary of the Treasury Shultz to Nixon, undated but probably 18 July 1972, FRUS, 1969–76, vol. III, 'International monetary policy'.

[35] Memo from Shultz to Nixon, undated, July 1972, FRUS, 1969–76, vol. III, 'International monetary policy'. Burns described how the policy was arrived at in Memo of conversation between Burns and Kissinger, 25 July 1972. Burns found Connally very difficult to work with and complained that he alone had had to hold the Smithsonian Agreement together.

[36] Information memo for the record, meeting of Schmidt and Kissinger, 20 July 1972, FRUS, 1969–76, vol. III, 'International monetary policy'.

the Snake) London hosted a meeting of G10 deputies to decide how to move forward on international monetary reform. The meeting agreed to widen the discussions to a Group of 20 and that the IMF should take a greater leadership role in coordinating meetings. This referred the G10 back to its original role of administering the GAB and the allocation of SDRs and left international monetary problems to a much more diverse group, reducing even further the chances for coherent proposals. James describes how the deliberations merely prolonged the stalemate between the United States and Europe. The final report of the Committee of 20 was submitted only in June 1974, by which time the international monetary system had already been transformed.

When advising Nixon that he intended to fall out of the Snake and float the pound in June 1972, Heath urged the president to move more urgently towards more radical and long-term changes to the international monetary system.[37] Nixon responded positively (in a letter drafted by Volcker) that 'against the background of current events I do think that the time is ripe for engaging in open-minded and candid exploration of certain basic alternatives with our closest partners. We should no longer be inhibited by the fear that certain approaches can be unthinkingly damned by some as too "radical" a departure from the past.'[38] This reflected the US Treasury's view that greater flexibility in exchange rates should be the goal of the ongoing discussions for international monetary reform.[39] Indeed, Shultz, who had taken over from Connally in May 1972, was in favour of a floating US dollar.[40] In the second half of 1972 the US Treasury, under Shultz, began to formulate an imaginative and comprehensive proposal for international monetary reform ('Plan X') based on greater flexibility for all exchange rates, prescribed circumstances when floating would be allowed and a system of monitoring movements in foreign reserves as a presumptive indicator for changes in exchange rates. Foreign exchange would be downgraded in primary reserves, which would comprise SDRs, gold and the IMF quota.[41] Trade and monetary issues would also be more closely linked. The outline of the plan was described in speeches by Shultz and Nixon at the IMF

[37] Telegrams from Heath to Nixon, 24 and 26 June 1972, NARA, Nixon Presidential Materials, NSC files, Country Files – 'Europe, UK', vol. VII, 9/71–9/72.

[38] Nixon letter to Heath, 10 July 1972, NARA, Department of Treasury, Files of Under Secretary Volcker: FRC 56 79 15, 'UK British float'.

[39] Recommended premises and objectives of the UK in forthcoming reform negotiations, 5 June 1972, FRUS, 1969–72, vol. III.

[40] Information memo for the record, meeting of Schmidt and Kissinger, 20 July 1972, FRUS, 1969–76, vol. III, 'International monetary policy'.

[41] Paper prepared in the Department of the Treasury, major elements of plan X, 31 July 1972, FRUS, 1969–76, vol. III, 'International monetary policy'.

meeting in September 1972, and was received with some relief that at least the United States was willing to take a leading role in international monetary reform.[42] In the end, however, events prompted pragmatic solutions that outpaced the complicated multilateral attempts to achieve a more deliberate and planned reform. For sterling, the key turning point was the decision to float the exchange rate in June 1972.

Floating the pound, June 1972

After the devaluation of sterling in 1967 and the temporary floating of the Deutschmark there was much wider academic and political discussion on the subject of greater flexibility for exchange rate parities, though few in the official and banking spheres were yet willing to advocate freely floating exchange rates. In the UK Treasury, contingency planning identified operational procedures for a float should sterling come under external pressure in a plan code-named Hecuba in 1968 and 1969 and later a plan dubbed Palinarus in 1970.[43] These efforts were basically technical investigations designed to collect a cache of operational guidelines for various contingencies rather than policy recommendations, but they show the readiness to consider these options within the UK Treasury as the pegged exchange rate regime weakened. US officials also considered the possibility of a sterling float at the time of the European exchange crisis in May 1969, which eventually resulted in the revaluation of the Deutschmark and the depreciation of the French franc. Paul McCracken, the CEA chairman, recommended that the United Kingdom should be encouraged to hold its exchange rate stable but that, if necessary, the United States should offer support in the event that sterling needed to be floated. The possibility of a sterling float at this stage met with hostility elsewhere in the administration, especially from Kissinger and Fred Bergsten, Kissinger's assistant for international economic affairs at the NSC, who successfully persuaded Nixon that this should not be mentioned in any correspondence with the British.[44] Nevertheless, the climate for greater flexibility and 'transitional floating' within the pegged exchange rate system continued to develop.

In January 1970 the United States announced again that it supported discussions on limited flexibility within the IMF and G10, and these

[42] Information memo from Hormats to Kissinger, 3 October 1972, FRUS, 1969–76, vol. III, 'International monetary policy'.

[43] TNA T312/2908.

[44] Action memo from Kissinger to Nixon, 7 May 1969. The memo was drafted by Bergsten. NARA, Nixon Presidential Materials, NSC Files, Subject Files, Box 309, 'Balance of payments'.

discussions began in April.[45] At the end of May 1970 the Canadian dollar floated due to upward pressure on the exchange rate, and it stabilised in June at a level about 5 per cent above the previous par rate. Within the IMF and outside, a consensus began to grow that some form of greater flexibility would allow prompter, more frequent and therefore less politically and economically damaging exchange rate changes to occur. A report by the executive directors of the IMF, circulated at the beginning of September 1970, made cautiously approving noises about the potential benefits of a greater frequency of changes in exchange rates to allow for incremental movements rather than large destabilising shifts after speculative pressure had built up. The report also noted the recent usefulness of 'transitional floating' within the pegged rate regime for currencies to find their level before re-pegging. In early May 1971 a massive capital outflow from the United States prompted the Deutschmark again to float temporarily, and on 19 July 1971 William Dale, the US executive director to the IMF, made a statement that the United States supported the use of floating exchange rates as a transition between par values.[46]

Despite EEC commitment to stable pegged exchange rates, the evolution of official and academic ideology over exchange rate flexibility and the successful 'transitional floating' of the Deutschmark made it easier for the United Kingdom to consider a wider range of options when pressure mounted on sterling in the summer of 1972. There had been several precipitating factors increasing speculative pressure in the spring of that year. The current account was in surplus, but injudicious comments by the Chancellor of the Exchequer, Anthony Barber, in his budget speech at the end of March hinting at a possible devaluation damaged confidence.[47] On 15 June news of a possible dock strike was announced in the afternoon, which, coupled with remarks by Denis Healey, the Labour Party's shadow chancellor, about the prospects for a devaluation, sent the market into a spiral. On 15 June EEC central banks bought $59 million worth of sterling to support the Snake in their first intervention that

[45] Memo of a conversation at Camp David between Treasury Secretary Kennedy, Volcker and other US Treasury representatives and Giscard d'Estaing, French minister of economy and finance, Wormser, governor of the Banque de France, Larre, director of the Treasury, 3–5 May 1970; NARA, Department of the Treasury, Files of Under Secretary Volcker: FRC 56 79 15.

[46] US$1 billion flowed into West Germany on 4 May and European foreign exchange markets were closed from 5 to 10 May 1971. Telegram from the Department of State to certain posts, 26 July 1971, NARA, RG 59, Central Files, 1970–73, FN 10.

[47] Heath criticised Barber for his comments in a meeting on Wednesday 21 June. Meeting at 10 Downing St., TNA T354/275.

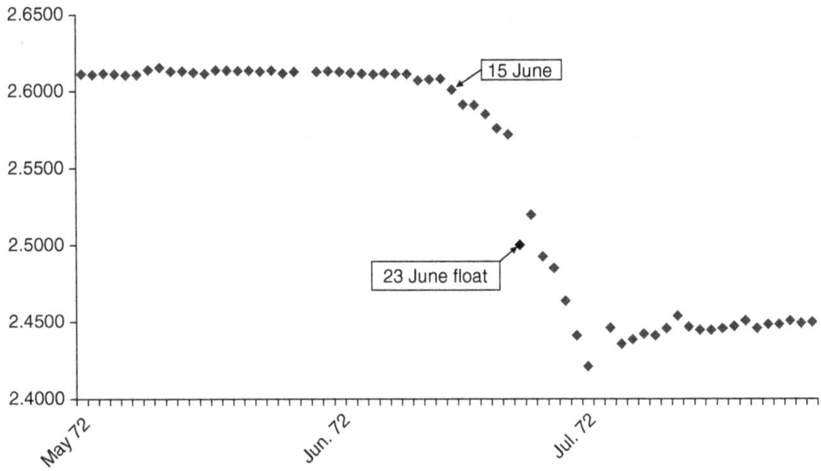

Figure 9.1 Daily exchange rate, US dollar/pound, 1 May–31 July 1972
Note: Rates are noon buying rates in New York.
Source: Federal Reserve statistical release, 1989.

month, and overnight the Bank of England spent $8 million in New York. The next day EEC central banks had to buy $504 million and the Snake margin was at its maximum 2.25 per cent.[48] Figure 9.1 shows that the pressure began in earnest on the exchange rate from 15 June and then mounted, until sterling was allowed to sink on 23 June to $2.50 from its earlier parity of $2.60. The rate then stabilised at about $ 2.45 during July and August.

At the beginning of June the Treasury had anticipated problems with regard to the public borrowing requirement as the projected deficit ballooned. Since money supply was growing quickly, as was private credit, the Treasury advised that interest rates should be raised in order to restore confidence in the government's ability to contain inflation and thus enhance demand for longer-term gilts.[49] The mounting exchange crisis on 20 June strengthened the case for a rise in bank rate, and the possibility of changing the sterling exchange rate was first discussed in a meeting of the Chancellor, the chief secretary to the Treasury, Patrick Jenkin, and the Minister of State in Barber's room at the House of

[48] Foreign exchange market evening report, 15 and 16 June 1972, TNA T354/275.
[49] Paper by A. M. Bailey on monetary policy – a draft note for the prime minister to be considered by the Chancellor of the Exchequer, 8 June 1972, TNA T354/275.

Commons on that afternoon. Sir Douglas Allen (the permanent secretary to the Treasury), Sir Alan Neale (second permanent secretary to the Treasury for finance), Sir Donald MacDougall (chief economic adviser), Christopher Fogarty and F. Cassell (of the Treasury staff) were also in attendance to prepare for Barber's meeting with the prime minister about monetary policy the next day.[50] This tentative discussion about changing the sterling exchange rate led to the commissioning of a flurry of papers in the Treasury to clarify various issues related to floating and devaluation.

During trading on 20 June the Snake margin grew to the maximum 2.25 per cent spread against the dollar, with sterling the weakest, at –0.75 per cent (closely followed by the Italian lira, at –⅝ per cent), and the franc and Deutschmark the strongest, at +1.5 per cent.[51] EEC intervention to help sterling amounted to $496 million by the French, Belgian and West German central banks (the Norwegian central bank also contributed), creating a forward liability that would be due for settlement by the Bank of England at the end of July. This brought the cumulative monthly liability from EEC intervention to $1.104 billion. UK reserves fell by $12 million to $8.343 billion, leaving a net accumulation in the reserves during June as a whole of $1.193 billion. Sterling closed half a cent down from the previous day at $2.5852.

During trading the next day there was a struggle to keep sterling within the 2.25 per cent margin, and after 4:00 p.m. it fell sharply to 1⅛ per cent below par, which stretched the Snake twenty-five points beyond the 2.25 per cent margin after the continental European markets closed.[52] EEC central banks intervened with a further $216 million, and UK reserves fell another $10 million. The pressure was clearly persisting, and the accumulated end-month liability to the EEC at the end of 21 June was now $1.32 billion. Nonetheless, this was almost within the net accumulation of UK reserves during June of $1.183 billion.

At his meeting with Edward Heath at 4:30 p.m., after the Continental markets had closed, Barber proposed raising the bank rate to 6 per cent, both to check the growth of domestic credit and to stem the outflow of dollars in the foreign exchange market. Along with an announcement of an increase in car registrations, and falling unemployment, this was predicted to have a helpful impact on confidence, which he believed was at the heart of the crisis. Echoing the circumstances of 1967, Barber concluded that, 'if no action was taken, it would be widely

[50] Note for the record by C. W. Fogarty, undated and added to the file after the event. There was no formal record of this meeting; TNA T354/275.

[51] Foreign exchange market evening report, 20 June 1972, TNA354/275.

[52] Foreign exchange market evening report, 21 and 22 June 1972, TNA T354/275.

assumed that the Government was not intending to defend the present exchange rate'.[53] Heath resisted Barber's proposal. He did not see a problem in the rapid rise in the money supply per se, merely that too much money was going into the property market, thus fuelling inflation. Increased consumer lending, meanwhile, was in line with government policy. Eventually he was convinced, however, that the alternatives of making a further call for special deposits or requiring banks to keep a minimum proportion of their assets in gilt-edged securities would not be feasible, and he approved the announcement the following day of a one percentage point rise in bank rate.

Barber then turned to exit strategies for the current exchange crisis. He preferred to float sterling, at least temporarily, rather than devalue to another pegged rate, which was unlikely to inspire much confidence 'unless it was combined with some definite action on inflation'. There was a danger that a float could 'get out of control' or even that the rate might float upward after a time, with damaging consequences for export competitiveness. Even with a float, the Bank of England and the Chancellor agreed that a statutory prices and incomes policy would be required to regain international confidence, but Heath countered that the experiences of the last ten years showed that such a statutory policy was unlikely to command credibility. Jeremy Morse of the Bank of England suggested that sterling would probably settle at a nominal rate of about \$2.40 (an 8 per cent depreciation, back to the pre-Smithsonian US dollar rate) if an effective anti-inflationary policy accompanied the float.[54] To avoid the trigger for payments under the Sterling Agreements guarantee, the rate needed to stay above \$2.376. Floating the exchange rate would contravene agreements the United Kingdom had with the IMF and the EEC, but Barber believed his European colleagues would accept a *temporary* float, although there might be difficulties if the rate was not fixed again by the time the country joined the EEC at the beginning of 1973. The Treasury's case for 'fundamental disequilibrium' to justify a change of parity to the IMF was that the current account needed to be in surplus by about £400 million to finance structural net foreign capital outflows, but this was unlikely to be met over the next few years because of the eroding price competitiveness of British exports and payments due to be paid to the EEC on accession.[55] The meeting closed without a decision having been made.

[53] Meeting at 10 Downing St. between Heath, Barber, Sir Douglas Allen, Sir Donald MacDougall and C. J. Morse; TNA T354/275.

[54] This was also the view of the Treasury. A. H. Lovell, 'A temporary float', 21 June 1972, TNA T354/275.

[55] Lovell to A. K. Rawlinson, 21 June 1972, TNA T354/275.

Overnight intervention in New York on 21 June amounted to $79 million. The exchange rate opened in London on 22 June at $2.571 and slumped to $2.5635 in the early morning before rallying by mid-morning. At 10:30 a.m. Sir Douglas Allen convened a meeting at the Treasury, at which it was decided to recommend to the Chancellor that the exchange market be closed and European central banks be advised to stop supporting sterling, thus introducing a floating exchange rate.[56] Jeremy Morse was also consulted and then Allen and A. K. Rawlinson, a senior Treasury official, went to no. 11 to meet with Barber, who was called out of the Cabinet meeting. Barber realised that closing the market would commit the government either to float or to devalue, and he hoped to avoid this by waiting to see if the bank rate announcement had any impact. It was planned to reassess the situation at 2:30 p.m.

In the event, raising the bank rate to 6 per cent at noon had only a marginal effect, and Barber, Allen, Sir Donald MacDougall, Morse and various Treasury officials met as planned at 2:30 p.m.[57] Barber was still reluctant to close the market and thereby commit to changing the exchange rate, since he had publicly denied any intention to devalue. We must suspect that this helped in the decision to float, as Barber would not have to contradict himself by changing the formal parity, although the broader consensus in the Treasury and the Bank was also moving in that direction as the afternoon wore on. Allen and MacDougall argued that the decision had to be taken in the national interest rather than on political grounds. The Treasury view was that there was a consensus in Europe that the sterling rate would need to be changed 'in due course' and that, 'if a change had to be made, it would be better to make it soon while some cushion of reserves remained'.[58] Morse dismissed the idea of merely leaving the Snake, since the only slightly wider Smithsonian margins would also be unsupportable. Barber concluded that the immediate decision was whether to close the market immediately or to wait until the evening. The meeting agreed that, in order to avoid the appearance of panic, any announcement should be in the evening, subject to the approval of the prime minister.

The meeting then discussed whether to float or to devalue sterling. The preference for a float was reinforced by a telephone call on the afternoon of 22 June from Sir Alan Neale, who was in meetings in Luxembourg. His European colleagues had all indicated that they would prefer London

[56] Rawlinson, 'The decision to float', 28 June 1972, TNA T354/275.

[57] Note of a meeting in Barber's room, Treasury Chambers, 22 June 1972, TNA T354/275.

[58] Ibid.

to 'declutch' rather than 'change gear'.[59] This lifted the threat of political obstacles to floating in Europe and made it an easier option. Sir Alan also observed that devaluation to a new parity would require much firmer commitments on wage restraint to ensure confidence, but not much could be done to contain inflation through, for example, a wage freeze as the unions would not agree. A key consideration was that Heath would not be convinced of the need for a draconian basket of accompanying measures, but with a float 'it was easier to justify the absence of accompanying measures against inflation'.[60] There was a danger that the float would turn into a continuous slide, but, on the other hand, MacDougall worried that the rate would not fall far enough to correct the balance of payments in the medium term. Moreover, the Americans were expected to prefer a float to a devaluation because it would generate less pressure on the US dollar.

Although it was not openly discussed, devaluation would also be embarrassing to Barber, and there were hints that 1967 was in the minds of officials. Unlike the infamous claims after the 1967 devaluation, this time the Treasury's draft announcement that was prepared for a possible devaluation concluded that 'the pound in your pocket is worth less – there is no escaping that fact'.[61] A floating rate would allow Barber to express confidence that the Smithsonian parity was appropriate but that short-term speculation had forced a temporary float 'as an alternative to wasting more resources in order to convince the holders of sterling about the appropriate exchange rate'.[62] This was particularly disingenuous, given the consensus that $2.40, not $2.60, was the equilibrium exchange rate. The meeting concluded that Barber should recommend to Heath that the markets be closed on 23 June and that sterling should float freely (or sink freely) until it reached $2.40.

Rather as an afterthought, it was agreed that new exchange controls would have to be introduced overnight against the sterling area to contain capital outflows through this 'loophole'. This effectively ended the sterling area system that had been operating since 1945, although the level of exchange control within the sterling area remained lower than for the rest of the world until 1974. Tight restrictions were imposed on outward portfolio investment in the sterling area but there were higher

[59] 'Rawlinson, 'The decision to float'.

[60] Note of a meeting in Barber's room, Treasury Chambers, 22 June 1972, TNA T354/275.

[61] Rawlinson to Sir Douglas Allen, enclosing draft statements for a float and for a devaluation, 21 June 1972, TNA T354/275.

[62] Note of a meeting in Barber's room, Treasury Chambers, 22 June 1972, TNA T354/275.

allowances for emigrants and for sterling companies borrowing in the United Kingdom compared to the non-sterling area.[63] The Treasury had been planning for imposing exchange control on the sterling area since March 1969, when large portfolio flows to Australia attracted its attention. Despite resurfacing repeatedly between 1969 and 1971 in the context of Britain's applications to the EEC, the plans had been rejected because of the threat to the Sterling Agreements if Australia and other sterling area members retaliated by diversifying reserves.[64] By June 1972 it was evident that the sterling area system had been so changed by the Sterling Agreements and the pragmatic acceptance of the benefits of greater exchange rate flexibility by most countries that these considerations receded into the background. The end of the sterling area system of exchange control became a footnote to the retreat of sterling rather than a crucial element.

At 4:00 p.m. on 22 June the market closed at the same rate as the previous day ($2.5765) but at huge cost in terms of EEC intervention (plus Norway), which reached $1.229 billion from France, Norway, Belgium and West Germany. In addition, UK reserves were run down by $106 million. The accumulated end-month liability to the EEC was now $2.549 billion against a net increase in reserves during June of $1.077 billion. Barber, Allen, MacDougall, Armstrong and Morse went to no. 10 at 4:15 p.m. and put their recommendations.[65] Heath asked about the source of the pressure and expressed optimism about achieving a voluntary prices and incomes policy, which would help dampen inflationary expectations. He agreed to announce the closure of the market and the float on the morning of 23 June before the markets opened.[66]

The reaction of the EEC and the United States to the news that sterling would float out of the Snake temporarily was generally supportive. As noted above, the EEC's preference was established before the decision was made but the United States was not consulted beforehand. In Washington, the Earl of Cromer, the British ambassador and former governor of the Bank of England, informed James Robertson, the Fed's vice-chairman, and Volcker together.[67] He noted that 'it was clear that the assumption

[63] R. S. Symons, 'Exchange control 1959–1972: UK attitudes and actions', Treasury Historical Memorandum no. 23, April 1975, TNA T267/34.

[64] TNA T312/2909. Rawlinson was consistently in favour of imposing exchange controls on the sterling area.

[65] Note for the record by R. T. Armstrong, 3 July 1972, TNA T354/275.

[66] Rawlinson, 'The decision to float'.

[67] Telegram from Earl of Cromer in Washington, 23/6/72, TNA T354/275. Cromer had not been able to reach the secretary of the Treasury, George Shultz, or Arthur Burns, chairman of the Federal Reserve. Cromer was governor of the Bank of England from 1961 to 1966.

that the US would prefer a float to a downward step change was correct'. Schweitzer, managing director of the IMF, was also sanguine 'and said that he did not see that we had any alternative'. All were concerned that other countries might choose to follow sterling in a float, in particular Italy, Norway and Denmark, which would undermine its effectiveness.

President Pompidou's message to Heath was cordial but concluded rather ominously:

> I am convinced that a regime of fixed rates of exchange, in addition to the fact that it will favour the development of trade and investment, also constitutes one of the indispensable conditions for the proper functioning of the Common Market, which GB is to join on 1 January 1973. Such a regime also seems to me to constitute the foundation of all progress in European monetary cooperation and all developments in the reform of the international monetary system whose necessity, as you yourself have observed, has been demonstrated by recent events.[68]

In other words, floating was not the policy of a good European.

The run on sterling was much greater than had been anticipated during a 'contingency' exercise conducted as recently as May 1972. This exercise assumed that the market expected a devaluation, and predicted that in the first month of pressure a total of £425 million in currency would flow out of the reserves for reasons other than normal current account transactions, rising to £3 billion within three months as both private and official sterling assets were sold. In the event, £1.14 billion flowed out in June before the closure of the exchange markets on 23 June. Clearly, the Treasury was not prepared for the liquidity of the market and therefore for the speed of the withdrawal, particularly with regard to overseas sterling area holdings, which were believed to pose a medium-term rather than a short-term threat.

From table 9.1 it is clear that the drain from the sterling area was much higher than had been anticipated, both on official and on private account. The total identified sterling area drain amounted to £325 million compared with an anticipated £75 million. This was the greatest miscalculation in the exercise.

Three sterling countries were primarily responsible: Kuwait, Malaysia and Singapore. The Persian Gulf territories were among the largest sterling holders as a result of rising oil revenues, and in May 1972 they held about £200 million in excess of their minimum sterling proportion as set by the Sterling Agreements, and they ran down their sterling balances by £225 million during June. Moreover, Kuwait borrowed £21 million

68 Letter from Pompidou to Heath, 7 July 1972, TNA T354/275.

Table 9.1 *Analysis of the June crisis of 1972 (£ million)*

	One-month estimate	Three-month estimate	Actual June 1972
Foreign-owned sterling assets			
Official OSA	50	500	165
Private OSA	25	150	75
NSA	200	800	175
Sterling borrowed from UK banks by OSA			85
Sterling borrowed from UK banks by NSA			65
Other sterling assets (gilt-edged and company securities)	25	200	0
Bank switching	100	100	200
Company-sector transactions			
Repayment of Eurodollar borrowing	0	200	0
Inter-company accounts	0	200	375
Balancing item (leads and lags)	0	500	
Other residents' transactions			
Hedging remittances to OSA	25	300	0
Stockbuilding	0	50	0
Total	425	3,000	1,140

Source: Memo by D. H. Curzon, FPB [Forum for Private Business] division, UK Treasury, for Boothroyd, 10 August 1972, PRO T354/275.

in sterling in June, which was much higher than the country's usual monthly borrowing, suggesting that it was speculative.[69] The rundown of sterling reserves by Malaysia and Singapore was of a different character, since they were not merely reversing accumulations of sterling made earlier in the year. They were among the most reluctant holders of sterling, for the reasons discussed in chapter 5, and their negotiations with London over MSPs had been bitter right from the beginning in 1968. Together, these states withdrew £50 million of bank deposits and borrowed a further £20 million from UK banks, amounting to a net outflow of £70 million. Most other sterling area countries (including Australia) held their official sterling reserves about constant through the crisis. The Treasury's judgement after the fact was that 'we clearly underestimated the reaction of the more sensitive OSA holders'.[70] During the first five

[69] Memo, 28 July 1972, BE 4A100/4.

[70] Memo by D. H. Curzon, 10 August 1972, TNA T354/275. Most of the increase in borrowing was by Singapore (£16 million); memo, 28 July 1972, BE 4A100/4.

months of 1972 Malaysia reduced its sterling reserves by £26 million, lowering the sterling proportion from 49 per cent to 41 per cent. After sterling floated on 23 June, diversification to European currencies accelerated, and by 10 July 1972 the proportion of Malaysia's sterling was below the 36 per cent MSP threshold, and the country abandoned its Sterling Agreement.[71]

The other major error in the estimate was the speed and scale of foreign companies running down short-term claims on their UK subsidiaries and associates. Such transfers amounted to about £375 million, or as much as the drain to the OSA. These claims had been built up in the last quarter of 1971 during the uncertainty over the US dollar, and then they were reversed in June 1972. It was not possible to distinguish these flows from leads and lags, but the Treasury believed that leads and lags could not be accumulated quickly enough to be responsible for this outflow. The spread of multinational companies in the 1960s thus challenged the international monetary system. The third substantial drain was London banks switching their assets from sterling to foreign currencies. This accounted for £200 million, or 20 per cent of the outflow.

As noted above, one of the historic by-products of the decision to float was the imposition of exchange controls on the overseas sterling area. The list of 'scheduled territories' that comprised the sterling area was contracted to Ireland and the Channel Islands. This was done without consultation and received little more than a passing reference in the Chancellor's announcement. The telegram advising the OSA of the float merely noted that the 'extension of exchange control to sterling area countries is an inescapable necessity during this period of floating rates in order to prevent disruptive outflows of UK resident funds'.[72] Before the announcement, Wiggins of the Treasury had advised Rawlinson that the crisis would be an ideal time to announce new controls, as it would not attract much attention.[73] In addition, it was 'better to have only one row with the Overseas Sterling Area rather than two'. Finally, the EEC would be enthusiastic about such a change, since it was very sensitive to any policies that favoured the sterling area.

The reaction from many parts of the sterling area was remarkably sanguine. New Zealand and Australia had been pegged to the US dollar rather than sterling since the Smithsonian Agreement of December 1971, to limit the range against the US dollar to +/–2.25 per cent, rather than

[71] The Bank of England reported that £40 million was transferred by Malaysia to deposit at European commercial banks, half in Germany and a further £15 million in Switzerland. D. Wiggins to J. G. Littler, 10 October 1972, TNA T312/2968.

[72] Telegram from Douglas-Home to Canberra and Wellington, 23 June 1972, TNA T354/275.

[73] A. J. Wiggins to Rawlinson, 21 June 1972, TNA T354/275.

a possible +/–4.5 per cent if the peg had been to sterling. The increasing amount of dollar-denominated debt and international trade had eroded the relevance of the peg to sterling for these countries. Sterling's float six months later seemed at first to justify their shift to a more stable anchor, although the sinking value of the US dollar soon created fresh inflationary pressures. Michael Wong, the chairman of the Monetary Authority of Singapore, expressed himself pleased, because the new exchange controls would prevent an inflow of capital into Singapore.[74] The float of sterling drove most sterling area governments to shift their peg to the US dollar in an effort to sustain some semblance of nominal exchange rate stability even while the pegged system crumbled. Malaysia and Singapore immediately moved to the US dollar as their reference currency, and Hong Kong followed in July.

Although the float was expressed as a temporary measure in June 1972, it was quickly apparent that refixing sterling would be difficult because of ongoing inflationary pressures. The rate fell below the $2.40 target on 19 October 1972, settling around $2.35 until the beginning of December, when it fell again to $2.34 and remained there until the end of the year. The initial deadline to re-enter the Snake was the beginning of January 1973, but in mid-December 1972 it was decided not to adhere to this timetable. Heath suggested a later deadline of April 1973, when the European Monetary Cooperation Fund was due to become active.[75] This delay had been anticipated in Europe and did not provoke adverse comment.

Throughout the post-war period floating sterling was considered a last resort, to be adopted only in the keenest of emergencies. This view prevailed in policy papers as late as the 1968 gold crisis. By 1972, however, the ideological basis and underlying structure of the international monetary system had changed so much that the sterling float was accepted without much internal opposition and provoked retaliation only from Malaysia. Economic ideology had changed quickly after the abandonment of the single fixed price of gold in 1968, and successful examples of 'transition' floating seemed to vindicate economists' growing theoretical support for floating rates. Furthermore, by 1972 the reserve role had been reduced substantially and the remnants tied up in formal agreements, although the 1972 crisis had shown sterling's continued vulnerability to overseas official and private holdings of sterling. In retrospect, the sterling float was the harbinger of the US dollar float less than a year later.

[74] Telegram from Kuala Lumpur to FCO, 23 June 1972, TNA T312/2967.

[75] Letter from Heath to Pompidou, 13 December 1972, TNA T354/276.

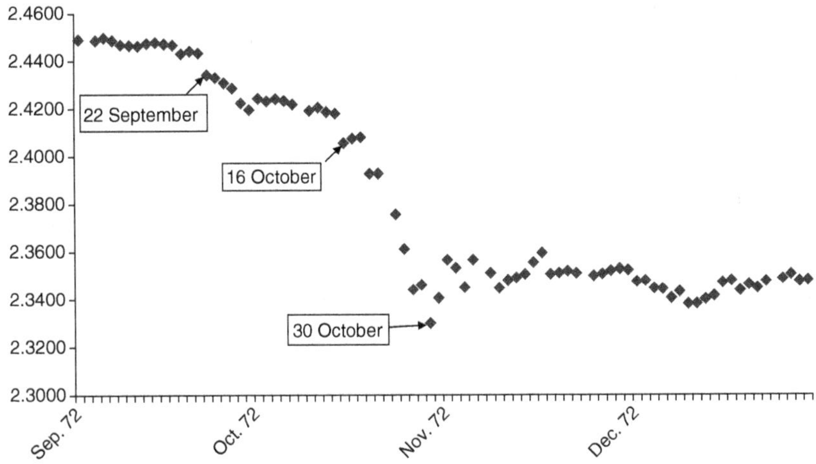

Figure 9.2 Daily exchange rate, US dollar/pound, 1 September–31 December 1972

The end of Bretton Woods, 1973–1974

Events in the international monetary system soon made the deadline for ending sterling's float obsolete. On 21 January 1973 Italy introduced a two-tiered exchange system with a pegged rate for commercial transactions and a floating rate for capital flows. This unsettled the markets, and the next day the Swiss franc floated upwards against the US dollar. A week later the US dollar itself came under enormous pressure when unfavourable balance of trade statistics for 1972 were published. On the morning of 1 February upward pressure on sterling drove the Bank of England to take in $30 million, and consultations began over how to deal with the crisis.[76] For Britain, the issue was complicated by the symbolism of holding the rate of $2.40/£1. Moving away from this target could herald calls from Europe to refix the sterling exchange rate into the Snake. In addition, if the Bank continued to take in dollars rather than letting sterling float upwards, it would have to consult with EEC partners, which would also raise the prospect of calls to refix. The next evening, at 6:00 p.m., Dieter Hiss of the West German Ministry of Finance called to 'consult' over the imposing of capital controls, which were announced later that evening.[77] The French and the Belgians believed that this

[76] Note for the record by D. J. Mitchell, second permanent secretary to the Treasury for overseas finance, 1 February 1973, TNA T354/62.

[77] Note for the record by Mitchell, 5 February 1973, TNA T354/62.

would not be enough to prevent a float of the Deutschmark and pressed, in the Monetary Committee meeting on 6 February, for a two-tiered exchange system separating official and commercial exchange rates, in order to prevent a general float that would forestall economic and monetary union.[78] The West Germans and the Dutch resisted this proposal as technically impossible.

By 9 February 1973 central banks had taken in $8.5 million to support the dollar and the crisis began to come to a head. The finance ministers of West Germany, France and the United Kingdom met in Paris to discuss tactics and options.[79] The Snake could float against the dollar, thus preserving exchange stability amongst the EEC countries, but this might be difficult for some to manage, such as the French franc and the lira. Sterling would probably be pulled up against the dollar as well, with detrimental effects on UK exports. Schmidt suggested a system of reserve pooling to come to the common defence of European exchange rates, but this was considered too generous an offer for the British to accept, since it would inevitably require a quid pro quo. If no arrangement could be found within the next few days, the Deutschmark would be forced into a temporary float, with damaging implications for the CAP and EMU. Volcker had just arrived in Bonn, but the American view was not yet clear and there were fears that there would be a renewed threat of import surcharges from Nixon.

On 10 February Schmidt phoned Barber to report on his private conversation with Volcker (even though Volcker had asked him not to).[80] The Americans proposed a 'big package' to defend the pegged rate system, comprising a dollar devaluation of 10 per cent and a yen revaluation of 20 per cent. Volcker wanted Schmidt to help convince the Japanese to adjust their parity and the French to accept the package, but Schmidt did not feel confident that this could be achieved. Schmidt's response to Volcker was to stall until the views of Barber and Giscard had been established. He told Barber that he and the West German Chancellor, Willy Brandt, still favoured a European solution rather than the American one, but that if the European proposal was not feasible then they might have to fall back on the Volcker plan. Barber and Schmidt agreed that Schmidt should now phone Giscard and warn him of Volcker's plan. This episode makes it clear that, with British membership of the EEC finally completed, the United Kingdom had returned to the core of decision-making, both within Europe and with the United States.

78 Note of the EEC Monetary Committee meeting, afternoon 6 February 1973. The United Kingdom's views on this were not invited because sterling was floating. TNA T354/62.

79 Note by Mitchell of the meeting in Paris, 9 February 1973, TNA T354/62.

80 Note for the record by A. M. Bailey, 10 February 1973, TNA T354/62.

Volcker met with Barber and O'Brien and various officials on the evening of 10 February 1973 to present his proposal.[81] The bilateral balance between the United States and Japan was at the heart of American balance of trade problems, but Volcker had been in Tokyo the previous week and found that the Japanese were unwilling to revalue against the dollar. They did, however, suggest that they might float if other currencies such as the Deutschmark floated. Volcker set out his proposal to devalue the dollar by 10 per cent and pressure the Japanese to revalue by 20 per cent. The United States would need an assurance that other currencies would not follow the dollar in a devaluation, and a specific undertaking from the British that they would allow sterling to float freely upwards. The European governments were given a deadline of only a few days to commit themselves. The alternative to this plan was a common Snake float against the dollar (including sterling), which would also be likely to prompt the yen to float, marking the end of the pegged rate system. The choice for the United Kingdom was, therefore, to fix the sterling rate against European currencies or to give the United States a commitment to allow sterling to climb freely against a depreciated dollar. Volcker indirectly threatened protectionism if his package was not accepted by concluding that 'at present the international monetary system was uneasily poised between openness and restriction' and that his proposal 'could be presented as a springboard for constructive trade negotiations'. He advised that Nixon had decided to introduce new trade legislation to allow import surcharges to be imposed when there was a deficit and to provide broad authority to negotiate tariff and non-tariff barriers. The announcement of these new laws would either follow or be simultaneous with the deal on exchange rates.

Once this meeting had concluded the key players moved on to Chequers, the official country residence of the prime minister, to discuss the options with Heath.[82] Heath reported that Brandt had told him that the French would not accept the US proposals and O'Brien reported on meetings in Basle at the BIS that afternoon at which it was clear that a common EEC float could not be arranged quickly. Because sterling could not be refixed realistically into the Snake within the next few days, it was agreed that the United Kingdom had to give its support to Volcker's proposals despite the French intransigence, and Barber relayed this decision to Volcker at about midnight. To encourage the French to accept the proposals, he also reported the British position to Giscard d'Estaing at nine o'clock the next morning, just before Volcker's meeting in Paris.[83]

[81] Bailey, note of a meeting at no. 11 Downing St., 10 February 1973, TNA T354/62.
[82] Note of a meeting held at Chequers at 10:30 p.m., 10 February 1973, TNA T354/62.
[83] Note for the record by Bailey, 11 February 1974, TNA T354/62.

In conversation with Schmidt, Barber explained that the United Kingdom could not commit itself to return to the Snake without considerable multilateral support to take account of overseas sterling liabilities, as moving in and out of the Snake was very costly.[84] Schmidt replied that he understood the British position and that the Volcker plan was acceptable to his government as a second best solution. Privately, Heath expressed great enthusiasm for the possibility of sterling going back into the Snake in exchange for transferring sterling liabilities to the EEC as a whole, noting that 'a time of crisis like the present gave an opportunity for major moves of this kind which could too easily be missed'.[85] After his meeting with Volcker, Giscard phoned Barber and invited him to dinner at his home in Paris that evening, along with Schmidt. Giovanni Malagodi, formerly a manager of Banca Commerciale Italiana, would join them after dinner, and then Volcker would be summoned. At this point the French were likely to accept the Volcker plan so long as the Japanese were prepared to revalue. Before leaving for Paris, Barber phoned the US Treasury secretary, George Shultz, to report on developments, noting that 'the US initiative in sending Mr Volcker on his round trip, beginning with the Japanese, had been enormously useful, and had given us and the other European Governments a much better appreciation of the options'.[86]

The dinner went as planned, and the French, Germans and British agreed to the US scheme.[87] Volcker returned to Washington the next day and Shultz announced the 10 per cent devaluation of the US dollar. As described by Solomon, Volcker 'had covered 31,000 miles, had run out of cigars and clean shirts, and had lost his hat in Tokyo', but he did manage to get the deal that Nixon, Shultz and Burns wanted.[88] At the dinner meeting in Paris, Giscard pressed Barber a bit over when sterling would be refixed, but Barber responded that uncertainty in industrial relations and the balance of payments made it impossible to tell, although he reassured Giscard that Britain was fully committed to progress towards EMU.

At the end of February the dollar gold price leapt to $90 per ounce, and on 1 March 1973 central banks took in $3.6 billion to support the newly devalued dollar exchange rate. The new rates were clearly not sustainable, and the London market was closed the next day. The EEC

[84] Note for the record by Bailey, 11 February 1974, TNA T354/62 [not ibid.].

[85] Note for the record of Chancellor's briefing meeting with the prime minister, 12 February 1974, TNA T354/62.

[86] Note for the record by Bailey, 12 February 1974, TNA T354/62.

[87] Note for the record, 12 February 1974, TNA T354/62.

[88] Soloman, *The International Monetary System,* p. 230. Solomon was adviser to the Federal Reserve Board during this period.

quickly rallied around with various proposals to discuss at a meeting on 4 March, including freezing all non-resident deposits to stop short-term capital flows, a two-tiered exchange rate within a common float, and the IMF's proposals to return to fixed parities. None of these were supported in London, due to the damage to the Eurodollar market in the City of London and their technical impracticality.[89] In the end, the major outcome of the meeting was a suggestion by West Germany that the EEC embark on the common float that had been rejected in February. The situation had not changed for the United Kingdom, however, and Barber claimed that sterling could not join unless there was support to help liquidate overseas holdings of sterling. Solomon notes that 'it seems unlikely that this was a serious demand', but we have seen that Heath and Barber certainly viewed the crisis as an opportunity to garner such support.[90]

Their views seemed vindicated by the European Council's simultaneous announcement on 11 March that the Snake would float free from the dollar and that the Council would study the problem of the sterling balances 'and the methods by which the Community could help to alleviate them'.[91] The European Commission was charged with making suggestions for short-term monetary support and a progressive pooling of reserves to help the United Kingdom, Ireland and Italy rejoin the Snake. This was an idea that the UK Treasury wanted to take forward immediately.[92] After a first flush of enthusiasm, however, the West Germans and the French lost interest in such a plan as the urgency for sterling to join the Snake receded. On 24 April Fogarty of the Treasury and Stanley Payton of the Bank of England met with their West German counterparts to discuss support for sterling's return to the Snake, but they encountered a hostile response. It was up to the United Kingdom to pursue domestic policies that would allow it to join the Snake in a sustainable way, just as other countries had overcome their domestic problems. The West Germans were particularly concerned not to increase international liquidity through new credit schemes to cope with reducing sterling's international reserve role.[93] Fogarty met with his opposite number in the French Ministry of Finance and received a similarly cool response. Although the French were more willing to consider new credit facilities for members rejoining the Snake, these would

89 Briefing papers for Chancellor's trip to Brussels, 3 March 1973, TNA T354/62.

90 Solomon, *The International Monetary System*, p. 232.

91 European Council announcement, 11 March 1973, TNA T354/62.

92 Telegram to D. P. Thomson, British embassy Bonn, from C. W. Fogarty, Treasury, 26 March 1973, TNA FCO 59/1060.

93 Talks of Fogarty (Treasury) and Payton (BE) with officials from German Ministry of Finance and Bundesbank, 26 April 1973, TNA T354/62.

not be big enough to deal with the sterling reserves.[94] Both the West Germans and the French were critical of the build-up in overseas sterling that had been allowed in 1971 and early 1972, and urged Britain to amend the Sterling Agreements to discourage further accumulations. Fogarty concluded that

> the proposals already before the Prime Minister ... now seem increasingly likely to be unnegotiable except perhaps by a major new political initiative.

With that, Heath's hopes for a European solution to the sterling balances as a quid pro quo for joining the Snake were dashed.

Meanwhile, after the announcement that the Snake would float, there was a round of extended G10 meetings to try to elicit from the Americans an undertaking to intervene in concert with members of the Snake to ensure 'orderly exchange markets'. The Europeans were not yet ready for a clean float, but at the deputies' meeting on 12 March Volcker refused to commit to intervention.[95] There was also debate over whether the intention of others to intervene should be made public. The BIS and Switzerland argued that this would merely draw in speculators to test the intentions of the authorities, while others argued that such publicity would stabilise the market. The British position was that, since the laissez-faire attitude of the Americans was destabilising, an announcement of their intentions would be helpful, although the guidelines for any intervention should remain secret.[96] In the end the communiqué of the conference did refer to intervention but not to collective intervention. Members agreed

> in principle that official intervention in exchange markets may be useful at appropriate times, to facilitate the maintenance of orderly conditions ... Each nation stated that it will be prepared to intervene at its initiative in its own market, when necessary and desirable, acting in a flexible manner in the light of market conditions and in close consultation with the authorities of the nation whose currency may be bought or sold.[97]

With this communiqué, the Bretton Woods system of pegged but adjustable exchange rates that had been established in 1945 finally came to an end. The lack of consensus over what form the international monetary system should take resulted in a compromise mixture of regimes, with pegged rates among most European currencies and developing countries

[94] Fogarty for the Chancellor, 'Rejoining the Snake: support facilities (including the sterling balance problem)', 27 April 1973, TNA T354/62.

[95] Note for the record by M. E. Hedley-Millar, 13 March 1973, TNA T354/62.

[96] Brief for the Chancellor of the Exchequer, for the G10 meeting on 16 March 1973, TNA T354/62.

[97] Quoted in Solomon, *The International Monetary System*, p. 233.

and floating rates for sterling and the US dollar. Sterling area countries shifted their peg from sterling to the dollar between 1971 and 1973, and then gradually to trade-weighted basket pegs (led by New Zealand in July 1974) in an effort to stabilise producer incomes. The new system was not viewed at the time, therefore, as the paradigm shift it is sometimes portrayed in hindsight – i.e. as a clean break from fixed to floating exchange rates. Sterling had been floating almost two years before the end of the Bretton Woods system while, on the other hand, many currencies maintained pegged exchange rates for many years afterwards. The Committee of 20 on the Reform of the International Monetary System was convened within the IMF to determine future directions, but its conclusions were in the end too vague to provide leadership. Guidelines to be followed while floating were adopted by members of the IMF in 1974, but it was not until 1978 that the IMF statutes were formally amended to allow members to choose their own exchange rate arrangements. The advent of floating rates for developed countries and a more generalised peg to the US dollar by developing countries that had used sterling did not immediately affect the currency distribution of reserves, which reflected the importance of sterling in trade and international borrowing as well as the continuation of the Sterling Agreements first forged in the summer of 1968.

Renewing the Sterling Agreements

The first renewal of the Sterling Agreements took place before the new exchange rates were set in Washington in December 1971. Under the renewed terms, the exchange guarantee was still set to be invoked if sterling fell below $2.376, but the Smithsonian rate increased the dollar/sterling exchange rate from $2.40 to $2.60, making it much less likely that the guarantee would be invoked, since the exchange rate could fall by 8.5 per cent before compensation would need to be paid. Countries holding large amounts of sterling, such as Malaysia, Singapore and Kuwait, assumed that the intervention rate would be adjusted, but they were disappointed. Barber considered changing the intervention rate to $2.60 at the time of the sterling float in June 1972, but this was roundly rejected by his staff, as it would cost the equivalent of about £200 million and would be viewed by the British public as 'in a sense a windfall gain to the overseas sterling area from the Smithsonian agreement'.[98] This decision generated very deep resentment in Malaysia and Singapore,

[98] Note of a meeting in the Chancellor of the Exchequer's room, 22 June 1972, TNA T354/275.

in particular, whose populations were already braced for the final withdrawal of British military forces.[99]

The Malaysian finance minister, Tan Siew Sin, wrote to Barber to request a change in the trigger rate on 12 February 1972 in terms that suggest he expected the request to be uncontroversial.[100] Singapore went a step further and requested a formal review of the entire Sterling Agreement, with a view to abandoning it. For the British this posed considerable risk, since, if Singapore dropped the agreement, it would have to be ejected from the sterling area, and exchange controls would need to be introduced between Singapore and Malaysia, which would be very difficult given the transferability of currencies between the two states. If, on the other hand, Malaysia followed Singapore in abrogating the agreement (which seemed likely), this would substantially reduce the proportion of total sterling covered by the agreements and thus mark 'the effective collapse of the structure of the Agreements'.[101]

Tan wrote to Barber on 21 April 1972 to complain: 'I must admit that until I received your reply, I felt that the amendment proposed by us should present no difficulty to you.'[102] He concluded that, if the amendment was not forthcoming, Malaysia needed more latitude with its reserves policy, warning that we 'may find it necessary to inform you that we have to reconsider our position in regard to the Agreement'. Barber responded rather equivocally, on 12 May, as speculative pressure was building against sterling. He asserted that 'Britain's external position is now stronger than for many years. There will naturally be fluctuations. Some things may go less well in the period ahead. Other things may go better.'[103] Just six weeks later sterling would float.

Malaysia's reaction to the float was the most negative and vociferous of all the sterling countries, as Tan accused the government of 'deliberate duplicity in having refused Malaysia's request for a new guarantee', and the Malaysians quickly ran down their sterling reserves below their MSP, thus abrogating the Sterling Agreement.[104] Wong of the Monetary Authority of Singapore told the UK high commissioner that his country no longer felt bound by the Sterling Agreement, although it did continue with it until it expired, unlike Malaysia. Singapore announced that it had lost the eqivalent of Singapore $45 million as a result of the float, but Tan

99 Schenk, 'Malaysia and the end of the Bretton Woods system 1965–72'.

100 Tan Siew Sin to Barber, 21 February 1972, TNA T312/2968.

101 Wiggins brief for Sir Alan Neale, 21 March 1972, TNA T312/2968. Bahrain and Kuwait were also expected to follow Singapore. Together, the four countries held 25 per cent of overseas-held sterling reserves.

102 Letter from Tan to Barber, 21 April 1972, TNA T312/2968.

103 Letter from Barber to Tan, 12 May 1972, TNA T312/2968.

104 Bank of England memo, 6 July 1972, BE OV44/245.

refused to reveal Malaysia's losses. On the basis of the amount of sterling in the reserves in May 1972, the losses were probably of the order of US$21 million, or Malaysian $59 million. Despite the float, most other signatories to the Sterling Agreements continued to see benefit in the exchange guarantee, and discussions for renewals began again in the autumn of 1972, in time for their expiry in September 1973.

Hong Kong, with one of the highest MSPs (originally 99 per cent, but reduced to 89 per cent in September 1971), was the most enthusiastic lobbiest for a new Sterling Agreement during 1972 and 1973. Crucially, the Hong Kong government had offered its own exchange rate guarantee for commercial banks' sterling assets after their devaluation/revaluation debacle of November 1967, and their ability to afford this guarantee depended on their own Sterling Agreement with the United Kingdom. In mid-September 1972 Philip Haddon-Cave, the Hong Kong financial secretary, was in London, where the Bank of England and UK Treasury urged him to cut the banks loose from the guarantee. He responded that 'we are trying to explain to Hong Kong banks that the Hong Kong government runs the place, but it is rather difficult'.[105]

Despite Hong Kong's importance as the largest holder of sterling, the United Kingdom continued to look to Australia as the bellwether for the Sterling Agreements. Without Australia on board, no progress was likely to be achieved with Malaysia, Singapore or New Zealand. As a colony, Hong Kong's bargaining power was limited, and the territory's pleas for a new agreement were ignored. As the sterling exchange rate plunged in October 1972 Barber finally confirmed that he was halting all negotiations for renewing the Sterling Agreements, since Australia and New Zealand had expressed their unwillingness to proceed at the recent IMF meeting in Washington.[106] Five days later, on 25 October, the sterling rate fell below the guarantee threshold and the clock started to tick on the thirty-day deadline before London would be due to pay compensation. Sterling did indeed stay below the threshold for more than thirty days in October/November 1972, costing the United Kingdom a total of £58 million in compensation to signatories of Sterling Agreements.[107]

At the end of October 1972 HSBC finally ran out of patience and announced that, without the underpinning of a new Sterling Agreement, it would diversify its own reserves (which amounted to

105 Haddon-Cave in London meeting with BE and Treasury, 18 September 1972, BE OV44/266.

106 Telegram from Chancellor of the Exchequer to OSA posts, 20 October 1972, TNA T312/2967.

107 Meeting on 26 August chaired by Sir Alan Neale, 27 August 1971. Prime minister's views recorded in a note from Armstrong to Ryrie, 20 September 1971, BE OV44/192.

about £300 million) by £10 to 15 million per month, starting in January 1973. The Hong Kong government feared that this would pull overall reserves into a breach of the Sterling Agreement, thus making them ineligible for the UK guarantee, which they relied on to compensate their domestic banks.[108] After some complicated negotiations, Barber agreed to a concession that Hong Kong's banks would be allowed to diversify up to £100 million over five months.[109] As it turned out, high demand for sterling from the Bank of China used up £90 million of HSBCs sterling reserves, and it did not diversify into other reserve currencies during the five-month period.[110]

All the same, a new Sterling Agreement was not forthcoming, and, after months of continued stalling in London, at the beginning of August 1973 the Hong Kong government itself finally ran out of patience and announced to the Bank of England that if a new sterling guarantee was not agreed within a week it would diversify official sterling assets down to 50 per cent of total reserves. At this point Hong Kong's sterling assets were £660 million, amounting to 88.6 per cent of its total reserves. The governor of Hong Kong, Murray MacLehose, also reported that compensating the commercial banks would cost the government £50 million, which would be paid at the end of September and would probably be immediately sold in London by the banks for other currencies.[111] Against the £50 million liability to Hong Kong banks, the government was eligible for payments of only £15.1 million from the United Kingdom under the guarantee.[112] MacLehose remarked that 'we have held on out of loyalty and in the expectation of definite proposals from HMG, and required the banks to do so too. Because the guarantee itself is now of so little value we have long passed the point of commercial prudence.'[113] He insisted that the MSP be reduced immediately to 70 per cent, to allow diversification, and then to 50 per cent after six months.[114] The British government reply invoked its imperial control by stating that 'we cannot endorse any diversification of your own official reserves', prompting

108 Governor MacLehose to FCO, 30 October 1972, BE OV44/266.

109 Payton note for Fenton and governors, 24 November 1972, BE OV44/267.

110 Payton note for the record, seen by O'Brien, 14 May 1973, BE OV44/267.

111 Telegram from Hong Kong, 26 July 1973, BE OV44/267. This compares to compensation paid to commercial banks after the 1967 devaluation of £10.6 million. Telegram from Governor Trench to Secretary of State for colonies, 17 January 1969, BE OV44/261.

112 Hong Kong received two interim payments, of £7,216,555 on 9 February 1973 and £7,776,064 on 12 April 1973. A final payment of £200,000 was pending settlement of the amount of eligible commercial bank sterling. 'Note on the sterling agreement', note by Overseas Office to Stone, 26 September 1973, BE OV44/268.

113 Telegram from governor of Hong Kong, 2 August 1973, BE OV44/268.

114 Ibid.

MacLehose and Haddon-Cave to set out for London.[115] When they left they were again empty-handed, to the dismay of the Hong Kong Legislative Council, which wrote in strong terms that it was 'gravely dissatisfied with the attitude of the British government over a matter which is of vital importance to the economy of Hong Kong'.[116]

As the deadline for the agreements to expire (24 September 1973) approached, pressure on the sterling exchange rate prompted the British government to announce a unilateral six-month extension for all the agreements on 6 September. This reassured the markets and avoided another round of prolonged bilateral negotiations. Goodstadt of the *Far Eastern Economic Review* reported this breakthrough as '[a] sweaty hand pushed a tatty piece of paper at Hong Kong Financial Secretary Philip Haddon-Cave when he stopped at Bahrain recently on a flight back from London'.[117] The new agreement differed from others by setting an upper limit on the amount of sterling that would be guaranteed (the amount held on 24 September 1973), thus reducing the incentive to accumulate new sterling. The guarantee threshold was set at $2.4213 (up from $2.37) and would be calculated as the average rate over the six months. The rate was breached as sterling floated down against the dollar from mid-October 1973, costing about £100 million in compensation.[118]

Although the Sterling Agreements were credited with limiting diversification and steadying confidence, the instability in the dollar/sterling exchange rate and high London interest rates made the sterling balances an expensive form of borrowing for the United Kingdom (and a lucrative investment for their holders).[119] Another consideration against renewing the agreements again was that oil producers were beginning to accumulate large balances, which were a new addition to the 'traditional' reserves that Britain felt an obligation to guarantee. In January 1974 Barber approached Australia and New Zealand to sound them out over a less formal arrangement to contain diversification of their reserves over the next two to three years without an exchange guarantee.[120] Although

115 Reply to Hong Kong, 2 August 1973, BE OV44/268.

116 Letter from P. C. Woo to Sir Hugh Norman-Walker (acting governor), transmitted in a telegram to the FCO, 28 August 1973, BE OV44/268.

117 Goodstadt, L., 'Greasy palms', *Far Eastern Economic Review*, 81(37), 1973, p. 55.

118 D. A. Walker, 'Post-election brief: official sterling balances', 19 February 1974, TNA T358/158. The average exchange rate from September to February was $2.34.

119 Ibid.

120 Barber to Heath, 18 February 1974, TNA PREM15/2056. Barber proposed this at the beginning of January 1974, and the Australian and New Zealand representatives were approached at the C20 meeting in Rome. Barber to Heath, 7 January 1974, TNA PREM15/2056.

they expressed sympathy with Britain's predicament, they were unable to commit themselves to any such scheme, so this approach was abandoned. Despite the drawbacks of the Sterling Agreements, Barber was convinced that the predicted pressures on the balance of payments over the next year made renewing them again unilaterally Britain's only option. The decision had to be taken quickly with the March 1974 deadline approaching, since 'speculation about the possibility of there being no guarantee will grow and could be damaging to sterling'.[121] Sir Douglas Allen expressed the threat in even stronger terms: '[C]ostly as the guarantees are, the effect on the foreign exchange market in the coming months if there are no arrangements for sterling is difficult to contemplate.'[122] Both the Treasury and the Bank of England, therefore, supported extending the agreements unilaterally for a further nine months, although with some changes to reduce the cost.

The timing of this decision was complicated by the dissolution of parliament, for a general election to be held on 28 February 1974, but the Bank of England and the Treasury believed the threat of a repeat of the disarray in the exchange markets in September 1972 caused by uncertainty about the renewal meant that a policy announcement had to be made before the election. Edward Heath was thus in the awkward position of having to decide whether to announce a policy that might have to be implemented by another government. In the end, he decided that the market was not expecting an announcement before the election and that it would merely make political capital for the Labour Party.[123] Instead, the outgoing Conservative government left behind its recommendation for another unilateral agreement for nine months from the end of March 1974. The guarantee threshold was expressed through the effective exchange rate rather than the bilateral US dollar exchange rate, to reduce the cost, and the minimum sterling proportions were further reduced by ten percentage points, to make the agreements more attractive to holders of sterling and to decrease the amount of sterling against which the United Kingdom would be liable for guarantee payments.[124]

The Conservatives lost the election, and Barber's successor as Chancellor, Denis Healey, was unenthusiastic about the sterling guarantees, but conceded that the agreements needed to be renewed until the end of 1974 because of the parlous balance of payments situation. He advised the new prime minister, Harold Wilson, that 'guaranteed sterling

[121] Barber to Heath, 18 February 1974, TNA PREM15/2056.

[122] Douglas Allen to principal private secretary to the Treasury, 8 February 1974, TNA T358/157.

[123] Heath to Barber, 20 February 1974, PREM15/2056.

[124] Walker, 'Post-election briefs: official sterling balances'.

is patently a very expensive way of borrowing and, for this reason, I would much like to get rid of guarantees altogether', but he accepted the recommendations left by the Conservative government and announced the renewal of the agreements on 15 March 1974.[125] In the end, no compensation was paid, since the effective exchange rate remained fairly stable through the rest of the year.

In October Healey told Wilson that the Bank of England agreed with him that 'we plainly should get off the guarantee hook if we can, and I have concluded that now is the time to do so'.[126] During 1974, as a result of the oil crisis, the geographical distribution of the sterling balances had shifted towards Nigeria and Saudi Arabia. The latter was not party to a sterling agreement, and the new inflows into Nigeria were not included in their guarantee agreement (which was benchmarked at the level in September 1973), so the agreements covered a smaller share of total sterling reserves. Ending them did not threaten market confidence as much as it would have a year earlier. Wilson agreed that the decision should be announced in the forthcoming budget on 9 November, and the Sterling Agreements were finally allowed to lapse at the end of December 1974. Elizabeth Hedley-Miller of the Treasury proudly claimed to have abolished both the sterling area and the sterling guarantees.[127] Ironically, on 10 December the Aramco Oil Group signed a new agreement with Saudi Arabia, under which it switched its settlements from sterling to the US dollar. This pushed the sterling exchange rate down temporarily on the eve of the expiry of the Sterling Agreements.[128] If this had been announced before the budget, the Sterling Agreements might have been renewed, since Wilson had noted in October that 'presumably if sterling is under pressure at the time of the Budget it might be necessary to think again'.[129]

Table 9.2 shows that the countries that signed Sterling Agreements did keep, on average, a much higher proportion of their reserves in sterling. Figures 9.3 and 9.4 show how the agreements operated in aggregate from 1968 to mid-1973, when the available data end. The sterling proportion of reserves for the signatories was fairly steady between 50 and 60 per cent, although the value of these reserves tripled. Sterling peaked at the

[125] D. W. Healey to Harold Wilson, 13 March 1973; Wilson minuted: 'I agree.' TNA PREM16/38.

[126] Healey to Wilson, 28 October 1974, TNA PREM16/38. A Treasury official reported meeting George Soros in October 1974, who believed that the agreements had been a major prop for sterling. Memo by D. A. Walker, 2 October 1974, TNA T358/163.

[127] Walker to Rawlinson at the IMF, 8 November 1974, TNA T358/163.

[128] Healey was in Saudi Arabia at the time and professed surprise at the announcement. Browning, P., *The Treasury and Economic Policy 1964–1985* (London: Longman, 1986), p. 64.

[129] Wilson minute on note from Healey to Wilson, 28 October 1974, TNA PREM16/38.

Table 9.2 *Share of sterling in foreign exchange reserves (percentage), 1968–72*

	Sterling Agreement countries	All countries
1968	57.9	20.0
1969	56.1	17.5
1970	53.7	5.2
1971	61.6	4.5
1972	54.5	4.7

Sources: 'Sterling Agreement countries' from BE EID15/7; 'All countries' from IMF, *International Financial Statistics, Supplement 1982* (Washington, DC: IMF, 1982).

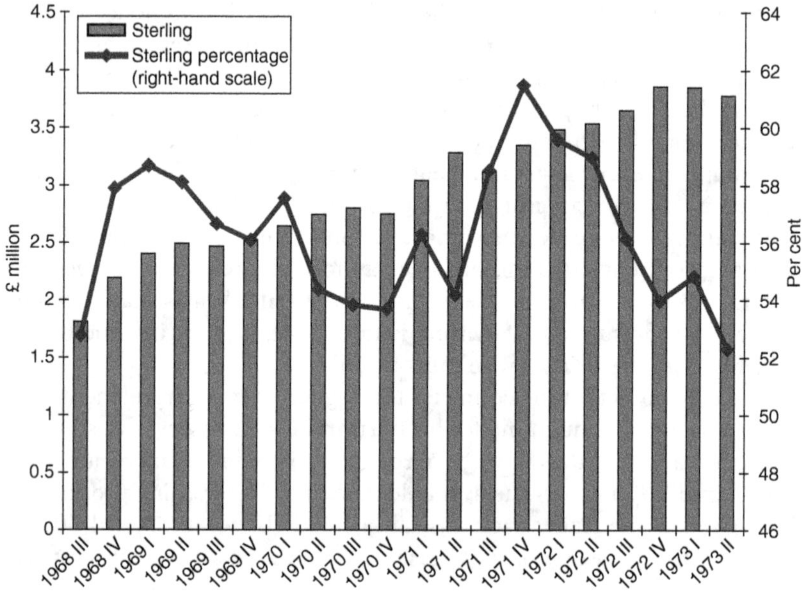

Figure 9.3 Sterling reserves of Sterling Agreement countries, quarter III 1968–quarter II 1973

time of the renewal in September 1971 but then declined steadily, falling from 62 per cent of total reserves to 52 per cent by mid-1973.

Figure 9.4 shows that the amount of sterling in these countries' reserves was about 8 per cent higher than the minimum agreed. After the MSPs were all reduced by ten percentage points in September 1971 the excess

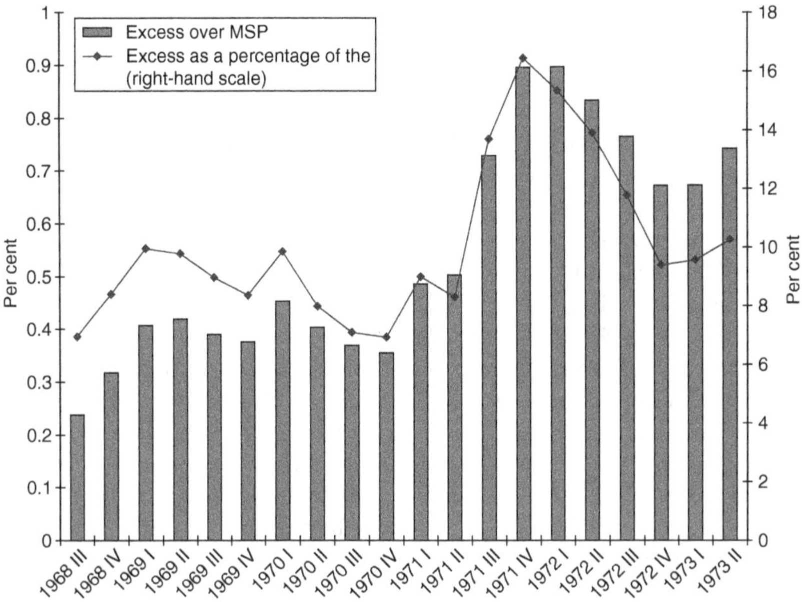

Figure 9.4 Sterling Agreement countries' excess over their MSPs, quarter III 1968–quarter II 1973

rose sharply, but sterling reserves were run down towards the new MSPs by the end of 1972. It took almost a year for countries to adapt to the lower MSPs, so sterling balances were probably larger than they would have been during this period. Countries had to keep a cushion of sterling reserves over MSP to ensure that seasonal fluctuations did not inadvertently cause them to breach the threshold, thereby denying them the right to the exchange guarantee, which accounts for the 8 to 10 per cent excess.

Of course, the aggregate data hide a variety of individual behaviour. Among countries for which data are available, Australia, India and Nigeria usually had the largest excess over MSP after 1971. India kept 26 per cent more of its reserves in sterling than required by their MSP, or £92 million over its minimum requirement. Australia was the other country contributing to the large amount of the excess, with £108 million over its requirement, but it exceeded its 36 per cent MSP by only three percentage points. Nigeria held an extra 6 per cent of its reserves in sterling but, because of its large reserves by this time, this amounted to £40 million. In sum, it is possible to see that most countries signing the agreements responded to changes in MSP, suggesting that the agreements did affect behaviour, although the limits were clearly not binding in many cases.

Conclusions

The collapse of the pegged exchange rate system based on the US dollar value of gold was widely predicted, but in the end it was rather prolonged and haphazard. The Nixon administration's confrontational approach to international monetary relations failed to deliver the profound reforms necessary to sustain a pegged rate system in an increasingly volatile international economy. The inflationary environment produced in the late 1960s was aggravated by a primary product boom at the beginning of the 1970s, which quickly pulled the Smithsonian compromise apart. Britain fell out of the Snake and the special international role of sterling was again invoked to distinguish the United Kingdom from the rest of Europe. Britain and sterling were relegated to the sidelines of negotiations when British governments concentrated on EEC accession, and the Americans found that bilateral negotiations with the French were the only way to overcome the deadlock with Europe. By the time of the crisis of 1973, however, the Heath government had been restored as a pivotal link between the United States and the rest of Europe as the consensus in favour of floating grew.

Throughout the 1960s and 1970s sterling assets held by overseas central monetary institutions were continually referred to as excessive and abnormal, and Britain struggled to restrain the use of sterling as a reserve asset. Economic development in east Asia in the 1960s and then Nigeria and the Middle East in the 1970s frustrated these efforts. Meanwhile, the G10 and the EEC continued to see sterling as an unnatural reserve asset prone to unpredictable and costly diversification that required multilateral support. Although sterling constituted a much smaller share of global reserves and the ratio of overseas sterling to UK reserves was falling, the surging nominal value of outstanding liabilities still concerned European and British policy-makers. We have seen that these liabilities were invoked as an excuse not to rejoin the Snake, thus giving UK governments greater flexibility over exchange rate policy after EEC accession. The expectation encouraged during the accession negotiations – that the United Kingdom would conform to European monetary norms – was not fulfilled, which suited the British governments of the day. The end of the Sterling Agreements ushered in a new stage for the management of the retreat of sterling with the final Group Arrangement in 1977, discussed in the next chapter.

10 Years of crisis 1973–1979

During the first two post-war decades the pegged exchange rate system was viewed as a necessary foundation for a smoothly functioning international economy. Politically, pegged rates did bring states together to promote coordination over their common interest in the management of the system. Economically, fluctuating exchange rates were deemed to increase uncertainty and add to the costs of international transactions and thereby inhibit global growth. As the 1960s progressed, the repeated shocks to confidence as exchange rates were forced to adjust, often under considerable market pressure with attendant overshooting, led to greater support for a more flexible structure, either through crawling pegs, wider ranges of fluctuation or floating. Chapter 9 showed how the strains in the system often generated conflict between states rather than cohesion, particularly in the case of France and the United Kingdom within Europe and between the United Kingdom and the United States.

The end of the constraints of the pegged rate system did not deliver greater cohesion or eliminate pressures on domestic economic adjustment. In Cooper's famous phrase, this was partly due to the 'size of the bumps in the road as well as the quality of the shock absorbers' during the 1970s. The new system had to cope with a series of challenges, including a commodity boom followed by two oil price shocks and the accumulation of huge sovereign debt burdens by developing countries. The oil crisis transformed the nature of sterling as a reserve currency, as it generated large accumulations by oil-producing countries while other countries ran down their reserves. The promise that the Sterling Agreements would remove the vulnerability that arose from the use of sterling as a reserve currency evaporated, since the rate of accumulation by Nigeria and Saudi Arabia was underestimated. Even so, the agreements were abandoned only at the end of 1974. It appeared that the multilateral approach to the retirement of sterling as a reserve currency had come to an end, having lost its rationale with the end of the pegged rate system.

The 1976 sterling crisis marked the first time that sales by central monetary institutions put the primary pressure on the sterling exchange rate rather than private holdings. Although the ratio of external sterling liabilities to UK reserves had fallen since 1945, the diversification of reserves as confidence in British economic management ebbed was still sufficient to prompt a sterling crisis, which was resolved only by a humiliating recourse to the IMF, with its attendant conditionality. The crisis also prompted the final multilateral effort to retire sterling as a reserve currency through the third Group Arrangement set up with the G10 central banks.

Sterling and the first oil crisis

At the beginning of the 1970s, when the international monetary system was in chaos, the value of sterling assets soared because of inflation and the global commodity boom. After dipping in 1967/8, sterling balances held in the Far East (mainly Hong Kong and Singapore) rose to £1.238 billion in 1971, and the boom in Australia and New Zealand boosted the total sterling held there to £1.124 billion by 1972. The sterling reserves of the overseas sterling area as a whole rose from a low of £1.65 billion in 1968 to £3.16 billion in 1972. This accumulation may have been encouraged by the minimum sterling proportions set by the Sterling Agreements as reserves rose, but these thresholds were rarely binding. The growth of sterling balances made the agreements very unwieldy, particularly after the change in parity with the US dollar after 1971. Nevertheless, during the crisis of June 1972 (which forced the sterling float) Malaysia, Singapore and Kuwait were the only countries whose speculative diversification of official reserves contributed to the pressure on the exchange rate.

The sterling assets of oil producers began to rise even before the oil crisis in the autumn of 1973. Figure 10.1 shows that there had already been three hikes in the price of oil even before the oil crisis began in October 1973, so that oil was already 43 per cent more expensive in September 1973 than it had been in 1970. This had important implications for the reserves of oil-producing countries and, because a proportion of the oil payments were denominated in sterling, caused a dramatic increase in sterling assets held in the Middle East and by Nigeria.

The sterling reserves of individual countries remain secret between the Bank of England and many of its customers, but, using Treasury archive data, table 10.1 shows the impact of the early price rises for Kuwait. By this time Kuwait was committed to an MSP of 22 per cent, but the country ended 1972 with almost 50 per cent of its reserves in sterling,

Table 10.1 *Kuwait's sterling balances as reported by the Ministry of Finance and Oil of Kuwait (£ million)*

	Nov. 1972	Dec. 1972	Jan. 1973	Feb. 1973	Mar. 1973	Apr. 1973
Total official reserves	956.624	943.946	1,092.562	1,054.912	1,018.259	1,152.347
Total sterling reserves	474.099	458.188	604.970	610.111	567.520	667.010
of which: equities	145.141	148.516	152.426	153.682	155.597	157.472
Sterling (%)	50	49	55	58	56	58
MSP = 22%	210.457	202.668	240.364	232.081	224.012	253.516
Amount of £ guaranteed	328.958	309.612	452.544	456.429	411.923	509.538

Source: TNA T358/38.

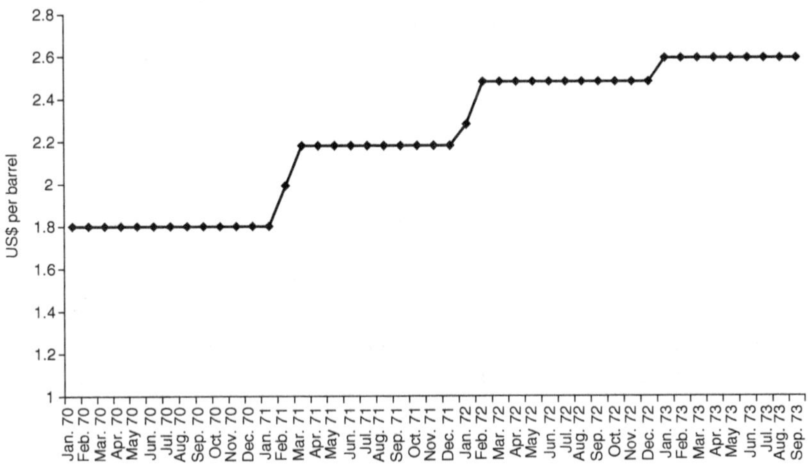

Figure 10.1 Official price of Saudi light oil, January 1970–September 1973

and this level rose further, to 58 per cent, by April 1973. This meant that the amount of guaranteed sterling rose by £200 million in the first quarter of 1973.

Table 10.2 shows the impact of the oil price at the end of the year on Nigeria's sterling balances, particularly in December 1973, when the sterling proportion soared to 71 per cent and the absolute value almost doubled. By September 1974 Nigeria still held 58.4 per cent of its

Table 10.2 *Nigeria's sterling balances (£ million), 1973–4*

	Sep. 73	Oct. 73	Nov. 73	Dec. 73	Jan. 74	Feb. 74	Mar. 74
Total reserves	140.18	152.30	145.23	211.72	261.43	352.16	539.38
Sterling reserves	80.94	90.33	83.41	150.81	168.69	220.97	323.82
Sterling (%)	58	59	57	71	65	63	60
MSP	54	54	54	54	54	54	54

Source: BE EID15/7.

reserves in sterling, amounting to £963 million, or almost one-third of the total sterling balances held by oil-producing countries in that year.

Oil-producing states received their royalty payments quarterly under formal contracts with oil companies, which determined the currency of payment in either sterling or US dollars. The sterling component was then either converted to other currencies or retained as official reserves. Sales of sterling by oil-producing states during this period were partly offset by accumulations of sterling by foreign oil companies in preparation for the next payment, so the potential impact of reserves diversification on the exchange rate was smoothed over the cycle. As contracts were renewed, a declining proportion of oil payments were due in sterling, since the dollar was the core currency for the oil industry, and states preferred to receive dollars rather than sterling even from British companies. For example, in July 1973, three months before the oil crisis began, Iran received its last oil royalties in sterling (£64 million) and all further payments were in dollars payable in New York. By the end of August 1973 Iran held only £13 million in sterling.[1]

The onset of the crisis in October 1973 exaggerated the impact of oil payments on sterling's reserve role. From the end of September 1973 to the end of April 1974, the price of Saudi light oil increased from \$2.59 per barrel to \$11.65, which was quickly translated into rises in reserves for oil-producing states.[2] In the first three months of 1974 the sterling assets of oil-producing countries increased by £250 million, but then, as the royalties related to the higher price came due, they accumulated a further £570 million in April alone. Sterling oil payments in April totalled £1.05 billion (£600 million by UK companies and £450 million by foreign

[1] Memo, 17 August 1973, BE 4A100/4.
[2] Data from US Energy Information Administration.

Table 10.3 *Denomination of oil revenues (£ million), first half of 1974*

	Sterling	Other	Percentage in sterling
Nigeria	450	800	36
Kuwait	530	800	40
Saudi Arabia	520	2300	18
Other	800	6200	11
Total	2300	10,100	19

Source: R. P. Fenton memo for C. McMahon, 22 July 1974, BE 4A100/5.

companies), so half the revenue was moved out of sterling almost immediately. The largest single recipient was Kuwait, with sterling receipts of £520 million out of total oil payment of £680 million, so 76 per cent of its oil payments were in sterling.[3] At the end of March Kuwait's sterling balances were £567 million, increasing to £910 million in April before falling back to £710 million in May, so only £200 million of the sterling payment was retained in official sterling assets. Other countries received more of their payments in other currencies. Saudi Arabia received only 19 per cent of its payments in sterling in January 1974, and this proportion fell to 10 per cent by September that year.[4] Due to the huge increase in the value of payments overall, however, the amount of sterling received by Saudi Arabia increased from £61 million in January to £196 million in September. Table 10.3 shows that Nigeria and Kuwait had the largest proportions of sterling payments, although not the largest total amounts. As a result, by June 1974 Kuwait's sterling balances amounted to £702 million and Nigeria held £627 million.[5]

These fluctuations caused considerable concern in London. The Bank of England was not sure what the oil-producing countries did with their sterling, but it was estimated that most went into the Eurocurrency market. Midland Bank reported that this was the case for Saudi Arabia in the first five months of 1974, although the Herstatt Bank crisis prompted clients to retain most of their sterling revenue in sterling in June 1974. Saudi Arabia's sterling holdings then increased by a further £440 million in August and September 1974, which was slightly more than their sterling oil revenue in these two months.[6] The Treasury took the opportunity

[3] Memo by R. P. Fenton for C. H. McMahon, 6 May 1974, BE 4A100/5.
[4] Memo, 8 November 1974, BE 4A100/5.
[5] These figures included official and private sterling assets. Brief for the Treasury, 27 June 1974, BE 4A100/5.
[6] Memo, 8 November 1974; H.W. Fleet memo, 10 July 1974; BE 4A100/5.

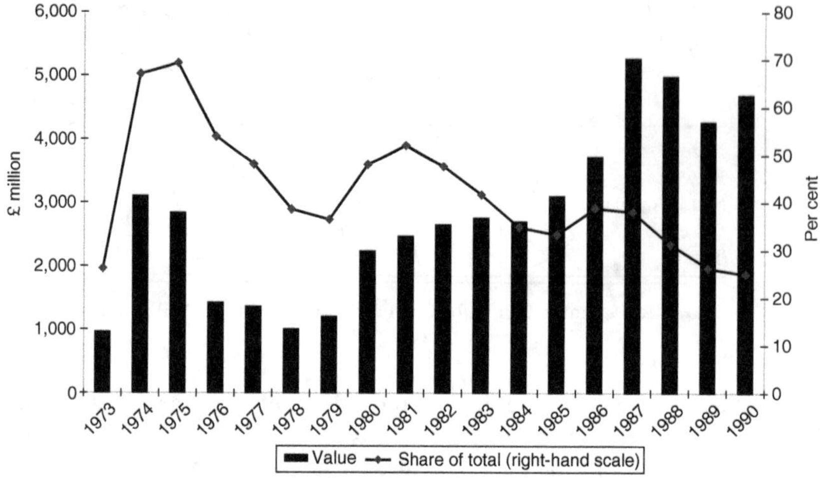

Figure 10.2 Exchange reserves held in sterling by OPEC central monetary institutions, 1973–90

to encourage Kuwait to invest in British real estate and equity, although in April 1973 almost a quarter of Kuwait's sterling assets were already in equity.[7] The Bank of England believed that Nigeria and the smaller Gulf states were more likely to keep their assets in sterling for longer because they lacked sophisticated investment advice, but they expected sterling to play a declining role in oil trade overall.

From 1973 the Bank of England began to publish the sterling balances of oil-producing countries separately, which showed that the sterling assets held by their central monetary institutions more than tripled between 1973 and the end of 1974, rising from £959 million to £3.2 billion.[8] This represented a rise from about a quarter of total overseas sterling liabilities to central monetary institutions to two-thirds in one year alone. Figure 10.2 graphs the series for 1973 to 1990, which clearly shows the impact of both the first and second oil crises on the value of sterling holdings and the proportion of sterling exchange reserves held by oil-producing countries. The effect of the first oil crisis on the distribution of sterling reserves is much greater than the second oil crisis, from 1979 to 1981, on account of the smaller proportion of the oil trade denominated in sterling by the

[7] Fenton memo for McMahon, 29 May 1974, BE 4A100/5.
[8] Bank of England, *Quarterly Bulletin*.

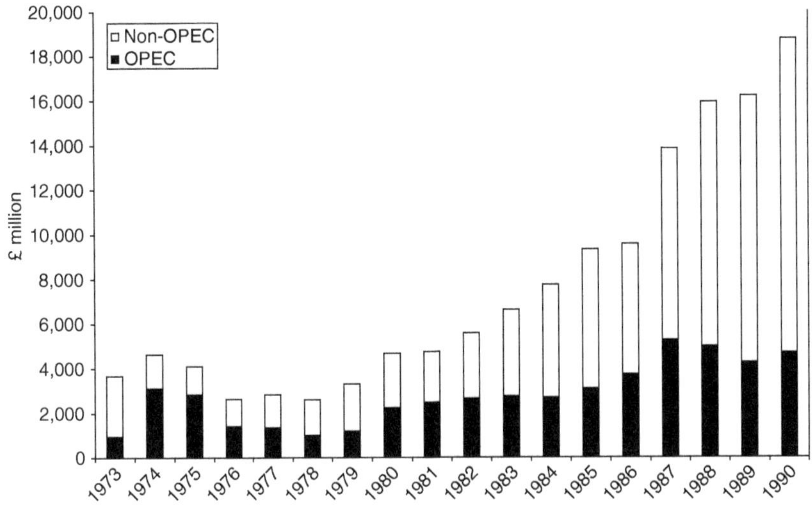

Figure 10.3 Exchange reserves held in sterling by central monetary institutions, 1973–90
Source: Bank of England Quarterly Bulletin.

end of the 1970s. Also clear is the dramatic fall in sterling held by oil producers' central monetary institutions in 1976, which prompted the sterling crisis of that year.

The largest decline in officially held sterling reserves was clearly among the OPEC countries in 1976, as figure 10.3 shows. From 1979, as the second oil crisis struck, the nominal value of sterling exchange reserves began to increase again, due to accumulations by OPEC and non-OPEC countries alike, although the oil-producing countries never restored their share of sterling reserves to the levels of 1974.

The IMF categorisation of global reserves shows more clearly the currency distribution of oil-exporting countries, in which the US dollar dominated, as figure 10.4 shows. Sterling's share began to decline in 1966 and then fell in the devaluation of 1967. Interestingly, at this time French francs replaced sterling reserves, as the dollar's share also declined. The sterling proportion recovered after the devaluation, peaking at 22 per cent of all reserves in 1971, before declining again, with a brief revival at the start of the oil price boom in 1973. As we have seen, the sterling denomination of oil revenues quickly declined, and OPEC countries diversified away from sterling and the dollar towards the Deutschmark and other currencies, including the Swiss francs and the yen.

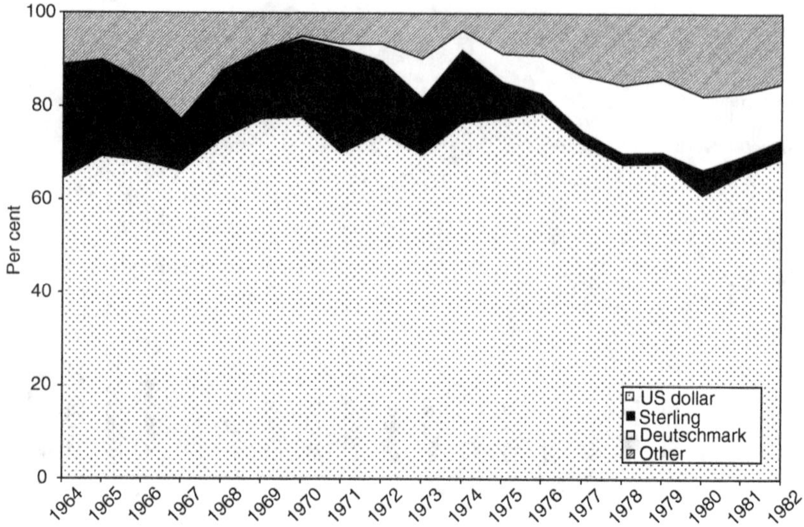

Figure 10.4 Composition of foreign exchange reserves of oil-producing countries, 1964–82

Figure 10.5 shows that the first oil crisis kept the ratio of official overseas sterling holdings above the level of Britain's own reserve assets, but that this ratio underwent a transformation during the later years of the decade. The 'overhang' was finally eliminated after 1976 with the end of sterling as a significant reserve asset.[9]

The nominal rise in sterling reserves after the Sterling Agreements had lapsed in 1974 prompted a variety of initiatives to reduce Britain's exposure to possible instability in these liabilities. In July 1975 the Cabinet asked the Chancellor to consider reintroducing guarantees for sterling balances to forestall diversification. The Treasury then considered a scheme to negotiate guarantees for the largest oil-producing holders of sterling (Nigeria, Saudi Arabia and Kuwait) and then to offer a unilateral agreement to other medium-sized holders, such as Brunei, New Zealand, Hong Kong and Ireland.[10] This would anticipate upcoming anti-inflationary policies planned in Britain, which might involve a further 30 per cent depreciation of sterling. On balance, however, the conclusion was that if the anti-inflationary policies worked there would be no need for a guarantee, but if they didn't work the guarantee would

[9] From 1950 to 1970 this ratio averaged about 3:1.

[10] Policy unit paper agreed by Treasury and Chancellor of the Exchequer, 7 July 1975, TNA PREM16/371.

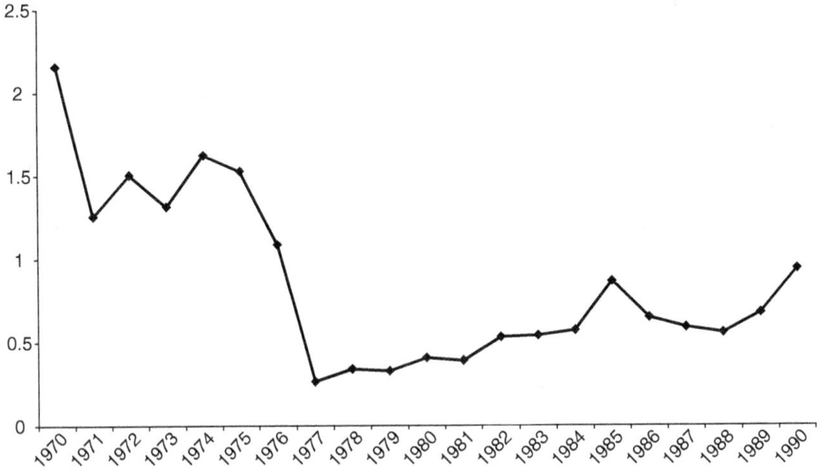

Figure 10.5 Ratio of UK sterling liabilities to overseas central monetary institutions to UK official reserves, 1970–90

be very expensive. It was noted that most speculative pressure did not in any case come from official reserves, and the negotiations themselves would make sterling vulnerable to speculation if they were not successful with one or more holder. Instead of undertaking these politically as well as economically risky initiatives, the Treasury advocated borrowing internationally, perhaps through the IMF, at lower interest rates to finance the diversification of overseas sterling reserves.

Andrew Graham, Wilson's economic adviser, disagreed with the Treasury view and encouraged the prime minister to solicit other opinions. He especially saw scope for encouraging oil-producing countries to maintain their substantial balances by offering them new exchange rate guarantees.[11] In response, Wilson asked Harold Lever, Chancellor of the Duchy of Lancaster (and former financial secretary to the Treasury) for his views, and set up a working group on the financing of the external deficit.

Lever had been lobbying Wilson since May 1975 to pay off sterling reserves with the proceeds of borrowing in other currencies.[12] He argued that sterling borrowing was expensive, despite the depreciation of the pound, because of high interest costs. Following the line of contemporary public analysis, he also blamed the disruptive 'stop-go' policies and

[11] Andrew Graham minute for prime minister, 11 July 1975, PREM16/371.

[12] Harold Lever paper for Barber and Wilson, 4 August 1975. This was a revised version of a proposal from 18 July 1975; TNA PREM16/371.

Britain's 'reputation for being prone to these policies' on the external constraint of keeping overseas holders of sterling happy to retain them. In addition, he reverted to the 1950s view that large sterling liabilities undermined confidence, since they were mostly short-term or liquid assets. While acknowledging that British interest rate policy could not be independent of international interest rates, he argued that the sterling balances constrained the flexibility of domestic policy. He therefore recommended that the United Kingdom's liabilities should be diversified away from sterling by borrowing more dollars on international markets, reducing interest payable on sterling balances to encourage diversification and using the borrowed dollars to replace some of the existing sterling reserves. This would turn short-term sterling liabilities into short-term dollar liabilities. Second, and even more ambitiously, he recommended a scheme to encourage UK banks to borrow dollars so that they could lend them to the Bank of England to replace some sterling liabilities. Rather than undermining London as an international financial centre, he argued that lifting the threat of a collapse of sterling caused by 'an excessive dependence on our sterling liabilities' would enhance the City's attractions.

Partly in response to Lever's proposals, David Walker, assistant secretary at the Treasury, began to develop a plan to stabilise Nigeria's sterling balances by issuing the country with an SDR-denominated bond payable in sterling that it would probably be more willing to hold than sterling securities.[13] The Chancellor, Denis Healey, was initially intrigued by this idea, which promised both to stabilise existing balances and potentially increase the government's ability to borrow, although the interest paid on such an instrument would have to be high enough to cover the expected depreciation of sterling. Negotiations might also prompt fears among creditors in the government's confidence in the future exchange rate.[14] Walker argued that Nigeria was the largest holder of sterling and was most likely to be responsive to the scheme, partly because 'Nigeria is newer to these investment questions, and less sophisticated than Kuwait, and Saudi Arabia, who may anyway have consciously placed a limit on UK paper of all kinds'.[15] As of May 1975 Nigeria held £1.5 billion in official sterling balances, out of a global total of £4.9 billion. Kuwait and Saudi Arabia together held £1.8 billion, so these three countries by themselves accounted for two-thirds of UK liabilities to overseas governments.[16] The reserve role of sterling had clearly been transformed as a result of the oil boom. Although the Treasury and Harold Lever were

[13] Letter to D. A. Walker from S. Payton (BE), TNA T358/219.
[14] Record of a meeting in Healey's room, Treasury, 5 August 1975, TNA T358/219.
[15] M. E. Hedley-Miller to Sir Derek Mitchell, 18 August 1975, TNA T358/219.
[16] Walker, 'A Treasury SDR bond', 15 August 1975, TNA T358/219.

firmly behind the plan, Healey chose to take the advice of the governor of the Bank of England, Gordon Richardson, that the threat to confidence outweighed the benefits of the scheme, but he asked that the proposal be developed to 'an advanced state of preparedness'.[17] It was to resurface in amended form as part of the third Group Arrangement, organised through the BIS in November/December 1976.

By September 1975 Healey agreed with both Lever and the Treasury that it was desirable to reduce sterling liabilities, but he saw no prospect for achieving this in the near future. Sterling reserves did pose a constraint on policy but, had they not been acquired, British governments and consumers would not have been able to finance their deficits to the same degree, and this would have posed a different kind of constraint on policy. On Lever's specific proposals, Healey believed that Britain was already borrowing as much as it could to cover the current account deficit, and the prospect of borrowing more to retire sterling liabilities was not attractive. On the other hand, the Bank of England and the Treasury were both against using British banks as a conduit for the Bank of England to borrow foreign currency from international capital markets. If it became public, it would be damaging to the United Kingdom's creditworthiness and would throw the independence and integrity of British banks into doubt.[18] Again, the threats to confidence outweighed positive initiatives to shore up the sterling balances against an uncertain future crisis.

The international environment for sterling in the first half of the 1970s was clearly very confused and volatile, though the effects were somewhat muted by the Sterling Agreements, which had minimised diversification away from sterling. The evidence of the excess of sterling over the statutory minimum sterling proportions suggests that the agreements were not binding in the early 1970s, but the impact of the oil boom revealed a shift in the nature of sterling as a reserve and transactions currency. Although sterling declined quickly as a petrocurrency, the absolute increase in the price of oil generated huge accumulations of sterling reserves by oil producers, which introduced a new element of uncertainty into the burden of Britain's overseas liabilities. On the other hand, the ability to increase short-term borrowing as a result of sterling's international role eased some of the pressures of adjustment for the United Kingdom. Within a few years, however, the pressure for adjustment had caught up with

[17] Note of meeting of Chancellor with governor of Bank of England, 24 September 1975, TNA T358/219.

[18] Healey's response to Lever's paper, 11 September 1975. The Chancellor's arguments were used to guide the prime minister in his preparation for the Cabinet discussion of the issue. Memo by John Hunt, 5 November 1975, TNA PREM16/371.

British governments, resulting in the crisis of 1976, which prompted the final BIS sterling support package.

Sterling and the 1976 IMF crisis

Although the details of the IMF negotiations have attracted considerable academic interest, there has not been a full exposition of the important Sterling Agreements that preceded and followed the conclusion of the IMF stand-by arrangement in December 1976.[19] As a result, the context in which the IMF negotiations took place is incomplete. The following analysis emphasises the importance of the negotiation of multilateral support for sterling through the BIS before, during and after the IMF loan for the successful conclusion of these talks. While the IMF loan caught the headlines and exerted more pressure on the Labour government to adapt its domestic economic policies to international opinion, the multilateral sterling facility of 1977 marked a further fundamental change in Britain's external economic policy and had a long-term impact on the role of sterling as an international currency.

As the effects of the oil crisis added to inflationary pressure in the British economy, in January 1974 the Conservative Chancellor of the Exchequer, Anthony Barber, predicted that the balance of payments deficit would worsen to about £4.5 billion to £5 billion, compared to his estimate in mid-December 1973 of £3 billion. Inflationary pressure meant that depreciation was not desirable. He therefore advised the prime minister that, although increased demand for sterling by oil surplus countries would help, 'it will not be good enough simply to rely on this happening on a sufficient scale to cover the deficit and keep up the exchange rate. We must be ready if necessary to defend the effective exchange rate at something like present levels, and this means being sure of having access to really big sums.'[20] The options were spending UK reserves (although selling more than £600 million, or about 20 per cent of the total, would impair confidence), borrowing on the Eurodollar market and approaching the IMF. EEC central banks did not have large resources and were believed unlikely to be willing to help, and the Fed swap with the United States was too short-term (twelve months maximum). Borrowing from

[19] The most thorough treatments are by Burk, K., and A. K. Cairncross, *Goodbye, Great Britain: The 1976 IMF Crisis* (New Haven, CT: Yale University Press, 1992), Harmon, M. D., *The British Labour Government and the 1976 IMF Crisis* (London: Macmillan, 1997) and Hickson, K., *The IMF Crisis of 1976 and British Politics* (New York: I. B. Tauris, 2005). For an insider's view, see Wass, D., *Decline to Fall: The Making of British Macro-economic Policy and the 1976 IMF Crisis* (Oxford: Oxford University Press, 2008).

[20] Barber to Heath, 7 January 1974, TNA PREM15/2056.

the IMF was appealing, since it would save about £75 million per year over borrowing on the Eurodollar market, as international interest rates were high. Moreover, Barber believed that the psychological impact of having a £1.5 billion IMF stand-by arrangement would boost confidence, making it less likely that it would have to be used. He also expected to be able to negotiate favourable terms with respect to conditionality and the letter of intent. Although the foreign secretary, Sir Alec Douglas-Home, wanted the topic to be discussed first with EEC partners, Edward Heath and Barber together decided that any approach to the IMF should be confidential.[21]

In the first few months of 1974, before the Labour government took power, the pound strengthened against the dollar. In a policy environment characterised by Wass as 'marking time', sterling stayed above $2.30 for the rest of the year, putting added pressure on the price competitiveness of British exports.[22] Harold Wilson's government increased spending despite the inflationary environment, but resisted depreciating the currency for fear of exacerbating inflation further. Sterling began to depreciate steadily from April 1975 as confidence in the government's policies weakened. In May 1975 an IMF team led by Alan Whittome, director of the Fund's European department, visited London for its annual consultations. The team members found officials and ministers much concerned with the domestic issues of high inflation and slow growth. They also sensed that ministers and officials alike had accepted the need for further depreciation of sterling to compensate for rising unit costs of production. This would sustain the competitiveness of British exports to resolve the current account deficit, a policy with which the IMF was content.[23] In July the government introduced a cap on wage increases to contain cost-push inflation but failed to make progress on public expenditure.

By July 1975 the pound was still depreciating and the 'gap' in the external balance for the rest of the year was anticipated to be only £500 million. Healey wanted to borrow this sum from Middle East surplus countries and/or Nigeria, or perhaps to sell the government's shares in British Petroleum to Germany (a scheme that was already under negotiation with BP). Officials from the Treasury were ready to visit Nigeria and the Middle East to test the waters on a potential loan, but it was decided that this initiative would have to be delayed until mid-October, when

[21] Sir Alec Douglas-Home to Heath, 11 January 1974. Heath minuted 'I'm sure the Foreign Sec. is right' but the decision not to inform the EEC ministers was taken at a meeting on 14 January 1974. Note by R. T. Armstrong, 16 January 1974, TNA PREM15/2056.

[22] Wass, *Decline to Fall*.

[23] W. John Woodley to managing director, 13 May 1975, IMF C/UK/810 'Mission Woodley and staff May 1975'.

Figure 10.6 Monthly official market exchange rate, US dollar/pound, January 1972–December 1977

Ramadan ended.[24] In the meantime, Harold Lever was in favour of selling the government's BP shares, but there was opposition from the minister for industry and the Paymaster General. At their meeting in early August, Healey authorised sending an envoy of two Treasury officials to the IMF that month to discuss the possibility of gaining access to credit through the IMF's oil facility, which aimed to recycle OPEC surpluses, and to a stand-by arrangement for the first credit tranche.[25] Interestingly, Healey also noted a *Financial Times* article suggesting setting money supply targets. Kit McMahon, an executive director of the Bank of England, and Lord Lever both 'doubted if this [money supply targeting] was really worthwhile'.[26] While the situation did not worsen, policy continued to muddle through, allowing the pound to depreciate from $2.15 at the end of July to $2.02 at the end of November, as shown in figure 10.6.

At a meeting in mid-December 1975 the Treasury warned Wilson that, although the depreciation of sterling from March to December had sustained the competitiveness of UK exports, the rate now threatened to break through the $2.00 barrier, which would require 'substantial intervention to maintain orderly conditions and underlines the need to supplement our modest resources by a drawing on the IMF so

[24] Record of a meeting in the Chancellor's office, Treasury, 5 August 1975, TNA T358/219.
[25] On the oil facility, see James, *International Monetary Cooperation*, pp. 316–18.
[26] Ibid.

that we can maintain an adequate intervention capability in the period ahead'.[27] In March 1976 the pound did break through the $2.00 barrier, prompting purchases totalling £916 million through the market, and a further £88 million in net off-market purchases of sterling, in the week from 5 to 11 March alone.[28] On 16 March Harold Wilson unexpectedly announced that he was resigning, and he was replaced as prime minister on 5 April by James Callaghan, who had been Chancellor during the devaluation of 1967. The turmoil continued as the markets lost further confidence in the government's policy, and by the beginning of June the Bank of England had spent over £3 billion defending the exchange rate, but it was unable to prevent it slumping below $1.70.[29]

On 1 June 1976 Johannes Witteveen, the managing director of the IMF, suggested to William Ryrie, second permanent secretary (domestic economy) of the UK Treasury, that the British should pursue a swap with the United States to bolster the reserves position and restore confidence. The IMF was still pushing for spending cuts that the Labour government was firmly resisting, and so direct recourse to the IMF was for the moment off the table. The idea of a more flexible instrument, such as a bilateral swap, was taken up with alacrity, and Gordon Richardson, the governor of the Bank of England, approached the chairman of the Fed, Arthur Burns, almost immediately to ask for a $3 billion Fed swap. Burns was not encouraging, suggesting that the amount was too high and that there would have to be strings attached to any arrangement given the risk that the United Kingdom might not be in a position to repay when the credit came due. He suggested that a swap would need to be underpinned by an undertaking from the IMF to cover the United Kingdom if it proved unable to repay. This potentially brought the British back to the problem of IMF conditionality and the need to cut public spending.

Instead of a bilateral arrangement, Richardson suggested negotiating through the BIS for $2 billion from the Fed plus $1 billion in a swap with European central banks. In addition, Healey asked Douglas Wass (his permanent secretary) and Richardson to consider quantitative targets for the money supply and special deposits by commercial banks to combat inflation. Healey phoned the new US secretary of the Treasury, William Simon, that evening and received more encouragement for a swap, although Simon warned that 'his [Simon's] own policy was not to

[27] The prime minister called a small meeting to discuss Treasury exchange rate policy (Chancellor of Exchequer, Lever, Crosland and Mrs Williams), 16 December 1975, TNA PREM16/796.

[28] Memo from Douglass Wass (permanent secretary to the Treasury) to the prime minister, 12 March 1976, TNA PREM16/796.

[29] Memo from Sir Kenneth Berrill to the prime minister, 3 June 1976, TNA PREM16/796.

give gratuitous advice to other Governments, but he wanted to pass on the feeling in some quarters that the UK had not done enough to get the fiscal area right'.[30] The British government would still have to give an undertaking to go to the IMF if it was unable to repay the swaps on maturity. With further reassurance from Healey that there would be no overshooting of the expenditure limits agreed for 1976/7, promises of cuts to reduce the deficit for the following year and hints that a money supply target was under consideration, Healey convinced Simon to agree that a Fed swap of $2 billion might be available on Monday 7 June.[31]

On Friday 4 June 1976 Healey and Callaghan met to discuss how to move forward.[32] There were four options: drawing further on the IMF, and becoming subject to conditionality, 'sweating it out' and waiting for the exchange rate to turn around; activating the swap with the Fed; or organising a 'soutien' with the EEC. The first option was quickly dismissed by both Healey and Callaghan, although it was supported by Richardson. Callaghan was particularly suspicious of Richardson's motives, 'which seemed simply designed to embroil the Government with the IMF for the specific purpose of enabling them to impose cuts in public expenditure'. He then cancelled a meeting with Richardson scheduled for later that day to discuss the sterling situation. Callaghan was also critical of the Bank's intervention policy: '[I]n his view the Bank had wasted USD3b of our reserves in recent months by their miscalculations over the effect of intervention and he thought more control [over the Bank of England] was needed.' As to the way forward, Callaghan had been advised by Kenneth Berrill, head of the Central Policy Review Staff, that the pound was undervalued at its current rate and that market sentiment would soon reverse the decline in the exchange rate, so he preferred the second option of waiting for the markets to turn around on their own.[33] He also worried that taking up the Fed swap would, perversely, have a detrimental impact on confidence, because the facility would have only a temporary effect – although Healey disagreed. At the end of the meeting a compromise was reached, whereby Callaghan was to put arrangements in place for a swap to be activated at an hour's notice. The decision would be taken either late Friday night or early Monday morning (7 June), before New York opened. In any case, it was agreed that Healey should make a reassuring speech in parliament on the Monday about the government's commitment to containing public spending and restraining

[30] Note for the record of a phone call at 9:00 p.m. 3 June 1976, TNA PREM16/796.
[31] Ibid.
[32] Note of a meeting between the PM and the Chancellor on 4 June at 10 Downing St., PREM16/796.
[33] 'The defence of sterling', Berrill to prime minister, 3 June 1976, PREM16/796.

the growth of the money supply. Callaghan ordered that there should be no mention of the swap facility and that the speech should be kept short so as to avoid provoking debate. If the markets showed continued pressure on sterling, the swap would be activated that afternoon. The Ministerial Committee on Economic Strategy would be informed at 10:00 a.m. and Healey would meet with the 'TUC/NEDC (National Economic Development Council) Six' before the formal announcement in the House. Finally, and rather casually, Callaghan expressed his desire for 'a long-term funding arrangement which would lead to substitution of the sterling deposits with e.g. SDRs. He thought it was time to get rid of the incubus of sterling as a reserve currency.' This sowed the seeds for the final BIS Group Arrangement.

Over the weekend Richardson arranged an offer of support from G10 (plus Switzerland) central banks over the telephone to supplement the Fed swap. The package added $2.3 billion to the bilateral swap with the Fed, totalling $5 billion (including $150 million from the BIS), available in three-month swaps renewable by mutual agreement for a further three months but with no maturity beyond 9 December 1976. Interest at the US Treasury bill rate was payable on all drawings. At the last minute the Banque de France joined, bringing the total available support to the equivalent of $5.3 billion. In line with Fed chairman Burns' conditions, the United Kingdom was committed to making drawings on the IMF if necessary to repay the swaps when they came due in early December. The arrangement thus offered a six-month breathing space, either to allow the markets to end their pressure on sterling (if the pressure was merely speculative, as Callaghan believed) or for the government to get its house in order before being forced to do so by the IMF (if the pressure was due to fundamentals, as Richardson believed). The timing of the eventual approach to the IMF was thus set by this multilateral swap arrangement in June 1976.

The swap facility was announced to the markets at 3:30 p.m. on Monday 7 June, in a way that blamed the depreciation on unwarranted speculative pressure outside the government's control:

> The financial authorities from the G10 and Switzerland, together with the BIS, noting that the recent fall in the value of sterling under exchange market pressure had led to disorderly market conditions which carried sterling to an unjustified level today agree, in the common interest of the stability and efficient functioning of the international monetary system to make available to the Bank of England a standby credit of in excess of US5b.[34]

[34] Telegram to R. Larre (BIS) from governor Richardson (BE), 7 June 1976, BISA LAR1 F01.

Table 10.4 *Contributions to the June 1976 stand-by credit*

	Amount (US$ million)	Share (%)
Belgium	200	3.8
Canada	300	5.7
France	300	5.7
West Germany	800	15.1
Japan	600	11.3
Netherlands	200	3.8
Sweden	150	2.8
Switzerland	600	11.3
United States	2,000	37.7
BIS	150	2.8
Total	5,300	100.0

Source: BISA, 'Draft annotated agenda for a meeting on the sterling balances at the Banque de France on 20th December 1976', DEA 4 7.18(12), 'Dealtry papers'.

Table 10.4 shows the contributions to the June 1976 stand-by credits. Ten days after this announcement the Bank of England had spent a further $600 million in spot interventions in the market, and it prepared to draw this amount from the swap facility, pro rata from each country. In addition, Richardson asked the BIS for extra support to cover part of the rollover of a further $450 million of short-date swaps that had been engaged to squeeze speculators. The BIS provided $388 million overnight at the end of June as window dressing in order to disguise the resultant fall in reserves, and thus freed the Bank of England from drawing even further on the swap facility.[35] By the end of the first three-month period, on 7 September, the Bank of England announced that it had drawn about 20 per cent of the total facility (equivalent to $1.03 billion), of which the United States had contributed $400 million.[36] A jump in the minimum lending rate (MLR) by one and a half percentage points to 13 per cent in September did not forestall a record fall of 4 per cent in the sterling exchange rate on 28 September, prompting Healey to approach the IMF formally for a $3.9 billion stand-by arrangement. This was followed by a further rise in MLR, to a record 15 per cent, on 7 October. The likelihood that the G10 credit would be repaid by the maturity on 9 December receded as sterling continued to come under pressure.

[35] Telephone conversations between R. P. T. Hall (BIS) and Sangster (BE), 17–30 June 1976, BISA LAR1 F01.

[36] Text of a message to participants in the June swap facility, note from Byatt (BE) to Hall (BIS), 3 September 1976, BISA 2/2 (5), 'Bank of England policy 1968–1982'.

Callaghan had underestimated the strength of the market's expectations about sterling, and the internal measures to contain inflation were too little, too late.

Through the autumn the Treasury and the Bank of England developed plans to gather medium-term multilateral support, to counteract the impact on the reserves of any future fall in official sterling reserves and to restructure these external liabilities. The plans culminated in the third Group Arrangement (discussed in the next section). These plans were disclosed at the same time as the IMF loan was beginning to be negotiated in October/November 1976, but they needed to await the approval of the IMF loan, since the Americans were adamant that the IMF conditionality terms needed to be successfully concluded before any longer-term support could be forthcoming. Conversely, however, it became increasingly clear that some announcement of longer-term support at the same time as the short-term IMF loan was a prerequisite to restoring market confidence. This led to complicated tactics on the part of the Americans, who offered their support for a longer-term facility as a carrot to encourage Callaghan to accept the short-term conditions on the IMF loan. It also complicated the planning for the long-term facility, as the negotiations for the IMF loan were protracted right up to the early December deadline.

The decision to approach the IMF having finally been made, formal negotiations began on 8 November in London. The path forward was anything but clear, and negotiations dragged on right to the deadline of the expiry of the June 1976 swap. Callaghan refused to consider the cuts to the public sector borrowing requirement (PSBR) and government spending that the Treasury and IMF recommended, and the United States and IMF remained intransigent over the need for the Labour government to take firm steps to contain inflation. Burns took a particularly hard line over the need to contain monetary expansion before any further support would be forthcoming from the United States, either directly or through the IMF. If an IMF loan could not be agreed by the deadline for repaying the swap, the Fed believed that the United Kingdom should be forced to repay the outstanding balance from reserves even at the expense of a large shock to the exchange rate.[37] The Fed was thus willing to call Britain's bluff over the collective importance of orderly exchange rates.

American doubts about the willingness of the United Kingdom to adapt its domestic policy were justified when, after weeks of negotiation,

[37] Note of a meeting between Henry Wallich (Fed) and A. Lamfalussy in Washington, 11–12 November 1976, BISA 7.18(14) LAR3, 'Third Group Arrangement sterling balances'.

the Cabinet rejected the IMF conditions on the PSBR on 23 November. The Cabinet refused to accept the IMF target cut of £2 billion from the total budget of £10.5 billion, and was willing to agree only to a cut of £1 billion in the PSBR, of which half would be met by the sale of the government's BP shares and the rest by a mix of tax increases and spending cuts. The Cabinet was convinced that any further spending cuts would increase unemployment and destroy the government's partnership with the trade unions.[38] Callaghan noted, when relating this outcome to Whittome and David Finch of the IMF delegation in London, that Len Murray, the general secretary of the TUC, had told him that if the PSBR was cut substantially 'the trade union movement would make a hell of a row', ultimately leading the TUC to break with the government.[39] Callaghan also warned that, in his view, a Conservative government would have even less success in retaining the cooperation of the unions, with disastrous results for the economy. Whittome replied that the PSBR targets set by the IMF were the minimum required to restore confidence in the government's policies and stem the slide of sterling in the exchanges. Callaghan threatened that 'an uncontrolled slide in sterling would be fatal in that the only outcome could be a siege economy'. Gerald Ford, the US president, rejected Callaghan's plea to intervene with Witteveen on Britain's side in the dispute but reasserted his readiness to consider longer-term support for running down sterling reserves once the IMF stand-by arrangement had been concluded.[40]

Tony Benn, the Secretary of State for energy, led the charge to reject IMF support, and he advocated withdrawing into protectionism rather than accepting the liberal economic ethos dictated by Washington. In essence, Benn was proposing a Callaghan 'shock' equivalent to Nixon's démarche of August 1971, but he was without the political clout to gather international support. Witteveen flew to London on Concorde on 1 December to aid the negotiations and reconfirmed his position that cuts of £1.5 billion to £2 billion from the PSBR (bringing the PSBR to below £9 billion in 1977/8) were a necessary prerequisite to a loan. This scale of reduction was required to restore confidence and contain inflation. This time Callaghan openly threatened him with protectionism, noting that, 'if it would keep the TUC in support of the Government's policies on wage restraint, then he would not shirk a protectionist approach and invoke Article Twelve of GATT'.[41] After reconvening in the afternoon,

[38] PM to Ford, telegram, 23 November 1976, TNA PREM16/802.

[39] Meeting of PM and CoE with Whittome and Finch, 23 November 1976, TNA PREM16/802.

[40] Telegram from Ford to Callaghan, 24 November 1976, TNA PREM16/802.

[41] Meeting of PM, CoE, Whittome with Witteveen, 1 December 1976, TNA PREM16/804.

agreement could still not be reached, and Callaghan closed the meeting by stating:

> If…there was no give in the IMF's position and if tomorrow the Chancellor had to say in Cabinet that the IMF wanted public expenditure cuts in 1977/78 of £2b as a prerequisite for the IMF loan, then he would lead the Cabinet to a conclusion that the right course was to go for a protectionist economy and the introduction of quota restrictions on imports forthwith.

An hour after this meeting President Ford called Callaghan, having learned of the impasse with the IMF from Helmut Schmidt.[42] Ford was particularly concerned at the prospect of the United Kingdom closing the foreign exchange market as well as imposing quantitative restrictions on imports. Callaghan described his meetings with Witteveen and the probability that the Cabinet would opt for protectionism if he insisted that a £2 billion cut was the only option. Ford agreed to 'talk to his people' to try to be helpful, and reassured Callaghan: 'I do want you to know that if we can get over this hump we are prepared to work with you on the sterling balance problem.' Longer-term support for sterling was clearly being used to sweeten the medicine of fiscal cuts in the short term.

The next day the Cabinet agreed to cuts of £1.5 billion in the PSBR (including the £0.5 billion of BP shares), but this move was rejected by Witteveen (who had since returned to Washington). Healey's response was that 'Dr Witteveen could take a running jump'.[43] Healey told Whittome that, 'rather than go down fighting the Labour Party, the Prime Minister would prefer that the government should fall because it was fighting the IMF. On that basis he might win an election, having advocated a switch of economic strategy which would enable Britain to go it alone.'[44] Despite this indignant tirade, the Treasury got down to formulating a compromise for larger cuts, contingent on economic growth reaching 3.5 per cent in 1978/9. In the end this was accepted by the IMF, along with an assurance that the United Kingdom would not allow rises in the exchange rate to erode the country's export competitiveness and that various financial indicators could be monitored by the IMF.

In real terms, the 1976 IMF rescue was not historically unprecedented, although it had a deep psychological impact on ministers and the public, and was the last major operation undertaken by the IMF for a developed nation. The stand-by arrangement, for $3.9 billion, was a large nominal amount, but it was equivalent to only $1.9 billion in 1956 dollars – a year when the United Kingdom had arranged $1.8 billion of support

[42] Conversation between PM and President Ford, 1 December 1976, TNA PREM16/804.
[43] Whittome meeting with CoE, 3 December 1976, TNA PREM16/805.
[44] Ibid.

through the IMF and the Export-Import Bank of the United States (of which $1.3 billion was from the IMF). In effect, the IMF loan could be viewed as merely a consolidation of the $5.3 billion in swaps that had been negotiated quickly over the phone in June 1976. The difference was the explicit nature of the conditionality, the prolonged and humiliating nature of the negotiations and the publicity that this generated for Britain's plight, both among the British public and overseas.

Throughout these tortuous and often hostile negotiations, in the background lurked Callaghan's vision of a longer-term solution to underpin the stabilisation of confidence in sterling. Since the liquidation of central banks' sterling reserves had increased the vulnerability of the exchange rate, a longer-term solution to prevent this kind of pressure in the future was clearly important to a sustained recovery. This diagnosis fitted with the view that sterling's weakness was a symptom not primarily of confidence in the Labour government's economic policy (which thus needed correcting) but of aberrations in the way that markets operated and the extraordinary external pressures on British policy. The last of these weaknesses – sterling being subject to special pressures because of the remnants of its reserve currency status combined with the accident of the oil crisis – was shared outside Britain and helped draw together a final multilateral initiative. A sterling safety net was the subject of ongoing discussion in Basle and with the US Treasury and Fed throughout the IMF negotiations, and, as we have seen, was prominent in discussions between Callaghan and Ford, who offered the prospect of US cooperation in a longer-term facility as an added incentive for Callaghan to meet the terms of the IMF loan.

As soon as the Cabinet had agreed the terms for the IMF loan, Callaghan wrote to Schmidt to stress the importance of a concurrent announcement of the sterling balances 'safety net'.[45] This would ensure the passage of the IMF loan through parliament and carry the trade unions by assuring them that speculative runs on sterling would not threaten the movement of resources into investment, exports and jobs. European central bankers had already moved the discussion of the 'safety-net' into the BIS, where a crucial meeting was scheduled for the weekend of 10–11 December. The safety-net's final formulation was thus timed to correspond with, and supplement, the announcement of the IMF loan.

The third Group Arrangement, 1976/7

The BIS had been consistently enthusiastic about offering its support for a long-term solution to sterling's problems. As early as the end of 1971,

[45] Text of a message from Callaghan to Schmidt, 9 December 1976, TNA PREM16/806.

after Geoffrey Rippon had assured the EEC countries that the United Kingdom intended to reduce official sterling balances and thus end sterling's reserve role, the BIS began to draft proposals for how it could facilitate this process. D. H. MacDonald's idea at this point was that the BIS itself would take over most official sterling reserves and offer a claim on the BIS for US dollars in return. The United Kingdom would then offer the BIS a dollar-denominated bond to the same value. In this way, sterling reserves would be shifted to dollar claims on the BIS, underpinned by a UK bond. Withdrawals would be financed by the BIS in the first instance from ready funds in the Eurodollar and US markets, but 'in order to cover the BIS liquidity needs (and to reassure the ex-sterling balances holders of the credibility of the BIS obligation) a group of countries would give the BIS a stand-by in US$ of an amount equal to, say, half of the balances taken over by the BIS'. Macdonald concluded that, 'basically, the idea is to use the market to turn into liquid US$ form the present sterling balances and to get the UK out of the reserve currency business. The liquidity guarantee from a group of countries is essential, but the aim would be not to have recourse to it.' In this way the plan corresponded to the 1968 Basle Agreement, whereby exchange guarantees were designed to obviate the need actually to draw on the BIS central bank facilities. The proposal was put to the Bank of England, which was positive, but the idea was not taken up in the monetary maelstrom of 1973/4.[46] Nevertheless, MacDonald's planning set the main building blocks for the 1977 third Group Arrangement.

The third and final BIS Group Arrangement to support sterling began to be considered in October 1976 and was finally concluded at the beginning of February 1977. The G10 (plus Switzerland) central banks approved a $3 billion medium-term facility (75 per cent of the value of the IMF loan), which would be available should official overseas sterling reserves fall below the £2.165 billion level of December 1976. The link to the IMF loan was made explicit because this Group Arrangement differed from the previous two by involving the IMF in its administration.[47] Witteveen, as director of the IMF, was given the task of ensuring that the British government conformed to the conditions of the stand-by arrangement and of advising the participating central banks if, in his view, policy had diverged from the terms of the stand-by. In such a case, access to the safety net facility would be suspended. The Group Arrangement thus reinforced the external surveillance and discipline of the IMF operation. As a condition of the safety net the United Kingdom

[46] D. H. MacDonald (BIS) aide-memoire on the sterling balances, 10 December 1973, BISA 1/19, 'Banking policy of the BIS notes 1970–1977'.

[47] Harmon, *The British Labour Government and the 1976 IMF Crisis*, pp. 225–6.

Table 10.5 *Numbers of countries with sterling reserves, 1968 and 1976*

Proportion of sterling in reserves (per cent)	December 1968	September 1976
1–10	0	10
11–20	0	6
21–30	2	3
31–40	1	0
41–50	5	1
51–60	2	0
61–70	5	0
71–80	3	0
81–90	6	0
91–100	7	0
	31	20

Notes: The 1968 figures cover 88.5 per cent of all official sterling and the 1976 figures 94 per cent. Only countries with holdings of £10 million and above are included.

embarked on a programme of trying to reduce the use of sterling as a reserve asset, by selling foreign-currency-denominated bonds in return for sterling reserves.

That Britain was still considered deserving of support to defend against the liquidation of overseas sterling liabilities despite the decline in sterling as a reserve currency and the advent of floating exchange rates is particularly striking and speaks to the priority given to stable exchange rates even in the environment of de jure floating rates. As Wass relates, the Treasury still considered that appealing to the collective interest in retiring sterling as an international currency and encouraging more orderly exchange rate dynamics were the two best prospects for engaging multilateral support for a final resolution of the sterling balances.[48] Certainly, the position of sterling had receded considerably since the last Group Arrangement. Table 10.5 shows the BIS calculations of the change in the use of sterling as a reserve currency between the 1968 Basle Agreement and the crisis of 1976. By the latter year only twenty countries had sterling holdings of more than £10 million and only one held close to 50 per cent of its reserves in sterling (New Zealand). Half the countries held less than 10 per cent of their reserves in sterling. This compares sharply with 1968, when twenty-three countries (74 per cent of those with at least £10 million) held over a half of their reserves in sterling.

[48] Wass, *Decline to Fall*, p. 242.

In response to Callaghan's desire during the crisis of June 1976 for a long-term solution to the sterling balances that would involve the substitution of sterling deposits with other liabilities such as SDRs, Healey initially proposed 'some form of safety net to underpin the sterling balances on the lines of the 1968 Basle facility'.[49] The success of the 1968 scheme in forestalling the liquidation of the sterling balances without requiring recourse to the support arrangements certainly recommended a repeated effort. An agreement through the BIS also fell outside the IMF's conditionality, which so plagued the Labour government at this time. As always, a medium-term scheme promised to relieve the pressure on policy-making posed by the threat of a conversion of the reserves and so free up the government's planning process. Potential obstacles included the fact that contributors would still need to be convinced by the government's monetary and fiscal policy commitments, and that these countries had only recently provided $5.3 billion in short-term stand-by credits, so they could not be approached again quickly. Nevertheless, in June that year Callaghan was advised to take up the idea speedily and raise it informally at the next summit meeting of the G5 scheduled for the end of that month in Puerto Rico. Harold Lever also pressed for an early start on an ambitious safety net of about $10 billion.[50] Healey resisted, however, on the basis that any multilateral approach had to await the outcome of the upcoming US and West German general elections. Callaghan acquiesced, and further planning was therefore delayed until September.[51]

By this time the external situation had weakened further, and plans were afoot to approach the IMF for a stand-by arrangement, with the public announcement coming on 29 September. A week earlier the Treasury presented its detailed proposals for a very ambitious $12 billion safety net for sterling, repayable over six years.[52] Healey supported the plan generally but did not want Callaghan to take his eye off the need for urgent short-term support in the form of an IMF stand-by arrangement, which would have to be negotiated first. Nevertheless, Callaghan raised the suggestion with President Ford when he called to tell him about the application to the IMF at the end of September.[53] He put two proposals to Ford: the IMF stand-by arrangement and a longer-term scheme for the sterling balances. Ford encouraged the first, but refused to commit

[49] Chancellor memo for the prime minister, 16 June 1976, TNA PREM16/797.
[50] BD to PM, 18 June 1976; Lever to PM, 9 July 1976; TNA PREM16/796.
[51] Correspondence between Healey and Callaghan, 26–9 July 1976, TNA PREM16/796.
[52] Healey to Callaghan, 22 September 1976, TNA PREM16/798
[53] Phone conversation between Ford and Callaghan, 29 September 1976, TNA PREM 16/798.

himself to the second. Wass interprets Ford's reluctance as a response to the increasing hostility of the Republican Party to providing financial support abroad. This was a particularly delicate time politically, with Ford engaged in the run-up to the 1976 presidential election, including the first televised presidential debate since 1960, to be held on 24 September. The preparation of a letter to elicit a firmer reaction from Ford on the safety net was overtaken by the collapse of the exchange rate, but Callaghan's enthusiasm for the idea kept it on the table despite the lack of interest from Healey and Ford.

In a meeting with Callaghan, Lever and others at no. 10 Downing Street on 6 October 1976, Healey opposed Callaghan's proposal to approach President Ford and Chancellor Schmidt formally with a safety net scheme. Callaghan's plan was still to arrange a $12 billion scheme repayable over six years, with a possible announcement as early as 16 October after discussion with Ford and Schmidt.[54] By this time the sterling rate had fallen to $1.64, and Healey was arguing that 'the major problem was a general lack of confidence in the adequacies of our policies, not the sterling balances', and so monetary policy should be tightened up both through an increase in interest rates and by calling in special deposits from banks. Furthermore, the reception by the United States to such an approach was likely to be negative and counterproductive. Edwin Yeo, US undersecretary of state for monetary affairs, had told Healey over the weekend that the United States would not consider a safety net 'until we [the United Kingdom] had got our policies right'. Nor was support likely from the newly re-elected Chancellor Schmidt, particularly if the proposal was linked to troop withdrawals. On the other hand, Lever argued, seductively, that the collapse of sterling was essentially speculative rather than caused by any 'inadequacies of government policy', and so the announcement of a safety net for sterling *was* an appropriate response. A stable exchange rate would be achieved only 'if substantial funds were available for support and there was an arrangement to deal with the sterling balance problem'. Both Lever and Callaghan refused to rely on domestic policy alone, for political reasons, since contractionary policies would provoke objections by the trade unions and the Labour Party. Callaghan suggested that Ford and Schmidt should be warned that the Labour government might well fall if support was not forthcoming. He suggested a compromise, of approaching the West German chancellor first rather than Ford, but Healey rejected this because of the danger of leaks from the West German side that would undermine the IMF negotiations. Callaghan conceded that 'he would not wish to go against the

[54] PM's brief for meeting with CoE on 6 October 1976, TNA PREM16/798.

Chancellor of the Exchequer's judgement', and he did not insist on a high-level approach to either the Americans or the West Germans. Wass relates, however, that on 10 October Schmidt raised the sterling balances in a private conversation with Callaghan at Chequers, and that Callaghan took strength from his positive attitude to a safety net scheme, although the decision ultimately rested with the Bundesbank, which had the resources.[55] Exploratory talks a week later with Karl Otto Pöhl, the West German state secretary to the Ministry of Finance, drew a less enthusiastic German response.

The Treasury moved forward with its planning for a safety net, and also with its proposal of August 1975 to issue SDR-denominated debt in exchange for official sterling reserves, particularly those of oil producers. The Treasury made another push to implement the SDR scheme on 21 October 1976, either along with or prior to the arrangement of a BIS 'safety net'.[56] By this time the Treasury argument was that the extra risk to sentiment had evaporated, since confidence was already so low. Moreover, such an initiative would strengthen the case for the safety net by showing Britain's willingness to take positive action to shore up sterling reserves. The two parts of D. H. MacDonald's 1973 scheme to end sterling's reserve role (funding the balances, underpinned by a multilateral stand-by arrangement) were thus being brought back together in the Treasury by the end of October 1976.

In a broadcast of the BBC programme *Panorama* on 25 October, the prime minister publicly raised the issue of the sterling balances and the need for international support, commenting that 'I would love to get rid of the reserve currency', perhaps by having the liabilities 'taken over in some form or other' by surplus countries such as West Germany, the United States and Japan.[57] On 28 October the US magazine *Business Week* leaked discussions between central bankers, reporting that the United Kingdom was negotiating a renewal of the Basle Agreement amounting to $10 billion in stand-by arrangements.[58] A week later, on 5 November, Brittan gave a detailed description in *The Financial Times* of the possibilities to be discussed in Basle, including another exchange guarantee and stand-by facilities. The pace was being forced at the British end through

[55] Wass, *Decline to Fall*, pp. 244–5.

[56] Derek Mitchell to principal private secretary to Chancellor of Exchequer, 21 October 1976, TNA T358/219.

[57] Dealtry note of a phone conversation with Mr McMahon, 26 October 1976, BISA DEA 4 7.18(12), 'Dealtry papers'. Excerpts from the interview are quoted in Wass, *Decline to Fall*, pp. 247–8.

[58] Reuters report, 28 October 1976, BISA 7.18(14) LAR3, 'Third Group Arrangement sterling balances'.

the media but American intransigence over discussing long-term support until the IMF loan had been concluded inhibited formal discussion among central bankers in Basle, and plans to discuss the matter in early November were postponed.[59] At this point the Treasury's expectation was that a safety net of about $5 billion would actually be sufficient, and that it could be combined with an SDR bond scheme for official sterling balances. The participation and leadership of West Germany, both on the Treasury and on the central bank side, was considered crucial, particularly if the Americans could not be persuaded to take part.[60]

In a set of papers for the central bank governors' meetings on 6–8 November, the Bank of England set out the problem of the sterling balances and addressed two potential solutions.[61] An important new concern was that, unlike in earlier crises, movements in official sterling reserves were contributing significantly to current problems. The level of reserves had increased sharply through the oil crisis, to a peak of £4.9 billion in March 1975, but then a persistent decline had set in. By the end of September official balances were down to £2.8 billion, having fallen by £1.3 billion since the start of the year, £900 million of which had been lost in the second quarter of 1976 alone, when sterling was under pressure. Private sterling balances, on the other hand, had remained stable at about £3.2 to 3.4 billion throughout 1976. Among official holders, four oil producers – Brunei, Kuwait, Nigeria and Saudi Arabia – together accounted for £1.4 billion, or a half, of total official sterling reserves. Only seven other countries had official holdings of more than £20 million.

In terms of solutions, the Bank of England examined two proposals: a safety net facility and a funding operation. The safety net would follow the pattern of the 1968 Basle Agreement: the United Kingdom could draw on stand-by funds in the event of a net decline in the overseas sterling reserves that had to be met by sales of the United Kingdom's own foreign exchange reserves. The new arrangement would operate without the exchange rate guarantee and minimum sterling proportions, which were no longer appropriate given floating exchange rates and the fact that most sterling balances now were in multifarious private hands rather than official reserves. This solution had the advantages that it required

[59] Lamfalussy note of a visit to Washington, 11–12 November 1976, BISA 7.18(14) LAR3, 'Third Group Arrangement sterling balances'.

[60] Note of meeting at no. 11 Downing Street: CoE, Wass, Derek Mitchell (Treasury), Lever, Richardson (BE), Kit McMahon (BE), 5 November 1976: Bank of England, www.bankofengland.co.uk/publications/foi/disc060519.htm.

[61] Bank of England paper 'Sterling balances', 5 November 1976, BISA 2/2n 1, 'Bank of England third Group Arrangement'.

no negotiation with sterling holders, could be related to state and private holders and, like the 1968 facility, would not prompt any net extension of credit to the United Kingdom if it were successful in restoring confidence. The second proposal was to offer to holders of large official sterling reserves medium- or long-term UK government US dollar bonds issued on market terms. Creditors would thus avoid exchange risk, at the cost of liquidity. In order to make the bonds attractive there would have to be some liquidity guarantee, not just marketability (since the latter would prompt a large discount if holders all began to sell on the market). The value of the bonds would be assured by a facility for the United Kingdom to have recourse to a support group of G10 central banks to liquidate them. The advantages of this approach were that activation of the facility would be unambiguous (when the bonds were cashed), a market interest rate and the liquidity guarantee should make the bonds attractive reserve assets, so they would be unlikely to be sold, and 'it would represent a positive and deliberate step towards a reduction in the reserve role of sterling'. The scheme would offer no protection from running down private balances, however, and there was no assurance that sterling holders would accept the bonds. Moreover, negotiations would be complicated and could potentially lead to a delay, which would be damaging to confidence. It was clear that the Bank preferred the safety net approach.

At the meeting in Basle the Americans were still unwilling to engage in discussion of a sterling plan until the IMF stand-by arrangement conditions had been agreed. As the negotiations in London foundered during November, Burns, as chairman of the Fed, resolutely refused to take part even in technical discussions in Basle until the IMF negotiations had been concluded, in order to put extra pressure on the British government.[62] Peter Ramsbotham, the British ambassador to the United States, noted that 'we argued at length but I am afraid he is incorrigible on this'.[63] Nevertheless, a committee of experts of the other participating central banks embarked on planning a medium- or long-term solution to the sterling balances problem. Callaghan remained impatient for progress that would allow a simultaneous announcement of the two branches of support, for the United Kingdom and sterling, so as to enhance confidence and, Wass asserts, to lessen the impetus for tough IMF conditionality.[64]

In mid-November Lever was sent to Washington to engage President Ford's support for Britain's resistance of the IMF, and he was finally

[62] Telegram from Ramsbotham, British embassy, Washington, to FCO, 23 November 1976, on discussion with Burns (Fed), TNA PREM16/802.

[63] Ibid.

[64] Wass, *Decline to Fall*, pp. 250–1.

successful in getting a positive reaction to the safety net proposals and a commitment to simultaneity if progress could be shown in the IMF negotiations, despite the continued opposition of Arthur Burns and William Simon (secretary of the Treasury). In the short term this contradicts Wass's conclusion that Lever's visit was counterproductive.[65] On 20 November Ford wrote to Callaghan that Lever's 'charm was in clear evidence and he, as usual, was a very able representative'.[66] With rather reserved support, he agreed that,

> in the expectation that your government will, as your message of November 17 suggests, come to substantial agreement on conditions deemed necessary by the Fund to achieve stability, I can assure you that we will, once such agreement has been reached, work sympathetically with you on a responsible way of addressing various aspects of the sterling balances and related concerns. Should a resolution be reached and we have confidence in prospects for success, it could be announced simultaneously with the announcement of your agreement with the Fund.

By this time, however, Ford had lost the 1976 presidential election to Jimmy Carter, and, although he remained in office until late January, his political capital was clearly waning.

On 15 November, with the IMF negotiations in progress in London, the head of the banking department of the BIS, Ricky Hall (who had been important in the development of the second Group Arrangement in 1968 while at the Bank of England), began a first draft of a formal proposal for a third Group Arrangement.[67] The paper began with the statement that 'the time is ripe to consider whether it is both desirable and feasible to negotiate with the Bank of England and with a supporting group of central banks an arrangement which would provide funds to finance a further drawing down of the sterling balances'. In making the case that a safety net was a necessary accompaniment to the IMF loan, it used the Bank of England's calculations of recent movements in sterling reserves to argue that, without a support mechanism, further drawings might rapidly eat up the proposed IMF stand-by arrangement of $3.9 billion. A new BIS facility would also have presentational advantages in terms of confidence if it could be announced soon after the IMF loan. Hall then set out versions of the Bank of England's two proposals, for a stand-by arrangement and a UK dollar-denominated bond. The bond issue would take time to negotiate with sterling holders

[65] Ibid., p. 252.
[66] Telegram from Ford to Callaghan, 20 November 1976, TNA PREM16/802.
[67] R. T. P. Hall paper, 'A possible third Group Arrangement concerning the sterling balances', 15 November 1976, BISA 2/2n 1, 'Bank of England third Group Arrangement'.

and could be concluded after the IMF stand-by arrangement had been announced, although the liquidity of the bonds would be underpinned by the safety net. A final draft was sent to the Bank of England on 25 November 1976.

With a meeting of central bank governors looming on 12–13 December, the BIS also prepared a paper for the G10 (plus Switzerland) central banks, which was completed on 9 December 1976, just after the IMF loan details had finally been agreed.[68] Even with the IMF support, additional action on the sterling reserves was justified, on the basis that 'it is now rather generally accepted that any significant further decline of the sterling exchange rate would impart a fresh inflationary impulse to British costs, prices and wages and would lead to a renewed weakening of confidence in sterling', which would create new disturbances in other exchange markets. The rationale was still, therefore, predicated on a call to respond to shared responsibility for burdens and threats to the international monetary system – a premise that had worn thin for the Americans. The paper argued strongly for a new arrangement, especially given the dip in reserves occasioned by the repayment of the June 1976 stand-by facility that had been made on 7 December. Drawing on the first tranche of the IMF loan would merely restore the reserves to the level before the repayment of these credits and would not resolve underlying weaknesses arising from further reductions in official sterling balances that threatened the reserves and undermined the sterling exchange rate. The paper then rehearsed the advantages and disadvantages of safety net facilities and the bond scheme along the lines of the British argument, but by this time it was becoming clear in London that, despite Ford's promises to Callaghan, it was not just the timing of a new initiative but its very principle that was the obstacle.

At a meeting on 6 December, Callaghan urged Richardson to persuade Karl Klasen, president of the Bundesbank, to support the safety net in principle publicly, so that Callaghan could allude to a pending sterling agreement when he reported to parliament on the outcome of the IMF negotiations, which he expected to do on 15 December.[69] Derek Mitchell, the second permanent secretary at the Treasury, reported that Karl Otto Pöhl had already confirmed the willingness of the Bundesbank to make such an undertaking. Callaghan was willing at this point to have an agreement that excluded the Fed, since he believed the United States would be unable to reject a fait accompli. Richardson was not as

[68] 'The sterling balances', 9 December 1976, BISA LAR3 7.18(4).

[69] Note of a meeting at no. 11 Downing Street, 7:00 p.m. 6 December 1976; Bank of England, www.bankofengland.co.uk/publications/foi/disc060519.htm.

optimistic and assured Callaghan that there was no possibility of a full agreement in Basle by 15 December.

Even after the conclusion of the IMF loan terms in London on 8 December, Burns remained hostile to the safety net scheme and resisted taking part in the BIS talks, while the US Treasury began to seek a bilateral agreement with the UK government rather than a central banking arrangement. On 11 December Mitchell reported from Washington that Burns 'regards the sterling balances as a UK problem, if it is a problem and all, and argued that unilateral guarantees were the obvious answer, if we could not adopt policies which would remove exchange rate instability'.[70] Any long-term support from the Fed would provoke criticism from Congress and threaten the independence of the Fed. Burns also bitterly resented the pressure being applied on him by President Ford to engage in the BIS discussions, supporting Wass's contention that Callaghan's manipulation of Ford was indeed counterproductive. Ford's promise to Callaghan that the United States would support the safety net if an IMF loan was concluded had little impact, given that he was a 'lame duck' president following his defeat in the presidential election by Carter. Callaghan hoped that Ford might at least leave a recommendation to Congress that the proposals be supported, but Edwin Yeo, undersecretary of state for monetary affairs, warned that the ensuing Congress debates would be 'brutal and humiliating for the UK'.

Mitchell met with Yeo the next day, when Yeo unexpectedly presented a scheme that had been developed in the US Treasury to deal with sterling reserves through a special trust fund at the IMF subscribed by surplus G10 countries plus Saudi Arabia, with drawings by the United Kingdom subject to IMF conditionality.[71] Yeo asserted that there was no hope of going through the BIS rather than the IMF and that he was offering bilateral US–UK negotiations on this scheme only. This did not meet Mitchell's remit for a scheme to be announced at the same time as the IMF loan, and it also cut directly across the negotiations about to begin in Basle, so he rejected this initiative. By this time, as the deadline for announcing the IMF loan drew near and with Congress due to rise on 15 December, thus effectively ending Gerald Ford's presidency, the British side began to panic that, without US support, the safety net might slip away. On 10 December Callaghan cabled Ford and pleaded that 'I cannot overstate how damaging it would be to our statement on

[70] Telegram from Sir Derek Mitchell to Chancellor of the Exchequer; initialled as read by Callaghan; TNA PREM16/807.

[71] Telegram from Ramsbotham in Washington to FCO, 12 December 1976, TNA PREM16/807.

Wednesday if we cannot then include a positive announcement that the US government together with the other governments concerned in the BIS have reached agreement in principle on an arrangement for dealing with the problem of the sterling balances'.[72] The next day, on the eve of the central bank governors' meeting in Basle, Callaghan phoned Chancellor Schmidt and urged him to call Ford and get him to move the US Treasury to accept the safety net, concluding forcefully that 'if they are not careful that bloody American Treasury is going to upset the whole of this packet'.[73]

At Basle Burns was able to accept a compromise that linked the safety net firmly to the terms of the IMF loan by including oversight by the managing director of the Fund. The safety net could then be interpreted as a further reinforcement to the United Kingdom's letter of intent to the IMF, since, if the managing director determined that the terms of the letter were not being followed, the safety net support would be suspended. This allowed agreement in principle to be confirmed among the G10 governors at their meeting on 13 December, and an ad hoc group of experts was formed to draft detailed proposals for both a safety net, to support reductions in the official sterling balances, and a dollar-denominated bond issue by the United Kingdom. The governors agreed that the safety net would be a facility made available by the BIS to the Bank of England, backed by a stand-by arrangement to the BIS by other central banks to be used if the BIS's own resources, or its access to funds on the market, were insufficient. At the same time, the UK government was required to phase out sterling as a reserve asset by offering a foreign currency bond, which would aim to reduce the official sterling reserves substantially. To emphasise that the facility was to be complementary to the IMF loan and would not undermine the commitments made by the Chancellor of the Exchequer in terms of monetary and fiscal restraint, the governors of the central banks sought to establish a direct link between the United Kingdom's right to draw on the BIS facility and the terms of the IMF loan. The governors also sought a commitment from the United Kingdom not to encourage the rebuilding of sterling reserves in the future. This allowed Callaghan to announce in parliament that support for the sterling balances was likely to be reached 'before too long' when he gave details of the IMF loan on 15 December, although the details were not agreed for almost another two months. Callaghan did not in the end achieve his goal of a set of firm proposals, but the details of the safety net and the

[72] Telegram from Callaghan to Ford, 10 December 1976, TNA PREM16/807.
[73] Transcript of phone call, Callaghan to Schmidt, 11 December 1976, TNA PREM16/807.

support of most of the BIS governors was known to the market by the time the IMF stand-by arrangement was announced.

The ad hoc group of experts held three meetings, on 20 and 22 December 1976 in Paris and on 9 January 1977 in Basle, to prepare detailed proposals for the governors. These meetings confirmed that the facility would refer only to reductions in official sterling reserves that caused an equivalent decline in the United Kingdom's own reserves. The facility would last for three years, and in the first two years the United Kingdom could draw on the funds only if it was still eligible to draw on the IMF loan. The United Kingdom would undertake to issue a foreign currency bond, and also to engage in bilateral discussions with the main holders of sterling so as to reduce their reserves to 'normal working balances'. The amount and the distribution of the stand-by arrangement, the baseline for measuring the sterling balances, and the mechanics of the link to the IMF loan conditions were left to the governors' meeting on 10 January. Witteveen, as IMF managing director, was invited to this meeting, in recognition of the prominent role the IMF would play in the arrangement.

The meeting of governors showed that the arrangement was by no means a done deal.[74] Burns presented a US paper that had been discussed and mostly agreed with Richardson and the Bank of England during December. It put greater emphasis on undertakings by the UK government to reduce the sterling reserves to working levels, so that there would be no need for a fourth Group Arrangement. More fundamentally, the paper suggested that the IMF managing director should regularly review the progress of the United Kingdom in reducing sterling's reserve role. The United Kingdom would become ineligible to draw on the BIS facility not only if it was ineligible to draw on the IMF loan but also if, 'in the judgment of the Managing Director', it was not making reasonable progress in reducing official sterling reserves. Richardson made it clear that the United Kingdom would make all *reasonable* efforts to reduce the sterling reserves but that it could not predict the holders' reactions to the bond offer. Moreover, he did not want to be pressed to define precisely what 'working balances' might mean in each instance. Finally, Richardson insisted that the managing director could take the monitoring role in a personal capacity, but that the executive board of the IMF (while approving this role) should not itself monitor Britain's progress. This proved a contentious point, as Burns sought to establish an independent role for Witteveen to decide when the arrangement

[74] Draft record of meeting of G10 (+Switzerland) central bank governors and managing director of the IMF, 10 January 1977, BISA 7.18(12) DEA4/6.

should be suspended, and the other central bank governors sought to retain control of the arrangement themselves. In the end a compromise was reached, which left the final decision on whether the arrangement should be suspended with the participating central banks. Witteveen subsequently made rather heavy weather of getting the executive board's approval, which was finalised only in March 1977 – a month after the stand-by arrangement had been implemented.

The meeting went on to set the baseline for the sterling balances at 8 December 1976 (£2.165 billion) and the total value of the facility at $3 billion, an amount deemed to be larger than the United Kingdom would need but sufficient to make it credible to the markets. The United Kingdom would not be eligible for financing any reductions in sterling reserves that merely shifted them from official to 'nominally' private hands. France and Italy declined to participate, on account of their own balance of payments problems. In a parting shot, Bernard Clappier, the governor of the Banque de France, chided Britain for not having made much progress in reducing sterling reserves since the commitment to the EEC five years earlier.

Officials and governors reconvened the next month, on 6 and 7 February, to finalise the details.[75] The Canadians proposed a baseline for UK reserves as well as overseas sterling balances, as they did not want to finance reductions in sterling balances if UK reserves were high. The UK reserves on 8 December (the baseline for sterling balances) were historically very low, at some $4 billion, however, which in fact made them a poor baseline from which to calculate reductions. On the other hand, by the end of January reserves had risen to $7.5 billion, which was considered too high by the Canadians and Americans. After much wrangling the governors agreed to a baseline amount of $6.75 billion. If the United Kingdom wanted to make a drawing when their reserves were higher than this level, they needed to convince the participating central banks that the increase was temporary and/or related to official borrowing. The US representatives also continued to press both for more discretion on the part of the IMF managing director and for any country to have the power to opt out of the facility if it thought that the United Kingdom was not adhering to the conditions, whatever the managing director thought. The latter proviso was included to satisfy domestic US opinion, but most other governors felt that it contravened the spirit of consensus in which the Basle meetings of the G10 traditionally operated. In the end, the formal letter from Zijlstra, as president of the BIS, had to accede that it was open

[75] Manuscript minutes by Dealtry, BISA DEA 4 7.18(12), 'Dealtry papers'.

to any central bank to withdraw in the event of a disagreement with the managing director. The final text of the third Group Arrangement was concluded on 8 February, for implementation that day.

The Bank of England subsequently made monthly reports to Witteveen on movements in official and private sterling reserves, reassuring him that there was no switching from official to private and that any increases were for specific purposes related to working balances. Like the second Group Arrangement, the third Group Arrangement fulfilled the ambitions of its founders and did not need to be drawn on. A total of £395 million worth of foreign currency bonds were sold to official holders, of which all but £2 million went to central monetary institutions. They were offered on 4 April (with a closing date of 14 April) in denominations of US dollars (with maturities from five to ten years), Deutschmarks, Swiss francs and yen (with a seven-year maturity). Originally the total was to comprise $750 million in US dollars and $250 million in other currencies, but in the end only $675 million worth were sold. This led to a one-off reduction in old sterling reserves in April 1977, but this was offset by an increase elsewhere, so the level of sterling balances actually increased by £115 million that month. Nonetheless, the sale of the bonds kept the level of official reserves from rising during the arrangement, with the result that the United Kingdom adhered to its obligations. In the first seven months of the arrangement official reserves fell by £322 million (including the sale of bonds), mainly due to a decrease by oil exporters that was not completely offset by an increase in other countries' balances. The entire decline, therefore, was covered by bond sales and not by calls on the UK reserves. In the second seven-month period, to February 1978, the decline was partially reversed, as oil exporters' sterling balances increased by £218 million. The net outcome for the period from December 1976 to February 1978 was a modest fall of £102 million in official sterling reserves. In 1977, as British foreign exchange reserves surged, the reduction in overseas sterling reserves finally pulled these liabilities below the level of UK nominal reserves. The 'overhang' identified in 1945 had finally disappeared – after thirty-two years.

This also marked the end of sterling's use as an important reserve asset, as figure 10.7 shows. By 1970 sterling already constituted less than 5 per cent of industrial countries' reserves, and this decline continued until the currency was no longer used as a reserve by these countries. The brief surge due to the oil crisis in 1974 is evident, but oil producers quickly reduced the share of sterling in their reserves as well. On the other hand, there was a small revival in the use of ster-

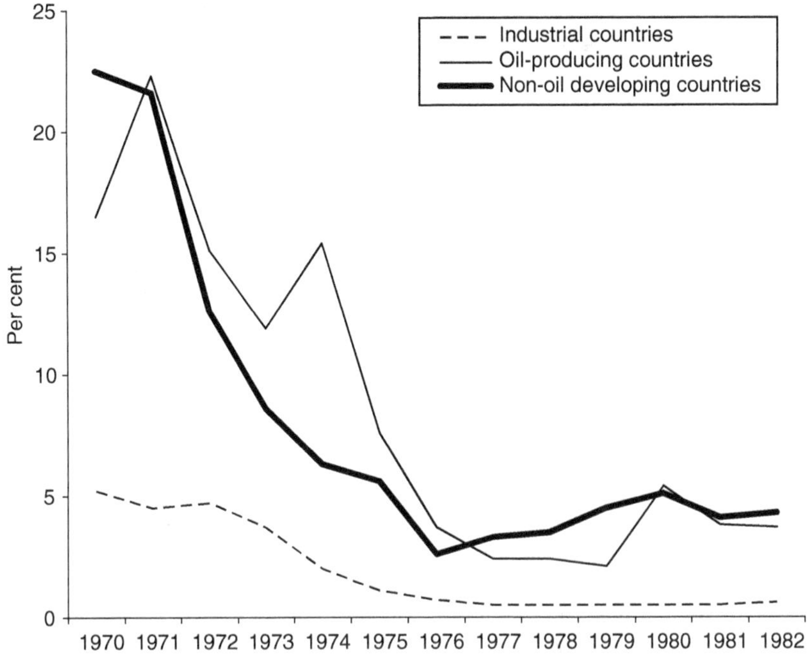

Figure 10.7 Sterling as a share of foreign exchange reserves, 1970–82

ling in the reserves of developing countries after the 1977 third Group Arrangement.

In the 1980s developing countries continued to use sterling as a reserve asset more than industrial countries, and by 1990 sterling's share had risen to 6.2 per cent of less developed countries' reserves, compared with a level of 3.2 per cent for all countries together. Nevertheless, the diversification of reserves away from the US dollar that began in the mid-1970s led to increases in the shares of the Deutschmark and the yen rather than a revival in the use of sterling.

Conclusions

The first oil crisis created a temporary resurgence in the importance of sterling as an international currency, briefly halting the decline that had begun at the end of the 1960s. The sterling share of oil revenues quickly fell away, however, and the share of sterling in the reserves of oil-producing countries dropped dramatically in parallel. Nonetheless, these accumulations did have longer-term implications for the management of the retreat of sterling, since the new holders, such as Nigeria and Saudi Arabia, were politically more difficult for the United Kingdom to deal with than other Commonwealth countries had been. While the relative importance of sterling declined, the absolute value of these obligations was historically high, which led to efforts to manage the increase. By the early 1970s British policy was clearly aimed at containing increases in overseas official holdings of sterling assets, partly because this was a relatively expensive form of borrowing compared with the Euromarkets, but also because the ratio of external assets to liabilities threatened to erode again. Middle Eastern governments were encouraged to make equity investments in Britain rather than to accumulate Treasury bills and other securities, but plans to manage Nigeria's sterling reserves proved more intractable.

The IMF loan of 1976 is often portrayed as the end of Britain's international economic leadership, as, for example, in the title of Burk and Cairncross's book *Goodbye Great Britain*. This chapter has argued that the IMF loan needs to be considered in the context of the Sterling Agreements that accompanied it and the rising value of overseas-held sterling as a result of the primary product boom of the early 1970s. The third Group Arrangement was almost as large as the IMF stand-by arrangement and was considered a vital element in a successful use of IMF resources. In the mind of James Callaghan in particular, but also within the BIS, the IMF loan itself was not seen as likely to be sufficient to overcome the market risks from the diversification of sterling or to restore confidence. As in previous crises since the 1950s, disorderly markets for sterling, it was argued, threatened the stability of the international monetary system as a whole and justified collective action. West German and BIS support for the British position was unable, however, to overcome the American reluctance to get involved yet again in a multilateral scheme to support the retreat of sterling as an international currency. Callaghan was able to convince President Ford to give assurances but these proved impossible to enforce against the intransigence of the Fed and US Treasury after the US elections in November 1976. In the end, Burns agreed – in principle – in time for Callaghan's announcement on 15 December only because the sterling support scheme operated as a further reinforcement to the terms of the IMF loan. As with other Group Arrangements, agreement was conditional on Britain reaching simultaneous agreements with other creditors to ensure that the safety net was not activated – in this case, the sale of foreign currency bonds to replace sterling reserves. From the beginning of 1977 sterling recovered, as planned, and so the rescue package was deemed a success. The management of the exchange rate continued to prove costly, however, and it was abandoned in mid-1977, when greater focus was placed on the domestic economy. By this time the exploitation of North Sea oil promised finally to release the British economy from a balance of payments constraint – but the international role of sterling was over.

11 The aftermath 1980–1992

The 1980s were dominated by the governments headed by Margaret Thatcher, which transformed the United Kingdom's domestic political landscape with a radical emphasis on liberalisation and privatisation. The last external capital controls were abandoned in October 1979 and the financial system was deregulated, culminating in 'Big Bang' in October 1986, which transformed the practice of trading in the City and restored its competitiveness through the 1990s. As chapter 10 showed, by the end of the 1970s sterling had effectively ended its role as an important reserve or commercial currency. Table 11.1 shows that, in the 1980s, sterling never accounted for more than 3 per cent of global foreign exchange reserves, falling behind not only the US dollar but also the Deutschmark and the yen as a reserve asset. Despite the stability in the share of total reserves, figure 11.1 shows that the real value, based on 1969 prices, increased in the 1980s after decreasing from 1975 to 1978.

While the story of the 1980s is not core to the narrative of managing sterling's retreat as an international currency, the continuing importance of sterling's exchange rate policy to Britain's changing place in the world does warrant a brief epilogue, culminating in the dramatic 1992 fallout from the Exchange Rate Mechanism. During these years sterling was defined variously as a petrocurrency, as a symbol of national independence and distinction from Europe and, for a brief period, as a European currency like those in the core of the European Community. These changing identities meant that sterling policy remained a key focus for the public debate within the United Kingdom over Britain's relationship with the evolving European Community and with the rest of the world. As in the 1950s, the debate revolved around how exchange rate policy delivered a solution to the policy trilemma, but by the 1980s the liberalisation of capital flows meant that the choice was between retaining policy sovereignty and aiming to retain exchange rate stability against core trading partners. This chapter gives a brief outline of sterling's progress during the 1980s, finishing with the exit from the ERM in 1992, which had a lasting legacy for the attitude of the British public and policy-makers to sterling as a European currency.

Table 11.1 *Share of national currencies in total identified official holdings of foreign exchange (per cent), 1979–90*

	US dollar	Deutschmark	Sterling	Yen	Other
1979	73.2	12.0	1.8	3.6	9.4
1980	68.6	14.9	2.9	4.3	9.3
1981	71.4	12.7	2.1	4.2	9.6
1982	70.5	12.3	2.3	4.7	10.2
1983	71.4	11.8	2.5	5.0	9.3
1984	70.1	12.6	2.9	5.8	8.6
1985	65.0	15.2	3.0	8.0	8.8
1986	67.1	14.6	2.6	7.9	7.8
1987	67.9	14.5	2.4	7.5	7.7
1988	64.7	15.7	2.8	7.7	9.1
1989	60.3	19.1	2.7	7.8	10.1
1990	56.4	19.7	3.2	9.1	11.6

Notes: European currency units (ECUs) issued against US dollars are included in the US dollar figures; ECUs issued against gold are excluded. Valued in SDRs.
Source: IMF, *Annual Report 1998* (Washington, DC: IMF, 1998).

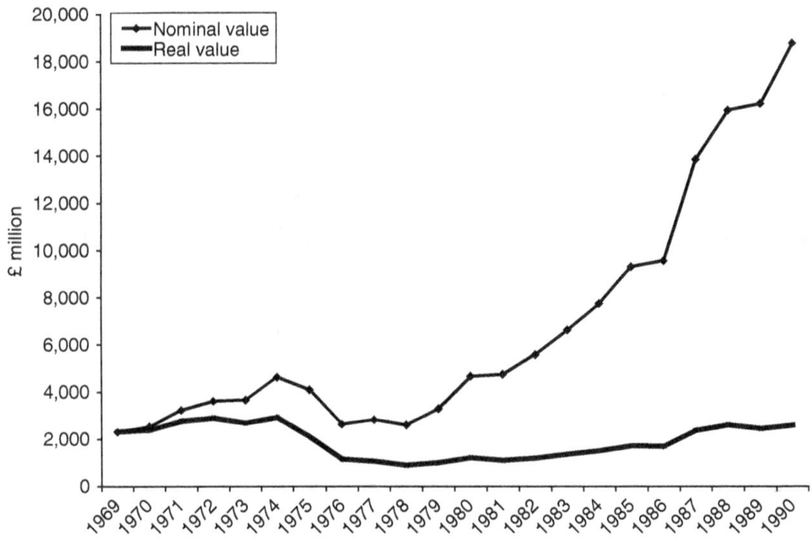

Figure 11.1 Real and nominal values of exchange reserves held in sterling by central monetary institutions, 1969–90

Sterling and North Sea oil

In the early 1980s the exploitation of North Sea oil seemed finally to release British governments from the constraint of precarious balances of current payments in a way that the advent of flexible exchange rates had not. A further outcome of the second oil crisis was that, just after the third Group Arrangement was concluded, finally eliminating sterling as a key reserve asset, the nominal value of sterling held by central monetary institutions in oil-producing countries rose rather than fell, as had been expected. The combined effect was a sharp appreciation of sterling from 1977 to 1980 that led to fears of a form of 'Dutch disease', with oil production draining away British industry's competitive power.[1] The appreciation was quickly reversed, however, and by the start of 1981 sterling began a precipitous decline. Nevertheless, the identification of sterling as a 'petrocurrency' meant that it continued to be viewed as having special characteristics as an international vehicle, which distinguished it from other European currencies in the minds of policy-makers. The exchange rate was determined not only by the United Kingdom's own economic performance but by fluctuations in global oil prices beyond British governments' control.

The first oil flowed from the North Sea in November 1975, allowing the industry to take advantage of the second global oil price shock, which resulted from the Iranian Revolution at the end of the decade. Oil prices began to rise sharply at the start of 1979 as the political situation in Iran deteriorated, with the price doubling to $38 per barrel by the peak, in December 1979. The price then gradually declined to pre-crisis level, before falling precipitously in 1985. By 1981 the United Kingdom was a net exporter of crude oil, and the balance of payments benefited from the rising world price, but the external balance was also vulnerable when the oil price collapsed in 1985. There is some debate about the importance of the oil boom on the sterling exchange rate compared to other factors, such as fiscal and monetary restraint and the depreciation of the US dollar.[2] Figure 11.4 shows that the exchange rate strengthened consistently from 1977, almost immediately after the conclusion of the third Group Arrangement and the IMF loan, which was before the oil could have had a substantial direct impact, although it did affect expectations.

[1] See, for example, Corden, W. M., 'The exchange rate, monetary policy and North Sea oil: the economic theory of the squeeze on tradeables', *Oxford Economic Papers*, 33(Supp.), 1981, pp. 23–46.

[2] Bean, C. R., 'Sterling misalignment and British trade performance', in R. C. Marston (ed.), *Misalignment of Exchange Rates: Effects on Trade and Industry* (Chicago: University of Chicago Press, 1988), pp. 39–76.

The IMF estimated that 56 per cent of the real appreciation of sterling was due to North Sea oil exploitation between 1977and 1981.[3] This included a 'petrocurrency' effect, of market expectations about the future current account balance owing to Britain's status as an oil exporter based on the present value of oil reserves. This effect is not the same as increased demand for sterling as a vehicle or reserve currency – the key elements that define an international currency. In this sense, the difficulties of managing the sterling exchange rate in the 1980s were not related to its use as an international currency but to the role of the United Kingdom as an oil exporter. That said, the exchange rate would be affected by oil companies' demand for sterling to pay taxes and royalties, although this must be netted against a drain of foreign exchange from repatriated profits. Government revenue from oil companies was divided into the petroleum revenue tax (PRT) on profits, royalties and corporation tax, of which the PRT formed the bulk. The annual total payments increased from £600 million in 1978/9 to £6.5 billion in 1981/2 and £12.2 billion in 1985/6.[4] Until 1977 the impact on the current account was negative, as oil production lagged behind costs in terms of imports of material and payment of services, but from 1978 the net surplus accumulated. After the oil price boom, the impact on the current account reached £3.8 billion, rising to £10.5 billion in 1982, and by 1984 oil production amounted to 6.5 per cent of GDP. Figure 11.2 shows the dramatic rise in the price of Brent crude oil in 1979/80 and the value of oil production from 1977 to 1985. Brent crude sold for $37 per barrel on average in 1981, but this fell 60 per cent to under $15 per barrel in the first quarter of 1986.

Figure 11.3 shows the National Institute for Economic and Social Research estimates for the impact of North Sea oil on the effective exchange rate during the oil boom of 1979/80. This includes the net impact on the current account balance and the impact of oil reserves on exchange rate expectations.

The appreciation effects were quickly overtaken from early 1981, when the oil price peaked and then began to fall while the US dollar began a dramatic appreciation. Figure 11.4 shows that, in February, sterling began a four-year decline against the dollar that led from a peak of $2.44/£1 to a low of $1.82/£1 a year later, and ultimately close to $1/£1 by 1985. This was reflected in a fall in the effective exchange rate index

[3] Bond, M. E., and A. Knoble, 'Some implications of North Sea oil for the UK economy', *IMF Staff Papers*, 29(3), 1982, pp. 363–97. The total real appreciation was 45 per cent from 1977 to the end of 1981.

[4] Hall, S., B. Henry and R. Herbert, 'Oil prices and the economy', *National Institute Economic Review*, 116, 1986, pp. 38–44.

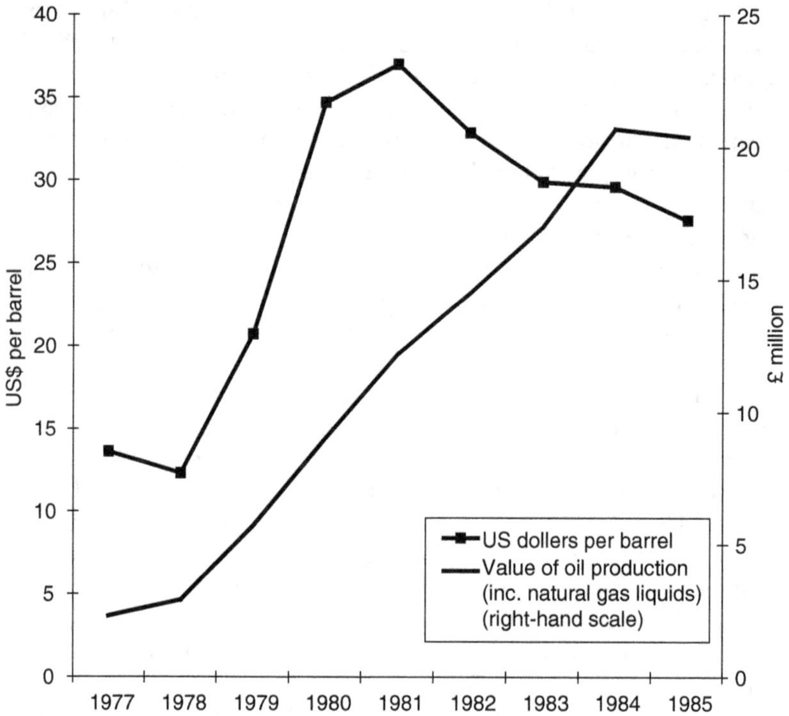

Figure 11.2 North Sea oil exploitation, 1977–85
Source: Hall, Henry and Herbert, 'Oil prices and the economy'.

from a peak of 140.5 in January 1981 to 102.81 in February 1985, as shown in figure 11.5.

Although the direct impact of North Sea oil on sterling's exchange rate was short-lived, the legacy was of longer duration. At the time of the sterling crisis of 1985 Thatcher emphasised that sterling's role as a petrocurrency distinguished the pound from other European currencies and ruled out membership of the Exchange Rate Mechanism, since the exchange rate was determined by global conditions outside Britain's control.[5] Her Chancellor of the Exchequer, Nigel Lawson, had a more realistic view of how long the petrocurrency status would persist, but the perception that North Sea oil made the United Kingdom, and therefore sterling, different from other European states continued to have an effect

[5] Lawson, N., *The View from Number 11: Memoirs of a Tory Radical* (London: Corgi Books, 1992), p. 495.

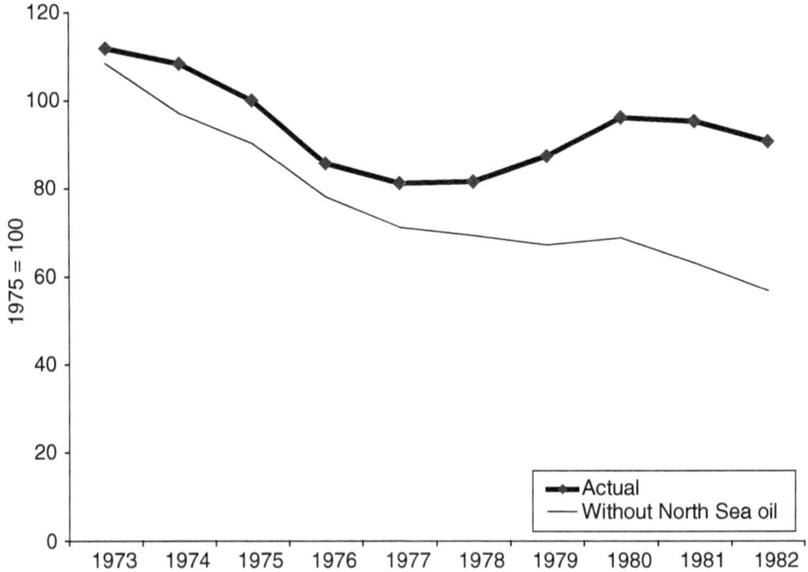

Figure 11.3 Impact of North Sea oil on sterling effective exchange rate, 1973–82
Source: Atkinson, F. J., S. J. Brooks and S. Hall, 'The economic effects of North Sea oil', *National Institute Economic Review*, 104, 1983, pp. 38–44.

Figure 11.4 US dollar/pound spot rate, end-month, January 1975–January 2005
Source: Bank of England statistical database.

Figure 11.5 Monthly effective exchange rate, January 1975–January 2005
Source: Bank of England statistical database.

in distinguishing Britain from its European partners. In the meantime, the focus turned to the seemingly inexorable appreciation of the US dollar in the first half of the decade.

Attempts to stabilise core currencies: the Plaza and Louvre Agreements, 1985–7

As is clear in figure 11.4, during the summer of 1984 sterling underwent a precipitous decline both against the dollar and in terms of the effective exchange rate. Lawson attributed this to ill-judged comments by the Bank of England combined with increased interest rates in the United States, but the fall of 1984/5 was evidently also part of a longer-term decline in sterling's exchange rate from its peak at the end of 1980.[6] In the United States, the administration of Ronald Reagan was pursuing a tight monetary policy, which, combined with a relatively loose fiscal policy, led to an appreciation of the dollar that exacerbated sterling's depreciation, as well as contributing to a global imbalance between persistent surplus and persistent deficit countries. While British governments nominally followed a monetarist policy guided only by monetary targets, the

[6] Ibid., pp. 461–3.

exchange rate was a secondary influence on interest rates, and was soon to become a more prominent target as Lawson lost faith in the efficacy of monetarism. In January 1985 Bernard Ingham, Thatcher's influential press secretary, tested the prime minister's single-target policy by hinting to the media that the government would not defend the pound, which further disturbed markets and forced Lawson to make public his commitment to the sterling exchange rate as an intermediate policy target. To defend the sterling exchange rate, the Bank of England arranged coordinated support for sterling from West Germany and Japan, and interest rates had been raised to 14 per cent by the end of the month.

As the dollar climbed, particularly against the yen, international political pressure grew on the American administration to manage what appeared to be a growing global imbalance. Policy in the United States, as the most powerful global economy, was not amenable to outside influences, however, and the Treasury secretary, Donald Regan, remained committed to a freely floating regime. In January 1985, just before the G5 finance ministers' summit in Washington, Lawson successfully urged Thatcher to use her personal relationship with President Reagan to encourage the American administration to abandon its policy of benign neglect. Reagan's response was non-committal, but it did open an avenue for Lawson to raise the issue at the upcoming meeting.[7] With the support of other G5 members, in particular France and West Germany, Regan was persuaded to agree to take action on the dollar exchange rate. The public communiqué for the meeting, anticipating the terminology used after future summits, noted that the G5 'expressed their commitment to work towards greater exchange market stability' by intervening in a coordinated way in the exchange markets. Almost immediately, from February 1985, the dollar finally began to weaken. In his March 1985 budget speech Lawson reiterated his own attitude to the exchange rate, that 'benign neglect is not an option' because large short-term fluctuations undermined inflationary expectations and made monetary policy less effective.[8] His progress towards explicit targeting of the exchange rate had begun.

The Plaza Agreement of September 1985 marked the formal beginning of coordinated efforts to stabilise the exchange rates of the major currencies, in particular the US dollar against the yen, in the expectation that, in the process, the exchange rates of the other core currencies would be stabilised. To some extent the United Kingdom was a side player in this summit diplomacy: a key member of the G5 but with little economic

[7] Ibid., pp. 472–5.
[8] Ibid., p. 476.

power to influence the major players. The British hoped to exert influence to adapt US policies to their own national interests, and the French unsuccessfully pressed their agenda to set target zones for core currencies, but the key negotiations were between the United States and Japan. The new US Treasury secretary, James Baker, was much more amenable to stabilising the dollar than his predecessor, because of his concerns over protectionist tendencies at home, which focused on the dangers of cheap Japanese imports. Depreciating the dollar against the yen offered an alternative to tariffs as a route to reducing Japanese competitiveness in the American market and to diffusing domestic political pressure to protect American jobs. In this sense, the Plaza Agreement was arguably a product of American domestic political expediency, combined with the Americans' ability to use the threat of trade restrictions to pressure Japan into action, rather than a result of multilateral negotiation. The private agreement between the representatives of all the countries as to their share of the proposed intervention against the dollar reflected the relative economic power of these states within the G5, with the United States and Japan taking on 30 per cent each, West Germany 25 per cent and France 10 per cent, but the United Kingdom only 5 per cent.[9] Paul Volcker later recalled that, after Baker's press conference announcing the intention to manage a depreciation, no official intervention was required to deliver the required result, since the market reacted appropriately to the finance ministers' intentions.[10] The dollar fell steadily over the following year and European reserves increased, although it is doubtful that this was heavily influenced by official intervention.

By the time of the G7 finance ministers' meeting in Paris in February 1987, the object of coordinated intervention was to stem the depreciation of the dollar rather than manage its decline, and the resulting Louvre Agreement sought to coordinate an appreciation of the US currency. This time, harnessing market sentiment proved more difficult, and the trade-weighted dollar rate continued to slide through the stock market crash of October 1987 until early 1988. Although ineffective in its main aim, the renewed commitment to stabilising core exchange rates provided the opportunity for Lawson to arrange for sterling to shadow the Deutschmark, in an effort to import sound economic policy and in anticipation of joining the ERM – a much-debated issue, discussed in the next section.

[9] Ibid., p. 536.

[10] Oral testimony by Paul Volcker, 'International monetary instability since 1968', witness seminar, 17 November 2008. Transcript available at Churchill Archives Centre, Cambridge.

The Plaza and Louvre Agreements are testament to the unwillingness of governments to accept persistent movements among the core exchange rates after the first era of floating in the 1970s. The 'disorderly' rates, typified by the appreciation and then the depreciation of the dollar, disrupted the ability of national governments to pursue their domestic policy targets, and this drew them to return to seek coordinated responses through high-level summits as they had during the 1960s, although on a narrower G5 basis rather than the G10. As in the 1960s, efforts to get the American administration to adapt internal policies to ensure greater stability in the longer term failed, although expansion in Japan laid the foundations for the asset market bust that heralded the 'lost decade' of recession in the 1990s. As in the 1970s, the power of central banks to influence the market proved inadequate once central bank resources were dwarfed by the private market.

In and out of the Exchange Rate Mechanism: failing to turn sterling into a 'European' currency

A month after defeating a vote of no confidence in parliament, a beleaguered prime minister, James Callaghan, announced in early December 1978 that the United Kingdom would not participate in the European monetary system, although sterling did form part of the valuation of the European currency unit at its core. This decision was the outcome of a range of factors. Britain had joined the EEC in January 1973, but the commitment did not carry full public or political support. The Labour Party, then in opposition, pledged to reopen negotiations to improve the terms of Britain's membership once elected and to hold a referendum. Harold Wilson's Labour Party was elected in February 1974 and promptly sought to improve the terms of the country's Common Market membership, although not enough to persuade the left wing of the party to support continued membership. A referendum duly took place in June 1975, in which two-thirds of the public who voted approved continued UK membership, but the issue remained politically divisive. A further consideration contributing to the decision not to join the ERM was the weakness of the Labour government, which was under pressure from its traditional supporters, as well as the Conservative opposition, over its efforts to restrain wage increases, which led to the infamous 'winter of discontent' during 1978/9. A system that effectively tied sterling to the Deutschmark was unacceptable to Callaghan, since it would spread deflationary pressure to the British economy, although he was sympathetic to the aims of exchange rate stability.[11] These economic and political circumstances all made 1978 an unpropitious moment to tie sterling into a pegged rate system with the rest of the EEC.

The early success of the ERM system and improvements in Britain's economic prospects led to a gradual change of view on the part of the incoming Conservative government of Margaret Thatcher. The United Kingdom's two-year association with the ERM from October 1990 is often seen as a policy mistake because of the disastrous and costly exit in September 1992, which has scarred the public psyche and contributed to the aversion to engage with more recent European monetary integration. Although the annual (ex-mortgage payment) inflation rate was reduced from 9.5 per cent in October 1990 to 3.6 per cent in October 1992, the recession and rising unemployment in 1991/2 contributed to the loss of credibility in the government's commitment to the peg, and ultimately to its abandonment.[12] In 1991 GDP fell by 1 per cent, and recovered only by 0.2 per cent in 1992, while unemployment rose from 1.7 million to 2.8 million.

In a lengthy investigation from October to December 1993, Stephen Davies, a senior Treasury official, used the Treasury files to compile a study of the reasons why Britain had joined the ERM, its operation and demise in a report intended for internal Treasury use.[13] His analysis reveals how the Treasury in particular viewed how sterling should and could be involved in the ERM. When the ERM was first created, in 1979, the Treasury was against joining because of the dangers to British economic performance posed by the external discipline required to retain exchange rate stability. In its view, Britain's fundamental problems of uncompetitive industry and inflationary expectations required a flexible exchange rate to achieve ongoing gains in price competitiveness. With an inflexible labour market, attempts to constrain inflation to an external target would be felt rapidly in output and employment, with dire economic and political consequences. The Treasury's viewpoint changed in line with developments in the competitive position of the British economy, as well as changes in the ideology underlying economic policy.

[11] Callaghan, J., *Time and Chance* (London: Collins, 1987), pp. 402–3.

[12] Masson, P., 'Gaining and losing ERM credibility: the case of the United Kingdom', *Economic Journal*, 105, 1995, pp. 571–82. For an account of the ERM experiment as a political disaster but an 'economic triumph', see Budd, A., *Black Wednesday: A Re-examination of Britain's Experience in the Exchange Rate Mechanism* (London: IEA, 2005). This volume also offers opposing views from Tim Congdon and Sam Brittan. For a more general survey of this period, see Stephens, P., *Politics and the Pound: The Tories, the Economy and Europe* (London: Papermac, 1997).

[13] ERM project paper, Stephen Davies, 21 December 1993.

During the first five years of the operation of the ERM British inflation was brought down close to the EEC rate, and when in 1985 the situation was reconsidered the Treasury came to the view that membership was likely and desirable in principle. Just before the G5 finance ministers' meeting in Washington in January 1985, discussed above, where the first commitment to a coordinated stabilisation of core exchange rates was agreed, Lawson met with his Treasury advisers to discuss using the ERM to contain sterling's volatility.[14] Thereafter, Lawson began his campaign to convince Thatcher that sterling should join the ERM, supported not only by his Treasury officials but also by key players such as Geoffrey Howe, the foreign secretary, and the Bank of England governor, Robin Leigh-Pemberton. In November 1985, at a special Cabinet meeting to discuss joining the ERM (which Leigh-Pemberton also attended), Thatcher threatened that, 'if you join the EMS, you will have to do so without me'. Lawson recalled this as 'the saddest event of my time as Chancellor and the greatest missed opportunity'.[15] Over the next few years the possibility was widely debated, and a consensus in favour of joining grew.

The outcome of the stalemate with the prime minister was a compromise in June 1989 that sterling would join once a set of circumstances known as the 'Madrid conditions' prevailed: freer exchange controls, greater market competition in Europe and a lower UK inflation rate. As Davies remarked, a wait and see approach was influenced by the lack of crisis, on the principle that 'a panacea is not necessary when there is nothing to cure', but the main obstacle was the prime minister's own intransigence over this issue of greater integration with Europe, together with fears that interest rates would become unstable under ERM pressure.[16] Ideological differences eventually drove Lawson and Howe to resign from the Cabinet in 1989 and 1990, respectively.

The new Chancellor, John Major, who took office in October 1989, did not share his predecessor's enthusiasm for the ERM, but external pressure to join the system from business and the Labour Party mounted. Major was also adrift in policy terms, as the credibility of monetary policy had been eroded through the end of the 1980s, making interest rate policy less effective. A new institutional departure was needed to restore confidence and credibility, and Davies notes the options considered by the Treasury included making the Bank of England independent or joining the ERM. During the summer of 1990 the Treasury's growth

[14] Lawson recalls this meeting happening on 11 January 1985. Lawson, *The View from Number 11*, pp. 485–7.

[15] Ibid., p. 499.

[16] ERM project paper, Stephen Davies.

forecasts for the British economy deteriorated while inflationary pressure continued. Thatcher was eventually convinced that interest rates could not be relaxed without joining the ERM, and Major was convinced that inflationary pressure meant that there should be no further depreciation of the exchange rate. On 3 October he wrote to the prime minister that entry to the ERM 'alone will allow us, once sterling is in place inside the mechanism, to reduce interest rates without any compromise to our monetary stance. I remain convinced that we could not contemplate an interest rate reduction outside the ERM.' Davies recalled that these arguments were clearly influential in changing Thatcher's mind. Major cut interest rates by one percentage point at the time of entry to the ERM.

Sterling entered the ERM on 8 October 1990 at the rate of DM2.95/£1, or about 70 pence to the ECU, which was criticised at the time and later as being too high and for contributing to the recession that followed.[17] In announcing the decision in parliament, Major noted that the market conditions for membership had all been met, in terms of the creation of the single market and financial market liberalisation, and that, while the UK inflation rate was still relatively high, it was predicted to converge towards the European level. In the press communiqué on 6 October 1990 announcing the par rates and the 6 per cent margin for fluctuation, the European Commission cautioned that UK membership would not be successful without more fundamental structural changes to enhance competitiveness, noting that 'participation in the exchange rate mechanism, provided that it is accompanied by the appropriate macroeconomic and structural policies and a rapid move to the narrow margins, will allow the UK to regain monetary stability, leading to strengthened growth and employment creation'. In the event, the Treasury's forecasts for growth and inflation – on which membership had been approved – both turned out to be too optimistic.

Along with the misreading of the economic context of membership, the monetary reunification of Germany was another factor weakening the system. The Treasury had first advised Major and Thatcher on the implications of German unification for the ERM in early February 1990, noting that the Deutschmark would probably become more unstable and that German interest rates would be likely to rise. The Treasury reassured policy-makers, however, that the implications of German monetary union would be clear well before sterling was likely to join, towards the end of 1990. Davies concluded that 'the Treasury does seem to have played down the relevance of German reunification to the prospects for the UK's ERM membership'.

[17] Critics at the time included the NIESR and Charles Goodhart.

As in previous moves to pegged systems, the exchange rate was chosen so as to correspond fairly closely to the rate that prevailed at the time, rather than on a sophisticated analysis of an equilibrium exchange rate. In May and August 1990 long-term trends in the effective exchange rate and the Deutschmark/pound exchange rate were plotted to determine an appropriate rate. These showed that an appreciation of sterling in the summer of 1990 had brought the level to or just above the average for 1980 to 1990 (DM2.99/£1), which was considered a benchmark, although this rate was significantly higher than the longer-run average from 1968. During September sterling weakened slightly, and the rate chosen by 4 October was that month's average, DM2.95/£1.

The first few months of sterling's membership in the ERM were rocky, as evidence of a looming recession encouraged journalists and economists to call for further interest rate cuts, but sterling's weakness in the ERM made these impossible without a rate realignment. From February 1991, however, the situation was ameliorated by the weakening of the Deutschmark, and interest rates were able to come down in a series of steps through the summer, weakening some of the public criticism of ERM membership. By late November, a year after membership, the economy began another downturn. A German interest rate increase on 19 December was followed by all ERM countries except for the United Kingdom, putting increasing pressure on sterling. The Conservative Party negotiated its way carefully through the election of April 1992, helped by the Labour Party's public commitment to remain in the ERM at a parity of DM2.95/£1, which steadied markets and expectations, both political and economic. During the summer of 1992, however, the housing market declined sharply and sterling hovered around its lower band, attracting speculators in anticipation of a devaluation. In July a 'senior official' of the Bundesbank suggested publicly that weaker currencies in the ERM would have to devalue, marking the beginning of a series of negative public statements coming from the German central bank as it lobbied for a general realignment, in order to relax pressure for cuts in German interest rates, which would increase inflation.

During mid-August the Bank of England was forced to intervene covertly in the foreign exchange market at a rate of about $150 million per day, and it warned that this could not be continued even for another month. If the market decided to test the government's resolve to defend the sterling exchange rate, the Bank warned that 'were that battle to be joined the potential offerings of sterling could substantially exceed our present gross exchange reserves'. Nonetheless, the Bank proposed to the Chancellor of the Exchequer, Norman Lamont, a scheme of starting with increased covert intervention up to $1 billion, to be followed by overt intervention of at least $2 billion, and eventually international borrowing, to defend the rate. The Bank of England accordingly stepped up its intervention, disguised from the market, culminating in a spend of $650 million on 24 August and a further $900 million the next day. This was not successful, and the Bank moved onto stage two of its plan, with a public intervention of about $1 billion on 26 August. On 5 September the European finance ministers and their central bank governors met in Bath, where the Bundesbank resisted strong pressure from Lamont and others to lower interest rates and relax pressure on those currencies at the bottom of their margins. On 14 September the Italian lira was devalued by 7 per cent, in a move widely interpreted as being forced by the Bundesbank as a quid pro quo for it reducing German interest rates. Lamont welcomed the move, and took the opportunity to reiterate his intention to hold the parity for sterling, rather optimistically observing: 'This demonstrates the benefits of the continuing close cooperation amongst Community countries. The UK government has repeatedly made clear that there is no question of any change in the central parity of the pound against the Deutschmark.'[18] Off-the-record remarks by Helmut Schlesinger, the president of the Bundesbank, the next day to reporters from *The Wall Street Journal* and the *Handelsblatt* suggesting he would have preferred a more general alignment undermined any semblance of returning market confidence when the *Handelsblatt* published his views on 16 September. By the end of the day, despite vigorous intervention, including about $31.4 billion by the Bundesbank itself, the battle to keep sterling in the ERM was finally abandoned.[19]

The cost of the ERM debacle was widely publicised as being anything between the £10 billion reported on 17 September 1992 in *The Guardian* newspaper to the £27 billion according to *The Independent*, triggering disgust over the apparently sanguine response of Norman Lamont, who subsequently recalled singing in the bath after the collapse and later claimed: 'Je ne regrette rien.' In studies laboriously undertaken in the years after the debacle, the Treasury came to the view that the actual cost of the 1992 'Black Wednesday' was more modest, taking into account the switch of reserves from foreign currency assets to sterling and the impact on net interest payable on reserves. The intervention to protect the pound on 16 September alone amounted to sales of $28 billion, bringing the total August/September operation to nearly $40 billion. During the rest of 1992 and 1993 the foreign currency position

[18] *International Herald Tribune*, 14 September 1992.

[19] Whitney, C. R., 'Bundesbank chief is at eye of currency storm', *New York Times*, 8 October 1992.

was gradually rebuilt, but in early 1994 the decision was taken to stop accumulating foreign exchange and to keep the reserves constant. From 1996 policy aimed to reduce the reserves gradually.

Calculating the cost of the ERM debacle was complicated by the change in the exchange rate itself, since the intervention had replaced foreign currency in the reserves with sterling. The immediate devaluation losses amounted to about £800 million, but from 1993 sterling began to appreciate, so that the cumulative loss fell from £785 million at the end of September 1992 to £122 million one year later. The cost calculated against what would have been the case if there had been no intervention amounted to £2.4 billion, or $4 billion, from 1 August to 1 October 1992, rather than the £10 billion to £27 billion quoted at the time. This assumed a counterfactual that none of the foreign exchange reserves had been sold and there was no loss attributable to the devaluation of sterling. The overestimates of 'losses' due to the crisis is based on a misunderstanding that, when foreign exchange is sold, this results in increased sterling assets in the reserves.

Table 11.2 shows the actual changes in the value of the reserves from August 1992 to April 1993. It is clear that the ERM crisis resulted in a shift of assets from foreign currency to sterling that included a substantial and prolonged short position in foreign currency. In the months that followed, sterling was slowly sold off and the short position was reduced. The cumulative losses in the dollar value of the reserves resulted mainly from the depreciation of sterling and the falling net return on reserve assets. The final row in the table shows the difference between actual reserves valued in dollars and a counterfactual of leaving the ERM on 1 August and so not engaging in any intervention and not accumulating any sterling assets. The estimates of reserve levels are on the basis of the returns on foreign exchange assets as they stood at 1 August 1992, and since there would be no sterling component the reserves would not have been affected by the sterling devaluation. On this basis, the Bank of England calculated that the best measure of the cost of the ERM debacle was $4 billion at the start of October, rising to $4.9 billion by April 1993 on account of earnings forgone and sterling's depreciation.[20]

A key element determining the cost is clearly the counterfactual. On a net basis, holding foreign exchange reserves assets was a costly business in the late 1980s, because of exchange rate movements. The depreciation of the Deutschmark, as well as net interest differentials, meant that, if the reserves had been invested in sterling assets instead of foreign currency

[20] Treasury paper, 'The cost of Black Wednesday reconsidered', 6 August 1997, www.hm-treasury.gov.uk/d/Cost_Black_Weds_reconsidered.pdf.

Table 11.2 *Cost of intervention, August 1992–April 1993*

	Aug. 1992	Sep. 1992	Oct. 1992	Nov. 1992	Dec. 1992	Jan. 1993	Feb. 1993	Mar. 1993	Apr. 1993
Actual total currency reserves	23.63	24.48	20.53	18.35	18.89	18.84	17.76	17.93	19.48
Foreign currency	23.63	16.90	–16.10	–13.00	–12.28	–10.50	–7.83	–7.85	–7.27
Sterling		7.58	36.63	31.35	31.17	29.34	25.59	25.78	26.75
Change from 3 August 1992		0.85	–3.10	–5.28	–4.74	–4.79	–5.87	–5.70	–4.15
Percentage change		3.6	–13.1	–22.3	–20.1	–25.4	–24.8	–24.1	–17.6
No intervention value of reserves	23.63	24.47	24.52	23.56	23.60	23.38	23.55	23.94	34.39
Loss compared to actual level of reserves		0.01	–3.99	–5.21	–4.71	–4.54	–5.79	–6.01	–4.91

Note: All figures are in billions of US dollars.
Source: Bank of England, 25 August 1993, document released under freedom of information (FOI) legislation; available at www.hm-treasury.gov.uk/d/cost_int_aug_93.pdf.

assets from 1987, their value would have been the equivalent of about $3 billion greater than they were at the beginning of August 1992.[21]

Conclusions

After the ending of sterling's status as an international currency, the management of the exchange rate and how sterling fitted into the international monetary system remained controversial. During the 1980s the freely floating system came into disrepute, as the dollar's instability and an unwillingness to see 'disorderly' exchange markets made it difficult for other countries to make their domestic economic policies effective. Efforts to manage the core currencies had mixed results. The EEC's reaction to the collapse of the pegged rate system was to develop structures that stabilised rates among themselves, and this had political as well as economic implications, particularly in the final push to economic and monetary union in the 1990s. For the British public and politicians, the commitment to the European project has not been enough to overcome nationalist independence, and so sterling has remained outside the system.

The debates over the ERM and the subsequent controversy over EMU show that sterling has continued to be viewed as distinct from other national currencies within Europe. This is not a reflection of sterling's role as an international currency but, rather, because the solution to the trilemma for British governments and the British public is not the same as for many other European states. Autonomy over exchange rate policy in order to ensure policy sovereignty has proved impossible to abandon in the British case. This is partly due to the scars left by the ERM crisis and public scepticism about the political dimensions of European integration, which have been reinforced by the fluctuations in the euro/pound exchange rate since 1999. The graphic examples of anti-European sentiment expressed through protecting the pound as a nationalist symbol included the 'Up yours Delors' cover of *The Sun* tabloid in 1989 and the rhetoric of the UK Independence Party in the 1990s. Although sterling's retreat as an international currency had been largely accomplished by the end of the 1970s, sterling's role as a symbolic as well as a practical expression of Britain's distinctiveness from the rest of Europe endures.

[21] Treasury paper, 10 December 1993, FOI release.

12 Summary and overview

The operation of the global economy still relies on a set of international currencies that are accepted as unit of account, means of exchange and store of value for a range of government and private purposes. The volume of foreign exchange reserves to world trade has decreased since the pegged exchange rate system was abandoned, which reduced the need for precautionary reserves. Innovation in reserve management with greater use of market resources has also reduced the need for central monetary institutions to hold owned reserves. Nevertheless, accumulations of large foreign exchange reserves by emerging economies such as China and Russia in the 2000s have to some extent reversed this trend. This has renewed questions about the costs and benefits of issuing an international currency, particularly in the context of the benign neglect of the United States towards its exchange rate and the growing global imbalance during the 2000s. The rise of the euro as a challenger to the US dollar has further increased interest in how international currencies emerge and how they can be replaced without disrupting the global economic system. The case of sterling in the post-war decades provides an opportunity to examine this process.

The case is particularly interesting because, like the dollar, the demise of sterling as a reserve and international transactions currency was widely predicted, although the process was slower than anticipated. Was this due to British government efforts to prolong sterling's role because it increased the capacity to borrow, because it enhanced Britain's international prestige or because it supported London as a centre for lucrative international finance? The argument presented in this book is that, from the 1950s, many British ministers and officials recognised that the burdens of sterling's role in terms of the cost of borrowing and confidence in the exchange rate outweighed the benefits of sterling as an international currency. Its role was prolonged by the structure of the international monetary system and collective global interest in its continuation rather than by positive action by the UK authorities. The retirement of sterling as a reserve currency was thus achieved through negotiated management among the developed and developing world rather than through market forces. The retreat as a commercial currency was achieved through exchange controls that encouraged the use of the dollar and the offshore Eurodollar market, which led to the displacement of sterling as the currency of the City. The reserve role was less easy to shed.

During the 1950s there were various plans to discourage the use of sterling as a reserve currency, by increasing exchange rate volatility or suspending the convertibility of overseas sterling reserves, but these plans were abandoned because they threatened Britain's political as well as economic relations with creditors, and because the retaliation and disruption to the international monetary system that would ensue would threaten the domestic priorities of full employment and price stability. In the early 1960s the future of sterling as a reserve currency became embroiled in the global efforts to reform the international monetary system, once it had become clear that the practice of using national currencies as international reserves in the pegged rate system was flawed. The accumulation of international reserves required persistent deficits to be run by issuing countries, which would ultimately undermine confidence in the national currencies' value. For sterling this was not such a threat, as the value of overseas sterling reserves did not increase, although the geographical distribution did shift dramatically. Rather than managing an increase in sterling reserves, British proposals aimed at replacing existing sterling reserves with some other form of asset that would not be directly issued by the United Kingdom. This would reduce the liquidity of these sterling liabilities and ultimately release the strain on the UK reserves of retiring outstanding liabilities as sterling reserves decreased, which they were expected to do. Meanwhile, British governments and central bankers were successful in using the vulnerability of sterling to systemic crisis arising from its role as an international currency to gather extraordinary credit from the United States, the IMF, the BIS and the G10.

The process of global reform was much more drawn out than expected, and in the end the solution was not radical enough to meet the task of retiring sterling. Instead, the 1968 Sterling Agreements built a system of bilateral commitments by holders of sterling to limit diversification in return for a guarantee of the dollar value of their reserves. This forestalled some diversification, although the minimum ratios were set lower than the status quo ante in many cases. In 1971 the imminence of UK accession to the EEC made it necessary to be publicly explicit that sterling's reserve role would be eliminated as soon as possible. Nonetheless, this proved elusive. Although sterling's share of international reserves fell sharply in the early 1970s, accumulations by oil producers left Britain vulnerable to diversification in 1976. This provoked a final multilateral package to replace sterling reserves with UK-issued foreign currency bonds. From the 1980s the liberalisation of exchange controls and diversification away from the dollar has increased the absolute value of sterling in international public and private reserves, but sterling's share in the total remains very small. While these are stock measures, the dominance of the dollar and the euro in foreign exchange market turnover suggests that sterling has only a marginal presence in international transactions. Current controversy over the sterling exchange rate and its position in the international monetary system are not about sterling's role as an international currency but as a domestic currency, in terms of unit of account, medium of exchange and store of value.

The shift from sterling to the US dollar, followed by the elimination of sterling as a major international currency, did result in periodic crises, international tensions and conflict over British domestic economic policy. It was not a painless transformation, therefore, partly because the alternative – the dollar – was not a safe haven during most of the 1960s. The commercial currency role was suspended unilaterally through a series of controls that were periodically intensified, with the justification that they helped to reduce outflows from the balance of payments. Although curtailing the international commercial role of sterling was not a formal policy goal, it was identified clearly as in the national interest despite attracting fierce opposition, particularly in the 1950s from the Bank of England. On the other hand, unilaterally withdrawing sterling as an international reserve currency was much more difficult, because it infringed on the sovereignty of other nations and affected the international monetary system as a whole, particularly in the 1960s, when many believed that there was inadequate international liquidity. Countries were still willing to accumulate assets in sterling during the 1960s despite its vulnerability because of the denomination of trade and debt in sterling and because many currencies remained pegged to sterling. By the early 1970s, however, sterling pegs were replaced by pegs to the dollar or currency baskets, and British trade and investment had declined relative to dollar-denominated activity (particularly oil). The sharp decline in sterling's share of reserve assets took place at a time of dramatic expansion in global reserves during the commodity boom and inflation. These factors eased the pressure on Britain from this final transformation, since the real value of existing sterling liabilities declined. Until 1976 the reduction of sterling as a reserve asset did not require the presentation in London of sterling reserves for exchange to dollars or other currencies, as the value of global sterling reserves was relatively stable. Rising international liquidity, inflation and international cooperation were the three cornerstones that eased the retreat of sterling from global to national status.

Sterling in the international system

At the end of the Second World War it was clear that the US dollar would be the dominant international currency in any global economic reconfiguration, and it became the core of the structure of the Bretton Woods system, with countries pegging their currencies to the dollar, which, alone, was valued directly in gold. Nonetheless, there continued to be a role for a secondary international currency to be used as a reserve asset, as an anchor currency and as a currency of settlement in the context of the restricted volume of dollar assets and gold anticipated in the immediate post-war period. This feature was exaggerated by the accumulation of inconvertible sterling assets among countries of the British Empire and Commonwealth as part of their war effort. Once it was clear that the bulk of these wartime balances would neither be cancelled nor liquidated, they would have to form part of these countries' foreign exchange reserves, and so be run down over time through current transactions. There was also space for a secondary commercial currency on account of the continued leadership of financial institutions in the City of London and the tight exchange controls imposed by most countries during the post-war reconstruction. In 1945 New York was not in a position to replace London as the world's premier international financial centre, despite the dominance of the American economy. Controls on foreign bank entry and other domestic regulations meant that New York was unable to compete with the scale and scope of London's institutional sophistication. A global role for sterling was thus part of the Bretton Woods system as it was conceived and formalised from 1944 onwards.

Once the Bretton Woods global solution was shown to have failed in 1947, though, with the indefinite postponement of current account convertibility, the world retreated into groups of monetary areas defined by exchange controls on both the current account and the capital account: the sterling area, the dollar area, the European Payments Union. In the early 1950s this new solution to international payments prolonged the important role of sterling for a wide range of emerging and less developed countries, and undoubtedly fostered the recovery of global trade. Already, however, industrialised countries in Europe clearly preferred to hold US dollars or gold as reserve assets, and trade between developed countries became increasingly settled in local currency or dollars rather than sterling.

By 1952 it was clear that the more developed states in the sterling area, led by Australia, would not be willing to continue to use sterling as their main international currency in the longer term, because of doubts over its value relative to the dollar and because these states were diversifying their trade and debt away from the United Kingdom. As a result, from early 1952 the independent members of the sterling area pressed for greater convertibility and diversified their foreign exchange reserves. By 1959, when current account convertibility for residents outside the sterling area arrived, the reserve role of sterling relied increasingly on less developed countries, oil producers and newly industrialising economies such as Hong Kong and Malaya. This evolution of sterling's global role was achieved without a major crisis for the United Kingdom because the absolute value of sterling held overseas was not reduced, so that, when diversification occurred, it did not pose a large net drain on the central reserves. Meanwhile, the real value of these liabilities and their value in relation to British GDP decreased markedly. By 1960, therefore, sterling's global role had been transformed, but it remained important enough for the stability of the pegged exchange rate system for Britain to gather multilateral support for the next stage of the retreat.

The 1960s have been identified as the key decade for the management of sterling's retreat as an international currency. In the end, this was a prolonged and complex process that was closely integrated into the more general management of international economic relations. As the pegged exchange rate system came under threat, the burden of sustaining sterling as an international currency became shared among the G10. The risk of a collapse of the sterling exchange rate if the reserve role ended abruptly posed dangers not only for Britain but for the system as a whole. This led to a sharing of the risks for sterling until more fundamental reforms could be agreed, alongside other initiatives, such as the Gold Pool to shore up confidence in the US dollar. Britain's very weakness thus proved an important source of power in negotiations with the United States, the IMF, the EEC and the G10. The skilful use of sterling's weakness and America's strategic troubles in south-east Asia to attract repeated short-term credit from President Johnson and, at the same time, to resist wider international pressure to restrain domestic credit and incomes is particularly illustrative of the self-awareness of this power and its successful exercise. British governments were also strategic in choosing their institutional partners and were able to evade the political as well as the economic pressures of IMF conditionality by operating through the less formal network of central bankers at Basle, who were unwilling to interfere in the national economic policies of others.

In return for sharing Britain's risk, eventually the G10 required a formalisation of the reserve role of sterling, achieved through the Sterling Agreements of 1968. These stabilised the situation by setting a floor for diversification, thereby reducing the risk of a rapid shift that could exhaust the Bank of England's reserves and lead to further calls for multilateral support. The US dollar exchange rate guarantee for sterling reserves in turn provided the holders with some initial security about their value, although this proved less valuable as the dollar weakened. Rather than undermining the impact of the Sterling Agreements, this trend made the dollar a less appealing alternative to sterling. We have seen that the Sterling Agreements were not uncontested and became a source of friction between the United Kingdom and countries with large sterling reserves. Nevertheless, they provided a framework within which to manage the gradual reduction of the sterling share of global reserves. As international liquidity expanded in the early 1970s, the commitments on a percentage basis failed to prevent new accumulations of sterling assets while total reserves were increasing, so a new element was included to cap the nominal value of sterling reserves.

After the devaluation of sterling in 1967 and the change in the US attitude with the arrival of President Nixon in 1969, patience began to wear thin in Washington and Europe, so the 1970s proved a much more difficult environment for Britain to operate in to gather multilateral support. The efforts of the IMF, the United States and the United Kingdom's European partners during the 1950s and 1960s to encourage British governments to pursue fundamental reform to restore competitiveness had failed, partly because the importance of sterling to the continuation of the pegged exchange rate regime meant that Britain was able to attract substantial rolling short-term credits. Domestically as well as externally, British governments were able to blame some of the weaknesses in Britain's economic performance on sterling's international role and the need to sustain the exchange rate. The advent of the floating exchange rate regime in 1972 did not relieve the pressures on British industrial competitiveness, however, which were supposed by some to have been caused by an overvalued pegged rate, and the problems of British industry were revealed to be much more fundamental. During the surge in international liquidity driven by the first oil crisis and inflation, sterling's share of global reserves fell sharply, but the 1976 crisis showed that Britain was still vulnerable to diversification. By the time of the final multilateral support scheme to manage the retreat of sterling as a reserve currency in 1976/7, the Americans were no longer content to leave the operation to the soft oversight of the BIS and demanded a political as well as an economic commitment enforced through the IMF. By linking the third Group Arrangement to the terms of the IMF stand-by arrangement and giving the managing director of the IMF oversight of Britain's compliance, the door to easy multilateral credit was finally closed. By 1977 sterling was no longer an important reserve currency even for poor countries, and the share of trade denominated and settled in sterling was marginal.

In the 1980s the exchange rate continued to be important to economic policy-making in the United Kingdom despite efforts to target the money supply, but, after a brief moment as a petrocurrency, sterling's global role was no longer a vital feature of international policy. The ERM experiment and its aftermath in the 1990s focused public attention once again on the trade-off between domestic policy sovereignty and exchange rate stability in the context of open capital markets, and the decision that was taken was to remain out of the formal process of monetary integration in the European Community. The initial appreciation against the euro led to some misgivings, but this was soon reversed. After 2001 the appreciation of sterling against the dollar, attributable to the Americans returning to benign neglect as part of their growth-oriented 'double deficit' strategy, was viewed with equanimity.

Sterling and Britain's place in the world

The evolution of sterling as an international currency was central to much of the repositioning of Britain in the global economy in the three deacdes after 1945. Although this book has argued that the commitment to restoring or sustaining sterling's global role was equivocal at best in the 1950s and had expired by the 1960s, the perpetuation of sterling's status did create a sense of 'exceptionalism' that had important implications for Britain's reorientation in the global system in this period. In the 1950s the sterling area was closely linked to the imperial and Commonwealth relations that Britain had developed in the early post-war period, although the hopes of some nostalgic commentators that the Commonwealth would become an ever tighter economic unit were not realised. Until 1952 the use of sterling as a reserve asset and common exchange controls defined an important element of Commonwealth and imperial cohesion, evidenced in annual finance ministers' meetings that aimed to develop common external targets. From this point, however, the enthusiasm for common sacrifice waned. As most colonies approached independence from the middle of the decade, the sterling held in their reserves became an element in Britain's management of the process of decolonisation, but never a primary driver. The sterling area system provided a context within which constitutional independence did not imply monetary independence as states made the transition from empire to Commonwealth. Even after most of the more established members of the sterling area had diversified their reserves, the poorer members continued to retain their links to sterling through the 1960s, partly out of inertia but also because of the high returns on sterling assets and the importance of the United Kingdom in their international trade and debt.

As an exception to the process of decolonisation, the rapid growth of Hong Kong led to reserve accumulations there that offset reductions in sterling held elsewhere. By the early 1970s sterling's reserve role came to rely on oil producers such as Nigeria and Saudi Arabia rather than on the traditional Commonwealth stalwarts.

Meanwhile, in the early 1960s British governments began their reorientation towards the EEC while still trying to sustain their bilateral relations with the United States, and sterling's exceptionalism had a role to play in this process as well. During the 1950s and 1960s British governments believed that the commonality of the United States and the United Kingdom as issuers of the two main reserve currencies could be developed to solidify the much-vaunted 'special relationship', particularly in negotiations with Europe over the reform of the international monetary system. In the end, though, they overestimated the strength of this feeling in Washington, as became evident with the rejection of the collective approach in 1952 and the unwillingness of the Americans to operate on a bilateral basis with the United Kingdom in G10 discussions from the mid-1960s. While transatlantic relations cooled in the 1960s and sterling became a source of conflict, Britain was still able to use American vulnerability to British strategic and sterling policy to exact repeated rounds of short-term credit.

The power of sterling's exceptionalism was also clearly apparent (and longer-lasting) in the case of Britain's relations with Europe. Although there were many obstacles to British accession to the EEC in the 1960s, both political and economic, fitting a global currency into the emerging plans for European monetary cooperation proved an important factor. By the time of the final discussions, the British government was forced to announce publicly its intention to rid sterling of its reserve status and to refashion it as a national currency similar to that of other European currencies. With some delay, sterling's reserve role was finally eliminated, though not without further multilateral support, but the British public have not been able to view their national currency in the same way as their European neighbours, and so sterling remains outside the core European monetary system. National policy sovereignty has proved too high a price to pay for further economic integration with Europe, and this hesitancy was only reinforced by the unhappy end of the experiment with ERM membership in 1992.

Sterling policy also influenced relations with other international organisations. Successive British governments were strategic in using the threat that a sterling collapse would pose to the global system to increase their influence, moving between different sets of actors to get multilateral support to reduce the perceived burdens of sterling's reserve role. There were some false starts and some fumbling in Anglo-American and European relations before a more effective strategy was adopted through the BIS. The Basle initiatives, aimed directly at reducing sterling's reserve currency role, were delivered by the Bank of England rather than the Treasury or the government, albeit with government approval and Treasury advice. The apolitical nature of this avenue suited Britain's creditors as much as British policy-makers themselves, since going to their respective parliaments for resources to repeatedly bail out the British had little appeal and less chance of success. The public were thus not as convinced of the importance of collective interest as were governments and central bankers. The process was helped by the fact that the BIS itself was keen to expand its role at this time, seeking out opportunities to take the initiative in offering its planning and technical support.

The IMF was much less welcoming, partly because of the greater transparency of its operations, as its resources were formally contributed by a much wider range of countries to which it was responsible. Nonetheless, in the 1950s and 1960s the United Kingdom was able to negotiate more lenient terms in the IMF than other states, by referring to its exceptional position as an issuer of a global currency, although the increasingly formal conditionality and publicity of the process meant that the IMF became a lender of *very* last resort for British governments. From the late 1960s the G10 increasingly linked their support through Basle with IMF stand-by arrangements. This served to underpin Britain's ability to repay short-term credits when they came due and increased the pressure on British governments to restrain inflation and credit expansion, in order to restore competitiveness in ways that would relax the likelihood of repeated calls for short-term credit. This process came to a head in the 1976/7 Group Arrangement, which most closely articulated the operation of the BIS and the IMF.

The development of British sterling policy

A key question, to which the answer is somewhat elusive, is one of timing. When did British governments begin to try to negotiate sterling's retreat to national status? There are clearly elements of this approach from the early 1950s, in plans within the Treasury to transform the sterling reserves held by overseas countries by replacing them either with longer-term securities or with assets denominated in another currency. The persistent concern over the 'sterling balances problem' shows that the Treasury clearly understood that the risks of operating a reserve currency – i.e. that short-term international liabilities would tend to exceed immediate liquid assets – were high for the United Kingdom, which had an economy that was more vulnerable to international trade and payments than the United States' and was suffering from waning international competitiveness. The emphasis on the 'overhang' of liabilities over assets persisted from the 1940s through to the 1970s, despite the early retirement of extraordinary wartime accumulations. The attitude within the Treasury shows that the use of sterling assets in other countries' reserves was viewed as a problem that required a solution rather than as a sign of Britain's global economic status, in spite of the public rhetoric to the contrary. The Treasury therefore acted in ways to reduce sterling's reserve role as early as the 1950s, although this was not formally acknowledged as a policy goal until the 1960s.

There undoubtedly was a perception that sterling's international status conferred prestige onto Britain, but this view was contradicted by persistent efforts to reduce overseas holdings of sterling. This inconsistency was rationalised by conceiving of the 'sterling balances' as an extraordinary outcome of Britain's indebtedness after the Second World War, long after these obligations had been exhausted in the early 1950s. By the mid-1950s sterling's international role was no longer a prime element in Britain's leadership of the Commonwealth but, instead, became a source of friction among its members, undermining British international prestige. We have seen, on the other hand, that sterling's status did provide some power (if not prestige) for British governments in their international negotiations with Europe, the United States and multilateral organisations such as the BIS and the IMF.

There is also evidence of hostility to the international commercial role of sterling early in the 1950s. The Treasury's actions contradict the public statements made repeatedly during this decade that emphasised the benefits of maintaining the international value and usefulness of the pound in order to promote the City of London (and vice versa). The policy of retaining – and, indeed, intensifying – controls on the commercial use of sterling is evidence that its international status was not a priority for the Treasury even in the early post-war decades. The failed plans to remove exchange controls on commercial current account transactions in the 1950s provide further evidence of where the government's priorities lay. The Robot plan would have eliminated sterling's reserve role by blocking the convertibility of sterling reserves while endeavouring to enhance its usefulness as a commercial currency through increased convertibility on the current account. The rejection of Operation Robot in early 1952 clearly set domestic price and employment stability above the promotion of sterling as a convertible international currency. The collective approach to convertibility, developed later in 1952, recognised that Britain could not act unilaterally in international monetary relations, but it also demonstrated a remarkable misjudgement of the power of the United Kingdom's leadership. Its abrupt rejection by the United States and western Europe clearly established that Britain would have to work within existing (and emerging) global structures and institutions rather than hope to lead in a new direction. The management of the end of sterling's role thus shifted to the European Community, the G10, the sterling area and the BIS from the early 1960s, but the hostility to relaxing exchange controls continued. Meanwhile, financial innovation to respond to the need for an international currency in London meant that the interests of the City were increasingly independent of sterling's international status. The rise of the Eurodollar market and the invasion of American and other international banks rejuvenated the City from the early 1960s onwards.

The indications that there were voices in the Treasury and the Bank of England explicitly calling for a reduction in sterling's international reserve status are unequivocal by the early 1960s, but the direct evidence of their influence is not as certain. Again, however, the actual management of the currency suggests a fairly persistent policy aimed at reducing this role. As the decade progressed, the importance of the Eurodollar market for the prospects of the City of London as an international financial centre and the changing nature of the City itself meant that even the Bank of England stopped lobbying so strongly for sterling's global status to be enhanced, although it did continue to press for the elimination of the controls on third-party commercial transactions. By 1963 the Bank of England began actively to encourage the offshore US dollar market, through the Eurobond and other innovations, and resisted EEC pressure to eliminate it. Bureaucratic politics certainly had a role to play in the management of sterling, as the relations between the Bank of England and the Treasury were affected by the different constituencies they served. The Bank responded to pressures from the City, and the Treasury was preoccupied with the near-term balance of payments outlook and employment.

Once the BIS had become the key route for reform, the retirement of sterling as a reserve currency in the 1960s and early 1970s required considerable cooperation, or at least commonality of purpose, between the Bank and the Treasury. The IMF and bilateral relations in which ministers and Treasury officials might hope to lead were gradually ruled out, because of the complexities of political relations and the need to get approval from parliaments that were not sympathetic to costly collective initiatives. The real clashes between the Bank and the Treasury arose from the controls on the commercial use of sterling, which undermined the range of activities in the City. In the end, Treasury priorities prevailed on the international commercial role, although the Bank found a way to serve its constituency by supporting the Eurodollar market and its attendant innovations, albeit at the cost of foreign domination of the market.

In terms of electoral politics, the demarcation between successive Conservative and Labour governments is not clear for the years from 1945 to 1964. Both parties sought to increase the current account surplus and foreign exchange reserves while pursuing expansionary policies to minimise unemployment. They also sought to retreat from the onus of issuing an international currency, although this was not consistently stated in policy terms. The rhetoric of the Conservative Party tended to engage more in nostalgia for the imperial past than was the case with the Labour Party, but controls on the external use of sterling as a commercial currency, the continuation of capital account exchange restrictions and the repeated plans to replace overseas sterling reserves with some other kind of asset all testify to the consistency of the underlying goal of relieving sterling of its international status.

From the mid-1960s prime ministers and their Chancellors had a more robust impact on the complexion of sterling policy as it was increasingly tied to high politics and longer-term strategic interests, particularly through Britain's relations with Europe and with the United States as relations with the Commonwealth ebbed. Harold Wilson's Labour governments, between 1964 and 1970 and again between 1974 and 1976, encouraged much more trade union influence in the process of policymaking. The ensuing stalemates over reducing inflationary pressure and implementing an incomes policy estranged him from his peers in the United States and the European Community. James Callaghan's personal influence over the process of devaluation and his lack of commitment to contractionary measures further frustrated international economic relations. When Edward Heath's Conservative administration (1970 to 1974) was challenged by external events it took bold action, including the decision to float the pound in 1972 and entering the Common Market in 1973. Of much greater significance for the global system as a whole at this time was the change from the relatively cooperative Kennedy and Johnson administrations to Nixon's uncompromising attitude, encouraged by his Treasury secretary, John Connally, from 1971, which pushed forward the reform of the international monetary system. The weak parliamentary position of the Labour governments from 1974 to 1979 coincided with a series of dramatic shocks to the international system, to which the government was politically ill-equipped to react. The result was the accumulation of debt and a loss of confidence in the country's economic future, which led to the 1976 sterling crisis. The Callaghan government was driven reluctantly to resort to the IMF and to Basle once again to shore up the reserves and restore global confidence, including a final initiative to eliminate the reserve role of sterling.

The abrupt change of direction under Margaret Thatcher's Conservative government (1979 to 1990) is commonly referred to as a 'revolution', which cast aside trade union influence, along with the commitment to welfare spending, and ushered in an era of monetarism. By this time, however, sterling's international role was no longer a preoccupation; its reserve role had ended and its commercial resurgence as a petrocurrency had been short-lived. The impact of movements in the exchange rate on the domestic economy continued to be influential, particularly given Thatcher's emphasis on low interest rates. She clung to the idea that sterling was distinct from other European currencies because of its international status as a petrocurrency in order to delay engagement with the ERM, but the debates over sterling policy were really focused on the exchange rate and external pressures on the balance of payments rather than sterling's global status. The tension as to whether to target the money supply or the exchange rate culminated in the departure of Nigel Lawson as Chancellor of the Exchequer, but the need for exchange rate stability and low interest rates led eventually to the Conservative Party's acceptance of the discipline of the exchange rate mechanism under John Major and Norman Lamont. Ultimately, however, the market (and Britain's European Community partners) lost confidence in the credibility of this commitment at the existing parity, and sterling floated again from 1992.

Conclusions

What does the experience of sterling's retreat suggest about the movement between key international currencies? Clearly, as Eichengreen has argued, there is space in an international system for more than one international currency even if one is dominant.[1] The experience of the pound and the dollar suggest that rivals can cause instability through shifting portfolios, but also that more than one international currency can enhance liquidity and diversify risk. There has been a persistent difference between the reserve portfolios of developing and developed economies, which in the early post-war years was partly influenced by traditional commercial relationships and oil exploitation. Even through the 1990s and 2000s the share of sterling in the reserves of less developed countries was two to four times the level of industrial countries, although this amounted to only about 4 to 5 per cent of the total. In the 1990s

[1] Eichengreen, *Global Imbalances and the Lessons of Bretton Woods.*

the distinct distribution of reserve assets was mainly due to the use of the ECU and the Deutschmark among EU countries in the context of the ERM. Since 2000 the euro has increased its share of global reserves in developing and richer economies alike. This suggests a second, and perhaps equally obvious, lesson from the case of sterling: that reserve portfolio choices are affected by the structure of the international monetary system. The pegged rate system founded on an ailing US dollar was critical to the explanation of why sterling persisted so long as an international currency.

The process of European monetary integration has had a profound impact on the demand for global currencies, but the euro has not yet come to rival the dominance of the dollar. In the 2000s the major effect has been the spread of euro holdings outside Europe, but this trend has been dwarfed by the accumulation of huge pools of dollar-denominated reserves in east Asia, particularly by China and Japan, which has increased the dominance of the US dollar as a global reserve asset. After diversifying into the Deutschmark and the yen in the early 1990s, by the end of the decade global reserves were once again dominated by the dollar, partly because of the prolonged downturn in the Japanese economy. By 2001 dollar assets comprised 71 per cent of identified global reserves (although the share of unallocated reserves had increased, particularly for developing countries). The subsequent depreciation of the dollar led to a decline in its share to 64 per cent in 2007, despite vigorous nominal accumulations in China and the Middle East. The euro's presence strengthened, reflecting both appreciation and accumulations, to 26 per cent at the end of 2007, while sterling moved into a distant third place behind these two currencies, with 4.7 per cent of global reserves, compared with 2.9 per cent for the yen.

In the 2000s, therefore, the US dollar remained the dominant international currency even though it had lost value relative to other currencies. The main alternative is the euro, but its prospects are weakened by the relatively shallow markets in euro assets and the fact that it is a currency without a government.[2] Some have predicted that, if the Eurozone expands to include the United Kingdom and others (thus making it a larger economy than the United States) and if the Americans do not stabilise the value of the dollar, the euro may (eventually) succeed the dollar as the world's main reserve asset.[3] Through most of the 2000s the global economic system has been robust to substantial shifts among reserve

[2] Cohen, B. J., 'Enlargement and the international role of the euro', *Review of International Political Economy*, 14(5), 2007, pp. 746–73. See also European Central Bank (ECB), *Review of the International Role of the Euro* (Frankfurt: ECB, 2007).

[3] Chinn and Frankel, *Will the Euro Eventually Surpass the Dollar?*

assets and to the dramatic decline in the value of the core international currency. The next test will be the response to the 2007–9 global financial crisis, which at first led to a flight to the yen and the US dollar that reversed much of the dollar's depreciation over the previous few years, but in the longer term may cause more major adjustment if the growth economies of east Asia run down their substantial dollar reserves.

A third insight is that, in the case of sterling, there was no single 'tipping point' at which countries replaced all their sterling reserves with other assets. Diversification in south Asia was offset first by accumulations in Australasia and colonial primary product producers in the late 1940s and early 1950s. Diversification in Australia and South Africa in the 1950s was offset by accumulations in east Asia and the Middle East, where sterling remained the key reserve asset through the 1960s, buttressed by the formalised Sterling Agreements. When the tipping point finally came, in the early 1970s, the real value of sterling reserves had been eroded by inflation, although the liquidation of reserves did cause a major external crisis in 1976 that required multilateral support. This experience suggests that the tipping point can be delayed and its impact ameliorated through international cooperation, and that in the meantime the shift in reserve assets may arise from a series of smaller adjustments.

Finally, the case of sterling shows that the key feature in the management of its retreat was the consensus that sterling's prospects were crucial to the stability of the global system as a whole. Here, the context of the Cold War in the 1960s was important, in that it prioritised continued prosperity and economic stability among capitalist countries. This led to cooperative (if at times reluctant) support in the exchange markets, and schemes that allowed the British deliberately to discourage accumulations and encourage gradual diversification without the risk of massive sterling sales exhausting the Bank of England's reserves or causing a collapse in the exchange rate. By the time that coordinated intervention had been negotiated to affect the dollar exchange rate in the 1980s, with the Plaza and Louvre Agreements, the resources of central banks were so small relative to the size of the market that the impact was probably negligible. Instead, the credibility of publicly announced intentions was more important, as the market anticipated policies aimed at moving the exchange rate. Even this tactic proved of weakening value by the time of the Louvre Agreement. The prospects for such a broad and powerful shared commitment in the current crisis, how influential it can be given the international financial environment, and the impact of the global political system (particularly with regard to China and Russia) have all yet to be determined.

To what extent can the process of the retreat from international status for sterling be deemed a success or a failure? In retrospect, the efforts in the 1960s to devise a new basis for a pegged exchange rate system were clearly a failure, but the process itself allowed the United Kingdom to gather considerable multilateral support to mitigate the risks associated with issuing a reserve currency. The pegged exchange rate system certainly inhibited national economic policy-making but the multilateral short-term credit attracted by sterling's international status lessened this constraint. The alternative, unilateral, course would have been to eliminate the reserve role by repudiating British government securities held overseas or opting out of the global pegged rate system to discourage the accumulation of sterling reserves. The first course was seriously considered only in the 1940s, and it was dismissed on political and moral grounds because most overseas sterling securities were held by poor dependencies and comprised a large element of war debt. In economic terms, repudiating government debt obviously damages the potential to borrow in the future. The choice to remain with a pegged exchange rate despite the constraint this imposed on domestic policy sovereignty was made because of the threat to domestic price stability and employment that could ensue from exchange rate instability. It was not sterling's international role that was the constraint but, rather, the inability of British governments to accept the costs of greater flexibility with thin reserves to moderate fluctuations. When sterling did finally float in 1972 the effects were not sufficient to relieve the problems of British industrial competitiveness. As in the 1950s and 1960s, the problems of competitiveness could not be solved by merely changing the relative prices of traded goods.

As it turned out, the British economy was able to sustain itself through the pegged exchange rate system with recourse to short-term credit while declines in sterling reserves in some areas were offset by accumulations elsewhere. This book has argued that this was not due to lucky accident but to the importance that the United Kingdom's partners accorded to the role that sterling played in the stability of the ailing pegged exchange rate system. Their commitment to the system's continuation and fears about the impact of its failure fostered multilateral support for the management of the retreat of sterling. From the 1950s there is evidence in the actions of policy-makers, and by the 1960s explicit protestations, that eliminating the reserve role of sterling was desirable, but it was not possible to do this unilaterally in the context of Britain's global economic and political situation. Britain was too weak economically to 'go it alone' if its actions provoked retaliation or if exchange rate volatility fed back to the domestic economy. This was determined in the early 1950s and set the course for the multilateral approach to reforming sterling's role.

As a result, it was not until the late 1970s, during the general floating regime, that sterling's reserve role was at the direct core of a crisis, when countries ran down their official reserves in anticipation of further depreciation. By this time sterling was no longer an important global reserve asset, and the ratio of overseas-held sterling to the foreign exchange reserves was much smaller than it had been during the Bretton Woods era. Meanwhile, the international commercial and financial role of sterling had retreated relatively painlessly through the process of international financial innovation. Nonetheless, the sterling crisis of 1976 provoked the kind of humiliating national exposure to external pressure that British governments had tried to avoid since 1945, so it can be said that British sterling policy did fail to avoid crisis. All the same, the success in delaying this outcome meant that the real value of these liabilities and the impact on the British reserves and on the British economy were much less than at any other time in the post-war period. Moreover, the precedent of multilateral cooperation over sterling meant that the global community came together one last time to mitigate the impact on Britain. To this extent, it would be difficult to claim that the prolonged retirement of sterling as an international currency was a policy failure. By engaging in the international economy and gathering multilateral support, the United Kingdom was able to share in the prosperity generated by the growth of trade and the acceleration of financial innovation during the 'long boom' of 1950 to 1973.

Bibliography

Aldcroft, D. H., and M. J. Oliver, *Exchange Rate Regimes in the Twentieth Century* (Cheltenham: Edward Elgar, 1998).

Alford, B., *Britain in the World Economy since 1880* (London: Longman, 1996).

Asbeek Brusse, W., *Tariffs, Trade and European Integration, 1947–1957* (London: Macmillan, 1997).

Atkinson, F. J., S. J. Brooks and S. Hall, 'The economic effects of North Sea oil', *National Institute Economic Review*, 104, 1983, pp. 38–44.

Bakker, A. F. P., *The Liberalization of Capital Movements in Europe: The Monetary Committee and Financial Integration 1958–1994* (Dordrecht: Kluwer Academic, 1996).

Bale, T., 'Dynamics of a non-decision: the failure to devalue the pound 1964–67', *Twentieth Century British History*, 10(2), 1999, pp. 192–217.

Bange, O., *The EEC Crisis of 1963: Kennedy, Macmillan, de Gaulle and Adenauer in Conflict* (New York: St Martin's Press, 2000).

Bangura, Y., *Britain and Commonwealth Africa: The Politics of Economic Relations 1951–75* (Manchester: Manchester University Press, 1983).

Bean, C. R., 'Sterling misalignment and British trade performance', in R. C. Marston (ed.), *Misalignment of Exchange Rates: Effects on Trade and Industry* (Chicago: University of Chicao Press, 1988), pp. 39–76.

Becker, W. H., 'The US and the search for a new monetary system', in H. Haftendorn, G. H. Soutou, S. F. Szabo and S. F. Wells (eds.), *The Strategic Triangle: France, Germany, and the United States in the Shaping of the New Europe* (Baltimore: Johns Hopkins University Press, 2006), pp. 189–206.

Bell, P. W., *The Sterling Area in the Modern World: Internal Mechanism and Cohesion 1946–1952* (Oxford: Oxford University Press, 1956).

Bernholz, P., 'The Bundesbank and the process of European monetary integration', in Deutsche Bundesbank (ed.), *Fifty Years of the Deutsche Mark: Central Bank and the Currency in Germany since 1948* (Cambridge: Cambridge University Press, 1999), pp. 731–89.

BIS, *Central Bank Survey of Foreign Exchange and Derivatives Market Activity 1995* (Basle: BIS, 1996).

Bond, M. E., and A. Knoble, 'Some implications of North Sea oil for the UK economy', *IMF Staff Papers*, 29(3), 1982, pp. 363–97.

Bordo, M. D., B. Eichengreen and D. Irwin, *Is Globalization Today Really Different than Globalization a Hundred Years Ago?*, Working Paper no. 7159 (Cambridge, MA: NBER, 1999).

Bordo, M. D., D. Simard and E. White, *France and the Bretton Woods International Monetary System: 1960–1968*, Working Paper no. 4642 (Cambridge, MA: NBER, 1994).

Bostock, F., and G. Jones, 'Foreign multinationals in British manufacturing 1850–1962', *Business History*, 36(1), 1994, pp. 89–126.

Boughton, J., 'Northwest of Suez: the 1956 crisis and the IMF', *IMF Staff Papers*, 48(3), 2001, pp. 425–46.

Boyle, K., 'The price of peace: Vietnam, the pound, and the crisis of the American empire', *Diplomatic History*, 27(1), 2003, pp. 37–72.

Brittan, S., *Steering the Economy: The Role of the Treasury* (London: Penguin Books, 1971).

Broadberry, S. N., and N. F. R. Crafts, 'British economic policy and industrial performance in the early post-war period', *Business History*, 38(4), 1996, pp. 65–91.

Browning, P., *The Treasury and Economic Policy 1964–1985* (London: Longman, 1986).

Budd, A., *Black Wednesday: A Re-examination of Britain's Experience in the Exchange Rate Mechanism* (London: IEA, 2005).

Burk, K., 'Witness seminar on the origins and early development of the Eurobond market', *Contemporary European History*, 1(1), 1992, pp. 65–87.

'Introduction', in K. Burk (ed.), *The British Isles since 1945* (Oxford: Oxford University Press, 2003), pp. 1–17.

Burk, K., and A. K. Cairncross, *Goodbye, Great Britain: The 1976 IMF Crisis* (New Haven, CT: Yale University Press, 1992).

Burn, G., 'The state, the City and the Euromarkets', *Review of International Political Economy*, 6(2), 1999, pp. 225–61.

The Re-emergence of Global Finance (Basingstoke: Palgrave, 2006).

Burnham, P., *Remaking the Postwar World Economy: Robot and British Policy in the 1950s* (Basingstoke: Palgrave, 2003).

Bussière, E., 'France, European monetary cooperation, and the international monetary system crisis, 1968–1973', in H. Haftendorn, G. H. Soutou, S. F. Szabo and S. F. Wells (eds.), *The Strategic Triangle: France, Germany, and the United States in the Shaping of the New Europe* (Baltimore: Johns Hopkins University Press, 2006), pp. 171–87.

Cain, P., and A. J. Hopkins, *British Imperialism: Crisis and Reconstruction 1914–1990* (London: Longman, 1993).

Cairncross, A. K., *Years of Recovery: British Economic Policy 1945–51* (London: Methuen, 1985).

The British Economy since 1945: Economic Policy and Performance, 1945–1995, 2nd edn (Oxford: Blackwell, 1995).

'From the Treasury diaries of Sir Alec Cairncross; four Anglo-French conflicts 1967–8', *Contemporary European History*, 6(1), 1997, pp. 117–31.

The Wilson Years: A Treasury Diary 1964–1969 (London: Historians' Press, 1997).

Cairncross, A. K., and B. Eichengreen, *Sterling in Decline: The Devaluations of 1931, 1949 and 1967* (Oxford: Blackwell, 1983).
Callaghan, J., *Time and Chance* (London: Collins, 1987).
Campbell, A., 'Anglo-French relations a decade ago: a new assessment', *International Affairs*, 58(3), 1982, pp. 429–46.
Camps, M., *Britain and the European Community 1955–63* (Princeton, NJ: Princeton University Press, 1964).
European Unification in the Sixties (Oxford: Oxford University Press, 1967).
Chinn, M., and J. Frankel, *Will the Euro Eventually Surpass the Dollar as Leading International Reserve Currency?*, Working Paper no. 11510 (Cambridge, MA: NBER, 2005).
'Why the euro will rival the dollar', *International Finance*, 11(1), 2008, pp. 49–73.
Choi, S. R., D. K. Park and A. E. Tschoegl, 'Banks and the world's major banking centers, 1990', *Weltwirtschaftliches Archiv*, 132(4), 1996, pp. 774–93.
'Banks and the world's major banking centers 2000', *Review of World Economics,* 139(3), 2003, pp. 550–68.
Clarida, R. H., *G3 Exchange Rate Relationships: A Recap of the Record and a Review of Proposals for Change*, Working Paper no. 7434 (Cambridge, MA: NBER, 1999).
Clark, P. B., and J. J. Polak, 'International liquidity and the role of the SDR in the international monetary system', *IMF Staff Papers*, 51(1), 2004, pp. 49–71.
Clark, R. J., 'The evolution of monetary and financial institutions', in D. R. Croome and H. G. Johnson (eds.), *Money in Britain, 1959–1969* (Oxford: Oxford University Press, 1970), pp. 131–49.
Clarke, W. M., *The City in the World Economy* (London: Pelican Books, 1965).
Cohen, B. J., *The Future of Sterling as an International Currency* (London: Macmillan, 1971).
'Enlargement and the international role of the euro', *Review of International Political Economy*, 14(5), 2007, pp. 746–73.
Cohen, S. D., *International Monetary Reform 1964–69: The Political Dimension* (New York: Praeger, 1970).
Coleman, J., *A Special Relationship? Harold Wilson, Lyndon B. Johnson and Anglo-American Relations 'at the Summit', 1964–1968* (Manchester: Manchester University Press, 2004).
Conan, A. R., *The Rationale of the Sterling Area: Texts and Commentary* (London: Macmillan, 1961).
Conservative and Unionist Party, *This Is the Road: The Conservatives and Unionist Party's Policy* (London: Conservative and Unionist Central Office, 1950).
United for Peace and Progress: The Conservative and Unionist Party's Policy (London: Conservative and Unionist Central Office, 1955).
Corden, W. M., 'The exchange rate, monetary policy and North Sea oil: the economic theory of the squeeze on tradeables', *Oxford Economic Papers*, 33 (Supp.), 1981, pp. 23–46.

Couve de Murville, M., *Une Politique Etrangère, 1958–1969* (Paris: Librairie Plon, 1971).

Daddow, O. J. (ed.), *Harold Wilson and European Integration: Britain's Second Application to Join the EEC* (London: Routledge, 2003).

Day, A. C. L., *The Future of Sterling* (Oxford: Clarendon Press, 1954).

De Paiva Abreu, M., 'Brazil as a creditor: sterling balances 1940–52', *Economic History Review*, 43(3), 1990, pp. 450–69.

De Vries, M. G., *The International Monetary Fund, 1966–1971: The System under Stress*, vol. I, *Narrative* (Washington, DC: IMF, 1976).

Dobson, A. P., *The Politics of the Anglo-American Economic Special Relationship, 1940–1987* (Brighton: Wheatsheaf, 1988).

Dooley, M. P., D. Folkerts-Landau and P. Garber, 'The revised Bretton Woods system', *International Journal of Finance and Economics*, 9(4), 2004, pp. 307–13.

Dow, J. C. R., *The Management of the British Economy, 1945–60* (Cambridge: Cambridge University Press, 1964).

Drummond, I. M., *The Floating Pound and the Sterling Area, 1931–1939* (Cambridge: Cambridge University Press, 1981).

Dumbrell, J., *A Special Relationship: Anglo-American Relations in the Cold War and After* (London: Macmillan, 2001).

Dumbrell, J., and S. Ellis, 'British involvement in Vietnam peace initiatives 1966–67: marigolds, sunflowers, and "Kosygin Week"', *Diplomatic History*, 27(1), 2003, pp. 113–49.

ECA, *The Sterling Area: An American Analysis* (Washington, DC: ECA, 1952).

ECB, *Review of the International Role of the Euro* (Frankfurt: ECB, 2007).

Economists Advisory Group, *An Economic Study of the City of London* (London: Allen & Unwin, 1971).

Eichengreen, B., *Reconstructing Europe's Trade and Payments: The European Payments Union* (Manchester: Manchester University Press, 1993).

From Benign Neglect to Malignant Preoccupation: US Balance of Payments Policy in the 1960s, Working Paper no. 7630 (Cambridge, MA: NBER, 2000).

Sterling's Past, Dollar's Future: Historical Perspectives on Reserve Currency Competition, Working Paper no. 11336 (Cambridge, MA: NBER, 2005).

Fforde, J. S., *The Bank of England and Public Policy, 1941–1958* (Cambridge: Cambridge University Press, 1982).

Fieldhouse, D. K., 'The metropolitan economics of empire', in J. Brown and W. R. Louis (eds.), *Oxford History of the British Empire*, vol. IV, *The Twentieth Century* (Oxford: Oxford University Press, 1999), pp. 88–113.

Fielding, J., 'Coping with decline: US policy toward the British defense reviews of 1966', *Diplomatic History*, 23(4), 1999, pp. 633–56.

Gavin, F. J., *Gold, Dollars, and Power: The Politics of International Monetary Relations, 1958–1971* (Chapel Hill: University of North Carolina Press, 2004).

Giavazzi, F., and A. Giovannini, *Limiting Exchange Rate Flexibility: The European Monetary System* (Boston: MIT Press, 1989).

Goodstadt, L., 'Greasy palms', *Far Eastern Economic Review*, 81(37), 1973, p. 55.

Gowland, D., and A. Turner, *Reluctant Europeans: Britain and European Integration 1945–1998* (London: Longman, 2000).
Gray, W. G., 'Number one in Europe: the startling emergence of the Deutsche Mark 1968–69', *Central European History*, 39(1), 2006, pp. 56–78.
Group of Thirty, *The Foreign Exchange Markets under Floating Rates* (New York: Group of Thirty, 1980).
Hall, S., B. Henry and R. Herbert, 'Oil prices and the economy', *National Institute Economic Review*, 116, 1986, pp. 38–44.
Hamilton, A., 'Beyond the sterling devaluation: the gold crisis of March 1968', *Contemporary European History*, 17(1), 2008, pp. 73–95.
Hannay, D. (ed.), *Britain's Entry into the European Community: Report by Sir Con O'Neill on the Negotiations of 1970–1972* (London: Frank Cass, 2000).
Harmon, M. D., *The British Labour Government and the 1976 IMF Crisis* (London: Macmillan, 1997).
Hazlewood, A., 'Sterling balances and the colonial currency system', *Economic Journal*, 62, 1952, pp. 942–5.
Helleiner, E., *States and the Reemergence of Global Finance: From Bretton Woods to the 1990s* (Ithaca, NY: Cornell University Press, 1994).
Hickson, K., *The IMF Crisis of 1976 and British Politics* (New York: I. B. Tauris, 2005).
Hinds, A., *Britain's Sterling Colonial Policy and Decolonization, 1939–1958* (London: Greenwood Press, 2001).
Horsefield, J. K., *The International Monetary Fund, 1945–1965: Twenty Years of International Monetary Cooperation*, vol. I, *Chronicle* (Washington, DC: IMF, 1986).
(ed.) *The International Monetary Fund, 1945–1965: Twenty Years of International Monetary Cooperation*, vol. III, *Documents* (Washington, DC: IMF, 1986).
James, H., *International Monetary Cooperation since Bretton Woods* (Oxford: Oxford University Press, 1996).
Jenkins, R., *A Life at the Centre* (London: Macmillan, 1991).
Jones, M., 'A decision delayed: Britain's withdrawal from south east Asia reconsidered, 1961–68', *English Historical Review*, 117, 2002, pp. 569–95.
Kaiser, W., *Using Europe, Abusing the Europeans: Britain and European Integration 1945–63* (London: Macmillan, 1996).
Kaplan, J. J., and G. Schleiminger, *The European Payments Union: Financial Diplomacy in the 1950s* (Oxford: Oxford University Press, 1989).
Kelly, J., *Bankers and Borders: The Case of American Banks in Britain* (Cambridge, MA: Ballinger, 1977).
Kenen, P. B., *The Role of the Dollar as an International Currency*, Occasional Paper no. 13 (New York: Group of Thirty, 1983).
Kerr, I. M., *A History of the Eurobond Market: The First 21 Years* (London: Euromoney, 1984).
Keynes, J. M., *The Economic Consequences of Mr. Churchill* (London: L. and V. Woolf, 1925).
Kindleberger, C., *International Money: A Collection of Essays* (London: Allen & Unwin, 1981).

Kitzinger, U., *Diplomacy and Persuasion: How Britain Joined the Common Market* (London: Thames & Hudson, 1973).

Klug, A., and G. W. Smith, 'Suez and sterling 1956', *Explorations in Economic History*, 36(3), 1999, pp. 181–203.

Krozewski, G., *Money and the End of Empire: British Economic Policy and the Colonies, 1947–1958* (New York: Palgrave, 2001).

Kunz, D. B., *The Economic Diplomacy of the Suez Crisis* (Chapel Hill: University of North Carolina Press, 1991).

Kynaston, D., *The City of London*, vol. IV, *A Club No More 1945–2000* (London: Pimlico, 2001).

Lawson, N., *The View from Number 11: Memoirs of a Tory Radical* (London: Corgi Books, 1992).

'Robot and the fork in the road', *Times Literary Supplement*, 21 January 2005.

Lee, D., 'Protecting the sterling area: the Chifley government's response to multilateralism 1945–49', *Australian Journal of Political Science*, 25(2), 1990, pp. 178–95.

Ludlow, N. P., *Dealing with Britain: The Six and the First UK Application to the EEC* (Cambridge: Cambridge University Press, 1997).

'A short-term defeat: the Community institutions and the second British application to join the EEC', in O. J. Daddow (ed.), *Harold Wilson and European Integration: Britain's Second Application to Join the EEC* (London: Routledge, 2003), pp. 135–50.

The European Community and the Crisis of the 1960s: Negotiating the Gaullist Challenge (London: Routledge, 2006).

MacDougall, D., and M. Hutt, 'Imperial preference: a quantitative analysis', *Economic Journal*, 64, 1954, pp. 233–57.

Maes, I., *Macroeconomic and Monetary Thought at the European Commission in the 1960s*, RSCAS Working Paper no. 2004/1 (Florence: EUI, 2004).

Masson, P., 'Gaining and losing ERM credibility: the case of the United Kingdom', *Economic Journal*, 105, 1995, pp. 571–82.

McKenzie, F., *Redefining the Bonds of Commonwealth, 1939–1948: The Politics of Preference* (Basingstoke: Palgrave, 2002).

McMahon, C. W., 'The UK's experience in winding down the reserve role of sterling', in Group of Thirty, *Reserve Currencies in Transition* (New York: Group of Thirty, 1982), pp. 42–9.

Meade, J. E., *UK, Commonwealth and Common Market* (London: IEA, 1962).

Milward, A. S., *The Reconstruction of Western Europe 1945–51* (London: Methuen, 1984).

The European Rescue of the Nation-State, 2nd edn (London: Routledge, 2000).

Moggridge, D. E. (ed.), *The Collected Writings of John Maynard Keynes* (Cambridge: Cambridge University Press, 1971).

British Monetary Policy 1924–31: The Norman Conquest of $4.86 (Cambridge: Cambridge University Press, 1972).

Morgan, K. O., *Callaghan: A Life* (Oxford: Oxford University Press, 1997).

Newlyn, W. T., and D. C. Rowan, *Money and Banking in British Colonial Africa: A Study of the Monetary and Banking Systems of Eight British African Territories* (Oxford: Oxford University Press, 1954).

Newton, S., 'The two sterling crises of 1964 and the decision not to devalue', *Economic History Review*, 62(1), 2009, pp. 73–98.
Nicholson, F., and R. East, *From the Six to the Twelve: The Enlargement of the European Communities* (London: Longman, 1987).
Obstfeld, M., 'International currency experience: new lessons and lessons relearned', *Brookings Papers on Economic Activity*, 1, 1995, pp. 119–220.
'The global capital market: benefactor or menace?', *Journal of Economic Perspectives*, 12(4), 1998, pp. 9–30.
Obstfeld, M., and K. Rogoff, 'The mirage of fixed exchange rates', *Journal of Economic Perspectives*, 9(4), 1995, pp. 73–96.
Obstfeld, M., and A. Taylor, *Global Capital Markets: Integration, Crisis and Growth* (Cambridge: Cambridge University Press, 2004).
O'Hara, G., 'The limits of US power: transatlantic financial diplomacy under the Johnson and Wilson administrations, October 1964–November 1968', *Contemporary European History*, 12(3), 2003, pp. 257–78.
Oliver, M. J., and A. Hamilton, 'Downhill from devaluation: the battle for sterling 1968–72', *Economic History Review*, 60(3), 2007, pp. 486–512.
Page, S. A. B., 'The choice of invoicing currency in merchandise trade', *National Institute Economic Review*, 98, 1981, pp. 60–72.
Pagedas, C. A., *Anglo-American Strategic Relations and the French Problem, 1960–1963: A Troubled Partnership* (London: Frank Cass, 2000).
Pain, N., 'The growth and impact of inward investment in the UK: introduction and overview', in N. Pain (ed.), *Inward Investment, Technological Change and Growth* (London: NIESR, 2001), pp. 1–33.
Parr, H., *Britain's Policy towards the European Community: Harold Wilson and Britain's World Role 1964–67* (London: Routledge, 2006).
Pecchioli, R. M., *The Internationalisation of Banking: The Policy Issues* (Paris: OECD, 1983).
Peden, G. C., *The Treasury and British Public Policy* (Oxford: Oxford University Press, 2000).
Peeters, T., 'EMU: prospects and retrospect', in M. T. Sumner and G. Zis (eds.), *European Monetary Union: Progress and Prospects* (London: Macmillan, 1982), pp. 1–17.
Polk, J., *Sterling: Its Meaning in World Finance* (New York: Harper, 1956).
Pollard, S., *Britain's Prime and Britain's Decline: The British Economy 1870–1914* (London: Edward Arnold, 1989).
Ponting, C., *Breach of Promise: Labour in Power, 1964–70* (London: Hamish Hamilton, 1989).
Pressnell, L. S., *External Economic Policy since the War*, vol. I, *The Post-war Financial Settlement* (London: HMSO, 1987).
Rajan, R., and L. Zingales, *Saving Capitalism from the Capitalists: Unleashing the Power of Financial Markets to Create Wealth and Spread Opportunity* (New York: Random House, 2003).
Reddaway, W. B., *Effects of UK Direct Investment Overseas: Final Report* (Cambridge: Cambridge University Press, 1968).
Rollings, N., *British Business in the Formative Years of European Integration, 1945–1973* (New York: Cambridge University Press, 2007).

Rooth, T., 'Imperial self-sufficiency rediscovered: Britain and Australia 1945–51', *Australian Economic History Review*, 39(1), 1999, pp. 29–51.

Roy, R., 'The battle for Bretton Woods: America, Britain and the international financial crisis of October 1967–March 1968', *Cold War History*, 2(2), 2002, pp. 33–60.

Schenk, C. R., 'The sterling area and British policy alternatives in the 1950s', *Contemporary Record*, 6(2), 1992, pp. 266–86.

'The origins of a central bank in Malaya and the transition to independence, 1954–60', *Journal of Imperial and Commonwealth History*, 21(2), 1993, pp. 409–31.

Britain and the Sterling Area: From Devaluation to Convertibility in the 1950s (London: Routledge, 1994).

'Closing the Hong Kong gap: Hong Kong and the free dollar market in the 1950s', *Economic History Review*, 47(2), 1994, pp. 335–53.

'Monetary institutions in newly independent countries: the experience of Malaya, Ghana and Nigeria in the 1950s', *Financial History Review*, 4(2), 1997, pp. 181–98.

'The origins of the Eurodollar market in London, 1955–1963', *Explorations in Economic History*, 35(2), 1998, pp. 221–38.

'The UK, the sterling area and the EEC, 1957–63', in A. Deighton and A. S. Milward (eds.), *Widening, Deepening and Acceleration: The European Economic Community 1957–63* (Baden-Baden: Nomos, 1999), pp. 123–37.

'Shifting sands: the international economy and British economic policy', in W. Kaiser and G. Staerk (eds.), *British Foreign Policy 1955–64: Contracting Options* (London: Macmillan, 2000), pp. 19–32.

'Sterling, international monetary reform and Britain's applications to the EEC in the 1960s', *Contemporary European History*, 11(3), 2002, pp. 345–69.

'The empire strikes back: Hong Kong and the decline of sterling in the 1960s', *Economic History Review*, 57(3), 2004, pp. 551–80.

'The new City and the state in the 1960s', in R. Michie and P. Williamson (eds.), *The British Government and the City of London in the Twentieth Century* (Cambridge: Cambridge University Press, 2004), pp. 322–39.

'Malaysia and the end of the Bretton Woods system 1965–72: disentangling from sterling', *Journal of Imperial and Commonwealth History*, 36(2), 2008, pp. 197–220.

'The evolution of the Hong Kong currency board during global exchange rate instability, 1967–1973', *Financial History Review*, 16(2), 2009, pp. 129–56.

Shannon, H. A., 'The British payments and exchange control system', *Quarterly Journal of Economics*, 63(2), 1949, pp. 212–37.

Shonfield, A., *British Economic Policy since the War* (London: Penguin Books, 1958).

'The economic implications of the Brussels breakdown', in K. Younger (ed.), *Implications of the Brussels Breakdown* (Oxford: Oxford University Press, 1963), pp. 15–23.

Singleton, J., and P. L. Robertson, *Economic Relations between Britain and Australasia 1945–1970* (Basingstoke: Palgrave, 2002).
Solomon, R., *The International Monetary System, 1945–81* (New York: Harper & Row, 1982).
Stephens, P., *Politics and the Pound: The Tories, the Economy and Europe* (London: Papermac, 1997).
Steuer, M. D., P. Abell, J. Gennard, M. Perlman, R. Rees, B. Scott and K. F. Wallis, *The Impact of Foreign Direct Investment on the UK* (London: HMSO, 1973).
Stewart, M., *The Jekyll and Hyde Years: Politics and Economic Policy since 1964* (London: J. M. Dent and Sons, 1977).
Stiglitz, J., *Making Globalization Work* (New York: Norton, 2006).
Stockwell, S., 'Instilling the "sterling tradition": decolonization and the creation of a central bank in Ghana', *Journal of Imperial and Commonwealth History*, 25(2) (special issue: *Managing the business of empire: essays in honour of David Fieldhouse*), 1998, pp. 100–19.
Strange, S., *The Sterling Problem and the Six* (London: PEP/Chatham House, 1967).
Sterling and British Policy: A Political Study of an International Currency in Decline (Oxford: Oxford University Press, 1971).
'Sterling and British policy: a political view', *International Affairs*, 47(2), 1971, pp. 302–15.
Sunderland, D., *Managing the British Colonial and Post-colonial Development: The Crown Agents, 1914–1974* (Woodbridge, Suffolk: Boydell & Brewer, 2007).
Tomlinson, B. R., 'Indo-British relations in the post-colonial era: the sterling balances negotiations, 1947–49', *Journal of Imperial and Commonwealth History*, 13(3), 1985, pp. 142–62.
Tomlinson, J., 'Economic growth, economic decline', in K. Burk (ed.), *The British Isles since 1945* (Oxford: Oxford University Press, 2003), pp. 63–90.
The Labour Governments 1964–70: Economic Policy (Manchester: Manchester University Press, 2004).
Toniolo, G., *Central Bank Cooperation at the Bank for International Settlements, 1930–1973* (Cambridge: Cambridge University Press, 2005).
UN Centre on Transnational Corporations, *Salient Features and Trends in Foreign Direct Investment* (New York: UN, 1983).
Vaisse, M., 'De Gaulle and the British "application" to join the Common Market', in G. Wilkes (ed.), *Britain's Failure to Enter the European Community 1961–63: The Enlargement Negotiations and Crises in European, Atlantic and Commonwealth Relations* (London: Routledge, 1997), pp. 51–69.
Wass, D., *Decline to Fall: The Making of British Macro-economic Policy and the 1976 IMF Crisis* (Oxford: Oxford University Press, 2008).
Wells, S. J., *British Export Performance: A Comparative Study* (Cambridge: Cambridge University Press, 1964).
Wilkes, G. (ed.), *Britain's Failure to Enter the European Community 1961–63: The Enlargement Negotiations and Crises in European, Atlantic and Commonwealth Relations* (London: Routledge, 1997).

Young, J. W., 'The Wilson government and the Davies peace mission to North Vietnam, July 1965', *Review of International Studies*, 24(4), 1998, pp. 545–62.

Young, S. Z., *Terms of Entry: Britain's Negotiations with the European Community, 1970–1972* (London: Heinemann, 1973).

Index

For EU product safety concerns, contact us at Calle de José Abascal, 56–1°, 28003 Madrid, Spain or eugpsr@cambridge.org.

www.ingramcontent.com/pod-product-compliance
Lightning Source LLC
LaVergne TN
LVHW011532200926
848484LV00001B/236
* 9 7 8 0 5 2 1 8 7 6 9 7 1 *